AUGUSTUS AT WAR

The Struggle for the *Pax Augusta*

LINDSAY POWELL

Foreword by
Karl Galinsky

Pen & Sword
MILITARY

First published in Great Britain in 2018 by
PEN & SWORD MILITARY
An imprint of
Pen & Sword Books Ltd
47 Church Street
Barnsley
South Yorkshire
S70 2AS

ISBN 978-1-78383-184-5

Typeset by Concept, Huddersfield, West Yorkshire HD4 5JL.
Printed and bound in England by TJ International Ltd, Padstow, Cornwall.

Pen & Sword Books Ltd incorporates the imprints of Pen & Sword Archaeology, Atlas, Aviation, Battleground, Discovery, Family History, History, Maritime, Military, Naval, Politics, Railways, Select, Social History, Transport, True Crime, and Claymore Press, Frontline Books, Leo Cooper, Praetorian Press, Remember When, Seaforth Publishing and Wharncliffe.

For a complete list of Pen & Sword titles please contact
PEN & SWORD BOOKS LIMITED
47 Church Street, Barnsley, South Yorkshire, S70 2AS, England
E-mail: enquiries@pen-and-sword.co.uk
Website: www.pen-and-sword.co.uk

In memoriam
Sonia St James
(1942–2015)
Friend and Muse

Contents

Foreword
by Karl Galinsky

War and military affairs were a major, if not the major, determinant of the man who gave his name to *Pax Augusta*. Espoused and promoted by Christians from early on, who saw divine providence at work in the birth of Jesus during the Augustan reign, the notion of the 'Prince of Peace' took hold and was not easily dislodged. Among secular scholars, it received its ostensible support by Augustus' advice to his heir Tiberius to 'confine the empire within its limits' (*consilium coercendi intra terminos imperii*; Tacitus, *Annals* 1.11) and the statement, if it was indeed made in those terms, resonated with Americans who found a kindred mentality in George Washington's farewell address that warned the United States to avoid foreign entanglements. That, of course, was not exactly what happened in subsequent American history, nor was it the case in Rome. The context in which Augustus issued that counsel, to put it charitably and realistically, points to some relativizing factors. It came after decades of war and conquest and it was given to a man who was Augustus' premier general and therefore knew about the limits of any such advice.

Still, the prince of peace image prevailed and, with it, the notion that Augustus' many wars – and there was no denying them – were basically defensive. That presumption began to be shattered in 1972 by Colin Wells' careful and detailed analysis of Augustus' frontier policy in Germany. On a more public and popular level, the perception that the *Pax Romana* was a matter of war surfaced in John Kennedy's landmark speech on his administration's strategy of peace in 1963; he eschewed 'a *Pax Americana* enforced on the world by American weapons of war.' What, then, did Augustus himself say about war and peace?

He could not have made himself clearer and there was no disconnect between actions and words. Much has been written about the purpose of the lengthy account of his deeds, *Res Gestae Divi Augusti*, the longest surviving Roman inscription that was set up in front of his Mausoleum in Rome and in various parts of the empire. But the title he chose says it all: *res gestae*, a long-standing Roman phrase, refers primarily to achievements in warfare. As is duly emphasized in the preamble, we are looking at 'the achievements of the deified Augustus, by which he made the world subject to the rule of the Roman people' (transl. A. Cooley). War and conquest were central. What about peace? He formulated it with unparalleled succinctness and precision: 'Peace was born from victories' (*parta victoriis pax*; *Res Gestae* 13). Peace, in Latin, means making a pact and you do so after warring the enemy down. Nothing sentimental here and, at the same time, Augustan monuments and art in Rome did not engage in extended sculptural glorifications of victorious Roman armies and defeated enemies – we are a century away from the Column of Trajan. The absence of such themes in his masterful deployment of the 'power of images' has tended to reaffirm the impression of Golden Age sweetness and light under Augustus, but why overload the message of peace through victories? He did not need to.

Did he need the army? It has often been claimed that when all is said and done, his power ultimately rested on the military. That certainly was true of his earlier incarnation as Octavian and, of course, as Augustus he resolutely remained as commander in chief. As in all things Augustan, there are numerous layers and facets here and Lindsay Powell does his customary superior work elucidating many of these aspects while having, as always, his boots on the ground. Augustus never had to use the army to put down a popular rebellion against his rule or one instigated by rivals, and it's simply wrong to situate the importance of the army there. Instead, its business was war and wars that went on for the entire duration of his reign, from 31 BCE to 14 CE. They are the subject of this book.

The end of the civil wars, with the conquest of Alexandria in 30 BCE, provided a major juncture. Here was an army of some half million soldiers that had been used to and for internecine war. One of the major accomplishments of the incipient emperor was to retire these troops – and it took a while – and replace them with an army that would resume fighting against external enemies. The resulting economy of force, now numbering some 300,000 soldiers, has rightly provoked the attention not just of Roman historians ancient and modern, but of specialists of military strategy, such as Edward Luttwak. In this book, Powell meticulously details and analyzes the composition, deployment, and actions of this army and provides a much needed resource of information that has no parallel in astute comprehensiveness.

There is so much more here, therefore, than a *catalogue raisonné* of the legions, their men, their leaders, their equipment, and so on. The central issue, as the title says, is Augustus at war, an essential and fascinating aspect of the man. Catapulted onto the stage of world history at the age of 18, his military résumé was as blank as his administrative one. Yet his success against Antony and others was largely due to his superior use of force and at the age of 33, he was 'in control of all affairs' as he put it in *Res Gestae* 34.1; the Latin phrase 'potens *rerum omnium*' again implies his dominance in the military realm, too. And he was not about to relinquish that ultimate power, even while re-involving the Senate and People in the government of the *res publica*. What followed was an elaborate game of strategy on several fronts. Military historians have tried to differentiate the unceasing sequence of Augustan wars in terms of conquest or consolidation. This can be matter of rich discussion and individual judgment though we can be reasonably sure that such semantics were probably of little import to the conquered.

Political considerations played a major role though, typically, in a more complex way than for the generalissimos of the Republic. During that era conquest and wars were driven greatly by the quest for individual glory and renown, to be memorialized by the victory temples that lined the triumphal route. Strategy was piecemeal and the resulting 'empire' was an amalgam of territorial acquisitions that had often been conquered impulsively. Augustus' strategy was more comprehensive. Certainly, he cast himself in the tradition of his Republican predecessors; military achievements were essential for maintaining his *auctoritas*, but – with some exceptions, such as the failed expedition to the south of the Arabian peninsula – a more cohesive overall framework evolved, parallel to that of making the provinces a more integral part of the empire in more than territorial ways. And there was a new twist: by agreement with the Senate, provinces that were certifiably pacified would return to senatorial control, along with the legions stationed in them. In other words, this would mean at least a technical loss of control by Augustus over those army contingents. It was paramount, therefore, from Augustus' perspective to demonstrate that the work of *pax Augusta* was never done and military actions needed to be ongoing. They were.

The end result, or bottom line, was that Augustus added more territory to the *imperium Romanum* than anyone before him. Fittingly, then, he took '*Imperator*', which was a statutory acclamation, as his first name; after all, there was no shortage of individuals called 'Caius'. This arrogation has enraged many a modern historian, but Powell's book perfectly illustrates why *imperator* – which was to become 'emperor' in later times – was more than a generic name for Augustus. His superb treatment shows Imperator Caesar Augustus in action and helps us understand the military Augustus and his times more clearly.

Karl Galinsky
Austin, Texas
October 2016

Preface

Spread to the regions of the East and of the West and to the bounds of the North and of the South, the *Pax Augusta* preserves every corner of the world safe from the fear of brigandage.

Diffusa in orientis occidentisque tractus et quidquid meridiano aut septentrione finitur, pax augusta omnis terrarum orbis angulos a latrociniorum metu servat immunes.

M. Velleius Paterculus, *Roman History* 2.126.3.

The years 31 BCE–14 CE, during which Augustus asserted his position as first man of the Roman Commonwealth, were celebrated by later historians and poets as a golden age when the world was secure. The term they coined for it, *Pax Augusta* – inaugurating a much longer epoch modern historians call the *Pax Romana* – is usually translated as 'the Peace of Augustus' or 'Augustan Peace', though 'Revered Peace' is perhaps more accurate. (There was even an altar, the exquisite *Ara Pacis Augustae*, in Rome that celebrated Augustus' safe return from the western provinces, lands he made peaceful.) The words evoke an epoch of uninterrupted peace across the vast Roman Empire, a serene period in which its citizens lived lives free of war and suffering. Today, one often reads in history books a line to the effect 'a 40-year period of peace took place under Augustus'. There is only one problem with this assessment. It is a fallacy – or at best a half-truth.

As I researched and wrote my biographies of Augustus' generals Nero Claudius Drusus (2011), Germanicus Caesar (2013) and Marcus Agrippa (2015), I was increasingly struck by the sheer number of military operations these and other field commanders were engaged in when it was supposed to be a world finally at peace. In fact, there were numerous skirmishes along the borders and punitive raids in response; but also insurgencies – acts of sedition, as the Romans called them – by supposedly conquered and pacified peoples, occurring in the same regions year after year, despite repeated efforts to crush them. Then there was the disenchantment of the rank and file of the army, whether stationed in the foothills of the Cantabrian Mountains of Spain or on the banks of the Danube or Rhine rivers. In Rome and other cities too, riots broke out periodically among ordinary citizens frustrated by natural and man-made disasters, and people died in them. In addition, Augustus actively waged war to acquire and conquer new lands. Using direct military force, Augustus nearly doubled the '*imperium* of the Roman People', as he himself called it – that portion of the world we now call the

Roman Empire. It was a greater accomplishment than that achieved by either Pompeius Magnus ('Pompey the Great') or the even more famous Julius Caesar (correctly Iulius Caesar), men widely regarded as among Rome's best generals. In most cases the Romans succeeded in retaining these annexed territories long after Augustus died. It was an astonishing achievement then and one that merits study today.

Amidst all this conflict, how could Augustus' apologists claim the world was really at peace? Lasting more than four decades, the 'reign' of Augustus was remarkable for being the longest in Roman civilization's entire 1,000-year long history. The man himself is an enigmatic, even a paradoxical, figure, and his motives are often obscure or opaque. When not presented in public as a *toga*-wearing magistrate or priest, Augustus is shown as a military commander.

One of the most instantly recognizable artefacts to survive from antiquity is the so-called statue of 'Augustus of Prima Porta'. (It was the centrepiece of the marvellous *Moi, Auguste, Empereur de Rome* exposition staged at the Grand Palais, Paris, which I was fortunate to attend in June 2014 in the bimillennary year of Augustus' death.) It is a puzzling sculpture. Discovered in 1863 on the Via Flaminia, it is presumed to have come from the nearby villa associated by some with Livia, Augustus' wife, though the exact location of the find spot is nowhere recorded. No one is quite sure when it was carved, but 4 CE seems likely, and it was probably a copy of an original in bronze cast around 20 BCE. Standing 2 metres (7 feet) tall, it survives as a bare white marble figure but in ancient times it was once painted to be lifelike. For all its magnificence, the image is a visual paradox. The youthful figure wears the anatomical cuirass and arming doublet of a senior officer. His raised right arm infers that he is acknowledging an acclamation from the troops, or that he is calling for silence and about to address them. Yet he seems curiously under-dressed for the occasion: there is no *parazonium* (an officer's sword) or spear – in fact, a weapon of any kind; his *paludamentum* (the cloak worn by a senior officer) is not attached to his shoulders, but decorously draped around his waist and over his left arm; rather than wearing elaborate boots, he is barefoot like an athlete, semi-divine hero or a god. Is he dressed for war, or is he dressed for peace? Is he the peacemaker who is always ready to make war? Or is he the warlord who is always ready to make peace?

How Augustus accomplished his rise and dominance has been closely studied by historians. The legal, political, literary and artistic life of the Roman world he 'ruled' over has been well researched by modern academics. Scholars have tended to view the military dimension of his reign, such as his relationship to the army, his generals and the campaigns they fought, largely as an adjunct to these other aspects – for example, see Sir Ronald Syme (1939 and 1986), Kurt A. Raaflaub (1979), Erich S. Gruen (1985), J.W. Rich (2003) or Fred K. Drogula (2015). I believe that to understand Augustus the man, and to fully account for his achievements, it is essential to study how he waged wars and managed the men who fought them. Events presented Augustus with often difficult choices, to which he had to respond. How he did so reveals much about him.

This book is not another biography of Augustus, though the life story of the man is part of it. Nor is it a political history, though politics does feature in it. Rather, it examines Augustus as commander-in-chief. What did *pax* mean for Augustus and the Roman People? Did Augustus have an 'imperial vision' for the Roman Empire? If he did, was it one of methodical expansion using war and diplomacy, or was it opportunistic – or, to put it another way, did Augustus have a 'grand strategy'? If so, did it begin as one or did it evolve over time? Which wars were ones of necessity and which of choice? What defined victory or a successful outcome? What kind of military leader was Augustus? How deeply was he personally involved in the management of war, in the setting of goals or formulation of strategies and tactics in regional and local campaigns and conflicts? Who were his generals and field commanders? How and why did he pick those individuals? How much authority did he delegate to his regional deputies? How did they perform in carrying out their duties? Did Augustus learn from military successes or setbacks and apply the lessons? How did Augustus present his military achievements to the Roman People? And finally, how successful was he in achieving the *Pax Augusta*?

I have wrestled for a long time on how best to present my findings and discussed different approaches with my friend and mentor, Karl Galinsky, who is the foremost scholar of Augustus. One approach would have been to devote chapters to the examination of specific themes, such as the army and reforms Augustus made to it, aspects of his leadership, the individual wars, the victory propaganda and so forth, and dive deep into each topic. The risk was that the resulting book would have been somewhat academic, repetitive and rather dry.

The approach I have decided to take is modelled on an 'after-action review' or AAR. This is a leadership and knowledge sharing technique widely used in modern military and government organizations to better understand events, activities or programmes. AARs can be helpful in identifying deficiencies, strengths and areas for specific improvement. They seek to answer several questions. What was expected to happen? What actually occurred? What went well and why? What can be improved and how? It provides a good, structured format to evaluate Augustus at war.

The start of an AAR is an accurate chronology of what actually happened. Chapters 1 through to 7 present a straight narrative account of the period beginning 1 January 31 BCE (a few months before the Battle of Actium) to 19 August 14 CE (when he died), and the events immediately following. The chapters mark the discrete periods of time when Augustus' legal military power to command his province (*imperium proconsulare*) was renewed. These intervals form natural beginnings and endings, like modern presidencies or terms in office of prime ministers. In these periods, Augustus had to deal with the issues as they arose – usually unexpectedly – and it is in studying his actions and reactions to events and crises that much can be learned. 'Hindsight is 20/20': Augustus neither had any idea that he would live as long as he did nor how his life would unfold after Actium. Throughout, I follow the dictum of investigative journalists, which is to 'work from the facts outwards: never a thesis inwards', letting the known facts speak for themselves. This is the unfolding story of Rome as a military power and the role war played in its often clumsy transformation from what modern historians call the Late Republic to the Early Empire, with all the twists and turns of an international thriller – and a cast of thousands.

Assembling a chronology and making sense of the whens, whos, whats, whys and hows was a crucial task in writing *Augustus at War*. For the events of history from 31 BCE to 14 CE, I closely studied written records by contemporary and later Roman historians for facts, supplemented by insights gleaned from archaeology, epigraphy, numismatics, prosopography and the visual arts. The material available to study today is challenging. Augustus is known to have written thirteen volumes of memoirs (Suet., *Div. Aug.* 85). Sadly, the ravages of time have been unkind to them; all are lost and only a few anecdotes and remarks have been preserved. Had they survived complete today, we might have been able to read first-hand about his personal ambitions or the aspirations he had for his nation, and from them assess how well he led his people through war to peace. What has come down to us is his own *Res Gestae*, literally meaning 'Things Done'. It is a formal – some say propagandistic – account of his deeds and one that has to be read with care. Yet it is a vitally important primary source from the star actor in the story, one told in his own words. I have included his *Res Gestae* in its entirety – both in Latin and in an English translation – as Appendix 1. The reader unfamiliar with this important document might wish to read this first before starting the main narrative.

Studying the accounts of Roman historians provides a survey of Augustus' world and the timeline of key events; but on matters of, say, his abilities as a leader or military strategist, they can sometimes come up short – not necessarily because they are bad researchers; rather it is the fact that the surviving material usually omits these aspects because ancient writers were not generally interested in them. Historical records of any age can never be completely trusted: every writer has an agenda, a purpose for writing, and writes to his strengths. The books of contemporary Titus Livius (Livy) – arguably Rome's greatest historian – covering the years of Augustus' principate end at 9 BCE. They survive as the *Periochae*, essentially short entries from an ancient library catalogue, the original texts having long since been destroyed. Velleius Paterculus, a commander who served under Tiberius Caesar and who had first-hand experience of combat in the Western Balkans, is often criticized as a sycophant – unfairly in my opinion – to the man who succeeded Augustus as 'First Man'. Several of the best ancient historians are weakest when explaining tactics or the details of battles, because they were not themselves military men or they deemed these minutiae to be unimportant to their narratives. They can also be selective about which events to include in their chronicles. In *Jewish Antiquities*, Josephus only focuses on events in Judaea. Others may conflate one event with another, or omit them altogether. Florus often does this. In the case of Cassius Dio's *Roman History*, which is the most complete and detailed source for the Augustan period but written 200 years later, the two surviving manuscripts have *lacunae* – gaping holes or tears – where entire years are missing: that history is literally lost to us. Thus a few militarily significant events could not be dated with complete certainty because of the unreliability or vagueness of the source material. Whenever this is the case, I have fully disclosed the problems of reconciling different dates in the endnotes. Suetonius gives us snippets of war stories and glimpses of several notable personalities in his biographies of Augustus, Tiberius, Caius (Caligula), Claudius and Nero, but usually does not tie them to a specific historical date.

The challenges of working with the extant sources were remarked upon by the prolific scholar Sir Ronald Syme in his paper 'Lentulus and the Origin of Moesia', published in 1934 in volume 24 of *The Journal of Roman Studies*. In his introduction he writes:

> The ancient evidence for the wars and conquests of Augustus is not only fragmentary: the fragments themselves are capricious and misleading. Chance and design have conspired to produce a like result; and the interested partiality of contemporary authorities has been nobly seconded by the ignorance or the indifference of subsequent compilers.

Commenting on the paucity of detail about campaigns and the commanders who led them, he goes on:

> They have been omitted, accidentally or even deliberately, and with them a large piece of history has either perished utterly or has narrowly escaped oblivion. What has survived in other sources is seldom detailed enough to fix the date and determine the significance of their exploits.

He died in 1989, aged 86. I never had the honour of meeting him, but as if warning me from the grave he offers this *caveat*: 'this being so, it is the duty of the historian, not merely to interpret what is recorded, but always to remember how little after all has been recorded'.

In Chapter 8, while heeding Sir Ronald's advice, I attempt to address the questions this book sets out to answer about leadership, strategy and operations, grouped into key themes and issues. In this assessment chapter the 'ABC' principles of the forensic scientist apply: 'assume nothing; believe nobody; check everything'. Informing my final assessment are the insights I have gleaned from several contemporary commanders, commentators, government officials and statesmen. I have talked with serving officers and soldiers as well as veterans who have seen combat first-hand. An avid viewer of *Charlie Rose* on PBS and *HARDtalk* on BBC World News, I have learned from interviews with high-ranking military and senior government professionals much about generalship, the pragmatics of field warfare, the management of large government organizations and the gentle art of diplomacy.

They remind us that there is a price to be paid in blood and treasure for peace; that despite the best preparations and advanced planning, heads of state and commanders-in-chief nevertheless still find themselves dealing with unexpected crises and have to make urgent decisions about whether to put men and matériel in harm's way; that the decision to go to war is never taken lightly; that intelligence upon which decisions are made is often incomplete and subject to bias and misinterpretation; that the narrow objectives of campaigns can quickly become subject to scope creep and morph into missions very different than originally envisioned; that policy agendas change; that sometimes the only choices are bad choices, but one still has to choose – 'doing nothing is not an option'; that the act of intervening in a conflict can change the situation on the ground and create new and unforeseen dangers and dilemmas; that picking allies and sustaining relationships with them through rewards and sanctions is fraught with difficulty and may not, in the end, support policy objectives; and that deciding when to suspend operations, and the manner of its doing, can have long-term consequences if the outcomes and timetable are not first fully considered. These test the mettle of men and women in leadership positions today. It was no different for Augustus or his deputies.

During the time Augustus ruled, many men served under him and in his name. Rather than interrupt the flow of the narrative with biographical backgrounds of the many supporting actors, I have assembled detailed profiles of more than ninety of his known colleagues, deputies and allies in Appendix 2. Their stories are as varied, interesting and astonishing as any group of high achievers and heroes, scoundrels and sons-of-bitches can be. Similarly, the composition and histories of the diverse military units they commanded are fascinating stories in their own right. Good and great, bad and ugly, Rome's war fighters were as much petulant as professional, each legion and cohort jealously guarding its traditions, rights and privileges. I have assembled these under Orders of Battle in Appendix 3. Even the coins the troops received in payment for service were a means for Augustus to shape opinion about his deeds, as Appendix 4 shows.

The astute reader might ask why I chose to cover the period 31 BCE–14 CE? Augustus died in 14 CE so that year marks the end of Augustus' reign. A traditional view for its start is 27 BCE (the date of the so-called 'First Constitutional Settlement') or – and that was Augustus' own view – 23 BCE (the date of the so-called 'Second Constitutional Settlement' when he assumed the tribunician power). These might be considered his *political* victories. Roman historians, however, dated his rule from the pivotal *military* victory at Actium (see, for example, Suet., *Div. Aug.* 8.3 and Dio, 56.30.5), representing a contiguous period of forty-five years. Again, Augustus himself refrained from doing so because – as you will read – that victory was won in a *civil* rather than a *foreign* war (an important distinction), even if war was formally declared only against Kleopatra.

Studying the Romans requires some effort on the part of a modern-day reader with respect to dates, titles and spellings of personal and place names. Writing about the ancient world involves making several editorial decisions and presentational compromises to make it intelligible. I have tried to be rational and consistent in my usage, but as the writer of this book they are, in the final analysis, *my* choices.

Chronology is one of them. The Romans had their own calendar using the names of each year's two consuls, and ancient historians routinely refer to dates in this way. For modern readers it is cumbersome and very confusing. Our own style of identifying years by serial numbers makes life so much easier! However, in respect of dates, I have adopted the increasingly accepted convention 'BCE' (before the Common Era) instead of B.C., and 'CE' (Common Era) for A.D. (*anno Domini*). The events in Augustus' life described in this book occur in both epochs. Thus Augustus received his honorary title in 27 BCE (27 B.C.) and died in 14 CE (A.D. 14). I am aware some readers find this format strange and foreign, but it is common in research literature. Popular classicist Mary Beard is on record in *A Don's Life* – her column for the *Times Literary Supplement* – on 26 September 2011 as stating the convention has been around for years and that about half of the academic papers published on ancient history display dates in this format.

Under each year I also include the names of the consuls appointed for the year. According to the Roman constitution, these two magistrates – elected from the members of the Senate in the autumn of the prior year – were the most senior in the *Res Publica*. Having completed their term in office, these men – now ex- or proconsuls – formed a bench of talent from which Augustus and the Senate chose governors of provinces and legates of the legions. Faced with a shrinking number of qualified men, Augustus encouraged consuls to resign midway through their terms in office to make way for other *consules suffecti*, suffect or replacement consuls. Election to the consulate was also a way for Augustus to recognize and reward men who had served him well or showed promise for future assignments. The observant reader will note the names of many military commanders among the lists of consuls during Augustus' principate in the course of reading the book.

The status-conscious Romans delighted in convoluted job titles. (That fact reveals something of the mindset of these status-conscious, legalistic ancient people.) The Glossary and Appendix 2 define the most important. There are generally no modern equivalents for Roman political, military and religious offices, so I have used the Latin style throughout. I do this to be accurate and authentic, not obscurantist. A case in point is how historians refer to Augustus as 'emperor'. It is an Anglicisation of *imperator*. To translate the word this way is a mistake, however. It simply means 'commander'. It was a spontaneous commendation from the soldiers – a Latin 'for he's a jolly good fellow' – as they, his countrymen, cheered their leader for bringing them victory on the battlefield. It was an honour to be proudly cited thus in the after-action report presented to the Senate, to add the title after his name and have it carved on inscriptions for posterity. Hence '*M ANTONIUS IMP*[*erator*]' which appears on coins from 41 BCE. It did not yet have the far-reaching regal or despotic connotation of 'emperor' promoted by Augustus' self-indulgent successors. His radical innovation was that from 38 BCE he audaciously adopted *imperator* as his own *first name*. Thereafter, he unabashedly used it on coins and inscriptions, consciously and purposely presenting himself as the nation's military *commander*: Imp. Caesar *Divi filius* Augustus.

Like their official titles, the Romans had long personal names to match, complete with filial connections. They generally had two parts, a forename (*praenomen*) and a family or clan name (*nomen genticulum*). From the later days of the first century BCE, it was becoming common to have three by adding a nickname (*cognomen*), which might describe a distinguishing feature. Victorious commanders in battle – the *imperatores* – might also be granted a honorific title (*agnomen* or *cognomen*) such as *Germanicus* for extraordinary action in Germania. Modern historians usually call Romans by this last name, hence Caesar for C. Iulius Caesar, or Augustus for Imp. Caesar *Divi filius* Augustus. (I have used Iulius for Julius and the abbreviated forms Imp. Caesar before 27 BCE, and Augustus thereafter in the text.) By tradition, Roman men and women in extended families often had the same name – Augustus was a particularly enthusiastic user, requiring his adopted sons to use the form Iulius Caesar so that they were clearly identified as part of the *gens Iulia*, while allowing them to keep their *praenomen*. Thus, Caius Vipsanius Agrippa and his brother Lucius became respectively Caius Iulius Caesar and Lucius Iulius Caesar; and Tiberius Claudius Nero became Tiberius Iulius Caesar. Tiberius' son was named after his younger brother, Nero Claudius Drusus, and to avoid confusion between the two men the uncle is often called Drusus the Elder, Drusus Maior or Drusus I, while the nephew is called Drusus the Younger, Drusus Minor or Drusus II. The reader will be forgiven for thinking that studying the *Domus Augusta*, the 'House of Augustus', can quickly become very confusing: it is, even for people intimately familiar with the Roman period. There is some relief for the reader in that I have omitted the father's name in all cases.

In some cases the Latin name has mutated into an Anglicism through common usage, such as Livy for Livius or Pliny for Plinius. For the names of ancient historians, I use the modern form throughout. For the protagonists in the story, however, I retain the original, authentic form. I know some readers dislike this approach, but I believe we owe it to the people of history to get their names right. It simply respects the names by which they themselves were known in their own time. Hence I use Marcus Antonius rather than Marc Antony or Mark Antony (popularized by William Shakespeare). Some names were actually Greek in origin, but were recorded with new phonetic spellings by Roman historians for their Latin-speaking audience, and thus found their way into later English translations and became the *de facto* spellings. Thus I call the Thracian king Roimetalkes not Rhoemetalces because this is faithful to the original spelling found on his coins and inscriptions. It is also why I use a 'K' in Kleopatra, which is the spelling in Greek – her first language – rather than Cleopatra, since the form with the 'C' was how her Roman *captors* spelled her name.

Where a place has a Latin name, I prefer to use it since the modern name creates a false impression of the scale and feel of the ancient place: hence Ara Ubiorum rather than Cologne, which at this time more likely looked like a town of the American Wild West. In other cases, where the modern place name is unfamiliar to a reader I use the ancient name, such as Antiocheia on the Orontes (in Roman Syria) rather than Antakya (now in Turkey). Some ancient places – especially in the eastern Mediterranean – have both Latin and Greek names, such as Laodicea and Loadikeia, in which case I tend to use the Greek form. The exceptions are Actium, Athens, Egypt and Rome, because to use Aktion, Athenae (or Athenai), Aegyptus and Roma would be unnecessarily pedantic; and places for which the ancient name is not known, where I use the modern name unless there is a well-known Anglicism. I have listed ancient and modern place names on page 325 for convenience.

The names and places used by the indigenous peoples who sided with or fought against the Romans are only known to us through Greek and Latin writings, and then but only by Romanized names. We do not know what Arminius of the Cherusci nation was called in his own language, or Marboduus of the Marcomanni. Few Germanic place names survive, though intriguingly the geographer Ptolemy lists several towns and even offers map co-ordinates for them. While attempts have been made to identify their precise locations, they are at best tentative.

The Latin version is used for Roman officer ranks, arms, equipment and battle formations throughout the text, since there is often no modern equivalent. The Romans were not as precise in naming things as we are today. That, too, is an insight into the Roman mind. Definitions of the commonly used technical terms are defined in the Glossary.

The symbol HS followed by a number is the Roman symbol for *sestertius*, a coin made of bronze or brass. A Roman soldier was paid a stipend of HS900 a year (see Appendix 3.3 and 4). Four *sestertii* was the equivalent of a silver *denarius* and twenty-five *denarii* equated to a gold *aureus*.

The job of a historian is to research, analyze and interpret events and the people who took part in them by studying a variety of historical documents and sources, and then to present as accurate and unbiased an account – warts and all – of his subject as possible for the reader. The task of a writer is to make the story compelling reading. I hope I have succeeded both as a historian and a writer in this new book.

To the shades of Imperator Caesar *Divi filius* Augustus and the men who served with him, I present this book. *Bene merenti fecit.*

Lindsay Powell
Leap Day, 2016
Austin, Texas

Acknowledgements

There are several people who deserve my thanks for helping me with this project.

My late friend Sonia St James (self-styled 'muse to creative minds') offered much appreciated encouragement throughout the project to her last days. To her I dedicate this book.

To my commissioning editor, Philip Sidnell at Pen & Sword Books, who responded enthusiastically to my proposal for this my fourth in a series of volumes on Augustus' generals, I shall again always be grateful. To the other hard-working members of the production team, Matt Jones and Dominic Allen at Pen & Sword, and Noel Sadler at Concept, I offer my sincere thanks for turning my virtual files into lovely printed pages.

I feel deeply honoured that Dr Karl Gaklinsky agreed to provide the foreword to *Augustus at War*. Floyd A. Cailloux Centennial Professor, University Distinguished Teaching Professor at the Department of Classics of The University of Texas at Austin, Karl is the world's leading authority on Augustus and his books have been on my bookshelf for years. Notable among them is his seminal work *Augustan Culture* (Princeton, 1996), my copy of which he kindly signed for me with the flattering inscription: 'For Lindsay, a cultured Augustan – K'. Since that initial meeting we have become good friends and discussed this project many times at Russell's Bakery in Austin, Texas, exchanging ideas and opinions about ancient and modern times over Schnecken and coffee. I know of no one more qualified to compose the opening remarks. For his kindness and encouragement I offer my sincerest thanks.

This book tells the story of Imperator Caesar *Divi filius* Augustus and his generals in both words and pictures. For helping me to illustrate the story, I offer my thanks to Shanna Schmidt of Harlan J. Berk, Chicago, and Richard Beale of Roma Numismatics Limited, London, for kindly providing images of coins. From the re-enactment world, I must thank Chris Haines MBE, Mike Knowles and members of The Ermine Street Guard, a registered charity – and of which I am proud to say I am a veteran member. For images of Roman portrait busts, I express my gratitude to Marie-Lan Nguyen, and to Jasper Oorthuys, editor-in-chief of the excellent *Ancient Warfare* magazine published by Karwansaray B.V. to which I am proud to say I am a regular contributor. I also thank Carole Raddato for allowing me the use of her photo.

War stories cannot be told without the aid of maps. I offer my sincere thanks to M.C. Bishop, who not only let me reproduce his exquisite scale maps of the forts from his book *Handbook of Roman Legionary Fortresses* (Pen & Sword, 2012), but also specially drew one for this volume. My thanks also to Carlos De La

Rocha of Satrapa Ediciones, whose work frequently appears in *Ancient Warfare* magazine, for letting me reproduce the map of Nero Claudius Drusus' military campaigns in Germania; and to Erin Greb, who did a marvellous job of producing the other maps in like style.

I have quoted extracts from several ancient authors' works whose voices lend authenticity to the narrative. For the translations I used: Augustus' *Res Gestae* translated by Frederick W. Shipley, in *Velleius Paterculus and Res Gestae Divi Augusti*, Loeb Classical Library, Harvard, 1924; Cassius Dio's Ρωμαϊκὴ Ἱστορία (*Romaikon Istoria*) translated by Herbert Balwin Foster in *Dio's Roman History*, Volume 4, New York: Pafraets Book Company 1905 and E. Cary based on the version by H.B. Foster in *Dio's Roman History*, London: William Heinemann, 1917; Florus' *Epitome de T. Livio Bellorum Omnium Annorum DCC* translated by E.S. Forster in *Florus: Epitome of Roman History*, Harvard: Loeb Classical Library, 1929; Horace's *Carmen*, *Ludi Saeculares* and *Sermones* translated by John Conington in *The Odes and* Carmen Saeculare *of Horace*, London: George Bell and Sons, 1882; Josephus' *Antiquitates Iudaice* translated by William Whiston in *The Genuine Works of Flavius Josephus*, New York: William Borradaile, 1824; Pliny the Elder's *Historia Naturalis* translated by John Bostock and H.T. Riley in *The Natural History of Pliny*, Volume 3, London: Henry Bohn, 1855 and *Pliny's Natural History* by Jonathan Couch for The Wernerian Club, London: Goerge Barclay, 1848; Plutarch's Οἱ Βίοι Παράλληλοι (*Oi Vioi Paralliloi*) translated by John Langhrone and William Langhorne in Plutarch's Lives, London: William Tegg, 1868; Strabo's Γεωγραφικά (*Geographika*) translated by Horace Leonard Jones in *The Geography of Strabo*, London: William Heinmann, 1930; Suetonius' *De Vita Caesarum* translated by Alexander Thomson in *The Lives of the Twelve Caesars*, London: George Bell and Sons, 1893; Tacitus' *Ab Excessu Divi Augusti* (*Annales*) translated by Alfred John Church and William Jackson Bodribb in *The Annals of Tacitus*, London: MacMillan and Co., 1906; Tacitus' *De Origine et Situ Germanorum* translated by R.B. Townsend in *The Agricola and Germania of Tacitus*, London: Methuen and Co., 1894; Vergil's *Aeneid* translated by Theodore C. Williams in *Vergil. Aeneid*, Boston: Houghton Mifflin Co., 1910; Velleius Paterculus' *Historiae Romanae* translated by John Selby in *Sallust, Florus and Velleius Paterculus*, London: George Bell, 1889; and Quintilianus' *Institutio Oratoria* translated by Harold Edgeworth Butler in *Quintilian. With An English Translation*, London: William Heinemann, Ltd. 1922. These were made accessible to me by the good people who digitized these texts and archived them online at *LacusCurtius*, *The Latin Library* and *The Perseus Digital Library*. Together these invaluable resources have transformed how a researcher can study the Greek and Roman texts.

Finally, I thank Austin Public Library service in Austin, Texas, for providing access to the phenomenal JSTOR.org ('journal storage') website, the digital library of academic journals, books and primary sources, which greatly facilitated my research for this book.

List of Illustrations

Figures

Maps

Orders of Battle

Key to Military Symbols

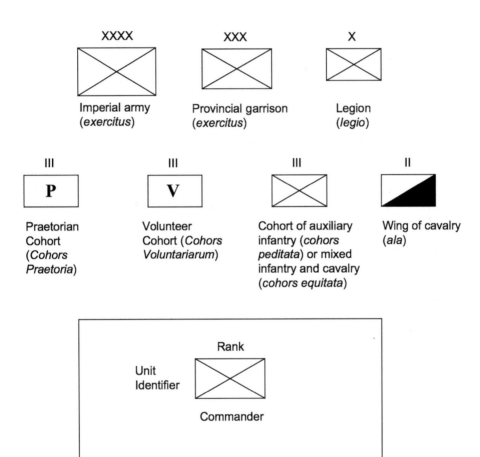

XXXX

Imperial army
(*exercitus*)

XXX

Provincial garrison
(*exercitus*)

X

Legion
(*legio*)

III

P

Praetorian
Cohort
(*Cohors
Praetoria*)

III

V

Volunteer
Cohort (*Cohors
Voluntariarum*)

III

Cohort of auxiliary
infantry (*cohors
peditata*) or mixed
infantry and cavalry
(*cohors equitata*)

II

Wing of cavalry
(*ala*)

Rank

Unit
Identifier

Commander

List of Tables

List of Plates

1. Marble portrait bust of Augustus Bevilacqua in the Glyptothek, Munich: Inv. No. 317. (Public domain)
2. Marble portrait bust of M. Agrippa from Gabii in the Louvre, Paris: Inv. No. Ma 1208/MR 402. (© Marie-Lan Nguyen/Wikimedia Commons/CC-BY 2.5)
3. Inscription in the *Forum Augustum*, Rome. (© Anthony M. from Rome/Wikimedia Commons/CC-BY 2.0)
4. Bronze *as* of Kleopatra VII: Svornos 1871. (Courtesy of Harlan J. Berk)
5. Silver *denarius* of *triumvir* M. Antonius: Crawford 517/2. (Courtesy of Roma Numismatics)
6. Wall painting from Herodium depicting a naval battle. Exhibit at the Israel Museum Collection, Jerusalem. (© Carole Raddato/Wikimedia Commons/CC-BY-SA 2.0)
7. Silver *denarius* of Augustus: *RIC* I 544/*BMC* 655. (Courtesy of Roma Numismatics)
8. Silver *denarius* of Imp. Caesar: *RIC* I 265a/*BMCRE* 625. (Courtesy of Roma Numismatics)
9. Silver *denarius* of Imp. Caesar: *RIC* I 264. (Courtesy of Roma Numismatics)
10. Silver *denarius* of Augustus: *RIC* I 99/*BMCRE* 399. (Courtesy of Roma Numismatics)
11. Silver *denarius* of Augustus: *RIC* I 136. (Courtesy of Roma Numismatics)
12. Silver *denarius* of Augustus: *RSC* 208. (Courtesy of Roma Numismatics)
13. Silver *denarius* of Augustus: *RIC* I 51. (Courtesy of Roma Numismatics)
14. Silver *denarius* of Augustus: *RIC* I 86a. (Courtesy of Roma Numismatics)
15. Silver *denarius* of P. Carisius: *RIC* I 4a. (Courtesy of Numismatica Mayor 25; Author's collection)
16. Silver *denarius* of P. Carisius: *RIC* I 7a/*BMC* 281. (Courtesy of Roma Numismatics)
17. Silver *denarius* of Augustus: *RIC* I 288/*BMC* 14. (Courtesy of Roma Numismatics)
18. Silver *tetradrachm* of Frâhata IV: Sellwood 58.9. (Courtesy of Roma Numismatics)
19. Re-enactor as a *legionarius* of the first century BCE. (Courtesy of The Ermine Street Guard)
20. Re-enactors as Roman legionary officers of the first century BCE/CE. (Courtesy of The Ermine Street Guard)

Chronology

31 BCE   ***Political events*:**
(*1 January*) Imp. Caesar consul (3).
Attempt to assassinate Imp. Caesar by Lepidus.
Imp. Caesar founds Nikopolis in Epirus.

***Military events*:**
Actian War (*Bellum Actiense*) – (*2 August*) Battle of Actium (*Bellum Actiacum*), Imp.
     Caesar with M. Agrippa defeats M. Antonius and Kleopatra in the Gulf of
     Ambracia.
Imp. Caesar acclaimed *imperator* (VI).

30 BCE   ***Political events*:**
(*1 January*) Imp. Caesar consul (4).
(*10 or 23 August*) Imp. Caesar founds Nikopolis in Egypt.
(*November/December*) *Lex Saenia*: adlects plebeians to the patrician class.

***Military events*:**
Alexandrian War (*Bellum Alexandreae*) – (*1 August*) Alexandria falls to Imp.
     Caesar's troops; Egypt annexed as a province Aegyptus.
Imp Caesar acclaimed *imperator* (VII?)

29 BCE   ***Political events*:**
(*1 January*) Imp. Caesar consul (5).
(*11 January*) Doors of Temple of Ianus closed.
Augustus *censor*, purges the Senate.
(*18 August*) Temple of Divus Iulius and Curia Iulia dedicated.
(*28 August*) Altar of Victoria dedicated inside the Curia Iulia.

***Military events*:**
Moesian War (*Bellum Moesum*), Year 1: M. Licinius Crassus campaigns against the
     Bastarnae, Moesi and other peoples.
African War: unspecified conflict after which L. Autronius Paetus is acclaimed
     imperator and awarded a full triumph.
Dacian War (*Bellum Dacicum*): Cn. Cornelius Lentulus campaigns against the
     Getae under King Cotiso.
Sarmatian War (*Bellum Sarmaticum*): Cn. Cornelius Lentulus campaigns in
     Sarmatia.
Cantabrian War (*Bellum Cantabricum*), led by Statilius Taurus.
(*13–15 August*) Caesar's 'Triple Triumph' for victories in Illyricum, Actium and
     Alexandria.
Revolts in Heroöpolis and Thebais, Egypt, in protest at treatment by tax collectors.
Cornelius Gallus sets Roman border between Egypt and Ethiopia at Meroë at the
     First Cataract; makes Ethiopia a Roman protectorate (*RG* 26.5).

28 BCE   ***Political events*:**
(*1 January*) Imp. Caesar consul (6) with Agrippa (2).
Restoration of *iura et leges populi Romani*.
Imp. Caesar named *princeps senatus*; appointed *censor*: first purge of the Senate.

Military events:

(*9 October*) Temple of Apollo dedicated on Palatinus Hill.

Moesian War, Year 2: M. Licinius Crassus campaigns against the Bastarnae, Moesi and other peoples; awarded a triumph by the Senate – claims the *spolia opima* denied by Augustus, offered a triumph *in lieu*.

(*26 May 26*) C. Calvisius Sabinus celebrates a triumph for victories in Hispania.

(*14 July 14*) C. Carrinas celebrates a triumph for victories over the Galli.

27–19 BCE	Augustus' First *Decennium*

27 BCE   **Political events:**

(*1 January*) Imp. Caesar consul (7) with Agrippa (3).

(*13 January*) Imp. Caesar granted control over a large *provincia* and permitted right to delegate its administration to *legati* (deputies); awarded *corona civica* for saving lives of citizens.

(*16 January*) Imp. Caesar granted title *Augustus* and right to display the *clipeus virtutis*; *imperium* confirmed for ten years.

Augustus goes to *Tres Galliae*, conducts census, holds assizes in Narbo.

Augustus falls seriously ill.

Military events:

Aquitanian War.

(*July*) Triumph of M. Licinius Crassus for victories against the Bastarnae. Moesi and 'other peoples'.

(*25 September*) Triumph of M. Valerius Messalla Corvinus for victories over the Aquitani.

26 BCE   **Political events:**

(*1 January*) Augustus consul (8).

Augustus in Hispania.

Military events:

Cantabrian War, Year 1: Three-pronged attack led by Augustus, P. Carisius and Antistius Vetus.

25 BCE   **Political events:**

(*1 January*) Augustus consul (9).

Augustus in Hispania.

Doors of Temple of Ianus closed for second time.

Foundation of *Colonia* Augusta Praetoria Salassorum.

Military events:

Cantabrian and Asturian War (*Bellum Cantabricum et Asturicum*), Year 2: P. Carisius defeats Astures, Antistius Vetus defeats Cantabri.

Salassian War: Salassi defeated by M. Terentius Varro. Watchtowers erected in Swiss Alps.

German War: M. Vinicius invades Germania; Augustus acclaimed *imperator* (VIII).

Thracian War: M. Licinius Crassus campaigns against the Thraci and Moesi.

24 BCE   **Political events:**

(*1 January*) Augustus consul (10).

Augustus falls seriously ill.

Tiberius *quaestor*.

Military events:

Revolt in Cantabria: defeated by L. Aelius Lamia.

Aelius Gallus moves east into Arabia; encounters the Nabataeans; army struck down with sickness; returns to Egypt.

23 BCE   *Political events*:
(*1 January*) Augustus consul (11).
Conspiracies of M. Primus (*proconsul* of Macedonia) and A. Terentius Varro
  Murena (*consul*).
(*June*) In Rome: Augustus resigns consulship; granted *tribunicia potestas* (the status
  and privileges – but not the burdens of the office – of a Tribune of the People).
  In provinces: Augustus' *imperium proconsulare* renewed for five years (extended
  to *maius*?); M. Agrippa granted *imperium* for five years.
Augustus falls seriously ill.

Military events:
Kandake of Kush invades southern Egypt; C. Petronius retaliates.
Frahâta of Parthia sends an embassy to Augustus requesting return of his son: he
  proposes a negotiated settlement.

22 BCE   *Political events*:
Augustus is offered, but refuses, powers of dictator and perpetual consulships,
  accepts *cura annonae*.
Augustus refutes unlawfully interfering in affairs of Macedonia.
Attempts to assassinate Augustus, by Ignatius Rufus, Murena implicated.

21 BCE   *Political events*:
Riots in Rome.
Augustus receives emissaries from Kandake of Kush, Ethiopia at Samos.
Augustus enslaves people of towns of Kyzikos, Tyre and Sidon for riot and
  unlawful killings of Roman citizens.
Augustus distributes territories among client kings.

Military events:
C. Petronius agrees peace treaty with Kandake of Kush.

20 BCE   *Political events*:
Augustus agrees to settlement with Armenia and Parthia: *aquilae* and *signa* lost at
  Carrhae 53 BCE returned to Tiberius.

Military events:
Agrippa in *Tres Galliae*; crosses Rhine?
(*12 May*) Augustus acclaimed *imperator* (IX).
Garamantian Campaign: *proconsul* of Africa L. Cornelius Balbus attacks Garamanti
  for raiding, and captures fifteen of their settlements.

19 BCE   *Political events*:
Riots in Rome.
(*12 October*) Augustus enters Rome with *aquilae* and *signa* from Parthia, granted
  additional privileges, *summum imperium auspiciumque*.
(*15 December*) Altar of Fortunae Reducis dedicated.

Military events:
(*27 March*) Triumph of L. Cornelius Balbus.
Gallic Revolt: M. Agrippa agreed to resettlement of Ubii on Roman terrritory;
  refuses triumphal honours.
Cantabrian and Asturian War: M. Agrippa restores morale to Roman army and
  leads troops to victory.

18–9 BCE   Augustus' Second ***Decennium***

18 BCE   *Political events*:
Augustus' and Agrippa's *imperium* renewed for five years.
Augustus purges the Senate.
Attempt to assassinate Augustus.

17 BCE	***Political events:***
	(*May–June*) Celebration of the *Ludi Saeculares*.
	(*4 June–15 July*) Augustus adopts sons of M. Agrippa, Caius and Lucius.
	Military events:
	Lollian Disaster (*Clades Lolliana*): M. Lollius defeated by an alliance of Tencteri, Sugambri and Uspetes, led by warlord Maelo, which invades Belgica and takes the *aquila* of *Legio* V *Alaudae*.
16 BCE	***Political events:***
	(*24 May*) Nero Claudius Drusus (the future Germanicus Caesar) born in Rome.
	Augustus and Tiberius travel to Gallia Comata, stay in *Colonia* Copia Felix Munatia.
	Tiberius appointed *Legatus Augusti Pro Praetore* of Gallia Comata and Belgica.
	M. Agrippa in Syria.
	Military events:
	P. Silius Nerva campaigns against Camunni, Vennii and Pannonii.
15 BCE	***Political events:***
	Augustus re-organizes the provinces of the Galliae and the Hispaniae.
	Procurator Licinius affair (?)
	Foundation of Augusta Vindelicorum.
	Military events:
	Alpine War (*Bellum Alpinum*): Nero Claudius Drusus leads campaign against the Raeti via the Reschen Pass; Raeti continue attacks in *Tres Galliae*: Drusus, joined by Tiberius with forces from Lugdunum, crush Vindelici.
	(*1 August*) Fall of *oppidum* of Genauni to Drusus.
	Norican War (*Bellum Noricum*): Drusus and Tiberius advance on the Kingdom of Noricum and annex it. Alpine nations provide auxiliary troops to Rome.
	Augustus acclaimed *imperator* (X).
	P. Sulpicius Quirinius campaigns against the Nasamones, Marmaridae and Garamantes in Cyrenaica.
14 BCE	***Political events:***
	Drusus appointed *legatus Augusti pro praetore* of *Tres Galliae*, relocates to *Colonia* Copia Felix Munatia.
	Military events:
	Drusus (?) subdues the Comati, Alpes Maritimae subjugated, made a prefecture.
	German War: Drusus begins preparations for invasion of Germania, befriends the Batavi, establishes military camps along the Rhine. Work begins on excavating the *fossa Drusiana*.
	Revolt of Scribonius: Agrippa squashes usurper's rebellion in the Cimerian Bosporus with help from Herodes and Polemon; refuses triumphal honours.
	Pannonian War (*Bellum Pannonicum*), Year 1: revolt of the Pannonii. M. Vinicius unable to contain the uprising.
13 BCE	***Political events:***
	(*1 January*) Tiberius *consul* (1).
	Augustus returns to Rome.
	Augustus' and Agrippa's *imperium* renewed for another five years.
	Augustus purges the Senate.
	(*4 July*) Senate votes to erect *Ara Pacis Augustae* in Rome.
	Theatre of Balbus opened.
	Census in *Tres Galliae* (?).

Military events:

Augustus makes reforms to pay, length of service and retirement benefits of the army.

Thracian War (*Bellum Thracicum*), Year 1: Raiskuporis I of Thracia slain in battle by Vologases, revolt of the Bessi.

Pannonian War, Year 2: M. Agrippa suppresses rebellion in Pannonia.

12 BCE   *Political events*:

Roimetalkes succeeds Raiskuporis as king of Thrace.

(*6 March*) Lepidus dies: Augustus appointed *Pontifex Maximus*.

(*? March*) M. Agrippa dies in Campania.

Consecration of Altar of *Roma et Augustus* at Condate, *Colonia* Copia Felix Munatia.

Nero Claudius Drusus appointed *praetor urbanus*.

Military events:

Thracian War, Year 2: L. Calpurnius Piso engages the Bessi.

Pannonian War, Year 3: Tiberius goes to Illyricum. Tiberius and Vinicius campaign against the alliance of the Breuci.

Homonadensian War: Quirinus wages war against the Homonadenses in Cilicia and Galatia.

Nero Claudius Drusus foils a rebellion in *Tres Galliae*.

German War (*Bellum Germanicum*), Year 1: Drusus launches an attack from Batavodurum against the Sugambri, Tencteri and Usipetes; takes fleet across Lacus Flevo; negotiates treaties with the Cananefates, Chauci and Frisii; navigates the Ems River and defeats the Bructeri in a river battle. On the return journey fleet is marooned on the Dutch coast, but rescued by the Frisii.

Augustus acclaimed *imperator* (XI).

11 BCE   *Political events*:

Drusus and Tiberius receive *imperium proconsulare*.

Senate decrees doors of the Temple of Ianus closed, but deferred.

Tiberius divorces Vipsania, marries Iulia.

Military events:

Pannonian War, Year 4: Tiberius campaigns against the alliances of Daesitiates and Breuci.

Thracian War, Year 3: L. Calpurnius Piso defeats rebels.

German War, Year 2: Nero Claudius Drusus returns to *Tres Galliae*; launches campaign from Vetera along the Lippe River; engages the Cherusci, Marsi and Usipetes; reaches the Weser River; and narrowly avoids defeat at Battle of Arbalo at hands of Cherusci.

Drusus' acclamation as *imperator* denied and claimed by Augustus (XII): Drusus granted an *ovatio* with triumphal ornaments instead.

10 BCE   *Political events*:

Augustus and Tiberius return to Lugdunum.

(*1 August*) Birth of Ti. Claudius Nero (future emperor Claudius) in *Colonia* Copia Felix Munatia; dedication of Altar of *Roma et Augustus* at Condate before an assembly of the Gallic tribal leaders. Nero Claudius Drusus returns to Rome with Augustus and Tiberius.

Military events:

Pannonian War, Year 5: final conquest by Tiberius.

German War, Year 3: Nero Claudius Drusus launches new phase of campaign from Mogontiacum; defeats the Chatti and Marcomanni; granted limited triumphal honours.

Dacian War (*Bellum Dacicum*)/Sarmatian War (*Bellum Sarmaticum*): Cn. Cornelius
Lentulus Augur engages the Daci and Sarmati.
Syllaeus/Nacebus challenge Herodes the Great.

9 BCE   ***Political events*:**
(*1 January*) Nero Claudius Drusus *consul*.
(*30 January*) Dedication of *Ara Pacis Augustae* in Rome.
Tiberius in Illyricum.
Nero Claudius Drusus' body carried to Ticinum, met by Augustus and Livia, and
on to Rome for state funeral, buried in Augustus' Mausoleum.

***Military events*:**
German War, Year 4: Nero Claudius Drusus launches second campaign from
Mogontiacum, reaches the Elbe River; erects an altar on the banks of the Elbe
River, turns back to the Rhine; fatally wounded in an accident.
Tiberius rides 200 miles in 24 hours by vehicle from Ticinum to join him. Thirty
days after the accident, Nero Claudius Drusus dies.
Augustus acclaimed *imperator* (XIII).
Tiberius acclaimed *imperator* (I).

8 BCE–3 CE   Augustus Third *Decennium*

8 BCE   ***Political events*:**
Augustus' *imperium* renewed for ten years. *Censor* with right to conduct a census.
Senate votes Drusus and his male descendants the *agnomen* 'Germanicus', erects
statues and a triumphal arch over the *Via Appia*. Rhine legions erect the
Tumulus (Cenotaph – the *Eichelstein*) honouring Drusus in Mogontiacum.
Reform of the calender, with month *Sextilis* renamed *Augustus*.

***Military events*:**
German War, Year 5: Tiberius in Germania Magna, negotiates a peace settlement
with all Germanic tribes; Maelo surrenders, Sugambri relocate to region around
Vetera, renamed Cugerni, and thereafter supply auxiliary cavalry to Rome.
Augustus acclaimed *imperator* (XIV).
Tiberius acclaimed *imperator* (II).
Polemon of Pontus engages the Aspurgiani in Phanagoria, is defeated, taken
prisoner and executed.

7 BCE   ***Political events*:**
(*1 January*) Augustus *consul* (11) with Tiberius (2)
Doors of the Temple of Ianus closed (?)

***Military events*:**
Tiberius celebrates *ovatio* in Rome for his victories in German War.

6 BCE   ***Political events*:**
Tiberius' *imperium* renewed, granted *tribunicia potestas* for five years; but withdraws
from public life unexpectedly, and retires to Rhodes.
Work begins on erecting the *Tropaeum Alpium* (La Turbie) marking the complete
subjugation of the Alps.

5 BCE   ***Political events*:**
(*1 January*) Augustus *consul* (12).
C. Caesar comes of age, designated *Princeps Iuventutis*.

***Military events*:**
Quirinius moves against the Homanadenses of Taurus.

4 BCE	***Political events*:**
	Death of Herodes (Herod the Great) in Jericho.
	Attempt to assassinate Augustus by Cn. Cornelius.
	***Military events*:**
	Revolts in Iudaea against Archelaos. Qunctilius Varus intervenes from Syria.
3 BCE	–
2 BCE	***Political events*:**
	(*1 January*) Augustus *consul* (13) for last time.
	(*5 February*) Augustus given accolade *Pater Patriae*.
	(*12 May*) Dedication of the *Forum Augustum* and Temple of Mars Ultor.
	L. Caesar comes of age, designated *princeps iuventutis*.
	Iulia arrested for adultery and treason, exiled to Pandateria; Tiberius divorces Iulia.
	***Military events*:**
	Augustus appoints two *praefecti* to command the *Cohortes Praetoriae*.
	Domitius Ahenobarbus intercepts Hermunduri, finds them land in vacated Marcomannic territory.
1 BCE	***Political events*:**
	(*29 January*) C. Caesar departs Rome to begin his mission to the East with *imperium proconsulare*.
	Doors of the Temple of Ianus closed for the third time?
1 CE	***Political events*:**
	(*1 January*) C. Caesar *consul* In Syria.
	Germanicus comes of age, assumes the *toga virilis*.
	***Military events*:**
	Marmaridian (Marmaric) War, Year 1: campaign against the Marmaridae on the frontier of Cyrenaica.
	German Revolt: L. Domitius Ahenobarbus, *legatus Augusti pro praetore* of Germania, suppresses revolt, crosses the Elbe, engages Hermunduri and negotiates settlement with Marboduus of the Marcommani; establishes an imperial cult altar and his headquarters at Ara Ubiorum.
	C. Caesar negotiates treaty with Frahâtak V of Parthia.
	Augustus acclaimed *imperator* (XV).
2 CE	***Political events*:**
	Death of C. Marcius Censorinus.
	(*20 August*) Death of L. Caesar at Massilia.
	Tiberius returns to Rome from Rhodes.
	***Military events*:**
	Armenian War (*Bellum Armeniacum*), Year 1: C. Caesar departs to intervene.
	Marmaridian War, Year 2: P. Sulpicius Quirinius, *proconsul* of Africa, defeats the Marmaridae.
	Sex. Aelius Catus oversees the transplantation of some 50,000 Getae across the Danube River to Macedonia.

3–11 CE   Augustus' Fourth *Decennium*

3 CE	***Political events*:**
	Augustus' *imperium* renewed for ten years.
	Iulia permitted to relocate to Rhegium.

Military events:
Armenian War, Year 2. Siege of Artagira.
(*9 September*) C. Caesar wounded at Artagira, Armenia.
Augustus acclaimed *imperator* (XVI).

4 CE **Political events:**
(*21 February*) Death of C. Caesar in Limyra.
(*26 June*) Augustus adopts Tiberius and Agrippa Postumus. Tiberius, adopts
   Germanicus.
Tiberius granted *imperium* and *tribunicia potestas* for five years.
C. Sentius Saturninus appointed *legatus Augusti pro praetore* of Germania.

Military events:
German Revolt: Tiberius campaigns in Germania, defeats the Bructeri, recalls
   Cherusci to loyalty.

5 CE **Political events:**
Earthquake strikes Rome. Tiber floods.
Famine in Rome.
Germanicus marries Vipsania Agrippina.

Military events:
Augustus reaches settlement with Senate over funding retirement bonus costs of
   soldiers.
German Revolt: Tiberius in Germania Magna, reaches the Elbe River.

6 CE **Political events:**
Famine continues in Rome; fire destroys parts of the city.
Germanicus appointed *augur*.
Germanicus and his brother Claudius sponsor games in honour of their father.
Birth of Nero Iulius Caesar (Germanicus' first son).

Military events:
Augustus establishes the *Aerarium Militare* to fund soldiers' retirement
   payments.
Numerous (unidentified) cities in revolt.
Brigandage rife in Sardinia.
Judaean Revolt: led by Iudas (of Gamala) the Galilean against the census, crushed
   by Quirinius.
Isaurian Revolt: in Asia Minor Cornelius Cossus (M. Plautius Silvanus?, *legatus* of
   Galatia-Pamphylia) squashes revolt of Isauri.
Gaetulican War (*Bellum Gaetulicum*): in Africa, *proconsul* Cossus Cornelius
   Lentulus defeats Gaetulici and Musulami: awarded triumphal ornaments and
   agnomen Gaetulicus.
Marcomannic War: Tiberius and C. Sentius Saturninus launch invasion of
   Bohaemium, but abort it when forces have to be redeployed to suppress major
   revolt in Illyricum (Dalmatia and Pannonia).
Batonian War (*Bellum Batonianum*) or Greater Dalmatian War or Great Illyrian
   Revolt, Year 1: Bato of the Breuci, Bato of the Daesidiates agree to work
   together.
In Rome Germanicus raises *Cohortes Voluntariarum*, marches to Illyricum.
Augustus acclaimed *imperator* (XVII).
Tiberius acclaimed *imperator* (III).

7 CE **Political events:**
Germanicus *quaestor*.

Military events:
Batonian War, Year 2: Tiberius and Germanicus with reserves in Illyricum. Battle at Mons Claudius, Volcaean Marshes.
Tiberius at Siscia.

8 CE

Political events:
Batonian War, Year 3: Tiberius and Germanicus in Illyricum.
(*3 August*) Pannonii submit after defeat at Bathinus River.
Bato of the Breuci murdered by Bato of the Daesidiates.
Augustus acclaimed *imperator* (XVIII).
Tiberius acclaimed *imperator* (IV).

9 CE

Political events:
Tiberius' *imperium* and *tribunicia potestas* renewed for five years.
Germanicus *praetor*.
Agrippa Postumus banished to Planasia.

Military events:
Batonian War, Year 4: Tiberius and Germanicus campaign in Illyricum. Bato of the Daesidiates surrenders, revolt squashed.
Augustus acclaimed *imperator* (XIX).
Tiberius acclaimed *imperator* (V), granted full triumph.
Germanicus acclaimed *imperator*, granted triumphal ornaments.
Varian Disaster (*Clades Variana*): P. Quinctilius Varus and *Legiones* XVII, XVIII and XIX annihilated at Teutoburg Pass by Germanic alliance forces led by Arminius.
Tiberius takes conscripts from Rome to Rhine forts.

10 CE

Military events:
Tiberius campaigns in Germania.

11 CE

Military events:
Tiberius campaigns in Germania with Germanicus on military exercises; celebrates Augustus' birthday (23 September) on German soil.
Augustus acclaimed *imperator* (XX).
Tiberius acclaimed *imperator* (VI).

12 CE

Political events:
(*1 January*) Germanicus *consul* (1)
(*31 August(?)*) Birth of C. Iulius Caesar (nicknamed 'Caligula', Germanicus' fifth son) in Antium.

Military events:
(*23 October*) Tiberius celebrates full triumph in Rome for victories in Illyricum ('Greater Dalmatian War').

13–14 CE   **Augustus Fifth *Decennium***

13 CE

Political events:
Augustus' *imperium* renewed; Tiberius' *imperium* made equal with Augustus'.
Germanicus made *Legatus Augusti Pro Praetore* in *Tres Galliae* and Germania.

Military events:
Gallic Revolt: Germanicus puts down insurrection in *Tres Galliae* (?), acclaimed *imperator* (I).
Augustus acclaimed *imperator* (XXI).
Tiberius acclaimed *imperator* (VII).

14 CE   ***Political events*:**
Census of Rome (4,190,117 recorded citizens).
(*19 August*) Death of Augustus at Nola.
(*? September*) Augustus' state funeral, cremation and burial in his Mausoleum.
Will of Augustus read in Senate by Drusus Iulius Caesar.
(*17 September*) Deification of Augustus. Tiberius assumes role of *princeps senatus*,
   aged 56.
Agrippa Postumus executed. Germanicus granted *imperium proconsulare*.
Germanicus appointed one of the first *Sodales Augustales*.

***Military events*:**
Mutiny of Rhine and Danube legions: Germanicus and Drusus Iulius Caesar
   negotiate settlements with the legions. Germanicus leads men on punitive
   expedition against the Marsi.

Roman Names

M. Caelius T. *f.* Lemonia Bononia

This is the official name of a centurion of *Legio* XIIX preserved on an inscription now in the Rheinisches Landesmuseum in Bonn, Germany (*CIL* XIII 8648; *AE* 1952). His name embodies the elements of Roman naming practice. It translates as 'Marcus Caelius, son of Titus, of the voting tribe of Lemonia, from Bononia'. Marcus is his forename (*praenomen*) by which his family and close friends called him. In inscriptions, public records and narrative texts it was abbreviated. The standard abbreviations for common *praenomina* were:

A.	Aulus	M'.	Manius
Ap.	Appius	P	Publius
C. *or* G.	Caius or Gaius	Q	Quintus
Cn. *or* Gn.	Cnaeus or Gnaeus	Ser	Servius
D.	Decimus	Sex	Sextus
L.	Lucius	Sp.	Spurius
M.	Marcus	T.	Titus
Mam.	Mamius	Ti.	Tiberius

Caelius is his clan or family name (*nomen genticulum*). Many of these clans, such as the Claudia and Cornelia, were famous old families of Rome with proud traditions. Then follows the filiation or patrymonic of the father's *praenomen*, whose full name would have been Titus Caelius. As a Roman citizen, his family was associated with one of thirty-five voting tribes: in elections Caelius voted with the Lemonian tribe. The final element is the place of his birth (*origo*) or domicile (*domus*), which is in this case Bononia, modern Bologna in Italy. Together, these distinguished this particular Marcus Caelius from another bearing the same name. To clearly tell men apart with the same name, with their warped sense of humour, Romans often adopted a third nickname (*cognomen*) such as Rufus 'red haired', Paulus 'shorty' or Brutus 'stupid'. Men who had achieved great victories in war might be granted use of a honorific title commemorating where they were won, such as *Africanus* meaning 'the African' (or 'of Africa') or *Germanicus*, 'the German' (or 'of Germania').

Let him who desires peace prepare for war.

Qui desiderat pacem, praeparet bellum.

P. Flavius Vegetius Renatus, *On Military Matters* 3 Introduction.

Chapter 1

Seek and Destroy

31–28 BCE

31 BCE

Imp. Caesar Divi *f.* III	M. Antonius M. *f.* III
suff.	M. Valerius M. *f.* Messalla Corvinus
suff.	M. Titius L. *f.*
suff.	Cn. Pompeius Q. *f.*

It was no ordinary New Year's Day. Something was very amiss. When Imperator Caesar *Divi filius* (plate 1) swore his oath as consul, the members present in the Senate House in Rome could not fail to notice that the curule chair beside his was vacant.[1] In the *Res Publica* (the name by which the Romans proudly called their commonwealth) there should always be two consuls. It was a check and balance against the tyranny of rule by one man born of popular revolution and the overthrow of kings centuries before. This day, however, his colleague, M. Antonius (plate 5), elected to the office the previous autumn, was tarrying in Greece.

Once the younger and older man had been friends, bound in a mutual pact of vengeance. Over the months following the assassination of C. Iulius Caesar on the Ides of March 44 BCE, the two men joined with M. Aemilius Lepidus, a former commander of the deceased *dictator*. They were colleagues in a self-appointed commission of 'Three Men for the Restoration of the Commonwealth'.[2] Working together as *triumviri*, they had divided up the world among themselves, raised armies and hunted down the assassins to a mosquito-infested marsh close to Philippi and killed them in two battles; but over ten subsequent years the three men had become estranged.[3] Power had seduced their better natures. Iulius Caesar's legal heir had ambitions to be pre-eminent in Rome, and soon ousted Lepidus, but in his way was Antonius.[4] Meanwhile the East had beguiled his partner in power. The perception among his enemies in Rome was that Antonius had abandoned his responsibilities as an officer of the state and turned away from the Roman People. Matters culminated when it was discovered that he had had a scandalous affair with the queen of Egypt, Kleopatra VII (plate 4), and wedded her, despite already being married – in fact to Octavia, the well-liked sister of *triumvir* Imp. Caesar.[5] It was a personal slight to him, but not reason enough to go to war.[6] The insulted brother-in-law shrewdly looked elsewhere for his *casus belli*. In his eagerness for glory, Antonius had led military expeditions against Parthia in Armenia – campaigns not sanctioned by the Senate but bankrolled by the Egyptian queen, and which, moreover, had spectacularly failed with great loss of Roman lives.[7] Antonius had also divided up among his illegitimate children territories that properly belonged to the Roman state and that were officially due for assignment to Roman senators by lot.[8] Caesar expressed his views about these and other complaints in writing; Antonius responded in like manner.[9] The letters exchanged between the two men became ever more vitriolic, finally spilling over into open hostility.

The *toga*-clad men sitting in the *Curia Iulia* that cold January day already had an idea of what lay ahead: it was to be all-out war between the adversaries for a final resolution and the future of the '*imperium* (sovereignty) of the Roman People' (map 1). The victor would take all. Unlike his rival in the Orient, the 31-year old Imp. Caesar had wasted no time. For several months, and with consummate skill, he had been executing his strategy to win the hearts and minds of his countrymen, some with charm, others with coercion. In the spring of the previous year he had required the whole civilian population of Italy to swear the *sacramentum* (a military oath of allegiance to him personally), in effect amalgamating the Roman state into himself – tactfully, the members of Antonius' hereditary family were exempted from taking it.[10] Sensitive to how the public might perceive the coming struggle, Caesar sought to avoid the appearance of a conflict between fellow Roman citizens. It was the Egyptian regent who provided both the pretext and focus for Caesar's belligerence. Finally, in October, among the charges laid against Antonius *Imperator* was that he had allowed himself to be seduced by a woman – and not a Roman woman, but worse, a foreigner. She had demanded the Roman Empire from the besotted, drunken *triumvir*, he asserted, as payment for her favours.[11] It was a sham. 'These proceedings,' writes Dio, 'were nominally directed against Kleopatra, but really against Antonius.'[12] He was stripped of his authority.[13] Now, at the age of 52, he was just a private citizen once more. He would not be consul this year – or ever again.

With his military offensive legitimated by due process of law, Imp. Caesar invoked the favour of the gods too; he was, after all, as coins and inscriptions proclaimed, *Divi filius*, 'son of a god' – specifically the divine Iulius Caesar.[14] For full effect, he re-instituted an ancient rite in which a fetial, dressed in priestly garb, intoned a declaration of war, melodramatically striking an iron-tipped spear smeared with blood into a patch of ground designated enemy territory at the Temple of Bellona.[15] With the sworn support of the People and the Senate, and the blessings of the Roman gods, how could Caesar now lose?

Some 1,250 kilometres (777 miles) away in Athens, and oblivious to the rapidly unfolding events in the West, Antonius still believed himself the legitimate co-consul. In his own mind he had no reason to think otherwise. Reduced in number, purged of rogues and dominated by friends of his young rival, nevertheless Antonius had many sympathisers in the Senate; they despised the arrogant young upstart who, in their view, had undeservedly inherited the dictator's name. Over the last several years they had worked to promote Antonius' interests while he was away from Rome, and to undermine his rival's. It had culminated in 32 BCE when one of the year's consuls, C. Sosius, had denounced Imp. Caesar before the Conscript Fathers.[16] Caesar had not been there to face the accusations personally, but upon his return to Rome he convened a meeting of the Senate to

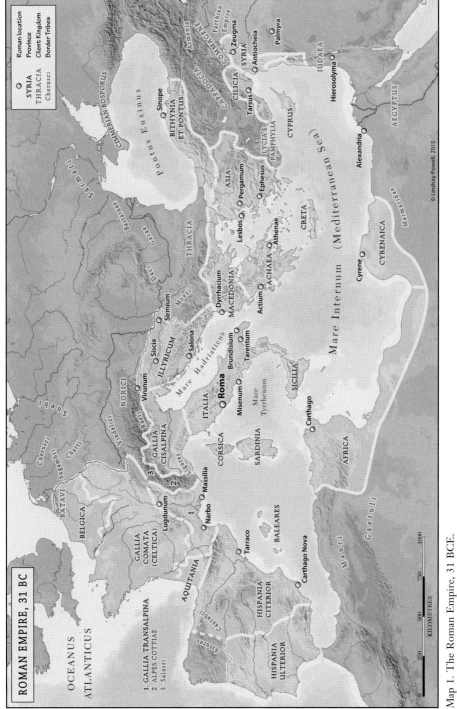

ROMAN EMPIRE, 31 BC

1. GALLIA TRANSALPINA
2. ALPES COTTIAE
3. Salassi

○	Roman location
SYRIA	Province
THRACIA	Client Kingdom
Cherusci	Border Tribes

© Lindsay Powell, 2015

Map 1. The Roman Empire, 31 BCE.

raise the matter. In the high-ceilinged chamber, he seated himself provocatively on a chair beside the two consuls, taking the precaution of bringing loyal soldiers who had daggers concealed in the folds of their togas.[17] At that extraordinary session he promised the next time they met to bring documents proving beyond a doubt Antonius' indiscretions. He also invited any man present who felt insecure to feel free to leave the city and join his champion. Many did – some 200 of the 900 senators fled, Sosius and his co-consul Cn. Domitius Ahenobarbus among them.[18] To emphasize the fact of Antonius' public ostracism, in Rome another man was elected to take his seat. M. Valerius Messalla Corvinus was the same age as Imp. Caesar. He had already proved loyal to him in battle and was considered a colleague who could be trusted to remain loyal in politics. Corvinus would be the first of many such career advancements that year to the highest office for services rendered – or expected. The die was cast. There would be no second throw.

The man who had brazenly taken *imperator* (plate 3) – meaning 'commander' – as his first name was no novice in war. He had personal experience of battle, and scars to prove it. Born on 23 September 63 BCE, his military career had not begun auspiciously, however. He had had the opportunity to learn first-hand from one of the greatest generals of all time when Iulius Caesar invited him as his great nephew, then just 16 years old, to join him in his campaign against the sons of Pompeius Magnus in Spain in 46 BCE. By an accident of timing, the teenage tyro had arrived too late – after the conflict had already concluded.[19] The second opportunity – the chance to accompany Iulius Caesar in a war against the Getae and Parthians in 44 BCE – had ended before it had even started when the great commander was cut down on 15 March.[20] But the young man quickly showed some of the promise the older relation had seen in him. A few months after the assassination, he successfully raised his own legions from among veterans who had served his great uncle and, at the Senate's insistence, had taken them into action against the then outlaw M. Antonius at the Battle of Forum Gallorum and siege of Mutina in April 43 BCE.[21] He commanded those troops against the rebel L. Antonius at Perusia (modern Perugia) in 41 BCE and at Fulginiae (Foligno) the following year, and against the renegade Sex. Pompeius in Sicily in 36 BCE.[22] He had led campaigns to quell rebellions in Illyricum and shown courage when he personally led charges at the sieges of Metulus in 35 BCE and Setovia in 34 BCE, and had sustained serious injuries in the attacks.[23]

Yet those campaigns had also revealed to him his limitations as a field commander. He was not a tough, 'lead from the front' warrior like Iulius Caesar. He was not even widely regarded as a 'man's man'. Sex. Pompeius taunted him as effeminate and M. Antonius mocked him for having won the favour of Iulius Caesar through 'unnatural relations'; another rumour suggested he had sold his body to one of the dictator's commanders while in Spain.[24] Of course, these allegations may have been nothing more than slanders by his enemies in an attempt to belittle him in the eyes of the public. Physically, he was considered short at 5 foot 9 inches in height, but thought handsome, with clear, bright eyes, curly blondish hair and in his comportment he carried himself gracefully.[25] However, his physical health was his weakness. Suetonius reports that he was not very strong in his left hip, thigh and leg, and even limped slightly at times.[26] 'In the course of his life,' writes his biographer, 'he suffered from several severe and dangerous illnesses.'[27] Embarrassing for him as a general was that he frequently became sick *before* battle, causing him to have to be carried back to his tent to recover while the fighting raged – a fact his enemies remorselessly exploited.[28]

His great strengths were his deep ambition, unyielding tenacity and ruthless intelligence. He had the ability to assess complex problems, to think strategically and operate tactically – whether it was manipulating the law, political connections, public relations or religion – and he knew how and when to use war, or the threat of it, to advance his cause. He also had the foresight to know he could not fight wars on his own, and, unlike his great uncle, that when he had won he could not run the empire by himself alone.

He had one capacity that would prove increasingly important and help to account for his exceptional achievement: he could consistently pick good men as personal advisors and for command positions. Regardless of background or class, and even if they had once served his enemies, it was ability that mattered most to him. He developed this talent early in his life. In his teens he had surrounded himself with a small, tight group of friends – Iulius Caesar had even complimented him on the quality of his companions, because they were observant young men and strove to attain excellence.[29] He understood the value of sound advice borne of experience. He was mentored by his great uncle, who saw potential in the young man, and in the months after his murder – when he was just 19 years old – by the commander's own close advisers too, in particular the Jewish financier and former consul (40 BCE), L. Cornelius Balbus (Balbus the Elder), and Iulius Caesar's private secretary and biographer, C. Oppius.[30] Few men alive at the time knew the dictator's mind so well as those two men. He had also received guidance from the foremost statesman M. Tullius Cicero (*cos.* 63 BCE) and his fellow triumvirs, Antonius and Lepidus – at least until he considered that advice was no longer useful. Caesar did not make friends easily, but when he did he remained stubbornly loyal to them; what he could not tolerate was betrayal.[31]

The events of 31 BCE would be the greatest test yet of those abilities. By the start of the new year, Caesar had his hand-picked military leadership team already in place. He had delegated overall strategic command of the anticipated war against Antonius and Kleopatra (*Bellum cum Antonio et Cleopatra*) to his best friend and confidant M. Agrippa (plate 2).[32] With thick eyebrows, short tousled hair and a fine aquiline nose, his pleasant facial features belied his ability to conceive cunning solutions to complex problems, and a willingness to selflessly risk his own life in pursuit of them. He was among the last of the small group which had been with young Caesar at Apollonia when news had reached him of his great uncle's murder.[33] Since then Caesar had come to trust him absolutely and he now ranked foremost among his generals. A man of almost the same age, Agrippa's humble – likely plebeian – background was well known and despised by the Roman aristocracy of old patrician families; in large part it was because he was a *novus homo*, a man lacking the prestige of coming from a family from which a member had served as a consul.[34] Yet in the previous decade, over several campaigns in different theatres of war, he had displayed a flair for battle. Indeed, to the chagrin of many senators, Agrippa had demonstrated many of the qualities the same supercilious aristocrats championed in a war hero and aspired to publicly display themselves. Practicality, preparation, persistence and unpretentiousness were the hallmarks of his leadership style.[35] By now he was a battle-hardened commander with a formidable reputation. He had quelled a rebellion in Aquitania and was only the second man since Iulius Caesar to cross the Rhine River with troops, for which actions he was granted a triumph (the highest military honour the Roman Commonwealth could grant a citizen) yet declined to celebrate it in deference to his friend, who was enjoying less success in his own campaign against Sex. Pompeius.[36] Crucially for the coming war against Antonius (fig. 1), Agrippa had proved he could defeat an opponent at sea. Five years earlier he had led Imp. Caesar's fleet to victory in two battles off the coast of Sicily against the same Pompeius whose piratical attacks on shipping carrying the grain that fed Rome's poor had posed an existential threat to Caesar's precarious political position. His definitive victories there had won him a unique award of a naval crown, specially created for him by his grateful friend.[37] All the more remarkably, Agrippa had taught himself the art of fighting on water and beaten a resourceful and much more experienced practitioner of it. Caesar now gambled his entire future upon the abundant talents of Agrippa.

Like Caesar, Agrippa was a thinker and a planner. In the closing months of 32 BCE he had reviewed the military situation to formulate his military strategy. Intelligence reports revealed that Antonius had established garrisons in many towns and shore forts along the coast of Greece, as far east as *Colonia* Laus Iulia Corinthiensis (modern Corinth), and that he had moved at least part of his fleet and land army to Kerkyra (Corfu), the westernmost Greek island (map 2).[38] The deployment could be interpreted as defensive, but more likely it suggested that

Figure 1. *Triumvir* M. Antonius paid his troops with silver coins struck at a military mint. This specimen calls out *Legio* V. The sleek warship, powered by oars, is shown with mast down and sail furled.

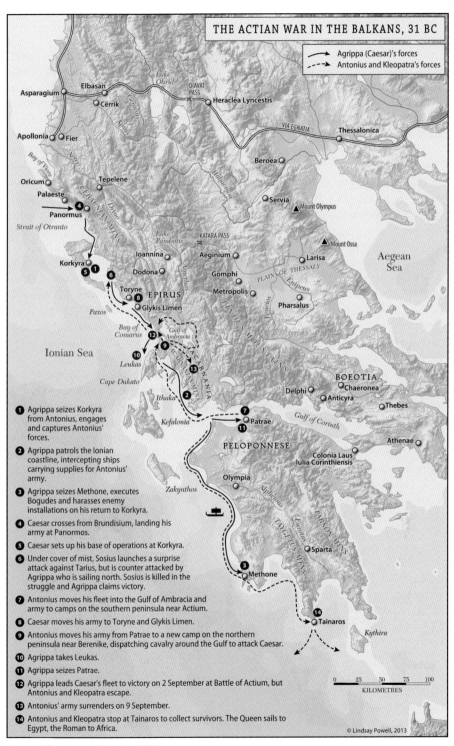

THE ACTIAN WAR IN THE BALKANS, 31 BC

→ Agrippa (Caesar)'s forces
⇢ Antonius and Kleopatra's forces

Asparagium
Elbasan
Cërrik
Lake Ohrid
DIAVAT PASS
Heraclea Lyncestis
VIA EGNATIA
Thessalonica
Apollonia
Fier
Beroea
Bay of Vlora
Oricum
Palaeste
Tepelene
Servia
Mount Olympus
Panormus
Strait of Otranto
Lake Pambotis
KATARA PASS
Mount Ossa
Aegean Sea
Korkyra
Ioannina
Aeginium
Larisa
Dodona
Gomphi
PLAIN OF THESSALY
Toryne
EPIRUS
Metropolis
Pharsalus
Glykis Limen
Paxos
Bay of Comarus
Gulf of Ambracia
PINDUS MOUNTAINS
Ionian Sea
Leukas
Cape Dukato
BOEOTIA
Chaeronea
Delphi
Anticyra
Ithaka
Thebes
Kefalonia
Patrae
Athenae
PELOPONNESE
Colonia Laus
Iulia Corinthiensis
Olympia
Zakynthos
Sparta
TAYGETUS MTNS
Methone
Tainaros
Kythira

1. Agrippa seizes Korkyra from Antonius, engages and captures Antonius' forces.

2. Agrippa patrols the Ionian coastline, intercepting ships carrying supplies for Antonius' army.

3. Agrippa seizes Methone, executes Bogudes and harasses enemy installations on his return to Korkyra.

4. Caesar crosses from Brundisium, landing his army at Panormos.

5. Caesar sets up his base of operations at Korkyra.

6. Under cover of mist, Sosius launches a surprise attack against Tarius, but is counter attacked by Agrippa who is sailing north. Sosius is killed in the struggle and Agrippa claims victory.

7. Antonius moves his fleet into the Gulf of Ambracia and army to camps on the southern peninsula near Actium.

8. Caesar moves his army to Toryne and Glykis Limen.

9. Antonius moves his army from Patrae to a new camp on the northern peninsula near Berenike, dispatching cavalry around the Gulf to attack Caesar.

10. Agrippa takes Leukas.

11. Agrippa seizes Patrae.

12. Agrippa leads Caesar's fleet to victory on 2 September at Battle of Actium, but Antonius and Kleopatra escape.

13. Antonius' army surrenders on 9 September.

14. Antonius and Kleopatra stop at Tainaros to collect survivors. The Queen sails to Egypt, the Roman to Africa.

0 25 50 75 100
KILOMETRES

© Lindsay Powell, 2013

Map 2. The Actian War, 31 BCE.

Antonius intended an amphibious invasion of Italy. With Antonius representing a threat to the security of the homeland, Agrippa wasted no time and immediately dispatched a small flotilla across the Adriatic Sea to block him. Any element of surprise was lost when Antonius' scouts situated off the Caraunian Mountains spied Agrippa's ships coming. That might have been his chance to knock Agrippa out of the war, but Antonius then made a serious tactical blunder. Believing these vessels were the vanguard of Caesar's main fleet, he advanced no further and withdrew to set up his winter quarters at Patrae (modern Patras).[39] Agrippa immediately grasped the island from the clutches of the *triumvir*. The windfall gain of Kerkyra gave Imp. Caesar's force a vital forward base from which to launch operations along the Greek coast. Agrippa wasted no time and 'pursued and routed the fugitives in a naval battle, and finally, after accomplishing many acts of the utmost cruelty, came back to Caesar'.[40]

In the spring of 31 BCE Antonius moved his fleet again, this time into the relatively shallow waters of the Gulf of Ambracia. He established a camp to control access to it on the southern peninsula near a small hamlet called Aktio; it is better known by its Latin name Actium.[41] Measuring 40km (25 miles) long and 15km (9 miles) wide, Antonius' first impressions of the Gulf of Ambracia must have been that it was a safe harbour for his and Kleopatra's combined fleet. In the meantime, Agrippa was not a man to sit idle. Over the months following that initial encounter at Kerkyra he had led patrols, scoured the Ionian Sea for the transports moving slowly under the weight of foodstuffs and munitions destined for Antonius' forces, and captured many of them.[42] To further weaken the renegade *triumvir*'s position, Agrippa landed an army at Methone (modern Methoni), a coastal town with stout defences located on the southwestern-most tip of the Peloponnese, which was a first port of call for ships arriving from Asia, Egypt and Syria. Antonius' ally, Bogudes, king of Mauretania, was in charge of the stronghold. Agrippa besieged it. The town soon fell and Bogudes was captured and executed.[43] Heading north again, Agrippa's attack fleet hunted for enemy vessels and bases on the Greek mainland, constantly degrading his opponent's resources and causing Antonius no little concern.[44] Commanding a group of Antonius' ships was Sosius, a man with previous experience of war fighting who knew what he was doing. In a fog-enshrouded dawn skirmish, he ambushed Caesar's ships commanded by L. Tarius Rufus, but failed to capture him. Then, by chance, returning from Methone, Agrippa intercepted Sosius and engaged him in a fight, but Antonius' man yet again evaded capture.[45]

In Italy, Imp. Caesar was greatly encouraged by the reports he received of Agrippa's successful hunter strategy. Leaving Rome in the care of his trusted political advisor C. Cilnius Maecenas, he relocated to the city of Brundisium, which was a vital seaport for travellers to the East. There he addressed many of his supporters, impressing on them that he had the largest and most loyal constituency among the Roman people sympathetic to his cause.[46] By March or April of 31 BCE, the main body of his army and navy was assembled at Brundisium, while other units were at Tarentum. Caesar led his force across the Adriatic Sea, unopposed, to the island of Kerkyra. Finding the main city of Corcyra abandoned, he occupied it, anchoring his ships in the adjacent Fresh Water Harbour. From here Actium was just 150km (93 miles) to the southeast. He intended to sail directly to Actium, but a storm blew up, preventing him from landing there.[47] When calm seas returned, Caesar finally gave the order for his main force to cross to the Gulf of Ambracia. He hoped to capture Antonius' fleet undamaged.[48]

Antonius had now been at Actium for weeks. After an initial survey, he had taken what seemed the prime position on the southern promontory and established his army camp close to the hamlet, which was also a place sacred to the god Apollo.[49] The longer he remained there, the more apparent it became to him that his choice of location was a liability; as much as protecting his fleet, the shape of the bay also worked to trap his ships inside.[50] Its narrow opening to the Ionian Sea – a mere 700-metre wide channel between Actium on the south and Berenike (modern Berenikea) on the north – formed a bottleneck which Caesar's fleet could blockade at will. The southern promontory projected northwards into the channel formed by the curve of the opposite shore. In the meantime, his troops had erected watchtowers on each side of the spur of land at the entrances of the channel and stationed ships in between to patrol it.[51] Antonius may have planned for the battle with Caesar to take place earlier in the year, but it was not to be.

Antonius had installed his men 'on the farther side of the narrows, beside the sanctuary [of Apollo], in a level and broad space', but as a long-term base of operations the site:

> was more suitable as a place for fighting than for encamping; it was because of this fact more than any other that they suffered severely from disease, not only during the winter, but much more during the summer.[52]

Malaria and dysentery are suspected of spreading misery among his troops. Agrippa's ongoing attacks on Antonius' supply ships succeeded in denying Antonius' men much-needed fresh provisions. The morale of the ordinary soldiers, which had been high at the beginning of the year, was sapped by the rising heat and worsening living conditions.[53] Flies constantly irritated the men, buzzing around their eyes and lips, congregating when they relieved themselves in the makeshift latrines, then landing on their food as they ate. Logistics could yet make or break Antonius. As long as he held on to the Gulf of Corinth, grain and other supplies brought from the parts of Greece still loyal to him could sustain his troops and keep them loyal.[54] As a precaution, he also required his allies and client kingdoms in the East to provide equipment for his campaign.[55]

In May or June, Caesar finally landed his troops on the shores of Epirus 'and took up a position on high ground there from which there is a view over all the outer sea around the Paxos islands and over the inner – Ambracian – gulf, as well as over the intervening waters'.[56] By design or good fortune, it was an excellent location: his men enjoyed clean water from the nearby springs and Louros River and a continuous supply of fresh provisions could land from Italy; in contrast to Antonius' men Caesar's were in good health and high spirits – and likely to remain so.[57] Caesar quickly established a defensible position, constructing entrenchments down to the outer harbour called Comarus (Komaros).[58] From there the ships could assemble on the Ionian Sea to blockade the enemy fleet. There is an apocryphal story that ships were also active on the other side in the Gulf. Writing some two centuries after the battle, Dio recounts that it was said Caesar had ordered many of his triremes (three-banked warships) dragged over land:

> using newly flayed hides smeared with olive oil instead of runways, yet I am unable to name any exploit of these ships inside the Gulf and therefore cannot believe the tradition; for it certainly would have been no small task to draw triremes over so narrow and uneven a tract of land on hides. Nevertheless, this feat is said to have been accomplished in the manner described.[59]

The *Bellum Actiense* (Actian Campaign), as it would come to be known, would comprise both land and sea operations. While Agrippa took personal charge of the fleet, he needed a trusted deputy to lead the army. He chose T. Statilius Taurus. He was a man five or six years his senior and, like himself, a *novus homo*. They had served as consuls together in 37 BCE – Agrippa's first – and developed a good, robust working relationship. Taurus was a showier personality than his superior, but he was as dedicated to fulfilling his mission and just as courageous. In 36 BCE he had seen action in the war against Sex. Pompeius, commanding a fleet of ships on loan from Antonius off the coast of Africa, for which he likely received an acclamation from his soldiers as *imperator* – one of three he would receive during his lifetime. His was no small challenge. The men under his direct command at Actium – some 80,000 infantry and 12,000 cavalry – would face Antonius' numerically superior force of 120,000 foot soldiers and 12,000 mounted troops led by P. Canidius Crassus.[60] His opponent was a battle-tested commander, wielding great influence over Antonius. Canidius had served under Lepidus in the Gallic War in the 50s BCE and taken leadership roles under Antonius in wars in Armenia and, most recently, Parthia.[61] He boasted that he had no fear of death.[62] That claim would be tested.

The tactical details of the campaign still had to be worked out. Agrippa joined Caesar at his *praetorium* tent in the hilltop camp and, together, they worked on the battle plan. This was their first real opportunity to deal Antonius a knockout blow. Antonius soon realised this too. In an effort to tip the odds in his favour, he moved some of his troops across the strait and set up a second camp directly facing his opponent, and then ordered his cavalry to ride around the Gulf to attack Caesar from the east.[63] While Caesar's men laboured on their ditches, palisades and watchtowers, Antonius' troops attacked. The target of highest value was Caesar's supply of fresh water. An army without fresh drinking water could soon be broken. Plutarch reports that Caesar showed great skill in enclosing his sources of potable water behind secure barriers to deprive the enemy of it, since there were so few places around to find it and the water from what ones there were tasted bad.[64] He responded by dispatching troops to Achaea and Macedonia to draw Antonius away.[65] Taurus showed initiative and daring too when he made a sudden charge on Antonius' cavalry, defeated it, and also won over Philadelphus, king of Paphlagonia, and his soldiers to Caesar's side.[66]

The weakness of Antonius' stratagem was revealed. His troops were now split on both sides of the Gulf and weakened by it. Exploiting the division of the enemy's forces, Agrippa made 'a sudden dash with his fleet'.[67] At the same time, Antonius' navy was effectively trapped in the Gulf of Ambracia while Agrippa's ships were free to traverse the adjacent Gulf of Corinth at will and patrol the coast of the Peloponnese, where they continued to harass their adversary's men and sank his warships and grain transports. Many of the targets were of high strategic value, which Antonius could ill afford to lose. 'Finally, right before the eyes of Antonius and his fleet,' writes Velleius Paterculus, Agrippa scored a series of tactically important blows: he 'had stormed Leucas (Levkas)', capturing a number of enemy ships; 'had taken Patrae', Antonius' winter quarters, by beating Q. Nasidius in a sea-fight; 'seized Corinth', Antonius' provisioning centre; 'and before the final conflict had twice defeated the fleet of the enemy'.[68] Laying due south of Actium, the island of Levkas was a significant win for Agrippa. Stationing warships there and in the Bay of Gomaros to the north, he could establish a blockade or launch an attack on any ships of Antonius' fleet attempting to enter or leave the strait.

While engagements occurred at sea, Imp. Caesar tried to provoke Antonius to fight on land. According to Dio's account, he would not oblige him:

> Caesar constantly drew up his infantry in battle order in front of the enemy's camp, often sailed against them with his ships and carried off their transports, with the object of joining battle with only such as were then present, before Antonius' entire command should assemble. For this very reason the latter was unwilling to stake his all on the cast, and he had recourse for select days to feeling out his enemy and to skirmish until he had gathered his legions.[69]

This may not be the whole truth. The later report of Orosius presents a different picture in which 'Antonius decided to hasten the beginning of the battle', but 'after quickly drawing up his troops, he advanced toward Caesar's camp but suffered defeat'.[70] Three days later, having failed to make any significant impact on his opponent, Antonius abandoned his second camp on the Epirot side of the Gulf and withdrew under the cover of darkness to his main base near Actium.[71]

In the wake of this tactical setback, Antonius called a council of war: he urgently needed a new plan. In his headquarters tent the Egyptian queen seemed more of a hindrance than a help. According to Dio, Kleopatra – who was allegedly unsettled by bad auguries – had convinced him that they should entrust the strategic positions to garrisons and let the main force depart to Egypt with herself and Antonius.[72] Her subliminal fears seemed to affect Antonius, who began to suspect members of his leadership team of plotting against him. He summarily tortured many and executed several, among them Iamblichus, king of a tribe of the Arabians, and handed over senator Q. Postumius to be torn apart.[73] In the last weeks of August, Antonius suffered several high-profile defections. They included the client Galatian kings Amyntas, who had been sent into Macedonia and Thrace to recruit mercenaries, and Deiotaros II (Deiotarus); and the Romans

Q. Dellius, who had served him in his war against Parthia, and Domitius Ahenobarbus, the proud ex-consul, allegedly smarting from unrelenting verbal abuse hurled at him by the queen.[74] Though deeply upset by Ahenobarbus' betrayal, Antonius respected the man enough to arrange for his personal effects and slaves to be sent over in another boat.[75]

The adversaries had been playing a high-stakes waiting game for several months. 'The two leaders neither were dismayed nor relaxed their preparations for war,' writes Dio, 'but spent the winter in spying upon and annoying each other.'[76] This stalemate served neither side's interests and could not last indefinitely. Either they must fight or they must withdraw. According to Dio's account, Caesar's plan was to allow his adversaries to sail out of the strait, then chase after them with his swifter fleet and capture Antonius and Kleopatra with as little bloodshed as possible.[77] They would make fine trophies in the victory parade he envisaged himself celebrating in Rome – and he needed their treasure.[78] The level-headed Agrippa expressed his fear that their opponents would get away and be able to regroup and fight another day; accepting the advice of his close friend, Caesar withdrew his plan.[79]

Imp. Caesar would certainly have interrogated the defectors from Antonius to better understand his adversary's intentions. The mission objectives of Antonius and Kleopatra are hard to determine from the extant accounts. They have been passionately debated by historians, ancient and modern, for years. Some – mostly the ancient writers and historians writing before the nineteenth century – are convinced that he was determined to win *this* battle just as he would any other he had fought in during his career, putting his faith in his heavy warships and loyal troops.[80] Others – mostly twentieth-century historians – are willing to dismiss the ancient historians and, instead, believe that his goal was to withdraw from the confines of the Gulf of Ambracia with as many ships and men as possible, taking as much treasure as could be carried, and to hold a last stand somewhere else.[81] Another, hybrid interpretation advances Antonius as approaching the mission pragmatically: fighting for victory as the primary, but difficult to achieve objective, with a break-out in force as the more likely achievable outcome.[82] The ancient historians all agree on one thing: the disagreement in Antonius' war council. Dio describes a debate about whether to stay and fight or to withdraw. Kleopatra won with the argument proposing that she and Antonius should escape to Egypt, leaving the troops behind to continue the fight.[83] Plutarch reports that Canidius pleaded with Antonius for Kleopatra to be asked to leave so that his commander could fight a decisive battle on dry land (perhaps in Macedonia or Thrace); but the queen argued for a sea battle, implying that her secret motive was to slip away under sail when the opportunity arose, and her paramour agreed.[84] In fact the treasure had already been loaded aboard the Egyptian vessels, with sails stowed in the event they could make a dash for open sea. We will probably never know with certainty what Antonius' plan was on the eve of battle, but it is clear that he would be the one to pick the day and time.

On 29 August, a deep depression settled over the Ionian Sea and adjacent Gulf of Ambracia, bringing with it a severe storm.[85] Rain cascaded over the entrance flaps of the commanders' goatskin tents, confining the frustrated leaders inside. Strong winds and choppy waves tossed around the ships of both sides, damaging many, though it appears Agrippa's ships anchored off Gomaros Bay fared better than Antonius'. The storm continued into a second day, then a third and a fourth. When the commanders awoke on the fifth day, they found, instead, a gentle breeze and a calm sea. 'Then came the day of the great conflict,' writes Paterculus, 'on which Caesar and Antonius led out their fleets and fought, the one for the safety, the other for the ruin, of the world.'[86] It was 2 September 31 BCE, a date that would be memorialized as pivotal in the history of the Roman Empire.[87]

The precise number of ships in the opposing navies continues to provoke argument amongst modern scholars. This is because the ancient sources themselves do not agree. Plutarch reports that Agrippa had 250 ships.[88] Orosius details 230 'beaked ships' – referring to the cast bronze rams (*rostra*) affixed to the prow at sea level – plus thirty 'without beaks' and some triremes comparable with the swift Liburnian type of vessel, which Imp. Caesar had brought over with him from Italy (but he excludes from this tally the advance force of Agrippa).[89] Florus states that he had 400 ships.[90] He explains:

> Caesar's ships had from two (*biremes*) to six (*hexeres*) banks of oars and no more; being, therefore, easily handled for any manoeuvre that might be required, whether for attacking, backing water or tacking.[91]

The design of these ships was similar to those used so effectively by Sex. Pompeius in Sicily to harass the coast of Italy.[92] Agrippa had been deeply impressed by the tactical fighting skills of the renegade son of Pompeius Magnus. Learning from his victories at Mylae and Naulochus five years earlier, he had revised his strategy for naval warfare and replaced the equipment with the smaller, but more agile and swifter vessels for the anticipated conflict with Antonius.[93] When not ramming and sinking enemy ships, these were platforms delivering marines who would clamber aboard the disabled vessel to fight as they would on land. According to Orosius, the decks ferried the men of eight legions, not counting the five Praetorian Cohorts – a number which is substantially more than the 20,000 heavily armed men plus 2,000 archers in Plutarch's account.[94] Smaller boats carried Caesar's friends relaying messages between the ships while in action.

The ancient sources are even more divided on the number of ships in Antonius' fleet than they are of Caesar's. According to Plutarch, Antonius brought 500 ships with him to Actium.[95] Florus states that in battle he had 'less than 200 warships', but Orosius gives the precise number as 170.[96] The differences in the counts might be explained by the fact that Antonius was forced to burn a number of the Egyptian ships because their crews had died from disease or left through desertion, and he did not want them falling into enemy hands, saving just sixty of the best (being a mix of triremes and *dekeres*, and not all of his ships were harboured in the Gulf of Ambracia).[97] Additionally, some ships had been lost – perhaps to Agrippa's patrols – and the recent storm had sunk several more.[98]

Unlike Agrippa, Antonius had no expertise in naval warfare. His fleet comprised large, heavy, multi-banked fighting platforms, among some of the biggest sailing craft of the ancient world. They included 'many vessels of eight (*okteres*) and ten (*dekeres*) banks of oars'.[99] Ironically, it seems his choice of vessel was based on studying Agrippa's victories over Sex. Pompeius where he had deployed enormous warships and large numbers of marines aboard them.[100] Antonius had apparently failed to understand that the key difference between the victor and vanquished in 36 BCE was not so much the size of the hardware as the innovative use of the war machines with which Agrippa had equipped them, combined with the talent of its admiral and the quality of the troops.[101] Florus confirms the larger size of Antonius' ships, adding that:

> their size compensated for their numerical inferiority [to Agrippa's]. For having from six to nine (*enneres*) banks of oars and also rising high out of the water with towers and platforms so as to resemble castles or cities, they made the sea groan and the wind labour as they moved along. Their very size, indeed, was fatal to them.[102]

The decks were packed with troops, and to enable his soldiers to 'fight from walls, as it were' he equipped these floating fortresses with 'lofty towers'.[103] Antonius ordered the masts and sails to be taken aboard the ships, not left on land – against the urgings of his captains – telling them 'that not one fugitive of the enemy should be allowed to make his escape'.[104]

The actual number of ships Antonius was able put to sea on 2 September may not, therefore, have been significantly different from Agrippa's – perhaps as few as 170 vessels, but probably not more than 230.[105] The composition of the fleets and warships of the opposing sides differed greatly, however, Agrippa having invested in smaller, lighter and more agile craft, Antonius in substantially bigger, but heavier and slower vessels.

The day of the great battle began well before dawn for Agrippa and Caesar. Agrippa had formed the fleet in the Ionian Sea into a line directly facing the strait of the Gulf of Ambracia at a distance, Dio says, around eight furlongs – approximately a mile – from the enemy.[106] Agrippa had taken up a position on the left wing with L. Arruntius.[107] Once sympathetic to the assassins of the late dictator (who after the signing of the Treaty of Misenum had switched his allegiance to Imp. Caesar's caucus), Arruntius was considered an illustrious man, but not much is known about his skills as a combat leader.[108] Having exchanged some final words with his admiral, Caesar moved down the line of warships on a small boat, encouraging his soldiers and sailors as he passed them.[109] Caesar boarded his own flagship on the right wing of the line with his *legatus* M. Lurius.[110] A native of the Balkans, Lurius was the former proconsul of Sardinia who had showed his mettle in the war against Sex. Pompeius. Agrippa was counting on him to do so again.[111] All that was now left to do was to wait for Antonius to make *his* move.

The hours passed by agonisingly slowly, forcing Agrippa's men to expend energy by using their oars to hold their ships steady in position.[112] But Antonius *was* preparing for battle. His fleet was forming up in front of the strait, riding up and down with the gentle waves.[113] From a row-boat he too was haranguing his soldiers, exhorting them to fight as though they were on land, while ordering his captains to hold their ships at the mouth of the strait and take the blows from the oncoming enemy vessels. There was a surreal, even festive, air to the proceedings. Antonius had decorated his warships 'in pompous and festal fashion' while he himself had donned 'a purple robe studded with large gemstones, a curved scimitar hung at his side and in his hand he gripped a golden sceptre'.[114] The soldier had turned showman, intent on making a spectacle of himself.

Like his more modest opponent, Antonius had also sub-divided the command of his fleet. Many were former allies of the men who had struck down Iulius Caesar or had joined the renegade Sex. Pompeius. In charge of the right wing was L. Gellius Publicola, a colourful character who had supported the assassins immediately after the Ides of March before himself entering into nefarious plots to kill the principal conspirators; he narrowly managed to escape with his life, finally defecting to the triumvirs and being rewarded for it with the consulship of 36 BCE.[115] The ships in the centre were jointly commanded by M. Insteius, who had accompanied Antonius on his campaigns against the Dardani nation (39–38 BCE), and M. Octavius, a distant cousin to Imp. Caesar, but sympathetic to the assassins, had seen action against his living relation in Illyricum (35–34 BCE) and was one of the few on the team who actually had some experience of commanding a navy.[116] Behind them were massed the ships of the Egyptian fleet led by Kleopatra aboard the *Antonius*, her 'golden vessel with purple sails'.[117] On Antonius' left wing was C. Sosius, the consul of 32, the outspoken critic of Imp. Caesar and a man with a grudge.[118] The ships of the line were arranged in close formation, with little margin for error.[119]

Having waited for several months in increasingly desperate conditions, Antonius' men were restless for battle.[120] When he judged the moment to be right, Antonius relayed by trumpet to order Sosius to advance against Imp. Caesar and M. Lurius.[121] As the oarsmen strained, the massive ships slowly cut a path through the water. Informed of the movement, Agrippa gave the pre-agreed signal for his entire line to row in *reverse*, taking it further out into the Ionian Sea.[122] His fleet now formed a wide concave arc. As far as can be ascertained from the sources, Agrippa's strategy seems to have been to draw Antonius out from the Gulf and only after he was on open sea to bring his left and right wings forward to encircle him in a naval equivalent of Hannibal Barca's brilliantly successful manoeuvre at Cannae.[123] However, Antonius appears to have anticipated this was exactly what his adversary was planning to do. Advancing his left wing first, he may have intended to break the integrity of his enemy's single line, hoping to wreak havoc with his bigger fighting platforms.[124]

The morning had already passed when, between the fifth and sixth hours – approximately 11.56am–12.56pm – a wind began to rise from the northwest from the Ionian Sea.[125] It still to this day starts to blow down from the west daily around 11.30am.[126] The poet Vergil calls it the *Iapyx*; it builds in strength through noon, changing direction to west-northwest, becoming a force 3–4 sailing breeze, causing the waves to become agitated between 2.00pm and 3.00pm, before dying out after sunset.[127] Agrippa was counting on it to arrive on time. This wind would propel Agrippa's small ships forward – and work against his opponent's. Now with the wind against them, Antonius' galleys moved, propelled by banks of oars – slowly at first, but steadily gaining speed – towards his enemy's centre.

According to Orosius, battle was joined during the sixth and seventh hours – approximately 12.56pm–1.56pm.[128] The ensuing clash is described by Plutarch:

> Though the struggle was beginning to be at close range, the ships did not ram or crush one another at all, since Antonius', owing to their weight, had no impetus, which chiefly gives effect to the blows of the beaks, while Caesar's not only avoided dashing front to front against rough and hard bronze armour, but did not even venture to ram the enemy's ships in the side. For their beaks would easily have been broken off by impact against vessels constructed of huge square timbers fastened together with iron. The struggle was therefore like a land battle; or, to speak more truly, like the storming of a walled town. For three or four of Caesar's vessels were engaged at the same time about one of Antonius', and the crews fought with wicker shields and spears and punting-poles and fiery missiles; the soldiers of Antonius also shot with catapults from wooden towers.[129]

Agrippa intended his warships to move at speed to ram and sink his opponent's; in contrast, Antonius planned to use the higher elevation of his vessels to shoot long-range missiles and cast-iron grapnels to pick off crews and seize his adversary's ships.[130] 'On the one side,' writes Dio:

> the pilots and the rowers endured the most hardship and fatigue, and on the other side the marines; and the one side resembled cavalry, now making a charge and now retreating, since it was in their power to attack and back off at will, and the others were like heavy-armed troops guarding against the approach of foes and trying their best to hold them.[131]

After the initial impact, it was not clear who had the advantage.[132] Locked in a bloody embrace in the centre, each captain manoeuvered his ship to strike the knockout blow. Agrippa gave the order for his left and right wings to move forward. Made aware of this move on his right side, Publicola slipped off some of the ships from his main formation to avoid being encircled and prepared to engage Agrippa head-on. The unintended result was a split in the centre bloc, creating a gap in the battle line.[133] While Arruntius' vessels collided with those of M. Octavius and M. Insteius, behind them the captains of sixty of the Egyptian ships now ordered their crews to hoist their sails and, as the wind picked up, they plunged through the opening in the line.[134] The crews of both Agrippa's and Antonius' ships watched the colourful ships sailing through in astonishment. Antonius interpreted the move to mean his queen was leaving the battle and, perhaps in a panic, he followed her aboard a *quinquereme*.[135] The *Iapyx* was now blowing at full strength. Agrippa's ships responded to block the way and the rest of Antonius' fleet found itself trapped. When Antonius' boat was close enough to Kleopatra's flagship, he clambered aboard and made straight for the prow.[136] Capturing the *Antonius* and its important cargo would be a major prize for

Caesar. Before the battle, Agrippa likely gave an order for Antonius' and Kleopatra's ships to be taken because 'at this point, Liburnian ships were seen pursuing them from Caesar's fleet, but Antonius ordered the ship's prow turned about to face them, and so kept them off'.[137] All his admiral could do now was trust that his officers would carry out their pre-assigned orders.[138]

Having broken free of Agrippa's line, the Egyptian ships veered hard southeast. With the wind filling their sails, they slipped away at speed, taking the Roman commander, queen and treasure with them. The effect on Antonius' men who were left behind was devastating. Had Antonius abandoned them? Some crews sought to follow after their commander, throwing overboard anything to lighten their weight, but they were unable to keep up.[139] Agrippa, however, held his nerve; tempting as it was to go in pursuit, he was not about to let his opponent's main fleet get away. The battle raged with increasing violence:

> For Caesar's men damaged the lower parts of the ships all around, crushed the oars, snapped off the rudders, and climbing on the decks, seized hold of some of the foe and pulled them down, pushed off others, and fought with yet others, since they were now equal to them in numbers; and Antonius' men pushed their assailants back with boathooks, cut them down with axes, hurled down upon them stones and heavy missiles made ready for just this purpose, drove back those who tried to climb up, and fought with those who came within reach. An eye-witness of what took place might have compared it, likening small things to great, to walled towns or else islands, many in number and close together, being besieged from the sea. Thus the one party strove to scale the boats as they would the dry land or a fortress, and eagerly brought to bear all the implements that have to do with such an operation, and the others tried to repel them, devising every means that is commonly used in such a case.[140]

Agrippa's and Caesar's flagships were now just two vessel amongst many in the general mêlée upon the Ionian Sea (plate 6). The captains of their fleet 'scattered at their will the opposing vessels, which were clumsy and in every respect unwieldy, several of them attacking a single ship with missiles and with their beaks, and also with firebrands hurled into them'.[141] Hoping to capture Antonius' ships undamaged, and the men aboard them, Caesar wanted to avoid using firebrands, even calling out to Antonius' troops to lay down their arms now that their commander had fled, but that was now an unattainable goal.[142] 'Now another kind of battle was entered upon,' writes Dio:

> where the assailants would approach their victims from many directions at once, shoot blazing missiles at them, hurl with their hands torches fastened to javelins and with the aid of engines would throw from a distance pots full of charcoal and pitch. The defenders tried to ward these missiles off one by one, and when some of them got past them and caught the timbers and at once started a great fire, as must be the case in a ship, they used first the drinking water which they carried on board and extinguished some of the

conflagrations, and when that was gone they dipped up the sea-water. And if they used great quantities of it at once, they would somehow stop the fire by main force; but they were unable to do this everywhere, for the buckets they had were not numerous nor large size, and in their confusion they brought them up half full, so that, far from helping the situation at all, they only increased the flames, since salt water poured on a fire in small quantities makes it burn vigorously. So when they found themselves getting the worst of it in this respect also, they heaped on the blaze their thick mantles and the corpses, and for a time these checked the fire and it seemed to abate; but later, especially when the wind raged furiously, the flames flared up more than ever, fed by this very fuel. So long as only a part of the ship was on fire, men would stand by that part and leap into it, hewing away or scattering the timbers; and these detached timbers were hurled by some into the sea and by others against their opponents, in the hope that they, too, might possibly be injured by these missiles. Others would go to the still sound portion of their ship and now more than ever would make use of their grappling-irons and their long spears with the purpose of binding some hostile ship to theirs and crossing over to it, if possible, or, if not, of setting it on fire likewise.[143]

Wherever fires raged, men suffered terribly from inhaling choking smoke or, becoming engulfed in flames, suffered terrible burns or, having leaped overboard to save themselves, sank under the weight of their sodden clothing or armour and drowned.[144]

The battle raged on through early evening according to Orosius' account.[145] 'The contest continued to so late an hour,' writes Suetonius, 'that the victor passed the night on board.'[146] Florus is more precise: only after Antonius' fleet was 'most severely damaged by the high sea' did his men finally give up the fight at the tenth hour – around 4.16pm.[147] At daybreak next morning, Caesar felt able to declare victory his.[148] Some would reckon the years of his reign from this moment.[149] As the sun rose on the morning of 3 September, the survivors could survey the gruesome carnage of the previous day's battle. It is graphically – if poetically – evoked by Florus, who writes:

> The vastness of the enemy's forces was never more apparent than after the victory; for, as a result of the battle, the wreckage of the huge fleet floated all over the sea, and the waves, stirred by the winds, continually yielded up the purple and gold-bespangled spoils of the Arabians and Sabaeans and a thousand other Asiatic peoples.[150]

Agrippa had successfully completed his mission and won the battle for Caesar. By one account he had captured 300 of his enemy's ships, which is likely an exaggeration.[151] Yet victory had come at a heavy price. The casualties on Caesar's side were 12,000 dead and 6,000 wounded – and of them 1,000 died later despite receiving medical care; of Antonius' men, some 5,000 had lost their lives.[152] On land, Antonius' nineteen legions of men-at-arms standing undefeated in battle,

and 12,000 cavalry, could not accept that their commander had simply abandoned them. As late as seven days after the Battle of Actium, they still believed
that he would make a surprise *deus ex machina*-style appearance and lead them to
victory.[153] Only when Canidius Crassus was found – despite his boast – to have
proved a coward and deserted them (he had sneaked away under the cover of
darkness) did the men finally capitulate and offer their unconditional surrender to
Imp. Caesar.[154] When captured, Canidius was summarily executed.[155] Ex-consul
Sosius fled the region and went into hiding, but he too was soon discovered and
taken captive.[156] When Arruntius, a man well-known for his old-time dignity,
advocated on the prisoner's behalf for his life, Imp. Caesar showed clemency
(*clementia*) and pardoned him.[157] But Caesar needed to make examples of some
and there were other retributions. The client kings who had aligned with
Antonius were punished by confiscations of their lands and titles; cities saw their
privileges withdrawn; Roman senators and *equites* were either fined, exiled or
executed.[158] On the fates of Antonius' other legates (L. Gellius Publicola,
M. Insteius and M. Octavius), history is silent: they may have died in the battle.

If the Actian campaign had been won, while the antagonists were still on the
run the larger war against Antonius and Kleopatra had not. Capturing the fugitives now became the regime's top priority. Agrippa dispatched part of his fleet in
pursuit of them.[159] For the time being the defeated *triumvir* and the queen had
managed to evade the pursuers, who finally gave up the chase and returned to the
security of Comarus harbour. Any last remaining pockets of resistance had also to
be flushed out: Caesar could not afford a repeat of the type of insurgency led by
Sex. Pompeius five years earlier.[160] Remnants of Antonius' army were retreating
to Macedonia, where they might regroup and stage a last stand. Agrippa intercepted them and, to everyone's relief, received their surrender without bloodshed. He took the enemy's fortified coastal locations, encountering no opposition
in the process. Crucially, he secured for his commander-in-chief *Colonia* Laus
Iulia Corinthiensis, which Iulius Caesar had refounded as a colony of army
veterans just months before his assassination; it had been the only Greek city to
shut its gates to his official heir.[161]

Imp. Caesar wanted to return to Italy without delay, but there was much to do
locally before he could leave. He decided to stay in Athens for the remainder of
the year, conducting affairs of state from there and hoping to discover Antonius'
whereabouts.[162] He soon learned how his adversary had abused the free Greek
communities.[163] To pay for his war effort, Antonius had ravaged them, confiscated their money, slaves and animals; their citizens – among whom was
Plutarch's own uncle, Nikarchos – had even been forced to carry heavy loads of
grain upon their backs like slaves to Antikyra and load up the vessels bound for
Antonius' camp at Actium.[164]

With a clear eye to shaping his legacy, he founded a new city on the site of his
army camp and populated it with the inhabitants of smaller settlements in the
surrounding region.[165] The name he gave to this place was Nikopolis, 'Victory
City', in honour of his success at Actium. The centrepiece, to be erected upon the
highest point above a grove sacred to Apollo (Imp. Caesar's patron god), was a

war memorial adorned with the spoils of the Actian War (plate 8).[166] Games dedicated to Apollo Actius were inaugurated, to take place every five years, and ground was broken for a gymnasium and stadium to be built to host the athletic competitions.

When the *Antonius* sailed away, it took not only Kleopatra but also the treasure Caesar had hoped to use to pay his troops. He had insufficient funds to cover his financial obligations to them from his own resources. His problems were now exacerbated by the fact his ranks were swollen with men from Antonius' legions: an additional nineteen legions now swore allegiance to him, bringing the total to almost sixty.[167] His own men had remained loyal to him through the long, hard years of campaigning, not entirely out of selfless service – though undoubtedly there were men among them who believed in Caesar's cause – but for the regular pay. They also had hopes to be rewarded with distributions from the rich pickings of Egypt. The seeming lack of activity since the day of the Battle of Actium led many soldiers to question whether this would actually happen at all. Trying to avoid a showdown, Caesar played for time. Statilius Taurus' officers managed to keep the rank and file in check. Most of the veterans (men who had served sixteen years) faced demobilization anyway, but when they realized they were not going to receive any cash payment or grant of land for their service to help them into retirement, they began to protest.[168] With much at stake, Caesar could ill afford a mutiny. Fearing the resentful mood might spread to all the men, he needed someone to repatriate the legions to Italy and resettle the men without delay.[169]

Caesar required a strong authority figure. Agrippa was an ex-consul who carried high status and was a decorated commander. Crucially, he had *imperium* (military power based in law). Maecenas, Caesar's present deputy in Rome, a member of the *ordo equester*, did not.[170] Yet the two men complemented Caesar's skills and temperament well and formed his personal, but unofficial, council of advisors (*consilium*). Where Agrippa brought experience and judgment in management and military matters, Maecenas provided the connections and deft-touch Caesar needed to get political things done. Caesar empowered *both* men to speak and act for him in his absence.[171] The unglamorous task of transporting the troops to Italy and demobbing them fell to Agrippa. Over the subsequent months of autumn and winter, Agrippa would write frequently to Caesar; he urged him to return to Italy to deal with matters which required his personal presence.[172] The fact he was making these direct requests strongly suggests that, despite his status and authorization, he was struggling to deal with the grievances of the veterans and concerned that control of the situation might be lost if Caesar did not return and assert his authority. Even after the conclusive result at Actium, Rome was not a safe place for M. Agrippa. As Caesar's senior representative, he faced real personal danger. A plot to assassinate Imp. Caesar, led by the son of the former *triumvir* Aemilius Lepidus, had been exposed this year and quelled by Maecenas.[173] Someone with the motive and the means could also attempt to assassinate Caesar's right-hand man at any moment. With Caesar away, the men growing impatient and the end of the year approaching, Agrippa would have to do the best he could with what he had.

30 BCE

	Imp. Caesar *Divi f.* IV	M. Licinius M. *f.* Crassus
suff.		C. Antistius C. *f.* Vetus
suff.		M. Tullius M. *f.* Cicero
suff.		L. Saenius L. *f.* (Balbinus)

Caesar finally relented to Agrippa's written pleadings and agreed to return to the homeland.[174] He had, in any case, been elected as consul for the year 30 BCE, his fourth term in that high office.[175] Before leaving Athens, he delegated to others the important mission of finding Antonius, whose whereabouts were still unknown.[176] Caesar was greeted on the quayside at Brundisium by a large delegation. Agrippa, Maecenas, members of the Senate and the *equites*, along with other high-status people, joined in a public display of support for the victor of the Actian War.[177]

While ensuring the security of Roman territory and its people continued to be the priority, and even though the war with the treacherous queen and renegade *triumvir* was not yet over, many army units still needed to be drawn down and redeployed. At Brundisium, after a strategic military review, 'he assigned different legions to posts throughout the world'.[178] Solving the challenge of resettling the troops to be demobbed, however, was uppermost on Caesar's mind. With him he had brought chests of money with which to settle the outstanding debt of the disaffected veterans; to the men who had loyally served him, he also granted the allotments they were promised.[179] He found the plots of land in Italy by confiscating property held by friends and allies of Antonius, but he was careful to compensate those negatively affected with other land in Dyrrhacium, Philippi and elsewhere, promising payment to those unsuccessful in getting alternative accommodations.[180] Caesar's policy decision had unintended consequences. He discovered that he was spending more cash than he had available. To raise funds he announced that he had put up for auction his own property, as well as that of his friends.[181] Although no buildings found new owners and no money actually ever changed hands, it demonstrated Caesar's willingness to go to this length to deal with the matter and it did succeed in buying him valuable time. He might have chosen, at this time, to punish those who had not supported him, but he did not. He issued to those who had received amnesty the right to live in Italy, and to the people who had sworn the *sacramentum* but failed to come out to greet him in Brundisium he issued a general pardon.[182]

Caesar urgently needed to find the treasure smuggled away by Kleopatra. Just a month after having landed in Italy, he boarded a ship and sailed again for Greece.[183] From there he went first to Asia Minor and then to Syria, settling local affairs as he went.[184] In the meantime, Caesar sent Cornelius Gallus to Africa. An *eques* (a man of the *Ordo Equester*), Gallus was an educated man – he had the same tutor as the poet Vergil – and he could be trusted to carry out his orders. Almost as soon as he had landed he received the surrender of Antonius' commander, L. Pinarius Scarpus, and his four legions stationed at Cyrene – all without a fight.[185] Now Antonius made a move. On Egypt's western border with Libya at Paraetonium (modern Mersa Matruh), he intercepted Gallus. After a skirmish,

Antonius was defeated, and when he retreated to Pharos, Caesar's deputy overwhelmed him a second time.[186]

In Egypt, Kleopatra was desperately rallying her army in readiness for a last stand. All men of military age were conscripted, including her own son, Caesarion, and Antonius' son, Antyllus.[187] 'Their purpose,' writes Dio:

> was to arouse the enthusiasm of the Egyptians, who would feel that they had at last a man for their king, and to cause the rest to continue the struggle with these boys as their leaders, in case anything untoward should happen to the parents.[188]

Meanwhile, she sent out emissaries carrying peace proposals intended to be read by Caesar, and money to bribe his allies.[189] To him she sent her golden crown and sceptre, and her throne too: if she was willing to hand him the symbols of her rule, perhaps he would be merciful.[190] She did this, however, without first consulting Antonius. Caesar saw an opportunity:

> Caesar accepted her gifts as a good omen, but made no answer to Antonius; to Kleopatra, however, although he publicly sent threatening messages, including the announcement that, if she would give up her armed forces and renounce her sovereignty, he would consider what ought to be done in her case, he secretly sent word that, if she would kill Antonius, he would grant her pardon and leave her realm inviolate.[191]

Secret negotiations between the foes continued.[192] Kleopatra promised money. Antonius too appealed to Caesar's better nature, reminding him of their family ties. One of the surviving murderers of Iulius Caesar who had been living with Antonius was handed over in exchange for sparing the queen's life, but Imp. Caesar summarily executed him. Antonius sent his son bearing gold, but Caesar returned him – alive but empty-handed and without an answer. Publicly he maintained his posture that Kleopatra should surrender unconditionally: he feared that she might escape and launch an insurgency in another part of the Roman world.[193] Privately he appealed to her vanity, sending his freedman Thyrsus with a message that he loved her just as much as the rest of mankind, but that she should leave Antonius and keep her money safe.[194]

When Caesar took Pelusium on the eastern side of the Nile delta (or the garrison there simply surrendered to him), he had gained an important foothold in Egypt.[195] His men and matériel were now just a week's march away from the Egyptian capital. When Caesar arrived outside the city founded by Alexander III of Macedon, but weary from the journey, Antonius and a unit of cavalry attacked him and prevented him from taking it.[196] Loyalties were tested. Valerius Maximus preserves the story of Maevius, a centurion in Imp. Caesar's army. At Alexandria he was ambushed and taken captive. Presented to Antonius, he was asked what should be done with him? 'Kill me!' he replied unflinchingly, 'because neither the benefit of life nor the sentence of death can stop me from being Caesar's, or becoming yours.'[198] Impressed by his resolution, the renegade commander spared his life.

The first battle of the Alexandrian campaign (*Bellum Alexandreae*), which Caesar had led, had been fought and lost. Antonius then tried to win over Caesar's men with a direct appeal. Over the camp's palisade he shot arrows, attached to which were papyrus pamphlets promising 6,000 *sestertii* to every man who joined him.[199] Caesar turned Antonius' appeal to his own advantage. He assembled his troops and from a tribunal read out the message himself, and proceeded to belittle the old commander's attempt to lure away his men.[200] They remained loyal.

On 1 August, Alexandria fell to Imp. Caesar. Egypt's fate was sealed. From that time the date would hold special significance for Caesar:

> The day on which Alexandria had been captured they declared a lucky day,
> and directed that in future years it should be taken by the inhabitants of that
> city as the starting-point in their reckoning of time. [201]

In learning the story of their 'Year 0', future generations of Alexandrians would be reminded of the victory of the Roman commander and the folly of the Egyptian queen.

Left without an army, Antonius took refuge in the few ships he had remaining from his navy. He fell into a depression and began to ponder staging a last battle at sea or even escaping to Hispania Ulterior.[202] According to Dio's account, the queen had secretly intervened and caused his sailors to desert him while she withdrew to her mausoleum.[203] The broken Roman commander now suspected her of betraying him; nevertheless he suggested he might consider taking his own life if it would mean his wife (the queen) could live.[204]

The true story of the final hours of Antonius and Kleopatra may never be known with certainty. On 10 August, he died from a self-inflicted wound and it was reported that she died from poison – legend has it from the bite of an asp – though professional assassination is equally plausible.[205] Imp. Caesar allowed their bodies to be prepared, embalmed and buried in the queen's mausoleum.[206] He spared the children of Antonius' marriage to both Fulvia and Kleopatra, except two. Caesarion (allegedly the lovechild of Iulius Caesar and the queen) was captured while trying to flee to India via Ethiopia and was executed; Antyllus, who was betrayed by his tutor, was beheaded.[207]

The ancient kingdom of the pharaohs had become the property of the younger republic of the Roman People (plate 7).[208] Egypt produced one of Rome's most important strategic resources – grain. Caesar needed a man he could trust to administer it. His most important duty would be to ensure an uninterrupted flow of grain shipped from its warehouses so that the hungry poor of Rome could have their daily bread.[209] Caesar placed Cornelius Gallus in charge of the new province as its first *Praefectus Aegypti*. Gallus had proved loyal in recent weeks, and was available at the time and place Caesar needed him. From that time on the position would always be filled by *praefectus*, a man of equestrian social rank. As an additional precaution, no men of senatorial rank were allowed entry to the country unless with the explicit permission of Caesar.[210] In support of him, two or three legions would be stationed in the province, *Legiones* III *Cyrenaica*, XII *Fulminata* and XXII *Deiotariana*.

While in Alexandria, Caesar viewed the preserved body of Alexander the Great. Already three centuries old, it had been mellified and lay in a sepulchre preserved in a sarcophagus of glass, alabaster or quartz crystal.[211] 'After gazing on it,' writes Suetonius, Caesar 'showed his respect by placing upon it a golden crown and strewing it with flowers; and being then asked whether he wished to see the tomb of the Ptolemies as well, he replied, "My wish was to see a king, not corpses".'[212] If the rumour preserved in Dio's account is true, when Caesar actually touched the body a piece of the nose broke off.[213]

The war against Antonius and Kleopatra was now officially over. With several legions at his disposal, rather than let the men spend their time in idleness he assigned them to labour-intensive projects to improve Egypt's infrastructure:

> To make it more fruitful and better adapted to supply the city [of Rome] with grain, he set his soldiers at work cleaning out all the canals into which the Nile overflows, which in the course of many years had become choked with mud.[214]

The victor also requested a lasting monument to be built to mark his achievement. 'Caesar founded a city there on the very site of the battle,' records Dio, 'and gave to it the same name and the same games as to the city he had founded previously.'[215] As he had done beside Actium in Epirus, so at Alexandria in Egypt he founded Nikopolis, a second 'Victory City'. Located a few miles east of the old city, when completed the new one would feature state-of-the art architecture, manicured gardens, precincts, an amphitheatre, a gymnasium and a stadium to host quinquennial games.[216] In time it would prove so popular that the old buildings of Alexandria would fall into disrepair.

The last item for which Caesar had waged war was gold. In that regard the former queen had, unwittingly, been most helpful. 'In the palace quantities of treasure were found,' writes Dio:

> for Kleopatra had taken practically all the offerings from even the holiest shrines and so helped the Romans swell their spoils without incurring any defilement on their own part. Large sums were also obtained from every man against whom any charge of misdemeanour were brought. And apart from these, all the rest, even though no particular complaint could be lodged against them, had two-thirds of their property demanded of them. Out of this wealth all the troops received what was owing them, and those who were with Caesar at the time got in addition 1,000 *sestertii* on condition of not plundering the city.[217]

Caesar knew full well that to leave debts unsettled could turn a friend into a foe. Those who had advanced him loans would soon be repaid in full. To both the senators and the *equites* who had actively participated in the war large sums would also be given as rewards. Rome and its temples too would be adorned from the proceeds of the war spoils (*ex manubiis*) of Egypt to maintain the goodwill of the gods.[218] In Rome the Senate voted him both a triumph and sacrifices.[219] In no hurry to return home, Caesar chose to remain in Egypt for the rest of 30 BCE.

The annexation of Egypt brought not only vast natural resources and unfathomable wealth, it greatly added to the size of the Roman Empire. Rome''s dominions now bounded the largest part of the Iberian Peninsula, Gaul, Italy below the Po River, the western Balkans, all of Greece, parts of Anatolia, Syria, tracts of North Africa and all the islands scattered across the Mediterranean, known to the conceited Romans simply as *Mare Nostrum*, 'Our Sea'. Rome's southernmost limit was now set at the First Cataract on the Nile River. A Roman garrison would soon have to be established in the Dodekashoinos on the border with Ethiopia. Enormous numbers of Roman troops had been withdrawn from the other territories to participate in the contest between the two men fighting to rule the Roman world.[220] The few military units still stationed in the provinces continued their regular duties as best they could. Some even excelled. In Gallia Comata, the army of C. Carrinas, a man who had a history of underperformance but whose services Caesar had retained as its governor, scored two great successes. He completed a punitive campaign against the Germanic nation of the Suebi, who had crossed the Rhine River and raided into his province to rampage through its largely unprotected settlements, and also quelled a revolt of the native Morini in Belgica.[221] In the Iberian Peninsula, C. Calvisius Sabinus led operations with distinction. In Africa, proconsul L. Autronius Paetus dealt with an unspecified challenge by military force. All three men's achievements were recognised when the Senate voted them triumphs.[222]

In northern Greece, the proconsul of Macedonia, M. Licinius Crassus, lived up to the reputation for courage of the greatest of Rome's military heroes. The grandson of the man who invaded Parthia and lost his life, and the eagle standards of his legions too, may have felt he had something to prove.[223] On the northern border of his province lived the Bastarnae and, beyond the Danube River, the Daci.[224] The Bastarnae were a people from Scythia (a region that would now be southwestern Russia) who had migrated west and crossed over the river into the territory already occupied by several native tribes, principally the Dardani and Triballi, and collectively called Moesi.[225] The Roman perspective was that as long as the Bastarnae did not encroach on Roman territory or attack one of their allies, they would not interfere.[226] However, when the Bastarnae crossed the Haemus (an unidentified mountain range in the Balkans) into the region of Thracia ruled by Sitas, the blind king of the Dentheleti, who was an ally, the Romans were obliged to intervene.[227] 'Chiefly out of fear for Macedonia,' writes Dio, Crassus went out to meet them.[228] Extraordinarily, 'by his mere approach he threw them into a panic and drove them from the country without a battle'.[229] Seeing an opportunity, he pursued them as they retreated. He took the region called Segetica and, having invaded the plains south of the Danube, ravaged the country and staged an assault on one of the main strongholds.[230] According to Florus:

> One of their leaders, after calling for silence, exclaimed in front of the host, 'Who are you?' And when the reply was given, 'We are Romans, lords of the

world.' 'So you will be,' was the answer, 'if you conquer us.' Marcus Crassus accepted the omen.[231]

The Moesi repulsed his vanguard, believing it was the entire force, and made a sortie from their fortification. It was a tactical mistake. Crassus brought up reinforcements, pushed back the enemy, then besieged and destroyed the stronghold. The Bastarnae halted their retreat at the Cedrus (Tsibritsa) River.[232] Having witnessed what Crassus had done to the Moesi, they sent emissaries to Crassus with a petition for him not to pursue them because they had done the Romans no real harm. Again Crassus saw an opportunity. He received the envoys, telling them he would give them an answer the following day, but in the meantime he treated them to his hospitality and interviewed them as they drank copiously.[233] From the inebriated guests the proconsul learned about their true intentions. Forearmed with this intelligence, that night he led an assault against the enemy under cover of darkness:

> Crassus moved forward into a forest during the night, stationed scouts in front of it, and halted his army there. Then, when the Bastarnae, in the belief that the scouts were all alone, rushed to attack them and pursued them as they retreated into the thick of the forest, he destroyed many of them on the spot and many others in the rout which followed.[234]

Their retreat was blocked by waggons and pack animals they had parked at their rear.[235] Women and children were trapped between them and, in the general mêlée which followed, were slaughtered.

During the bloody struggle Crassus displayed *virtus*, the attribute of selfless courage or manliness, which the Romans greatly respected in their leaders. He had personally sought out Deldo, king of the Bastarnae, to engage him in a duel; the two commanders fought and, after a fierce struggle, the Roman slew his royal opponent.[236] As was his right, he stripped the armour from the dead war chief and claimed it as *spolia opima*, 'rich spoils'. By tradition he could look forward to the honour of taking these and dedicating them in the Temple of Iupiter Feretrius. He would be only the fourth man in history to do so.[237] Only two men since the city's legendary founder Romulus had been deemed worthy: A. Cornelius Cossus in either 437 or 426 BCE, and M. Claudius Marcellus in 222 BCE.[238] *Virtus* was shown by other ranks too:

> No little terror was inspired in the barbarians by the centurion Cornidius, a man of rather barbarous stupidity, which, however, was not without effect upon men of similar character; carrying on the top of his helmet a pan of coals which were fanned by the movement of his body, he scattered flame from his head, which had the appearance of being on fire.[239]

Without their leader, the resistance broke. Some Bastarnae perished when they took refuge in a grove, which the Romans then set on fire; others rushed into a fort, where they were butchered by Crassus' troops; yet others drowned when they leaped into the Danube, or died of hunger when they were separated from each other and scattered across the country.[240] There were survivors, however. They rallied and staged a last stand.[241] Crassus besieged them for several days but the defenders inside held out and the frustrated Roman commander reluctantly withdrew. Finally, with the addition of troops of Rolis (Roles), king of the Getae nation, Crassus' army tried again and this time sacked the stronghold. The captives were distributed as war booty (*praeda*) among the soldiers for use as slaves.[242] For leading them to this victory, his troops may have acclaimed him *imperator*.[243]

Crassus then turned his attention to the neighbouring Moesi. 'Partly by persuasion in some cases,' writes Dio, 'partly by terrifying them, partly also by applying force, he subdued all except a very few, though only after great hardships and dangers.'[244] But he was running out of time. The Roman campaign season generally lasted from the spring through to late summer. Autumn was already upon him and winter now approaching, yet Crassus was still far from the safety of the permanent base in his own province. He needed a place where his men could build a fortified camp as a refuge to replenish their supplies and repair their kit. Marching south, the Roman lines entered Thracia.[245] The Thraci were Roman allies and Crassus reasonably assumed he was in friendly territory. The inhabitants, however, interpreted his uninvited presence as hostile and attacked his men, resulting in casualties on both sides. Out of options, proconsul Crassus had to remain there until conditions allowed him to move on unhindered. Meantime, a messenger succeeded in reaching Rome with a report of the year's campaign. The Senate was pleased with his review.[246]

On the eastern border there was a move to seek a diplomatic settlement. Two years earlier, while the triumvirs were engaged in war, a man named Tiridates had led a rebellion against Fraat (Phraates), king of Parthia, Rome's rival in the orient. Both men had sought an alliance with Imp. Caesar, but he had resolutely maintained his neutrality, favouring neither side.[247] Dio comments that 'his excuse was that he was busy with Egypt, but in reality he wanted them, in the meantime, to exhaust themselves by fighting against each other'.[248] Tiridates' revolt had since failed and the rebel had fled behind the Roman frontier to seek sanctuary in Syria. Caesar sent emissaries to Fraat seeking an accord. Agreeing not to back Tiridates, the Roman leader permitted him to remain in Syria; as a mark of his good faith, Fraat gave Caesar one of his own sons as a hostage to take back with him to Rome.[249]

Imp. Caesar may have been away awhile from the centre of Roman politics, nevertheless his supporters were advancing his agenda in the Senate House and Popular Assemblies. Suffect consul L. Saenius sponsored a *senatus consultum* (a decree of the Senate) intended to increase the number of patrician families after their decimation during two Civil Wars and the subsequent purges.[250] Approved into law by popular vote in a *lex curiata* (a law of confirmation), the *Lex Saenia* adlected plebians, raising them to patrician status.[251] It would soon prove to be very useful to Caesar. One of the early beneficiaries was Statilius Taurus. This year his loyal friend and deputy began work on the first purpose-built stone amphitheatre in Rome to display gladiatorial and hunting combats, which, up to

that time, had taken place in the *Forum Romanum*, with wooden stands temporarily erected for spectators. He paid for the building with his share of the booty
from the Actian War.[252] It proved a popular investment as 'because of this he was
permitted by the people to choose one of the praetors each year'.[253]

29 BCE

	Imp. Caesar *Divi f.* V	Sex. Appuleius Sex. *f.*
suff.		Potitus Valerius M. *f.* Messalla

As the winter receded, the legions and their commanders prepared to address
dangerous threats to security within and along the empire's borders. One of
them, M. Licinius Crassus, was still encamped in Thracia, well outside his
province, and he was eager to reach home. The Bastarnae had been constantly
watching the invader safely from a distance. They were smarting from the loss of
their king and the humiliation of their defeat. Their ire was directed at Sitas and
the Dentheleti, whom they blamed for their predicament.[254] Crassus was again
obliged to come to the aid of Rome's ally:

> Thus it came about that Crassus reluctantly took the field; and falling upon
> them unexpectedly after advancing by forced marches, he conquered them
> and imposed such terms of peace as he pleased.[255]

Once more in the full thrust of war, Crassus moved to punish the Thraci nation
for their belligerence and what he saw as a betrayal. Information reached him
that the host was fortifying its position and spoiling for a fight.[256] Crassus obliged
and marched his men to meet them. The ensuing campaign was hard-fought: the
Thraci were formidable fighters and the Romans encountered stiff resistance
wherever they encountered them. The Maedi and Serdi tribes were finally beaten,
and their captives punished by having their hands cut off. The Odrysae were
spared the bloodshed because of their unswerving track record of service to
the god Dionysus; indeed they were awarded lands confiscated from the Bessi
tribe who had defied the proconsul.[257]

Also appealing for assistance was Rolis, king of the Getae, who had earlier
helped Crassus defeat the Bastarnae. It was an internal matter in which the king
found himself challenged by a certain Dapyx, another king of the Getae, but,
having been approached by an ally, Crassus responded. What followed was a
sordid affair of treachery and double-dealing:

> By hurling the horse of his opponents back upon their infantry he so
> thoroughly terrified the latter also that what followed was no longer a battle
> but a great slaughter of fleeing men of both arms. Next he cut off Dapyx,
> who had taken refuge in a fort, and besieged him. In the course of the siege
> someone hailed him from the walls in Greek, obtained a conference with
> him, and arranged to betray the place. The barbarians, thus captured, turned
> upon one another, and Dapyx was killed along with many others. His
> brother, however, Crassus took alive, and not only did him no harm but
> actually released him.[258]

In its wake came a series of brutal actions designed to break the will of the Getae who supported Dapyx. The rebels had taken refuge with their belongings and livestock in a subterranean cave system called Keiris (Ciris). It provided Crassus with an opportunity for a textbook blockade. Roman soldiers located all the ways in and out of the cave and sealed them with walls of stone. The people trapped inside were gradually starved into submission and their increasingly agonized cries to be released were heard.[259] Emboldened by his success, the pro-consul marched his army against other tribes in the federation making up the Getae nation. Genucla, the most strongly defended fortress of the kingdom of Zyraxes, became Crassus' next target. He learned that the military standards (*signa*), which the Bastarnae had seized from C. Antonius (the governor of Macedonia in 59 BCE) in a battle near the city the Istrians built upon the river, were held there.[260] It was another opportunity to cover himself in glory. The assault was made both by land and from along the Danube. Zyraxes was not at the fortress. As soon as he had heard of the Romans' approach, it seems the king had left urgently to meet the Scythians and seek an alliance with them, but failed to return in time to lead the defence.[261] In a relatively short siege, and despite strong opposition from the defenders, Crassus finally captured the stronghold and recovered the standards.

After two campaigns, Crassus had added, perhaps unintentionally, the region of Moesia as a new territory to the empire of the Roman People. The conquered people, however, did not kowtow. They rebelled against their would-be sub-jugator. Even reduced in numbers, they remained a formidable opponent. Only by co-ordinating their tactical operations did the combined efforts of Crassus' deputies eventually quell the uprising. Crassus himself had to deal with violent protests from the Artacii and other nations:

who had never been captured and would not acknowledge his authority, priding themselves greatly upon this point and at the same time inspiring in the others both anger and a disposition to rebel. He brought them to terms, partly by force, after they had made no little trouble, and partly by fear for their countrymen who were being captured.[262]

The campaign had lasted two seasons and forced Crassus' army to stay in enemy territory through a difficult winter. The proconsul had waged war on his own initiative, as he was entitled to under the terms of his *imperium*, but the acclamation and claim over the *spolia opima* did not sit well with Imp. Caesar.[263] In the late 30s BCE, the young heir to the dictator had visited the Temple of Feretrius beside the *Capitolium*. By then the building was already in a precarious state (part of the roof was damaged and letting in rain).[264] Inside the decaying building he read the 'inscription on the linen breastplate (*thorace linteo*)' of Cossus, which was already four centuries old.[265] Inspired by what he saw, he had vowed to restore the building, the repairs to which may have begun in 32 or 31 BCE.[266] Crassus' military achievement collided head-on with political expediency. His claim posed an awkward predicament for Imp. Caesar. Allowing Crassus to make his dedication in the temple, and thus take his place beside Rome's three other timeless heroes, could be seen as undermining his own carefully crafted posture as Rome's pre-eminent commander of the modern era. Imp. Caesar insisted that the rules had to be followed. He had inherited the exclusive right granted to Iulius Caesar, in 45 or 44 BCE, of 'dedicating *spolia opima* in the shrine of the Iupiter Feretrius just as if he had slain a commander of the enemy with his own hand'.[267] Since Crassus did not report to him and operate under his auspices (*auspicia*), the proconsul would not be permitted to deposit the spoils. Furthermore, Crassus' entitlement to use the designation *imperator* was also disputed. The man who had assumed the honourary title as his first name quietly saw to it that the claimant could not keep that either.[268] (Caesar assumed the title for himself, counting it as his seventh acclamation.)[269] For his indisputable valour and exemplary field leadership, Crassus was, however, permitted a full triumph and sacrifices.[270]

Meanwhile, in Belgica proconsul M. Nonius Gallus quelled an uprising of the Treveri, a nation living beside the Moselle River which had nominally been conquered by Iulius Caesar in the 50s BCE but was still under arms two decades later.[271] For his successful action against them, his troops acclaimed him *imperator*.[272] In the mountains of northern Spain too, local tribesmen continued to resist Roman attempts at full conquest of the Iberian peninsula. When not interrupted by civil wars between their own leaders, a succession of legates had endeavoured to complete the conquest begun in 218 BCE, but each had found themselves fighting motivated insurgents.[273] The end to the project remained elusive. Statilius Taurus was now in charge of operations there, making slow but steady progress against the Astures, Cantabri and Vaccaei.[274] Dio writes:

> There were also numerous other disturbances going on in various regions; yet inasmuch as nothing of importance resulted from them, the Romans at the time did not consider that they were engaged in war, nor have I, for my part, anything notable to record about them.[275]

Imp. Caesar himself was needed in Rome, where he had been elected consul for the year, to restore a much-needed sense of stability amongst the war-weary populace. By the spring, Caesar's business in Egypt was done and it was time to leave. He would never return. In readiness for his arrival in Italy in August the Senate had voted a cornucopia of awards and honours for him. It granted him a full triumph for his victory over Kleopatra in the Actian War, and another for defeating the Egyptian army in the Alexandrian War.[276] It further decreed that he should be allowed to wear the laurel crown and *toga picta* of the victorious *triumphator* at *all* public festivals, not just on the day of his triumph.[277] The Senate consented to erect arches (*iani*) adorned with trophies, one in Brundisium where he had re-entered the homeland and one in Rome's *Forum Romanum* (plate 11), taking care not to mention in the entablature inscriptions that Roman lives had been sacrificed on Antonius' side.[278] The bronze *rostra* of the warships captured at Actium would be affixed to the foundation slab of the shrine of Iulius Caesar in the city and a festival would be held every four years in honour of his heir. There would be a general thanksgiving on his birthday – 23 September – and another on the anniversary of the announcement of his victory. When he entered the city it was decreed the Vestal Virgins, the Conscript Fathers and the people with their wives and children should go out as a throng to greet him.[279] Decorations of wreaths or crowns (*coronae*) – the equivalent of modern medals – of various kinds, bronze statues and other lesser public honours were awarded to him.[280] The priests and priestesses were required to pray for him and at all banquets, be they public or private, everyone present was obliged to pour a libation to him.[281] The only honour Caesar expressly declined was the one requiring that the whole population of the city should go out to meet him on his arrival; he was never one for grand receptions.[282]

One honour particularly pleased Imp. Caesar. That was the decree requiring the bronze doors of the Temple of Ianus Quirinus to be closed. Shutting the double doors of the home of the ancient god with two faces on 11 January advertised to the world that all wars had ceased; it was an exceedingly rare event and that it could happen on account of Caesar's actions reflected very well on him personally.[283] Connected with its closure was the honour of performing the *augurium salutis*, a rite that could only be observed on the day of each year upon which no Roman army was actively engaged in war fighting, or the preparation for war.[284]

Silver coins poured out of the mint at Brundisium and from the Temple of Iuno Moneta in Rome, spreading news of Imp. Caesar's victory at Actium. Exquisitely cut portraits of Caesar on the obverses, and images of a naval war trophy or winged Victory standing on a ship's prow on the reverses, communicated the message to the widest audience as the *denarii* passed through people's hands.[285] The contributions of his leadership team were individually and publicly recognized too. 'Caesar bestowed eulogies and honours upon his deputies, as was customary,' writes Dio, 'and to Agrippa he further granted, among other distinctions, a dark blue flag in honour of his naval victory.'[286] It was a unique honour. The choice of a vividly coloured ensign (*vexillum*) – blue to signify the sea – may have been determined by the fact that Agrippa had already received the *corona classica* or *corona navalis* (the golden crown surmounted with ships' beaks) for his victory over Sex. Pompeius at Mylae and Naulochus in 36 BCE.[287] Agrippa received other honours as well, but Dio, who is our primary source on these matters, does not specify what they were.[288] Caesar may have given Agrippa a share of the treasure removed from Egypt and he may also have received an estate there.[289] Caesar gave away valuable property in Rome. For the joint use and enjoyment of Agrippa and Messalla, he donated the house of M. Antonius on the Palatinus Hill.[290] It may have been at this time that four columns (*columna rostrata*) incorporating bronze beaks and anchors of warships captured at Actium were erected in Rome in honour of Caesar and Agrippa.[291] Proud of their role in fighting for Imp. Caesar's naval victory, several regular soldiers adopted the war title *Actiacus* as their *cognomen*.[292] The commander-in-chief and his deputies refrained from doing so. Only *Legio* XI is recorded to have taken the battle honour.[293]

The high point of the year was to come in the summer. For three days (from 13 until 15 August) Imp. Caesar celebrated not one, but three military celebrations.[294] Each was a full triumph (*pompa triumphalis*) – a combination of ticker-tape parade and carnival, with a solemn religious rite concluding the event. Leading the procession, and displayed as war trophies, were the war spoils and paintings or dioramas of battles displayed on wheeled floats, accompanied by trumpeters and dancers, and high-value captives, bound in chains. Painted sign boards (*fercula*) explained the exhibits to the curious crowds. Following behind them was Caesar the *triumphator*, a laurel crown upon his brow, his face and arms daubed in purple dye, as was the custom, and carrying a sceptre (plate 9). He wore, not military panoply, but the purple *toga picta* elaborately embroidered with stars and draped over the *tunica palmata*, bearing fine stitch work of victory palms. He rode in a high-sided chariot decorated with a gilt laurel crown and winged victories (plate 10). Standing behind him in the chariot, a public slave held a golden crown above his head and periodically uttered in his ear the phrase 'look behind you: remember you are a man'.[295] Making the occasion a family affair, his nephew M. Claudius Marcellus (son of his sister Octavia) and oldest stepson Ti. Claudius Nero (by marriage to Livia Drusilla) rode the flanking horses, and his daughter Iulia and youngest stepson Nero Claudius Drusus stood beside him in the *triumphator*'s chariot.[296] Massed ranks of soldiers marched behind them, singing bawdy songs. Along the route crowds cheered their hero. The procession wound its way round the city, through the *Forum Romanum* along the *Via Sacra*, and finally up to the *Capitolium*, where sacrifices were made to Jupiter, king of the Roman pantheon, in the climax of the proceedings.

On the first day he celebrated the victories of 35 and 34 BCE in Illyricum.[297] The second celebrated the Actian War, during which Agrippa must surely have made an appearance; but the most spectacular of the three days was saved until last.[298] This honoured Caesar's victory in the Alexandrian War, and with it the annexation of Egypt. In the absence of the living queen, a wax effigy of Kleopatra was carried on a couch. Her surviving children – the 10-year-old twins Alexander Helios and Kleopatra Selene II and 6-year-old Ptolemaeus Philadelphus – walked in the vanguard with other enchained captives and carts heaped up with war spoils.[299] Caesar rode in his chariot and after him came his fellow-consul Sex. Appuleius and the other magistrates, along with the senators who had participated in the campaign, each wearing their purple-bordered togas.[300] Alexander, the brother of Iamblichus, was led in his triumphal procession and afterwards put to death because he had secured his realm as a reward for accusing Caesar.[301] In contrast, when Rolis, king of the Getae, visited Caesar he was treated as a friend and ally on account of his service to the Romans.[302]

On 18 August, Caesar dedicated the new Temple of Iulius Caesar and the renovated *Curia Iulia*.[303] These buildings reinforced his public support of the emerging cult of *Divus Caesar*, the popular Roman military hero deified by decree of the Senate thirteen years earlier; they were subtle, but ever present, reminders of the personal connection between the god Iulius and his mortal heir.[304] Ten days later, a statue of *Victoria* (the angel-like winged goddess of victory in battle) was installed inside the new Senate House, 'thus signifying that it was from her that he had received the empire'.[305]

With the wealth of Egypt finally in his possession, Imp. Caesar paid off his own debts and cancelled the financial obligations on the Treasury (*Aerarium Saturni*) incurred prior to 2 September 31 BCE.[306] He gave to each citizen – adult and child – 400 *sestertii*.[307] So much gold bullion and coin was brought to the city that inflation spread through the economy, making money for loans easy to find but driving up the prices of basic commodities and property.[308] The result of the sequence of spectacular celebrations and the distributions of largesse was, writes Dio, that 'the Romans forgot all their unpleasant experiences and viewed his triumph with pleasure, quite as if the vanquished had all been foreigners'.[309]

As for M. Antonius, by decree he was declared *damnatio memoriae*, his name being scratched from the roster of Roman citizens.[310] His birthday – 14 January – was declared an unlucky day on which to conduct business, and male members of *gens Antonia* were forever barred from using the *praenomen* Marcus.[311] His statues were also removed – the head of one was even re-carved to become the likeness of M. Agrippa, the man who had defeated him at Actium.[312]

28 BCE

Imp. Caesar *Divi f.* VI   M. Agrippa L. *f.* II

On 1 January 28 BCE, Imp. Caesar was sworn in as consul for his sixth time, alongside Agrippa for his second.[313] Caesar publicly demonstrated his own loyalty to his best friend 'for he always paid exceptional honour to Agrippa'.[314] From that time on, of the twenty-four *fasces* – each an axe in a bundle of rods borne by a paramilitary bodyguard (*lictor*) – given to Caesar as consul he re-assigned half of them to Agrippa, signifying that he considered the two consuls were of equal status.[315] Furthermore, he provided Agrippa with a *praetorium* tent similar in size and design to his own, so that when they were on campaign together they would be seen by the troops as equals, and he instructed that the night watchword was to be given out by both of them.[316]

Fourteen months after the end of the Civil War, Imp. Caesar's intentions were still unclear. The army and navy, even with their reduced size and with the exception of a few legions commanded by proconsuls, were still under his direction. His vision for Rome seems to have been to create a system of government that would prevent a few powerful oligarchs with their own private armies from ever again wreaking destruction upon the Commonwealth, but one also capable of running a worldwide empire and keeping it secure. It could not be an autocracy; there would neither be a king – a *rex*, as in Rome's earliest times, before their expulsion – nor a perpetual *dictator* – as Iulius Caesar had briefly become before his assassination.[317] Both were anathema to Romans. The byword was *restituta*: it would be a *restoration* of the *Res Publica*.[318] To emphasize the point, a gold coin minted this year announced that 'he restored the laws and rights to the Roman People' – the 'he' being the Imp. Caesar, whose laureate head was shown on the reverse side.[319] Outwardly, the Roman Commonwealth would retain its essential character as a democratic nation of free citizens working together in the Senate and Popular Assemblies to ratify laws, elect their peers for public office and hold them accountable for their actions after completion of their terms. What made it different from pre-Civil War days was that Imp. Caesar's men now managed the key institutions which decided who was granted *imperium*.[320]

In the Senate, Caesar was appointed as *princeps*, a largely honorary but traditional position indicating he was the leading man among the Conscript Fathers; crucially, in this role he could speak first on matters in the House, and thus set the tone of the ensuing discussion.[321] He and Agrippa were also granted the powers of *censor* – but not actually the office – with which to conduct a count of the Roman population for taxation purposes but, as importantly, to review the membership of the Senate.[322] They set to work to downsize it by as much as two-thirds, from 1,000 men to eventually just 300 – the number it had originally been when first convened centuries before.[323] They rewarded their own loyal followers and admitted as members many of the patrician families newly created under the *Lex Saenia*.[324] To prevent senators from meddling in the affairs of the provinces and the army, any member wishing to travel outside Italy – except Sicily and Gallia Narbonensis – would have to ask permission first from Caesar.[325] However, to reassure those senators who had been loyal to M. Antonius that there would be no retaliation against them, Caesar burned all the private correspondence with the late *triumvir*, ensuring their contents were kept secret forever.[326]

Restoration came to Rome's cityscape too. Before a campaign, a commander would pray, ask his chosen god to bless his military endeavour and promise upon his successful return that he would erect an altar and offer sacrifice in gratitude. A great victory, however, called for a temple. Over the centuries, Rome's public spaces had become crowded with them. Many had fallen into dereliction from years of neglect of their upkeep. In an act of piety (*pietas*), this year Caesar commenced an ongoing programme of repairs to these temples – eventually eighty-two in all.[327] Apollo (Imp. Caesar's personal favourite god) received particular attention. He dedicated a temple to him on the Palatinus Hill beside his own house – the *Palatium* – complete with a colonaded square and a library.[328]

The victory honours extended to Caesar went beyond bricks and mortar. During the period of *postbellum* euphoria, the Senate had voted games to be held in his honour (for his victory at the Battle of Actium) and of Apollo Actius.[329] The first of these athletic and blood sport events (called Circensian Games) was held this year, at which Imp. Caesar and Agrippa attended in person.[330] Presented within a specially constructed wooden stadium erected for the purpose in the *Campus Martius*, boys and men of the nobility took part in a gymnastic contest, and gladiatorial combats were fought between captives.[331] The festivities lasted for several days. When Imp. Caesar was unexpectedly taken ill, his right-hand man, M. Agrippa, continued attending to represent them both.[332]

Several victorious commanders returned this year to Rome to celebrate their achievements in grand fashion. On 28 May, C. Calvisius Sabinus celebrated his full triumph for success in Hispania Citerior.[333] On 14 July, it was the turn of C. Carrinas for his actions against the Morini and Suebi. On 16 August,

L. Autronius Paetus rode the *triumphator*'s chariot along the *Via Sacra* for his victory in Africa.

In Egypt, Cornelius Gallus faced his first test when the inhabitants of Heroöpolis rebelled. The Pithom of the Hebrew Bible, it was now a large city east of the Nile Delta, located near the mouth of the Royal Canal which connected the Nile River with the Red Sea, and thus was of strategic importance. Gallus arrived with a small number of soldiers and quickly retook the city.[334] A dispute over taxation, which turned violent in the Thebaïd, was also met by force and quelled by the *Praefectus Aegypti*. Taking advantage of the instability, the Meroites invaded from Ethiopia. In a withering counteroffensive, Gallus recaptured five cities – Boresis, Koptos, Keramike, Diospolis Megale (Thebes) and Ophieon – in just fifteen days of battles and then crossed the border at the First Cataract.[335] He drove the Ethiopians back to their city of Pselchis (Ad-Dakka) on the Nile. Receiving the king at Philae, Gallus established a new buffer zone below the First Cataract, called *Triacontaschoenus Aethiopiae* (meaning 'The Thirty Miles of Ethiopia'), over which the Meroite regent ruled, but from that time on as a client of the Roman People.[336]

Elsewhere around the empire, Roman troops in their winter camps performed their normal policing and security duties, while others repaired their equipment and practised their fighting skills with wooden swords and wicker shields. It seemed that, for the first time in years, most of the people of the empire – but especially those in the Italian homeland – had enjoyed a year of relative peace.

Chapter 2

Command and Conquer
27–19 BCE

27 BCE

Imp. Caesar *Divi f.* Augustus VII   M. Agrippa L. *f.* III

In January, Imp. Caesar's consulship was renewed for the seventh time, Agrippa's for the third.[1] Caesar now faced a difficult and consequential decision. He had won the civil war and was the commander-in-chief of the majority of the armed forces. If the Roman world was at peace (or at least no longer consumed by a worldwide conflict) and there were no existential threats to its security, his mission had been accomplished. Should not Caesar now renounce his military command and restore full control of the army to the Roman People, as he had their laws and rights?[2] The stakes were high, both to him personally and to the *Res Publica*, but he was above all a practical politician. He and his close advisers had thought long and deeply about the matter, and had reached an agreement on a plan. On 13 January, it was presented to the Senate. That day Imp. Caesar read from a prepared statement.[3] To the great surprise of many of those present in the *Curia Iulia*, Caesar announced his resignation from the Senate.[4] His supporters, who had been told in advance, responded with rehearsed pleas for him to stay on.[5] The members not in the know were suddenly uncertain about what to do. No one wanted to see a return of conditions that could lead to another civil war.[6] Caesar's supporters now executed their plan. As an inducement to retain his service, several senators moved to offer him *imperium proconsulare* (proconsular military power) over Rome's provinces, save for the homeland of Italy, giving him what was in effect his own personal super *provincia*.[7] Caesar accepted. It was tantamount to a *coup d'état*, but through careful stage-management there had been no violence.[8] To ensure his own blood would not be spilled in the days following, Caesar's very first act was to secure a decree giving the men who would serve as his bodyguard double what was paid to the regular soldiers.[9]

Imp. Caesar had a more nuanced plan for the management of the world 'under the sovereignty of the Roman People', as he called it.[10] He revealed his idea when the Senate reconvened on 16 January. The empire was to be divided into pro-consular and propraetorian territories, which Strabo calls respectively 'Provinces of the People' and 'Provinces of Caesar'.[11] Strabo, a contemporary who lived through the reforms, explains that Caesar kept:

> to himself all parts that had need of a military guard (that is, the part that was barbarian and in the neighbourhood of tribes not yet subdued, or lands that

were sterile and difficult to bring under cultivation, so that, being unprovided with everything else, but well provided with strongholds, they would try to throw off the bridle and refuse obedience), and to the Roman people all the rest, in so far as it was peaceable and easy to rule without arms.[12]

The Senate would retain control of the mainly prosperous territories around the Mediterranean Sea, those being Africa, Numidia, Asia, Greece with Epirus, Illyricium and Macedonia, Sicily, Crete and the Cyrenaica portion of Libya, Bithynia and Pontus which adjoined it, Sardinia and Hispania Ulterior (map 3).[13] In keeping with the traditions of the *Res Publica* – that he was so keen to present as 'restored' – the governors of these provinces would be proconsuls, picked annually by lot by the Senate, as they had for centuries. The crucial innovation was the partnership struck between himself and the Senate. By *Lex de Imperio* for a period of ten years, Imp. Caesar agreed to take sole responsibility for the propraetorian provinces.[14] In his *provincia* he now had direct control of Hispania Citerior, the three Gallic provinces of Aquitania, Gallia Comata (also known as Celtica) and Belgica, Narbonensis, Coele-Syria, Syria, Cilicia, Cyprus and newly acquired Aegyptus (fig. 2).[15] Pacification continued to be the priority in these regions. The majority of the legions – twenty-two of the twenty-eight – and the auxiliary units were stationed in these territories, effectively giving Imp. Caesar command of the army (*exercitus*).[16] It was not by coincidence. He had already made the crucial decisions about legionary deployments in 30 BCE, very likely with this long-range goal of his control of them in mind.[17]

Crucially, Imp. Caesar was granted the right in law to appoint the men to run them. These men were his hand-picked legates, each one deputized to act in his name and serve him for a period of three years.[18] They were selected from among the ex-consuls, ex-praetors or ex-quaestors, or one of the positions between *praetor* and *quaestor*.[19] Their official title, *legati Augusti pro praetore*, indicated they were subordinate to Imp. Caesar (operating under his auspices and deriving their *imperium* from him) and they could not claim the glory or spoils they won in carrying out their duties.[20] (These would accrue to Caesar.) Moreover, the commander-in-chief could take over at any time or appoint any of his chosen friends or family to do so. Dio reports:

> The following regulations were laid down for them all alike: they were not to raise levies of soldiers or to exact money beyond the amount appointed, unless the Senate should so vote or the emperor so order; and when their successors arrived, they were to leave the province at once, and not to delay on the return journey, but to get back within three months.[21]

His *legati* were required to wear the panoply of a military officer, in contrast to the proconsuls who wore the national attire of a civilian *toga* with the purple strip.[22] Their rank was junior to the governors of proconsular provinces too, and to emphasize the fact, they had five rather than a full complement of six lictors.[23]

Grateful for his generosity and willingness to term-limit his powers, the Senate sought a suitable title for him in recognition. Imp. Caesar knew not to demand

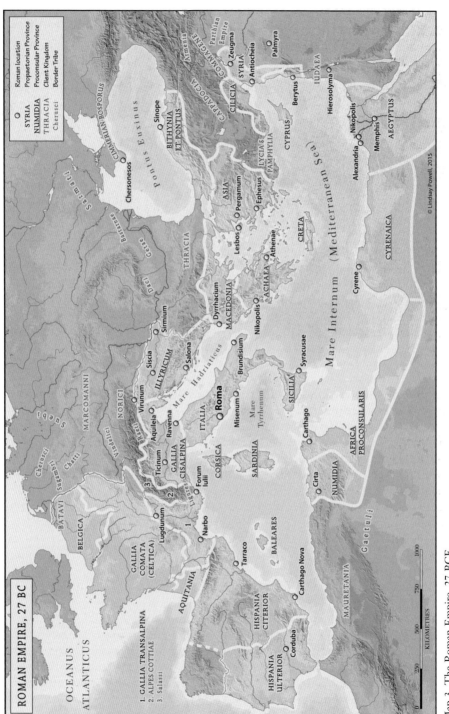

ROMAN EMPIRE, 27 BC

	Roman location
SYRIA	Propraetorian Province
NUMIDIA	Proconsular Province
THRACIA	Client Kingdom
Cherusci	Border Tribe

1. GALLIA TRANSALPINA
2. ALPES COTTIAE
3. Salassi

© Lindsay Powell, 2015

Map 3. The Roman Empire, 27 BCE.

Figure 2. Augustus presented himself as a commander-in-chief, taking *Imperator* as his first name. He counted the imperatorial acclamations of his deputies as his own (see *Res Gestae* 4).

the title of *dictator perpetuo* as his great uncle had. Dio records that Caesar was rather keen on the name Romulus, after the city's legendary founder; sensitive to its negative associations with royalty, however, he desisted from pushing the matter.[24] At the suggestion of Munatius Plancus – a crafty man who had switched sides many times during his career before settling on Caesar's – the Senate unanimously voted him the honorific title *Augustus*, a word meaning 'the revered one'.[25] The name did not carry any inherent hard power – he already had abundant *auctoritas* (the prestige or personal influence derived from his victories, political achievements and legacy as heir of Iulius Caesar), as well as legal military power (*imperium*) conferred on him by virtue of being an elected consul of the *Res Publica*. Yet it did come with the soft power derived from its religious connotation, indicating that a person so named was sacred or worthy of worship.[26] From that day forth it was the name by which he was called – and is still best known today.[27]

Imp. Caesar *Divi filius* Augustus was also voted a slate of new honours, many using ancient symbols designed to evoke old traditions borne of success in war. By ending the conflict he had saved the lives of countless fellow citizens (expressed on coins and inscriptions by the phrase *ob cives servatos*) (plate 12), in recognition of which he was permitted to grow a laurel tree outside his house on the Palatinus Hill, while from his front door he could hang a crown made of leafy oak twigs, emblems of peace and victory, images that were promoted on coins (plate 13).[28]

The Senate also granted him the right to display a round 'Shield of Virtue' (*clipeus virtutis*) (plate 14) in the *Curia*, upon which were inscribed his cardinal virtues of 'courage, clemency, justice and duty'.[29] It hung close to the statue of winged Victory.[30]

While political control of the army transferred peacefully in Rome, her troops were engaged in the bloody business of combat operations elsewhere. Shrewdly, Caesar Augustus decided it would be wise to absent himself from Rome for a while. Shortly before 4 July, leaving Rome in M. Agrippa's care, he headed north by land. Augustus was keen to make his mark on the world. He had ambitions for conquest beyond the present borders of Empire. In his chronicles Dio records:

> He also set out to make an expedition into Britannia, but on coming to the provinces of Gallia lingered there. For the Britons seemed likely to make terms with him.[31]

Years before, Iulius Caesar had launched two amphibious campaigns to the island, in 55 and 54 BCE. Neither amounted to much more than raids, but he won great notoriety as the first Roman to traverse the British Ocean and gained political capital from the story.[32] By actually conquering Britannia, Augustus would achieve something his adoptive father had not.[33]

The chance for glory had to be offset by the need for pragmatics. The deceased commander had failed to begin, let alone complete, the process of pacification of the Gallic territories that he had spent a decade conquering. In 27 BCE, 'the affairs of the Gauls were still unsettled, as the civil wars had begun immediately after their subjugation', writes Dio.[34] The security of the people of the provinces had remained precarious for a generation. The presence of a semi-permanent Roman army in the region is implied, but the historical sources give no indication as to the number, type or whereabouts of units. The confederacy of fourteen nations forming the Aquitani (between the Garonna and Liger rivers) had rebelled while Agrippa had been governor in 39/38 BCE, and had been quelled by him.[35] In 27 BCE they rose up again. M. Valerius Messalla Corvinus (consul of 31 BCE) was dispatched to deal with the problem; with him was Albius Tibullus, a young officer who 'was his tent companion in the war in Aquitania and was given military prizes'.[36] Indeed, Corvinus would celebrate his success with a triumph in fine style in Rome on 25 September this year.[37] But there had been other sporadic uprisings since in Belgica, and incursions by Germanic bandits from across the Rhine.[38]

After war came the opportunity to make peace. The Romans had a plan for post-war pacification.[39] Independent tribes would be transformed into urban Romanized communities with a national identity. Army surveyors would mark out the foundation of new towns in which to resettle the people from their hilltop strongholds. The leading families would be assimilated into the political system modelled on the institutions of the *Res Publica*. It began with a *census* to assess the size of the population and its wealth in coin and ability to produce grain, fruit, hides and the basic necessities. This would, in part, pay in coin and kind for the army based there to defend it.[40] The information-gathering process took time and was conducted by the staff of the *legatus Augusti pro praetore*. Augustus likely wintered at *Colonia* Copia Felix Munatia (modern Lyon). It was the leading city of the Gallic region, from which metalled roads built by Agrippa radiated and along which troops and officials could move unhindered.[41]

On 25 July, M. Licinius Crassus celebrated his triumph for his victories in Thracia and the territory that would later become known as Moesia (see Table 6). Also this year, Polemon Pythodorus of Pontus was recognized as an ally of the Roman People.[42] He was among the first of many allied kings who had supported M. Antonius now seeking to reconcile with the victor of the Battle of Actium and 'First Man' in Rome.

26 BCE
Imp. Caesar *Divi f.* Augustus VIII   T. Statilius T. *f.* Taurus II

Having played a crucial part at Actium and recently performed with distinction in the Iberian Peninsula, Statilius Taurus was rewarded with a second term as consul alongside Augustus, now serving his eighth term.[43] On 26 January, Sex. Appuleius (*cos.* 29 BCE) celebrated his triumph in Rome for victories in Hispania Citerior.[44] Meanwhile, Augustus sought an opportunity for military glory for himself. Remote Britannia might provide it. In assessing the chance of success, he may have hoped for a quick campaign to take the island, or at least to make all or parts of it a client kingdom, but the politics were complex: there were numerous tribes – some pro- and others anti-Roman – many of which were warring with each other. Kings Dumnobellaunus and Tincomarus are known to have sought the friendship of the Romans, and likely met Augustus in person.[45] His attempts at diplomacy with the Britons, however, failed when the people with whom the Romans were negotiating refused to agree terms.[46] The information that has come down to us is too cryptic to determine the extent and seriousness of Augustus' ambitions for annexing the land over the ocean.[47] The conquest of Britannia would have to wait. There were other matters now needing his urgent consideration.

Satisfied that public affairs in Aquitania, Gallia Comata and Belgica were under control, Augustus proceeded to the Iberian Peninsula, intending to 'establish order there also'.[48] Augustus arrived in Segisama (Sasamon, west of Burgos) and made it his forward base of operations.[49] Roman forces had been active for almost a decade in the region between the Basque Country and Cantabria (as the recent discovery of a military installation at Andagoste (Cuartango) shows), but they had failed to stop the violent resistance of the local people.[50] Despite Statilius Taurus' successes in the region three years before, the Astures and the Cantabri in the north and northwest of the peninsula continued to resist full annexation.[51] They also represented a threat to territory recently acquired by Romans, for 'not content with defending their liberty, they tried also to dominate their neighbours and harassed the Vaccaei, the Turmogi and the Autrigones by frequent raids'.[52] Banditry (*latrocinium*) was a particular problem:

> There was a robber named Corocotta, who flourished in Iberia, at whom he [Augustus] was so angry at first that he offered a million *sestertii* to the man

that should capture him alive; but later, when the robber came to him of his own accord, he not only did him no harm, but actually made him richer by the amount of the reward.[53]

Augustus decided that only a full-blooded military campaign using overwhelming force would finally break these unyielding peoples and that he, personally, would lead it.[54] In preparation for the campaign, he assembled an immense force, including *Legiones* I *Augusta*, II *Augusta*, IIII *Macedonica*, V *Alaudae*, VI *Victrix*, VIIII *Hispana*, X *Gemina* and XX[55] (see Order of Battle 1). They were supported by auxiliary cavalry from *Ala Augusta*, *Ala* II *Gallorum*, *Ala Parthorum* and *Ala* II *Thracum Victrix Civium Romanorum*; and auxiliary infantry from *Cohors* II *Gallorum* and *Cohors* IV *Thracum Aequitata*.[56] The total land force deployed was up to 52,000 troops. The number of enemy troops they would face is not recorded.

Augustus had with him two experienced *legati*.[57] The first, C. Antistius Vetus (serving with him as suffect consul in 30 BCE), was the former proconsul of Gallia Narbonnensis who had lost the war with the Salassi; nevertheless, he brought experience of mountain warfare and, perhaps, now older and wiser, sought an opportunity to redeem himself.[58] He now replaced Sex. Appuleius as *legatus Augusti pro praetore*.[59] The second legate, P. Carisius, had served in the war against Sex. Pompeius in Sicily on Imp. Caesar's side, and was eager to take on a senior command role.[60] Also accompanying Augustus was Ti. Claudius Nero (his stepson by Livia) and M. Claudius Marcellus (his nephew by his sister Octavia); both aged 16, they were beginning their military careers as *tribunus militum*.[61]

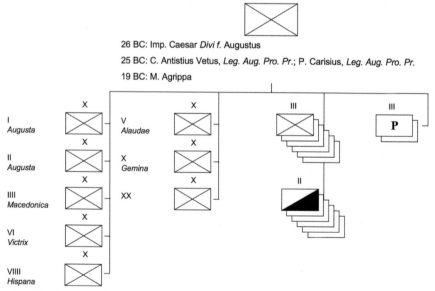

Order of Battle 1. Cantabria and Asturia, 26–19 BCE. Several units of ethnic *auxilia* are recorded as having served in Hispania including *Cohors* II *Gallorum* and *Cohors* IV *Thracum Aequitata* as well as *Ala Augusta*, *Ala* II *Gallorum*, *Ala Parthorum* and *Ala Thracum Victrix C.R.*

Over many years the warriors of the two aboriginal peoples had proved very able to resist the Romans. From strongholds in the hills and valleys of the craggy Cantabrian Mountains, they forced a guerrilla-style war upon an enemy trained to fight set-piece battles on open plains.[62] The trouser and tunic-wearing warrior of the Astures and Cantabri preferred light equipment optimized for ambuscades and skirmishes. He fought with either a leaf-shaped dagger (*pugio*) a short, straight double-edged stabbing sword (*gladius hispaniensis*) or a curved, single-edged *falcata*, or more commonly with darts or spears; he defended himself with a buckler (*caetrae*) – concave in shape and made from wood and leather, two feet in diameter – or a rectangular *scutum*; and on his head wore a leather hood to cover his long hair or, if he could afford one, a bronze helmet.[63] The Cantabrians alone among the Celt-Iberian peoples used the double-headed axe (*bipennis*).[64] Their cavalry were renowned for their tight formation fighting, notably the *circulus Cantabricum* in which a single file of riders rode in a circle while launching a volley of missiles; and the *Cantabricus impetus*, a fast, massed charge at the enemy troops.[65] An infantryman might ride into battle seated behind a cavalryman and dismount to engage the opponent on foot.[66]

While Dio writes 'Augustus himself waged war upon the Astures and upon the Cantabri at one and the same time,' in practice he treated them as two separate targets.[67] The first mission was to reduce to submission the Cantabri. In a co-ordinated three-pronged offensive, he led one of the army groups from Segisama in the south, while Vetus and Carisius commanded the other two (map 4).[68] The first recorded battle of the campaign was fought under the walls of Attica or Vellica (modern Helechia), 5 miles south of the base of *Legio* IIII.[69] It was a swift victory. Beaten, the Cantabri grudgingly withdrew to Mons Vindius or Vinnius (possibly Peña Santa) – described as 'a natural fortress' – in the expectation the Romans would not to follow them into the mountains, where they could exploit the terrain to their advantage.[70] The enemy the Romans faced was agile, cunning and resilient. Dio writes:

> But these peoples would neither yield to him, because they were confident on account of their strongholds, nor would they come to close quarters, owing to their inferior numbers and the circumstance that most of them were spear-throwers, and, besides, they kept causing him a great deal of annoyance, always forestalling him by seizing the higher ground whenever a manoeuvre was attempted, and lying in ambush for him in the valleys and woods.[71]

Despite the massive resources Augustus had deployed, the campaign was not delivering the results he sought. Vindius only fell to him when the people trapped inside began to starve and surrendered.[72] He opened a new front on the northern side when he ordered transports to sail from Aquitania with troops – perhaps of *Cohortes Aquitanorum Veterana* formed from men of the fleet at Forum Iulii – who 'disembarked while the enemy were off their guard'.[73] At the city of Aracillum or Racilium (possibly modern Aradillos or Espina del Gallego), the rebels held

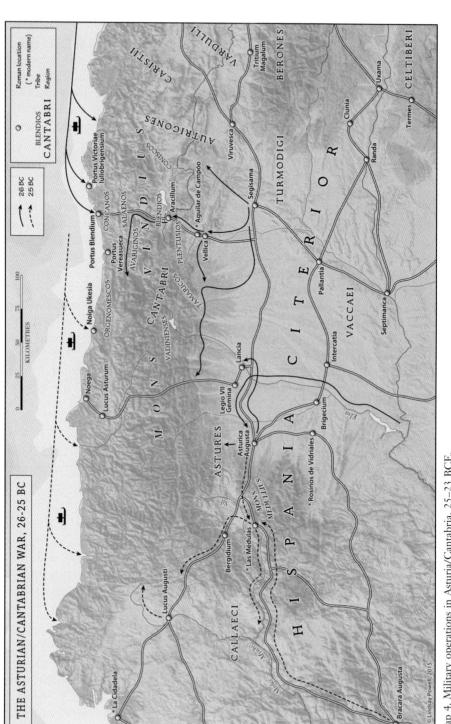

Map 4. Military operations in Asturia/Cantabria, 25–23 BCE.

out, before finally succumbing to Augustus' troops.[74] With Roman forces now advancing upon the rebels on several sides, they gradually 'enclosed its fierce people like wild beasts in a net', as one historian described the attack.[75] The war began to turn in the Roman commander-in-chief's favour. Indeed it may have been during this campaign that *Legio* VIIII received its honorific title *Hispana* or *Hispaniensis* for victory in battle. Archaeological investigations demonstrate the intensive use of artillery (both large and small calibre) to overwhelm the native defenders of the hilltop stronghold at the *oppidum* of Monte Bernorio.[76]

When not assessing military strategies and tactics, Augustus attended to official matters. His mind also turned to a new project by P. Vergilius Maro – not a military man but a poet of high regard from Mantua. He had come to the *princeps*' attention through his close friend Maecenas, who was patronizing poetic talents for his amusement and edification. Impressed by his work thus far, Augustus had commissioned Vergil to compose an epic poem two years earlier. Called the *Aeneid*, it would describe the flight of the warrior Aeneas from Troy after its fall to the Greeks and his epic journey to Italy, ultimately leading to the foundation of Rome.[77] The mythological story greatly appealed to the *princeps*. It would be an allegorical narrative for the new age of renovation and restoration he was pioneering, glorifying old Roman values and appealing to the nation's belief in its exceptionalism. Augustus was impatient to see evidence of progress on it even as he was fighting the Cantabri. He:

> demanded in entreating and even jocosely threatening letters that Vergil send him 'something from the *Aeneid*'; to use his own words, 'either the first draft of the poem or any section of it that he pleased'.[78]

The harassed poet obliged and from then on sent him regular instalments.

In Egypt, allegations of serious misconduct were being levelled against the equestrian official Augustus had personally appointed in 30 BCE. Cornelius Gallus had seemed like a good choice for *Praefectus Aegypti* at the time, but the trappings of near absolute power and the sycophancy shown by the Egyptian bureaucrats had corrupted his good judgment, and accentuated his natural arrogance and determination:

> He indulged in a great deal of disrespectful gossip about Augustus and was guilty of many reprehensible actions besides; for he not only set up images of himself practically everywhere in Egypt, but also inscribed upon the pyramids a list of his achievements.[79]

Gallus' comrade and closest friend Valerius Largus informed Augustus of the man's indiscretions and bizarre behaviours.[80] Emboldened by the informant, others soon came forward with their own examples of the prefect's impropriety and overindulgence. The Senate voted to arraign him to face charges in Rome, urging that his punishment should be exile and the confiscation of his assets.[81] Gallus could not look to Augustus for help: he had committed the cardinal sin of betraying the *princeps*' trust and friendship. He knew his career was over.

Before the decree of the Senate was even served and took effect, Gallus ended his own life.[82]

Largus was an ambitious man who thought that he would assume Gallus' office. He was, in fact, becoming powerful by attracting a large following.[83] However, a certain Proculeius:

> conceived such contempt for Largus that once, on meeting him, he clapped his hand over his nose and mouth, thereby hinting to the bystanders that it was not safe even to breathe in the man's presence.[84]

It was a calculated and very public snub. The choice of successor was not Largus' decision to make, but that of Augustus, and he had already chosen another man. The new *Praefectus Aegypti* was C. Aelius Gallus.[85] He took over the position this year. Thereafter Largus vanishes from recorded history.

25 BCE

Imp. Caesar *Divi f.* Augustus IX   M. Iunius M. *f.* Silanus

In the western Alps, the Salassi nation rose up in revolt. This Iron Age 'Celtic' people occupied a strategically important position: they mined gold and levied tolls on the road between Gallia Narbonensis and Gallia Cisalpina, but they also engaged in banditry, all of which drew the interest of the Romans.[86] An attempt to subjugate them in 35 BCE by the then proconsul of Gallia Narbonensis, C. Antistius Vetus, and another by Messalla, had both failed.[87] To deal with the ongoing problem, this time Augustus dispatched A. Terrentius Varro. Nothing is known of his background; he seems, however, to have been a competent field commander.[88] Geography largely determined how he would have to run his campaign. The Salassi lived in a deep glen at the confluence of the Buthier and the Dora Baltea, at the intersection of the Great and Little St Bernard routes, accessible only by passes which they themselves controlled, including the main road from Italy.[89] Varro employed a multi-pronged attack approach, invading their territory at different points simultaneously.[90] It worked: in Livy's economical phrasing, 'the Salassi, an Alpine people, were subdued.'[91] They had been unable to meet their opponents either with sufficient numbers or to unite together to repel them. In a single campaign, Varro had won an important victory for Augustus.[92] Their punishment was heavy:

> After forcing them to come to terms he demanded a stated sum of money, as if he were going to impose no other punishment; then, sending soldiers everywhere ostensibly to collect the money, he arrested those who were of military age and sold them, on the understanding that none of them should be liberated within twenty years.[93]

The prisoners of war were taken to nearby Eporedia (modern Ivrea) – Strabo claims 36,000 were captured, of which 8,000 were men at arms – and sold as slaves.[94] Where Varro had struck his camp he founded a new *colonia*, a city for some 3,000 retiring soldiers, among them Praetorians in whose honour it was granted the name Augusta Praetoria Salassorum (modern Aosta).[95] The presence of so many veterans would help keep the peace in the region and ensure the all-important road through the western Alps stayed open.

Further north, perhaps in retribution for the actions of C. Carrinas back in 30 BCE, Roman traders travelling on the Right Bank of the Rhine found themselves under attack, taken prisoner and brutally executed.[96] The new proconsul of Gallia Comata and Belgica, M. Vinicius, led a punitive raid into Germania Magna. No details survive of the course of the campaign, nor from where along the river it was launched, but it was considered a success. His troops acclaimed Augustus as *imperator*, who counted it as his eighth cumulative award.

In the Iberian Peninsula, the war of conquest began anew. As he so often did during a military campaign, Augustus fell ill. Dio suggests over-exertion and anxiety, while Suetonius says 'he was in such a desperate plight from abscesses of the liver', though it is entirely possible that it was typhus.[97] He was moved urgently from the war zone to Tarraco (modern Tarragona) on the Mediterranean coast, where he remained in the care of his wife, Livia, and personal physician, Antonius Musa.[98] He would remain there for several months in intensive care. Augustus had pushed himself too far. He would never again lead a military campaign in person. From now on he would rely completely on his *legati* to fight his wars for him.

'Meanwhile,' writes Dio:

> Caius Antistius fought against them and accomplished a good deal, not because he was a better commander than Augustus, but because the barbarians felt contempt for him and so joined battle with the Romans and were defeated. In this way he captured a few places, and afterwards Titus Carisius took Lancia, the principal fortress of the Astures, after it had been abandoned, and also won over many other places.[99]

Florus elaborates on the events leading to the siege of Lancia. Carisius' army had pitched three marching camps over the winter beside the Astura (Esla) River.[100] The Astures came down from their snow-capped mountain retreats *en masse* and, dividing into three groups, settled close to the Romans in preparation for an all-out attack.[101] Outnumbered, the Romans faced annihilation, but their luck held. Having been forewarned by the Brigaecini – whose act was seen as treachery by the Astures – Carisius arrived just in time with reinforcements. Carisius engaged the enemy in the open and defeated them, and though he took casualties, the addition of the relief troops turned the odds firmly in the Romans' favour. The Astures withdrew to stage a desperate last stand:

> The well-fortified city of Lancia opened its gates to the remains of the defeated army; here such efforts were needed to counteract the natural advantage of the place, that when firebrands were demanded to burn the captured city, it was only with difficulty that the general won mercy for it from the soldiers, on the plea that it would form a better monument of the Roman victory if it were left standing than if it were burnt.[102]

The last recorded battle in the *Bellum Cantabricum et Asturicum* is the siege of Mons Medullius (possibly Peña Sagra) 'towering above the Minius [Miño] River'.[103] To seal in the rebels, the Roman army surrounded it with a continuous earthwork comprising a ditch and palisade 15 or 18 miles long.[104] The blockade then began. Time was on the side of the Romans. With supplies unable to get in and all routes of escape cut off, the defenders trapped inside were eventually forced to submit. Once in Roman hands, Carisius erected the traditional *tropaeum* of a victor. On a tree trunk staked in a mound covered with round shields, daggers, swords and double-headed axes captured from the Astures, hung the bloody panoply of an unnamed, vanquished rebel commander.[105] The proud *legatus Augusti* later commemorated the sacred victory monument on coins (plates 15 and 16).[106] The veterans (men who had served sixteen years or more) of *Legiones* V *Alaudae*, X *Gemina* and XX were honourably discharged and settled in a new *colonia*, founded – most likely by Carisius – especially for them with grants of land in the newly conquered region, at Augusta Emerita (modern Mérida).[107]

There were also developments in the kingdoms of the allies. King Iuba II (plate 24) was a handsome man in his mid-20s, clean-shaven with short hair, who had an inquiring mind and a talent for writing. After his capture by Iulius Caesar he had been educated in Italy. Since then he had become a good friend of his heir, ruled a kingdom in Africa. He was asked to yield parts of Gaetulia and Numidia to the Romans in exchange for Mauretania and lands formerly ruled by Bokchus and Bogud.[108] He complied without contest. In the East, Amyntas, king of Lycaonia and Galatia, unexpectedly died. An ambitious regent, he had been waging a war against bandits from the Homonadeis nation living in his kingdom and may have been killed in an ambush or a plot.[109] Formerly an ally of M. Antonius, he had switched his allegiance to Augustus and since proved loyal to him. By prior agreement, his kingdom was to pass into the possession of the Roman People as a Province of Caesar. Rome now had a major territory right in the centre of Asia Minor. Its first governor was M. Lollius, a promising and ambitious *novus homo* from a plebeian family who had fought with Caesar at Actium.[110] As *legatus Augusti pro praetore*, he began the process of integrating the territory into the Roman Empire, which included assimilating its army. It was reconstituted as *Legio* XXII *Deiotariana* (named after Amyntas' antecedent Deiotarus II). The city formerly known as Antiocheia was refounded in the new province as a *colonia* called Caesarea for Roman veterans of *Legiones* V *Gallica* and VII.[111]

Though Augustus himself ended the year in uncertain health, the Senate received with delight his reports of successes across his *provincia*:

> A triumph, as well as the title, was voted to Augustus; but as he did not care to celebrate it, a triumphal arch was erected in the Alps in his honour and he was granted the right always to wear both the crown and the triumphal garb on the first day of the year.[112]

While Roman soldiers fought in far-away lands, the doors of the precinct of Ianus in Rome had stayed open. With the campaign season's victories and the ending of wars, Augustus closed them for the second time.[113]

24 BCE

Imp. Caesar *Divi f.* Augustus X   C. Norbanus C. *f.* Flaccus

Augustus recovered sufficiently to leave Tarraco and depart for Rome.[114] The Roman Senate and People expressed their relief when he reached the city:

> Various other privileges were accorded him in honour of his recovery and return. Marcellus was given the right to be a senator among the ex-praetors and to stand for the consulship ten years earlier than was customary, while Tiberius was permitted to stand for each office five years before the regular age; and he was at once elected *quaestor* and Marcellus aedile.[115]

As the next *legatus Augusti pro praetore* of Hispania Citerior he appointed, according to one source, L. Aelius Lamia, to another L. Aemilius Paullus Lepidus (*cos.* 34 BCE).[116] The contemporary historian Velleius Paterculus describes Lamia as 'a man of the older type, who always tempered his old-fashioned dignity by a spirit of kindliness'.[117] His mild nature would be tested by both the rugged Cantabrian Mountains and its tough, resourceful peoples. To prove they were still unbeaten, the Astures and Cantabri rebelled once again. They hatched an elaborate, but cruel, subterfuge:

> Sending word to Aemilius, before revealing to him the least sign whatever of their purpose, they said that they wished to make a gift to his army of grain and other things. Then, after securing a considerable number of soldiers, ostensibly to take back the gifts, they conducted them to places for their purpose and murdered them.[118]

Lamia (or Lepidus) now showed how tough-minded a *vir antiquissimi* could be. He ordered his troops to devastate the rebels' lands and mete out harsh punishments to anyone taken captive. To ensure no future revolts, the hands of all the prisoners of war were cut off. Within the year the revolt was over.[119]

In Egypt, the new *Praefectus Aegypti* had initiated a war against neighbouring Arabia Felix.[120] According to Strabo, who knew Gallus and may have been a friend, Augustus personally authorized the expedition:

> He was sent by Augustus Caesar to explore the tribes and the places, not only in Arabia, but also in Aethiopia, since Caesar saw that the Troglodyte country which adjoins Aegyptus' neighbours upon Arabia, and also that the Arabian Gulf, which separates the Arabians from the Troglodytes, is extremely narrow. Accordingly he conceived the purpose of winning the Arabians over to himself or of subjugating them.[121]

There were economic attractions to annexing the territory. The Arabians were wealthy from trading in spices, gold, silver and gemstones with merchants in the Near East, northern and eastern Africa and even India.[122] It was a prize worth having and, so he thought, ripe for the taking.

Gallus assembled an expeditionary force of 10,000 infantry, comprising men of the Roman garrison of province Aegyptus and of allies – 500 Jewish troops were provided by Herodes, and 1,000 Nabataeans arrived from Petra with their administrator, Syllaeus.[123] Expecting to engage the enemy on the sea, the prefect invested in eighty vessels (biremes, triremes and light boats) built at the shipyard at Kleopatris (or Arsinoê, modern Suez), located on a canal which connected the Nile River to the Gulf.[124]

Setting off in early summer, Gallus met no opposition initially, and when he did encounter resistance his army was able to overwhelm and defeat the attackers.[125] Gallus had been assured by Syllaeus that he would provide whatever guidance he could.[126] By his personal assurances he had won the complete confidence of the Roman commander.[127] Unknown to the *praefectus*, however, Syllaeus was operating duplicitously. Strabo surmises that he intended to reconnoitre the lands they entered so that he could later annex them for his own nation of Nabataea.[128] To that end he took the expeditionary force on a long detour down the coast, where there were no natural harbours for the ships to berth but, instead, shallows and reefs or strong tides that presented real dangers to them. By the time the expeditionary force reached the entrepôt of Leukê Komê (meaning White Village) a fortnight later, several of the ships had already been lost to accidents, not to warfare.

The soldiers had suffered too. The harsh terrain, the fierce heat of the sun and the poor quality of the potable water took a heavy toll on his men, to the extent that he lost the larger part of his army to sickness.[129] Dio describes the symptoms:

> [they] attacked the head and caused it to become parched, killing forthwith most of those who were attacked, but in the case of those who survived this stage it descended to the legs, skipping all the intervening parts of the body, and caused dire injury to them.[130]

A cure proved to be a blend of olive oil and wine – taken orally and applied as an ointment – but few had access to the remedy. Strabo provides an alternative interpretation: the men suffered from *stomacacce*, a form of paralysis around the mouth, and *scelotyrbe*, lameness of the legs – both afflictions allegedly being caused by consuming the local water and herbs.[131] So many men were afflicted with ailments that Gallus had to suspend operations for the rest of the season until they could recover.

Finally, after several weeks had passed, his men had recuperated and Gallus ordered them to march on. They now entered regions of the Arabian Peninsula where there was no water and all supplies had to be carried on camels' backs. Syllaeus' connivance took the Romans on a roundabout journey until thirty days later they reached the country of Aretas, a kinsman of a certain Obodas, where they were able to replenish basic provisions.[132] For the next fifty days they trudged over tracts of desert before reaching Negrani (Negrana), a municipality set in a lush landscape. Its king, Sabos, seeing the large army marching towards the settlement, had apparently fled and left it undefended. Gallus seized the town; but the king returned six days later, bringing with him an army of his own. The two opposing forces met at the river and fought. Strabo states that the Arabians took 10,000 casualties to only two Roman. He explains that the Arabians' weapons – bows and arrows, spears, swords, slings and double-headed axes – and their combat skills were no match for the Romans' equipment. The Romans then besieged Asca, which had also been abandoned by its king, and took it too. After acquiring nearby Athrula, Gallus installed a garrison which foraged for provisions, including grain and dates. His army then moved on Marsiaba, which belonged to the Rhammanitae nation, who were subjects of a certain Ilasarus. After six days the city still would not fall to Gallus and, with his water rations depleting, he was forced to suspend the siege.[133]

When interrogated, the prisoners his men had captured informed him that the lands that produced the famous spices he had come to find were just two days' march away. The secret was out. He now realized that Syllaeus had duped him into wandering around the peninsula for almost six months in search of them. He quickly formulated his own plan to return to Egypt without the Nabataean's help. The march back took just sixty days. Reaching the Myus Harbour, the few remaining Roman survivors who had endured the campaign's hardships marched to Coptus and finally arrived at Alexandria. Remarkably, of the expeditionary force which had left half-a-year before, only seven men were lost to fighting, the rest having died from sickness, hunger or fatigue.

Strabo did not blame Gallus for the failure. He writes, 'indeed, if Syllaeus had not betrayed him, he would even have subdued the whole of Arabia Felix.'[134] Perhaps echoing Gallus' own words, Strabo explains, 'this expedition did not profit us to a great extent in our knowledge of those regions, but still it made a slight contribution.'[135] Dio offers a more generous assessment:

> These were the first of the Romans, and, I believe, the only ones, to traverse so much of this part of Arabia for the purpose of making war; for they advanced as far as the place called Athlula [modern Baraquish in Yemen], a famous locality.[136]

Augustus himself presented the venture as a great imperial success.[137]

While Aelius Gallus was away, the imperial province of Aegyptus also came under surprise attack. An army of 30,000 of the Kushite (or Nubian) kingdom of Meroë in Ethiopia led by King Teriteqas invaded *Triakontaschoenus Aethopiae* and crossed the Roman Empire's southernmost border at the First Cataract (map 5).[138] They reached the Island of Elephantine in the Nile and sacked the city of Syene, taking captives. They pulled down a bronze statue of Augustus and hauled its head away, burying it in the steps of a victory temple they erected at Meroë.[139] Notwithstanding the positive spin on the failed campaign in Arabia Felix, Gallus' high-profile career was over; his replacement, C. Petronius, was already on his way.[140] The Nabataean Syllaeus was tried in Rome for betraying his friendship with the Romans, as well as other crimes, and beheaded.[141]

23 BCE

	Imp. Caesar *Divi f.* Augustus XI	A. Terentius A. *f.* Varro Murena
suff.	L. Sestius P. *f.* Quirinalis	Cn. Calpurnius Cn. *f.* Piso

Augustus' health had not improved since leaving Tarraco. Although voted the consulship for the eleventh time, he felt so sick that he decided it would be wise to

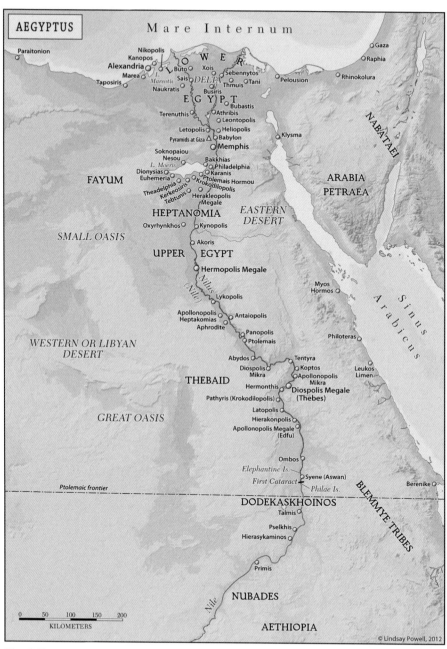

Map 5. Egypt.

make arrangements for the transfer of his responsibilities over his *provincia* and the armed forces in it. He convened a private meeting of magistrates, the leading senators and equestrians.[142] Resigning the consulship, he gave the suffect consul Cn. Calpurnius Piso 'the list of the forces and of the public revenues written in a book, and handed his ring to Agrippa'.[143] Many began to believe the worst, that he had just days to live. There were speculations about who would succeed him: would it be his nephew, Marcellus, or his right-hand man, Agrippa? Then, having tried everything else but failed to find a cure, his personal physician Antonius Musa put his patient on a course of cold treatments. To everyone's surprise – and relief – Augustus staged a near-miraculous recovery.[144]

His young nephew Marcellus, however, was not so fortunate. Despite treatment administered by Musa, he died – perhaps from typhus – at Baiae (modern Baia), aged just 19.[145] He was given a public funeral in Rome with eulogies and his ashes were placed in Augustus' own mausoleum.[146] During a subsequent private reading of Books 2, 4 and 6 of the draft *Aeneid* to the imperial family, the teenager's mother Octavia fainted at hearing the name of her son.[147]

Agrippa, the 40-year old man now popularly regarded as Augustus' successor, left Rome and took up an assignment supervising the provinces in the East. His seemingly hasty departure led some to wonder about the state of his relationship with the 'First Man' in Rome.[148] Agrippa set up his office in Mytilene rather than at Antiocheia in Syria, the preferred base of visiting Roman officials when in the region – a decision that only added to the speculation about his mission.[149]

An embassy from Parthia arrived in Rome to meet with Augustus.[150] It had been sent by Frahâta (Phraates) IV (plate 18), who requested that Augustus return his son in involuntary exile in the city. His captor, Tiridates II, had briefly occupied the Parthian throne at the time of the Battle of Actium but been ousted by Frahâta and fled, seeking sanctuary among the Romans in 26 BCE; he had taken Frahâta's son with him as a hostage.[151] Augustus refused the king's demand, but, seeing an opportunity, suggested that he could consider an exchange of the Parthian prince for the captured *signa* and survivors from the defeat of M. Licinius Crassus at Carrhae in 53 BCE and of M. Antonius in 40 and 36 BCE in the region.[152] Romans could accept tactical defeats, but the loss of the legionary *aquila* was considered *graves ignominias cladesque* – 'a grave and severe disaster' – leaving the nation feeling *infamia*, 'shame' or 'humiliation'.[153] With this diplomatic trade Augustus saw a chance to expunge the stain on the country's honour and raise his own prestige. The emissaries promptly left to present the Roman leader's counteroffer to their king. It would be months before they crossed the border of the Parthian Empire.

In Hispania Citerior, Carisius was asserting his position as Augustus' deputy in the region. The mint in the new *colonia* at Emerita poured out silver coins to fill the veterans' purses, each bearing his name and title, as well as images of rebel arms and equipment captured in the recent war.[154] Where he had shown foresight in saving a community of Astures in the aftermath of battle, he now manifested signs of blindness in his dealings with the same people in peacetime. Unwittingly, he was sowing seeds for a new crop of discontentment.

In Italy Tiberius (plate 23), now 19 years old, served out his term as *quaestor*.[155] One of his tasks was:

> the investigation of the slave-prisons throughout Italy, the owners of which had gained a bad reputation; for they were charged with confining not only travellers, but also those for whom dread of military service had driven to such places of concealment.[156]

A stern disciplinarian, Augustus had no tolerance for deserters.[157]

22 BCE

M. Claudius M. *f.* Marcellus Aeserninus   L. Arruntius L. *f.*

For the first time in eight years, Augustus did not hold the consulship. By unfortunate coincidence, the conditions in the homeland were dire this year: in Rome, the Tiber had flooded its banks, inundating parts of the city, while a pestilence had spread throughout Italy and famine gripped the population.[158] Connecting Augustus' decision not to stand as consul with the nationwide affliction, many people urged him to assume the powers of *dictator* (awarded to a single individual only at a time of emergency). The Senate objected. For refusing to accede to their wishes, a mob locked them in the *Curia* while the People voted in their Assembly for the proposition to make it law.[159] Augustus adamantly refused to accept the plebiscite, tearing at his clothes to express his exasperation at the People's persistence, though he relented to their wishes that he accept the post of commissioner for the grain supply.[160]

Augustus' patience was tested again this year when a case went before the courts which seemed to challenge the transparency with which he applied his war-making powers. The proconsul of Macedonia, M. Primus, had initiated an unauthorized war against the Odrysae.[161] When called to explain himself, Primus said he had made war with the approval of Augustus, but then later changed his story to say it was consul M. Claudius Marcellus who had authorized it. Hearing his name was being dragged through the courts, Augustus appeared in person. The *praetor* presiding over the case put the question directly to the *Princeps Senatus*: had he authorized the war? Augustus replied he had not; Macedonia was a proconsular not a propraetorian province, which mean he had no authority over it. Dio records the ensuing *contretemps*:

> And when the advocate of Primus, Licinius Murena, in the course of some rather disrespectful remarks that he made to him, enquired: 'What are *you* doing here, and who summoned you?' Augustus merely replied: 'The public weal'.[162]

Many of the bystanders laughed at the retort. On a vote of the jury Primus was acquitted. The verdict upset many in the aristocracy, however. Plots to assassinate the *princeps* were hatched. One, an amateurish affair in which the outspoken Murena was himself implicated, was discovered and the conspirators were tried in secret.[163] Another, conceived by senator Ignatius Rufus, also ended badly for the would-be assassin.[164]

Augustus left Rome and departed for Sicily, taking Tiberius with him.[165] On the island he established a *colonia* for retired soldiers at Syracusae (modern Siracusa).[166] He was aware that he needed to show progress was being made in pacifying his *provincia*. To that end he returned to the Senate both 'Cyprus and Gallia Narbonensis as districts no longer needing the presence of his armies', but in the process gained Illyricum.[167] In Hispania Citerior, however, his army was still essential. Peace in the north of that country remained as elusive as ever. Rome's old enemies, the Astures and Cantabri, rebelled once again.[168] Dio ascribes the cause of their uprising this time to the excesses and cruelties of Carisius. He had been joined by C. Furnius, a man who had impressed Augustus when, years before, he appealed to him in person to save the life of his father, a known supporter of M. Antonius.[169] His boldness and filial loyalty earned him the *princeps*' respect and a place among the ex-consuls.[170] He was now to show some of that boldness in the Iberian Peninsula. If the warriors of the mountains thought he would be easy to beat, they soon discovered he was as resolute as his colleague in breaking their will.[171] He had briefed himself well on the situation among the tribes. In tandem the Roman commanders used a divide and conquer strategy. Furnius engaged the rebels, working with Carisius to reduce the Astures further west.[172] The Astures, in response, besieged one of the Roman army camps, hoping to destroy the men within its wooden palisade. They were unable to take it, and later were themselves defeated in open battle. Through attrition, their national resistance collapsed. Many were taken as prisoners of war. The Cantabri fought on desperately until, resigned to imminent defeat, many took their own lives by sword, poison or immolation rather than be captured by the Romans and sold as slaves. The legates also subdued the Gallaeci in the far northwest of the Iberian Peninusla.[173]

In Egypt, C. Petronius was determined to re-establish Roman control over *Triakontaschoenus Aethopiae*, which had been invaded by Teriteqas two years before. Three legions and several cohorts of auxiliaries were under his direct command. From them he drew some 10,000 infantry and 800 cavalry. Eschewing the 'lightning war' strategy of his predecessor Cornelius Gallus, Petronius took a more diplomatic approach.[174] Leading the Meroites was Amanirenas Kandake (Queen Candace). She might be the widow of Teriteqas. Strabo characterizes her as 'a masculine sort of woman, and blind in one eye' – a description which probably owes more to a Roman stereotype of barbarian queens in general than an accurate portrait of her.[175] Petronius sent envoys to demand to know why the Ethiopians had started the war and to request the return of the stolen goods and prisoners. The Ethiopians replied that the nomarchs (the local senior officials who administered the *nomes* into which Egypt was divided) had wronged them. The Roman emissaries explained that they did not rule the country but Caesar did. The Ethiopians then asked for three days to deliberate the issue. Growing impatient at the delay, Petronius forced them to engage him in battle. The

Ethiopian warriors – carrying axes, pikes and swords and defending themselves with large oblong shields covered with ox hide – retreated when faced with the heavily armed and well-equipped Roman alliance troops. Casualties were light, however. Some made their way to Pselchis. Others fled to a nearby island in the Nile or into the desert. The rest were taken alive, forced on to rafts and ships and sailed up river to Alexandria. Petronius then moved on Premnis (present day Qasr Ibrim) and captured it.

From her location near the royal capital Napata (modern Karima in Northern Sudan), Kandake sent her own ambassadors to Petronius to negotiate a truce.[176] She offered to return all the Roman prisoners and booty. The prefect gave his answer in fire. Roman troops poured into Napata, snatched its treasures, took its inhabitants as slaves and razed the city. Kandake's son, Akinidad, only just managed to evade capture.[177] As further punishment, Petronius imposed a tribute on the Ethiopian nation.[178] The *praefectus* could have marched still further south, but the practicalities of waging a war in a foreign country factored into his calculus. Instead he ordered his troops to turn around and march home. *En route* they improved the fortifications at Premnis in *Triacontaschoenus Aethopiae* and installed a garrison there with enough supplies to support 400 men for two years. When finally back in the provincial capital, Petronius sold most of the captives but, eager to avoid his predecessor's fate, he sent a thousand of them to Augustus.

21 BC

   M. Lollius M. *f.*   Q. Aemilius M'. *f.* Lepidus

At the beginning of the year riots broke out in Rome when the public, believing one of the two curule chairs was intended for Augustus, was disappointed to learn that he had declined it and that the position was actually still open for election.[179] M. Lollius, recently returned from a successful tour of duty in province Macedonia and now rewarded with a consulship, found himself unexpectedly, and rather awkwardly, serving alone. Two men, Q. Aemilius Lepidus and L. Silvanus, bitterly contested the open consulship. Lollius appealed to Augustus to return to settle the matter, but he refused and summoned the rival candidates to meet him in Sicily.[180] Following a stern lecture from him, the chastened senators returned to Rome. When they arrived, riots more violent than the first erupted, only ceasing when Lepidus was finally chosen and sworn in.

Augustus expected trouble in his own *provincia*, which is why he had an army, but not at home. Dio writes:

> Augustus was displeased at the incident, for he could not devote all his time to Rome alone and did not dare leave the city in a state of anarchy; accordingly, he sought for someone to set over it, and judged Agrippa to be most suitable for the purpose.[181]

M. Agrippa could always be relied upon to carry out his assigned duty unquestioningly and efficiently. It was time to recall him from the East and publicly recognize his special status. Binding his best friend and the Roman Empire's finest commander closer to him, Augustus offered Agrippa his only daughter, Iulia Caesaris, to be his wife; they were married that year.[182] But even the popular Agrippa could not quell the civil unrest in Rome when a protest erupted on the city's streets over the election of the *Praefectus Urbi Feriarum Latinarum Causa* (the official who represented both consuls at the Latin Games held in the Alban Hills).[183] Agrippa was in no mood to compromise. To settle the matter, he suspended the election altogether and the year passed with the post of Prefect of the City remaining vacant.

The populations of other cities were restless too, using different ways to express their grievances. Augustus decided he was needed in the East (map 6). In his entourage were Tiberius and a young man from Cremona, P. Quinctilius Varus, serving as his *quaestor*.[184] Over the winter of 22/21 BCE, Augustus sailed from Sicily to Greece and visited Sparta and Athens. The Athenians had no particular love of the Romans, having suffered abuses under Sulla, Iulius Caesar and his legate Q. Fufius Calenius, and resentments still festered.[185] Augustus was also conscious that the Athenian populace had supported Antonius during the Actian War. When he arrived in Athens there was an act seemingly calculated to cause him personal offence. According to a modern reconstruction of the events recorded by Dio, a statue of Athena on the Acropolis, which had been erected facing the east, was found to have been deliberately turned around to face the west, that is, in the direction of Rome; provocatively, blood had been sprinkled from the mouth and down the front of the statue to create the impression that Athena, the patron goddess of Athens, had spat blood at the Romans.[186] Augustus' response was typically thoughtful but deliberate. He hurt the Athenians in a way they understood – financially. He took from them the administration of Aigina and Eretria, from which they received tribute, and he forbade them to make anyone a citizen in exchange for their money.[187] He himself spent part of the winter on Aigina (where he wrote that he was angered by the Athenians' welcome) and part on Samos.[188]

During his sojourn on Samos, he received a deputation of Ethiopians. Following her defeat by C. Petronius in Egypt the year before, an outraged Amanirenas Kandake had rallied her people for a counteroffensive. With thousands of warriors, she had marched on Premnis. According to Strabo, Petronius arrived at the fortress before she did and was ready for them.[189] In the meantime, he strengthened its defences, making it virtually impregnable to the lightly equipped Ethiopian army. When her emissaries approached the Romans to parlay, they were told to petition Augustus. They proclaimed they did not know who or where *he* was. Petronius provided them with an escort and delivered them to Samos, where Augustus was residing. He listened to their pleas and acceded to them, even remitting the tribute which Petronius had imposed.

There was, as yet, still no word from the king of Parthia in response to his diplomatic counteroffer. In the spring, Augustus travelled through Bithynia and Asia Minor.[190] Appalled to discover that the citizens of Kyzikos (Cyzicus), a major town of Mysia in Anatolia, had rioted, flogged and summarily executed several Roman citizens, he condemned the inhabitants of the city to slavery.[191]

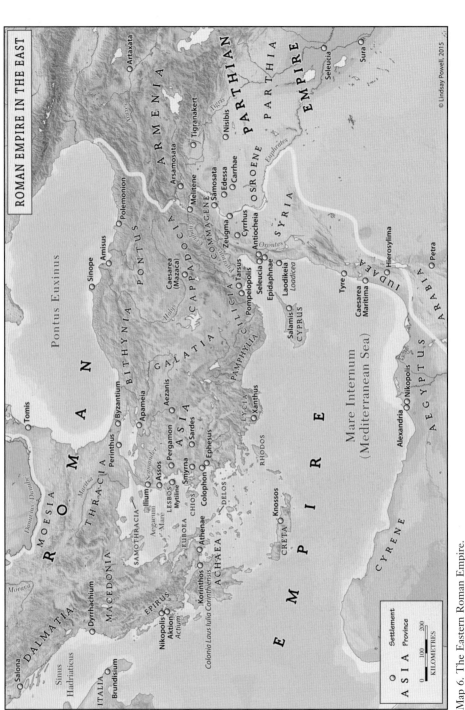

Map 6. The Eastern Roman Empire.

Arriving in Syria and learning that the people of Tyre and Sidon had rioted violently there too, and with loss of life, he responded with the same harsh punishment.[192] Among the kings and potentates loyal to Rome, Augustus re-assigned territories following the death of Archelaos the Mede who had ruled them: Iamblichus, the son of Iamblichus, received his ancestral dominion over the Arabs; Tarcondimotus, the son of Tarcondimotus, was given the kingdom of Cilicia, which his father had once held.[193] To Herodes he entrusted the tetrarchy of a certain Zenodoros; and to one Mithridates, though still only a boy, he gave Commagene, because its king had put the boy's father to death.[194] It was shrewd politics. As their *patronus*, Augustus would sponsor and represent each client king's causes – and, should they arise, grievances – in the Senate or courts in Rome; in return they would support him with troops and matériel as and when called upon to supply them, saving the Romans the additional expenditure.

In Rome, on 12 October, L. Sempronius Atratinus drove a gilded chariot in celebration of his full triumph for victories in Africa through the streets of the city to cheering crowds of onlookers.[195]

20 BCE

M. Appuleius Sex. *f.*   P. Silius P. *f.* Nerva

In Syria, Augustus received emissaries from Armenia. They requested his help to replace the incumbent king, Artaxes, with his brother, Tigranes, who had been a refugee in Rome for a decade.[196] Augustus agreed to the demand. Assigned the unusual, and potentially risky, mission of taking an army to assist in the ousting of the king of Armenia was his stepson Tiberius.[197] Even as Roman troops marched into the country, the Armenians themselves murdered their king.[198] Tiberius finally reached the capital city and personally crowned Tigranes (fig. 3).[199] The installation of a pro-Roman regent in Armenia tipped the balance of power in the

Figure 3. Determining the fate of Armenia was a key point in negotiations between Augustus, his envoy and the Parthian 'king of kings'. On this coin Augustus claims 'Armenia Captured' for the Roman People (see *Res Gestae* 27 and 29).

region. Word reached Tiberius that the king of Parthia – apparently 'awed by the reputation of so great a name' – was prepared to accept the terms of the settlement proposed three years before.[200] Augustus' stepson now unexpectedly found himself responsible for overseeing the historic recovery of *signa* and war prisoners in a formal ceremony, which took place on the banks of the Euphrates River (plate 17).[201] His stepfather was delighted:

> Augustus received them as if he had conquered the Parthian in a war; for he took great pride in the achievement, declaring that he had recovered without a struggle what had formerly been lost in battle.[202]

After such a success it was time to leave the East. Reaching Samos, Augustus decided to spend the winter there. While residing on the Aegean island he received several foreign leaders and even a guest from India.[203]

C. Petronius, the man who had dealt successfully with an invasion of Ethiopians, had since become unpopular in his own province. A 'countless multitude of Alexandrians rushed to attack him with a throwing of stones', writes Strabo, but the mob was no match for well-armed and trained soldiers, and 'he held out against them with merely his own bodyguard, and after killing some of them put a stop to the rest'.[204]

Along the southern border of neighbouring province Africa, the Garamantes raided into Roman-held territory. Determined to stop the incursions, the *proconsul* L. Cornelius Balbus, son of the Jewish financier and consul, launched a punitive campaign against them.[205] By temperament an extrovert, he was an attention-seeker given to carrying out acts of bravado. Against the backdrop of the Libyan desert, his dash and daring were on full display. The commander and his legion pursued the enemy to its strongholds to the south. Together they captured fifteen settlements, including Garama (Gherma), 'the most famous capital of the Garamantes'.[206] The Senate was impressed by his exploits, not least because he was not even a Roman, but a native of Hispania Ulterior. Pliny notes that:

> Cornelius Balbus was honoured with a triumph, the only foreigner indeed that was ever honoured with the triumphal chariot, and presented with the rights of a Roman citizen; for, although by birth a native of Gades, the Roman citizenship was granted to him.[207]

The award was both deserved and overdue.

19 BCE

        C. Sentius C. *f.* Saturninus   Q. Lucretius Q. *f.* Vespillo
suff. M. Vinicius P. *f.*

The year started badly. Fighting broke out between gangs of supporters for different candidates for the consulship. C. Sentius Saturninus had secured one *sella curulis* in the Senate House, but the other remained vacant when Augustus declined to accept it.[208] Fear gripped the city as thugs committed murders. Sentius was assigned a bodyguard, but he refused it. The Senate dispatched two envoys, accompanied by two lictors each, to seek Augustus' counsel.[209] Augustus chose one of the two men before him, Q. Lucretius Vespillo, which proved a popular choice.

With calm restored in Rome, on 27 March the extrovert Cornelius Balbus, now proudly Roman after his naturalization, celebrated his triumph.[210] It was a spectacular event, combining the familiar trappings of the standard military procession augmented this time with the exotic spoils of the African continent. Its unfamiliar place names were painted upon *fercula* to inform and impress the crowds as the triumphal parade passed by:

> There is also this remarkable circumstance, that our writers have handed down to us the names of the cities above-mentioned as having been taken by Balbus, and have informed us that on the occasion of his triumph, besides Cidamus and Garama, there were carried in the procession the names and models of all the other nations and cities, in the following order: the town of Tabudium, the nation of Niteris, the town of Miglis Gemella, the nation or town of Bubeium, the nation of Enipi, the town of Thuben, the mountain known as the Black Mountain, Nitibrum, the towns called Rapsa, the nation of Discera, the town of Decri, the Nathabur River, the town of Thapsagum, the nation of Tamiagi, the town of Boin, the town of Pege, the Dasibari River; and then the towns, in the following order, of Baracum, Buluba, Alasit, Galsa, Balla, Maxalla, Cizania, and Mount Gyri, which was preceded by an inscription stating that this was the place where precious stones were produced.[211]

Midway through the year, M. Vinicius, the man who had led a successful raid into Germania, was elected suffect consul; he replaced C. Sentius Saturninus, who had reportedly carried out his duties in the severest way.[212] In Macedonia the new proconsul, M. Lollius, following a successful term as governor of Galatia-Pamphylia, came to the assistance of his neighbour, Roimetalkes of Thracia (plate 25), who was involved in a war against the Bessi nation.[213] By working together the two men defeated their common foe.

At about the same time, news arrived of strife in the Gallic provinces (map 7). Without specifying which nation, Dio says the Galli were quarrelling amongst themselves, and the situation was made worse by raids of Germanic war bands from the Rhineland.[214] With Augustus still in transit from the East, Agrippa felt obliged to go to the region in person to deal with it. Having reached *Colonia Copia Felix Munatia* to assess the situation, Dio cryptically states that Agrippa 'put a stop to those troubles'.[215] The fact is all the more remarkable because Agrippa had not participated in active combat since he had faced the forces of M. Antonius and Kleopatra in 31 BCE.

Solving the ongoing Germanic menace required a different approach. The Rhine River was a permeable natural barrier. There was still no standing army on the left bank to intercept brigands (*latrones*) when they raided Roman territory in search of rich pickings. As he had done twenty years before, Agrippa travelled to the border country to assess the situation for himself. He found the Ubii once

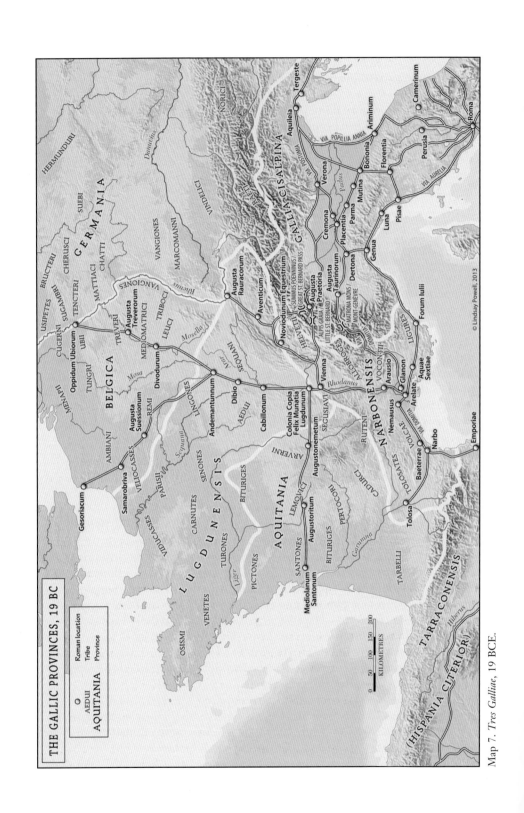

Map 7. *Tres Galliae*, 19 BCE.

again attacked at their rear by the Suebi, who were moving ever southwestwards and encroaching aggressively on the territory of their neighbours.[216] The Ubii sent a deputation to their Roman allies to plead with them to provide sanctuary. Agrippa made an extraordinary decision. 'By their own consent,' writes Strabo, 'they were transferred by Agrippa to the country this side of the Rhenus.'[217] He founded for them a settlement called *Oppidum* Ubiorum (the precursor to modern Cologne). There were conditions attached, however. The Ubii would be relocated specifically to assist the Romans in guarding that section of the Rhine.[218] It may have been at this time that work also began on an urban settlement for the Treveri nation, whose *territorium* extended between the Rhine and Maas rivers.[219] Later called Augusta Treverorum, the new city was established on the banks of the Mosella (Moselle) River (and would become modern Trier).[220] In combination with the Ubii, some 190 kilometres (118 miles) to the north, Agrippa had effectively established a buffer zone between the people across the Rhine and the Galli to the south, where local allies – rather than Roman troops – provided the soldiers to defend their land from invaders from the north. At least one *Cohors Ubiorum Peditum et Equitum* and one *Ala Treverorum* are known.[221]

Just as the northern border seemed settled, bad news reached Agrippa from the Iberian Peninsula. The Cantabri were in revolt yet again. Dio reports:

> It seems that the Cantabri who had been captured alive in the war and sold, had killed their masters in every case, and returning home, had induced many to join in their rebellion; and with the aid of these they had seized some positions, walled them in, and were plotting against the Roman garrisons.[222]

True to his character, Agrippa immediately departed for Hispania Citerior to evaluate the situation for himself with the *Legatus Augusti Pro Praetore* of Hispania Citerior, P. Silius Nerva.[223] What he found was an army demoralized in spirit, fatigued from endless fighting and on the verge of mutiny. When ordered to fall-in, 'his soldiers would not obey him', writes Dio.[224] Now 44 years old, this was the first recorded time in his life that Agrippa had faced open insubordination by his own troops. Even before he could fight the rebels, he first had to restore discipline and revitalize the morale of his own men – and do so quickly. He adopted a 'carrot and stick' approach and applied it with his usual patience and persistence.[225] 'Partly by admonishing and exhorting them and partly by inspiring them with hopes,' writes Dio, 'he soon made them yield obedience.'[226]

Now he could turn his attention to the enemy in the foothills. The details of the ensuing war of 19 BCE are entirely lost. The sources imply that it was one of the toughest wars Agrippa ever fought. 'In fighting against the Cantabri,' writes Dio, 'he met with many reverses.'[227] His opponents were battle-hardened and motivated, 'for not only had they gained practical experience, as a result of having been slaves to the Romans, but also despaired of having their lives granted to them again if they were taken captive'.[228] There is a story of a mother, who seeing her husband and sons chained and fettered ready for transportation, grabbed a sword and slew them all; another prisoner, summoned before his drunken captors, threw himself upon a pyre.[229] Faced with this kind of desperate courage, Agrippa 'lost many of his soldiers' and his opponents 'degraded many others because they kept being defeated'.[230] He was particularly disappointed by the performance of *Legio I Augusta*. Its inability to beat its adversary led Agrippa to strip the unit of the honorific title given it by Augustus – a deeply humiliating act for the troops, who had probably won it for gallantry during the campaign of 26–25 BCE.[231] Yet Agrippa was a determined man who would never give up if there was a chance of success. 'Finally Agrippa was successful,' records Dio, and 'he at length destroyed nearly all of the enemy who were of military age, deprived the rest of their arms, and forced them come down from their fortresses and live in the plains.'[232] Writing at the time of these events, Strabo noted the achievement:

> At the present day, as I have remarked, all warfare is put an end to, Augustus Caesar having subdued the Cantabri and the neighbouring nations, amongst whom the system of pillage was mainly carried on in our day.[233]

For winning the last *Bellum Cantabricum*, the Senate voted Agrippa a triumph.[234] While the Roman Commonwealth was grateful to the commander, his own reaction hints that he was not particularly proud of the victory:

> Yet he sent no communication concerning them to the Senate, and did not accept a triumph, although one was voted at the behest of Augustus, but showed moderation in these matters as was his wont.[235]

He did, however, accept a *corona muralis*, the military honour of a crown decorated with turrets, awarded to the first man to scale the wall of a besieged city.[236] On coins and statues, Agrippa would now be shown wearing it in combination with his *corona navalis*.[237] His defeat of the Cantabri ended a struggle to conquer the Iberian Peninsula that had lasted two centuries. In gratitude, three altars were dedicated to Augustus on a promontory (perhaps Cape Finsiterre or on Monte Louro) in northwestern Hispania Citerior, called the *Sestianae* after the man who set them up: L. Sestius Quirinalis Albinianus (suffect consul of 23 BCE) may have replaced P. Carisius as *legatus* in the region in 19 BCE.[238] Cohorts of troops recruited from the Astures, Cantabri and Gallaeci nations entered the service of the Roman army from this time.[239]

Arriving in Athens on their return from the East, Augustus and his entourage happened to meet the poet Vergil. He was editing the final version of his *Aeneid*.[240] There was only one copy of the epic poem in existence and Augustus was acutely concerned to own it lest anything unfortunate should happen either to the great work or its author.[241] He convinced the poet to accompany him back to Italy, ensuring that the boxes containing the handwritten scrolls were kept secure on the return journey. At Megara, the 51-year old poet, who was known to have a weak constitution, caught a fever.[242] His condition worsened as the ship sailed across the Adriatic Sea. Upon landing at Brundisium, on 21 September he died. Vergil had left clear instructions with his executors for his poem to be burned upon his death, but Augustus countermanded the order, arranging for it to be published instead, even with the incomplete edits.[243] The *Aeneid* was too important a document to the leader of the Roman world to consign to oblivion. Among many evocative scenes, in particular, in Book 1 of the great work were the climactic words spoken by Jupiter to the itinerant hero Aeneas:

> To these I give no bounded times or power,
> but empire without end. Yea, even my Queen,
> Juno, who now chastiseth land and sea
> with her dread frown, will find a wiser way,
> and at my sovereign side protect and bless
> the Romans, masters of the whole round world,
> who, clad in peaceful toga, judge mankind.
> Such my decree![244]

Hearing that Augustus was in Italy, a group of praetors and tribunes left the city to greet him in Campania, the first time it had been done. [245] On the night of 12 October, Augustus entered Rome bringing with him the precious *Aeneid* and the *signa* received from the Parthian king.[246] The next day, he ordered sacrifices to be made. His arrival from Asia was an occasion for public celebration. The Senate voted him several honours, all but two of which he refused.[247] Firstly, he accepted an altar to Fortuna Redux to be erected beside the Temple of Honour and Courage (*Honos et Virtus*) at the *Porta Capena* (fig. 4), which was dedicated on 15 December of that year; and, secondly, he permitted the day of his return to be celebrated as an annual holiday, which came to be known as the *Augustalia*.[248] Augustus 'rode into the city on horseback and was honoured with a triumphal arch'.[249] Not since Actium had he felt such a deep sense of military accomplishment. A series of coins issued at the time expresses the *princeps*' evident pride in the result, achieved entirely without bloodshed.[250]

The recovered *signa* were taken to the *Capitolium* and placed in the old Temple of Mars Ultor (fig. 5).[251] It would suffice for the time being, but such important

Figure 4. Returning from the East in 19 BCE, the Senate voted Augustus an altar to Fortuna Redux (the goddess who oversaw safe returns from dangerous journeys) beside the Porta Carpena, Rome. The annual *Augustalia* was held to mark the occasion.

Figure 5. The military standards that were recovered from Parthia under Augustus' auspices in 20 BCE were kept temporarily in the round Temple of Mars Avenger in Rome while the *Forum Augustum* was constructed.

artefacts would need a grander home for their display and veneration. Augustus chose this year to break ground on a vast, new precinct behind the *Forum Romanum* and adjacent to the *Forum Iulium*. He paid 100 million *sestertii* to buy the land from its private owners, but soon discovered that even he could not acquire all the land he wanted for the project.[252] It would take years to complete the construction work on the landmark project.

Horace, now the favourite poet and a friend of Augustus, expressed in verse the celebratory mood of the times:

Thy age, great Caesar, has restored
To squalid fields the plenteous grain,
Given back to Rome's almighty Lord
Our *signa*, torn from Parthian fane,
Has closed Quirinian Ianus' gate,
Wild passion's erring walk controll'd,
Heal'd the foul plague-spot of the state,
And brought again the life of old,
Life, by whose healthful power increased
The glorious name of Latium spread
To where the sun illumes the east
From where he seeks his western bed.[253]

Among rewards and recognitions issued, he promoted Tiberius to the rank of ex-*praetor* and to his younger brother, Nero Claudius Drusus, he granted the privilege of standing for public office five years earlier than stipulated – the same gift given to his older brother five years previously.[254]

Under his auspices, Augustus and his subordinates had achieved much over the previous decade. Cyprus and Gallia Narbonensis, now pacified, had been passed over to the Senate to administer. The project to subjugate the entire Iberian Peninsula had finally been completed after two centuries of struggle. New territory had been added in the Italian Alps and in Anatolia. Enemies who had invaded from the Rhineland and Ethiopia had been punished. A rebellion had been quelled in Aquitania. Roman troops had explored deep into Arabia. Under the *Pax Parthorum*, Rome's eastern nemesis changed from an ongoing threat into a partner in peace. Augustus had been acclaimed an unprecedented nine times. Yet there was still much to be done. Across the German Ocean the island of Britannia beckoned, and in the Orient lay other prizes:

> O shield our Caesar as he goes
> To furthest Britannia, and his band,
> Rome's harvest! Send on Eastern foes
> Their fear, and on the Red Sea's strand![255]

The deployment of the army reflected the strategic imperatives of the previous decade (table 1). There was a high concentration of manpower in the West: nineteen legions (67 per cent) out of twenty-eight were spread between the Iberian Peninsula, Gaul and the Balkans. With the subjugation of the Astures and Cantabri, resources could be redirected to military projects elsewhere. Where was yet to be decided.

In the meantime, Augustus consolidated his own position politically under the guise of ensuring social cohesion:

> And inasmuch as there was no similarity between the conduct of the people during his absence, when they quarrelled, and while he was present, when they were afraid, he accepted an election, on their invitation, to the position of supervisor of morals for five years, and took the authority of *censor* for the same period and that of consul for life, and in consequence had the right to use the twelve *fasces* always and everywhere and to sit in the curule chair between the two men who were at the time consuls.[256]

Table 1. Dispositions of the Legions, Summer 19 BCE (Conjectural).

Province	Units	Legions
Hispania Citerior	8	I *Augusta*, II *Augusta*, IIII *Macedonica*, V *Alaudae*, VI *Victrix*, VIIII *Hispana*, X *Gemina* and XX
Aquitania / Gallia Comata (Celtica) / Gallia Belgica	3	XVII, XIIX, XIX
Gallia Cisalpina	4	XIII *Gemina*, XIV *Gemina*, XVI *Gallica*, XXI *Rapax*
Illyricum	4	IIII *Scythica*, VIII *Augusta*, XI, XV *Apollinaris*
Galatia-Pamphylia	2	V, VII
Syria	3	III *Gallica*, VI *Ferrata*, X (*Fretensis*)
Aegyptus	3	III *Cyrenaica*, XII *Fulminata*, XXII *Deiotariana*
Africa	1	III *Augusta*

Sources: Appendix 3; Lendering (Livius.org); M'Elderry (1909); Mitchell (1976); Sanders (1941); Šašel Kos (1995); Syme (1933).

Augustus' power was now confirmed as *summum imperium auspiciumque*, superior to all other consuls, proconsuls or magistrates of equal rank to his.[257] He could intervene in any and all provinces of the Empire – even those under the management of the Senate – and exercise supreme military command there.

At the end of December, however, Augustus' ten-year *imperium* over his vast province would expire and with it control of the army.[258] The question for Augustus and the Senate was what would happen next?

Chapter 3

On the Offensive
18–14 BCE

18 BCE

　　P. Cornelius P. *f.* Lentulus Marcellinus　　Cn. Cornelius L *f.* Lentulus

Pacifying the Roman world was still a work in progress. The Conscript Fathers accepted the fact that there were still regions of the world 'that had need of a military guard' and, unhesitatingly, they granted Augustus *imperium* for five more years to continue the work.[1] Certain powers were also granted to Agrippa to match those of the *princeps* for five years.[2] Augustus is reported by Dio as having remarked at the time that the interval – called a *lustrum* – would be long enough for them to carry out their duties.[3]

Augustus embarked on another purge of the Senate.[4] He could not take chances with the body's composition. Not only did he need to be sure he had enough members to support his legislative programme, but he also required a wide bench of talent from which he could choose his future provincial and legionary legates. Many senators were upset by the proposed reduction in membership and some even refused to resign.[5] Undaunted, the *princeps* set up a board of thirty commissioners to select the best men by lot, but ways were soon found to circumvent the process and affect the supposed randomness of the results.[6] One senator, Licinius Regulus, was particularly incensed at being struck off when, in his opinion, other less-qualified men – including his own son – still retained their seats. In a dramatic protest he 'rent his clothing in the very Senate, laid bare his body, enumerated his military campaigns, and showed them his scars'.[7] Recognizing mistakes were being made and that talented men were being lost to chance or corrupt practice, Augustus intervened; he picked candidates himself and, while letting others go, allowed many who had been disbarred to return to the House.[8]

His mishandling of the selection process deeply offended many, to the extent that some, as before, contemplated committing murder. Augustus had become increasingly concerned about attempts on his life and had already taken to wearing a cuirass or mail shirt underneath his tunic as a precautionary measure, even when he attended sessions of the Senate.[9] Plots to assassinate Augustus and Agrippa were, allegedly, discovered.[10] Executions followed in a few cases.[11]

17 BCE

　　　　C. Furnius C. *f.*　　C. Iunius C. *f.* Silanus
　suff.　　　　　　　L. Tarius Rufus

It was the long-established tradition that, after battle, a victorious commander retained the larger share of the captured plunder (*praeda*) – baggage, cash, precious artifacts and enslaved prisoners of war – of the defeated enemy and dispersed a portion among their troops as he pleased.[12] The promise of booty was one of the reasons men went on campaign.[13] Augustus sought to channel some of the rewards of conquest conducted in his name for the public good and, this year, 'commanded those who celebrated triumphs to erect out of their proceeds (*ex manubiis*) some monument to commemorate their deeds'.[14]

In the last week of May, heralds wandered the streets of Rome inviting the citizens to a once-in-a-lifetime's spectacle. The *Ludi Saeculare* (games held at 110-year intervals, then reckoned to be the maximum length of a man's life) were to be presented.[15] The last 'Century Games' had been hosted in the 140s BCE, but at Augustus' insistence they were scheduled for this year, with the consent of the Senate.[16] On 31 May, as its *magister* or director, Augustus led the members of the *Quindecemviri Sacri Faciundis* (charged with consulting the Sybilline Books (*Libri Sybillini*) of prophecy for Rome) in a distribution to the People of items of torches, brimstone and pitch used for ritual purification. After sunset, beneath a full moon, the Commission of Fifteen Men and guests gathered on the *Campus Martius*: C. Sentius Saturninus, M. Claudius Marcellus Aeserninus, M. Fufius Strigo, D. Laelius Balbus, M. Agrippa, L. Marcius Censorinus, Q. Aemilius Lepidus, Potitus Valerius Messalla, Cn. Pompeius, C. Licinius Calvus Stolo, C. Mucius Scaevola, C. Sosius, C. Norbanus Flaccus, M. Cocceius Nerva, M. Lollius, L. Arruntius, C. Asinius Gallus, Q. Aelius Tubero, C. Caninius Rebilus and M. Valerius Messalla Messalinus.[17] Members of this élite college had helped Augustus acquire or renew supreme power, at various times governed his provinces and commanded his armies. Sacrifices were offered to the ancient Moerae, hymns were sung, a theatre piece was performed and a special banquet was laid on.

The Games would last three days. On 1 June, the pageant officially began. Sacrifices were offered to Jupiter Optimus Maximus and games were held for Apollo and Diana. On the second day there were sacrifices to Juno Regina and the Magna Mater. On the third and final day, in the climax of the celebration, a choir sang a hymn specially written and scored for the occasion by Horace. In this 'Poem of the Century' (*Carmen Saeculare*), the voices of twenty-seven boys and twenty-seven girls filled the precinct of the Temple of Apollo, addressing him alone of the pantheon:

> God, grant to our sons unblemish'd ways;
> Grant to our old an age of peace;
> Grant to Romulus' race power and praise,
> And large increase![18]

The poet wrote of how, with the Sun god's blessing, Rome's enemies were now vanquished:

> Now Media dreads our Alban steel,
> Our victories land and ocean o'er;
> Scythia and India in suppliance kneel,

So proud before.
Faith, Honour, ancient Modesty,
And Peace, and Virtue, spite of scorn,
Come back to earth; and Plenty, see,
With teeming horn.[19]

In a crescendo, the young voices appealed to the god to continue to promote the Romans' well-being through eternity:

Lov'st thou thine own Palatial Hill,
Prolong the glorious life of Latium and Rome
To other cycles, brightening still
Through time to come![20]

The Games triumphing the Roman achievement concluded. The crowds dispersed, buoyed by the inspirational themes of the evening, and abuzz with stories they would one day tell their grandchildren.

On a day sometime between 14 June and 15 July, Augustus adopted Agrippa's two sons with the full consent of their father. [21] The older boy, just weeks from his third birthday, would assume the name C. Iulius Caesar Augustus *filius*, and his brother – barely a year old – would become L. Iulius Caesar Augustus *filius*. The *princeps* would now assume responsibility for their education and advancement in Roman society. Seen as his successors, the young boys were wildly popular with the Roman People and expectations for them ran high.

The months passed peaceably until, in the late summer, reports reached Rome from the *legatus Augusti pro praetore* of a military disaster in Belgica. The incumbent governor, having assumed the province from Agrippa in late 19/early 18 BCE, was M. Lollius. This high-performer in the league of provincial governors had stumbled – badly.[22] An alliance of Germanic tribes on the right bank of the Rhine had crossed the river and raided his province. Florus writes:

The Cherusci, Suebi and Sugambri had begun hostilities after crucifying twenty of our centurions, an act which served as an oath binding them together, and with such confidence of victory that they made an agreement in anticipation of dividing up the spoils.[23]

Of them, 'it was the Sugambri, who live near the Rhenus, that began the war' under the leadership of their chief Maelo.[24] As well as booty, the Sugambri – who, in Iulius Caesar's day, had united with the Suebi, Tencteri and Usipetes – were looking for a new homeland.[25] The new alliance crossed the Rhine on boats and rafts and advanced deep into Belgica. It ambushed a unit of Roman cavalry, which was out on a routine exercise.[26] Chasing down the Roman fugitives, the Germanic warriors then collided with Lollius riding at the head of his legion coming the other way. In the ensuing battle, the men of *Legio* V *Alaudae* witnessed their prized *aquila* standard stolen away.[27] Having only three years before recovered the *signa* lost during Rome's historic defeats in Parthia, it was an acute embarrassment to Augustus to see an eagle lost by one of his own handpicked legates operating under his auspices. Incensed by the inexcusable failure, he prepared to visit the province in person. There would have to be consequences.

16 BCE

	L. Domitius Cn. *f.* Ahenobarbus	P. Cornelius P. *f.* Scipio
suff.		L. Tarius Rufus

In the spring, leaving Statilius Taurus as *praetor urbanus* in charge of affairs in Rome, Augustus travelled north to Gallia Comata with Tiberius by his side.[28] 'The greatest of the wars which at that time fell to the lot of the Romans,' writes Dio, 'and the one presumably which drew Augustus away from the city, was that against the Germans.'[29] What many were beginning to call the *Clades Lolliana*, (the 'Disaster of Lollius') was to Augustus' knowledge still unresolved.[30] When he reached *Colonia* Copia Felix Munatia, he learned the full facts from the legate himself:

> He found no warfare to carry on; for the barbarians, learning that Lollius was making preparations and that the emperor was also taking the field, retired into their own territory and made peace, giving hostages.[31]

Among those preparations may have been the erection of a small military outpost on the Rhine at Neuss, at the end of the Roman road from Copia Felix Munatia.[32] The locations of the main legionary garrison in the region have still not been definitively identified, but the 16-hectare winter camp with its extensive outer system of ditches at Folleville in the Somme Valley in Belgica may date to this time.[33] Reflecting that the event was more humiliating than serious, Augustus turned his attention instead to pursuits that did not require force of arms.[34] He likely now began reorganizing the territories of Aquitania, Celtica and Belgica, which had largely remained unchanged since Iulius Caesar left them in 51 BCE, and among which the chiefs of the sixty or so nations frequently squabbled.[35] Augustus reduced the territory encompassed by Gallia Comata, renaming it Lugdunensis (map 3), hiving off parts to the other two provinces and enlarging them in the process. The regional grouping would henceforth be referred to as *Tres Galliae* – or 'The Three Gauls' – but they would remain as Provinces of Caesar.

Lollius' fate was also decided. He had been in the role of governor for almost two years. While one source describes him as a model of reliability and a man immune to greed, another portrays him quite differently, as crafty and deceitful.[36] Augustus determined that a new leader was needed to carry through his provincial reforms without the risk of further embarrassment. He relieved Lollius of his command and replaced him with his own stepson.[37] Lollius would never again serve as a provincial governor, and from this moment on the man would harbour a deep grudge against Tiberius.

If calamity had been avoided on the northern frontier, it was more than offset by violent disturbances elsewhere.[38] In Central Europe, the Alpine nations of the Camunni and Vennii raised their shields and spears against the Romans; they were quickly subdued by the intervention of P. Silius Nerva, who could draw on experience of fighting a war in mountainous terrain with M. Agrippa in northern Spain.[39] Nothing is preserved in the extant accounts about the course of his successful campaign. In the Western Balkans, seeing an opportunity for gain, the nations of northern Illyricum, in concert with the Norici in the eastern Alps, overran the Roman settlements at Istria.[40] Emboldened by his recent victory, Nerva and his legates engaged the Balkan warriors who, now faced with a superior opponent, put down their arms and came to terms again. Fighting without their alliance partners, the Norici suspended hostilities and quickly agreed a pact with the Romans too.[41] Meanwhile, in neighbouring Macedonia the Dentheleti and the Scordisci roamed the land, leaving destruction in their wake, while in Thracia L. Caninius Gallus – who is not recorded as having fought a war before – assisted the Roman ally Roimetalkes in his struggle against the Sarmatae, and succeeded in driving them from his kingdom and back across the Danube River.[42]

Agrippa, meanwhile, was heading east to take up another assignment and had reached Athens by the onset of winter.[43] *En route* he had stopped off at *coloniae* – Augusta Buthrotum (Butrint) in Epirus, Augusta Aroe Patrensis (Patras) founded for the veterans of *Legiones* X *Fretensis* and XII *Fuliminata*, and Laus Iulia Corinthiensis (Corinth) in the Peloponnese – to meet with city officials and veterans.[44] The stalwart commander was now constantly suffering severe pain in his legs.[45] He had been living with the condition for years but had kept his ailment secret from Augustus. The loyal commander, now 49 years old, did not want to distract his friend or give him cause to worry, but on his way to Asia Minor he discreetly visited shrines of gods associated with healing, hoping to reduce his discomfort or find a cure.

15 BCE

M. Livius L. *f.* Drusus Libo   L. Calpurnius L. *f.* Piso (Pontifex)

In the West, Augustus toured the Iberian Peninsula, making a point to visit the *coloniae* where veterans of the recent war were settling down and creating new lives for themselves.[46] As he had done in *Tres Galliae*, he reorganised the region, creating three new provinces out of the old two.[47]

Hispania Tarraconensis was fashioned out of Hispania Citerior, incorporating the newly conquered territories of the Astures and Cantabri.[48] This became the permanent base of the *Exercitus Hispanicus.* In the homeland of the Astures, *Legio* VI *Victrix* was stationed at Legio (modern León); *Legio* X *Gemina* was billeted at Astorga, and IIII *Macedonica* at Herrera de Pisuerga (Palencia) among the Cantabri – all fortresses apparently being founded after the war at strategic locations to facilitate communications and troop movements.[49] Atlantic-facing Lusitania, also a Province of Caesar, was delimited in the north by the Douro River and in the east side its border passed through Salmantica (Salamanca) and Caesarobriga (Talavera de la Reina) as far as the Anas (Guadiana) River.[50] Its capital was the *colonia* Augusta Emerita (Mérida). Baetica, the third administrative entity, was to be a 'Province of the People' governed by a proconsul from its capital at Corduba (modern Córdoba).[51] A new road, the *Via Augusta*, was constructed across the Iberian Peninsula to connect the Gallic border of Tarraconensis with the Pillars of Hercules at Gades; at the crossing of the Baetis River on the borderline of Baetica, a bridge with an arch was erected (the *Ianus Augusti*) bearing an inscription which marked the starting point for the distances on the milestones along the road.[52]

Native resistance having been broken, the Romans could begin full economic exploitation of the region. A reported 20,000 pounds of gold were extracted from mines each year, some of which would be used to pay the army.[53] The farmers of Baetica would grow rich providing the Roman army with olive oil as far away as Germania.[54] Many local men of military age chose to make careers for themselves in the Roman auxiliary army and followed the *signa* of the *Alae Asturum* and *Cohortes Asturum et Callaecorum*.[55]

In Gallia Cisalpina (the region of northern Italy beyond the Po River and south of the Alps), the native people – in particular the Raeti – were unwilling to accept the encroachment of Roman settlers who had made homes in numerous *coloniae* and *municipia* and constantly traipsed through their territory.[56] Their response was to attack the travellers – behaviour that was to be expected of barbarians, notes Dio – but the cruelty of some acts allegedly committed by the Raeti shocked even the Romans. It was reported they slew not only all their male captives who were old enough to bear arms, 'but also those who were still in the women's wombs, the sex of whom they discovered by some means of divination'.[57] Augustus now had his *casus belli*, if he needed one. The Romans had engaged the Raeti before: L. Munatius Plancus had fought them around 43 BCE, eliminating them as a threat to Gallia Narbonensis and Comata.[58] This new war would be one of outright conquest.

Tiberius was already developing an acumen for military affairs. His younger brother was as yet untried. This was his opportunity to learn the arts of war. Augustus chose the 23-year old Nero Claudius Drusus (plate 26) to command the campaign in the Alps.[59] Paterculus describes Drusus as:

> A young man endowed with as many great qualities as men's nature is capable of receiving or application developing. It would be hard to say whether his talents were better adapted to a military career or the duties of civil life.[60]

To succeed in the coming war, he would have to be a fast learner.

No doubt guided by Augustus and his older brother, Drusus assembled his expeditionary army. He began the campaign on the northeastern side of the Italian peninsula, moving from the Veneto to the foothills of the Dolomites (map 8).[61] He engaged the Carni as well as certain tribes of the Norici, among them the Taurisci, and made safe the area around the city of Aquileia and its important port on the Adriatic Sea.[62] Moving inland, he encountered the Breuni, Genauni and the Ucenni nations.[63] It was 'near the Tridentine mountains', Dio writes, that Drusus clashed with a detachment of Raeti warriors 'which came to meet him'.[64] His men easily overwhelmed the lightly armed fighters.[65]

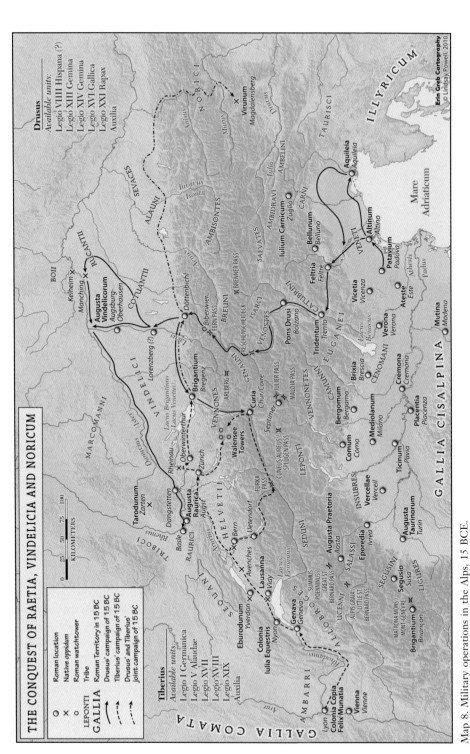

Map 8. Military operations in the Alps, 15 BCE.

Drusus' army then marched north following the direction of the adjacent valley into the Alps. The course of the future *Via Claudia Augusta* suggests he chose the Reschen (or Reschen-Scheideck) Pass, which follows the course of the Adige (or Etsch) River.[66] The ability to use river craft for at least part of the outbound journey may have swayed Drusus' decision to take it over the alternative Brenner Pass.[67] On the south side, the pass was wide, level and ideal for marching legionaries, their pack animals and waggons. Rising over the main chain of the Alps, the Reschen Pass connects the Inn River valley in the northwest with the Vinschgau valley in the southeast. Polybius describes this pass – as he does all the others traversing the Alps – as 'excessively precipitous'.[68] The young commander may have been the first to establish a permanent crossing over the Adige at Bolazano, known from Roman sources as *Pons Drusi* ('Drusus' Bridge').[69] From here the Reschen Pass formed a corridor of approximately 160 Roman miles (240 kilometres) from *Pons Drusi* to the foothills of the Schwäbisch-Bayerisches Alpenvorland along which to move his men and matériel.[70]

In contrast, the northern side of the pass formed a narrow and steep bottleneck, nowadays called the Finstermünzpaß (1,188 metres), which would slow down their advance. Roman troops faced a tough ascent crossing the streams in the valleys without the benefit of military roads and bridges. With the Romans in hot pursuit, the Raeti retreated up the pass. They resorted to ever more desperate measures. When they had used up their arsenals, records Florus, the women used their own children as weapons, smashing their heads against the ground and flinging their limp bodies at the approaching Romans.[71] Drusus' army systematically defeated them. Units of troops were stationed along the route of the Roman advance to relay communications back and forth.[72] In just a few weeks, Drusus' expeditionary force emerged victorious into the foothills of the Schwäbisch-Bayerisches Alpenvorland. Receiving the news that Drusus had defeated the Raeti and that they had been 'repulsed from Italia', Augustus rewarded him with a promotion to *praetor* – the magistracy ranked just below consul.[73]

The fleeing Raeti spread into neighbouring Gallia Lugdunensis. Augustus dispatched his elder stepson with an army and orders to quell the Alpine nations once and for all.[74] Tiberius, likely following the course of the Rhône River (Rhodanus) or the Jura Mountains, succeeded in subjugating the Alpes Poeninae and all the access routes from the west. He may have split his troops and taken the Rhine route via Walensee, or additionally the Valais over the Furka Pass.[75] Meanwhile, Drusus' men marched from their new positions along the River Lech to the source of the Rhine, or followed the Danube to its source.[76] Dio writes that 'both leaders then invaded Raetia at many points simultaneously, either in person or through their deputies', inferring that the brothers were executing a pre-agreed, co-ordinated plan.[77] They fought in pitched battles that saw heavy losses among their opponents, but few Roman casualties.[78] When Tiberius reached a major lake, he took the shortest route, ordering his men to construct boats with which they launched an audacious amphibious operation to reach the other side, crossing the water and taking their opponent completely by surprise.[79]

Even the boldest of the Raeti nations, the Cotuantii and Rucantii, could not muster the forces to repel the invader.[80] Attacked on all sides, their resistance finally collapsed.[81]

Keen to ensure a lasting peace would follow, Tiberius and Drusus were determined to prevent the survivors from reuniting and fighting against them at a later time. As A. Terentius Varro Murena had done with the Salassi:

> because the land had a large population of males and seemed likely to revolt, they deported most of the strongest men of military age, leaving behind only enough to give the country a population, but too few to begin a revolution.[82]

Many of the deportees would serve in the Roman army with new units of *Cohortes Raetorum*.[83] Tiberius gave out decorations to legionaries who had demonstrated valour during the campaign.[84]

By the summer, the Claudius brothers had begun operations in the Alpenvorland, reaching as far north as the banks of the River Danube. Facing them now were the tough warriors of the Vindelici nations, Iron Age Celtic people who were particularly feared for their brutality and cruelty. The Clautenatii, Licatii and Vennones were reputed to be the boldest and bravest of them.[85] Living in organized communities, many had settled in fortified cities or *oppida*.[86] Roman troops were trained for siege warfare using a variety of techniques and technologies. By such means, Drusus' men stormed 'many towns and strongholds' with ruthless efficiency.[87] The date of the siege against the stronghold of the Genaunes is known.[88] Their citadel is recorded as having fallen to Drusus on 1 August – an auspicious date as fifteen years earlier, on the same day, the then Imp. Caesar had taken Alexandria from Kleopatra.[89] The resistance of the Vindelici ceased.[90] Several *Cohortes Vindelicorum* came into service after this date. Tiberius distributed more awards for distinguished service to men of the legions.[91]

The Roman army continued its eastward march. In its sights was Noricum, a kingdom which had co-existed peacefully with the Romans since establishing formal relations in 186 BCE, but had upset the arrangement the year before when it had stirred up unprovoked trouble.[92] Its principal city was Virunum, a formidable *oppidum* atop the Magdalensberg.[93] Below it, on a south-facing terrace, was an entrepôt where Romans traded for resin, pitch, torches, wax, cheese and honey, as well as gold and high quality iron ingots called *ferrum Noricum*.[94] The attack seems to have taken the Norici by surprise. Feared warriors in their own right, Florus writes that they had fooled themselves into thinking that their natural mountainous defences would be deterrent enough against the Romans, who 'could not climb their rocks and snows'.[95] They were wrong to think so. The gates of Virunum were breached and the kingdom of Noricum fell to the Romans. In a single summer campaign the brothers had subjugated the region.[96] The requirement for payment of tribute annually was imposed on them as punishment for their audacity.[97] Soon men of military age began serving with the *Alae* and *Cohortes Noricorum*.[98]

In his stepsons, Augustus had two young men he could promote as all-Roman heroes.[99] New coins were struck showing the figure of Augustus in a *toga* seated on a curule chair upon a raised dais, his right arm reaching down to receive olive branches from the two armed figures of Drusus and Tiberius wearing military cloaks (plate 27).[100] The legend '*IMP X*' below attested to the acclamation by the troops of Augustus as *imperator* for a total of ten times. In his fourth *Carmina*, published two years later, Horace extolled:

> What honours can a grateful Rome,
> A grateful Senate, Augustus, give
> To make thy worth through days to come
> Emblazon'd on our records live,
> Mightiest of chieftains whomsoe'er
> The sun beholds from heaven on high?
> They know thee now, thy strength in war,
> Those unsubdued Vindelici.
> Thine was the sword that Drusus drew,
> When on the Breunian hordes he fell,
> And storm'd the fierce Genaunian crew
> E'en in their Alpine citadel,
> And paid them back their debt twice told;
> 'Twas then the elder Nero came
> To conflict, and in ruin roll'd
> Stout Raetian kernes of giant frame.
> O, 'twas a gallant sight to see
> The shocks that beat upon the brave
> Who chose to perish and be free!
> As south winds scourge the rebel wave
> When through rent clouds the Pleiads weep,
> So keen his force to smite, and smite
> The foe, or make his charger leap
> Through the red furnace of the fight.[101]

The young Drusus, in particular, had demonstrated *virtus* in the best tradition of his ancestors:

> So look'd the Raetian mountaineers
> On Drusus: whence in every field
> They learn'd through immemorial years
> The Amazonian axe to wield,
> I ask not now: not all of truth
> We seekers find: enough to know
> The wisdom of the princely youth
> Has taught our erst victorious foe
> What prowess dwells in boyish hearts
> Rear'd in the shrine of a pure home,
> What strength Augustus' love imparts
> To Nero's seed, the hope of Rome.[102]

The brothers seemed invincible in the face even of the most brutal and savage of foes:

> What will not Claudian hands achieve?
> Iove's favour is their guiding star,
> And watchful potencies unweave
> For them the tangled paths of war.[103]

Tiberius had proved his ability to get results once again. After just a year in the governor's role, Augustus charged Tiberius with taking command of Illyricum, where the nations were restless.[104] In the new year his younger brother would replace him as *legatus Augusti pro praetore* for *Tres Galliae* – a significant promotion for a man who barely a year before had no military experience at all.

Operations were suspended in the region. Roman armies, or those of their allies, now controlled most of the main passes throughout the Alps.[105] To ensure their gains were secure, the legions and *auxilia* would spend the winter in newly conquered Raetia and Vindelicia.[106] The site of the camp located at the convergence of the Lech and Wertach rivers and on the Singold would become the *civitas* capital of the Vindelici and be given the official name Augusta Vindelicorum in honour of the *princeps*. *Legio* XIX, under the command of P. Quinctilius Varus, the former *quaestor* of Augustus, established a fortress further west at Döttenbichl in Oberammergau (fig. 6).[107] An auxiliary fort may have been established at Strasbourg on the Rhine at the head of the Vosges Mountains to defend the interior of Gallia Lugdunensis.[108]

In North Africa there was military activity too. This year P. Sulpicius Quirinius had assumed his post as proconsul of Creta et Cyrenaica, one of the Provinces of the People.[109] He is described by one Roman commentator as 'an indefatigable soldier'.[110] If he was looking for a war to wrap himself in glory, he found one. The Nasamones, a nomadic tribe of Berbers, provided the opportunity

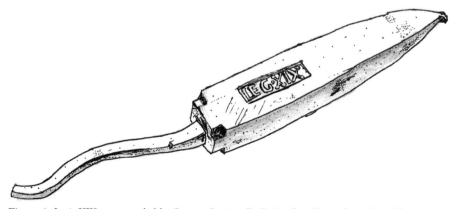

Figure 6. *Legio* XIX, commanded by *Legatus Legionis* P. Quinctilius Varus, brought artillery on the campaign to complete the conquest of the Alps in 15 BCE. This catapult bolt, bearing the legion's index number, was used in anger.

in Cyrenaica. No details of the conflict survive, only that he successfully subjugated them.[111] In the Sahara Desert, Quirinius also battled the Marmaridae and Garamantes, previously beaten by Cornelius Balbus in 20 BCE. He 'might have returned with the title of *Marmaricus*', writes Florus, 'had he not been too modest in estimating his victory'.[112] Having proved himself 'by his zealous services', however, Quirinius had impressed his colleagues and would win a consulship.[113] Valour and victory on the battlefield still counted in the race for political office.

On his second mission in the orient, Agrippa finally arrived at Antiocheia. On his way he founded a new *colonia* at Alexandria Augusta Troadis (modern Eski Stambul in Turkey).[114] Having reached Syria, he soon departed to the colony of veterans of *Legiones* V *Macedonia* and VIII *Augusta* at Iulia Augusta Felix Berytus (modern Beirut) to meet with officials.[115]

14 BCE
M. Licinius M. *f.* Crassus Frugi   Cn. Cornelius Cn. *f.* Lentulus (Augur)

While Augustus was busy in the West, his associate Agrippa was on a state visit to Iudaea, enjoying the hospitality of King Herodes. The two statesmen were becoming firm friends. During the return sailing to Lesbos, Agrippa was made aware of the deteriorating political situation in the kingdom of the Cimmerian Bosporus on the northern shores of the Euxine (Black) Sea.[116] Immediately following the death by suicide of King Asander, a man named Scribonius, claiming to be the son of Mithradates VI of Pontus, had assumed the throne and declared that he had received the kingdom legitimately from Augustus.[117] Agrippa refused to accept this version of events and determined that direct intervention was needed. He sent instructions to Polemon, the king of Pontus and the Roman ally closest to the trouble spot, to move quickly to expel Scribonius. Furious at the pretender's audacity the people of the kingdom had, meanwhile, assassinated him. The crisis was already over when Polemon berthed his ships at the dock at Tanaïs. Polemon's arrival now led to anxiety that he would lay claim to the kingdom himself, and the local people resisted his involvement in what they considered an internal matter.[118] That fear was realized when fighting ensued and Polemon sacked the city; yet unbowed, the people continued their resistance.[119]

Having reached Mytilene in the spring, Agrippa departed for the Bosporus with a fleet of ships to personally take charge of operations. Before he left, he wrote to Herodes with a request for ships, crews and troops. The king of Iudaea responded without hesitation, but when his fleet, delayed by winds at Chios, reached Lesbos he discovered the Roman commander's ships had already left for the Cimmerian Bosporus.[120] Herodes finally caught up with Agrippa at Sinope in Pontus (Sinop on Cape Ince, Turkey).[121] Agrippa was delighted by the king's arrival.

In the Cimmerian Bosporus, Polemon was struggling to contain the problem he had largely created himself. He fought the rebels in a battle but they would not submit to him.[122] Only when Agrippa came to Sinope with the purpose of conducting a campaign against them and news of his imminent arrival in the Bosporus reached the rebels did they finally lay down their arms and surrender to Polemon.[123] Dio's account infers that Agrippa's formidable reputation alone was enough to break the resistance and that he did not need to make the journey across the Black Sea. Orosius, however, clearly states that he *was* actually involved in fighting, writing: 'Agrippa, however, overcame the Bosporani and, after recovering in battle the Roman *signa* formerly carried off under Mithridates, forced the defeated enemy to surrender.'[124] The outcome was that Agrippa brokered a new settlement between the warring factions. Dynamis (the widow, first of Asander and later Scribonius) was to become Polemon's wife; and the Cimmerian Bosporus was re-affirmed as a client kingdom of the Roman Empire, required to provide men to serve in the Roman army.[125] Augustus approved.[126] Agrippa also bound neighbouring Cheronesos (now Crimea) to the Cimmerian Bosporus, thereby securing control over the entire peninsula for Rome.[127]

Just as he had done after the *Bellum Cantabricum et Asturiucum* five years previously, Agrippa sent his official after-action report not to the Senate, but directly to Augustus. The ramifications of his decision were far-reaching. 'In consequence,' writes Dio, 'subsequent conquerors, treating his course as a precedent, also gave up the practice of sending reports to the public.'[128] Nevertheless, for his successes the Senate still voted Agrippa a triumph – and, as before, he declined it, though the sacrifices offered to him did take place. That decision was consequential too. 'For this reason – at least, such is my opinion,' remarks Dio, 'no one else of his peers was permitted to do so any longer either, but they enjoyed merely the distinction of triumphal honours.'[129]

Tiberius returned to Rome while the legions under his command marched out of the foothills of the Alps to the western Balkans. M. Vinicius had recently assumed from him his post of *legatus Augusti pro praetore* of Illyricum.[130] The units would reinforce the four legions already in the region, where the Breuci and Dalmatae had taken up arms.[131] 'Caesar [Augustus] sent Vinnius to subdue them,' writes Florus (who calls the conflict the *Bellum Pannonicum*), 'and they were defeated on both rivers.'[132]

As the new governor of *Tres Galliae*, one of Nero Drusus' first tasks was to undertake a census of the population.[133] To bind them closer to Rome, and thus neutralize them as a threat to internal security, he established a council of the sixty Gallic nations called the *Concilium Galliarum*.[134] This consultative body would meet annually at *Colonia* Copia Felix Munatia, at a new complex to be the focus of the cult of Roma and Augustus, the foundations of which were laid this year. In addition to the normal duties of a propraetorian legate, he was given care of the mint which had been set up in the city. It met the ongoing need for production of silver *denarii* to pay the soldiers of the legions stationed in the West. The facility came with its own high-security detail, a unit of the *Cohortes Urbanae*, complete with an officer holding a key to the prison.[135]

Augustus had appointed his stepson expressly to prosecute his war of conquest of Germania.[136] The commander-in-chief's intent is summed up by Florus:

> Since he was well aware that his father, Caius Caesar, had twice crossed the Rhenus by bridging it and sought war against Germania, he had conceived the desire of making it into a province to do him honour.[137]

The preparations would be extensive and cover a wide front; the planning would be thorough and take up to two years to complete. The theatre of operations was to be a vast tract of land from the Rhine to the Weser or Elbe rivers, encompassing many kinds of terrain and an unknown number of tribes and nations between them. As he had done in the *Bellum Cantabricum et Astricum*, Augustus would bring to bear overwhelming force upon the enemy. With the Astures and Cantabri finally quelled, there was an opportunity to dilute the heavy concentration of military assets in the Iberian Peninsula. Several of the eight legions stationed in Hispania Tarraconensis could now be drawn down and redeployed where they were needed in Illyricum and *Tres Galliae*. *Legiones* XIV *Gemina* and XVI *Gallica* marched to join I, V *Alaudae*, XVII, XIIX and XIX already stationed in *Tres Galliae*.[138]

The immediate task was to move them to new locations along the Rhine. The siting of the military camps makes it is clear the invasion plan was well conceived. From the outset, Drusus intended to dominate the river by controlling all lines of communication along it.[139] According to Florus, he established over fifty military bases (*castella*) on the river, though modern archaeology has yet to find all of them.[140] He mentions bridges (*pontes*) being constructed at Borma or Bonna (perhaps Bonn) and Gesoriacum (identified with uncertainty as Boulogne) and that Drusus 'left fleets (*classes*) to protect them'.[141] At key strategic points along the lower and middle Rhine, five new legionary fortresses were built at Batavodurum (Nijmegen-Hunerberg), Vetera (Xanten), Novaesium (Neuss), *Oppidum* Ubiorum (Cologne) and Mogontiacum (Mainz).[142] To facilitate the movement of men and matériel, a military road connected the bases with the provincial command at *Colonia* Copia Felix Munatia.[143] Smaller forts for auxiliary units and supply dumps were constructed along this road at Andernach, Argentorate (Strasbourg), Asciburgium (Asberg), Bingen, Bonna, apud Confluentes (Koblenz), Speyer and Urmitz.[144]

Mogontiacum, built on a 40-metre high rise above the river, was the most southerly fortress of the new Rhine offensive line.[145] Two legions, possibly XIV *Gemina* and XVI *Gallica*, shared this basecamp. It controlled a network of suppliers whose commodities were essential to the war effort. At Weisenau, about 3.5 kilometres (2 miles) south of Mogontiacum, another military installation has been identified on an escarpment overlooking the Rhine River.[146] About 2 kilometres (1 mile) downstream at Dimesser Ort was a harbour.[147]

Some 200 kilometres further down river from Mogontiacum stood *Oppidum* Ubiorum. It was the burgeoning market town of the Ubii nation, founded when Agrippa granted them sanctuary on the Roman side of the Rhine in 39/38BCE or 20/19BCE.[148] The Roman army had bases here at different times over several years, but which were probably located away from the civilian settlement. The new installation may have been the new winter camp of *Legio* XIX, which was earlier based at Dangstetten, and possibly shared it with *Legio* XVII.[149]

Located about 50 kilometres northwest of *Oppidum* Ubiorum, the original outpost of Novaesium (called 'Neuss A' by modern archaeologists) was now redeveloped into a full-size winter camp (or 'Neuss B').[150] Polygonal in shape with a V-profile ditch, it enclosed an area of at least 27 hectares, large enough for one legion.[151] It may have been home to *Legio* XVII or XVIII.[152] A wooden bridge was constructed to carry the military road uninterrupted over the marshy Meertal to the northwest.[153]

Laying 65 kilometres down river on the Fürstenberg was Vetera (meaning 'the Old One').[154] It was located opposite the Lippe River (Lupia). Traces of ditches and earthen rampart indicate it may have been large enough to house two legions, the most likely candidates being V *Alaudae* and XVIII.[155]

The penultimate fort in the chain of military bases was Batavodurum. Located 2 kilometres east of modern Nijmegen at a place called Hunerberg, the legionary camp occupied an escarpment above the floodplain of the Waal River (Vahalis).[156] At 42 hectares, it was large enough for two legions (map 9). It may have been the winter camp for *Legiones* I *Germanica* and V *Alaudae*.[157] Unusually, the fortress lay outside the Roman Empire in the *territorium* of the Batavi, whose permission must have been sought before construction work could begin.[158] These native

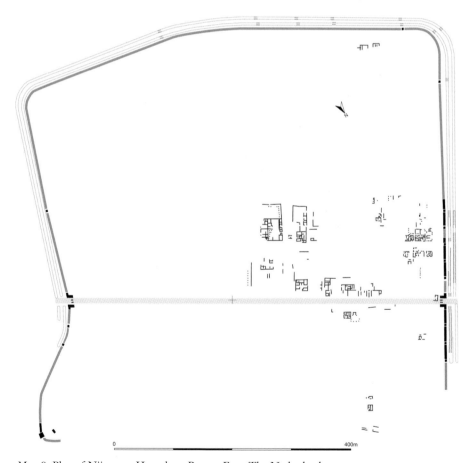

Map 9. Plan of Nijmegen-Hunerberg Roman Fort, The Netherlands.

warriors would be part of Drusus' expeditionary force. Honoured allies to the Romans, they were fine horsemen known for their ability to cross rivers in full armour.[159] It was widely believed that, like the best weapons, they were only to be used in times of war.[160] The exquisite quality of the armour and equipment found at the site emphasizes the high value the Romans placed on their Batavian allies. Several *Alae Batavorum* and at least nine *Cohortes Batavorum* are recorded.[161]

The locations of the military installations suggest the region had been well-surveyed by the Romans in advance of the campaign and that they were intended to be the embarkation points for invasion routes into Germania.[162] From Batavodurum, the army could approach from the west, moving northeast towards the Ems River (Amisia) and then to the Weser River (Visurgis). From its bases further along the Rhine, the army could follow its tributaries, reaching, first, the Weser River and then the Elbe River. From Vetera, the army could thrust into Germania following the course of the Lippe. From Novaesium, there was potential for a direct line of attack up the Ruhr River (Rura). From *Oppidum* Ubiorum, Roman forces could go north to the Ruhr or march south to the Sieg. From Mogontiacum, the army could move along the Main River (Moenus) and then march across to the Saal River (Sala), a tributary of the Elbe.

An amphibious landing to deliver Roman troops into Germania using its rivers from the north must have been part of the original strategic concept for the campaign right from the start. The North Sea (*Mare Germanicum*) was treacherous and dangerous to a flotilla of small ships carrying men and matériel sailing out via the mouths of the Rhine or Waal rivers. The audacious option chosen required one or more canals to be excavated between the River Rhine and the large inland sea called Lacus Flevo (formerly the Zuider Zee, nowadays the Ijsselmeer) to allow a fleet to sail into the relatively protected and calmer Wadden Sea, and thence reach the estuary of the Ems. The 'Drusus Canal' (*fossa Drusiana*) system was, by Suetonius' account, located beyond the Rhenus and took 'immense exertion' to build.[163] It comprised an *agger* (a word translated variously as 'embankment' or 'rampart') and other associated structures referred to as *moles* ('dams' or 'dykes').[164] Nearby was the last fort in the chain, Fectio (Vechten), which is known from inscriptions to have been a naval base.[165] Work also began on a fleet of hundreds of ships and barges that would ferry the troops and matériel across the sea and directly into the war zone.

One last corner of the southwestern Alps held out against Rome. No details of the campaign or who led it survives – though Drusus would seem the likely candidate. Dio writes only that in 'the Alpes Maritimae, inhabited by the Ligures who were called Comati, and were still free even then, were reduced to slavery'.[166] The courage of these mountain warriors was channelled into new *Cohortes Ligurum*, which entered service soon thereafter.[167]

Just as the great project to annex Germania was about to begin, Augustus' legal power to do so was due to end. The five-year extension to his *imperium* granted in 18 BCE would expire at the end of December. To complete the task he would need the Senate to ratify another *lustrum*.

Chapter 4

Into the Unknown
13–9 BCE

13 BCE

   Ti. Claudius Ti. *f.* Nero I   P. Quinctilius Sex. *f.* Varus

When the road to Italy became passable in the spring, Augustus set off for Rome. He was confident that affairs in the Hispanic and Gallic provinces were settled and that Drusus was fully capable of leading the coming invasion of Germania.[1] Already in the city of seven hills his brother Tiberius had been sworn in as consul alongside P. Quinctilius Varus, the former legate of *Legio* XIX who had served with him in the Alps two years before.[2] Augustus himself arrived in Rome at night – which was his usual practice – to avoid the unwanted attention of senators and common people; and when it was revealed he had come home he declined a proposal for an altar to be placed in the *Curia Iulia* to commemorate his safe return (*adventus*).[3] The following day, he welcomed guests at his home on the Palatinus Hill for the customary *salutatio*. After the morning's social obligations were dealt with, he climbed the steps to the *Capitolium*, where he removed the laurels from around his *fasces* and placed them in gratitude upon the knees of the statue of Jupiter in the temple.[4]

As *princeps*, Augustus convened a session of the Senate to discuss important business. His time away from Rome and in the company of his *legati* had allowed him to think deeply upon many matters of state. Finding his voice to be hoarse, he passed the handwritten speech to the *quaestor* who read it aloud on his behalf.[5] He gave the Conscript Fathers an account of his recent tour of his *provincia*. Then he presented a proposal for reforms to army terms of service, pay and retirement benefits. His purpose was clear: explicitly defining the conditions and rewards of life in the military would mitigate against the risk that soldiers might contemplate mutiny as a means to negotiate improvements to their lot.[6]

Firstly, he reduced the years of service in the *Cohortes Praetoriae* from sixteen years to twelve, and set the number at sixteen for the legions and auxiliaries.[7] Secondly, he made adjustments to salaries and the cash lump sum paid at the end of their service instead of the land grant, which the regular troops were always demanding.[8] Dio comments:

> These measures caused the soldiers neither pleasure nor anger for the time being, because they neither obtained all they desired nor yet failed of all; but in the rest of the population the measures aroused confident hopes that they would not in future be robbed of their possessions.[9]

The proposal was accepted.

Witnessing the rate of progress in quelling the unruly territories by the armies operating under Augustus' auspices, many senators might have imagined they would soon see the return of more Provinces of Caesar into their care. In optimistic mood, on 4 July the Senate voted for an altar to *Pax Augusta* – 'the revered pact' or 'August Peace'.[10] It would be erected on ground a mile outside the *pomerium* beside the *Via Flaminia* and become a prominent feature of the Field of Mars. The ceremony to consecrate the ground for the altar was held the same year.

Augustus initiated another purge of the Senate.[11] In the aftermath of the Civil War, the Senate had seen its numbers shrink drastically. The financial qualifications to enter the body had been reduced to HS400,000 to allow less wealthy men to join, but over a decade the Senate membership had grown and the asset limit was again raised to HS1,000,000 to reduce the number eligible. However, the substantial increase had succeeded too well; now many gifted, but impoverished, younger patricians failed the wealth test while others who were qualified pretended they were below the limit in order to avoid joining.[12] If Augustus did nothing his talent pool was at risk. To address the matter he took direct action:

> Augustus himself made an investigation of the whole senatorial class. With those who were over 35 years of age he did not concern himself, but in the case of those who were under that age and possessed the requisite rating he compelled them to become senators, unless one of them was physically disabled. He examined their persons himself, but in regard to their property he accepted sworn statements, the men themselves and others as witnesses taking an oath and rendering an account of their poverty as well as of their manner of life.[13]

His timely intervention would create opportunities in public service for a new generation to replace the one loyal to Augustus that was aging and taking a less active role in public life – older men like Cornelius Balbus, Norbanus Flaccus, Valerius Messalla Corvinus, Silius Nerva and Statilius Taurus.

The most distinguished member of this old guard, M. Agrippa, returned this year from his mission in the East. His *imperium* was authorized for another five years along with Augustus', 'entrusting him with greater authority than the officials outside Italia ordinarily possessed'.[14] There could be no doubting now among detractors – and there were many in the ranks of *nobiles* – that Agrippa was Augustus' right-hand man, the one he trusted above all others (fig. 7).[15]

While work on the infrastructure for the coming *Bellum Germanicum* proceeded apace, a year into Drusus' governorship of *Tres Galliae*, a violent conflict erupted involving the Aquitani in the Pyrenees. A military response was required and one ensued, the details of which are entirely lost.[16]

In Thracia, a political assassination upset the fragile peace in the kingdom friendly to Rome.[17] A priest of the cult of Dionysus named Ouologaisis (Vologaesus) of the Bessi nation gained a popular following by practising clairvoyance.[18] Inspired by him, his adherents rebelled and in the ensuing chaos King Raiskuporis (Rhascuporis) I, son of Kotys I, was killed. Playing on his reputation for having a supernatural power, he stripped Roimetalkes (Rhoemetalces) I – the

Figure 7. M. Agrippa was Augustus' right-hand man and closest friend. The man who brought him victory at Actium continued to command in other campaigns around the world until his death.

victim's uncle – of his army without a battle. This was a catastrophe, for, as Florus records, 'he had accustomed the barbarians to the use of military standards and discipline and even of Roman weapons'.[19] Their training alone should have taught them to stand their ground; instead they deserted their ensigns. In pursing the Thracian king, Ouologaisis crossed into the Chersonese, where he wrought havoc. Separately, but at the same time, the Sialetae nation was running amok in Macedonia, its governor apparently absent.[20]

Meanwhile, the impact of M. Vinicius' victory in Illyricum proved short-lived. The confederacy of the nations of the northern Balkans rose up again. Alerted to the fact that his legate was seemingly unable to contain the insurrection, Augustus sent his 50-year-old best friend to supervise combat operations.[21] Agrippa departed for the war zone in spite of the fact that it was already winter. His reputation went before him. 'The Pannonii became terrified at his approach,' writes Dio, 'and gave up their plans for rebellion.'[22] There was no reason for him to stay any longer than absolutely necessary. Hardly had he arrived when he began making his preparations to return home.

12 BCE

	M. Valerius M. *f.* Messalla Barbatus Appianus	P. Sulpicius P. *f.* Quirinus
suff.	C. Vagius C. *f.* Rufus	
suff.	C. Caninius C. *f.* Rebilus	L. Volusius Q. *f.* Saturninus

In the early weeks of the new year, M. Agrippa embarked on the journey back to Italy.[23] He did not stay in Rome, however, but proceeded directly to his summer house in Campania. Shortly after arriving, he fell ill and took to his bed.[24] His adjutants sent a message to Augustus requesting him to come urgently. When the *princeps* finally arrived he found him already dead.[25] Tragically, Fate had intervened to prevent the old friends from exchanging final words. Augustus personally arranged for the body to be carried to Rome, where it was laid in repose. Following a grand funeral procession, which moved through the city to the *Forum Romanum*, he gave the eulogy himself, part of which has survived.[26] After the corpse had been cremated, the urn containing the ashes was placed in Augustus' own mausoleum, despite Agrippa having already build a sepulchre for himself on the *Campus Martius*.[27]

Agrippa's sudden death was a devastating loss to Augustus personally, but also to the *Res Publica*. He had been Augustus' best friend for over thirty years, his most trusted political associate and the nation's greatest military commander. Augustus urgently needed a new 'right-hand man'. He found him in his eldest stepson, Ti. Claudius Nero (plate 23).[28] In many ways he was like the late Agrippa – a battle-tested field commander, a proven diplomat, and he was self-disciplined, hardworking, trustworthy, modest and reliable. To cement the relationship, Augustus required Tiberius to divorce his present wife (a daughter of Agrippa) and marry Augustus' daughter, Iulia (now the widow of Agrippa).[29] The forced separation from the woman he loved affected him deeply.[30] Despite his protests, Tiberius resentfully complied.[31] Between grieving for Agrippa and marrying Tiberius, Iulia Caesaris gave birth to a son named M. Agrippa (better known to History as Agrippa Postumus).[32]

Tiberius' combat leadership skills were soon pressed into action when the nations of northern Illyricum rebelled again.[33] He did not yet have the name recognition of Agrippa with its pacifying effect among these people, which meant he would have to go and wage war against them in person. To assist him he was able to call up on the Scordisci, long-term allies of the Romans (and one of the largest tribes in the western Balkans) as well as neighbours of the rebels.[34] The warriors of the two nations were similarly equipped and fought in similar fashion.[35] The armed Scordisci, Roman legions and auxiliary cohorts together unleashed a brutal counteroffensive. The alliance proved highly effective. 'Tiberius subdued them,' writes Dio, 'after ravaging much of their country and doing much injury to the inhabitants.'[36] As he had with the Raeti, 'he took away the enemy's arms and sold most of the men of military age into slavery, to be deported from the country'.[37] The annual demand of payment of tribute was imposed on those remaining.[38] Eager for news of the campaign, Augustus had, in the meantime, relocated to Aquileia.[39] Receiving the report of the successful outcome of the war, the Senate voted Tiberius a full triumph. For Augustus, however, giving the highest military award to the 30-year-old commander was too much too soon: he did not permit his stepson either to accept or celebrate it. Instead, 'he granted him the triumphal honours'.[40]

In *Tres Galliae*, Tiberius' 26-year-old brother was about to launch his invasion of Germania with his massive army (see Order of Battle 2). Intelligence reached him that several of the Gallic chieftains were planning a rebellion, apparently in concert with certain Germanic nations led by the Sugambri.[41] Drusus had to move quickly or his invasion plan would be in jeopardy. He contrived to invite the leaders of the sixty nations to a special meeting of the *Concilium Galliarum* at *Colonia* Copia Felix Munatia. The ploy worked and the rebellion was

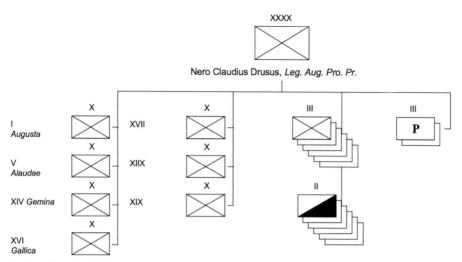

Order of Battle 2. Germania, 12–9 BCE. Units of ethnic *auxilia* are recorded as having served in Germania, including *Cohors Batavorum, Cohors Canninefatium, Cohors Raetorum, Cohors Vindelicorum* and *Cohors Ubiorium*. There were also *alae*, including *Ala Frisiavonum*.

extinguished before it could take place. Meanwhile, he waited for the Germans to cross the Rhine and, when they did, repulsed them. With his rear secure, Drusus now gave the order to proceed with the war. Two years in the planning, the *Bellum Germanicum* had begun.

The opening move of the first year's offensive was a punitive attack on the perpetrators of the *Clades Lolliana* of 17 BCE and the recently failed Gallic revolt (map 10). The Roman incursion was launched from the legionary base at Batavo-durum. In the spring, the expeditionary force crossed the Rhine and marched south along the right bank of the river, then veered left into the country of the Usipetes and their target, the Sugambri.[42] Drusus' men were ordered to devastate their countryside (*vastatio*). The destruction of their agricultural capability – forcing the tribe to make repairs or risk losing their crops later in the harvesting season – would ensure they could not be active participants in the war this year.

The main thrust of the campaign was directed at the nations on the west coast of Europe. Dio writes that Drusus now 'sailed down the Rhine to the ocean'.[43] The newly constructed *fossa Drusiana* provided safe passage for the fleet of trans-ports into Lacus Flevo, which, in Drusus' time, was about half the size of the modern IJsselmeer. The ships were rowed by the legionaries themselves, who had to take care to navigate as they went.[44] Oak trees lined the banks of the lake. Many had been toppled by high winds and floated in the lake, posing a danger to the lightly built Roman craft.[45] Making landfall each night on the voyage allowed the men and animals time to rest and recuperate for the next leg of the journey.

En route, Drusus made contact with the local inhabitants of the region. There was much to be gained by making an ally out of an adversary: he could provide men to supplement the army; pilots to navigate unfamiliar seas; and translators to aid in understanding other tribes. The local people were the Cananefates and

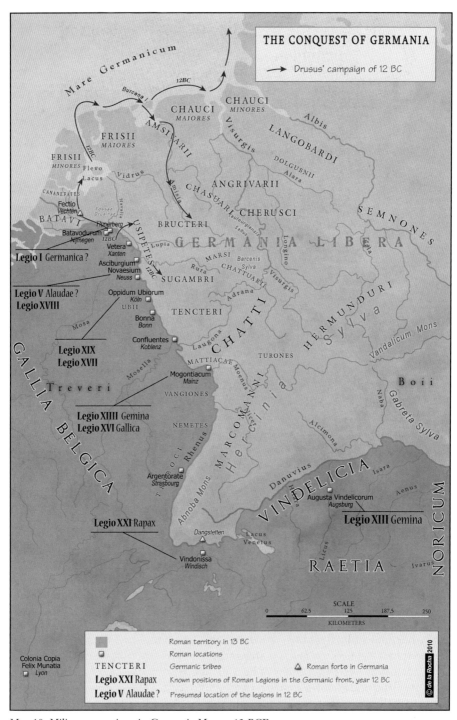

Map 10. Military operations in Germania Magna, 12 BCE.

Figure 8. Nero Claudius Drusus presents Germanic prisoners of war and hostages to Augustus, who is seated, in a scene on a silver cup. Unconditional surrender was a prerequisite for a declaration of victory.

Frisii. Drusus 'won over the Frisii', writes Dio, and signed a treaty with them (fig. 8).[46] During this and subsequent campaigns, men of the Frisii served with the Romans as auxiliary infantry in the *Cohors Frisiavonum*.[47] From now on they would provide tribute (*tributum*) in the form of cow hides for the Roman army.[48]

From the relative calm of Lacus Flevo, Drusus' fleet sailed into the region now called the Wadden Sea. Drusus 'subjugated, not only most of the tribes, but also the islands along the coast', writes Strabo, 'among which is Burchanis, which he took by siege'.[49] Reaching the Dorlar Estuary, the fleet berthed and its crews disembarked. A few ships, however, sailed on to Jutland, apparently on a voyage of exploration, making Drusus 'the first Roman general to sail the northern Ocean'.[50] He might have gone further:

> Drusus Germanicus indeed did not lack daring; but the Ocean barred the explorer's access to itself and to Hercules. Subsequently no one has made the attempt, and it has been thought more pious and reverential to believe in the actions of the gods than to inquire.[51]

The Roman navy had never sailed this far north – and would never again.

The main body of the expeditionary force disembarked at the Ems (Amisia) River.[52] Drusus then 'invaded the country of the Chauci', the people who lived in what is now called Lower Saxony (Niedersachsen), who were regarded as the noblest Germanic people, but were impoverished by living on the coastline.[53] His fleet sailed down the Ems until it reached the land of the Bructeri, where a battle was fought on the river. Roman ships came under attack from missiles lobbed from the banks and small boats. The outcome was 'Drusus won a naval victory over the Bructeri', writes Strabo, probably with some hyperbole (plate 28).[54] On the return, Drusus' captains misjudged the tides and several ships of his fleet ran aground on the mudflats of the Wadden Sea.[55] His new allies proved their worth when the Frisii helped rescue the stranded vessels and the army was able to reach its camps along the Rhine before winter set in.[56] Minor setbacks notwithstanding, Augustus' youngest stepson was proving to be a living example of the best of Roman values. Upon his arrival in Rome, in recognition of his bold endeavours, Drusus was promoted to *praetor urbanus*.[57]

In the same year, M. Iulius Cottius, who was king of the Ligures (a nation inhabiting the mountainous region of the western Alps known as the Alpes Cottiae), agreed a treaty with Augustus. He was son of King Donnus, who had initially opposed, but later made peace with, Iulius Caesar.[58] Cottius – and his own son of the same name after him – would continue to retain power at his seat at Segusio (Susa), but as client kings of the Romans. Crucially, this secured the road between Augusta Taurinorum (Turin) and Brigantium (Briançon), connecting Gallia Cisalpina to Narbonensis.[59]

In stark contrast, the situation in Thracia was worsening. To avert disaster, Augustus ordered L. Calpurnius Piso (plate 22), *Legatus Augusti Pro Praetore* of Galatia-Pamphylia, to march against the rebels.[60] Consul of 15 BCE, Piso had the complete confidence of the *princeps*: he was from an old plebeian family promoted to the patriciate, an independent-minded man whose virtue, tact and personal achievements were widely praised.[61] Velleius Paterculus had kind words for him:

> All must think and say that his character is an excellent blend of firmness and gentleness, and that it would be hard to find anyone possessing a stronger love of leisure, or, on the other hand, more capable of action, and of taking the necessary measures without thrusting his activity upon our notice.[62]

When the rebels learned that Piso was approaching, afraid of certain defeat they retreated homeward.[63] In his war against Ouologaisis and the Bessi, the Roman commander initially suffered reverses, but true to his character he would not give up until he had achieved his mission. The fortune-telling usurper had not, apparently, foreseen his own defeat.

At home, Augustus sponsored traditional paramilitary exercises. This year the *Lusus Troiae* coincided with the dedication of the Theatre of Marcellus.[64] To be held every four years, these 'Troy Games' were a display of mock combat routines performed on horseback by freeborn equestrian Roman boys of different ages in the *Circus Maximus*.[65] Also known as Circensian Games, they were Augustus' favourite public spectacle, 'thinking that it was a practice both excellent in itself, and sanctioned by ancient usage, that the spirit of the young nobles should be displayed in such exercises'.[66] A particular crowd-pleasing attraction was C. Caesar, the 9-year old adopted son of Augustus, who took part in them for the first time. Embarrassingly for Augustus, during the show 'the joints of his curule chair happening to give way, [and] he fell flat on his back'.[67]

11 BCE

Q. Aelius Q. f. Tubero   Paullus Fabius Q. f. Maximus

With the western sector of Germania invaded and treaties signed with several of its peoples, in the second year of the *Bellum Germanicum* Drusus opened up a new

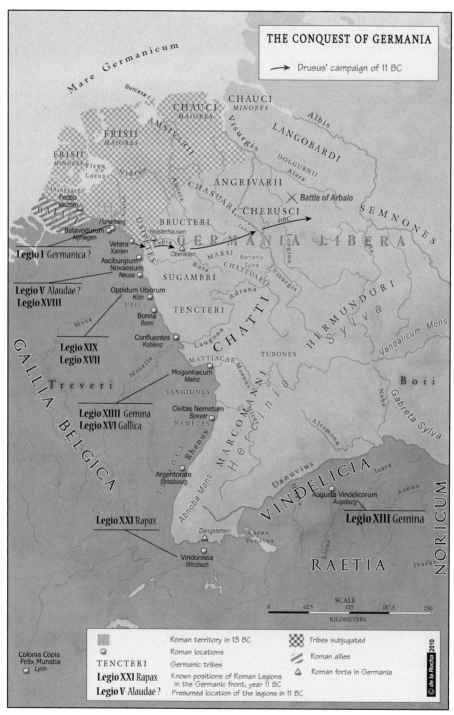

Map 11. Military operations in Germania Magna, 11 BCE.

front. At the start of spring his army crossed the Rhine again, but marched into the central region of Germania, beginning with the territory of the Uspietes (map 11). Their resistance collapsed quickly and, having received their surrender, the Romans marched on. As the Romans approached, the Sugambri raised no opposition. They were not there but, in fact, away raiding the lands of the neighbouring Chatti nation to the east. Dio reports that the Sugambri were angry at them for having refused to join their alliance against the Romans, and 'seizing this opportunity, Drusus traversed their country unnoticed'.[68]

As he advanced towards the Weser River (Visurgis), temporary marching camps, semi-permanent garrison forts and supply dumps were erected at intervals of roughly 18 kilometres – or a day's march – along the course of the Lippe River. Located 36 kilometres (22 miles) from Vetera on the north bank of the river was Holsterhausen, a marching camp roughly rectangular in shape with a V-shaped ditch and encompassing a space of 50 hectares, able to accommodate up to two legions and auxiliaries.[69] Some 54 kilometres (36 miles) east of Vetera lay Haltern. The site was initially occupied with a temporary camp covering 34.5 hectares – enough space for two legions – and a fortlet upon a hill called the Annaberg.[70] Some 15 kilometres (9 miles) east of Haltern stood Olfen. Storing food and matériel was the likely purpose of this fortified site of 5 hectares, large enough for one or two cohorts.[71] Nearby, the river was crossed by a bridge; Dio refers to it when writing that Drusus 'bridged the Lupia and invaded the country of the Sugambri'.[72] The chain of installations continued up river, but the forts were now sited on the opposite bank. At Beckinghausen, a small fort of 1.56 hectares with triple ditch on the three sides facing inland was erected, its purpose perhaps being to receive supplies delivered by boat for transportation overland.[73] Just 2 kilometres (1 mile) southeast of it – and some 90 kilometres (56 miles) from Vetera – was the fortress at Oberaden. Roughly oval in shape, at 56 hectares it was an enormous fortress, able to house up to two legions and auxiliaries (map 12).[74] This year Roman engineers began to lay out the foundations of its essential infrastructure, such as water tanks and the main internal buildings which would, over the next two seasons, be fabricated of wood. The strongly constructed defences and gates at Oberaden indicate the Roman high command intended the army to stay a while.[75]

Elsewhere, above the Wetter – a tributary of the Main River – in the territory of the Mattiaci, a supply dump was erected on the edge of a plateau at Rödgen.[76] Within its polygonal plan encompassing 3.3 hectares, three large granaries were installed to store grain and other commodities shipped up river from Mogontiacum (map 13). This would ensure the army advancing northeast towards the upper section of Weser was fed and equipped.

Progress through Germanic territory was swift. One curious incident that unsettled the military high command – so much so it was considered important enough to be recorded by several Roman historians – involved a portent:

> In Germania in the camp of Drusus a swarm of bees settled on the guy ropes and posts of the tent of Hostilius Rufus, *praefectus castrorum*.[77]

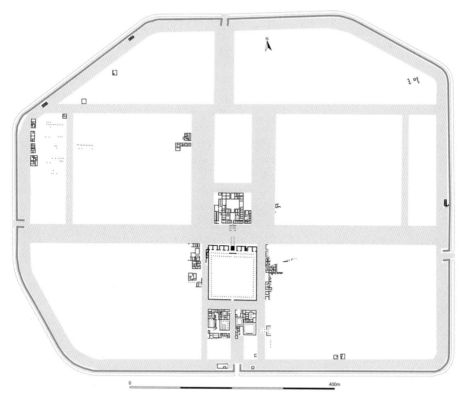

Map 12. Oberaden Roman Fort, Germany.

The *augur* interpreted the phenomenon as a bad omen and predicted a coming ambush;[78] but when, and where? The forewarning was obscure, as was so often the case with omens. Just as the campaign season was drawing to a close, the army reached the Weser.[79] Far into enemy country, Drusus' supplies were now running perilously low. Wise counsel prevailed and he gave the order for the march home.[80]

The columns of his expeditionary force, extended over many miles, came under constant attack. Exploiting the element of surprise, the Germans rushed out from the cover of forest and dense undergrowth to strike at soldiers, pack animals and the others who followed the Roman army to war. Germanic warriors fought both on foot and horseback. Their preferred weapon was the *framea*, which, according to Tacitus, was a spear with a 'narrow and short head'.[81] It could be thrown long distance, or thrust or swung at close quarters and, in the trained hands of an experienced warrior, could inflict damage even against a heavily armoured legionary wearing chain mail (though the new articulated plate armour afforded better protection).[82] Nevertheless, the Romans pushed ahead. At a place called Arbalo, Drusus' army came under the most intense attack of the campaign. It was a pass that forced his troops to march along the bottom of the narrow

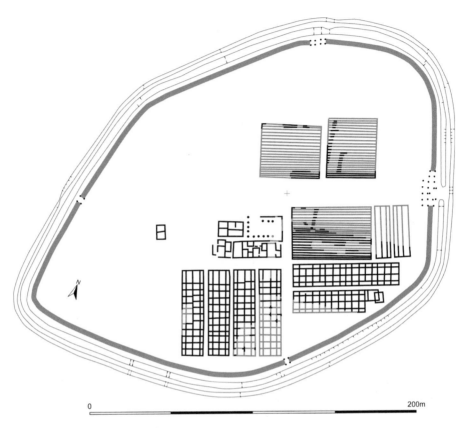

Map 13. Rödgen Roman Fort, Germany.

defile. The Germans blocked off his escape routes, front and rear, and used the higher ground to devastating effect. Pressed together and burdened by their carry packs (*sarcinae*), the Roman legionaries struggled to deploy in formation and use their *pila* or *gladii*. Dio writes that 'once they shut him up in a narrow pass and all but destroyed his army', but then, almost as suddenly as they had staged their offensive, it seems the Germans had a last-minute change of heart:

> They would have annihilated them, had they not conceived a contempt for them, as if they were already captured and needed only the finishing stroke, and so come to close quarters with them in disorder. This led to their being worsted, after which they were no longer so bold, but kept up a petty annoyance of his troops from a distance, while refusing to come nearer.[83]

The Germans let pass the opportunity to destroy the invaders. It was an unexpected stroke of good luck for Drusus. The Romans claimed the battle as a success on account of their prowess in the arts of war. Indeed, polymath and former military officer Pliny the Elder praises 'commander Drusus when he gained the brilliant victory at Arbalo', adding that it is:

a proof, indeed, that the conjectures of soothsayers are not by any means infallible, seeing that they are of opinion that this is always of evil augury.[84]

For their part, the common soldiers enthusiastically acclaimed their 26-year-old legate as *imperator*.[85]

Strategically, it was important that Drusus establish a permanent military presence in the region and 'to secure the province he posted garrisons and guard-posts all along the Mosa, Albis and Visrurgis'.[86] He erected a new fort at the confluence of the 'Lupia and Elison rivers' (known by the name Aliso) and a second one in the territory of the Chatti (whose location is still disputed).[87] Units previously headquartered on the Rhine now began relocating to the forward operating base at Oberaden.[88] It was the first time that garrisons of Roman troops would spend an entire winter in their cramped goat skin tents (nicknamed *papiliones*, 'butterflies', by the soldiers) on German soil.

The news of Drusus' achievement was well received in Rome:

> For these successes he received the triumphal ornaments, the right to ride into the city on horseback, and to exercise the powers of a proconsul when he should finish his term as *praetor*.[89]

However, Augustus refused to allow Drusus to keep the appellation of *imperator* – just as he had done with his older brother.[90] The victory at Arbalo had been won under his auspices and, as was his privilege, the *princeps* added it to his own list of acclamations, which had grown to a cumulative total of twelve.

This year, Tiberius was once again called upon to intervene in Illyricum. While he and the larger part of his army was away, first the Dalmatae on the coast, and later the tribes collectively known as Pannonii in the hinterland, revolted.[91] No details of the war have come down to us, save a general description. Dio writes only that Tiberius swiftly returned to the region and made war upon both of them simultaneously, dividing his time between one front and then the other. It was a validation of the Senate's decision in 22 BCE to transfer the province to Augustus, 'because of the feeling that it would always require armed forces both on its own account and because of the neighbouring Pannonii'.[92]

In Thracia, Piso recovered from his early setbacks and succeeded in conquer-ing both the Bessi and the neighbouring nations who had taken part in the rebellion.[93] To break the revolt, the resourceful commander had applied a variety of approaches, including compromise:

> At this time he reduced all of them to submission, winning over some with their consent, terrifying others into reluctant surrender, and coming to terms with others as the result of battles; and later, when some of them rebelled, he again enslaved them.[94]

Florus recounts the same events of the *Bellum Thracicum* with his customary dramatic imagery:

> Though subdued by Piso, they showed their mad rage even in captivity; for they punished their own savagery by trying to bite through their fetters.[95]

Summing up the campaign, which took three years to conclude, Paterculus writes with a somewhat broader perspective:

> As *legatus* of Caesar [Augustus] he fought the Thraci for three years, and by a succession of battles and sieges, with great loss of life to the Thraci, he brought these fiercest of races to their former state of peaceful subjection. By putting an end to this war he restored security to Asia and peace to Macedonia.[96]

For these successes the Senate voted him thanksgivings (*supplicationes*) and *ornamenta triumphalia*, but not a full triumph.

The positive news flow kept Augustus' popularity high among the Roman People. The Senate remained under his close scrutiny. He conducted a census of the population and, having carried out an audit of attendances of sessions of the house, ruled that the Senate could pass legislation with fewer than the required quorum of 400 members.[97] The People insisted on paying for statues of Augustus to be erected in the city, but he declined the offer, preferring instead to see the money invested in images of the divine trio of *Salus Publica*, *Concordia* and *Pax* – 'Public Heath', 'Harmony' and 'Peace'. When his sister Octavia died that year, she was accorded a public funeral in Rome. Both Drusus and Tiberius gave eulogies.[98]

10 BCE
   Africanus Fabius Q. f. Maximus   Iullus Antonius M. f.

In high spirits, Augustus travelled back to *Colonia* Copia Felix Munatia in *Tres Galliae*, accompanied by Drusus and Tiberius.[99] The steady stream of good news from around the empire encouraged the Senate to vote to consider closing the doors of the Temple of Ianus Quirinus, which had remained open since the last time they were shut in 25 BCE; but then Augustus received reports that 'the Daci, crossing the Ister on the ice, carried off booty from Pannonia, and the Dalmatae rebelled against the exactions of tribute'.[100] Tiberius immediately left to lead the campaign to quell the insurgents.[101] The qualification that 'wars had ceased' was not, finally, met. The temple doors would have to stay open.

Drusus departed for Mogontiacum to continue his war in Germania. His objective this season was the subjugation of the Chatti (map 14).[102] Dio reports that, in a volte-face to their position of the previous year, the Germanic nation had combined forces with the Sugambri. They lived in the area between Elder, Fulda and upper reaches of the Weser rivers in what is now Hessen on the edge of the Black Forest. It was a region notorious to the Romans for being inhabited by exotic, even mythical creatures.[103] The Chatti had a reputation as formidable foot soldiers who, like the Romans themselves, were well organized, planned their actions strategically, fought in formations and erected camps while on campaign.[104] They, and their neighbours the Tencteri, would now feel the cold, sharpened edges of Roman steel.[105] Among important people (*primores*) fighting with the Romans over there were Avectius and Chumstinctus, both tribunes from the Belgic nation of the Nervii, about whose exploits nothing survives beyond a cryptic reference in the synopsis of Livy's now lost books of Roman history.[106]

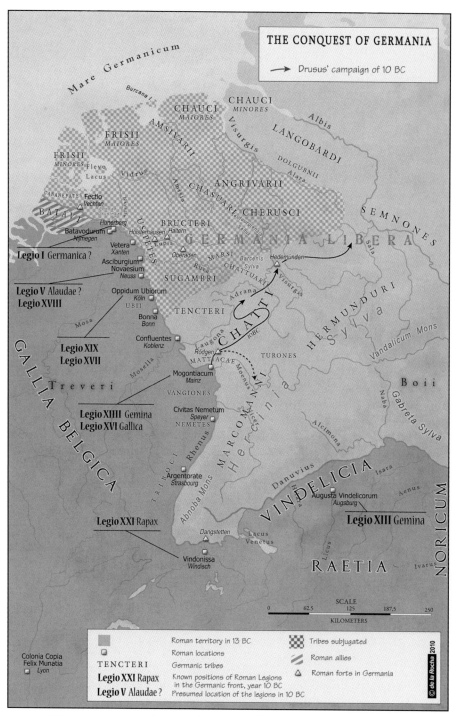

Map 14. Military operations in Germania Magna, 10 BCE.

On the battlefields of Germania, Drusus led from the front like the commanders of old. Inspired by the example of his distant ancestor M. Claudius Marcellus, he often charged the war chiefs opposing him at great personal risk to engage them in one-to-one combat in the hope of winning the *spolia opima*.[107] The ambiguity of Suetonius' language leaves open the possibility that he achieved the rare honour, last claimed by M. Licinius Crassus in 29 BCE.[108]

By the end of the campaign season, Drusus' army had reached the northeastern corner of the territory of the Chatti. Some 240 kilometres (149 miles) away from Mogontiacum, on a bend in the Werra River at Hedemünden near Göttingen, he erected a new fort large enough for a single cohort.[109] The archaeological site has produced a *cornucopia* of iron objects left by the troops based there, including *hasta*-heads (spear-heads), ballista bolt-heads, *dolabra* (axes), nails, chains, hooks and even tent pegs with rings for tying leather straps to. The find of iron fetters betrays the presence of slavers: the P-shaped design of the restraint meant the prisoner had to keep his arms high across his chest where they could be seen, to avoid neck ache. These merchants in human lives (*lixae*) were making profits from the Roman army on active campaign.

From his base in Gallia Lugdunensis, Augustus eagerly awaited his stepson's progress reports.[110] In the summer, Drusus and Tiberius handed over their respective campaigns to their *legati* and returned to *Colonia* Copia Felix Munatia. On 1 August, the new cult complex to *Roma et Augustus*, begun two years before, was officially opened in the presence of the *princeps* himself.[111] It marked an important stage in the transformation of the sixty conquered territories into three pacified provinces sharing a common future. Here the *Concilium Galliarum* would gather each year under the auspices of the tutelary goddess and its imperial patron, chaired by one of its own members as chief priest, and hold sacrifices at the great altar beneath columns topped with winged Victories and celebrate gladiatorial games at the adjacent amphitheatre – potent symbols of Roman culture combined by design to promote a burgeoning cult of victory.[112] It was hoped that by bringing the people together, intertribal war could be avoided. It was an important milestone in the history of the lands conquered by Iulius Caesar four decades before, whose pacification was since made possible by his adopted son and heir.

North of the Danube River, bands of Daci under their king, Cotiso, raided unopposed into Roman-held territory. These fearsome warriors were notoriously difficult to beat.[113] Nevertheless, 'Caesar Augustus resolved to drive back this people.'[114] He dispatched Cn. Cornelius Lentulus Augur, consul of 14 BCE and now *Legatus Augusti Pro Praetore* of Thracia Macedoniaque, to lead operations.[115] Details of the *Bellum Dacicum* are sparse, but what survives hints at a hard-fought defensive war. The Roman force faced a motivated and numerically large opponent. Strabo reports that even in his day the Daci could field an army of 40,000 warriors.[116] Florus writes:

> Lentulus pushed them beyond the further bank of the river; and garrisons were posted on the nearer bank. On this occasion then Dacia was not subdued, but its inhabitants were moved on and reserved for future conquest.[117]

He also turned his attention to the neighbouring Sarmatae, who rode the Hungarian Plain unchecked and crossed the Danube at will on their horses. Lentulus' mission was to prevent further incursions. It is not clear from Florus' account that he succeeded here either, when he writes with contempt of the Sarmatae, 'so barbarous are they that they do not even understand what peace is'.[118]

Leaving *Colonia* Copia Felix before the onset of winter, Augustus and his stepsons returned to Rome. For Drusus, what awaited him there was the turning point of his career.

9 BCE
Nero Claudius Ti. *f.* Drusus   T. Quinctius T. *f.* Crispinus Sulpicianus

On 1 January, Nero Claudius Drusus, now in his 29th year, was sworn in as consul with his colleague T. Quinctius Crispinus.[119] Over the last seven years he had proved the rightness of Augustus' instinct that the young man had the natural courage and aptitude to be a fine field commander. Drusus was impatient to return to Germania, but before he could leave there was a formal matter to attend to in Rome. On 30 January – the birthday of his mother, Livia Drusilla – the *Ara Pacis Augustae* was finally ready for its official dedication.[120]

Some three-and-a-half years in the making, it was an expression in marble and paint of the aspiration of the age. It had been voted for by the Senate on the safe return of Augustus from his tours in the West in 13 BCE.[121] Erected on the field of the war god, the altar to Peace was highly visible. Measuring 11.6 metres (38 feet) by 10.6 metres (35 feet), the re-assembled sacrificial altar stood on a raised podium within a sacred enclosure in the style of a *templum*, approached by ten steps on the west side (fig. 9). On the exterior wall of the enclosure, above a lower panel decorated with volutes of acanthus, a procession was depicted in half-relief. The élite of Roman society are shown here: the Vestal Virgins, members of the religious colleges and their retinues of attendants, the consuls accompanied by their lictors carrying their *fasces*, and many other state officials. On the south side (plate 30), at the front of the procession was Augustus, shown as *Pontifex Maximus*. Further down the line stood a man, covered (*velatus*) with his toga. This was M. Agrippa.[122] A boy in a tunic stood behind him clutching the edge of his toga while looking up at the lady behind – who may be Livia Drusilla.[123] This boy may be C. Caesar or Lucius.[124] The frieze on the north side showed the same procession but seen from the other side (plate 31). Among the people, Iulia was shown with a boy – perhaps L. Caesar.[125] Augustus' trusted deputies, Tiberius, Drusus, L. Domitius Ahenobarbus and Sex. Appuleius, were represented too. These men's military victories were helping to establish the *Pax Augusta*.

Shortly after the ceremonials had concluded, and despite the occurrence of many ominous portents reportedly seen in Rome, Drusus set off again to lead the fourth year of the *Bellum Germanicum*.[126] He launched the offensive from Mogontiacum (map 15). Crossing the Rhine, Drusus' expeditionary force entered Germania through the lands of the Chatti, for the first time cutting a path through the *Hercinia Sylva* (Black Forest), fabled for its impassability and bizarre

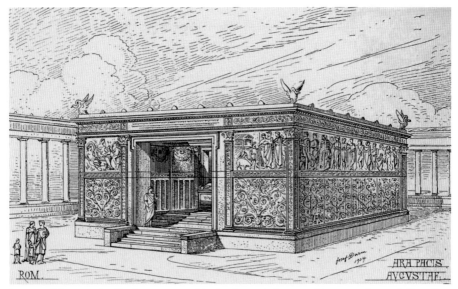

Figure 9. The exquisite *Ara Pacis* was voted by the Senate in honour of Augustus. It was dedicated on 31 January 9 BCE, the birthday of Augustus' wife, Livia.

flora and fauna.[127] The army cut a pathway through and advanced swiftly north-east to engage the confederacy of the Suebi.[128] Drusus met fierce resistance at every step, 'conquering with difficulty the territory traversed and defeating the forces that attacked him only after considerable bloodshed'.[129]

The Roman invaders then entered the territory of the Cherusci, a nation of tough warriors, before reaching the Weser River. Marching further, the army eventually arrived at the west bank of the Elbe River.[130] The Roman commander was eager to cross. He tried but, for reasons not explained in the surviving accounts, he failed in the attempt. It was late in the campaign season and he could not dawdle this far from the army's winter camps on the Lippe and Rhine. While he decided what to do, he ordered his men to erect a victory trophy, 'a high mound adorned with the spoils and decorations of the Marcomanni'.[131] Known as the *Tropaeum Drusi*, it was the most northerly Roman-built structure up to that time; its map coordinates are recorded in Ptolemy's *Geography*.[132] Then a story began to circulate that Drusus had had a strange encounter:

> For a woman of superhuman size met him and said: 'Where, pray, are you hastening, insatiable Drusus? It is not fated that you shall look upon all these lands. But depart; for the end alike of your labours and of your life is already at hand.'[133]

As a chronicler, Dio was unwilling to discount the tale, but he remarked that Drusus departed with apparent haste from the region. On the march back there were other strange – some said supernatural – occurrences that unsettled the soldiers.[134]

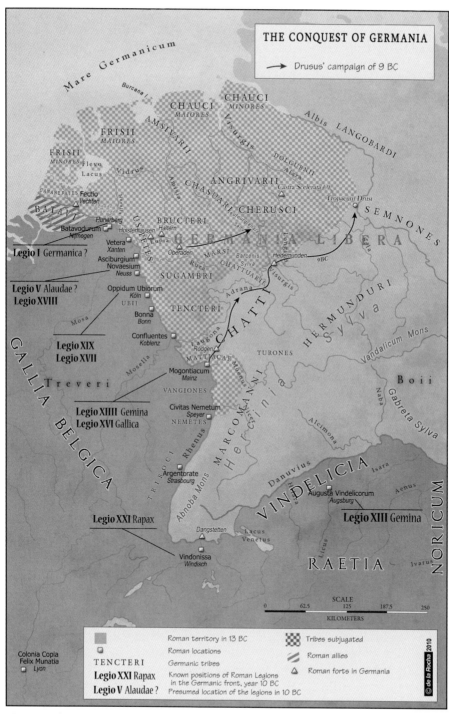

Map 15. Military operations in Germania Magna, 9 BCE.

While riding on the return journey, Drusus fell – or was struck off – his horse which, in turn, fell upon him and broke his leg.[135] The commander now mortally wounded, the army's retreat was halted somewhere between the 'Albis and Salas' Rivers.[136] A profound sense of gloom and foreboding settled over the already nervous troops. The marching camp they erected that night came to be called *Castra Scelerata*, the 'Accursed Fort'.[137] A messenger was immediately dispatched to inform Augustus. He had already moved to Ticinum (modern Ticino) in Gallia Cisalpina to be closer to the war zone and receive reports of progress. In the meantime, Tiberius had joined him from another tour of duty in Illyricum.[138] Receiving the news of his brother's fall, he raced to be with him, in so doing setting the land speed record of the ancient world.[139] He arrived just in time to exchange some final words. After a fever lasting thirty days, Drusus died.[140] Tiberius arranged for the body to be prepared for transportation. It was carried by the military tribunes and centurions on the first stage of the journey – the German nations even suspended hostilities to let them pass – as far as the army camp at Mogontiacum, and then conveyed by road to Italy.[141] As the body approached each city, the leading men came out to take their turn to carry it.[142] Each step of the way, Tiberius walked at the head of the column, an act regarded by Valerius Maximus as a supreme example of *pietas*, 'devotion'.[143]

The cortège finally reached Rome in the winter. Received by the *scribae quaestorii* (the most important of the magistrates' assistants), the body was laid in state.[144] On the day of the funeral, the first eulogy was delivered by Tiberius in the *Forum Romanum*.[145] The second was pronounced by his stepfather Augustus. Still holding legitimate *imperium* and technically at war, he was not permitted within the *pomerium* of the city so his funerary oration was delivered in the largest available building outside it, which was the *Circus Flaminius*.[146] He is reported to have told the hushed audience that he 'prayed the gods to make his Caesars [Caius and Lucius] like Drusus, and to grant him, when his time came, as glorious a death as they had given that hero'.[147] The funeral bier was then carried upon the shoulders of men of the *Ordo Equester* to the *Campus Martius*.[148] After the body was cremated, the ashes were placed in the Mausoleum of Augustus, alongside those of Marcellus, Agrippa and Octavia.[149]

It was a poignant way to end what had been a glorious five years of Augustus' latest extended *imperium*. The *Ara Pacis Augustae* had been built as a symbol of the ending of wars in the West and the safe return of the man responsible for it. The future of the *Tres Galliae* now seemed secure. His great project to annex Germania, to which he had committed fully a third of his legions and several of which were presently stationed beyond the Rhine, was still unfinished – and now missing its field commander. The indispensable Agrippa, too, was gone. The timing could not be worse. On the night of 31 December, the power, which would permit the *princeps* to complete it, would expire.

Chapter 5

Trouble in the East
8 BCE–2 CE

8 BCE
    C. Marcius L. *f.* Censorinus   C. Asinius C. *f.* Gallus

No longer imbued with war-making powers, Augustus was free once again to cross the *pomerium* and enter the city. Contrary to custom, he took the laurels from his *fasces* carried by his lictors into the Temple of Jupiter Feretrius as an offering.[1] He was in a sombre mood and emotionally wrought. 'He himself did not celebrate any festival in honour of the achievements,' writes Dio, 'feeling that he had lost far more in the death of Drusus than he had gained in his victories.'[2] There were those – mostly opponents of the regime – who saw foul play at work in his stepson's death. Drusus had been known to some for his outspoken view that his stepfather should relinquish his powers and let the Senate and People's Assemblies rule unfettered, as they had in the old days.[3] That opinion allegedly made him the object of suspicion by Augustus. Suetonius reports that there was a rumour that he had recalled Drusus from his province and, when he did not immediately obey the order, Augustus had him poisoned. The biographer himself doubted the truth of the allegation. Malicious chatter notwithstanding, Augustus' personal feelings towards his stepson were well known. He had even announced in the Senate that he loved Drusus so dearly while he lived, he always named him joint-heir along with his sons, Caius and Lucius. In a moment of solitude, secreted away in the private office he called *Syracusa* on the top floor of his home, Augustus composed a laudatory inscription in verse which he placed on Drusus' nîche in his Mausoleum, and began to write a prose memoir of the young man's life.[4]

Separately, the Senate voted Nero Claudius Drusus (plate 29) several posthumous honours, including a marble arch adorned with trophies to straddle the *Via Appia*, and the honorific war title *Germanicus* which could be inherited by his descendants.[5] His eldest son, Nero, shortly after adopted the title as his own *praenomen*.[6] At the fortress of Mogontiacum on the Rhine, the men of the legions who had proudly served with Drusus raised their own tribute to his memory:

> The army reared a monument in his honour, about which the soldiers should make a ceremonial run each year thereafter on a stated day, which the cities of Gallia were to observe with prayers and sacrifices.[7]

(The stone core of the cenotaph still stands in Mainz and is known as the *Drususstein*.)[8]

In this collective mood of reflection and introspection, the Senate willingly granted Augustus the *imperium proconsulare* for another five years.[9] He accepted, 'though with a show of reluctance', since he often publicly expressed his intention to resign it.[10] The urgent priority now was finishing the war in Germania. He dispatched his right-hand man Tiberius to complete the work begun by his brother.[11] Paterculus writes of the 34-year-old commander that 'he carried it on with his customary valour and good fortune'.[12] Tiberius had matured into a formidable, but almost boorish, man with an intense personality and intimidating presence. He would stride with his head bent forward, wearing a stern expression on his face, and avoided conversation while walking; he displayed austere manners and had a preference for discipline that seemed better suited to the army camp than the dinner party.[13] Augustus often tried to excuse his stepson's mannerisms by declaring that they were natural failings, and not intentional, yet he was in no doubt of his abilities as a general.

Leaving with Tiberius was Augustus' adopted son C. Caesar (plate 36) – just 14 years old – who would see the Roman army in action for the first time.[14] Arriving in Germania, the nations of the Rhineland sought terms with Tiberius rather than go to war – all, that is, except the Sugambri.[15] Augustus would not accept a truce with the Germans unless they were part of it. 'To be sure, the Sugambri also sent envoys,' explains Dio:

> but so far were they from accomplishing anything that all of these envoys, who were both many and distinguished, perished into the bargain. For Augustus arrested them and placed them in various cities; and they, being greatly distressed at this, took their own lives. The Sugambri were thereupon quiet for a time, but later they amply requited the Romans for their calamity.[16]

Tiberius led his army across the country, crossed the Weser River, fighting battles and skirmishes with few casualties on his side, 'for he made this one of his chief concerns'.[17] The Sugambri then sought their revenge for past humiliations. They attacked the Romans, but in the engagement were decisively defeated. War chief Maelo surrendered unconditionally and Tiberius transplanted 40,000 prisoners from Germania, settling them in Belgica in the vicinity of Vetera on the Rhine.[18] From that time large numbers of able warriors served in the Roman army with several *Cohortes Sugambrorum*, which would became known for their valour.[19]

There are hints, too, that Tiberius used the year to consolidate the Romans' gains in the region. The fortress at Oberaden on the Lippe River was abandoned and a new base was established further down river, about halfway to Vetera.[20] It marked a more cautious strategy for Germania. Located at Haltern, the site had previously been occupied and the Annaberg may still have been operational at this time.[21] Beside the river, a new legionary fortress was erected with a double ditch all around (map 16).[22] Its principal interior buildings were eventually fabricated in wood.[23] The Roman army intended to stay.

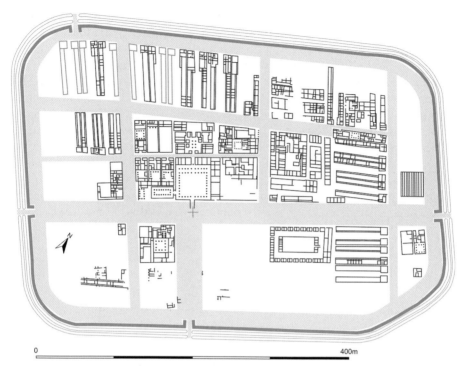

0   400m

Map 16. Haltern Roman Fort, Germany.

Augustus was delighted with his stepson. He promoted Tiberius to commander of operations in Germania, permitted him to use the appellation *imperator* –
though he did add one more acclamation to his own total – and approved him for
a second triumph, opting not to celebrate it himself.[24] Additionally, he arranged
that Tiberius would be given one of the two consulships for the following year.
Augustus also rewarded the troops with cash because C. Caesar had taken part in
exercises with them (plate 38).[25]

C. Cilnius Maecenas, the cultured equestrian, died this year; he was in his late
sixties. In concert with Agrippa, he had provided Augustus with valuable counsel
over three decades and poets to sing the praises of the new age of glory and peace;
he was also a calming influence in moments when the *princeps* raged out of
control.[26] On military and political affairs, the *princeps* would now have to rely
more than ever on his other long-standing, but aging friend T. Statilius Taurus
and the young, but promising, Tiberius.

7 BCE

Ti. Claudius Ti. *f.* Nero II   Cn. Calpurnius Cn. *f.* Piso

On New Year's Day, consul Tiberius and his colleague Cn. Calpurnius Piso convened the Senate in the *Curia Octaviae*, because it was located outside the
pomerium.[27] He announced that he would repair the Temple of Concord so that

he could inscribe both his and his brother's names on it, and then proceeded to celebrate his triumph.[28] Afterwards he gave the customary banquet to the Senate at the *Capitolium*.

The consul might have hoped to serve out his term peaceably in Rome, but later in the year, when a messenger delivered the news that there was disturbance in Germania, he was obliged to take the field. The details of his manoeuvres are entirely lost. The historian Dio writes cryptically that 'nothing worthy of mention happened in Germania'.[29] Yet a passing tale preserved by Suetonius may relate to an event involving Tiberius during this year's campaigning:

> But in the very hour of victory he narrowly escaped assassination by one of the Bructeri, who got access to him among his attendants, but was detected through his nervousness; whereupon a confession of his intended crime was wrung from him by torture.[30]

At the end of the year, Rome's riparian frontier in the north stretched from the English Channel, along the Rhine and Danube rivers to the Black Sea. After years of bitter fighting, the myriad nations of Germania, Illyricum and Thracia Macedoniaque were peaceful. Augustus could now make the case to close the doors of Ianus' temple for the third time.[31]

6 BCE

D. Laelius D. *f.* Balbus   C. Antistius C. *f.* Vetus

C. Antistius Vetus, the *legatus* who had faithfully served Augustus in the war against the Astures and Cantabri, was sworn in as consul.[32] Many clamoured for Caius, the oldest son of Augustus, to be made consul too, but he – and his brother – were too young even to enroll in the army. It was a quandary for their adoptive father. Augustus was increasingly concerned about the boys. His heirs apparent were behaving like spoiled brats, not at all in the mould of their natural father M. Agrippa or the *exemplum* Nero Claudius Drusus Germanicus.[33]

Augustus believed he could still rely on his stepson Tiberius. He was granted the tribunician power for five years, and assigned responsibility for Armenia.[34] The frontier in the East was coming under pressure. The kingdom was slipping from under Roman influence since the death of Tigranes III and his succession by the pro-Parthian Tigranes IV; Augustus now sought to see Artavasdes III replace him.[35] But the *princeps* was unprepared for his stepson's reaction. Tiberius announced he was retiring from public life and sailed away to Rhodes as a private citizen, leaving his wife and retinue behind, taking only his astrologer Thrasyllus with him.[36] Why he did so has perplexed historians, both ancient and modern, who have offered different explanations: he may have decided to remove himself so Caius and Lucius could grow into their roles out from under his shadow; or he was irked that the inexperienced but popular sons of Augustus were receiving all the attention; there were even rumours that the *princeps* had ordered him to leave. The true motive for his action remains a mystery. The stark reality for Augustus was that he now found himself without his right-hand man and completely reliant on his *legati*.[37]

One of these, C. Sentius Saturninus, having completed his tour in Syria, may have transferred this year to *Tres Galliae* and Germania as *legatus Augusti pro praetore*.[38] In his new role he was placed 'in charge of expeditions of a less dangerous character' compared to the ones Tiberius undertook himself, writes Velleius, though he provides no specifics.[39] The inference is that the army under Saturninus was engaged in routine policing duties, laying down the road network and town street plans that were essential to the pacification of a new province.[40] He was ideally suited to the project, being not a warmonger but a man of purposeful action and foresight, equally comfortable in a combat role as he was in cultural pursuits.[41] He was the friendly face of pacification.

In the southwest corner of the Alps on the *Via Iulia Apta*, which ran from Italy to Gallia Narbonensis, crossing the highest ridge of Mount Agel and following a natural depression some 500 metres up, a monument was nearing completion. It could be seen by anyone using the road, which ran along its west side. Within a temple-like precinct, the *Tropaeum Alpium* (at what is now La Turbie) stood nearly 50 metres (164 feet) high.[42] It was Roman 'wedding cake' architecture at its finest. Upon a podium stood a rotunda of twenty-four Doric columns (plate 32), forming a colonnade around a core containing twelve nîches – perhaps for statues of gods or military commanders – topped by a cone-shaped roof, upon which stood a statue of Augustus. The view from this point looked far into Italy and beyond Antibes. In expertly carved lettering, originally gilded or painted, an inscription on the base read:

> To Imperator Caesar *Divi filius* Augustus, Pontifex Maximus, acclaimed *imperator* fourteen times, in the seventeenth year of his holding the tribunician power, the Roman Senate and People, in remembrance that under his command and auspices all the Alpine nations, which extended from the Upper Sea to the Lower, were reduced to subjection by the Roman people. The Alpine nations so subdued were: Triumpilini, Camuni, Venostes, Vennonenses, Isarci, Breuni, Genaunes, Focunates, four nations of the Vindelici, Consuanetes, Rucinates, Licates, Catenates, Ambisontes, Rugusci, Suanetes, the Calucones, Brixentes, Lepontii, Uberi, Nantuates, Seduni, Varagri, Salassi, Acitavones, Medulli, Uceni, Caturiges, Brigiani, Sogiontii, Brodiontii, Nemaloni, Edenates, Esubiani, Veamini, Galliae, Triulatti, Ecdini, Vergunni, Eguituri, Nementuri, Oratelli, Nerusi, Velauni, and Suetri.[43]

It marked the end of the great effort expended by Roman armies over several decades to subjugate the forty-four nations who inhabited the Alps – a banner in gleaming white limestone (with architectural details popping out in colour) celebrating a 'mission accomplished'.[44] Completed between 1 July 7 BCE and 30 June 6 BCE, its dedication coincided with the creation of three new districts: Alpes Maritimae, Alpes Cottiae and Alpes Graiae. Thanks to Caesar Augustus, the *Summa Alpe* (Europe's highest mountain range) was finally under the *imperium* of the Roman People. It would now be much harder for the pesky bandits who preyed on traders and officials to operate there.

5 BCE

	Imp. Caesar *Divi f.* Augustus XII	L. Cornelius P. *f.* Sulla
suff.	L. Vinicius L. *f.*	
suff.	Q. Haterus	C. Sulpicius C. *f.* Galba

The number of proconsuls and *legati* available to govern the provinces and command the legions was falling short of the ongoing need; consuls were encouraged to serve for a few months and then resign to make way for suffects.[45] Augustus became consul for the twelfth time after an interval of eighteen years.[46]

With Tiberius in self-imposed exile, Augustus now needed to find ways to rapidly advance his two sons. It was an important time for C. Caesar. He came of age this year and his name and tribe were registered at the public records office. He was also appointed to a priesthood.[47] As a special honour, Caius was appointed *princeps iuventutis*, 'the first of the youth', which gave him command of one of the six *turmae* of *iuniores*.[48] Largely honorific, nevertheless it placed the young man in a position of having to manage a structured organization and observe its traditions. The role would require him to learn how to lead, master horsemanship and prepare his men for the *transvectio equitum*, the public paramilitary ceremony – revived by Augustus – held annually on 15 July of each year.[49] Lucius, however, was still too young for a formal public role.

In Galatia-Pamphylia, the new *Legatus Augusti Pro Praetore*, P. Sulpicius Quirinius, assumed command. It was a troubled region. A coalition of bandits, called Homonadeis, were operating freely in Cilicia and challenging the internal security of the province.[50] With *Legiones* V *Macedonica* and VII *Macedonica*, Quirinius set out to crush them. He besieged several of their strongholds, starved the inhabitants into submission and took 4,000 prisoners, whom he resettled in the neighbouring cities, leaving no one in the country who could take up arms against him while he was governor.[51]

Activities to pacify Germania continued apace. Haltern was now in operation as a permanent fortress, large enough for a single legion – most likely XIX – with an adjacent dock on the Lippe River to receive cargoes shipped from the bases on the Rhine.[52]

4 BCE

	C. Calvisius C. *f.* Sabinus	L. Passienus Rufus
suff.	C. Caelius	Galus Sulpicius

In March, King Herodes died in Jericho.[53] In his last years he had suffered terribly with an affliction – possibly chronic kidney disease complicated by Fournier's gangrene.[54] He was buried in the Herodion, the hilltop fortress he had built for himself near Hierosolyma.[55] His death marked the end of an era. In Herodes, Augustus had found a staunch ally, a true philo-Roman.[56] His death created unwelcome uncertainty on Rome's eastern frontier. Augustus discussed the succession with his friends and advisors, and approved the late king's will and testament.[57] It was decided that Herodes' realm would remain an independent kingdom, but it would now be divided up among his sons. To Archelaos

(Archelaus) as ethnarch ('national leader') was given Samaria and Iudaea; to Herodes Antipas as tetrarch went Galilee and the east bank of the Jordan; and to Philippos as tetrarch were assigned the Golan Heights in the northeast.

The transition of power between the heirs was not achieved peacefully, however. Archelaos, who arranged his father's funeral, soon faced protests in the streets of Hierosolyma.[58] The new king tried using persuasion on the crowds, but when his commander entered the Temple compound he was pelted with stones even before he could speak to the protesters. Subsequent attempts at mediation also failed. By the time of Passover – the seven days of the 'Feast of Unleavened Bread' on the fifteenth day of the month of *Nisan* – their number had grown considerably. Archelaos was worried by the developing situation:

> and privately sent a tribune, with his cohort of soldiers, upon them, before the disease should spread over the whole multitude, and gave orders that they should constrain those that began the tumult, by force, to be quiet. At these the whole multitude were irritated, and threw stones at many of the soldiers, and killed them; but the tribune fled, wounded, and had much ado to escape so. After which they betook themselves to their sacrifices, as if they had done no mischief; nor did it appear to Archelaos that the multitude could be restrained without bloodshed.[59]

The protests reached a new level of violence,

> so he sent his whole army upon them, the infantry in great multitudes, by the way of the city, and the cavalry by the way of the plain, who, falling upon them on the sudden, as they were offering their sacrifices, destroyed about 3,000 of them; but the rest of the multitude were dispersed upon the adjoining mountains: these were followed by Archelaos's heralds, who commanded everyone to retire to their own homes, whither they all went, and left the festival.[60]

The king urgently needed help to contain the sedition. There were three legions in neighbouring Syria under the command of P. Quinctilius Varus. Having completed a successful term as proconsul of Africa between 8 and 7 BCE, Augustus had appointed him to replace Sentius Saturninus as *legatus Augusti pro praetore*.[61] Varus received the king's formal request for assistance and proceeded to Caesarea Maritimae, the great port city built by the late Herodes on the Mediterranean coast, taking one legion with him.[62] The *procurator* of Syria, a certain Sabinus, had already arrived. He intended to go to Iudaea to secure the cash and valuables of the late King Herodes' estate that had been bequeathed to the Romans and which, as the official responsible for collecting taxes and duties, was his responsibility. He was instructed by Varus to remain there. In the meantime, Sabinus met Archelaos and his entourage at the port before the royal party departed for Rome.

With the king out of the way, Varus now marched on Hierosolyma with his army to quash the forces of revolt.[63] Having entered the city and taken the royal palace, he stationed his legion there to secure it. With order restored, Varus then left for Antiocheia.[64] The heavy-handed actions of the *procurator* following the legate's departure, however, incited yet more trouble. Keen to complete his mission, Sabinus used men of Varus' legion in the city and his own armed guards to attempt to force open the various strongholds at which the nation's wealth was kept and to take it. Incensed by the provocations, crowds came down from Galilee, Idumaea, Jericho and Perea to join the people of Hierosolyma, and settled in three large camps outside the city. The Romans now found themselves besieged by angry protesters. Unable to deal with the rapidly deteriorating situation, Sabinus dispatched a courier to Varus with a message to come urgently to his aid. Josephus describes the scene:

> As for Sabinus himself, he got up to the highest tower of the fortress, which was called Phasaelus (it is of the same name with Herodes' brother, who was destroyed by the Parthians) and then he made signs to the soldiers of that legion to attack the enemy; for his astonishment was so great, that he dared not go down to his own men. Hereupon the soldiers were prevailed upon, and leaped out into the temple, and fought a terrible battle with the Jews; in which, while there were none over their heads to distress them, they were too hard for them, by their skill, and the others' want of skill, in war; but when once many of the Jews had reached the top of the cloisters, and threw their darts downwards, upon the heads of the Romans, there were a great many of them destroyed. Nor was it easy to avenge themselves upon those that threw their weapons from on high, nor was it more easy for them to sustain those who came to fight them hand to hand.[65]

In the general confusion, several buildings, including ones around the Temple with their fabulous contents, were set alight. Trapped inside, some soldiers and rebels burned to death.[66] Nevertheless, Sabinus found the treasure he was so determined to take.

Among the rebels were men of Archelaos' own army, but the toughest of them were the 3,000 from Sebastia who remained on the side of their Roman ally and were present at Hierosolyma.[67] Commanding the infantry was a man named Gratus, while in charge of the cavalry was another called Rufus. Their loyalty and troop numbers tipped the balance in favour of the defenders. The besiegers, whose progress now slowed, changed tack and tried to negotiate with the Romans. They proposed to let Sabinus go if he would leave the city and take the legion with him. The *procurator* did not trust the Jewish emissaries, however, and refused to leave, preferring to hold out until Varus arrived with soldiers.

The turmoil in Hierosolyma created a window of opportunity for other troublemakers to promote their own agendas. In Idumaea, some 2,000 veterans of Herodes' army re-formed and mounted attacks against men of Archelaos' army.[68] In Galilee, at Sepphoris, writes Josephus:

> There was one Iudas (the son of that arch-robber Hezekias, who formerly overran the country, and had been subdued by King Herodes); this man got no small multitude together, and broke open the place where the royal

armour was stored, and armed those about him, and attacked those that were so earnest to gain the dominion.[69]

In Perea, one of the king's own servants, Simon, staked his own claim to the kingdom.[70] Described as a tall and handsome man, he broke into the palace at Jericho with a gang of armed men and stole its contents before setting the building on fire. The rebels would have succeeded in spreading the chaos wider had not Gratus arrived with archers from Trachonitis. The usurper Simon tried to escape through a narrow pass, but pursued by Gratus and his mounted contingents he was intercepted. With a swipe of his sword, Gratus slashed Simon's neck and killed him.

In Emmaeus, a shepherd named Athrongeos claimed to be a king.[71] Reportedly a strong, fearless man, he appointed his four brothers to be generals and commanders with him. Together they gathered armed men and overran the country:

> killing both the Romans and those of the king's party; nor did any Jew escape him, if any gain could accrue to him thereby. He once ventured to encompass a whole troop of Romans at Emmaus, who were carrying corn and weapons to their legion; his men therefore shot their arrows and darts, and thereby slew their centurion Arius, and forty of the stoutest of his men, while the rest of them, who were in danger of the same fate, upon the coming of Gratus, with those of Sebastia, to their assistance, escaped. And when these men had thus served both their own countrymen and foreigners, and that through this whole war, three of them were, after some time, subdued; the eldest by Archelaos, the two next by falling into the hands of Gratus and Ptolemaios.[72]

Receiving Sabinus' message, Varus commanded his two other legions with four *alae* of horse to march south to Ptolemais.[73] He issued orders for the auxiliaries sent by the allied kings and city governors to meet him there. As he passed through the *colonia* of Berytus, 1,500 legionary veterans volunteered to join him. Arriving at Ptolemais, where he found Aretas the Arabian (who had brought with him a large number of infantry and cavalry), Varus split his army into two groups. The first he placed under the command of his friend Caius (whose *nomen genticulum* is not recorded) and dispatched him to Galilee. Caius defeated all those whom he encountered and captured the city of Sepphoris, razed it and enslaved its inhabitants. Varus himself led the second army group. He marched to Samaria where, because he learned that the city had not participated in the troubles, he left it unharmed, and pitched his camp instead at a nearby village called Aras. He then marched on to the village of Sampho, another fortified place, which was plundered for its treasures and set alight by the Arabian allies. When its inhabitants evacuated their town, Emmaus was also burnt on the orders of Varus.

The hinterland quelled, Varus could turn his attention to Hierosolyma itself, which was still under siege.[74] When he was spied on the horizon leading his army, the protesters outside the city abandoned their camps and quickly dispersed. The citizens who had been trapped inside the walls came out and warmly welcomed the *legatus Augusti*. He was met by a number of officials, among them Joseph (the first cousin of Archelaos), Gratus and Rufus, and the men of the legion who had stood firm during the unrest. As for Sabinus, afraid to present himself to Varus, he had already slipped away to Caesarea. Now in control of the city, the Roman commander ordered mopping up operations:

> Varus sent a part of his army into the country, against those that had been the authors of this commotion, and as they caught great numbers of them, those that appeared to have been the least concerned in these tumults he put into custody, but such as were the most guilty he crucified; these were in number about 2,000.[75]

Varus was informed that there were still 10,000 men at arms in Idumea.[76] He also learned that the Arabian troops did not act like regular auxiliaries in the field and were engaged in a private war of retribution borne of their deep hatred of Herodes, and were laying waste to the country. The Roman commander immediately ordered them to withdraw, deploying his own soldiers instead to carry out the mission to seek out and destroy the remaining rebels. Heeding the advice of Achiabus (Herodes' first cousin), many insurgents surrendered themselves to the Romans. Varus showed them clemency, forgiving the majority for their offences, but arrested their commanders and sent them to Augustus to be examined by him in person. (The *princeps* would later forgive all, except the king's relations who had engaged in a war against a king of their own family and had them executed.) Satisfied that he had settled matters at Hierosolyma, Varus left the single legion he had originally assigned to it as a permanent garrison and returned to Antiocheia on the Orontes with the rest of the army.

In Germania, the process of pacification continued apace. This year trees were felled to produce the timber used in the construction of buildings being erected in a new town at Waldgirmes.[77] Located on a spur of land along the Lahn River, the settlement or entrepôt featured a *forum* with *basilica* and at least twenty-four houses or shops. Here Roman and German merchants peaceably traded goods together within a secure area bounded by a double ditch and palisade. Gateways on three sides and a watchtower on the fourth imply the presence of a military guard detail in case of trouble.

3 BCE

L. Cornelius L. *f.* Lentulus   M. Valerius M. *f.* Messalla Massallinus

L. Cornelius Lentulus and M. Valerius Messalla Messallinus were sworn in as *consules ordinarii* for the year.[78] Lentulus served the full year and drew the lot in the autumn that won him the proconsulship of Africa the following year.[79] Messallinus, son of the Messalla Corvinus famed for his oratorical skills, had done nothing in his military career that merited recording by the historians and, indeed, he may have advanced through the *cursus honorum* with help from his esteemed father. He was known personally to Augustus, having been a member of the *collegium* of the *quindecimviri sacris faciundis* responsible for the Sybilline

Books since 21 BCE, and had attended the *Ludi Saeculares* in 17 BCE.[80] With mentoring, the 40-year old could yet prove his worth as a commander in the field.

Agrippa Postumus was now old enough to be enrolled among the young men of military age.[81] Strangely, he was not accorded the same honours as his older brothers.[82]

No record of any wars fought this year survives.[83]

2 BCE

	Imp. Caesar *Divi f.* Augustus XIII	M. Plautius M. *f.* Silvanus
suff.		L. Caninius L. *f.* Gallus
suff.	C. Fufius Geminus	
suff.	Q. Fabricius	

There was more churn in the consulships to create more ex-consuls for provincial, legionary and other leadership appointments. Augustus, now a man of 60 years of age, started the year as consul for the thirteenth time.[84] He yielded it to C. Fufius Geminus, who in turn resigned after a few months in office to be replaced by Q. Fabricius. Augustus' colleague was *novus homo* M. Plautius Silvanus, who resigned in favour of L. Caninius Gallus. Among this group, after Augustus only Gallus had earned military distinction, having 'conquered the Sarmatae ... and driven them back across the Ister' in 17/16 BCE.[85] As one of the three commissioners responsible for the mint in Rome in 12 BCE, he had ensured that Augustus' successes in Germania were promoted on the coinage.[86]

Apparently unprompted, the Popular Assembly unanimously voted Augustus an accolade.[87] On 5 February, now ex-consul Valerius Messalla Messallinus spoke in the Senate proposing the same motion, which is recorded verbatim by Suetonius:

> 'Good fortune and divine favour attend you and your house, Caesar Augustus; for thus we feel that we are praying for lasting prosperity for our country and happiness for our city. The Senate in accord with the People of Rome hails you "Father of the Fatherland".' Then Augustus, with tears in his eyes, replied as follows (and I have given his exact words, as I did those of Messalla): 'Having attained my highest hopes, Conscript Fathers, what more have I to ask of the immortal gods than that I may retain this same unanimous approval of yours to the very end of my life?'[88]

The title *Pater Patriae* had been granted to only a few other men in Rome's past, but most significantly to its legendary founder Romulus.[89] It was the honour Augustus was most proud of.

L. Caesar was now in his fifteenth year. On 17 March, he put away the *bulla* of his boyhood and donned the *toga virilis*. He would now be eligible to begin his public career. He received the honours that had been granted to his popular older brother, including the post of *princeps iuventutis*.[90] Unlike Caius, however, he was appointed as *augur*, an ancient priesthood that interpreted the god's opinions by studying the behaviour of birds.[91] With his older sibling, Lucius organized this year's *Lusus Troiae*.[92] Their youngest brother M. Agrippa (Postumus), now aged 10, would join them and perform mock military exercises in this, his first Circensian Games.[93]

On 12 May occurred the long-awaited dedication of the *Forum Augustum*.[94] Almost two decades in the making, it was a meeting place fit for the people of a world power. Rectangular in shape, measuring about 125 metres (410 feet) long and 90 metres (295 feet) wide, it featured the innovation of two large semi-circular apses – one on each of the southeast and northwest sides and one at the northeast end – to provide additional space (map 17).[95] The precinct was sur-rounded by a wall. At the northeastern end it stood nearly 36 metres (118 feet) high and was constructed of peperino (a light, porous volcanic rock) to protect it against fire – a regular occurrence in Rome – and to block out the view behind of

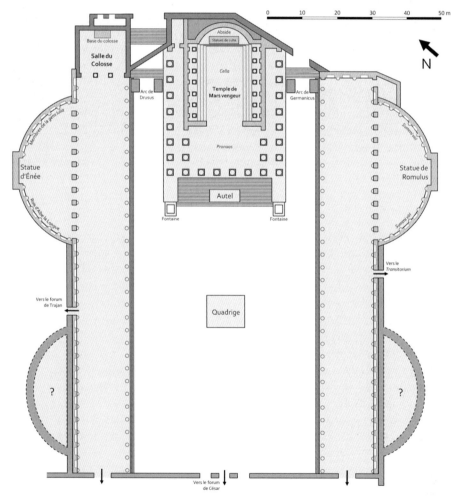

Map 17. Ground plan of the *Forum Augustum*.

Figure 10. The Temple of Mars Avenger (*Templum Marti Ultori*) was the centrepiece of the *Forum Augustum* in Rome. The military ensigns recovered from Parthia were kept here along with the sword of Iulius Caesar.

the neighbourhood, which was comprised of ugly low-grade residential buildings. Directly in front of it stood the Italic-style podium temple to the god of war and vengeance, *Marti Ultori*, vowed by Imp. Caesar *Divi filius* at the Battle of Philippi forty years before (fig. 10).[96] Financed through funds raised from sales of spoils from the war in Egypt, Germania, Hispania and Illyricum, there had been unforeseen architectural and construction delays; even though the temple was still not finished Augustus insisted the forum be officially opened.[97] The final touches could wait. The central figure of its pediment – supported by columns topped with Corinthian capitals – Mars the Avenger, flanked by other gods and goddesses, with Aeneas carrying his father in the lower left corner and Romulus bearing a trophy in the lower right.[98] In front of the temple on a plinth was mounted a *quadriga* driven by Augustus (dedicated by the Senate to him).[99]

The complex itself was an architectural wonder – state of the art for the time – incorporating many varieties and colours of marbles for the pavements, columns and statues (plate 35). Pliny the Elder considered the *Forum Augustum* to be one of the most beautiful buildings in Rome in his day.[100] The edifice formed a backdrop for other decorations weighty with meaning and significance.[101] Many fine art works were displayed in it, among which were two large paintings of Alexander the Great by the celebrated Apelles, inviting comparison with the Roman sponsor of the new *Forum*.[102] Covered porticos of thirty columns each lined the two longest sides of the *Forum*, forming a Roman 'Hall of Fame'. Erected along them were bronze statues of *summi viri* ('topmost men'), and all the *viri triumphatores* ('men of triumph'), from the legendary founder Aeneas and Romulus to Augustus' time, chosen either for their civic or military virtues.[103] The name and career history (*titulus*) of each was engraved on the plinth and a description of his achievements (*elogium*) carved on a marble slab was fixed to the wall below.[104]

On this spring day, the inauguration of the *Forum* was accompanied by great ceremonial. Augustus and his two adopted sons proudly led it. Both young men had been granted the right to consecrate the Temple of Mars Ultor 'and all such buildings' for this purpose.[105] As the new *princeps iuventutis* (plate 37), Lucius and his *turma* – bearing spears and shields – presented a mounted pageant before the assembled array of *aquilae* and *signa cohortis* which had been brought down from their temporary home.[106] Joined now by his older brother, Caius, and father Augustus, the family observed a lustration with sacrifices at the altar in the precinct to consecrate and cleanse it. The *suovetaurilia* involved the sacrifice of a pig (*sus*), a sheep (*ovis*) and a bull (*taurus*) with a ritual incantation to *Mars pater*.[107] The litany having been delivered perfectly word-for-word and the omens having been declared favourable, the dignitaries may then have accompanied the military standards as they were carried in solemn procession to their new home within the temple, where the sword of the avenged Iulius Caesar was also to be displayed.[108] They were placed before the giant statues of Mars (plate 34), Divus Iulius and Venus, which stood in an apse inside the sacred space, their polished metal surfaces reflecting the flickering flames and bathed in the hues of glowing embers from the tripods that illuminated the interior of the building.

Once the formal opening ceremony was concluded, the crowds were treated to entertainments in the *Circus Flaminius*. There was a beast hunt that saw 260 lions slaughtered, and later in the programme the arena was flooded to create an environment in which thirty-six crocodiles could be slain.[109] Particularly memorable was 'the magnificent spectacle of a gladiatorial show [in the *Saepta*] and a mock naval battle' between combatants representing the Persians and the Athenians.[110] The choice of opposing sides was deliberate. The struggle between East and West continued to excite the Roman imagination. It was a reminder, too, that the non-aggression pact between Parthia and Rome was agreed under Augustus' auspices. (Faithful to historical events, the Athenians won).[111] Anticipating the popularity of these spectacles, Augustus stationed guards of the *Cohortes Urbanae* across the city to deter any robbers who might be tempted to break into the houses left unattended by their owners who were away at the games.[112]

The end of the momentous day marked the time for Caius to depart for his new assignment.[113] Now aged 17, he was old enough to see active service in the field. Initially he would serve with the legions on the Danube.[114] But if his father thought the placement on the front line would improve his command skills and toughen his spirit through exposure to army life, he was to be disappointed. Dio remarks that Caius fought no battles himself, not because there was no military action, but rather he was learning to command from behind in quiet and safety by delegating to others the dangerous undertakings.[115]

In Rome, Augustus made yet more adjustments to the military. In a significant change to the command structure of his own guard unit, he appointed two *praefecti* to command the *Cohortes Praetoriae*.[116] To the positions he appointed men of the equestrian order, known to be Q. Ostorius Scapula and P. Salvius Aper. Up to then, each of the nine *cohortes* of up to 1,000 men apiece had had its own *tribunus*. Augustus still allowed no more than three cohorts to be billeted in Rome – and even then they were scattered throughout the city – at any one time, the rest being stationed around Italy.[117] Ever mindful of costs, Augustus struggled with the expense of keeping the field army.[118] He introduced a bill in the Senate proposing that a budget of sufficient amount, rolling from year to year, should be created, in order that the soldiers would be assured of receiving their pay and bonuses without the need to raise additional monies from other sources. The means for setting up such a fund were urgently sought.

1 BCE

	Cossus Cornelius Cn. *f.* Lentulus	L. Calpurnius Cn. *f.* Piso (Augur)
suff.	A. Plautius	A. Caecina (Severus)

Taking the oath on 1 January to faithfully serve the *Res Publica* as its consuls were Cossus Cornelius Lentulus and L. Calpurnius Piso. They would each step down to allow two *novi homines*, respectively A. Plautius, son of the *praetor urbanus* of 51 BCE, and A. Caecina Severus, to serve in high office.

Reports reached Augustus that the pro-Roman Artavasdes III had been deposed as king of Armenia and that the Parthians were supporting the rebels. [119] The apparent abandonment of their alliance with Rome meant that the peace along the eastern frontier, which had held for a generation and counted as one of Augustus' singular achievements, was now seriously at risk. He needed to ensure the kingdom stayed within the Roman sphere of influence as a buffer against Parthia's territorial ambitions. He felt he was too old to take the field himself: someone else would have to go and lead the Roman response if it came to war. Tiberius was unavailable. While Augustus could have chosen from among his best *legati*, he decided, instead, to appoint his own son C. Caesar to the combat leadership role.[120] Sending him would impress upon the Parthian king the gravity with which he viewed the infringement. The 19-year-old was given the special assignment as *Orienti praepositus* ('overseer of the East'), and to ensure he had the legal power to wage war in Augustus' name, Caius was voted the *imperium pro-consulare* which had been forfeited by Tiberius.[121] He was also made consul designate for the following year. It was an extraordinarily fast career advancement for the young man.

Compensating for his inexperience in military and political affairs, Augustus assigned his son the services of an advisory body formed of official 'advisors and guides'.[122] Chief among them was M. Lollius, the former governor of Galatia and Macedonia, and the same man who had been responsible for the eponymous disaster in Gaul in 17 BCE.[123] The other notable was P. Sulpicius Quirinius, the ex-consul who had distinguished himself in wars in Cyrenaica and Cilicia. Also travelling with them were M. Velleius Paterculus, the historian who was then a serving *tribunus militum*, and L. Aelius Seianus, son of the *Praefectus Praetorio* who likely marched with the one, or more likely two, Praetorian Cohorts that would guard the *princeps*' son for the duration of the assignment.[124] While in Syria, Caius could also draw upon the expertise and local knowledge of the *legati* of the legions and *praefecti* of the auxiliary units stationed in the province. Caius left Rome on 29 January. Travelling by ship, he stopped at several ports on the outbound journey before reaching Syria.[125]

In the western Balkans, L. Domitius Ahenobarbus (cos. 16 BCE) was now *Legatus Augusti Pro Praetore* of Illyricum.[126] While active along the Danube, he intercepted the Hermunduri nation, which had migrated from its homeland in search of a new place to live.[127] Ahenobarbus found them land in the territory of the Marcomanni, who had since migrated to Bohaemium (modern Czech Republic). Once satisfied they would remain there, he proceeded north and crossed the Elbe River, achieving what Nero Claudius Drusus Germanicus had not.[128] He encountered no resistance from the local people – indeed, he even established friendly relations with them.[129] To mark his achievement, he set up an altar to Augustus on the bank of the river.[130]

1 CE

	C. Caesar Aug. *f.*	L. Aemilius Paulli *f.* Paullus
suff.		M. Herennius M. *f.* Picens

Despite being thirteen years younger than was required, C. Caesar was elected as consul.[131] There was a practical reason for his promotion. As consul, his stature was greatly enhanced as a negotiator with the Parthians. The young man received the confirmation while at his field headquarters in Syria.[132] His colleague back in Rome was L. Aemilius Paulus, one of whose ancestors stood with the famous Scipiones against Hannibal Barca of Carthage.[133]

Learning that Caius was in the border region, a diplomatic spat ensued between Augustus and Frahâtak V.[134] The Parthian king sent envoys to Rome with a message politely, but firmly, requiring the return of his brothers as a prerequisite for a peace settlement. Dio explains that Augustus sent him a reply, addressing the recipient simply as 'Phrataces', purposely omitting the royal title of 'king'. In the letter he required the Parthian to lay aside the royal name and to withdraw from Armenia. Frahâtak wrote back in a generally supercilious tone, addressing Augustus simply as 'Caesar' and calling himself 'King of Kings'. Tigranes, who was the hostage of Augustus, refrained from sending any envoys. However, when the pro-Parthian king Artabazus fell ill and died, which meant his rival had been removed, Tigranes sent gifts to Augustus and petitioned him for the kingship of Armenia. Influenced by these considerations, and at the same time fearing a war with the Parthians, Augustus accepted the gifts and released him with high hopes to Caius in Syria.

The presence of Augustus' own son so close to the international frontier had the desired effect on the Parthians. Frahâtak V, the son of King Frahâta (Phraates) III from whom, eighteen years earlier, Tiberius had received back the *signa*, sought to de-escalate the spiraling diplomatic crisis by withdrawing his troops from Armenia.[135] A summit conference was held to craft a new treaty between the two superpowers. Velleius Paterculus witnessed the event himself and writes:

> On an island in the Euphrates, with an equal retinue on each side, Caius had a meeting with the king of the Parthians, a young man of distinguished presence. This spectacle of the Roman army arrayed on one side, the Parthian on the other, while these two eminent leaders not only of the empires they represented but also of mankind thus met in conference – truly a notable and a memorable sight.[136]

The Parthians agreed to renounce their claim on Armenia on the condition that the king's brothers – his four sons – remained outside his realm.[137]

Either during the dinner before the talks were scheduled to take place, or following the formal negotiations, Frahâtak revealed that Lollius had been taking bribes from the Parthians, which was consistent with his reputation for avarice and underhandedness.[138] It was a deeply embarrassing admission. Here was evidence from the highest level source that one of Augustus' trusted deputies was working as a double agent. He was promptly recalled to Rome to face charges. Rather than suffer the humiliation of a trial and almost certain exile, or possibly worse, Lollius took his own life. Caius immediately replaced him with P. Sulpicius Quirinius, whose loyalty was unimpeachable.[139]

C. Caesar's letter announcing the news of the new pact with Parthia was read out in the Senate by Lucius, a task he always enjoyed.[140] It was likely for this achievement – a victory over Parthia without shedding Roman blood – that Augustus received his fifteenth acclamation.[141]

Then came a dramatic and unforeseen setback. Tigranes was struck and killed by unnamed 'barbarians'.[142] As an ally under treaty, the Romans were obliged to respond. The inexperienced young Caius suddenly and unexpectedly found himself having to deal with an international crisis.[143]

Elsewhere in the Roman world there were military adventures. L. Caesar was preparing to embark on his trip to Hispania Taraconnensis to be trained for the first time with the legions.[144] In one of the provinces of North Africa (presumed to be Cyrenaica), there were raids by bandits or a military invasion.[145] The anticipated violence of the ensuing Marmaric War appears to have been sufficiently intense that soldiers had to be called in from neighbouring Egypt to supplement the local force. The arrival of an unnamed tribune from a *Cohors Praetoria* – perhaps one accompanying L. Caesar – marked the turning point in the struggle to regain control.[146] The anonymous *tribunus militum* was so successful in leading the troops to expel the enemy that no senator governed the cities in the Roman province for several months.

Senator Domitius Ahenobarbus had since transferred from a successful tour in Illyricum to Germania as *legatus Augusti pro praetore*.[147] The new governor

inherited a province that had remained largely trouble-free since Tiberius' punitive expeditions, and he could pursue policies and activities consistent with pacification. One of his first decisions was to move the provincial capital from the army
base at Vetera to the civilian settlement at Oppidum Ubiorum on the Rhine,
where an altar to the cult of Augustus was being erected and on account of which it
became known as Ara Ubiorum.[148] In the west of the province, he constructed a
corduroy road of wooden planks laid over marshland in the country of the
Cherusci called the *Pontes Longi* ('Long Bridges').[149] That Ahenobarbus tried to
secure the return of certain exiles of the Cherusci nation through intermediaries,
but had failed in the attempt, is revealed by Dio.[150] The negotiations may not have
been helped by his reputation for haughtiness, extravagance and cruelty, or his
complete disdain for social rank and good manners.[151] An unintended consequence of this diplomatic defeat was that the other Germanic nations, who took it
as a sign of Roman weakness, apparently now felt contempt for them too.[152] The
'barbarians' had proved that the Romans were not, after all, invincible.

2 CE

	P. Vinicius M. *f.*	P. Alfenus P. *f.* Varus
suff.	P. Cornelius Cn. *f.* (Lentulus) Scipio	T. Quinctius T. *f.* Crispinus Valerianus

In the East, Ariobarzanes II prepared himself to be crowned king of Armenia, but
while he was the choice of the Romans his subjects-to-be felt very differently.[153]
The Armenian people rose up in protest at the imposition of a man they did not
want as their ruler, perhaps incited to do so by the Parthian king.[154] C. Caesar
was now obliged to enter Armenia with his army and come to Ariobarzanes' assistance, a situation which could yet escalate into a full-blooded war with Parthia.[155]

Shortly before 1 July, having been away for eight years, Tiberius returned to
Rome; he was still a private citizen.[156] Why he chose that moment to return is
unclear. In his account, Dio ascribes the change of heart to Tiberius' interest in
astrology, through which he had foreknowledge of the fates of Augustus' sons,
while Suetonius mentions C. Caesar's association with the disgraced M. Lollius
(the *princeps*' own appointee) as being a clear factor in his favour.[157] Tiberius
could be strong willed, but never a traitor. The intervention of his mother, Livia,
may also have played a role.[158]

On 20 August, L. Caesar, while on his way to begin his military service in the
Hispaniae, died at Massilia (modern Marseille).[159] His was not a heroic death;
the cause is simply described as 'a sudden illness'.[160] He may have contracted
an infection on one of the missions to many places Dio alludes to.[161] His body
was prepared for transportation by sea to the port at Ostia, where it was received
by military tribunes and thence conveyed to Rome.[162] A state funeral was held
for the youngest of Augustus' adopted sons, whose ashes were placed in his
mausoleum.[163]

As Tiberius had done with the Sugambri in 8 BCE, the praetorian-grade proconsul of Macedonia, Sex. Aelius Catus, oversaw the transplantation of some

50,000 Getae across the Danube River.[164] They were granted land in Thracia, with whose inhabitants they shared a common language. In time this community would come to be called Moesia.

At the end of another five-year period, the primary task of the *princeps* in his province was still incomplete. Under his auspices, Roman armies had largely been successful in maintaining the security of the empire from threats, both from within and without, even at the cost of the life of his stepson. While the pacification of Germania was progressing and order had been restored to Cilicia and Iudaea, on the eastern edge of the empire Armenia was in revolt and there was now the real possibility of an all-out war with Rome's longstanding rival. Though in mourning for the death of his adopted son, Augustus was the only man with the ability and experience of managing the military resources needed to ensure the integrity of Rome's borders, but his legal power to do so was due to end.

Chapter 6

World in Tumult

3–12 CE

3 CE

	L. Aelius L. *f.* Lamia	M. Servilius M. *f.*
suff.	P. Silius P. *f.*	L. Volusius L. *f.* Saturninus

The Senate renewed Augustus' proconsular command powers for another ten years.[1] Dio remarks that he accepted this, his fourth ten-year term, under compulsion. He had mellowed with age – he would be 66 at his next birthday in September – and acted largely out of concern to retain the goodwill of the Senate. Weighing on his mind, however, was the proxy war with Parthia. He waited eagerly for news from the eastern front, where C. Caesar was now engaged in full combat operations in Armenia.[2] The expeditionary force had taken up a position at the strategically important fortress city of Artagira (or Artageira).[3] It was one of several fortified sites around the country at which the royal treasure of Tigranes II and Artavasdes of the Artaxiad dynasty had been hidden.[4]

There are several versions of the events.[5] In the account of Strabo, who wrote closest to the time of the events, a governor named Adon (or Addon), who had been appointed by the ousted Armenian king, is responsible for defending the stronghold.[6] Adon proves loyal to the old king and will not yield Artagira to the Romans. Caius then lays siege to the walled fortress. In Dio's version of the story, written almost two centuries after the war, Adon lures Caius into approaching the city's walls on the pretence he will reveal to him the Parthian king's secrets – presumably of the whereabouts of the king's valuables – but double-crosses the Roman and succeeds in wounding him.[7] The Roman army then besieges Artagira. In his account of the *Bellum Armeniacum*, Florus introduces another character:

> For Donnes, whom the king had appointed governor of Artagera, pretend-ing to betray his master, attacked the [Roman] commander while he was examining a document, which he had himself handed to him as containing a list of the treasures, and suddenly struck him with his drawn sword. Caesar recovered from the wound for the time being … His barbarian assailant, beset on all sides by the angry soldiers, made atonement to the still surviving Caesar; for he fell by the sword, and was burnt upon the pyre on which he hurled himself after he was stabbed.[8]

In Rufus Festius' even later telling, this same Donnes is described as having been appointed by King Arsaces as the commander of all forces in Parthia.[9] They may all contain elements of truth.

After a long siege, the Romans finally stormed the fortress, captured its commandant and pulled down its walls.[10] The soldiers hailed both Augustus and Caius as *imperator*.[11] The rebellion having been crushed, the pro-Roman Ariobarzanes II of the Arsacid dynasty was finally enthroned as king of Armenia.[12] When he unexpectedly died shortly after, he was succeeded by Artabazus, another Arsacid, with Augustus' full blessing.

The young Roman commander was, however, wounded. The *Fasti Cuprenses*, a Latin inscription found at Cupra Marittima listing Roman consuls, gives the authorized, matter-of-fact version. It states:

> C. Caesar, son of Augustus ... on 9 September was struck down waging war in Armenia against the enemies of the Roman People while he was besieging Artagira, a town of Armenia.[13]

He was not dead, but he was badly injured and his wound caused him to fall seriously sick.[14] He would not have lacked for medical care. As a member of the *princeps'* family, he would have had a personal physician, but he could also call on the services of the professional *medici* of the legions who were skilled in treating combat traumas of many kinds.[15] However, Dio notes that Caius' health was not known for being particularly robust and the ensuing fever clouded his normally clear thinking.[16] In this unsettled frame of mind, Caius wrote to his father pleading to be relieved of his duties and to be allowed to retire as a private citizen. Augustus reluctantly agreed to his request on the condition that he should immediately return to Italy. Perhaps the young man was delirious; some rest and recuperation might restore his faculties, he thought. The injured commander made his preparations to leave. With winter approaching, Quirinius supervised the withdrawal of Roman troops from Armenia; he was temporarily appointed *Legatus Augusti Pro Praetore* of Syria until his official replacement, L. Volusius Saturninus (*suff.* 12 BCE), arrived.[17]

4 CE

	Sex. Aelius Q. *f.* Catus	C. Sentius C. *f.* Saturninus
suff.	Cn. Sentius C. *f.* Saturninus	C. Clodius C. *f.* Licinius

In the new year, his condition worsening, C. Caesar boarded a merchant ship bound for Lykia (Lycia). Reaching Limyra on the southern coast of Asia Minor on 21 February, Caius died.[18] He was just 23 years old. A cenotaph was erected on the Limyrus River to commemorate his brief life.[19] At *Colonia* Obsequens Iulia Pisana (modern Pisa), as likely happened in other communities, the town council decreed that the proper rites must be observed, that matrons should lament his passing, and the doors of temples, public baths and shops must be shut as the women wailed.[20] Like his younger brother nineteen months before, Caius' body was brought under military escort provided by the *Cohortes Praetoriae*, which had accompanied him on the mission. The cortège was received by the magistrates of the cities it passed through *en route* to Rome. There a state funeral was held. A period of mourning was declared. The casket containing his ashes was placed in the Mausoleum of Augustus. The silver shields and spears the two brothers had each received on achieving the age of military service were hung side by side in the *Curia Iulia*.[21] It was a poignant memorial to the lives of two young Romans who had once offered so much hope and promise.

In the deaths of Caius and Lucius, Augustus had lost not only his sons and heirs, but the next generation of military leaders as well. His response was typically practical. On 26 June, Augustus adopted Tiberius and M. Agrippa (Postumus), but required Tiberius also to adopt his nephew Germanicus as his son.[22] Responding to the surprise development, Tiberius publicly announced '*hoc rei publicae causa facio*' – 'this I do for sake of the Commonwealth'.[23] Now fully rehabilitated, Tiberius' tribunician power was restored for ten years.[24] Formally a member of *gens Iulia*, he assumed the new name Ti. Iulius Caesar Augustus *f.*; in turn his natural son changed his to Drusus Iulius Caesar (Drusus the Younger), and his adopted son similarly became Germanicus Iulius Caesar.

Augustus also set up a new commission to examine the qualifications of senators, which saw several expelled.[25] To replenish its thinning ranks with younger and abler talent, he assisted several impoverished men so that they had the wealth to meet the admission requirements.[26] These developments offended some. There were several plots to assassinate him – the one alleged to have involved Cn. Cornelius, the son of the daughter of Pompeius Magnus, may have taken place this year.[27] Augustus did not press charges against him and even nominated Cornelius for the consulship.[28]

That summer, the Germanic nations, peaceful for a decade, broke into revolt. Augustus dispatched Tiberius with orders 'to pacify Germania'.[29] Somewhat ironically, his last active combat command prior to his self-imposed exile had been in the same region in 7 BCE. Details of the campaign come to us from the account written by Velleius Peterculus, who served with Tiberius, both as *praefectus equitum* and *legatus legionis*.[30] He writes as an eyewitness that, on his arrival in *Tres Galliae* and Germania, Tiberius was warmly received by old soldiers, *evocati* and veterans who had served with him before:

> Indeed, words cannot express the feelings of the soldiers at their meeting, and perhaps my account will scarcely be believed – the tears which sprang to their eyes in their joy at the sight of him, their eagerness, their strange transports in saluting him, their longing to touch his hand, and their inability to restrain such cries as 'Is it really you that we see, commander?' 'Have we received you safely back among us?' 'I served with you, Commander, in Armenia!' 'And I in Raetia!' 'I received my decoration from you in Vindelicia!' 'And I mine in Pannonia!' 'And I in Germania!'[31]

It was time to go on the offensive. Velleius' account indicates that Tiberius began his punitive campaign against the Germanic nations of the western and central sectors, seemingly following his younger brother's plan of 12 BCE.[32] In charge of one of the army groups he put the newly appointed *Legatus Augusti* Sentius Saturninus – relieved from his consulate by suffect Clodius Licinius – who had previously served as a *legatus legionis* in Germania under his father, and

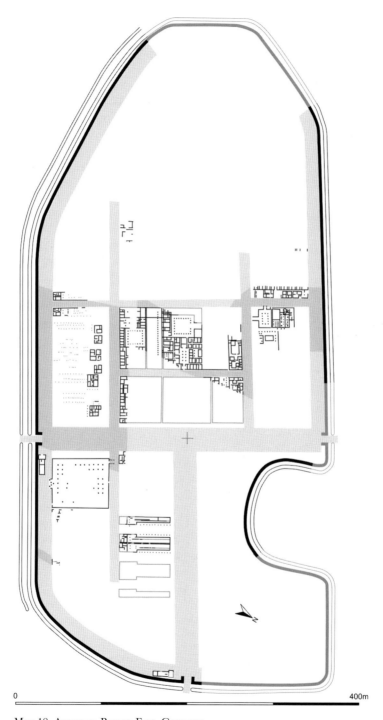

Map 18. Anreppen Roman Fort, Germany.

0   400m

thus was quite familiar with the terrain.[33] The two commanders coordinated their operations, attacking on multiple fronts. The Cananefates and Cherusci – both former allies – were beaten, along with the Attuari and Bructeri. Tiberius' forces crossed the Weser River and marched deep into territory on the other bank.[34] Near the Weser, temporary or semi-permanent camps were established at Minden and Hameln. Traces of a Roman marching camp with evidence for some thirty baking ovens have also been found at Barkhausen, Porta Westfalica that has produced military finds contemporary with this period.[35]

Unusually for a Roman military campaign, the war lasted into the month of December. Before his departure for Rome, Tiberius 'pitched his winter camp at the source of the Lupia, in the very heart of the country', evidently reversing his earlier defensive posture.[36] On that river, a new forward military base, located some 100 kilometres (65 miles) east of Haltern, or 185 kilometres (114 miles) from Vetera, was founded at Anreppen.[37] At 23 hectares, the oval-shaped fortress was large enough for a single legion and contained all the standard interior military buildings, each constructed of wood, including an outsize *principia* or headquarters, as well as a *praetorium* or house for the resident commander (map 18). From Anreppen, the military road apparently continued further east in the direction of modern Paderborn, where another fort is suspected.[38]

5 CE

L. Valerius Potiti *f.* Messalla Volesus	Cn. Cornelius L. *f.* Cinna Magnus
suff. C. Vibius C. *f.* Postumus	C. Ateius L. *f.* Capito

Encouraged by his success the previous year, Tiberius eagerly returned to Germania in the spring.[39] In this second phase of the relaunched *Bellum Germanicum*, he escalated the war, taking it to the nations of the central, northwestern and eastern sectors. Under his command were five legions: *Legiones* I, V *Alaudae*, XVII, XIIX and XIX (table 2). Recorded as engaged in this season were the Chauci, the Langobardi and, after he crossed the Elbe River, the Semnones and

Table 2. Dispositions of the Legions, Spring 5 CE (Conjectural).

Province	Units	Legions
Hispania Tarraconensis	4	II *Augusta*, IIII Macedonica, VI *Victrix*, X *Gemina*
Germania	5	I, V *Alaudae*, XVII, XIIX, XIX
Raetia	2	XVI *Gallica*, XXI *Rapax*
Illyricum	5	VIIII *Hispana*, XIII *Gemina*, XIV *Gemina*, XV *Apollinaris*, XX
Thracia-Macedoniaque	3	IV *Scythica*, VIII *Augusta*, XI
Galatia-Pamphylia	2	V *Macedonica*, VII *Macedonica*
Syria	4	III *Gallica*, VI *Ferrata*, X (*Fretensis*), XII *Fulminata*
Aegyptus	2	III *Cyrenaica*, XXII *Deiotariana*
Africa	1	III *Augusta*

Sources: Appendix 3; Lendering (Livius.org); Mitchell (1976); Šašel Kos (1995); Swan (2004), table 5, p. 165; Syme (1933 and 1986).

Hermunduri.[40] Having the advantage of offence, Tiberius was the subject of an attack only once, during which he inflicted major casualties on the unnamed enemy.[41] Tiberius replicated his brother's use of a fleet to support the expeditionary force, sailing transports down the Elbe River, 'and after proving victorious over many tribes effected a junction with [Ti.] Caesar and the army, bringing with it a great abundance of supplies of all kinds'.[42] The troops celebrated the progress with acclamations for Augustus (his seventeenth) and Tiberius (his third).[43]

The commander-turned-historian relates a curious story of an encounter between Tiberius and an awestruck German:

> We were encamped on the nearer bank of the aforesaid river, while on the farther bank glittered the arms of the enemies' troops, who showed an inclination to flee at every movement and manoeuvre of our vessels, when one of the barbarians, advanced in years, tall of stature, of high rank to judge by his dress, embarked in a canoe (made as is usual with them of a hollowed log) and, guiding this strange craft, he advanced alone to the middle of the stream and asked permission to land without harm to himself on the bank occupied by our troops and to see Caesar. Permission was granted. Then he beached his canoe, and, after gazing upon Caesar for a long time in silence, exclaimed: 'Our young men are insane, for though they worship you as divine when absent, when you are present they fear your armies instead of trusting to your protection. But I, by your kind permission, Caesar, have today seen the gods of whom I merely used to hear; and in my life have never hoped for or experienced a happier day.' After asking for and receiving permission to touch Caesar's hand, he again entered his canoe, and continued to gaze back upon him until he landed upon his own bank.[44]

The second campaign was a successful one for the adopted son of Augustus. In lofty language, Velleius Paterculus writes:

> All Germania was traversed by our armies, races were conquered hitherto almost unknown, even by name ... All the flower of their [Germanic] youth, infinite in number though they were, huge of stature and protected by the ground they held, surrendered their arms, and, flanked by a gleaming line of our soldiers, fell with their leaders upon their knees before the tribunal of the commander.[45]

In contrast, unimpressed by the Roman commander's comings and goings, Dio writes that:

> expeditions against the Germans also were being conducted by various leaders, especially Tiberius. He advanced first to the river Visurgis and later as far as the Albis, but nothing noteworthy was accomplished at this time.[46]

Tiberius led his expeditionary force back to its camps in time for winter. For some units this would mean breaking new ground. During the campaign he had developed a strategic plan for the conquest of the remaining lands of Germania under the control of the Marcomanni. In readiness for its execution, two new legionary bases were established. In what is now Bavaria, located 147 kilometres (91 miles) east of the Rhine, a camp was pitched at Marktbreit on a meander in the Main River, and buildings of timber were erected inside it (map 19).[47] Another even larger camp, containing an area of almost 58 hectares, was dug on an escarpment overlooking the Danube River at Carnuntum (or Karnuntum near modern Vienna, Austria).[48] While the legionaries toiled, Tiberius travelled to Rome – but he would be back.

M. Agrippa (Postumus), Augustus' 18-year-old adopted son, had since become eligible for military service. While he was enrolled among the youths of military age, he had still not been accorded the same honours and privileges as his brothers, even after their deaths.[49] The reason why is still debated.

If Agrippa was unhappy at his adoptive parent's treatment of him, it was nothing compared to the deep dissatisfaction felt among the regular troops. At issue was the compensation and terms of their service:

> The soldiers were sorely displeased at the paltry character of the rewards given them for the wars which had been waged at this time and none of them consented to bear arms for longer than the regular period of his service.[50]

It was important to address this issue without delay. After the mass discharges in 14 BCE, the disgruntled men protesting their pay in 5 CE were the ones who had

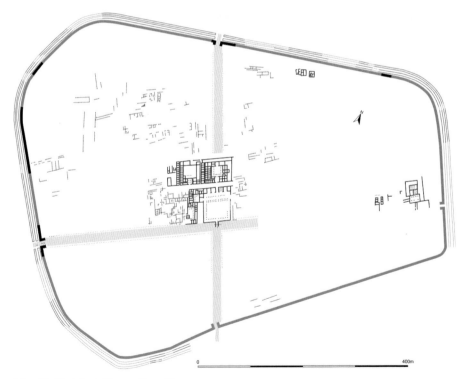

0   400m

Map 19. Marktbreit Roman Fort, Germany.

replaced them, agreeing to serve for sixteen years.[51] Now many were overdue for retirement and a new intake of recruits had to be found to fill their ranks. They in turn might be dissuaded from joining if they heard the complaints from the veterans. Augustus had last reviewed army remuneration and retirement benefits in 13 BCE. Now it was for the Senate to find a solution:

> It was therefore voted that 5,000 *drachmai* [HS20,000] should be given to members of the *Cohortes Praetoriae* when they had served sixteen years, and 3,000 *drachmai* [HS12,000] to the other soldiers when they had served twenty years.[52]

For both the *praetoriani* and *caligati*, this meant serving an additional four paid years, but by offering a large cash bonus at the end of their terms the Senate had sweetened the deal and helped Augustus avert a potential crisis of confidence in the ranks. Upon the unswerving co-operation of the army, the security of the empire – and Augustus' leadership position – relied.

6 CE

	M. Aemilius Paulli *f.* Lepidus	L. Arruntius L. *f.*
suff.		L. Nonius L. *f.* Asprenas

Of the three consuls appointed for the year, two were related to men who had served with Augustus in wartime. The suffect consul L. Nonius Asprenas, nephew of P. Quinctilius Varus, was now well-positioned for a future military post of his own.[53] Varus himself assumed command of Germania from Sentius Saturninus, whose military acumen was being deployed elsewhere.[54] Varus' mission from Augustus was clear: to expedite the process of pacification of the Germanic nations, including the levying of taxes upon them.[55] After two decades of conquest, the province was now a fist-shaped spur of territory extending northeast from the Rhine and bounded by the free, allied nations along the North Sea coast and Elbe and Main Rivers.[56] Varus deployed detachments from the five legions and several auxiliary cohorts under his command across the region, and embedded them with the Germanic communities as peace-keepers, police and road-builders:

> Soldiers of theirs were wintering there and cities were being founded. The barbarians were adapting themselves to Roman ways, were becoming accustomed to holding markets, and were meeting in peaceful assemblies.[57]

Germania was a bright spot in a darkening geo-political sky. This year the carefully constructed world order managed together by Augustus and the Senate came under threat. 'During this period,' writes Dio:

> many wars also took place. Brigands overran a good many districts, so that Sardinia had no senator as governor for some years, but was in charge of soldiers with knights as commanders. Not a few cities rebelled, with the result that for two years the same men held office in the provinces which belonged to the People and were appointed instead of being chosen by lot; of

course the provinces which belonged to Caesar were, in any case, assigned to the same men for a longer period.[58]

In Africa, old tensions burst into a new violent conflict. The Isauri raided into Roman territory, initially ravaging settlements, but quickly escalating into a full-blooded war.[59] Only when military resources were ranged against them were the tribesmen finally driven out. The neighbouring Gaetuli of Numidia also chose this moment to rebel against their king, Iuba II.[60] This highly educated man had proved a reliable ally – perhaps too willing to kowtow to the Romans in the eyes of his subjects. His alignment with Augustus was at odds with the independence-mindset of many in his kingdom who saw an opportunity to challenge their regent. His early attempts to contain the rebellion failed. The insurgents then took their fight to the Roman province of Africa, destroying property and killing many of its people. Proconsul Cossus Cornelius Lentulus (consul 1 BCE), an impoverished patrician with a distinguished pedigree, led a campaign against them. He had a single legion under his command – *Legio* III *Augusta*. No details of the war have come down to us, yet Dio's cryptic description that the Romans took heavy casualties fighting the rebel army is significant. The lightly armed Gaetuli, it seems, were initially able to inflict damage upon the better-equipped legionaries. Dogged determination and unbending discipline, however, finally extinguished the menace in Africa and Numidia. Receiving Lentulus' after-action report that order had been restored to the region, the Senate awarded its man triumphal ornaments and the unique war title *Gaetulicus*.[61]

In the East, Herodes' successor was proving to be a thoroughly incompetent ruler.[62] It was decided – almost certainly with Augustus' consent and, perhaps, at his instigation – to remove Archelaos beyond the Alps to Vienna (modern Vienne, France), essentially banishing him.[63] This was more than regime change: his realms of Idumaea, Iudaea and Samaria were now to be annexed and merged together as a new Province of Caesar.[64] The office of *Praefectus Iudaeorum* was created and an *eques*, one Coponius, was appointed to it, reporting to the *Legatus Augusti Pro Praetore* of Syria, P. Sulpicius Quirinius.[65] Establishing direct Roman authority over Iudaea quickly proved problematic. The attempt by the new *procurator*, Cyrenius, to conduct a census to assess the tax base of the province was met initially with vocal resistance, until the high priest Joazar persuaded the people to comply. Most, but not all, followed his counsel:

> Yet was there one Iudas, a Gaulanite, of a city whose name was Gamala, who, taking with him Sadduc, a Pharisee, became zealous to draw them to a revolt, who both said that this taxation was no better than an introduction to slavery, and exhorted the nation to assert their liberty.[66]

Iudas' protest was religious rather than political, one based on renouncing worldly infatuation with material goods in favour of developing a spiritual life. According to Josephus, this new doctrine rapidly swept across the nation, though the author of the *Acts of the Apostles* in the New Testament states only 400 people joined the man's cause.[68] However, the intensity of the following led to conflict with the authorities. Josephus mentions great robberies and assassinations of unnamed officials. That the other Roman historians make no mention of them infers that they were skirmishes or minor infractions.[68] The sedition was quelled within the year. The fate of Iudas of Gamala is not recorded by Josephus, but the *Acts* states he was killed and his followers then dispersed.[69] Quirinius could continue the assimilation of the new territory at will.

The nascent province between the Rhine and Elbe rivers, meanwhile, remained a work in progress. The damaged relations with the native peoples of Germania, who had revolted the year before, needed to be repaired. Trust had to be re-established. There also remained an ever-present threat the Romans perceived as existential, one that could yet destabilize the balance of power in the region. The land north of Noricum, beyond the Danube, was occupied by the Marcomanni. They were led by a respected but feared king, Marboduus. He was an intelligent man who had been educated in Rome as a private individual rather than as a hostage, and been befriended – like Iuba II – by Augustus.[70] Around 10 BCE, Marboduus rejoined his people, who were then living close by the Main River, and assumed the highest social position among them.[71] He formed alliances with neighbouring nations and tribes and convinced them to relocate away to territory further east, in the region of Bohaemium (Bohemia in the modern Czech Republic), to avoid encroachment by, and conflict with, the Romans.[72] He knew how effective they were at war. He had learned the lessons of military science from living for some sixteen years among the Romans – perhaps from service with the *auxilia* – and applied them to his own army, organizing and training his own soldiers like theirs. By 6 CE he had an armed force approaching 70,000 infantry and 4,000 cavalry.[73]

Tiberius had conceived his invasion plan of Bohaemium as part of his greater mission to pacify Germania the previous year, or even earlier (fig. 11).[74] The scale of the operations and number of units involved imply careful preparations undertaken over many months.[75] The strategic plan called for a two-pronged attack to surround, cut-off and crush the Marcomanni. The army group under Tiberius' command would strike directly north-northwest from Carnuntum on the Danube, resourced with troops drawn from Raetia and others provided by *Legatus Augusti* M. Valerius Messalla Messallinus of Illyricum; simultaneously, Sentius Saturninus would lead his army group east from Mogontiacum and forts within province Germania along the Main River, march through the territory of the Chatti and cut a pathway through the dense *Hercynia Silva*.[76] Up to twelve legions and an unspecified number of auxiliary cohorts of infantry, *alae* of cavalry and mixed units were in position, perhaps representing a combined force of 80,000 men – the largest deployment for a single campaign since the Cantabrian and Asturian War of 26 BCE[77] (see Order of Battle 3).

The order for the advance was given:

> Caesar had already arranged his winter quarters on the Danubius, and had brought up his army to within five days' march of the advanced posts of the enemy; and the legions which he had ordered Saturninus to bring up,

Figure 11. After Agrippa's death, Tiberius became Augustus' right-hand man. A talented commander, he fought many wars for the *princeps* and was popular with the soldiers.

separated from the enemy by an almost equal distance, were on the point of effecting a junction with Caesar at a predetermined rendezvous within [a] few days.[78]

Roman finds on the left bank of the Danube and its confluence with the March River approximately 10 kilometres (6 miles) east of Carnuntum at Bratislava-

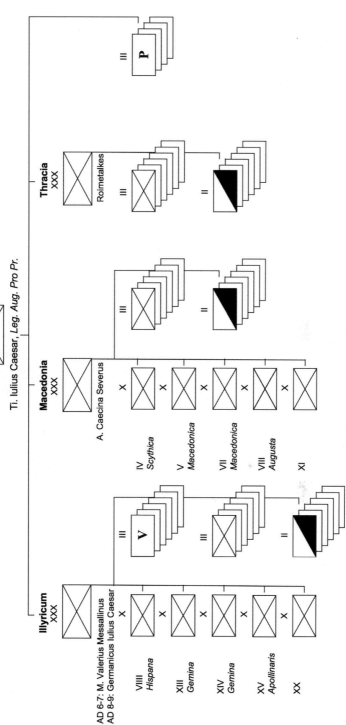

Order of Battle 3. Illyricum, 6–9 CE. Units of ethnic *auxilia* are recorded as having served in Illyricum.

Devín may mark the actual crossing point of Tiberius' army group.[79] Following the course of the March, it moved inland at a steady pace in search of its target.[80]

Then the unexpected happened. Far behind the advancing Roman columns, the supposedly pacified people of the north of Illyricum rose up in revolt.[81] The long-simmering frustrations borne of Roman occupation, heated by perceived abuses concerning tribute obligations, now boiled over. The chief of the Breuci of the Pannonii confederacy – a man named Bato – led his people in a direct assault against the Roman town of Sirmium.[82] No one was spared from the violence:

> Roman citizens were overpowered, traders were massacred, a large detach-ment (*vexillatio*) of veterans stationed in the region, which was most remote from the commander, was exterminated to a man.[83]

The inhabitants withstood Bato's onslaught, but the brazen attack could not go unpunished. Closest geographically and able to deal quickest with the insur-rection was A. Caecina Severus, *Legatus* Augusti *Pro Praetore* of neighbouring Thracia Macedoniaque. He led the counterattack and soon 'everywhere was wholesale devastation by fire and sword'.[84] He engaged the rebels at the Drava River, and in the mêlée the Breuci suffered heavy casualties and were eventually forced to retreat, but not without first inflicting damage upon the Romans. The rebels' audacious resistance proved a great draw for the discontented, and more men soon swelled the ranks of the insurrectionists.[85]

As a defeated people, the nations of Illyricum were required to pay tribute. One of the possible causes of the rebellion was the additional demand of a conscrip-tion levy imposed by the Romans upon the male populations of the subject nations of Illyricum for the war against Marboduus.[86] As subjects, they were obligated to provide men for the *auxilia* and serve alongside Roman troops when required. In preparation for the *Bellum Marcomannicum*, propraetorian legate Messallinus had issued an edict for all able-bodied men to present themselves for duty.[87] Dio reports that when the auxiliaries assembled together they realized just how large a force and how strong in arms they were; then one of them, Bato of the Daesidiates nation – a man with *maxima auctoritas* or 'greatest prestige', according to Velleius Paterculus – took the lead to openly incite rebellion.[88] Their choice was either to put their lives at mortal risk in a war that they did not themselves want in order to benefit the Romans, or to fight the Romans and by doing so liberate their own homeland from the oppressors. Many decided to join him. Bato's highly moti-vated force promptly defeated the first Roman troops sent against it.[89]

The rebel army quickly swelled to 90,000–100,000 infantry and 9,000 cavalry.[90] Little is known about their organization or mode of fighting, but of the Iapodes tribe, who lived in the far northwestern corner of Illyricum, Strabo writes that 'they are indeed a war-mad people', noting 'their armour is Celtic, and they are tattooed like the rest of the Illyrii and the Thraci'.[91] The most widely used offensive weapon was the long, heavy spear (*lancea*, *sibyna*) with a flat leaf-shaped bronze or iron blade at the tip.[92] Warriors of the Illyrii used arms and armour derived from Greek models, preferring the curved, single bladed *machaira* or the *sica*, a short curved sword the Romans associated with assassins.[93] Noted for their horsemanship, many warriors of the Western Balkans often rode into battle, dismounted and continued to fight on foot.[94] Small-scale ambuscades and surprise attacks on troops on the march were common tactics.

Separately, Bato and the men of the Daesidiates moved on *Colonia* Martia Iulia Salona, hoping to take the city from which the Romans administered the province. The trapezium-shaped stronghold on the Dalmatian coast was fortified with stout walls and towers.[95] The details of the attack on the city of Salona are lost to us. The defenders managed to hold their town and, in the ensuing battle, Bato himself was wounded when struck by a stone, perhaps launched from a Roman sling or *ballista*.[96] The rebel leader wounded, the siege collapsed and the retreating insurgents fanned out along the Dalmatian coast, wreaking havoc on the unprotected communities and settlements as they passed through. At Apollonia they engaged the Romans again, initially seeming to suffer defeat before snatching an unexpected victory.[97]

The *princeps* feared Illyricum could yet be lost, and 'such a panic did this war inspire that even the courage of Caesar Augustus, rendered steady and firm by experience in so many wars, was shaken with fear'.[98] Emergency measures were implemented:

> Troops were accordingly levied: all the *veterani* were everywhere called out; and not only men, but women were compelled to provide freedmen for soldiers, in proportion to their income. The *princeps* was heard to say in the Senate, that, unless they were on their guard, the enemy might in ten days come within the sight of the city of Rome. The services of Roman senators and *equites* were required, according to their promises, in support of the war.[99]

Tiberius was officially placed in command of counterinsurgency operations.[100] He was faced with a major dilemma: either to continue with the mission in Germania, but divert resources to quell the insurgency; or to suspend operations altogether, deal with the rebellion in Illyricum as the priority and return to the invasion another season.[101] He settled for a truce with Marboduus and began a full tactical withdrawal of his forces and their redeployment to the Western Balkans.[102] It was a victory of sorts. Recognizing that the enemy had been forced to make a pact with the Romans, Tiberius and Saturninus were both granted triumphal honours, the former also being awarded a consulship.[103] But greater perils lay ahead that would test both commanders' skills.

While Tiberius organized the withdrawal of his army from the right bank of the Danube, Messallinus left with a small detachment from *Legio* XX (map 20); Tiberius would follow with the main army group as soon as he could.[104] In this first year of war, eight legions – equivalent to 40,000 men at full strength – plus an unknown number of auxiliary cohorts were committed.[105] The *Bellum Delmaticum* – also known by its other moniker *Bellum Batonianum*, the 'War of the Batos' – would later be considered 'the most grave conflict since Rome's struggle with Carthage'.[106]

Despite still recovering from his injury, Bato of the Breuci nevertheless led his force in person to intercept Messallinus. The insurgents gained the upper hand in open battle, but lost their advantage when later ambushed by the Romans.[107] Bato realized he could not decisively beat the Romans with his small force. He needed many more men. The obvious man to approach was Bato of the Daesidiates, who was achieving results through his own efforts in the south of the country.[108] The two chiefs met and agreed to cooperate and share the war command. They assembled their combined army north of the city of Sirmium on a mountain called Mons Alma (Fruška Gora), hoping to exploit the advantage and protection offered by high ground. To beat them, the Romans would have to fight uphill.

Severus had, meanwhile, set off from newly incorporated Moesia, counted a Province of Caesar. Before leaving, he had sought assistance from Rome's ally Roimetalkes to augment his numbers.[109] Responding quickly to the request, the king actually managed to bring his lightly armed, but tough Thracian units in theatre *ahead* of the Roman commander. The rebels resisted the Romans on the first assault but, under the additional numbers from Roimetalkes' army, they eventually crumbled. Hardly had Severus celebrated his victory when he discovered he had problems of his own. The Daci and Sarmatae had taken advantage of his absence and invaded his province unopposed; at the same time, the Dalmatae entered the territories of their neighbours in Illyricum and stirred up revolt there.[110] The legate of Moesia had no choice but to return urgently and regain control of it.

Tiberius and Messallinus arrived in Illyricum. They set up their operational headquarters at Siscia with the resident garrison commander M'. Ennius; soon they found themselves trapped within its stout walls and under a sustained rebel assault.[111] Despite the setbacks, there were Roman successes. Eager to take part in the campaign, the former cavalry commander and *quaestor* designate for 7 CE, Velleius Paterculus, set off from Rome.[112] He had accepted the post of *legatus* assigned to Tiberius and duly arrived in Siscia with reinforcements.[113] Messallinus and his army found themselves surrounded by a greater number of enemy soldiers, but Roman discipline held and the enemy was routed, with 20,000 fleeing the field.[114] When news of his victory reached Rome, Messallinus was accorded the honour of triumphal ornaments.[115]

By this time the rebels had learned the wisdom of not engaging the Romans in open battle. Instead they used their knowledge of terrain, skills with light arms and agility to wage a guerrilla war, which greatly disadvantaged the heavily armed legionaries.[116] They successfully stretched their resistance into the winter, when the legions normally retired to camp, and even invaded the neighbouring Roman province of Macedonia, causing destruction wherever they went.[117] Once they reached Thracia, their south and eastward advance was blocked by Roimetalkes, assisted this time by his brother Raskiporis (Rhascyporis).[118] Faced with inclement weather, the rebel army retreated to the hills of Illyricum, from where they launched hit-and-run raids upon the Romans at will.

Augustus watched the 'War of the Batos' from afar with deepening concern.[119] He had personal experience of the terrain and the enemy from his two tours in

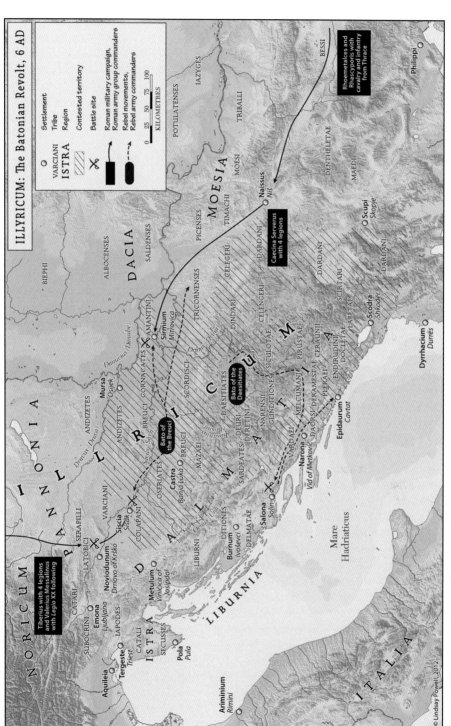

Map 20. Military operations in Illyricum, 6 CE.

Illyricum forty-two years before, and even sustained injuries in combat during them.[120] Dio writes that he believed that the campaign should have been over quickly and suspected that Tiberius was deliberately impeding progress so that he could have an army under his direct control.[121] Yet the letters he sent to Tiberius – at least the examples preserved by Suetonius – show that the *princeps* actually extolled his virtues as a consummate general, praised his prudence and emphasized that the fate of the nation depended on his continuing good health and prudent decision-making:

> Farewell, Tiberius, most charming of men, and success go with you, as you war for me and for the Muses. Farewell, most charming and valiant of men and most conscientious of generals, or may I never know happiness.
>
> I have only praise for the conduct of your summer campaigns, dear Tiberius, and I am sure that no one could have acted with better judgment than you did amid so many difficulties and such apathy of your army. All who were with you agree that the well-known line could be applied to you: 'One man alone by his foresight has saved our dear country from ruin.'[122]

This time of crisis should have been the opportunity for his youngest adopted son M. Agrippa (Postumus), now eligible for military service, to prove himself. Instead he spent his time fishing, drinking, bickering and acting in ways others interpreted as depraved or mad.[123] When he argued that he had been denied his natural father's – that is M. Agrippa's – inheritance and denigrated Livia, Augustus finally disowned, disinherited and banished him to the small island of Planasia off Corsica.[124]

There was only one close relative left whom the *princeps* could turn to. He ordered Germanicus Caesar – then holding the junior rank of *quaestor* – to assemble an army and go to assist Tiberius.[125] This was the 21-year-old's first chance to gain military experience and to prove his mettle; he was two years younger than his father Nero Claudius Drusus had been when he set out on his first mission.[126] Germanicus grasped the opportunity eagerly. From the outset he faced two formidable challenges. Firstly, he had no training in military matters. Secondly, he had to build his army from scratch by himself. A levy (*dilectus ingenuorum*) of the free-born citizen population called by Augustus produced the men, supplemented with *liberti* (freedmen, manumitted or former slaves) and slaves whose freedom had been bought expressly to recruit them into military service.[127] Nothing is recorded of the organization of his *Cohortes Voluntariorum*, or how they were equipped or trained, but at the end of the year his irregular army – perhaps numbering *Cohortis Apulae Civium Romanorum* and I *Campana* among them – was ready for active deployment.[128] Intending to reach the war zone in time for the new campaign season, Germanicus led his men out of Rome, almost certainly accompanied by two cohorts of *Praetoriani* for his own protection.

The fact that Augustus resorted to conscription confirms the real anxiety he felt at the worsening situation in the Western Balkans. Velleius Paterculus describes him as visibly 'shaken with fear'.[129] Ever mindful of the delicate state of public finances, to pay for Germanicus' conscript unit Augustus levied a 2 per cent tax on the sale of slaves and redirected funds from the budget for scheduled gladiatorial games.[130] Furthermore, Augustus suspended the annual *transvectio* review of the equestrians in the *Forum Romanum*.[131]

The turbulent events of 6 CE highlighted not only the vital role the army played in maintaining the security of the *imperium* of the Roman People, but also the precariousness of its funding. The army now comprised twenty-eight legions. The annual operating cost in salaries, equipment, animals and supplies was now immense.[132] To pay for the programme, Augustus made the first contribution that year to a military fund, the *Aerarium Militare*, with a commitment to make annual deposits in future.[133] He accepted voluntary contributions from allied kings and certain confederate communities, but he took nothing from private citizens – although, according to Dio, a considerable number made offers of their own free will, or so they said.[134] Even with his generous deposits, withdrawals from the account would exhaust the monies in short order. More cash was needed. Augustus encouraged the Senate to propose ways and means to ensure the *Aerarium* would be properly funded and invited them to write down their ideas and submit them for his consideration.[135] He already knew, of course, how he would do so. The method had been used before and later been suspended:

> At all events, when different men had proposed different schemes, he approved none of them, but established the tax of 5 per cent on the inheritances and bequests which should be left by people at their death to any except very near relatives or very poor persons, representing that he had found this tax set down in Caesar's memoranda.[136]

To administer the fund, a board was appointed of three ex-consuls, chosen by lot, to serve a term of three years; they would be entitled to two lictors each and to request any assistance they deemed necessary.[137] With their help, Augustus was able to reduce several types of expenditure or to cut them altogether.

Security at home also received the *princeps'* attention. This year, during which the citizens of the city of Rome suffered through a combination of severe famine and devastating fires, Augustus founded the *Vigiles Urbani*, the 'City Watch', as a paramilitary firefighting force.[138] Commanded by an equestrian *Praefectus Vigilum* whom he personally appointed, the 6,000 men filling its ranks were recruited from among freedmen.[139] The *Vigiles* also served as the city's night watch and helped the *Cohortes Urbanae* to enforce public order, arrest thieves and capture runaway slaves.[140] Funded by a tax on the sale of slaves, the *Vigiles* had barracks located in the city and proved very popular with the citizens.[141]

7 CE

Q. Caecilius Q. *f.* Metellus Creticus Silanus	A. Licinius A. *f.* Nerva Silanus
suff.	[-]. Lucilius Longus

Germanicus and his cohorts of volunteers reached Illyricum in time for the new campaign season. Roman forces were now deployed right across the region, intent on quelling the Great Illyrian Revolt (map 21). Tiberius, Messallinus and their men were still unable to leave Siscia. From the neighbouring provinces, A. Caecina Severus and M. Plautius Silvanus marched with five legions, bringing the total under Tiberius' command to '10 legions, more than 70 auxiliary cohorts, 10 *alae* of cavalry and 10,000 veterans and, in addition, a large number of volunteers and numerous cavalry of the [Thracian] king' – a combined force of some 145,000 men, equivalent to almost half of Roman troops on active service.[142] 'Never,' writes Velleius Paterculus, 'had a greater army been assembled in one place since the civil wars.'[143] Caesar Augustus was determined to destroy the opposition once and for all.

The Romans may have believed that, with such resources, victory was assuredly theirs. They had underestimated the guile of their adversary. The legions brought by Caecina Severus and Silvanus, augmented by Roimetalkes and his Roman-trained Thracian infantry and cavalry, however, found themselves surrounded by the rebels.[144] In the ensuing battle – the location of which is unknown – the cavalry of the Thraci was routed, the auxiliary infantry and cavalry were chased away and even among the legionaries 'some confusion took place'.[145] The Roman casualties included a *tribunis militum*, *praefectus castrorum*, *primus pilus* and other centurions of the legions and several *praefecti* of auxiliary cohorts.[146] It was a shambles. In the heat of battle the centurions – the backbone of the Roman army, who could be relied upon to keep cool heads – applied the basic combat doctrine and maintained unbending discipline with cold efficiency. Paterculus writes in praise of the rankers:

> The courage of the Roman soldiers, on that occasion, gained them more honour than they left to their officers, who, widely differing from the practice of the commander-in-chief [Tiberius], found themselves in the midst of the enemy, before they had ascertained from their scouts in which direction they lay.[147]

They saved the day. 'The legions, encouraging one another, made a charge upon the enemy,' Paterculus writes, 'and, not content with standing their ground against them, broke their line, and gained an unexpected victory.'[148]

Severus followed the course of the Bosut River (a tributary of the Sava now in eastern Croatia) and marched right into a trap. The combined forces of the two Batos rushed upon his marching camp near the Volcaean Marshes, near the site of later Cibalae (Vinkovici).[149] Dio writes that the rebels 'frightened the pickets outside the ramparts and drove them back inside'.[150] However, once behind the turf rampart surmounted by its fence of sharpened stakes (*sudes*) lashed together, the Roman soldiers' resolve returned; with their centurions barking orders at them, they stood their ground and gradually repulsed the besiegers. Learning from this and other incidents, the Romans adapted their tactics. They divided into their cohorts and centuries so 'that might overrun many parts of the country at once'.[151] These smaller detachments would form, in effect, a mobile army.

Tiberius finally broke out from Siscia and began his advance to the east. He quickly contained many rebels in the area between the Drava and Sava rivers at

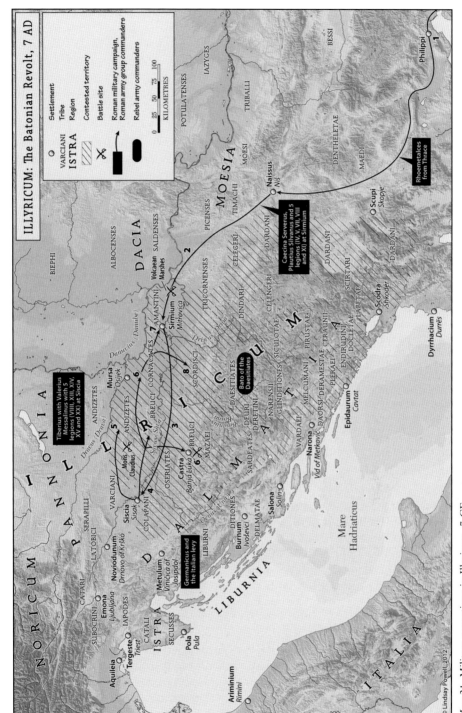

ILLYRICUM: The Batonian Revolt, 7 AD

	Settlement
VARCIANI	Tribe
ISTRA	Region
	Contested territory
	Battle site
	Roman military campaign, Roman army group commanders
	Rebel army group commanders

0 25 50 75 100
KILOMETRES

Tiberius with Valerius Messalinus with 5 legions (VIII, XIII, XIV, XV and XX) at Siscia

Germanicus and the Italian levy

Caecina Serverus, Plautius Silvanus and 5 legions (IV, V, VII, VIII and XI) at Sirmium

Rhoemetalces from Thrace

Bato of the Daesitiates

Map 21. Military operations in Illyricum, 7 CE.

© Lindsay Powell, 2012

Mons Claudius (Papuk Hills).[152] The Augustan military camp at Obrežje along the Sava River may date from this action.[153] Having made such little progress against the insurgents, this small victory was important to boosting morale of his men.[154] Germanicus' army also enjoyed success when he clashed with the Mazaei nation.[155] Listed as Pannonii by Strabo, the Mazaei lived on the transitional grassy plain upon which Banja Luka now stands in modern Bosnia-Herzegovina.[156] The enthusiasm of the young commander and the effectiveness of his soldiers' training proved decisive. Germanicus 'conquered in battle and harassed the Mazaei', writes Dio.[157] His army remained in the country in sight of the Dinaric Alps through the winter in case of a counterinsurgency. Whether Germanicus stayed or returned to brief Augustus is not disclosed in the extant records. In his eagerness for news of the war, Augustus had relocated to Ariminum (modern Rimini).[158] Tiberius likely stayed there with the *princeps*, discussing military strategy with him until the spring of the following year.

Having completed his proconsulship in Africa, Cossus Cornelius Lentulus Gaetulicus returned to Rome. There this noble and respected man celebrated his well-deserved triumphal ornaments.[159]

8 CE

| | M. Furius P. f. Camillus | Sex. Nonius L. f. Quinctilianus |
| *suff.* | L. Apronius C. f. | A. Vibius C. f. Habitus |

The *Bellum Batonianum* entered its third year. Germanicus Caesar and his troops continued their operations by moving into the mountains (map 22). Their target was Splanaum – or Splonum to the Romans – on the Dalmatian side of the Dinaric Alps.[160] It was a populous region and the centre of mining in Illyricum, producing ores for the precious metals industry.[161] Splonum's remote location, strong fortifications and 'vast number of defenders' posed a considerable challenge to the young man and small army.[162] Given that time was not on the novice commander's side, blockading the defenders – in the hope of starving them out – was not an option. Having brought with him a quantity of siege weapons, Germanicus attempted a direct assault. However, even 'high technology' tension and torsion weapons did not give the Romans the decisive tactical edge they needed in this remote situation. Finding 'he had been unable to make any headway either with engines or by assaults', the Roman attackers had reached a stalemate.[163] Frustrated, one Pusio:

> a Germanic horseman, hurled a stone against the wall and so shook the parapet that it immediately fell and dragged down with it a man who was leaning against it. At this the rest became alarmed and in their fear abandoned that part of the wall and ran up to the citadel.[164]

The audacious act changed the odds. Through the breach, the besieging troops poured into the fortress. The Roman troops exacted a terrible revenge. A last stand by the defenders would be futile. Shortly after they surrendered the citadel and themselves.[165]

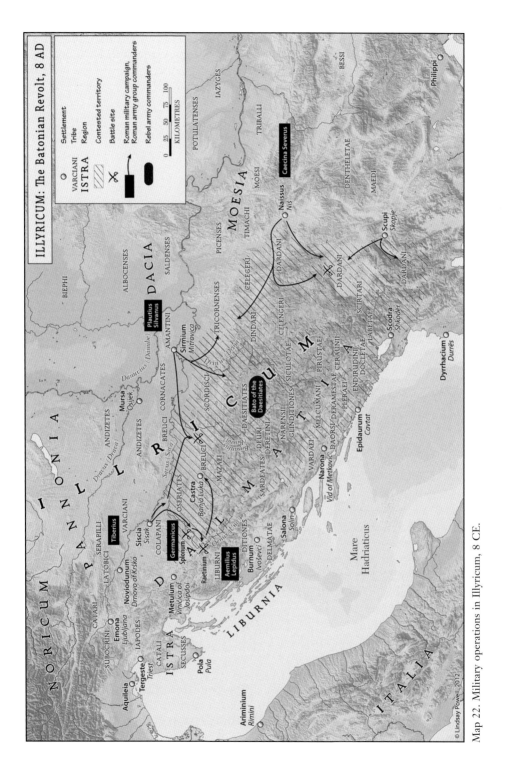

Map 22. Military operations in Illyricum, 8 CE.

Germanicus advanced deeper into rebel-held territory with his irregular troops. On the way they captured several strongholds; the fall of Raetinum is recorded in gruesome detail by Dio.[166] He writes:

> The enemy, overwhelmed by their numbers and unable to withstand them, set fire of their own accord to the encircling wall and to the houses adjoining it contriving, however, to keep it so far as possible from blazing up at once and to make it go unnoticed for some time; after doing this they retired to the citadel. The Romans, ignorant of what they had done, rushed in after them, expecting to sack the whole place without striking a blow; thus they got inside the circle of fire, and, with their minds intent upon the enemy, saw nothing of it until they were surrounded by it on all sides. Then they found themselves in the direst peril, being pelted by the men from above and injured by the fire from without. They could neither remain where they were safely nor force their way out anywhere without danger. For if they stood out of range of the missiles, they were scorched by the fire, or, if they leaped back from the flames, they were destroyed by the missiles; and some who got caught in a tight place perished from both causes at once, being wounded on one side and burned on the other. The majority of those who had rushed into the town met this fate; but some few escaped by casting corpses into the flames and making a passage for themselves by using the bodies as a bridge. The fire gained such headway that even those on the citadel could not remain there, but abandoned it in the night and hid themselves in subterranean chambers.[167]

By the next day, the charred ruins of Raetinum had fallen to Germanicus.

Despite having a proven talent for combat command and a formidable force of ten legions, Tiberius nevertheless suffered setbacks.[168] As the war dragged on seemingly without end, his often idle troops became restless in the humid heat of the Balkan summer. Facing the possibility of outright mutiny, Tiberius urgently needed a new strategy that could break the impasse and bring his troops victory. His answer was to realign the expeditionary army. 'He made three divisions of them,' writes Dio, 'one he assigned to Silvanus and one to Marcus Lepidus, and with the rest he marched with Germanicus against Bato.'[169] For Germanicus, who now led his own army group comprising legions and auxiliaries as well as his own irregular unit, this was a major promotion and a public recognition of his military achievement.

The rebels were restless too. They began to squabble among themselves and committed acts of treachery against each other. Having betrayed a certain Pinnes with the connivance of members of the tribe, Bato of the Breuci now ruled alone over the nation. The two leaders of the Great Illyrian Revolt had since become estranged and grown deeply suspicious of each other. There was a struggle and the Breucian was betrayed by his own people; he was handed over to Bato of the Daesidiates and summarily executed.[170] Many of the Breuci rightly felt betrayed and raged against their former allies.

The division among the rebels created just the opportunity the Romans needed. *Legatus* Silvanus now launched an offensive against them. Disunited and taken by surprise, the opposition collapsed. He defeated the war-weary Breuci and their allies, writes Dio, 'without a battle'.[171] The disaffected warriors of north Illyricum soon sued for peace. On 3 August, they surrendered to Silvanus at a place on the Bathinus (Bosnar?) River.[172] Bato of the Daesidiates, however, would not yield. The men still loyal to him retreated to the passes leading to the relative safety of their homeland in central Illyricum, ravaging the surrounding lands as they moved and resisting Roman attempts to defeat them for several months more.[173]

Quelling the rebellion in Illyricum had become a protracted, grinding struggle of asymmetric warfare. The theatre of operations now concentrated on the lands of the Perustae, Daesidiates and Dalmatae, but the jagged hillsides and craggy vales of central Illyricum were unsuited to Roman tactics and equipment.[174] While the rebels were dispersed in smaller bands, the Romans were forced to waste time and effort tracking them down. However, many retreated to their fortified places, confident they could wait out the inevitable oncoming storm. The Romans were experts in siege craft. Strongholds that had earlier successfully held out against Tiberius and his deputies' armies began to fall, one by one, including Seretium, which had resisted the Romans right from the beginning. Silvanus and Lepidus rapidly overwhelmed the insurgents they encountered too.

Tiberius and Germanicus had to work harder for their victories. Bato of the Daesidiates had since moved his base of operations to Andetrium (Muč), a fort built on a rocky escarpment with steep sides not far from Salona, surrounded by a fast-moving stream.[175] All attempts by Tiberius to capture it by direct means had so far failed. Anticipating a siege, Bato had wisely stocked provisions there; he could endure a blockade for some considerable time – time that Tiberius did not have. When the Romans tried to scale or undermine the walls, the defenders pelted his men with rocks and projectiles, and launched hit-and-run raids on his wagon trains carrying essential supplies. 'Hence Tiberius,' writes Dio, 'though supposed to be besieging them, was himself placed in the position of a besieged force.'[176]

The odds of a successful counteroffensive to reduce Andetrium gradually turned in the Romans' favour. They had clear superiority over the rebels in one key respect: supply chain management. Able to draw upon the resources of the empire during the last winter, the Romans had replenished their combat units' stocks of food and matériel, though the supply of grain remained an ongoing issue.[177] In contrast, the years of war had taken its toll on the rebels. Unable to tend to their fields, beyond the special arrangements Bato had made at fort Andetrium, the rest of the rebel army, lacking food and the means to treat wounds, went hungry and many succumbed to disease.[178] Fear also permeated their ranks. Were they to surrender, these deserters from the auxiliary units of the Roman army could not expect to be shown mercy by the Romans; they saw to it that those intent on laying down their arms – such as one Scenobardus – were prevented from doing so.[179]

Encamped in his *praetorium* tent on the plain beneath the walls of Andetrium, Tiberius was deeply frustrated. Incensed at their commander's apparent indecision, his troops were rioting and shouting protests loudly. The commander needed to contain the unrest, and quickly reassert his authority. Yet it was against his nature to make rash decisions. He was, above all, a strict disciplinarian. He mustered the men. From a tribunal he addressed them, rebuking some, but staying calm as he delivered his speech.[180] Bato heard the noise and, from his place on the parapet, watched the Roman army standing to attention before its commander with growing unease. He feared an imminent attack and ordered his men to retreat into their fort for safety.[181] He dispatched a herald to Tiberius with a request for terms.[182] The Roman commander now had the rebel leader exactly where he wanted him. Yet Tiberius would not negotiate with the rebel leader and, instead, rallied his men for a direct attack on the fort.[183] Bato had correctly read his adversary's intentions.

The legionaries formed up in their centuries and cohorts. Arrayed in a *quadratum* (a dense square or rectangle formation), his men advanced towards the fort. At first they marched at a steady walking pace, and then, as they approached the walls, picked up speed into a trot, breaking into a charge only when they reached the rocky ascent. The rebel soldiers deployed outside the walls rained down missiles upon the advancing Romans – Dio lists rocks, slingshot, wagon wheels, carts and circular chests loaded with rocks.[184] For a while it seemed the rebels were winning, and the men watching the battle from the top of the circuit wall cheered on their side. The Romans sustained casualties, but for Tiberius it was a calculated risk, and he now sent up reinforcements.[185] Seeing the addition of new troops, the insurgents panicked. In the chaos of battle, the rebels inside closed the gates of the fort; many still fighting outside now discovered they could not retreat to safety.[186] In desperation they tried to escape up the mountainside, throwing down their cumbersome weapons and shields. The Romans continued their relentless chase into the forests. When the soldiers found the enemy, they slew them like hunted prey.[187] Witnessing the fate of their kinsmen and assessing the situation to be hopeless, the men inside Andetrium capitulated. In the confusion Bato escaped. Disappointed that he had not captured his opponent, Tiberius spent the days immediately after the siege in arranging the affairs concerning those who had surrendered to him.[188]

9 CE

	C. Poppaeus Q. f. Sabinus	Q. Sulpicius Q. f. Camerinus
suff.	M. Papius M. f. Mutilus	C. Poppaeus Q. f. Secundus

On New Year's Day, the '*imperium* of the Roman People' was at its greatest extent (map 23). In the forty years since Actium, Augustus and his team of commanders had added nearly double the territory of the empire. Yet problems remained within its extended borders and the legions were arranged in strategic clusters rather than strung along the frontier (table 3).

Having demonstrated success in command, Germanicus Caesar now took a prominent role in the prosecution of the war against the remaining rebels in

Table 3. Dispositions of the Legions, Summer 9 CE (Conjectural).

Province	Units	Legions
Hispania Tarraconensis	4	II *Augusta*, IV *Macedonica*, VI *Victrix*, X *Gemina*
Germania	8	I *Germanica*, V *Alaudae*, XIII *Gemina*, XIV *Gemina*, XVI *Gallica*, XVII, XIIX, XIX
Pannonia	4	VIII *Augusta*, VIIII *Hispana*, XV *Apollinaris*, XX *Valeria Victrix*
Dalmatia	2	VII *Macedonica*, XI
Moesia	2	IV *Scythica*, V *Macedonica*
Syria	4	III *Gallica*, VI *Ferrata*, X (*Fretensis*), XII *Fulminata*
Aegyptus	2	III *Cyrenaica*, XXII *Deiotariana*
Africa	1	III *Augusta*

Sources: Appendix 3; Hardy (1889), p. 630; Lendering (Livius.org); Syme (1933 and 1986).

Illyricum (map 24).[189] He laid siege to an important stronghold called Arduba.[190] There Germanicus' army faced defenders protected within thick stone walls surrounded almost entirely by a fast-flowing river.[191] Faced with this seemingly impregnable fortress, his numbers, which were greater than those of the besieged, did not give him any tactical advantage. It was the people inside Arduba who, unexpectedly, tipped the odds in his favour. Many desperately wanted to surrender and avoid an uncertain fate. Their anguished pleas were spurned by women loyal to the rebellion, who swore liberty or death over surrender and ignominy. Those trying to escape were obstructed by others determined to remain inside. Fighting broke out among the two opposing sides. Some escapees reached the Roman line and offered their unconditional surrender, but those still in the town chose to end their lives, either throwing themselves onto bonfires or hurling themselves into the river.[192] Satisfied the siege was over, Germanicus put Postumius in charge of mopping-up operations and left to rejoin his adoptive father.[193] Learning the fate of Arduba, other strongholds still in rebel hands promptly offered their own surrender.

Bato was still free and negotiating terms with Tiberius.[194] Bato sent his son Sceuas with an offer of surrender in exchange for a pardon. This time Tiberius agreed.[195] It seems he had learned from previous failures of post-war policy in Illyricum following the *Bellum Pannonicum*.[196] On a late summer evening, Bato set off for the Roman camp. On his arrival next morning, he was taken under armed escort and presented before Tiberius as the assembled Roman troops watched. But Bato surprised his captors. He now displayed the courage and dignity the Romans respected in a defeated enemy. He kneeled before the Roman commander, who was seated upon a tribunal, and laid down his arms at his feet; he spoke in defence of his fellow rebels, pleaded for clemency for his men, but asked no special treatment for himself.[197] Bowing his head, he bared his neck ready for the *coup-de-grâce*. The order was stayed. Germanicus declared victory for the Romans, and the troops vociferously acclaimed Tiberius – shouting '*Imperator!*' – for his achievement; it was his sixth accolade. The long and brutal 'War of the Batos' was finally over.

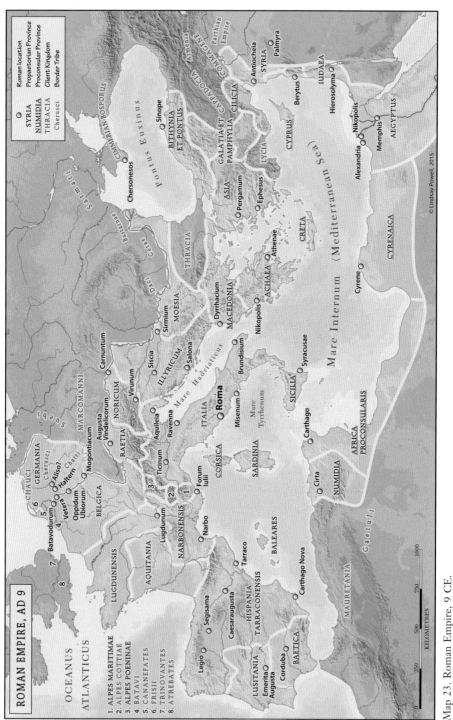

ROMAN EMPIRE, AD 9

Roman location
SYRIA Propraetorian Province
NUMIDIA Proconsular Province
THRACIA Client Kingdom
Cherusci Border Tribe

1. ALPES MARITIMAE
2. ALPES COTTIAE
3. ALPES POENINAE
4. BATAVI
5. CANANEFATES
6. FRISII
7. TRINOVANTES
8. ATREBATES

OCEANUS
ATLANTICUS

Sarmatia
Suebi
CHAUCI
GERMANIA
Cherusci
Chatti
MARCOMANNI
BELGICA
Batavodurum
Vetera
Aliso?
Haltern
Oppidum
Ubiorum
Mogontiacum
LUGDUNENSIS
Augusta
Vindelicorum
Lugdunum
Forum
Iulii
AQUITANIA
Narbo
NARBONENSIS
Tarraco
BALEARES
HISPANIA
TARRACONENSIS
Caesaraugusta
Segisama
Legio
LUSITANIA
Emerita
Augusta
Corduba
BAETICA
Carthago Nova
MAURETANIA
Gaetuli
CORSICA
SARDINIA
Cirta
NUMIDIA
Carthago
AFRICA
PROCONSULARIS

RAETIA
NORICUM
Virunum
Carnuntum
Siscia
Sirmium
ILLYRICUM
Salona
MOESIA
Aquileia
Ticinum
Ravenna
ITALIA
Misenum
Roma
Mare
Tyrrhenum
SICILIA
Syracusae
Brundisium
Dyrrhacium
MACEDONIA
Nikopolis
ACHAEA
Athenae
CRETA

Mare Hadriatcus
Mare Internum (Mediterranean Sea)
Cyrene
CYRENAICA

CIMMERIAN BOSPORUS
Pontus Euxinus
Chersonesos
Sinope
BITHYNIA
ET PONTUS
THRACIA
Daci
Getae
Bastarnae
CAPPADOCIA
COMMAGENE
Armenia
Parthian Empire
GALATIA ET
PAMPHYLIA
CILICIA
ASIA
Pergamum
Ephesus
LYCIA
CYPRUS
Antiocheia
SYRIA
Palmyra
Berytus
IUDAEA
Hierosolyma
Nikopolis
Alexandria
Memphis
AEGYPTUS

KILOMETRES
0   250   500   750   1000

© Lindsay Powell, 2015

Map 23. Roman Empire, 9 CE.

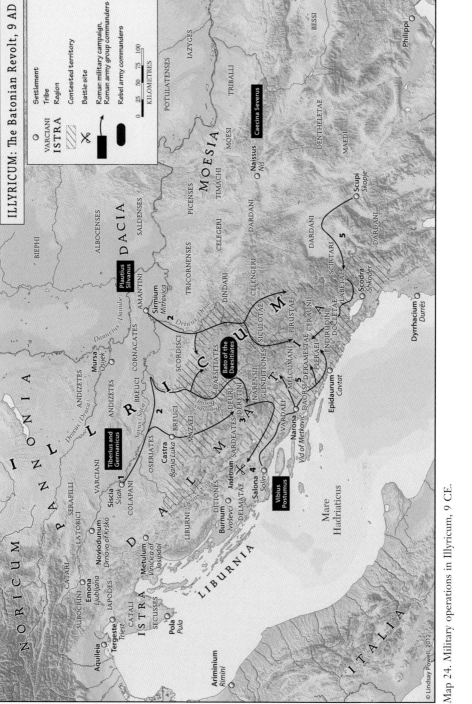

Map 24. Military operations in Illyricum, 9 CE.

Receiving the news in Rome, some senators were eager to award Tiberius a new and distinctive accolade. Among the titles proposed were *Pannonicus* ('Conqueror of Pannonia'), *Invinctus* ('Invincible') and *Pius* ('Pious'); all were overruled by Augustus.[198] A triumph would be adequate reward, he said.[199] Moreover, it would be shared by his subordinates who had shown valour during the four-year-long campaign.[200] As for Bato, he would be exhibited as a human trophy during the celebration for the amusement of the Roman People lining the procession route.

While the Romans celebrated the end of rebellion in the Western Balkans, they were taken by complete and utter surprise by the start of a new one in the lands across the Rhine River they thought pacified.[201] The ringleader of the German rebellion was Arminius, a hostage from 7 BCE who, after being taken to Rome, had been promoted into the *Ordo Equester* and given command of his own unit of Cherusci nationals, perhaps seeing service in the Western Balkans.[202] His motives are unclear. Roman authors speculated that to Arminius it may have appeared that if the Romans could oppress the people of Illyricum through the imposition of tribute and taxes, and commit abuses while collecting them, they could – and likely would – do so in Germania; there could be no end to Roman tyranny as long as they were in his country. In his conspiracy he was assisted by his father Segimerus (or Sigimer).[203] Together they secretly assembled an alliance of several Germanic nations – among them the Angrivarii, Bructeri and Marsi. They agreed a plan to destroy the Roman army as it passed through their lands *en route* to its winter camps along the Lippe and Rhine rivers. How many men Arminius' alliance was able to put into the field is not recorded, but one reasoned, conservative estimate is 15,000 men.[204]

His summer campaign concluded, *Legatus Augusti Pro Praetore* P. Quinctilius Varus ordered his army to return home. He had with him three legions, three *alae* of cavalry and six *cohortes* of auxiliaries[205] (see Order of Battle 4). At full strength that would represent 22,752 men at arms; however, the force was likely significantly smaller, perhaps as few as 14,000 men.[206] It was no small force to defeat but, as the Germans had seen on several previous occasions, including Arbalo in 11 BCE, the Roman army was most vulnerable on the march.[207] In his favour, Arminius could count on the trust and complacency of the Roman commander, which he and his complicit father had carefully nurtured in recent days.[208] As far as Varus was concerned, Germania was at peace. So convinced was he of it that when informed by Segestes – 'a loyal man of that race and of illustrious name' and Arminius' father-in-law – about the conspiracy he chose to ignore the warning.[209] Reassured, Arminius could move forward with his plot.

On a predetermined date, Varus received a report of 'an uprising, first on the part of those who lived at a distance from him'.[210] Then, as the Roman column marched out from its summer camp, Arminius rode up to Varus with a request to excuse his *ala*, giving as his reason the need to ride ahead to assemble their allied forces.[211] Varus agreed. The column moved on. In his account of the battle, Dio criticizes Varus for poorly organizing his column and baggage train.[212] Normally non-combatants would follow the army, but, he says, traders, slaves, women, children and the wagons were mixed up with his troops and arranged in no particular

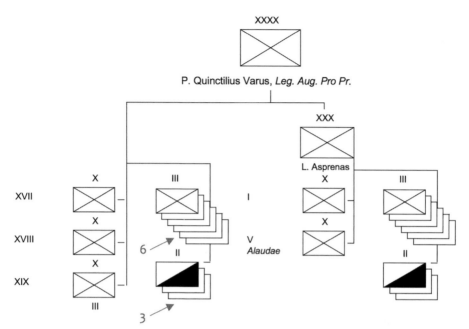

Order of Battle 4. Germania, 9 CE. In addition to two legions, Asprenas had an unknown number of ethnic *auxilia*, *alae* and *cohortes* under his direct command.

order.[213] Ahead lay uncharted territory and there was no road to lead them through it.[214] In Tacitus' account (and only his), the region of hills and forests is called *Saltus Teutoburgiensis* – located perhaps in the vicinity of Kalkriese near modern Osnabrück, though there are several other candidates.[215] Legionaries in the vanguard had to fell trees to clear a way forward and erect simple bridges over rivers too deep to cross by foot. Late in the afternoon, the men established a camp for the night for their comrades arriving at the end of their march.

At dawn the following day, the reveille sounded, the troops awoke, ate, kitted up and broke camp. Varus had yet to receive word from Arminius and his Cherusci auxiliaries, but he was not unduly worried. Unbeknownst to the commander, the Germans had slaughtered the Roman soldiers billeted at the road stations and staging posts embedded in their communities.[216] The warriors of the Germanic alliance then assembled at their designated places along the anticipated route of the Roman soldiers' march and waited, hidden among the trees and undergrowth, ready to strike.[217] That afternoon, exploiting the element of surprise, they launched an enfilade of *frameae* and stones upon the unsuspecting legionaries and non-Germanic auxiliaries.[218] The Germans rushed upon the Romans in their disorganized line. Some swung their long spears in a menacing wide arc like a scythe to cut at legs and ankles, while others used theirs to thrust and stab, forcing their opponents to step back to avoid the deadly blows.[219] Other German warriors wielded single-edged iron swords, which they used to slash and chop their opponents' unprotected arms and legs. Finding themselves attacked, the unarmed civilians sought what cover they could find amidst the unfolding terror. The infamous Battle of Teutoburg Pass – also known as Teutoburg Forest – had begun.

Arminius' rebels now sealed off Varus' escape route, leaving him only one direction of travel: forward and deeper into their trap.[220] The legionaries attempted to defend themselves and stand their ground. Those that could threw their *pila* and formed up with their *gladii* drawn, gripped close to their bodies, and their shields held high so that only their eyes were visible. Their armed resistance became harder when, according to Cassius Dio, a strong wind blew up and it began to rain heavily.[221] Roman troops and their equipment quickly became sodden. The soldiers struggled to hold their *scuta* steady, made heavier by the rain-soaked protective leather covers (*sarcinae*), as the wind buffeted them like kites. The Romans took casualties while inflicting few in return.[222]

Varus ordered a camp to be pitched. Scouts identified a clearing on a rise among the trees.[223] While some troops dug with their entrenching tools, others fought, all of them operating under a constant hail of slingshot and spears.[224] Almost as suddenly as it had started, the German attack ceased. Relieved, the Romans filed in behind their hastily dug entrenchments, which were large enough for all three legions.[225] In his *praetorium* tent, the senior officers met with Varus that evening. Arminius was still absent, presumed delayed by rebels or missing in action.

At dawn on the third day of the German revolt, the Romans evacuated their camp, intent on getting some distance between them and the enemy's forces.[226] The priority was to reach the fort called Aliso as fast as possible. Varus ordered the wagons to be burned and to leave behind any *impedimenta* that could not be destroyed.[227] The unencumbered army emerged out of the forest into open country. But the Germans were waiting for them and attacked anew. They maintained their assault throughout the day. Varus' men reached the end of the open plain. Ahead of them was more dense forest. Their only choice was to enter it. Germanic warriors lay in wait to attack them once within. The legionaries and auxiliary infantry tried to form up, but in the confined spaces between the trees their own cavalry only hampered their manoeuvres.[228] Without supplies and entrenching tools, the men tried to establish a defensible space as best they could. Varus and his officers assessed their desperate situation. L. Eggius, one of the *praefecti castrorum*, proposed surrender, but he was pointedly overruled.[229]

The fourth day began with more heavy rain and a gale-force wind.[230] Now lost deep inside the territory of the Bructeri, the soaked and exhausted Roman troops came under attack once more.[231] In the ensuing struggle Eggius fell.[232] Perhaps on this day too 53-year-old centurion M. Caelius of *Legio* XIIX perished.[233] The contemporary general-turned-historian Paterculus records how Numonius Vala, *legatus* of one of the three legions, attempted to break out with his scouts; he and his men were surrounded by Germans and cut down.[234] He also cites one Caldus Caelius, who, having been taken captive and realizing the terrible fate that awaited him, used the prisoner's iron chain around his neck to strike a fatal blow to his head.[235] Legionary standard bearer Arrius is reported as having grabbed the *aquila* from off its pole to avert the disgrace of it falling into the enemy's hands.[236] Tucking the venerated eagle into his tunic, he managed to hide in a marsh for a while before finally being discovered.[237] One officer, Ceionius, believing he might be shown mercy by his captors, surrendered; his fate is not recorded, but blood offerings and human sacrifice were widely practised among the Germanic peoples.[238] Florus preserves the story of one legionary who, having had his tongue cut out, saw it waved in front of him by the German torturer. 'At last, you viper,' the German is alleged to have said, 'you have ceased to hiss.'[239] The victim's lips were then sewn together.

Seeing all was lost, Varus committed suicide along with many of his deputies.[240] To prevent its desecration, Varus' adjutants attempted to burn their commander's body, but they only partially succeeded. The Germans found the charred corpse, cut off the head and presented it to Arminius.[241] He sent it to Marboduus of the Marcomanni, hoping he would join the cause and declare war on the Romans. However, the king remained true to the treaty he had signed with Tiberius. He sent the head to Augustus.[242] The war spoils were divided among the rebel alliance partners. The prized *aquila* of *Legio* XIX went to the Bructeri, with the other two given to the Chauci and Marsi.[243]

Remarkably, despite the relentless onslaught, there were survivors. Many were enslaved by their Germanic captors, but some had their eyes gouged out or hands cut off.[244] The Germans quickly occupied all of the Roman installations across the country – all but one: Aliso.[245] There the *Praefectus Castrorum* (or *Primuspilus*) L. Caecidius opened the gates to refugees while using archers to prevent the enemy from coming too close to the perimeter wall.[246] Surrounded by German rebels, the people inside, hoping relief would come, were now trapped.[247] The besiegers set up pickets on the military road along the Lippe to the Rhine to stop anyone who might try to escape. Caecidius conceived clever ruses to deceive the Germans and to buy more time for his few armed men and many frightened civilian guests.[248] Concerned that the Germans might take the stacks of wood his soldiers had stocked outside the wall and use it to set fire to his fort, he dispatched his men in different directions; they pretended to search for fuel, while actually retrieving the timber before it could fall into enemy hands.[249] Faced with dwindling supplies, he tried to convince the Germans that the Romans had sufficient food to withstand a blockade:

> They spent an entire night leading prisoners round their store-houses; then, having cut off their hands, they turned them loose. These men persuaded the besieging force to cherish no hope of an early reduction of the Romans by starvation, since they had an abundance of food supplies.[250]

When a storm blew up a few nights later, Caecidius seized the opportunity and led the people out of the camp.[251] Now beyond the perimeter wall, the anxious escapees faced great dangers:

> They succeeded in getting past the foe's first and second outposts, but when they reached the third, they were discovered, for the women and children, by

reason of their fatigue and fear as well as on account of the darkness and cold, kept calling to the warriors to come back.[252]

Instead of pursuing them, however, the Germans stayed and plundered the abandoned fort.[253] Their distraction allowed the fittest Romans to get some distance away. The horn-players with them sounded the signal for a march at *plenus gradus* ('full step'), causing the enemy to think that relief troops were on their way. Through his cunning and courageous actions, Caecidius won 'with the sword' the safe return of the refugees to the winter camps on the Rhine.[254] Coming to their aid was Varus' nephew, L. Nonius Asprenas.[255] His timely intervention also prevented other German tribes, who were wavering in their loyalty, from defecting to Arminius' side.[256] The former suffect consul of 6 CE still commanded *Legiones* I and V *Alaudae* – the only two legions now standing between the Germanic rebels and the Roman homeland.

News of the loss of three legions and the hurried evacuation of Germania reached Tiberius by messenger just five days later.[257] Arriving at Ara Ubiorum, Tiberius quickly ordered guard details to be posted along the bank of the Rhine to intercept any German invaders attempting a crossing.[258] Deputising Germanicus as commander on the frontier, Tiberius rode off to Rome to determine with Augustus what to do next.

When Augustus was informed of the calamity, his reaction was one of shock and dismay. His worst fears had been realized. He is reported to have torn at his clothes and exclaimed: 'Quinctilius Varus, give me back my legions!'[259] Fearing his German bodyguard might turn on him, he dispatched the *Germani Corporis Custodes* 'to certain islands' where they could do him no harm, and required 'those not under arms to leave the city'.[260] His reaction was driven, according to one source:

> not only because of the soldiers who had been lost, but also because of his fear
> for the Germanic and Gallic provinces, and particularly because he expected
> that the enemy would march against Italia and against Rome itself.[261]

He also took the additional precaution of extending the terms of the provincial governors to ensure the allies continued to work with men they knew and remained loyal.[262]

News of the catastrophe – which rapidly acquired the moniker *Clades Variana*, the 'Varian Disaster' – spread far and wide, and terror of barbarians of all kinds gripped the population of Rome. Augustus ordered the *Cohortes Urbanae* to maintain patrols (*excubiae*) throughout the city during the night to reassure the city dwellers and to prevent any unrest.[263] Illustrating how grave the public perceived the situation, even the religious festivals were temporarily suspended.[264] However, Augustus solemnly vowed to hold games to Iupiter Optimus Maximus in return for his help to avert the dire situation facing the *Res Publica*.[265]

When Tiberius reached Rome, he decided not to celebrate his full triumph but, nevertheless, insisted on wearing the embroidered purple garments of the *triumphator*.[266] Tiberius ascended a tribunal erected in the *Forum Romanum* and took his place beside Augustus, sitting between the two consuls, while the members of the Senate stood alongside. Tiberius addressed the assembled crowd with carefully chosen words. He was then escorted to pay the required religious observances at the *Capitolium*. It was a public display of solidarity between Augustus and his most senior field commander, and also a reminder to the people that despite a military setback, the *pax deorum* – the sacred pact between the Roman state and its gods – still prevailed.[267]

The urgent need was to boost the drastically reduced numbers of troops on the Rhine, now Rome's *de facto* border in the north. Having already conscripted men of military age to fight in Illyricum just three years before, there were fewer available this time who could be called up to defend the Fatherland.[268] Nevertheless, he issued instructions for a another *dilectus ingenuorum* to fill the ranks of new volunteer cohorts. His call to action met with passive resistance:

> When no men of military age showed a willingness to be enrolled, he made them draw lots, depriving of his property and disfranchising every fifth man of those still under 35 years of age and every tenth man among those who had passed that age. Finally, as a great many paid no heed to him even then, he put some to death. He chose by lot as many as he could of those who had already completed their term of service and of the freedmen, and after enrolling them sent them in haste with Tiberius into the province of Germania.[269]

Ever the disciplinarian, faced with a particularly recalcitrant equestrian who had chopped off his two young sons' thumbs so that they could not hold a weapon, it is reported that a furious Augustus confiscated the man's estate and sold it, along with the former owner, at auction.[270]

As soon as the fresh units of *Cohortes Voluntariorum* were trained and ready, they would accompany Augustus' most trusted commander and join his grandson.[271] But so shaken by the dire turn of events was Augustus, who was normally fastidious about his appearance, that he did not shave or cut his hair for months.[272] Every year thereafter he would mark the anniversary of the disaster at *Saltus Teutoburgiensis* as a day of sorrow and mourning.[273] Yet, despite the calamity, still loyal to his deputy, Augustus honoured Varus by arranging the burial of his head in the tomb of his family.[274]

10 CE

P. Cornelius P. f. Dolabella   C. Iunius C. f. Silanus
suff.   Ser. Cornelius Cn. f. Lentulus Maluginensis   Q. Iunius C. f. Blaesus

The new year passed, and so too did the immediate crisis. The feared invasion of Germanic warriors into Italy did not occur.[275] Indeed, it seemed there had been no movement at all among the Germans. Cautious but pragmatic as usual, after having dedicated the Temple of Concord in Rome in his and his brother's names, on 16 January Tiberius set off for the front.[276] He did not lead an army into Germania, however, 'but kept quiet, watching to see that the barbarians did not cross; and they, knowing him to be there, did not venture to cross in their turn'.[277] Tiberius would bide his time and use it to formulate a new military strategy.

Several Roman troops were still being held captive by the Germans, who now realized that the men's lives could be traded for cash. Their relatives willingly paid the ransoms and received back their loved ones. Yet in a cruel twist, the survivors of the *Clades Variana* suffered a second humiliation. The Roman authorities intervened and insisted that the freed hostages were never to be permitted to return to Italy.[278] They were considered cursed and might bring bad luck to the *Res Publica* if they were allowed to step on the sacred soil of the Fatherland.

In the spring, Germanicus returned to Rome, but Tiberius remained with the army on the Rhine.[279] He led it in a campaign into Germania, involving an invasion both by land and sea. No details of it survive, except that in the *Caesia Silva*, or 'Caesian Forest', located between Lacus Flevo and the Lippe River, Tiberius ordered his men to construct a barrier (*limes*) of a trench and palisade.[280] It was the first time the Romans erected a continuous defensive border in Germania to demarcate enemy territory from theirs; it has yet to be identified by archaeologists. This and other locations were garrisoned, though it is unclear if these were on the right bank of the Rhine.[281]

With the loss of three legions, others would be redeployed to the Rhine to replace them. At around this time the riparian corridor running along the left bank of the river to the North Sea was stripped from Belgica and redesignated as two smaller jurisdictions. Germania Superior enclosed the territory from the source of the river in the Alps as far south as the territories of the Helvetii and Rauraci, and west to Confluentes (modern Koblenz), with Mogontiacum as its administrative centre. [282] Four legions were stationed in the new military district. *Legiones* XIV *Gemina* and XVI Gallica shared the base at Mogontiacum. *Legio* II *Augusta* occupied Argentorate (Strasbourg) and XIII *Gemina* Vindonissa (Windisch). Neighbouring Germania Inferior bounded the lower section of river, with Ara Ubiroum as its principal city. *Legio* V *Alaudae* billeted with XXI *Rapax* at Vetera along with men of the *Classis Germanica*, while I *Germanica* and XX *Valeria Victrix* shared the based at Ara Ubiroum – the legionary fortresses at Nijmegen-Hunerberg and Novaesium having been abandoned when the army transferred to Oberaden until it too was evacuated.

On his return journey, while passing through *Tres Galliae*, Tiberius quelled a dispute among the Viennenses 'by restraint rather than by punishment'.[283] The lessons learned in Illyricum had proven useful once again. There was also much to do to restore the prosperity and good will of the peoples of the Western Balkans. In the aftermath of bloody insurrection, as in the Iberian Peninsula and along the Rhine, Illyricum was subsequently divided into two smaller provinces.[284] The coastal region (covering all of the Dinaric Alps) became Dalmatia, administered from Salona. Two legions, VII *Macedonica* and XI, were jointly stationed at Tilurium (Gardun near Trilj), though VII may have shared the fortress at Burnum (Kistanje) with *Legio* XI – the evidence is unclear.[285] The inland region up to the Danube River was designated Pannonia and administered from Carnuntum on the Danube or Sirmium. Three legions had their bases in the province: VIII *Augusta* was stationed near Poetovio (Ptuj), VIIII *Hispana* at Siscia (Sisak) and XV *Apollinaris* at Carnuntum.

11 CE

	M. Aemilius Q. *f.* Lepidus	T. Statilius T. *f.* Taurus
suff.	L. Cassius L. *f.* Longinus	

German territory on the right bank of the Rhine continued to be the object of punitive expeditions. Germanicus, now acting as proconsul, accompanied Tiberius in a modest military action. Dio writes that they only 'overran portions of it', adding:

> They did not win any battle, however, since no one came to close quarters with them, nor did they reduce any tribe; for in their fear of falling victims to a fresh disaster they did not advance very far beyond the Rhine.[286]

The troops acclaimed Augustus *imperator* for the twenty-first time and Tiberius for his sixth. On 23 September, they celebrated the birthday of Augustus with a horserace held under the direction of the legionary centurions on German soil. Once the games concluded, they all returned to the Roman side of the river.

Sensitive to maintaining good relations with Rome's provincial peoples, among several edicts Augustus issued this year was one relating to practices of governors seeking to thwart prosecution for maladministration at the end of their terms in office:

> He also issued a proclamation to the subject nations forbidding them to bestow any honours upon a person assigned to govern them either during his term of office or within 60 days after his departure; this was because some governors by arranging beforehand for testimonials and eulogies from their subjects were causing much mischief.[287]

12 CE

	Germanicus Ti. *f.* Caesar	C. Fonteius C. *f.* Capito
suff.		C. Visellius C. *f.* Varro

In the year Germanicus Caesar became consul, Augustus wrote a letter commending his grandson to the Senate and the latter to Tiberius; unable to make himself heard in the Senate House, the letter was not read by Augustus but by Germanicus himself, as was now the usual practice. 'After this,' writes Dio, 'the emperor, making the German War his excuse, asked the senators not to greet him at his home or to feel hurt if he did not continue to join with them in their public banquets.'[288]

Upsetting the normal life of Rome, the Tiber burst its banks and inundated parts of the city, including the *Circus Maximus*, where the annual *Ludi Martiales* were due to take place on 12 May. Instead, the clatter of horses' hooves echoed on the polished marble slabs of the open space of the *Forum Augustum*, where excited spectators watched and cheered from temporary wooden stands erected along the porticos.[289]

One of the undoubted high points of the year was Tiberius' triumph. Originally awarded in 9 CE, it had been postponed by the terrible events at *Saltus Teutoburgiensis*.[290] On 23 October, crowds lined the city's streets to cheer the 53-year-old commander during his celebratory parade (fig. 12).[291] Sharing the glory were Germanicus and the other *legati*, including Velleius Paterculus and his brother, who had been awarded triumphal ornaments.[292] The last time Tiberius had been so honoured was on a cold New Year's Day in 7 BCE as a reward for his earlier victories in Germania.[293] The seemingly interminable series of rainy days broke, and that day the sky was, at last, clear and serene.[294] Tiberius entered the city on a glittering *quadriga*, wearing the embroidered garments of the *triumphator*, his head crowned with laurel and his face daubed with red dye.[295] The spectators were eager to see the man who had 'reduced to complete subjection all Illyricum, lying between Italia, the kingdom of Noricum, Thrace, Macedonia, the Danube River and the Adriatic Sea'.[296] Where the *Via Sacra* turned beside the Temple of Saturn and ascended the hill to the *Capitolium*, Tiberius stepped down from his four-horse chariot and knelt at Augustus' feet in homage and fealty.[297] Special coins, and, perhaps, the cameo called the *Gemma Augusta*, were produced to commemorate the occasion.[298]

One of the star attractions of the triumphal procession was Bato, the captive war chief of the Daesidiates. The man who had defied the Romans for four years, but surrendered with humility, did not face long-term incarceration at the Tullianum jail, or a humiliating death by strangulation which had been the grim end of Vercingetorix at Iulius Caesar's triumph in 46 BCE.[299] After the public celebration of Tiberius' victory, Bato instead retired to Ravenna to live a comfortable, but quiet, life in exile.[300]

After all the sacrifices and prayers of thanks, a feast was offered to the public, its abundance laid out before them on a thousand tables. In addition to this culinary

Figure 12. For breaking the rebellion in Illyricum in the war of 6–9 CE, Tiberius was awarded a full triumph. It was delayed by the 'Varian Disaster' and was finally celebrated on 23 October 12 CE.

largesse, Tiberius gave each freeborn man 30 *sestertii*. On this day too he dedicated, in his and his deceased brother's names, the Temple of Concordia, which had been paid for by the spoils of the Pannonian War.[301] The young men Augustus had adopted would also not be forgotten. Eight and ten years respectively had passed since the deaths of the commanders C. and L. Caesar. They were finally honoured with the dedication of the *Porticus Iulia* that was under reconstruction in the *Forum Romanum* following a fire.[302]

The last decade had been a gruelling test of endurance for Rome's aging commander-in-chief. His choices of deputies had largely proved sound. The majority of his *legati* had performed and prevailed in the face of diverse and difficult challenges. His two surviving relations, Tiberius and Germanicus, had both proved to be natural leaders on the battlefield. Only Varus had truly failed in his mission. Augustus bore responsibility for its consequences and felt them personally. Yet, notwithstanding the terrible loss of life and land, he was still the man the Roman Senate and People trusted to ensure the security of their dominions.

Chapter 7

Toeing the Line
13–14 CE

13 CE

C. Silius P. *f.* A. Caecina Largus   L. Munatius L. *f.* Plancus

'With seeming reluctance,' writes Dio, 'Augustus accepted a fifth ten-year term as head of the *Res Publica*.'[1] The burdens of acting commander-in-chief weighed heavily on his septuagenarian shoulders. More than ever he relied on his deputies and the assistance of senators and equestrians for the day-to-day running of public affairs. Hard of hearing and unable to project his voice far, he now received diplomatic embassies from communities and kings accompanied by three consulars who, 'sitting separately, gave audience to such embassies and answered them, except in matters in which the final decision had of necessity to be rendered by the Senate and Augustus'.[2]

It was clear to many that Tiberius was the uncontested heir apparent come the inevitable time that Augustus died. This year the Roman Senate and People voted him *imperium* equal to Augustus 'in all provinces and armies'.[3] They also renewed his *tribunicia potestas* for another five years, to take effect the following year.[4] For maturity, talent and experience in military matters, as well as international diplomacy and domestic politics, he had no rivals. Augustus' adopted son had been a loyal deputy from the first days he had entered the army as a *tribunus militum* in Hispania Citerior at the age of 16, and had been fighting his wars around the world in a great many of the years since.[5]

During the rotation of governorships, Augustus' adopted grandson, Germanicus Caesar, was assigned *Tres Galliae* and the recently formed Germania Inferior and Germania Superior as *legatus Augusti pro praetore*.[6] In the early months of the year, he arrived with his wife, Agrippina, children and slaves at the official residence at *Colonia* Copia Felix Munatia, the home of Agrippa, Augustus, Tiberius and his father before him. Soon after, he initiated a census of the Gallic population.[7] The *Tabula Siarensis* mentions cryptically that he 'set Gallia in order'.[8] There is a hint in the extant records of incursions by Germans raiding across the Rhine into Roman territory; in another account, Germanicus is reported as having won a great victory over Germans living between the Alps and Pyrenees.[9] More than that is not known. Wherever the military engagement occurred, it was the likely occasion when he garnered his first imperatorial acclamation.[10]

Germanicus had a greater mission, however, than to administer the sixty Gallic nations and ensure the security of the expat Roman citizens living among them. He had been given explicit instructions by the *princeps* 'to finish the remainder of the war in Germania'.[11] Augustus wanted the lands across the Rhine River back under Roman control. The Roman ghosts exiled at the Teutoburg Pass must be avenged.

14 CE

Sex. Pompeius Sex. *f.*   Sex. Appuleius Sex. *f.*

While Germanicus worked on his campaign plan, Tiberius decided to return by sea to Illyricum 'to strengthen by peace the regions he had subjugated in war'.[12] Augustus intended to accompany him as far as Beneventum on the *Via Appia*, whence Tiberius would continue on to Brundisium, but he was detained in Rome to hear disputes in court and had to let his adopted son travel on alone.[13] Having completed his business in the city, the *princeps* headed south to Campania.[14] 'As he sailed by the Gulf of Puteoli,' Suetonius relates:

> it happened that from an Alexandrian ship which had just arrived there, the passengers and crew, clad in white, crowned with garlands, and burning incense, lavished upon him good wishes and the highest praise, saying that it was through him that they lived, through him that they sailed the seas, and through him that they enjoyed their liberty and their fortunes.[15]

In late July, he relaxed on the island of Capreae (Capri).[16] After four days there, he returned to the mainland and reached Neapolis (modern Naples) in time to attend games held in his honour on 1 August.[17] In the meantime, his bowels were causing him intermittent, but nevertheless great, discomfort.[18] Feeling unwell, he went inland to the tranquility of his natural father's old villa at Nola and retired to the same bedroom in which he had slept.[19] He sent instructions for Tiberius to be recalled from his mission.[20] In his private room, Augustus spoke with his friends, exchanged pleasantries and then dismissed them.[21] He died on 19 August, having lived seventy-five years, ten months and twenty-six days; had he lived an additional thirteen days, he would have been able to mark the fortieth anniversary of his victory at Actium.[22] Livia and Tiberius made arrangements to transport the corpse to Rome.[23]

Forty *praetoriani* carried out the body of the deceased commander-in-chief to public view.[24] As had been done for Nero Claudius Drusus Germanicus, M. Agrippa, C. and L. Caesar before him, the bier with the body of Augustus was carried by the leading men of each city as it passed through during the day, and then laid in the basilicas or temples at night.[25] At Bovillae, the *equites* took charge of the corpse and conveyed it after dark into Rome – as Augustus had preferred to travel in life – placing it in the vestibule of the *Palatium*.[26]

On the following day – perhaps 4 September – the Senate met, convened by Tiberius using his authority as tribune.[27] Most of the senators sat in their usual seats, but, out of respect, the consuls sat below, one on the praetors' bench and the other on the tribunes'.[28] Augustus' will was brought from the House of the Vestals and read aloud by Polybius, an imperial freedman, since it was not considered proper for a senator to do so.[29] In addition to distributions to members of his family and friends, there were gifts for the soldiers: Augustus left HS1,000 to each of the men of the Praetorian Cohorts, HS500 to each of the *Vigiles*, and to those in the legions he bequeathed HS300 apiece – a disbursement of HS37 million in total.[30] Several sealed annexes to the will in scroll format were then brought in and read by Tiberius' own son, Drusus Iulius Caesar.[31] The first set out clear instructions for the funeral.[32] The second contained the full text of his lifetime's deeds – the *Res Gestae* – which was to be reproduced and displayed later as cast bronze plaques in front of his mausoleum.[33] The third was a '*breviarium* of the whole empire'.[34] Written 'in his own hand', it:

> contained an account of military matters, of the revenues, and of the public expenditures, the amount of money in the treasuries, and everything else of the sort that had a bearing upon the administration of the empire.[35]

He had left the empire and its army in good health (map 25, table 4).

The state funeral combined ancient tradition with military pomp in the style of a triumph, outdoing even Sulla's for its magnificence.[36] A wax effigy of Augustus dressed in the clothes of a *triumphator* lay on a couch of ivory and gold, adorned with fabrics of purple and gold; it was mounted on the funeral bier over the coffin containing his decaying body.[37] From Augustus' house it was carried down the hill by *designati* (the magistrates designate for 15 CE), followed by images of the great and good – beginning with Romulus – and placed on the *rostra* in front of the Temple of *Divus Iulius*.[38] There the younger Drusus read a prepared eulogy, customarily delivered by a nearest male relative.[39] Then, from the old speakers' *Rostra* at the other end of the *Forum Romanum*, his father spoke to the crowd over the body. Tiberius praised Augustus' virtues, described how in his many public offices he had served the *Res Publica* and talked of the victories which had brought glory to the Roman People.[40]

The bier was then lifted up and carried by the *designati* to the head of the funeral procession.[41] By decree of the Senate, the golden statue of *Victoria*, which Augustus had erected in the *Curia Iulia* after his victories at Actium and

Table 4. Dispositions of the Legions, Summer 14 CE (According to Tacitus).

Province	Units	Legions
Hispania Tarraconensis	3	IV Macedonica, VI *Victrix*, X *Gemina*
Germania Inferior	4	I *Germanica*, V *Alaudae*, XX *Valeria Victrix*, XXI *Rapax*
Germania Superior	4	II *Augusta*, XIII *Gemina*, XIV *Gemina*, XVI *Gallica*
Pannonia	3	VIII *Augusta*, VIIII *Hispana*, XV *Apollinaris*
Dalmatia	2	VII *Macedonica*, XI
Moesia	2	IV *Scythica*, V *Macedonica*
Syria	4	III *Gallica*, VI *Ferrata*, X *Fretensis*, XII *Fulminata*
Aegyptus	2	III *Cyrenaica*, XXII *Deiotariana*
Africa	1	III *Augusta*

Sources: Appendix 3; Hardy (1889), p. 631; Lendering (Livius.org); Ritterling (1925); Syme (1933; 1986); Tac., *Ann.* 4.5.

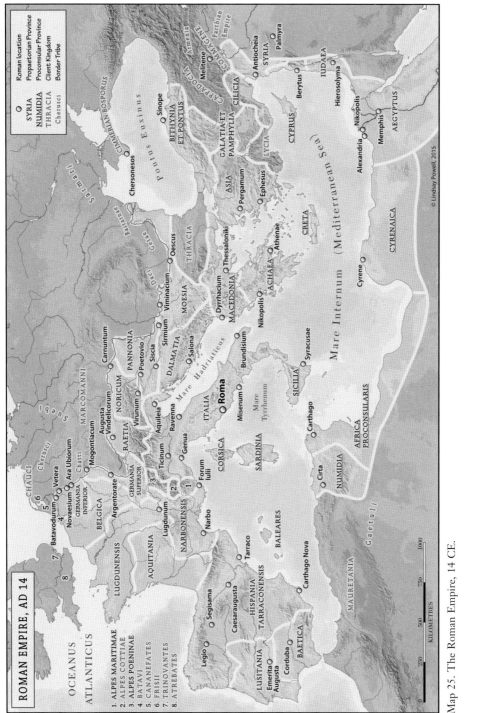

Map 25. The Roman Empire, 14 CE.

Alexandria, was placed first in the line.[42] On their way along the *Via Sacra* to the *Campus Martius*, they were followed by the images of the ancestors, the family mourners, priests, state officials and a golden statue of Augustus mounted on a triumphal four-horse chariot.[43] An *imago* of Pompeius Magnus was also included, as well as figures to represent all the nations he had acquired. The procession passed through the *Porta Triumphalis* – symbolically moving in the reverse direction taken by a commander celebrating his triumph, indicating that he was leaving the world where civil law ruled and out beyond the city's ancient walls where military law applied.[44]

Having arrived at the crematory erected beside the Mausoleum, the bier was lifted onto the awaiting pyre.[45] All the priests of the colleges encircled it, and then the cavalry and infantry of the Praetorian Cohorts performed a final *decursio* for their commander.[46] After their parade, they tossed the military awards they had received from Augustus – their *armillae*, *phalerae*, *torques*, *coronae* – upon the heap.[47] With flaming torches in hand, a group of centurions lit the combustible material and the body was soon engulfed by fire.[48] Livia remained at the site for five days with the leading *equites*, who wore unbelted tunics and went about barefoot; then they gathered up the bones into a casket and placed it inside the tomb Augustus had built for himself and his family.[49]

This was a delicate, potentially high-risk, moment in the long history of Rome. As a precaution – just as his forebear had done before him – Tiberius surrounded himself with 'a guard of soldiers' against any attempt on his life.[50] Some in the Senate urged him to assume the position of first man, but he refused the title of *princeps*.[51] In front of Augustus' golden statue of Victory in the *Curia*, several senators implored Tiberius to rule.[52] He was an autocrat in all but name, having already the same political and military powers as the late Augustus, vested in him by successive decrees of the Senate and sanctioned by the People's assemblies – and to acquire them he had been promoted by Augustus.[53] With reluctance, Tiberius gradually yielded to the entreaties of the Conscript Fathers – but two years would pass before he felt his position as the first citizen of the *Res Publica* was secure.[54]

Tiberius sent news of Augustus' death to the *legati Augusti*, legionary commanders, auxiliary prefects and the allies; having the *imperium proconsulare maius*, he was still in charge of the Provinces of Caesar and the armed forces there. Any potential threat to his position from Agrippa evaporated with his death by the tribune appointed to guard over him; despite the man's claims, Tiberius denied issuing the order for his execution.[55] A man called Clemens, who was the slave of the late Postumus, gathered together a mob intent on avenging his master's death, but he was intercepted and liquidated.[56] L. Scribonius Libo, one of the *nobiles*, was alleged to have secretly hatched a plot to lead a revolution, but it amounted to nothing.[57] The other potential challenger was Tiberius' adopted son, Germanicus Caesar, who was still in *Tres Galliae*. A deputation was sent to him in *Tres Galliae* to formally deliver the news of Augustus passing, to convey its condolences and assure his fidelity.[58]

Germanicus' loyalty was never in doubt. It was tested soon after Augustus' death. While the *Legiones* II *Augusta*, XIII *Gemina*, XIV *Gemina* and XVI *Gallica* of Germania Superior under C. Silius remained steadfastly true to their military oath, the troops at the army bases in Germania Inferior under A. Caecina Severus – the suffect consul of 1 BCE and former *legatus Augusti* of Moesia – protested and mutinied[59] (see Order of Battle 5). Accompanied by his adjutants, Germanicus immediately set off to deal with the insubordination of *Legiones* I, V *Alaudae*, XX *Valeria Victrix* and XXI *Rapax*, who were in their summer camps (*in aestivis*).[60] Several centurions had been assaulted and their bodies cast into the Rhine River by the mob for having run what amounted to protection rackets – assigning less arduous duties to those who had paid bribes, while those who objected felt the vine staff.[61] One named Septimius had pleaded with Caecina for his life but, fearful of repercussions if he did not surrender the man, the legate refused: the centurion was summarily executed by his captors. The senior officers, including the *praefectus castrorum*, meanwhile, had been arrested and confined. There was even talk of a march on Ara Ubiorum to sack it and then raid into Belgica.[62]

Germanicus' arrival at the joint camp of *Legiones* I and XX was met with a frosty welcome.[63] Almost ignored as he entered the camp, he climbed up onto the tribunal at the centre of the enclosed space and called the men to order. They milled around in disarray. Germanicus insisted that the legionaries form up in their centuries and cohorts. The men refused, protesting their rough treatment at the hands of cruel centurions, while others complained they were still obligated

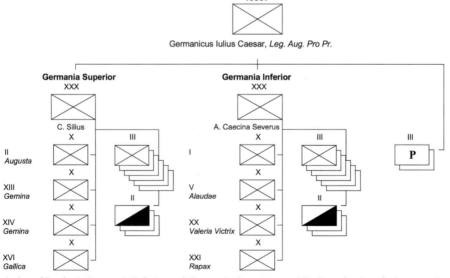

Order of Battle 5. Germania Inferior and Germania Superior, 14 CE. Several units of ethnic *auxilia* are recorded as having served under Germanicus Caesar, though it is unclear into which provincial command they reported in AD 14: *Cohors Batavorum*, *Cohors Gallorum*, *Cohors Raetorum*, *Cohors Vindelicorum* and probably *Cohors Sugambrorum* and *Cohors Ubiorium*. There were other *alae*, including Chauci and possibly Cananefates.

to serve even though they had completed their contractual terms of service, and all were angry at the poor rates of pay.[64] Some were in a wretched state, with teeth missing and joints worn out by years of toil. The reality was that most had joined the legions, not out of love of their country or fervour to live a military life, but because it was a stable job with an income, there were prospects of a share of booty and a bonus at the end of their career. For years these men felt they had been abused, and now was the time for action.

Eventually the men lined up. Germanicus appealed to their better natures, but when one soldier called upon him to be the successor of Augustus in place of Tiberius, the young commander leapt down from the tribunal and firmly rejected the plea.[65] He had no wish to be *princeps*, he said, and every intention of staying loyal to his adoptive father. Returning to the subject of the men's grievances, he offered honourable discharges for those who had served twenty years, releases with conditions for those with sixteen years, and settlement of outstanding pay and bonuses for all.[66] The mutinous troops of V and XXI rejected the deal out-right. Fomenting the discord among the ordinary soldiers of these two units was 'a rabble of city slaves' who had been freed and conscripted into the *Cohortes Voluntariorum*.[67] Germanicus eventually acceded to their demands for better compensation – using money from his own and officers' savings – and agreed to improved terms and discharges for those eligible veterans.[68] Satisfied with their new deal, the troops assembled and marched to their winter camps (*in hiberna*) carrying the pay chests, with a humiliated Caecina riding at the head of his column.[69]

On the Danube, the legions were in a state of mutiny too.[70] Receiving the news of Tiberius' succession, the *Legatus Augusti Pro Praetore* Iunius Blaesus had allowed discipline to slip.[71] One *caligatus* named Percennius incited his peers to strike over terms of military service. Blaesus' appeals for order contained the situation only when he agreed to consider their grievances and sent his son, a *tribunus militum*, to Rome with the mutineers' demands.[72] A particular focus of the soldiers' rage was the brutal way *Praefectus Castrorum* Aufidienus Rufus treated the troops; he was a stern disciplinarian who had risen through the ranks.[73] The troops constructing roads and bridges in Nauportus beat up the senior officer and ridiculed him.[74] When those soldiers returned to camp, they were arrested, flogged and imprisoned, while inciting the others to violence.[75] Outnumbered, the officers and centurions lost control of the situation. The mutinying troops freed the prisoners, ejected the tribunes and the camp prefect and plundered the baggage of the fugitives. They also killed Lucilius, a centurion the soldiers nick-named *Cedo Alteram* ('Bring Another') because, when he had smashed one vine-staff (*vitis*) on a man's back, he would shout out his demand for a replacement.[76] At the climax of the troubles, two legions, VIII and XV, drew swords against each other, the former demanding the death of a centurion nicknamed Sirpicus, while the men of the other defended him.[77] The situation was only calmed when the soldiers of *Legio* VIIII intervened.

Tiberius ordered his son to break the mutiny.[78] When Drusus reached the camp, the troops initially disrespected his rank, but he managed to get their attention.[79] He addressed them, talked of their pay and conditions, and tried to appeal to their sense of patriotism, but the men reacted violently and he had to withdraw for his own safety.[80] It was a lunar eclipse, which occurred at the same time, that allegedly prevented further conflict.[81] Interpreting it as a bad omen caused by their own insubordination, sanity gradually returned and the mutiny ended.[82] The instigators were identified, taken into custody and executed by centurions and soldiers of the *Cohortes Praetoriae* who had accompanied Drusus to the frontier.[83]

In Germania Inferior, the situation that seemed to have been contained now spiralled out of control. A deputation led by Munatius Plancus had arrived in Ara Ubiorum, where Germanicus had retired for the night.[84] A mob of angry soldiers surrounded the visitors, believing them to have come to revoke their agreement, then stormed the building in which Germanicus slept, and demanded to be given the legionary eagle standard. In one account, they seized his wife Agrippina and his young son Caius.[85] Having heard the commander plead for their release, the men let his wife go, but insisted on keeping the boy as a hostage. Withdrawing with their hostage, the men encountered the visitors from Rome. To avoid being assaulted, Plancus fled to the camp of *Legio* I and hid in the strong room of the base's *principia*.[86] He would have been killed had not the legion's *aquilfer* Calpurnius intervened to stop them.

Next day, Germanicus addressed the soldiers again from the tribunal and berated the troops, in particular of *Legio* XX who he said had disgraced themselves with their behaviour.[87] Plancus and his deputation were allowed to leave under escort of a cohort of auxiliaries rather than the customary legionary *ala* – since the citizen riders had sided with the mutineers. Agrippina was to follow with her child and relocate for their safety to Augusta Treverorum. As retold by Tacitus, when the men watched Germanicus tearfully embrace his family and bid them farewell, the men responded. The emotional scene caused many to question how they had reached this low point.[88] Germanicus continued with his speech. By the end of it he had persuaded the men to suspend their action. The ring-leaders of the mutiny in *Legio* I were quickly identified and brought before the legionary legate. In a makeshift court under martial law, when each man was charged a military tribune turned and asked the soldiers if he was guilty. If affirmed, the defendant was thrown off the tribunal and stabbed to death by the men standing ready below.[89]

Among *Legiones* V and XXI, the justice meted out was particularly brutal. Germanicus agreed a plan with Caecina to arrest the men behind the mutiny.[90] Caecina discreetly issued orders by letter to his officers that the loyal men were to turn on the others who had led the mutiny. But the plan backfired. The tribunes moved ahead without Caecina being present and gave the signal for the assassinations to begin. Several fought back and killed their attackers, so that the blood of the innocent and guilty alike was spilled. When Germanicus finally arrived at the camp, he was mortified by the scene of slaughter that he found.[91]

With order re-established, Germanicus needed a target to restore – and prove – the men's sense of duty. In the late summer, Germanicus took his men across the Rhine in a punitive raid. Accompanied by Caecina Severus, he led a force of 12,000 men drawn from *Legiones* I, V, XX and XXI, along with twenty-six cohorts of auxiliaries and eight *cohortes equitata*.[92] Novellius Torquatus Atticus was military tribune of the *vexillatio* comprising these four legions.[93] Cutting their way through the *Caesia Silva*, they reached the fortified entrenchment constructed by Tiberius four years before and set up camp.[94] From there they sacked villages of the Marsi. Germanicus was in no mood to take prisoners. To stir up the Roman fighting spirit, German blood would be spilled. His soldiers slaughtered any men, women and children they found without mercy.[95] Back in their bases on the Rhine, the re-energised troops, eager for another chance at glory, spent the winter preparing for a new war against the Germanic peoples the following year.[96]

Germanicus returned to Rome to a hero's welcome. Despite being ordered to remain in barracks, the *praetoriani* still turned out in force to greet him.[97] He presented the soldiers' demands to his adoptive father. Tiberius agreed to the increase in pay to the armies of Germania and Pannonia, but insisted on keeping the extended service term at twenty years.[98] As Augustus had done decades before, Tiberius Caesar needed to establish his legitimacy by asserting unequivocally that he was the commander-in-chief.

Chapter 8

Assessment

In the beginning there was war. To the Romans it was the prerequisite for peace. Augustus was clear about what *pax* meant to him: 'peace, secured by victory'.[1] The Latin word *pax* derives from the verb *pacere*, meaning 'to pacify' or 'to subdue'. After a struggle, one party must stand tall, the other must submit. The derivative *pactio* means a bargain or agreement or contract. The defeated must keep their word. Winning wars required mastery of many skills. To achieve victory, and so accomplish a sustainable peace, Augustus had to be effective both as a military leader and as a manager of war.

Augustus as Military Leader

Modern historians have struggled to describe the kind of leader Imp. Caesar *Divi filius* Augustus was. They have variously called him an 'autocrat', 'between citizen and king', a 'monarch', a 'military dictator', 'Rome's first emperor', even a 'warlord', and his form of rule a 'military regime' or a 'monarchy'.[2] None of these titles adequately encompasses his unique leadership position in Roman society and arguably even obscures it because each comes with its own baggage acquired from use over the subsequent centuries. Augustus was not an elected *magistratus* and he did not hold the official title of the 'proconsul of the *imperium* of the Roman People'.[3] Augustus referred to himself as *imperator*, the explicitly military title meaning 'commander' – adopting it as his *praenomen* as early as 38 BCE – and also as *princeps*, a reference to his primary position in the Senate and Roman society.[4] Contemporaries often called him a *dux*, 'leader'.[5] His rise to power was based on victories over his opponents and his enduring rule depended on command of the army. The Roman Commonwealth had always been a compromise between a democracy and a paramilitary regime, its elected magistrates holding term-limited *imperium*, its consuls empowered to lead its citizen militia to battle, its electorate even willing to allow a temporarily appointed *dictator* to govern the nation during an existential crisis. Thus, 'commander-in-chief' or 'single dominant military leader' would seem to come closest to accurately describing Augustus' place in Roman society.[6]

There was no military academy for officers in Rome. The Romans believed that leadership could not be taught, but could only be learned. Augustus, like all his peers, would have learned the arts of generalship and war from reading, observing and, above all, by doing it. Ancient historians certainly recognized good military leadership when they saw it. The Greek and Roman works of history are filled with exemplars, from Leonidas of Sparta to Claudius Marcellus.[7] These men displayed courage or manliness (*virtus*) in abundance. *Virtus* was 'nearly the most important thing in every state, but especially in Rome', writes Polybius, observing the rise of the Romans as a military power in the Mediterranean in the second-century BCE and attempting to explain it to a Greek audience.[8] There were digests – didactic compilations – in which their authors quoted examples of generalship and military strategy from history; and there were handbooks on military science, drill and tactical aspects of combat such as fighting formations, deceptions and siege warfare.[9] Augustus could have also studied the memoirs of great Roman commanders, such as Sulla and Marius, or their and others' war reports.[10]

Most remarkably, in his youth Augustus had access to arguably the ancient world's greatest practitioner of military science, C. Iulius Caesar. The older commander had seen potential in his great nephew and encouraged him as he grew up to take an active role in the army. We can only guess at the kinds of conversations and exchanges these two men had, and how much his young relative learned from the genius of military leadership, strategy and tactics. After Caesar's death, the teenage heir did not lack for advisors. He had access to men who had known Caesar well, such as L. Cornelius Balbus, C. Oppius and for a time the dictator's erstwhile right-hand man, M. Antonius. Later, among his own peers, Augustus could draw on the abundant talents of his friends M. Agrippa and Statilius Taurus. But Augustus was no 'armchair general'. To this learned knowledge he could add personal experience and the judgment that it afforded. He had already demonstrated years after 44 BCE the innate leadership attributes of character, intellect and presence in different measures.[11] Expressed in modern terms, he showed warrior ethos, confidence, military bearing, resilience, mental agility and other qualities marking him out as an effective leader of *some* merit, despite his political enemies' attempts to belittle his talents. He even had real scars to prove he had been in battle. Augustus was, in every way, a military leader. People followed him. He never gave up. Yet he was also aware he had shortcomings.

Then as now, being a military leader did not mean always having to lead troops on the front line. Leadership is a broader concept. In the absence of a definition of leadership in the military and its attributes from an ancient writer, we must look to a modern authority. The Army of the United States defines leadership as 'influencing people by providing purpose, direction, and motivation, while operating to accomplish the mission and improve the organization'.[12] As the leader, Augustus could only succeed through the appeal of his vision and by inspiring and motivating those around him that the 'whats' and 'whys' were important enough to commit to.

The sources of Augustus' influence were emotional, legal and religious. He had inherited from Iulius Caesar a powerful name. 'Caesar' evoked strong emotions: admiration and loyalty in some, fear and loathing in others. It was further enhanced after the dictator's deification by the bond he styled as *Divi filius*, which he included in his amended name.[13] (It was hard to argue with the 'son of god'.) Through his adoption into *gens Iulia*, he could trace his ancestry back through time along a direct line to Iulus (Ascanius), Aeneas and to Venus.[14] Over the 40s and 30s BCE, through his own deeds – by successfully confronting the assassins, then overcoming those who stood against the Triumvirate and ultimately his rivals in it too – he built up immense *auctoritas*. It had connotations of *auctor*, a leader able to wield influence though the qualities of his intellect or military force.[15] The agreement with the Senate in 28 and 27 BCE granted him his legal military power – renewed and extended in 23 BCE as *imperium proconsulare maius* – to command in his province. After 19 BCE, the *summum imperium auspiciumque* formally established him as the supreme commander over all others of nominally equal rank anywhere. The honorary title *Augustus*, meaning 'revered one' and implying he was worthy of veneration, only added to his already substantial aura.

Even before he received his title Augustus, Imp. Caesar cleverly – it might be said cunningly – tapped into the Romans' profound reverence for tradition (*mos maiorum*) and piety (*pietas*) to sanctify the beginning and ending of his wars. Supplementing the long-honoured rites, he reintroduced other long-abandoned rituals. Thus, to validate his action against Antonius and Kleopatra, in 31 BCE he reinstated the ancient ceremony undertaken by a fetial priest, who struck an iron-tipped spear in the ground of the Temple of Bellona while intoning the declaration of war. Having defeated them, in 29 BCE, he restored the *augurium salutis*, a ceremony which publicly affirmed that the nation was no longer at war or preparing for one. The last time it had been done was in 63 BCE – co-incidentally the year of Augustus' birth. Also in 29 BCE, he closed the doors of the Temple of Ianus Quirinus. They had last been shut in 235 BCE to celebrate the end of the First Punic War. Augustus would often look to the past to find a solution to a modern problem.

Augustus provided purpose and long-range direction. After the murder of Iulius Caesar in 44 BCE, his 19-year-old legal heir sought justice for the crime. He was explicit about that goal very early in his quest and applied himself with a stubborn singularity of mind to achieving it. To invoke a divine sponsor for his enterprise, he created an avatar of the Roman god of war, calling him *Marti Ultori*, 'Mars the Avenger'. Not having all the military resources to complete the task alone, Imp. Caesar joined with M. Antonius and Aemilius Lepidus in a Commission to Restore the Commonwealth from the men who they claimed had hijacked it and rained destruction upon it. Soon after the assassins had been killed at Philippi in 42 BCE, frictions emerged between the members of the Triumvirate, which led inevitably to civil war.[16] Caesar unceremoniously relieved Lepidus of his command. Antonius, despite his strange behaviour, was still popular with large segments of the Roman People and Senate. In 31 BCE, under the guise of a foreign war, Imp. Caesar set as his new goal to eliminate the Egyptian queen, the patron funding her Roman consort. He portrayed her as a threat to the integrity of the *imperium* of the Roman People, her lover as a victim of her guile. When Antonius did not leave her, he became a legitimate target. Caesar required all Italy to swear an oath to him before he went to war. Victory for him at this phase in his career was to remove Antonius and Kleopatra permanently.[17] At Actium on 2 September, his opponent fled and a year later he was dead by his own hand – and the queen too.

Imp. Caesar was now the undisputed leader of the *Res Publica*, with an immense army under his command to impose his will.[18] Remarkably, he did not march on Rome and impose a junta. It is not clear what he had envisaged beyond that point. In his *Res Gestae*, the victor states simply, 'when I had extinguished the flames of the Civil War, after receiving by universal consent the absolute control of affairs, I transferred the Commonwealth from my own control to the will of the Senate and the Roman People'.[19] He had avenged his adoptive father and he restored the *Res Publica* to its rightful masters. But was that really all he ever intended to do?

Initially, it seems, he was not interested in ruling over the entire Roman Empire. Such an ambition would not have been consistent with his professed commitment to a *Res Publica restituta*. Through the years 28 and 27 BCE, Imp. Caesar worked with the Senate to decide who controlled which regions of the Roman world and who commanded the army units within them. It was a political negotiation. His carefully stage-managed resignation in 27 BCE permitted an agreement – a pact – to be reached between the two parties. It granted him, now hailed as Augustus, for a period of ten years a *provincia* (meaning both territory and a duty).[20] The presence of the army was required there because the province covered regions not yet pacified, or the nations adjacent to them had not yet subjugated, or the lands themselves were deemed difficult to cultivate, or a combination of these problems. Conveniently, there was a precedent. In the *Lex Gabinia* of 67 BCE, the Senate had granted Pompeius Magnus a *provincia* for three years to defeat the pirates operating at will in the eastern Mediterranean Sea. This extended term saved him the need to return to the Senate each year to renew his power.[21] It was the vast size of Augustus' province, combined with the decade-long duration of his *imperium*, that made his situation so novel and unprecedented.

In his *provincia* (comprising Hispania Citerior, Aquitania, Gallia Comata, Belgica, Narbonensis, Coele-Syria, Syria, Cilicia, Cyprus and newly acquired Aegyptus), Augustus had free rein to conduct affairs as he saw fit. It was a military matter. This arrangement also presented him with an opportunity. So long as there remained unsubdued peoples and unpacified regions, a military guard would be required – and a leader to command it. Waging war would become a central policy tool to ensure Augustus *remained* Rome's commander-in-chief. Thus in his account of his deeds Augustus writes, 'wars, both civil and foreign, I undertook throughout the world, on sea and land'.[22] He knew well that every victory brought glory (*gloria*) and honour (*decus*) to the Roman People, which augmented his personal prestige (*auctoritas*) and worthiness (*dignitas*) in Roman society – just as had been the case with all successful commanders in the heyday of the *Res Publica*, from Cornelius Scipio Africanus to Iulius Caesar.

The question inevitably arises as to whether Augustus, as leader, had an explicit grand strategy. The term is defined as an overarching collection of policies, plans and directives that encapsulate the state's conscious effort to mobilize the diplomatic, economic, military and political resources to advance and achieve its national interest.[23] It is difficult to answer definitively because of the opaqueness of the decision-making process at the time and the type and quality of the records still available to us today. Writing two centuries after Augustus' death, even Dio himself recognized the challenge of understanding how decisions were made:

> Formerly, as we know, all matters were reported to the Senate and to the People, even if they happened at a distance; hence all learned of them and many recorded them, and consequently the truth regarding them, no matter to what extent fear or favour, friendship or enmity, coloured the reports of certain writers, was always to a certain extent to be found in the works of the other writers who wrote of the same events and in the public records. But after this time most things that happened began to be kept secret and concealed, and even though some things are perchance made public, they are distrusted just because they can not be verified; for it is suspected that everything is said and done with reference to the wishes of the men in power at the time and of their associates. As a result, much that never occurs is noised abroad, and much that happens beyond a doubt is unknown, and in the case of nearly every event a version gains currency that is different from the way it really happened. Furthermore, the very magnitude of the empire and the multitude of things that occur render accuracy in regard to them most difficult.[24]

However, there is a 'paper trail' of inscriptions, coins, letters, legal sources and Augustus' own *Res Gestae* which expresses, justifies or celebrates imperial actions, even if the component parts were produced many years after the original policy decisions were taken; to which can be added archaeological evidence, which can indicate troop movements, type of units deployed and duration of stay.[25] Indeed these underpin the research of the preceding chapters. From such sources the diplomatic and military policies can, within limits, be inferred, implied or extrapolated.

Modern scholars have long debated whether the Romans at any time had a long-term military strategy. They certainly understood the concept of 'a plan of the whole war'.[26] Based on their actions prior to the first-century BCE, however, it seems unlikely that they had one for building a transcontinental empire. The Roman People largely acquired their overseas dominions by accident and opportunism rather than through any grand design for world conquest. Roman citizens engaged in foreign wars primarily to defend their territorial acquisitions – the first war with Mithridates being something of an aberration.[27] Rarely too did the legions fight to prevent an existential strategic threat – the three wars against Carthage being the notable exceptions.[28] Yet fighting was in the Romans' blood, a trait of their national character. Almost every year from 219–70 BCE the men of the Commonwealth marched off to war in their centuries and maniples, led by their praetors or consuls citing some justification or other for doing so.[29] In the century Augustus grew up in, however, it was individuals with private armies seeking glory, prestige and booty for *themselves* – men such as Licinius Crassus, Pompeius Magnus and Iulius Caesar – who promoted the agenda for war.[30]

The opening line of the monumental inscription, written by Augustus in his seventy-sixth year of life and displayed outside his mausoleum, declares 'the deeds of *Divus Augustus*, by which he placed the whole world under the sovereignty of the Roman People'.[31] This statement refers to the world subject to Roman rule in 14 CE, the product of a restless ambition tempered by a lifetime's lessons in the pragmatics of diplomacy and war. Harder to gauge is how Augustus saw the world after his victories at Actium and Alexandria, and how this informed his military strategy for the coming decades. It has long been hotly debated by modern historians.[32] Several have argued that the frontiers of the Roman Empire evolved without any planning and that there was no strategic thinking behind where they lay.[33] Some have interpreted the evidence to understand his approach either as evolving over time and not shaped by a unifying global strategic vision, or as a series of responses regulated by cautious pragmatism to events as they arose.[34] These interpretations present Augustus as a more passive actor than the evidence from his deeds suggests he actually was. Augustus was most definitely not a pacifist.[35]

In his ground-breaking – but controversial – study, Edward Luttwak, a writer on strategic defence, attempted to synthesize military actions under Augustus into a cogent theory.[36] He portrayed Augustus as a vigorous, proactive commander-in-chief unleashing wars of conquest in pursuit of establishing a defensible, 'scientific' frontier supported by an economy of force.[37] Annexing the viable states of allies was not part of Augustus' grand design; it was unnecessary because, in awe of their Roman patron, these allies were kept in virtual subjection.[38] The army formed a protective circle around Rome, but was concentrated in multi-legion groups, uncommitted to the defence of any particular region, that could be assembled *en masse* to conduct campaigns, then drawn down and redeployed elsewhere. The benefit of such a flexible, mobile approach, Luttwak argued, is that troops could be moved without risking the security of the whole empire.[39] The model goes a long way to explaining Augustus' grand design, though it is still problematic.

The issue of borders is complex and discussion in the literature often centres around whether they were marked, fixed and defended frontiers where the army patrolled and collected customs duties.[40] The eminent Sir Ronald Syme saw Augustus' interest in conquering Germania as driven by the need to set a northern frontier to the empire along the Elbe and Danube Rivers, a hypothesis soundly disputed by Colin Wells, who had reviewed the available archaeological evidence.[41] One historian has pointed out that the Roman Empire did not have borders in the modern sense but, in fact, existed within fuzzy intermediate 'frontier zones' that were neither fixed nor uniform.[42] Yet Augustus did perceive frontiers of some kind. In 14 CE he wrote, 'I extended the boundaries (*finitima*) of all the provinces, which were bordered (*fines*) by races not yet subject to our *imperium*.'[43] If there is a single word that encapsulates that goal that shaped his policy and to which he devoted resources it is *enlargement*.[44] As the poet Vergil's Jupiter succinctly instructed Aeneas, Romans were not to be limited by the constraint of a border, but to wield power without end – *imperium sine fine*. Augustus was able to claim a direct connection with Aeneas.[45] From the historical survey in the preceding chapters, it is clear that military actions were purposely launched by Augustus to push out the frontiers of his *provincia* – in Hispania Citerior,

Arabia, the Alps and Germania – and where he could not, he enforced the existing ones, such as when his treaty partner Parthia attempted to bring Armenia into its sphere of influence.[46] At the same time his *legati* were empowered – often working in tandem with allies and other *legati* – to deal with brigandage, foreign invasion and revolt in accordance with their duty of ensuring provincial *security*. All of these military actions aligned with Augustus' ongoing political aim. Within the bounds of each of the ten-year periods (*decennia*) that his *imperium* was legally in force, he and his subordinates were engaged in both defensive and offensive operations. These might be completed before the ten-year term ended, or if not – as, in fact, happened – the case would be made to the Senate to renew his *imperium* to pursue them in the next.[47]

In his first *decennium* of holding basic military power (27–19 BCE), Augustus' actions indicate a strategy aimed at removing immediate threats on the borders in the West and the East (table 5). There was interest in taking Britannia, but Augustus may have considered the island already part of the empire through treaties and friendship with British kings who had come to Rome in person and sought supplication from him. Augustus chose as his first military mission to finish the subjugation of the Iberian Peninsula, a project begun some 200 years before. He may have considered it an easy victory if overwhelming force was brought to bear. He laid out a plan to win, assembled a large army, chose the field commanders and coordinated manoeuvres with them. After leading the first thrust himself – cut short by sickness – a series of subsequent campaigns concluded by M. Agrippa finally broke the resistance of the two last Ibero-Celtic nations of Astures and Cantabri. In the East, Augustus personally ordered *praefectus Aegypti* Aelius Gallus to invade Arabia Felix in an attempt to annex it for its access to the lucrative trade routes with the Middle East and India. It failed spectacularly, though Augustus still saw value in claiming credit for it. Augustus' major policy success of this period was to receive back from Parthia the *signa* lost by Crassus at Carrhae, achieving through diplomacy what M. Antonius had failed twice to do with armed force. Of the fifteen documented conflicts during this period, four were to quell revolts in conquered territories and four were responses to invasions into Roman-occupied space by foreign tribes. His *legati* led actions to address specific threats in Africa, the Alps and Aquitania. On account of victories in the field, Augustus could demonstrate he was making progress in pacifying his *provincia* – and as proof returned to the Senate the management of Cyprus and Gallia Narbonnensis – but more time was needed to complete the project and he gained restless Illyricum. By 19 BCE, he had consolidated his military and political primacy over the consuls and all other magistrates in the *Res Publica*.

The following year, the Senate renewed his *imperium*. The actions of the first half of his second *decennium* (18–14 BCE) indicate a continued commitment to conquest beyond the border of his province. If gaining more land in North Africa was of little value and the eastern border was claimed by Parthia, the open terrain on the right bank of the Rhine River now represented the best option for expansion. The trigger for action may have been the humiliation of Lollius in

Table 5. Wars of Augustus, 31 BCE–14 CE.

Years	Region	Commander	Enemy	Cause
31 BCE	Achaea (Actium)	Agrippa	Romans, Egyptians	Civil War
30	Egypt (Alexandria)	Imp. Caesar	Romans, Egyptians	Civil War
30	Gallia Comata	Carrinas	Morini, Suebi	Revolt, bandit raid
30–29	Macedonia, Thracia	Licinius Crassus, *Sitas, Rolis*	Bastarnae	Migrant invasion
29	Belgica	Nonius Gallus	Treveri	Revolt
29	Hispania Citerior	Statilius Taurus	Astures, Cantabri	Conquest
28	Egypt	Cornelius Gallus	Meroites	Bandit raid
27	Gallia Comata	Messalla Corvinus	Aquitani	Revolt
26–25	Hispania Citerior	Augustus Antistius Vetus	Astures, Cantabri	Conquest
25	Alps	Terrentius Varro	Salassi	Conquest
25	Gallia Comata	Vinicius	Suebi?	Bandit raid
24	Hispania Citerior	Aelius Lamia *or* Paullus Lepidus	Astures, Cantabri	Conquest
24	Arabia Felix	Aelius Gallus	Arabs	Conquest
24–25	Egypt, Ethiopia	Petronius	Nubians	Bandit raid
23?	Macedonia	Primus	Odrysae	Conquest
23	Hispania Citerior	Furnius	Astures, Cantabri	Revolt
23	Egypt, Ethiopia	Petronius	Nubii	Punitive strike
20	Africa	Cornelius Balbus	Garamantes	Bandit raid
19	Macedonia, Thracia	Lollius, *Roimetalkes*	Bessi	Bandit raid
19	Gallia Comata	Agrippa	Galli	Revolt
19	Germania	Agrippa	Suebi	Migrant invasion
19	Hispania Citerior	Agrippa	Astures, Cantabri	Revolt
17	Gallia Comata	Lollius	Sugambri, Suebi, Tencteri, Usipetes	Bandit raid
16	Alps	Silius Nerva	Camunni, Vennii	Revolt
16	Illyricum	Silius Nerva	Norici	Bandit raid
16	Macedonia	?	Dentheleti, Scordisci	Bandit raid
16	Thracia	Caninius Gallus, *Roimetalkes*	Sarmati	Migrant invasion
15	Raetia	Nero Claudius Drusus	Carni, Raeti	Conquest
15	Vindelicia, Noricum	Nero Claudius Drusus, Ti. Caesar	Vindelici, Norici	Conquest
15	Africa	Sulpicius Quirinius	Garamantes, Marmaridae, Nasamones	Bandit raid
14	Cimmerian Bosporus	Agrippa, *Polemon, Herodes*	Bosporani	Usurpation, Counter-insurgency
14–13	Illyricum	Vinicius, Agrippa	Breuci, Dalmati	Revolt
13–11	Thracia	Calpurnius Piso	Bessi	Revolt
13–11	Macedonia	Calpurnius Piso	Sialetae	Revolt
12–11	Illyricum	Ti. Caesar	Breuci, Dalmati	Revolt

Table 5. (*continued*)

Years	Region	Commander	Enemy	Cause
12–9	Germania	Nero Claudius Drusus	Sugambri, Chauci, Usipetes, Cherusci, Bructeri, Chatti, Suebi	Conquest
10	Thracia	Lentulus Augur	Daci, Sarmati	Bandit raid
8–7	Germania	Ti. Caesar	Sugambri, Bructeri	Conquest
5	Cilicia	Sulpicius Quirinius	Homonadeis	Revolt
4	Iudaea	Quinctilius Varus, *Archelaos*	Galileans, Idumaeans, Pereans	Revolt
2 BCE	Illyricum	Domitius Ahenobarbus	Hermunduri	Migrant invasion
1 CE	Africa	?	Marmaridae	Bandit raid
2–3	Armenia	C. Caesar, Sulpicius Quirinius	Armenians	Revolt
4–5	Germania	Ti. Caesar	Cananefactes, Cherusci, Attuari, Bructeri, Chauci, Langobardi, Semnones	Revolt
6	Africa	Cossus Lentulus, *Iuba II*	Isauri, Gaetuli	Bandit raid
6	Iudaea	Sulpicius Quirinius	Gaulanites	Revolt
6	Bohaemium	Ti. Caesar	Marcomanni	Conquest
6–9	Illyricum	Ti. Caesar, *Roimetalkes*	Breuci, Daesidiates	Revolt
9	Germania	Quinctilius Varus	Cherusci, Angrivarii, Bructeri, Marsi	Revolt
10	Germania	Ti. Caesar	Usipetes?	Punitive strike
11	Germania	Ti. Caesar	Usipetes? Marsi?	Punitive strike
13	Gallia Beligica? Alps?	Germanicus Caesar	Unidentified Germans	Bandit raid
14	Germania	Germanicus Caesar	Marsi	Punitive strike

Sources: Dio; Florus; Josephus; Livy; Orosius; Tacitus; Velleius Paterculus.

Tres Galliae by Germanic raiders in 17 BCE. Troops were drawn down from the Iberian Peninsula and transferred to *Tres Galliae*. Two years later, Augustus appointed a new generation of commanders – his own stepsons – to lead foreign wars to complete the annexation of the Alps, resulting in the subjugation of the Raeti, Vindelici and Norici. On the Rhine, massive investments were made in installations for legions and auxiliaries in preparation for a full-blooded invasion of Germania led by Nero Claudius Drusus. The German War was finally launched in the last half of Augustus' second decade of *imperium* (13–9 BCE). A well-planned and executed campaign moved men and matériel from the north-west coast of Europe through Germania each season, first to the Ems, then to the Weser and finally to the Elbe River. Meanwhile, bandits, rebels and foreign invaders kept the Roman army and forces of its allies busy in Africa, Cilicia,

Cimmerian Bosporus, Galatia, Illyricum, Macedonia and Thracia. As further evidence of progress with the project of pacification, the new province of Baetica, split off from Hispania Ulterior, was given to the Senate. Tragically, by the end of this period death had claimed the lives of both the greatest commander of his day, M. Agrippa, and the promising new military talent, Nero Drusus.

In his third *decennium* (8 BCE–2 CE), Augustus would look to Tiberius to take the lead in military matters. Germania was the priority. Tiberius picked up the campaign where his brother had left it and focused on the process of pacification by initiating civil settlement construction and road building, which continued over the next decade. The Sugambri, the cause of so many incitements, were transplanted on Roman territory. Following the death of pro-Roman Arta-vasdes III, Augustus became aware of Parthia's designs on Armenia. Augustus moved to thwart it. When Tiberius unexpectedly quit his responsibilities, Augustus chose his inexperienced adopted son, C. Caesar, to negotiate a non-aggression pact with Parthia. In this he succeeded. He also intervened to oversee the installation of a pro-Roman regent in Armenia. Meanwhile, the troublesome Getae were moved in their thousands to new land in Thracia.

The strategy of overseas expansion was to be continued in the fourth decade of *imperium* (3–12 CE), but its implementation was undermined by events. In the West, L. Caesar died while on manoeuvres. In the East, war in Armenia was abandoned when the Roman army's wounded leader, C. Caesar, resigned his command and later died on the journey home. A strategic withdrawal was the best option. Iudaea became a concern on account of the poor handling of internal security by the unpopular Archelaos – King Herodes' successor approved by Augustus. He acted decisively to seize the kingdom for his *provincia*, allowing him to intervene directly using troops from Syria should there be any future uprisings in this important district so close to the frontier with Rome's arch-nemesis. In the North, complete annexation of Germania seemed attainable. Now returned from self-imposed exile, Tiberius planned a massive thrust into Bohaemium to elimi-nate the Marcomanni, seen as the last major strategic obstacle to completing the conquest of the region. He assembled the largest force in Roman history to encircle and crush the enemy. The invasion had to be abandoned because of a major rebellion of auxiliary troops in Illyricum. Perceived as the gravest threat since the Punic Wars, military resources were hurriedly redirected, supplemented by a levy of citizens and freedmen mobilized from Italy. Illyricum was saved only after a war lasting four years. Within days of its conclusion, news arrived of a revolt in Germania. The land and people recently considered pacified there were completely lost. In panic, Augustus prepared for an invasion of Italy by Germanic nations. It did not come. Punitive raids across the Rhine led by Tiberius and Germanicus Caesar enforced the Romans' right of access, but no serious attempt to recover the former province would be launched for another five years. New Provinces of Caesar were created – Germania Inferior, Germania Superior, Moesia and Pannonia – and troops redeployed. Meanwhile, the Roman army and its allies successfully engaged bandits, rebels and foreign invaders in Africa, Cilicia, Iudaea and Sardinia.

In his last *decennium* (13–14 CE) of holding military power, Augustus adopted a much more cautious approach. An attempt at finishing the business in Germania was assigned to Germanicus Caesar. After a lifetime expending blood and treasure, Augustus set the limits to the *imperium* of the Roman People at their present positions, 'fenced in by the sea, the Ocean and long rivers'.[48] In the last clause of his handwritten *breviarum*, he insisted that his successor hold to that policy.[49] The goal of enlargement had finally been replaced by one of conservation and co-existence – or so we are led to believe by Tacitus.

Where Augustus could achieve his aim without bloodshed, and the calculus made sense, he took that option.[50] In Parthia, Rome had an adversary that matched her own prowess in war. Failure to understand this basic point meant several attempts to beat the Parthians in battle had failed disastrously. Iulius Caesar had a much better appreciation but was killed before he could execute the plan he had carefully detailed.[51] The pragmatic Augustus understood that the neighbour to the east was the permanent occupant and that a diplomatic settlement was the best result that could be achieved. Agrippa may have laid the diplomatic groundwork, which led to Tiberius receiving back the *signa*, *aquilae* and prisoners of war from the Parthian king in 20 BCE. It is worth noting that while Augustus was in the region he did not attend the ceremony in person. That way, the Parthian 'king of kings' could not claim the Roman leader had sought supplications from him. Frahâta's son was returned (along with the Italian-born slave Musa) in reciprocation.[52] Armenia remained a contentious issue. The spat between Augustus and Frahâtak showed both sides could play the diplomatic game, and its chief protagonists knew when to stop short of injurious insults. In 1 CE, the Parthian king finally met Augustus' envoy C. Caesar on an island in the middle of the Eurphrates in the ceremonies witnessed by Velleius Paterculus. Again Augustus was not there in person. The Romans now recognized the right of the Parthians to territory east of the Euphrates River. It was an important concession by the *princeps*. The parties also agreed that while Rome had an interest in nominating or approving the regent of Armenia, it did not require an army to be based there to enforce the terms. Should the situation call for armed intervention, Augustus had several legions (a quarter of his entire army) and auxiliary units stationed in Syria and Egypt. Augustus presented both achievements to his own people as great military victories – as demonstrations of his strength and resolve. In his *Res Gestae*, he specifically cites Armenia Minor, explaining that instead of annexing it into the empire after the assassination of its King Artaxes:

> I preferred – following the precedent of our fathers – to hand that kingdom over to Tigranes, the son of King Artavasdes, and grandson of King Tigranes, through Ti. Nero who was then my stepson; and later, when the same people revolted and rebelled, and was subdued by my son Caius, I gave it over to King Ariobarzanes the son of Artabazus, King of the Medes, to rule, and after his death to his son Artavasdes. When he was murdered I sent into that kingdom Tigranes, who was sprung from the royal family of the Armenians.[53]

Achieving victory, so that he could present it to the Senate and Roman People, is what mattered most to Augustus.[54] Tradition required that after battle the vanquished would engage in an act of unconditional surrender (*deditio*) and the victor would impose terms of a pact.[55] To the Romans, this act defined a successful outcome of war. As an assurance of trustworthiness, the defeated would be required to hand over hostages (*obses*) (plate 39) and weapons.[56] Their display was an essential aspect of celebrating victory. Celebrating the *Pax Parthorum*, Augustus enjoyed showing off the hostages he had received from the Parthian king.[57] Coins presented this same image of surrender: a defeated leader, often on bended knee, raising his arms in supplication, offering up a battle standard or a child. The defeated barbarian warrior with hands tied behind his back, sitting beneath a *tropaeaum*, was a common motif on triumphal arches or inscriptions gracing war monuments (see plate 33).[58] A dejected man and a distraught woman are shown in this pose in one of the scenes on the *Gemma Augustea* (plate 40), where a group of Roman soldiers erects the trophy, while others restrain a man and a woman by pulling on their hair. Once the decorated oak tree trunk is in position, these captives will join their countrymen in obeisance. Acknowledgement of the victor's supremacy and showing deference to him were crucial behaviours in this power transfer ritual. Rome would willingly make an ally of those who accepted their subjection, but would brutally crush a people who did not or displayed arrogance (*superbia*).[59]

Failure to uphold the terms of the pact was an injury (*iniuria*) to Rome, which would be met with revenge (*ultio*).[60] They were important reasons for waging wars of necessity – what the Romans called 'just war' (*bellum iustum*). Cicero explains, 'no war is just, unless it is entered upon after an official demand for satisfaction has been submitted or warning has been given and a formal declaration made.'[61] Notifying the enemy that a state of war existed between them and the Romans for a violation was the purpose of ancient fetial law and its officials (*fetiales*).[62] Their arcane rite of declaring war, which had fallen into disuse during the late first century BCE, was re-established by the then Imp. Caesar to validate his war against Kleopatra. Thus it could be said:

> [Augustus] never made war on any nation without just and due cause, and he was so far from desiring to increase his dominion or his military glory at any cost, that he forced the chiefs of certain barbarians to take oath in the temple of Mars Ultor that they would faithfully keep the peace for which they asked; in some cases, indeed, he tried exacting a new kind of hostages, namely women, realizing that the barbarians disregarded pledges secured by males; but all were given the privilege of reclaiming their hostages whenever they wished. On those who rebelled often or under circumstances of especial treachery he never inflicted any severer punishment than that of selling the prisoners, with the condition that they should not pass their term of slavery in a country near their own, nor be set free within thirty years.[63]

After beating the Salassi in 25 BCE, A. Terentius Varro sold 8,000 war captives as slaves. Ten years later, Nero Claudius Drusus and his older brother forcibly transplanted the strongest men able to bear arms among the defeated Raeti, leaving just enough to cultivate the land – although many opted to serve with the Roman army as auxiliaries. In 12 BCE, when victorious in battle over the Pannonii in Illyricum, Tiberius sold most of the men of military age into slavery and deported them from the country. Such brute-force examples of social engineering changed these vanquished societies forever.

Victory did not have to mean utter destruction for the losing side. Augustus could be generous and show clemency (*clementia*) to the defeated. In *Res Gestae*, he claimed to have spared the foreign nations which he believed could be trusted to uphold their terms, preferring to save rather than to destroy them.[64] Taking his lead, Augustus' subordinates too could be merciful. When the Astures surrendered their stronghold of Lancia in 25 BCE, the Roman commander P. Carisius responded to lobbying and agreed to spare their lives. Tiberius permitted 40,000 Sugambri to relocate to Roman territory in 8 BCE. This also explains Tiberius' response to Bato of the Daesidiates' surrender in 9 CE: having freely offered himself and asked for no special treatment, the captive rebel leader was displayed in triumph three years later, but he was spared execution, granted a pension and permitted to live his life in peace. Many newly conquered peoples showed their allegiance when recruited as paid troops in native *alae* and *cohortes*. This is how the Astures, Breuci, Cantabri, Frisii, Ligures, Norici, Sugambri, Vindelici and others found their way into the Roman army, which benefited from employing their distinctive fighting styles to its advantage.

In other cases, Augustus presented his success as recovering what had once been Roman, such as Cyrenae, Sicily and Sardinia.[65] The annexation of regions previously thought too remote or barbaric to be explored were a source of particular pride to him:

> I extended the boundaries of all the provinces, which were bordered by races not yet subject to our *imperium*. The provinces of the Galliae, the Hispaniae and Germania, bounded by the Ocean from Gades to the mouth of the Albis River, I reduced to a state of peace. The Alps, from the region which lies nearest to the Adriatic Sea as far as the Tuscan, I brought to a state of peace without waging on any tribe an unjust war.[66]

He claims credit for his deputy's explorations of, and exploits in, the furthest reaches of *barbaricum*:

> My fleet sailed from the mouth of the Rhenus River eastward as far as the lands of the Cimbri to which, up to that time, no Roman had ever penetrated either by land or by sea, and the Cimbri and Charydes and Semnones and other peoples of the Germans of that same region through their envoys sought my friendship and that of the Roman People.[67]

In contrast, he writes simply: 'Aegyptus I added to the *imperium* of the Roman People.'[68] The matter-of-fact reporting is astonishing for the absence of any embellishment.

Augustus' grand strategy – his military policy and its resourcing sustained over decades – did not evolve. It was the consistent use of 'just war'. In pursuit of it he was not reckless. Indeed he was calculating, erring on the side of risk aversion. Most of the conflicts fought under his auspices were wars of necessity, undertaken in response to real threats (such as insurrection) or in self-defence (such as against invasions). Few were wars of choice or aggression. A war of conquest took years to prepare, execute and complete, and incurred a great cost in men and *matériel*. The exigencies of fighting particular campaigns and missions on the ground required adaptation and change in pursuit of successfully achieving the overall military objective. The adversary's unconditional surrender was preferred over a policy of annihilation. Pacification could then follow through settler colonization, urbanization of native people, the inclusion of tribal élites into the Roman political system, the levying of taxes and tribute (which would include recruiting their warriors into the Roman army), and so on.

When he decided to embark on a just war Augustus had both the political will and ability to bring the military resources together to achieve a lasting victory. Compared to the consuls and praetors of earlier times, he had two distinct advantages. Firstly, the Senate granted him greatly extended periods of time in which to wield his military power, and renewed those terms when they expired. In turn the legates he personally appointed also served out field commands of several years. Thus Augustus could afford to take the long view. Secondly, the vast size of his province meant he could recruit the necessary numbers of men and animals and then replace his casualties campaign season after campaign season. As well as drawing upon contingents from treaty allies, he could further augment the ranks of his full-time professional troops – increasingly comprised of Romanized provincials rather than just Italians – with new units created from recently subjugated peoples.

A war of necessity could, however, become one of choice if 'scope creep' was allowed to cloud the clarity of the initial purpose. The *Bellum Germanicum* launched in 12 BCE was a response to invasions by coalitions of Germanic warriors raiding into Roman territory and the murder of Roman citizens peacefully trading across the Rhine. Subjugating the Sugambri, Tencteri and Uspietes might have been enough to address the military threat, but successive campaigns, driven by the irresistible chance for glory, lured the field commanders far beyond. A dictum of war is that it takes more combat power to hold an objective than to take it. It took the revolt of Arminius twenty-one years later to remind the Romans of the folly of carelessly applying the doctrine of *imperium sine fine*. If Augustus allegedly did temper his strategy within a year or two of his death, it was because he had finally come to realize there were limits to what he could do with the economy of force and budget under his control.

Augustus as Manager of War

Having assumed responsibility for a province, keeping it secure posed an immense challenge. Quoting an extract from the eulogy delivered by Tiberius at Augustus' funeral, Tacitus reports:

> Only the mind of the deified Augustus was equal to such a burden: he himself had found, when called by the sovereign to share his anxieties, how arduous,

how dependent upon fortune, was the task of ruling a world! He thought, then, that, in a community, which had the support of so many eminent men, they ought not to devolve the entire duties on any one person; the business of the *Res Publica* would be more easily carried out by the joint efforts of a number.[69]

In this rôle, he needed a different set of skills. Augustus could not be everywhere at once, making decisions on matters great and small. Spread over three continents, separated by great distances and facing issues in real time, made delegating responsibility to subordinates not only practical but essential.[70] As the military leader, his job was to inspire and motivate; his task as a manager was to plan, organize, coordinate and control. As the leader, Augustus had to take a long-range perspective; as a manager, the short-term would be more important, with a focus on the 'hows' and 'whens' needed to achieve results.

Structure follows strategy, according to modern management theory.[71] In the past, a governor (proconsul or propraetor) was assigned a territory by the Senate and was answerable to the Conscript Fathers at the end of his term. Augustus created a three-tier command structure to manage his *provincia*. Its purpose was to execute the process of pacification and to deal with military exigencies as they arose. He inserted himself at the strategic level. To each of the nine – later more – geographically-based operational commands within it, he appointed a pro-praetorian legate (*legatus Augusti pro praetore*). This officer was responsible in turn for the tactical level legions and auxiliary units stationed there.[72] Each *legatus* was semi-autonomous, empowered by Augustus to make decisions that affected his territory and army group. It was not actually a new approach. Pompeius Magnus had managed his extensive command when fighting the pirates this way, as had Iulius Caesar on a smaller scale in the Gallic War.[73] Under the terms of the *Lex Gabinia*, Pompeius could operate up to 50 miles inland from the coast. However, this meant his *provincia* (task or military duty) overlapped with other proconsuls' existing *provinciae* (territories). Rather than sub-divide his campaigns among the governors and be forced to act as a coordinator between them, he cunningly assumed overall strategic command and directed tactical operations through his own team of twenty-four *legati*, who were each imbued with *imperium* as provided for in the law.[74] In effect, Pompeius created for himself a three-year command of a 'super province', directing over the heads of the annually appointed proconsuls – a provision the Senate almost certainly would not have agreed to when passing the law.[75] The strategy had proved effective in crushing the menace of piracy. This precedent too was helpful to Augustus.

Governing an armed 'Province of Caesar' was a military assignment, and the job title and responsibilities reflected that fact. Augustus handpicked every one of the men for the posts of *legatus Augusti pro praetore*.[76] In contrast, the proconsul of a 'Province of the People' was chosen by lot from among ex-consuls.[77] In office, the *legatus* wore full military panoply, in contrast to the proconsul, who wore civilian attire of tunic and toga.[78] Keeping his province 'pacified and quiet' was the legate's most important task.[79] As a direct representative of Augustus, he had the necessary military *imperium* to command all the army units stationed in his *provincia*, with every commander of an auxiliary unit reporting to him.[80] The Roman army was not only the instrument of conquest and subjugation, but a province's *de facto* police force as well.[81] The *legatus* was invested with authority to exercise full powers at his discretion, including capital punishment.[82] His tour typically lasted three years (*triennium*), which was longer than the one-year term of the proconsul of a senatorial province.[83] He enjoyed a complement of five *fasces*-bearing lictors – one less than a proconsul, emphasizing his lesser status.[84]

The exception was Egypt. In 30 BCE, the then Imp. Caesar appointed a *praefectus Aegypti* to manage the province, command the army of occupation and report directly to him.[85] As Rome's strategically important breadbasket, Egypt had to be administered by someone who could never become a challenger to Augustus. Despite the indiscretions of the first man in that post, all subsequent appointments continued to be *praefecti*.[86] Similarly, after its annexation in 6 CE Iudaea would be governed by a *praefectus* who would report to the *legatus Augusti* of Syria.[87] *Praefecti* were recruited from among the *equites* to ensure that their allegiance lay with Augustus rather than with the Conscript Fathers. The appointment of equestrian superintendents in both jurisdictions signalled that they were lower status and relatively undesirable appointments compared to the provincial governorships given to senators, and that officers serving in these positions lacked both the *dignitas* and *auctoritas* of the *legati Augusti*.[88] Nevertheless, these postings represented the pinnacle of a career for an *eques*.

As a manager, selecting the right people for his organization was Augustus' most important task. His future success and reputation depended on the reliability of his subordinates in carrying out their broad mission. He had to trust them completely. Over forty-one years (27 BCE–14 CE), Augustus worked with three generations of men to run his province.[89] The first generation was comprised of men who had fought with him at Actium and Alexandria, or aligned with him even before these episodes. He picked them from all classes. He cared only for ability. Many were patricians, such as Paullus Fabius Maximus and L. Sempronius Atratinus. He also chose and advanced commoners, the *novi homines* like M. Agrippa, Sex. Appuleius, L. Autronius Paetus, C. Calvisius Sabinus and T. Statilius Taurus.[90] Remarkably, others had once been his enemies, like L. Domitius Ahenobarbus and M. Titius, but later defected to him. Individually, these men had a special bond with Augustus and would continue to enjoy his support and friendship (*amicitia*) for the rest of their lives. Many were accorded the special honour of being welcomed into the high status college of *quindecemviri sacris faciundis* headed by Augustus, whose members organized the *Ludi Saeculares* of 17 BCE.

The Actian War was the defining event that confirmed beyond a doubt the loyalty and stature of Augustus' greatest general. M. Agrippa was his paragon of a deputy. He personified honour, courage, commitment, and above all unswerving loyalty. His equal in age, he also matched him in experience and temperament. They had been through a lot together. Agrippa was disarmingly modest yet faithful, almost to a fault, putting his life in harm's way repeatedly in the service of his friend. His talents for organization and field combat leadership were without rival. Augustus trusted Agrippa so well he alternated command with him; when he went to the East his associate went West, and vice versa. T. Statilius Taurus was another loyal and talented commander upon whom he counted. Augustus could feel confident to leave Rome in his care as *praetor urbanus* in 16 BCE. Of these two men, Velleius Paterculus writes:

> In the case of these men their lack of lineage was no obstacle to their eleva-tion to successive consulships, triumphs, and numerous priesthoods. For great tasks require great helpers, and it is important to the *Res Publica* that those who are necessary to her service should be given prominence in rank, and that their usefulness should be fortified by official authority.[91]

The second generation comprised his own stepsons, Nero Claudius Drusus and Tiberius, and their contemporaries such as A. Caecina Severus, L. Calpur-nius Piso (Piso the Pontifex), Cossus Cornelius Lentulus Gaetulicus, P. Quinc-tilius Varus, C. Sentius Saturninus and M. Valerius Messalla Messallinus. The Claudius brothers both proved to have natural talent for command and were popular with their troops. When Agrippa died, Tiberius proved to be a risky, but ultimately fine surrogate. Younger, and with a history very different than Agrippa's, he was more temperamental and less imaginative. Yet he proved as dedicated and as reliable in military matters. Once rehabilitated from his retire-ment he returned to form, assuming the burden of command as Augustus aged – and never wavered.

The third generation of subordinates included C. Caesar, L. Caesar and Germanicus, whom Augustus mentored himself. They were starting their mili-tary careers when he was already in his sixties. 'The younger men had been born after the victory of Actium,' writes Tacitus, 'most even of the elder generation, during the civil wars; how few indeed were left who had seen the *Res Publica*.'[92] When the young Caesar brothers died prematurely, Augustus turned to Tiberius and Germanicus Caesar to promote his policy in the field.

Augustus was not coy about exposing his own family to death. To be successful in public life in Ancient Rome, a man had to able to display *virtus*, and that could only truly be earned on the battlefield, witnessed by his countrymen. Augustus understood the risks. With that in mind, he always maintained a fallback posi-tion. If he died, Agrippa could assume leadership. If Agrippa died, Tiberius could take over. Unfortunately for Augustus he had a large measure of bad luck, losing his nephew Marcellus, son-in-law Agrippa, stepson Nero Drusus and adopted sons Caius and Lucius. Yet of these, only two men actually died from wounds sustained in battle (Drusus and Caius) – the rest having fallen victim to sickness, ironically picked up while on, or travelling from, campaigning. His calculus was sound in that at the time of his death two men of outstanding talent (Tiberius and Germanicus) still remained to execute his grand strategy. Nevertheless, it was a high-risk approach to succession planning.

The last time Augustus led his troops in person on the battlefield was during the Cantabrian campaign of 26 BCE. Sickness caused him to withdraw, and he delegated prosecution of the war to C. Antistius Vetus and P. Carisius. Why he entrusted the field leadership of all future military operations to his deputies can only be surmised. His health and fitness were certainly factors in his decision. It was not age: Agrippa was older by several months and would be active in combat operations for years to come. It was not lack of self-confidence: he had that in abundance. Nor was it cowardice: he had put himself in harm's way often enough in his lifetime, even sustaining wounds in doing so. It is more likely that, ever the pragmatist, he recognised that his *legati* were now abler than he was at executing prolonged combat offensives. For the system to work Augustus had to step back and let the men he had picked get on with their jobs. He had empowered them to respond to security threats as they deemed appropriate. To be successful he had to resist the temptation of micromanaging them.

The majority of men who commanded in the wars fought on Augustus' behalf served as consul.[93] Keeping the bench of talent full was an ongoing challenge. His frequent censorial reviews of the Senate resulted in removal of many unsuitable men while revealing new potential candidates for command positions, men like C. Poppaeus Sabinus, P. Sulpicius Quirinius and L. Tarius Rufus.[94] Reducing the qualification age was another expedient Augustus tried in order to expose men to military service at a younger age than was customary:

> To enable senators' sons to gain an earlier acquaintance with public business, he allowed them to assume the broad purple stripe (*latus clavus*) immediately after the toga of manhood and to attend meetings of the Senate; and when they began their military careers, he gave them not merely a tribunate in a legion, but the prefecture of an *ala* of cavalry as well; and to furnish all of them with experience in camp life (*expers castrorum*), he usually appointed two senators' sons to command each *ala*.[95]

Commanding between 512 and 768 adult men would be a significant responsibility for a man in his late teens or early twenties and, doubtless, a life-transforming experience.

In parallel, he picked men of the *Ordo Equester* exclusively to fill vital positions of trust, notably the *praefecti* of Egypt, the Praetorian Cohorts and the *Vigiles*.[96] Augustus was eager to repurpose the faded order as a new military class. It was once formed of men equipped with horses at public expense to support the legions, but had long since become a 'club' of advocates and bankers eschewing the battlefield for the *basilica*. 'To keep up the supply of men of rank and induce the commons to increase and multiply', Augustus 'admitted to the equestrian military career those who were recommended by any town' in Italy.[97] Men who had served as centurions in the army could be promoted into the order.[98] To re-establish its prestige, he reintroduced the traditional *transvectio* parade after it had fallen into disuse.[99] Significantly, he appointed his own sons in turn to be *princeps iuventutis* ('the first of the youth'), ranked a *sevir turmae* in charge of one of the six *turmae* of *iuniores*.[100]

To foster a pro-military mindset in the younger generation, Augustus urged Roman boys to adopt the warrior's values of courage, honour and the rest. He encouraged participation in the traditional paramilitary exercises, which were performed for the public:

> he gave frequent performances of the Game of Troy (*Lusus Troioae*) by older and younger boys, thinking it a time-honoured and worthy custom for the flower of the nobility to become known in this way. When Nonius Asprenas was lamed by a fall while taking part in this game, he presented him with a golden torque and allowed him and his descendants to bear the *cognomen Torquatus.*[101]

Through his semi-autonomous *legati*, Augustus was able to develop, adapt and revise strategies for pacification and annexation in different theatres simultaneously. Remarkably, these were not career military men. During their working lifetimes they alternated between civilian and command positions. Rising through the *cursus honorum*, they could serve as a military tribune, prefect and legionary legate, and at other times work as a *quaestor* carrying out financial audits, an aedile arranging road repairs or as a *praetor* overseeing a case at a law court. When faced with military threats – banditry, migrant invasions, revolts – or leading wars of conquest, these men did so to the best of their abilities. During their terms, many *legati Augusti* would see just one combat season. The burden of fighting war did not fall on the shoulders of all legates equally, however. Several fought in multiple campaigns, notably: Agrippa (31, 19, 14 and 13 BCE); L. Calpurnius Piso (13–11 BCE); Nero Claudius Drusus (15 and 12–9 BCE); Sulpicius Quirinius (15, 5 BCE and 2–3 CE); and Tiberius (15, 14–13, 8–7 and 4–5 BCE, 6–9 and 10–11 CE). Of his *praefecti Aegypti*, Cornelius Gallus repulsed a bandit raid (30 BCE), Aelius Gallus fought a single war in Arabia Felix (24 BCE), but Petronius undertook campaigns over three seasons (25–24 and 23 BCE).

Suetonius provides a fascinating insight into the behaviours Augustus valued in his *legati*:

> He thought nothing less becoming in a well-trained leader than haste and rashness, and, accordingly, favourite sayings of his were: 'More haste, less speed'; 'Better a safe commander than a bold' [in Greek]; and 'That is done quickly enough which is done well enough.'[102]

His preference was clearly for level-headedness, preparedness, steadfastness and thoroughness. Consistent demonstration of these traits could take a subordinate far. It was an idea embodied in the Roman virtue of *moderatio* – the avoidance of extremes, the showing of restraint and the power of self-control.[103] Cicero regarded it as the appropriate quality for a man serving in public office.[104] Agrippa lived by it and so too did Tiberius.[105] In contrast, L. Domitius Ahenobarbus was the antithesis of moderation. His reputation for haughtiness, extravagance and indifference to pain and suffering was a liability. It hindered, for example, his ability to negotiate with the Germans for the return of prisoners in 1 CE. It extended to his taste for beast hunts and gladiatorial games, where he displayed 'such inhuman cruelty that Augustus, after his private warning was disregarded, was forced to restrain him by an edict'.[106] Yet despite his distasteful antics, Augustus could not dismiss or unfriend Ahenobardus; the man got results in Germania, for which he earned himself a triumph. There was still a place for such men in Augustus' military organization. He was not naïve. War was a dreadful business; he knew that from personal experience. Someone had to do the dirty work. To be successful he needed 'tough bastards' too who could commit detestable acts without flinching. Even cultured Germanicus authorized *vastatio* against the Marsi in 14 CE – not for any atrocity the Germanic nation had committed, but to restore morale among his troops. Like any manager today, Augustus did not like surprises. He would also introduce controls to change excessive behaviours, as shown by the mandated requirement for his subordinates to invest some of their war spoils in buildings and works that would benefit the public, not just themselves.

The majority of Augustus' *legati* performed their duties well, several with distinction. In an organization as large and enduring as Augustus', however, there were bound to be exceptions. M. Lollius was taken by surprise in 17 BCE when ambushed by Germanic raiders. It was, perhaps, more a case of accident than incompetence, but the loss of the *aquila* of *Legio* V *Alaudae* was unforgivable to the *princeps*. The track record of this enemy-turned-friend was, until then, unblemished. He had successfully managed the transfer of Galatia from the late king Amyntas' estate to the *imperium* of the Roman People. But the blunder in Belgica (or Gallia Comata) was an acute embarrassment to the man who had boasted the achievement of reclaiming the *signa* lost by Crassus at Carrhae just three years before. The *Tres Galliae* would be Lollius' last command. He was replaced by Tiberius. Lollius avoided the enmity of the *princeps* and later was appointed to accompany his adopted son to the East. It was then revealed that he had received bribes from the Parthians. From that moment nothing could save him. Redemption would take the form of a self-inflicted wound or a draught of poison. His ward too disappointed. C. Caesar proved inadequate to the high-profile command he had been given. Inexperience or unsuitability for the role combined with bad luck to expose him to mortal danger. Injured by a battle wound, his character buckled and he resigned his commission. He died on the journey home. In comparison, Quinctilius Varus was an accomplished field commander. He had served as a legionary legate in the Alpine War of 15 BCE and quelled a rebellion in Iudaea in 4 BCE as *legatus Augusti* of Syria. He should have been more alert in Germania. Ambushes were the ever-present danger to Roman troops on the march, yet he took no precautions. He even failed to heed a tip-off from reputable source and dismissed it. He lost his life to his own sword – and Germania with it. Thus Augustus suffered a second military humiliation by his own subordinates.

Roman commanders seemed to perform less well when they were acting on the defensive (reacting to a threat). Even a general as experienced as Tiberius could be caught out when marching full stride towards Bohaemium, when he learned of the uprising in Illyricum in 6 CE. Tiberius had fought several campaigns in the

Western Balkans and knew the people, so the unwelcome surprise is itself surprising. This likely points to a failure of ground intelligence gathering by the *legatus Augusti* of Illyricum, M. Valerius Messalla Messallinus. This was his first provincial command. The inexperience of certain *legati Augusti* in combat, however, was a weakness of the Augustan system. When Caecina Severus and Silvanus arrived with their contingent, the rebels were waiting for them. In the ensuing ambush, the casualties included a *tribunus militum*, a *praefectus castrorum*, a *primus pilus* and other centurions of the legions, plus several *praefecti* of auxiliary cohorts. Only the discipline and cool-headedness of the lower-ranking legionary centurions and the soldiers managed to turn the situation around and prevent it from descending into a complete rout. Having recovered, Severus promptly marched into a second trap at Volcaean Marshes when his camp was surrounded by rebels, but this time he managed to repel them.

The strength of the Augustan military organization showed itself when Tiberius could rapidly pull together resources from Moesia and Thracia to come to his assistance. It would seem from this example that the territory-based three-tier organization structure allowed communication to be routed directly to the neighbouring command rather than having to seek permission from Augustus first, which might cause serious delay. The arrangement was facilitated by personal relationships, which mattered very much in Ancient Rome. Throughout their careers, men of similar age competed for political appointments in the *cursus honorum*. From their first professional steps in public life they would have known of each other, either forming friendships or developing rivalries. While they would know each other's strengths (and weaknesses), as *legati* of Augustus each would come to a colleague's assistance when asked, as demonstrated in Illyricum in 6 CE.

Relationship-building extended to non-Romans as well. Allies played an important role in Augustus' strategy.[107] Though bound by treaty, the *princeps* respected the independence of his alliance partners. Many of their sons gained an education in Rome under Augustus' hospitality. Rome stood to benefit, of course. When the allied leader died, his territory might be bequeathed to the Roman People. This was the case with King Amyntas in 25 BCE. The realm passed peacefully into the control of the Roman People, overseen by Augustus' legate M. Lollius. In wartime, allies could be called on to provide troops. During the war of 6–9 CE in Illyricum, at the request of Caecina Severus, Roimetalkes brought his Thracian warriors to assist. It was a reciprocal arrangement. When Sitas, the blind king of the Dentheleti, requested help to fend off the Bastarnae in 30 BCE, M. Licinius Crassus was obliged to respond. The following year Rolis, king of the Getae, who had helped Crassus defeat the Bastarnae, himself called for assistance. When the king later visited Augustus, he was treated as a friend and ally on account of his service to the Romans. Agrippa formed a close friendship with the irascible King Herodes of Iudaea. When Agrippa (known to have a quick temper himself) needed help to suppress the Scribonian Revolt in the Cimmerian Bosporus in 14 BCE, he only had to write a letter to the regent and a fleet of ships and marines appeared, following him to Sinope. Agrippa had already requested another ally, Polemon Pythodoros, to go to the source of the trouble and contain it. On occasions the ally with a higher agenda could manipulate the unwary Roman commander. Petronius was thoroughly duped by Syllaeus, who was secretly working for the advantage of Nabateans, an act of treachery which cost several thousand Roman lives and the deceiver his head. Quinctilius Varus trusted the Cherusci-born Arminius (who, though a hostage, had been educated in Rome) and Segimerus too much and was tricked into leading his army into a fatal ambush in 9 CE.

Augustus understood the value of rewards and recognitions to encourage high performance by his team members. He had learned that powerful men do not respond to threats, so he appealed to their vanity. By carefully controlling the number and distribution of awards, he greatly increased their worth. Competition for prestige and public recognition had been one of the factors in Rome's military success. Under Augustus, commanders still competed hard for the distinction of a triumph. For a day a commander enjoyed the adulation and congratulations of his fellow citizens in a glittering military parade in the centre of Rome. Between 31 BCE and 14 CE, more than thirty triumphs were awarded and 'the triumphal ornaments to somewhat more than that number' (table 6).[108] About a third of these took place during the first decade of Augustus' *imperium*, the phase during which his generation occupied the highest positions of command. The most magnificent was, of course, Augustus' own triple triumph of 29 BCE, an event intended to rival Pompeius Magnus' and Iulius Caesar's, or outdo them. The other events rewarded the old guard for wars fought in Africa, Hispania Citerior, Macedonia, Thracia and *Tres Galliae*.[109] One was declined by the *triumphator* M. Agrippa himself, whose deeply ingrained sense of modesty prevented him from accepting. Eager to celebrate his, Sempronius Atratinus was the last *privatus* to be granted a full triumph with a *quadriga* in 21 BCE. In the next ten-year term, Agrippa turned down another triumph, while, at Augustus' insistence, one granted to Tiberius was downgraded to triumphal ornaments. His brother received an *ovatio*, which permitted him to ride a horse along the *Via Sacra*, along with triumphal ornaments. These men had grown up in a different era; they were young boys when Augustus celebrated his triumphs and had even taken part in them. They did not need such ostentatious enticements to perform in the field as the older generation of *viri triumphales* had, yet they were still highly attractive prizes to this younger generation of commanders eager for recognition.[110] In the third and fourth periods, the frequency of these distinctions changed from every two or three years to three to five. Tiberius was the last man to be honoured with a full triumph for crushing the revolt in Illyricum of 6–9 CE. It was postponed to 12 CE on account of the Varian Disaster.

The award of war titles (*cognomina*) was a rarer honour in Roman history. Augustus curtailed the practice further. Cossus Cornelius Lentulus was permitted the unique war name *Gaetulicus* in 6 CE for his victory over the African tribe, but

Table 6. Triumphs and Ornaments Awarded, 31 BCE–14 CE.

Year	Date	Commander	Award	Theatre of War
29 BCE	13 August	Imp. Caesar	*Triumphus*	Illyricum
	14 August	Imp. Caesar	*Triumphus*	Actium
	15 August	Imp. Caesar	*Triumphus*	Aegyptus
28	26 May	C. Calvisius Sabinus	*Triumphus*	Hispania
	14 July	C. Carrinas	*Triumphus*	Gallia
	16 August	L. Autronius Paetus	*Triumphus*	Africa
27	4 July	M. Licinius Crassus	*Triumphus*	Thracia Macedoniaque
	25 September	M. Valerius Messalla Corvinus	*Triumphus*	Gallia
26	26 January	Sex. Appuleius	*Triumphus*	Hispania
21	12 October	L. Sempronius Atratinus	*Triumphus*	Africa
19	27 March	L. Cornelius Balbus	*Ornamenta*	Africa
		M. Agrippa – *declined*	*Triumphus*	Hispania
14		M. Agrippa – *declined*	*Triumphus*	Cimmerian Bosporus
12		Ti. Caesar – *triumphus overruled by Augustus*	*Ornamenta*	Illyricum
11		Nero Claudius Drusus	*Ovatio* and *Ornamenta*	Germania
11 / 10		L. Calpurnius Piso	*Ornamenta*	Thracia Macedoniaque
7	1 January	Ti. Caesar	*Ornamenta*	Germania
3? BCE		P. Sulpicius Quirinius	*Ornamenta*	Cilicia
2 CE		L. Domitius Ahenobarbus	*Ornamenta*	Germania
4?		M. Vinicius	*Ornamenta*	Germania
6		Cossus Cornelius Lentulus (Gaetulicus)	*Ornamenta*	Africa
		L. Passienus Rufus		
7	1 January	Ti. Caesar	*Ornamenta*	Germania
9	*Postponed to 12 CE*	Ti. Caesar	*Triumphus*	Illyricum
		Germanicus Caesar	*Ornamenta*	Illyricum
		M. Aemlius Lepidus	*Ornamenta*	Illyricum
		A. Caecina Severus	*Ornamenta*	Illyricum
		M. Plautius Silvanus	*Ornamenta*	Illyricum
		M. Valerius Messalla Messallinus	*Ornamenta*	Illyricum
12	23 October	Ti. Caesar	*Triumphus*	Illyricum

Sources: Appendix 2; *Fasti Triumphales Barberini*; *Fasti Triumphales Capitolini*, Dio; Suetonius; Boyce (1942); Hickson (1991); Itgenshorst (2004); Wardle (2014).

Tiberius was denied one for Illyricum, which might have seen him called one of several names including *Pannonicus*. Nero Claudius Drusus posthumously received the title *Germanicus*. It was hereditary and adopted by his eldest son as his first name.

Another form of recognition Augustus tightly controlled was the acclamation. Traditionally it was in the gift of the soldiers after battle to shout out '*imperator*' in praise of their commander for leading them to victory. By 31 BCE, the then Imp. Caesar had himself received six acclamations, including one for Actium (table 7). The following year he picked up another in Egypt. That year he denied Licinius Crassus this honour – but offered him triumphal ornaments – yet the following

Table 7. Imperatorial Acclamations of Augustus and His Legates, 31 BCE–14 CE.

Augustus' Acclamation	Year	Acclaimed Legate	Campaign
VI	31 BCE	M. Agrippa	Actium
VII	30		Alexandria?, Aegyptus?
	30	M. Licinius Crassus – *declined by Augustus*	Moesia
	29	L. Autronius Paetus	Africa
	29	C. Nonius Gallus	Gallia
VIII	25		Germania / Gallia Comata
IX	20		Parthia, Armenia
X	15		Alps / Raetia
XI	12		Illyricum
XII	11	Nero Claudius Drusus – *declined by Augustus, reinstated posthumously*	Germania
XIII	9	Ti. Caesar I	Illyricum
XIV	8	Ti. Caesar II	Germania
XV	1 / 2 CE	C. Caesar I	Parthia and Armenia?, Arabia?
XVI	3	C. Caesar II	Armenia – Artagira
XVII	5 / 6	Ti. Caesar III	Germania
	6	L. Passienus Rufus?	Africa?
XVIII	8	Ti. Caesar IV	Illyricum – Bathinus River
XIX	9	Ti. Caesar V	Illyricum
XX	11	Ti. Caesar VI	Illyricum
XXI	12 / 13	Ti. Caesar VI	Germania
	13	Germanicus Caesar I?	*Tres Galliae?*

Sources: Appendix 2; Barnes (1974); Swan (2004); Wardle (2014), with author's revisions based on Dio and other Roman sources.

year he permitted L. Autronius Paetus and M. Nonius Gallus to retain theirs. From that time on, the acclamation was considered Augustus' privilege alone and the running tally was displayed on coins. The only exceptions were Tiberius, C. Caesar and Germanicus (Drusus having been denied his but allowed it posthumously), but in these cases the *princeps* also counted them towards his running total. By 14 CE, he had garnered an unprecedented twenty-one acclamations.[111]

The highest honour a Roman citizen could win in wartime was to take the *spolia opima* or 'rich spoils' of a defeated enemy leader. Courageous Roman commanders sought to emulate city founder Romulus' exploit of slaying King Acron by his own hand and stripping him of his blood-spattered panoply. It was an exclusive club, which made the prize extremely desirable. Only two men had since succeeded: A. Cornelius Cossus in either 437 or 426 BCE; and M. Claudius Marcellus in 222 BCE. Just two years after Actium, M. Licinius Crassus killed the king of the Bastarnae in combat when his army crossed the Danube River and it was intercepted by the Romans. Crassus claimed the right to deposit his *spolia opima* in the Temple of Jupiter Feretrius. For the heir of Iulius Caesar it posed an awkward political dilemma. He had inherited the dictator's rights to the practice and was the restorer of Jupiter's temple, yet at the time was still seeking to establish his credentials. He insisted that the rules had to be followed. Since Crassus did not report to him as his commanding officer, he could not authorize deposit of the spoils.[112] Crassus was offered a triumph instead. Two decades later, Augustus' own stepson Nero Claudius Drusus attempted to follow in the great tradition in the fields of valour of Germania. There is no record that he succeeded.

Augustus had a deep respect for the chain of command and believed that men should follow orders. He was known as 'a strict disciplinarian'.[113] Intended to enforce discipline (*disciplina*), martial law could be applied particularly harshly in the military zone (*militiae*) – on the march, in camp, on the battlefield – and the protections afforded citizens under civil law did not apply.[114] Suetonius provides several examples of Augustus' expectation of complete obedience and the punishments he meted out for violations:

> He dismissed the entire *Legio* X in disgrace, because they were insubordinate, and others, too, that demanded their discharge in an insolent fashion, he disbanded without the rewards which would have been due for faithful service. If any cohorts gave way in battle, he decimated them, and fed the rest on barley. When centurions left their posts, he punished them with death, just as he did the rank and file; for faults of other kinds he imposed various ignominious penalties, such as ordering to stand all day long before the legate's tent, sometimes in their tunics without their sword-belts, or again holding ten-foot poles or even a clod of earth.[115]

His deputies followed his example, as Agrippa did in the Cantabrian War of 19 BCE when he stripped *Legio* I of its honorfic title *Augusta*.

Unlike his mentor Iulius Caesar, Augustus believed there should be some distance between himself and the rankers. He preferred to address them as *milites* or 'soldiers', not by the more familiar *commilitiones* or 'fellow soldiers' – 'thinking the former term too flattering for the requirements of discipline' – and went so far as to instruct his own sons and stepsons to do likewise.[116] In reciprocity, he refused to be addressed by anyone as *dominus* – 'master' – because it inferred a servile relationship and he was 'only a man'.[117] 'As patron and master he was no less strict than gracious and merciful,' writes Suetonius, 'while he held many of his freedmen in high honour and close intimacy, such as Licinus, Celadus, and others.'[118]

Augustus was aware of the importance of kind words in encouraging high performance from his direct reports. The letters he wrote to Tiberius (quoted by Suetonius) reveal that. He could also show forgiveness when it was appropriate.[119] In his *Res Gestae* he writes that 'when victorious I spared all citizens who sued for pardon'.[120] Though replacing Lollius as *Legatus Augusti* in *Tres Galliae* after his embarrassing ambush, Augustus still had enough confidence in the man that he later appointed him as mentor to his adopted son C. Caesar on his mission in the East. When he learned that his slave Cosmus had spoken in most insulting terms of him, 'he merely put [the man] in irons'.[121]

In return Augustus demanded complete loyalty from his people, whether citizen, freeborn, freedman or slave. Disloyalty or treachery led to swift retribution. As soon as the same Lollius was discovered to have taken bribes from the

Parthians, he was recalled to Rome to face trial. Gallus, the *praefectus Aegypti*, met a similar end for his indiscretion. When freedman Thallus was discovered to have been paid a bribe of 500 *denarii* to betray the contents of a letter, Augustus ordered his legs broken.[122] While he could be clear-headed and calculating, he could also be highly emotional. He could explode into bouts of anger, especially with his close friends, and he lamented that he could not control it in their presence.[123] Most famously, on hearing the news of the disaster in Germania he cried: 'Quinctilius Varus give me back my legions!' In this regard, Maecenas was a moderating influence when the *princeps*' temper got the better of him.[124] His deputies were an assortment of temperaments: Agrippa was bashful, but impatient; Aelius Lamia kindly; Calpurnius Piso (Piso the Pontifex) willing to compromise; Cornelius Balbus showy; Domitius Ahenobarbus arrogant and cruel; Marcius Censorinus very likable; and Tiberius was brooding and intense, to describe but a few.

Augustus involved himself directly and personally in the planning of military affairs. Rome's enemies posed threats both within and without the border constantly. Immediately after Actium, military actions were *ad hoc*, mostly responses by local commanders to quell unrest among peoples already subject to Roman rule and to block raids by foreign invaders. His decision to redeploy legions in 30 BCE while in Brundisium indicates that he was ready to deal with the present threats to the nation's security. It also reveals that he was thinking longer-term and was positioning the troops where he needed them to be as part of a larger strategic plan.

Before committing to a military campaign, Augustus conducted what could be called a strategic risk assessment. Suetonius preserves his dictum of the 'golden fish hook' (*aureo hamo piscantibus*):

> He used to say that a war or a battle should not be begun under any circumstances, unless the hope of gain was clearly greater than the fear of loss; for he likened such as grasped at slight gains with no slight risk to those who fished with a golden hook, the loss of which, if it were carried off, could not be made good by any catch.[125]

To improve the chances of success in war, he believed in bringing overwhelming force (*vis maior*) to bear on an opponent. The campaigns in Cantabria (26–25 BCE), Germania (12–9 BCE) and Illyricum (6–9 CE) brought together some of the largest numbers of legions and auxiliary units ever assembled. The army groups might be split to execute pincer movements, as in the war planned against the Marcomanni (which had to be abandoned) or in the war against the Astures and Cantabria. In these actions, coordination between the commanders was crucial to ensuring the objective of encircling and crushing the enemy was achieved. Augustus also believed in patience. Actium was the epitome of this type of battle. Both sides faced each other on dry land for months before finally engaging upon the sea. A war might take years to accomplish the final goal – speed was secondary to quality of the result.

Comparing the campaign to annex Germania with the pacification of Illyricum makes for an interesting case study. In 27 BCE, there was no strategic imperative to acquire the lands east of the Rhine. Tacitus would later ask rhetorically:

> Who would leave Asia, or Africa, or Italia for Germania, with its wild country, its inclement skies, its sullen manners and aspect, unless indeed it were his home?[126]

Roman commanders were reluctant to involve themselves in protracted military engagement in what was for them the unknown. On two occasions (in 55 and 53 BCE), Iulius Caesar constructed a wooden pontoon bridge across the river and M. Agrippa followed him some years later (in 39/38 or 19/18 BCE). Neither general conducted their missions for conquest, but in response to pleas for intervention from the Ubii, an ally of the Romans. The ambush of Lollius in 17 BCE by Germanic bandits on Roman territory seems to have been the tipping point that caused Augustus to re-evaluate policy in the region. Augustus relocated to *Colonia* Copia Felix Munatia for some portion of the four years he was away from Rome, and took Tiberius with him. Having acquitted himself well in the *Bellum Alpium*, Nero Claudius Drusus was appointed to lead operations. Augustus would certainly have discussed the details of the invasion plan with them.

Successive explorations had established its boundaries:

> Germania is separated from the Galliae, Raeti and Pannonii by the rivers Rhenus and Danuvius; from the Sarmatae and Daci, by mountains and mutual dread: the rest is surrounded by an ocean, embracing broad promontories and vast insular tracts, in which our military expeditions have lately discovered various nations and kingdoms. The Rhenus, issuing from the inaccessible and precipitous summit of the Raetic Alps, bends gently to the west, and falls into the Northern Ocean.[127]

Before these wars, much less was known about it. Roman commanders had maps but their detail and accuracy at this period is generally believed to have been poor.[128] In the case of Germania, its scale confounded the geographers of the ancient world. To compile the current state of knowledge, Agrippa had assembled a team of Greek scholars to create a 'Map of the World' (*Orbis Terrarum*).[129] About Germania, Pliny the Elder writes:

> the dimensions of its respective territories it is quite impossible to state, so immensely do the authors differ who have touched upon this subject. The Greek writers and some of our own countrymen have stated the coast of Germania to be 2,500 miles in extent, while Agrippa, comprising Raetia and Noricum in his estimate, makes the length to be 686 miles, and the breadth 148.[130]

These woefully inaccurate measurements would undermine any serious military planning from the start. Compared to the combined measurement of the *Tres Galliae* (420 Roman miles long by 318 miles wide) in Agrippa's *Orbis Terrarum*, the whole of Germania was only eight times greater. It had taken the army of

Iulius Caesar just nine years to reduce these Three Gallic Provinces; the Iberian Peninsula had required two centuries. On the basis of these comparisons, the conquest of Germania seemed an attainable objective.

Germania was home to dozens of independent tribal nations or coalitions. They lived in scattered villages and hamlets in forest clearings or beside rivers, not in large *oppida* like the Iron Age people who inhabited Gallia Comata or Noricum. A campaign involving one large pincer movement would not work. Instead, the strategy for conquest was phased so that with each campaign season Roman forces attacked particular targets, took the territory, held it with a small garrison and returned during the next year to continue the progress. It was an incremental advance, hold and build strategy. To support these invasions, military installations were first erected along the Rhine from which invasions could be launched and supported by matériel delivered by river. It took two years (14–13 BCE) to build out the fortresses, a canal system and a fleet. Five legions (some drawn down from Hispania Taraconnensis) and several auxiliary *alae* and *cohortes* were moved in.

The initial phase of the *Bellum Germanicum* under Nero Claudius Drusus took four years (12–9 BCE), following the Lippe, Ems and Main, and a nominal frontier was established between the Weser and Elbe. The premature death of the commander did not halt operations. They were continued for two more years (8–7 BCE) by his brother. Some tribes were attacked and defeated (like the Bructeri, Sugambri and Usipetes) and their unconditional surrender received, while others (like the Cananefates, Frisii, Chauci and Cherusci) became allies. Hostages were taken – including one Arminius – to be educated in Rome. By 1 CE, the Elbe River had been traversed by the detestable Domitius Ahenobarbus. Meanwhile, the essential infrastructure of roads and urban settlements was developed by him and his successors, Sentius Saturninus (6–3 BCE or 3–5 CE) and Vinicius (2/3–4 CE). Uprisings were quelled by Tiberius, who used *vastatio* to bring the troublemakers to terms in 4 and 5 CE. Roman troops were stationed along the tributaries of the Rhine on the right bank and also embedded within Germanic communities to advance the process of pacification. Their geographical dispersion enabled a coalition of nations led by Arminius of the Cherusci to massacre the army of occupation in 9 CE. When Quinctilius Varus (the military governor since 6 CE) was lured into a trap and his army ambushed, the great project was interrupted. Having planned for so long and invested so much, little wonder Augustus mourned the loss. However, it was not abandoned. Germanicus was dispatched in 13 CE to recover the territory.

In contrast, Illyricum had been of interest to the Romans for centuries. The geography and demographics of the Western Balkans were relatively well understood in the first century BCE.[131] When it became a Roman province is not known with certainty, but by 59 BCE Iulius Caesar had been granted *imperium* to operate in the territory.[132] Under the terms of the Treaty of Brundisium, Imp. Caesar had control of it and in 35–34 BCE he undertook campaigns there in person with M. Agrippa. By 27 BCE, it was a *bona fide* province, but not part of Augustus' *provincia*. That changed in 22 BCE when the Senate gave it to him.

In 13 BCE, M. Vincius was faced with a rebellion among the people of the north of the territory (whom Dio collectively calls Pannonii). Agrippa was sent to assist. His arrival was sufficient deterrent for the rebels to seek terms. The following year, an insurrection broke out among the coastal nations (whom Dio calls Dalmatae). Tiberius was sent to quell it and took troops from the north of the country. The Roman army now absent, the Pannonii took the opportunity to cause mischief. Tiberius was able to call on the assistance of the Scordisci, who were allies, to ravage their country. Those taken prisoner were sold as slaves. But his harsh recourse only caused deep resentment. Tiberius would spend the next several campaign seasons in a deadly game of 'whack-a-mole' in attempting to pacify the province. Under terms of their treaty, the nations living in Illyricum were required to provide troops for the *auxilia*. When the *legatus Augusti* M. Valerius Messalla Messallinus issued the call to join the *signa* for the war against the Marcomanni, it seems that, unbeknownst to him, the leader of the Breuci refused. In 6 CE, this Bato led a direct assault against Sirmium. Other nations were inspired to join the rebellion. When he combined forces with Bato of the Daesidiates, who launched an attack on *Colonia* Martia Iulia Salona, the Romans faced the real possibility of losing Illyricum altogether. Legions already across the Danube River were redirected by Tiberius, who led the counter-insurgency. He coordinated the efforts of the commanders of Illyricum and Moesia, assisted by Thracian allies.

Perhaps the issue was Tiberius' inflexible approach? All he was doing was implementing the tried and tested military policy. In Illyricum in 12–9 BCE and Germania in 8–7 BCE and 4–5 CE, he had launched *vastatio* upon the native tribes for breaking their good faith treaty terms. By the time Varus had assumed command in Germania in 6 CE, the local people in general seemed ready again to engage in trade, adopt Roman law and pay taxes. The situation appeared similarly calm in Illyricum, but it was disrupted when the annual tribute was combined with a levy on the men for a war they did not want to fight. In Tiberius' view, their refusal to obey the call to arms and their violent insurrection could only be met with blood and steel. Though losing territory, the rebels could continue to wage a guerrilla war against the Romans for some time. The relentless action of the army of Tiberius and his deputies over four campaign summers only succeeded when the rebel leader himself saw no possibility for victory and surrendered. Tiberius' reaction was surprising. He spared Bato's life. A couple of years later, Illyricum was split into two smaller provinces and economic investment in the form of roads and towns followed – in Dalmatia under the enlightened management of P. Cornelius Dolabella. Both provinces were garrisoned. The Romans had finally found a way to work *with* the people of the region.

Taking advantage of the Romans' distraction in the Balkans, Arminius of the Cherusci led a revolt of nations in Germania that caught the *legatus Augusti* unprepared, despite being pre-warned. After the ambush at *Saltus Teutoburgiensis*, Rome still had allies across the Rhine, but it would take time for Augustus' organization to regroup and decide how best to respond. For the time being, Germania across the Rhine was lost. It survived only in the name of two military districts carved out of Gallia Belgica. Both were also garrisoned. There was no rush to regain the lands north of the Rhine as there had been to salvage those south of the Danube. Why? Illyricum was simply more important strategically. Nevertheless, in total thirteen legions – more than half of Augustus' entire citizen army – were now stationed just in the two Germanies, Dalmatia and Pannonia, to which can be added many more auxiliary units.[133] Whereas the legions along the Rhine and Danube were intended to intercept a Germanic invasion, those in the Western Balkans kept vigil against further internal unrest.

What if certain key events had unfolded differently? It is an interesting thought experiment in alternative history. If *legatus Augusti* Valerius Messalla Messallinus had better understood the mood among his provincials, he might have been able to pre-empt, prevent or crush the revolt of the Daesidates before it could spread and become a national insurgency. Tiberius might have delayed the invasion of Bohaemium or he could have proceeded, assured that the situation in Illyricum was contained. Had the pincer movement targeting Marboduus been successful, that, in turn, would have allowed the Romans to extend their reach up the eastern flank of Germania along the Elbe River. In this scenario, Arminius would have had to consider cancelling his revolt. Had the German chief then proceeded, the Romans would have been better positioned to deal with it by mounting a counterattack from the east; if Arminius moved ahead, he might well have been defeated, sooner or later. Similarly, if Varus had heeded the warning from Segestes and arrested Arminius and Segimerus, three legions and several auxiliary cohorts would have remained operational and he would have lived. There would likely have been more uprisings, but as in other parts of the empire, resistance was usually finally broken as long as the Romans could keep replacing their casualties. Recruiting auxiliaries from new allies in eastern Germania could have provided the necessary manpower to supplement the existing force. Either way, under these changed circumstances it is well within the realm of possibility that the pacification of province Germania could have continued, and its borders even expanded beyond the Elbe River to the Vistula. The Roman world, and indeed our own, would look very different.

Throughout this dynamic period of history – as it actually happened – Augustus was kept apprised by his commanders of the ongoing military situation and doubtless made strategy and policy recommendations. He regularly left Rome to set up his base of operations in Aquileia, Ticinum or other cities where he would be closer to the front and receive correspondence from his *legati*. During the War of the Batos:

> he was so vigorous when it came to directing campaigns against the enemy that he proceeded to Ariminum in order that he might be near at hand to give all necessary advice in regard to both the Dalmati and the Pannonii.[134]

Indeed his successor was publicly criticized for remaining in Rome while the Rhine and Danube armies mutinied, whereas, even in old age, Augustus always left the city to be closer to the conflict.[135] On his travels he was accompanied by his German bodyguard and *Cohortes Praetoriae* (see Appendix 3.1 and 3.2). Augustus spent time over the winter months reviewing the prior season's campaigning and discussing the next. He had a small personal staff of freedmen – some of whose names are known from Suetonius' account and cited above – who assisted him in processing his orders (*praescripta*, *mandata*), replies (*rescripta*) and executive summaries (*breviarii*). The remarkable fact is how few support staff Augustus had to run his office – perhaps no more than a handful of trusted assistants at any time.

This was possible because the bulk of the administration for management control purposes was done in the provinces. It was a decentralised model. The effectiveness of Augustus' control over his organization relied on accurate and comprehensive information about it being provided by his deputies. Crucially, each propraetorian legate was responsible for assembling an annual register (*pridianum*) of the strength of the units in his province as of 31 December. These reports were collated from information provided by army clerks at the camps (detailing each unit's location, date of arrival there, net numerical strength, as well as numbers of promotions and transfers in and out, casualties, new recruits, discharges and other relevant information) and summarised by the legionary staff (*officium*) seconded to the *legatus Augusti*. These registers provided statistical information about manpower resources that formed the basis for strategic and tactical planning.

To keep this information updated, Augustus regularly communicated with his subordinates. To facilitate the flow of information he set up a postal service:

> To enable what was going on in each of the provinces to be reported and known more speedily and promptly, he at first stationed young men at short intervals along the military roads, and afterwards post-chaises. The latter has seemed the more convenient arrangement, since the same men who bring the dispatches from any place can, if occasion demands, be questioned as well.[136]

There were times when secure communications were also required, as we know from allegedly secret *mandata* that he placed in safekeeping with L. Calpurnius Piso (Piso the Pontifex).[137] He was not comfortable speaking extempore to large crowds, and if he did have to speak publicly he composed his thoughts and wrote them down first.[138] If he needed the contents to be kept confidential, following the example of Iulius Caesar, he used a code. His chosen cipher was one with a shift of one whereby 'he wrote B for A, C for B, and the rest of the letters on the same principle, using AA for X'.[139] He used a signet ring containing an intaglio that could be pressed into a bead of wax affixed to his letters to prove they came from him:

> In passports, dispatches, and private letters he used as his seal at first a sphinx, later an image of Alexander the Great, and finally his own, carved by the hand of Dioscurides; and this his successors continued to use as their seal.[140]

When Augustus believed himself close to death in 23 BCE, he handed this ring to Agrippa. In 31 BCE, Augustus had given identical copies of his seal to both Agrippa and Maecenas so they could open documents written by him, amend them as they thought appropriate, and reseal them with his full authority.[141]

He was a meticulous record-keeper. He kept a record detailing the armed forces and public finances and guarded it carefully. He formally handed it to Calpurnius Piso (the suffect with whom he shared the consulate) at the same time he gave Agrippa his ring in 23 BCE. An updated version of this document (the *breviarum* in Suetonius' account), was produced during the reading of the will thirty-seven years later. Augustus was obsessive about dating his correspondence and 'always attached to all letters the exact hour, not only of the day, but even of the night, to indicate precisely when they were written'.[142]

At the end of a campaign season, a commander customarily submitted a war report to the Senate, which was read aloud by one of the officials. This practice ended abruptly when M. Agrippa presented his review directly to Augustus after his mission in Cantabria in 19 BCE.[143] Agrippa's action made clear that military matters conducted in Augustus' *provincia* were the privilege of the *princeps*, whose choice it was to share information with the Conscript Fathers, or not. Having official command of armed forces there from 27 BCE, it was a function of Augustus' organization to decide on the deployment of the army in ensuring security and relations with neighbouring nations. It was clearly effective and a fact recognized by foreign heads of state, who sent deputations to *him* and sought *his* friendship (whether from Ethiopia, India, Parthia or indeed the British kingdoms), not the Senate's.[144] Agrippa represented him in the East, as did Tiberius and C. Caesar, who met the Parthian king on the Euphrates River. Augustus maintained his active interest in international affairs even into his final years. When he was too frail to receive such delegations alone, he enlisted the support of consulars.

After the Actian and Alexandrian Wars, the number of legions in the victor's care, combining his own and those formerly under the command of M. Antonius, numbered more or less sixty. His decision to disband half of them was remarkable, yet it was in keeping with the traditional practices of the *Res Publica*. The Roman army before the first century BCE was essentially a citizen militia. When the Senate and Popular Assemblies voted for war, the citizens would form up in their centuries on the *Campus Martius* and swear the *sacramentum*, the solemn oath to follow the consuls, obey and execute the orders of the officers, never leave their posts or do anything illegal.[145] Grouped into legions, they marched to fight in the summer season and were disbanded when they returned in the autumn. In 31–30 BCE, demobilization was a pragmatic solution. Cutting the number not only reduced the threat posed to the *Res Publica* by such a large number of increasingly bored, restless and resentful men, it also slashed the crippling cost of paying them for their service, which the victor now bore. Yet it was more than just about the money. At the end of the war Imp. Caesar had a special relationship with the army – the shared values of loyalty, service and sacrifice. The manner in which he retired his men would be an opportunity for him to display his gratitude (or clemency in the case of the defeated troops) and to secure their continued support in retirement. The immediate challenge was to address the massive logistics and security problem. The ever-trustworthy M. Agrippa was assigned to take the demobbed troops to Italy and find them homes. Of the more than 300,000 men Augustus claimed to have resettled, some returned to the *municipia* from whence they originally came, while others were found homes in newly created cities for veterans (*coloniae*), as had been done in previous centuries.[146] Augustus boasts in the *Res Gestae* that he founded twenty-eight *coloniae* in Italy 'which have grown to be famous and populous during my lifetime' (table 8).[147] Others were located overseas as need dictated, in Achaea, Africa, Asia, Gallia Narbonensis, Hispania Citerior and Hispania Ulterior, Macedonia, Pisidia, Sicilia and Syria. The settlements of retired Roman troops would also play a vital role in pacifying these foreign territories, creating opportunities for Latin-speaking people to mix with the natives.[148] In time, a new generation of soldiers could be recruited from among the sons of these pro-military communities. In 29 BCE, the commander-in-chief gave just over a year's pay to each of the 120,000 qualifying

Table 8. *Coloniae* Established for Legionary Veterans by Augustus, 31 BCE–14 CE.

Colonia	Province	Date of Foundation
Venafrum	Italia, Regio I	Post Actium
Suessa	Italia, Regio I	Post Actium?
Luceria	Italia, Regio II	Pre 14 CE
Lucus Feroniae	Italia, Regio IV	Post Actium
Falerio	Italia, Regio V	?
Tuder	Italia, Regio VI	Post Actium
Fanum Fortunae	Italia, Regio VI	Before 25 BCE
Sutrium	Italia, Regio VII	?
Rusellae	Italia, Regio VII	?
Saena	Italia, Regio VII	?
Obsequens Iulia Pisana	Italia, Regio VII	Post Actium
Brixellum	Italia, Regio VIII	?
Placentia	Italia, Regio VIII	Post Actium
Brixia	Italia, Regio X	Post Actium
Ateste	Italia, Regio X	Post Actium
Augusta Taurinorum	Italia, Regio XI	Post Actium or later
Augusta Praetoria Salassorum	Italia, Regio XI	25 BCE
Augusta Aroe Patrensis	Achaea	Post Actium
Alexandria Augusta Troadis	Asia	15 BCE
Caesarea	Galatia-Pamphylia	25 BCE
Caesaraugusta	Hispania Tarraconensis	25–12 CE
Augusta Buthrotum	Illyricum	Before 25 BCE?
Augusta Emerita	Lusitania	25 BCE
Paxaugusta (Pax Iulia?)	Lusitania	15–14 BCE
Augusta Vindelicorum	Raetia	15 BCE
Syracusae	Siciliae	22 BCE
Iulia Augusta Felix Berytus	Syria	Post Actium

Source: Dio; Keppie (1984), pp. 77–114; Rich (2002), p. 140; Swan (2001), p. 342.

men – an astonishing HS120 million in total – as their share of the war spoils, injecting a huge infusion of cash into the economies of these new towns.[149]

The victor of the Civil War could now design the type of army he wanted to serve his military organization. He opted to stick with the tried and tested model and kept the legions formed of sixty centuries arranged in ten cohorts apiece, which had fought to victory on his own side (plate 20). However, many of his legions had suffered casualties or lost men to honourable discharge and were below full strength. Re-assigning men from other disbanded units to these legions would address that problem. In a few cases the commander-in-chief also blended two different legions together to make up their numbers, and identified them by the honorific title *Gemina*, 'Twin' (see Appendix 3.3). Altogether there would be a standing army of twenty-eight legions of professional troops, each *legionarius* receiving a regular stipend. Citizens and freeborn would be eligible to serve for a term fixed initially at sixteen years, with the option of being recalled for four more. The legionary serving a full term and discharged honourably (*honesta missio*) would be eligible to receive a *praemia* of a cash lump sum or land. Each legion would be commanded by a *legatus legionis* granted *imperium* in the manner pioneered successfully by Iulius Caesar.[150] Legions prior to him had no permanent commander.[151] The legate's position would not be an elected one. Augustus could not chance their loyalty to politics. He would personally appoint each legionary legate from Rome's senatorial class, typically ex-praetors and ex-quaestors, and they would be changed on a regular basis.[152] That way a commander could not become so comfortable in his position that he might be tempted to use the legion to challenge Augustus' deputy or even the *princeps*. The legionary legate's second in command, the *tribunus militum laticlavius* ('military tribune with the broadstripe') would also be handpicked by Augustus from among the sons of senators.[153] It would be the young man's chance to learn first-hand the arts of military command in readiness for a legateship of his own some day. His team of five *tribuni militum angusticlavii* ('military tribunes with the narrow stripe'), acting as adjutants, would be picked from the *Ordo Equester*.

In making these changes, Augustus had created Rome's first nationalized army.[154] It was a revolutionary development in the history of the *Res Publica*. The army was his creature, subordinated to his will. Indeed, he insisted that the men of the legions would swear the oath of allegiance to him personally every year.[155] Crucially, it made possible a new phase of pacification in his province – and expansion beyond it.

Establishing a nationalized army entailed heavy financial and administrative burdens. Fiscally conservative by nature, Augustus was particularly concerned about the financial viability of the army. The cost of a standing army was an immense burden on the public purse (*Aerarium Saturni*) – by one calculation representing 77 per cent of the Commonwealth's budget.[156] The annual cost is hard to determine accurately, but one reasoned estimate of the recurring annual expense of twenty-five legions after 9 CE (assuming there were 140,000 legionaries each being paid HS900 per year, and allowing for higher pay for officers) was HS150 million; plus there was HS40 million for the *Vigiles*, Praetorian and

Urban Cohorts, and perhaps HS120 million for the *auxilia*.[157] The cost each year of *praemia* to the honourably discharged added a further HS48 million and to auxiliary soldiers HS30 million more (assuming the auxiliaries received a retirement benefit). In total, Augustus needed an annual budget of HS350–400 million to service the cost in salaries and benefits or risk losing the loyalty of the troops. Much of this had to be managed in hard cash, since the Roman economy was a money economy.[158] Reducing actual outgoings were deductions for food, clothing and equipment, which meant troops were not always paid in full, and some payments were made in kind.[159] Nevertheless, when Augustus writes in *Res Gestae* that he assisted the Public Treasury with his own money four times with the sum of HS150 million, this would cover only about half the serving troops' salaries.[160] Yet the HS170 million in cash he contributed to the Military Treasury (*Aerarium Militare*), which he founded himself in 6 CE, only ensured that there would be just over two years' worth of cash in the fund to cover *praemia*.

Augustus knew well the dangers of running out of money. This concern had two consequences. Firstly, new sources of tax revenue would be needed. This was likely the reasoning behind levying the *centesima rerum venalium* (1 per cent tax on sales by auction) and *quinta et vicesima venalium mancipiorum* (4 per cent tax on the sale of slaves), and certainly the purpose of the *vicesima hereditatum* (5 per cent tax on inheritances).[161] Secondly, the army had to engage in periodic wars of conquest to find *praeda* – booty and slaves that could be sold to raise cash. It may explain why military campaigns to complete the conquest of Hispania Citerior (26–19 BCE) and to annex Noricum (15 BCE) were launched – the former provided rich sources of gold and silver, the latter gold and high-quality iron, among other valuable commodities.[162] Coincidentally, the decision not to reconstitute *Legiones* XVII, XIIX and XIX after the *Clades Variana*, notwithstanding any concerns with bad luck, saved the budget each year approximately HS18 million in salaries and HS6 million owed to retiring soldiers having completed twenty or more years. To Augustus, who was managing a tight budget, every *sestertius* counted. The loss of three legions and as many auxiliary units was an opportunity for retrenchment.

Augustus recognized that pay and conditions – length of service and retirement benefits – were potential sources of discontentment among the troops. There not having been a nationalized army before, Augustus was learning about such matters as they arose. His 'reforms' were attempts to deal with the issues.[163] Historically, legions were raised on an annual basis, but as the empire grew some units could serve away continuously and their men were effectively working open contracts.[164] Those signing up as legionaries in their twenties following Iulius Caesar's murder would leave in large numbers, starting with the demobilization after Actium – the same time that several *coloniae* were founded – while those enrolling to replace them would be discharged from 14 BCE onwards. The new regulations passed in time for that release date fixed the term for a newly enrolling legionary at sixteen years. When that group began to retire, starting in 2 CE, the revision to the army regulations was urgently needed. Augustus insisted the Senate deal with the matter. Their agreement to raise service to twenty years

206 Augustus at War

in 5 CE was already late. Lengthening years of service was efficient because men with experience stayed in the ranks longer, reducing the frequency of recruiting new troops and the time for training them. It was also cost-effective. The Senate agreed that a legionary was to be paid a discharge bonus of HS12,000. With sixteen years of service, a theoretical 155 legionaries would leave each legion every year at a cost of HS1.9 million; increasing the service term to twenty years reduced the number to 135 men and the cost to HS1.6 million, saving 15 per cent.[165] The actual number leaving would be further attritted by premature deaths in service from health conditions, disease and wounds received in combat – in other words, extending the term of service raised the likelihood that some men would not live to see retirement and collect their *praemia*.

However, the system was prone to inefficiency and abuse. Once, Imp. Caesar had begged men to join him in his quest for justice. For a price, many did so. From the moment he had won, the soldiers again became the subordinated.[166] Firstly, many soldiers were forced to stay on well after their official term had ended. The exigencies of war may have been one reason, but the cumbersome administration based on handwritten records probably contributed to delays in release from service. The personal records of a soldier were stored in the archive of the winter camp, and a prolonged campaign would separate the man from them and the information about his enrollment date. Measures had to be taken 'in order to keep them from being tempted to revolution after their discharge either by age or poverty'.[167] Secondly, Augustus had originally acquired land for his troops in Italy – up to 14.7 hectares per legionary.[168] The *Res Gestae* states he paid out HS400 million in tranches over the years 7, 6, 4, 3 and 2 BCE.[169] When that source was exhausted, he had to look elsewhere. It resulted in some men receiving near worthless allotments. The grant of land was eventually replaced with the cash lump sum, so the retiree could decide how best to provide for his senior years. The financial drain on the public purse led to Augustus setting up the separate *Aerarium Militare* in 6 CE. Thirdly, in some units grievances were compounded by discipline enforced harshly and unfairly, as in the shocking case of the centurion nicknamed *Cedo Alteram* ('Gimme Another'). Some soldiers paid centurions bribes to avoid unpleasant duties or take time off. Fourthly, troops expected quick victories and a share of the spoils. In these long drawn-out campaigns, wins were elusive, booty was scarce and sleeping under goatskin on uneven ground year after year sapped morale.

These feelings could be amplified by the relative isolation of army units from the rest of the population. Separated both physically by the location of their camps, and their different status as professional soldiers, legions could become inward-looking institutions, worlds unto themselves. In extreme cases, troops gave full vent to their grievances in mutinies. Augustus' best commanders – M. Agrippa (in northern Spain in 19 BCE) and Tiberius (in Illyricum in 8 CE) – both faced mutinous troops, despite the Roman army's reputation for discipline. For Agrippa, sitting below the Cantabrian Mountains, the solution was a mix of incentives and punishments that finally restored morale. For Tiberius, it was a rousing speech to his troops and a successful attack against the rebel stronghold of Andetrium which regained their confidence. In the weeks following Augustus' death, Tiberius' sons Germanicus and Drusus faced the full wrath of legionary soldiers frustrated by years of abuse. Only hard cash and firm commitments to re-introduce shorter, sixteen-year service terms could appease them and restore order.

Taken together, the reform measures – or more accurately *refinements* – went some way to addressing the concerns of the army rank and file but did not go far enough. Further, the great differential in pay, length of service and pension bonus between regular soldiers of the legions and guardsmen of the Praetorian Cohorts – which effectively bought the loyalty and protection of the *praetoriani* – brought with it risks of interference that would play out as an unintended consequence in later decades in the selection of emperors of Rome.

Augustus sought operational efficiencies in the professional army too. He is credited with having created the position of *praefectus castrorum*, the legion's third most important officer, appointed from the *Ordo Equester*.[170] Unlike the legate's and tribunes', his was a permanent job. It had to be. His responsibilities covered all the essential aspects involved in running a military base, from its location, ground plan and construction to office administration, from supply chain management to training of new recruits, from the maintenance of artillery to conducting sieges. He supervised the army on the march and its baggage train (*impedimenta*).[171] The position likely evolved out of a role performed by the *praefectus fabrum*, the officer in charge of camp workshops, of earlier times. The requirement for the new position likely arose as a natural consequence of establishing the nationalized, standing army. An incoming team of new commanding officers needed to rely on a professional who could run the unit without being told how. He would know its inner workings intimately, having been promoted from within the army. Aufidienus Rufus began his career as an ordinary soldier, serving in that capacity for several years, followed by promotion to centurion, before his appointment as *praefectus castrorum* of one of the Danube legions, where he is recorded in 14 CE.[172] He was a disciplinarian, which made him unpopular and a target during the mutiny. Resourcefulness could be a useful trait in this job, as L. Caecidius demonstrated when rescuing survivors fleeing from the Germans after the *Clades Variana*.[173]

The location of some installations indicates a desire by the military to assert control over access to space or a river.[174] In effect, where the *praefectus castrorum* set the location for a camp determined where the frontier lay. While campaigning troops would conduct operations from a summer camp (*in aestiva*), as for example in the early phases of the German War, they would withdraw to a winter camp (*in hiberna*).[175] Troops might then return the following year to the same location of the previous summer camp to launch a new thrust. This accounts for the multiple occupations at Haltern, Novaesium and other locations. Over successive phases of combat operations, the location of the winter camp could be moved up closer to the advancing theatre of war. Thus Vetera on the Rhine was superseded by Oberaden on the Lippe, then later itself replaced by Anreppen. As a result, in a multi-year war the frontier zone expanded and contracted with the seasons.

A chain of forts and supply dumps would be erected to keep the troops supplied. In Germania, many of the bases were erected beside rivers, where their function was associated with logistics, storing supplies received from the winter camp on the Rhine and distributing them to the summer camp on the front line. At these installations, Roman soldiers performed the functions of stevedores and quartermasters – all duties overseen by the *praefectus castrorum*. Transport by river was generally faster and safer than overland, an important consideration in a dynamic theatre of war where roads had not yet been laid down. Troops could also be moved by boat, as shown by the amphibious landings of Nero Claudius Drusus and Tiberius. The navy patrolled the rivers as well as acting as a coastguard (see Appendix 3.5).

Bases varied greatly in size and shape, depending on occupancy and terrain, and were not intended for permanent garrisons.[176] The archaeological evidence shows they ranged from the smallest fortlet of around 2 hectares to immense fortresses of 58 hectares – as large as fifty-four football pitches (table 9). During this period, the line of the perimeter embankment generally followed the contours of the ground – which was normally a high point in the landscape – so that no two ground plans are alike. The rectangular playing-card shape would come in later decades. As had been practice for years, internal layout placed the important buildings – the headquarters (*principia*), commander's house (*praetorium*) and tribunes' accommodations – in the centre, with the stores and barracks ranged in tidy rows to the front and rear of them.[177]

The fortresses of this period were often home to mixed units. Combining detachments of legions and auxiliaries under their flag standards (*vexilla*) was

Table 9. Comparison of Roman Military Installations and Garrisons.

Installation	Area (hectares)	Garrison
Carnuntum	58	2–3 legions plus *auxilia*
Oberaden	56	2 legions plus *auxilia*
Dorsten-Holsterhausen	50	2 legions plus *auxilia*
Nijmegen-Hunerberg	42	2 legions plus *auxilia*
Marktbreit	37	1–2 legions plus *auxilia*
Noevaesium	27	1 legion plus *auxilia*
Anreppen	23	1 legion
Haltern	18	1 legion or part thereof
Folleville	16	1 legion or part thereof
Dangstetten	13	1 legion or part thereof
Annaberg	7	1–2 cohorts
Olfen	5	1–2 cohorts
Hedemünden	4	1–2 cohorts
Rödgen	3	1 cohort
Beckinghausen	2	1 cohort

Sources: Bishop (2012); Delbrück (1990), p. 142; Keppie (1998); Kühlborn (2004); von Schnurbein (2000; 2002; 2004). For comparison, the maximum size of a football pitch is 120m × 90m. This is an area of 10,800m^2; 1 hectare = 10,000m^2. A full-size pitch could be 1.08 hectare.

another innovation pioneered under Augustus. These *vexillationes* provided a field commander with flexibility where a whole legion was not required or available, and they could be sized according to the needs of the mission. The *vexillarius* of 12,000 men commanded by *Legatus Augusti* Caecina Severus and military tribune Novellius Torquatus Atticus, and deployed in the punitive raid into Germania in 14 CE, included cohorts drawn from *Legiones* I, V, XX and XXI.[178] Such a detachment of veterans was formed to defend the city of Sirmium when it came under attack from rebels led by Bato of the Breuci in 6 CE.

Technical innovations to legionary arms and equipment occurred during Augustus' time as commander-in-chief. These were likely developed to address specific tactical threats, such as enemy weapons or fighting styles, by adding or modifying equipment as soldiers always do in wartime. Success with a new design would spread within one unit as men copied the idea. Perhaps with the approval of the *praefectus castrorum*, it could be deployed across a single legion and then replicated across an entire army group. This may explain the changes in head protection (*casis*, *galea*), particularly in the northern frontier region. Its design changed from the helmet made of bronze popularly known as the Montefortino (plate 19), in widespread use in 31 BCE, to the so-called Coolus style with a separate eye/brow guard to deflect blows to the face and a wider neck guard, and finally to the so-called Weisenau (or 'Imperial Gallic A') made of iron, with detailing at the front and back to strengthen the dome.[179] Body armour in common use among legionaries was a shirt of riveted links (*lorica hamata*) or scales (*lorica squamata*). From c. 15 BCE, a new form of articulated, segmented plate armour (the so-called *lorica segmentata*) was introduced (plate 21), and archaeological finds show that it was worn by some troops in the Alpine and German Wars.[180]

Roman soldiers faced an array of opponents fighting with different weapons and combat styles. Much as the Romans supposed themselves invincible, they were to learn the hard way under Augustus' auspices that not all barbarians were created equal. Far from being inept, their diverse enemies could be resourceful, skillful and *victorious*. A Cheruscan infantryman dressed only in textiles and carrying a crude wooden shield for protection made up for his poverty of armour with agility in the use of the *framea* and prowess in irregular warfare. The Cantabrian cavalryman charged with his compatriots arrayed in tight formation, and could turn in an instant to spear his opponent. Native war fighters trained long hours to master technique, becoming professionals in their own right. Eschewing the set-piece battle for guerrilla warfare, they could stall the advance of legionaries equipped and trained to fight on the open plain or to besiege a stronghold. In arid valleys, dense forests and rocky mountain ranges across Europe, they launched ambushes upon lines of marching Roman troops where they were at their most vulnerable. Sometimes their foes – like Arminius or Bato – were natives trained in Roman combat doctrine. They knew how to inflict maximum damage. Roman commanders – like Tiberius and his brother – were forced to rethink tactics to deal with their adversary. They knew they had to win. The recruitment of troops into native *alae* and cohorts not only placed large numbers of tribesmen where they could be controlled, but their myriad fighting

Table 10. Military Manpower, 31 BCE and 14 CE (Estimates).

Unit	31 BCE	14 CE
Germani Corporis Custodes	500?	500?
Cohortes Praetoriae	8,000	10,000
Legiones	300,000	150,000
Auxilia	80,000	150,000
Classes	75,000	45,000
Cohortes Ingenuorum / Cohortes Voluntariorum	5,000	23,000
Cohortes Urbanae	–	4,000
Vigiles Urbani / Cohortes Vigilum	–	6,000
Total	468,500	388,500

Sources: Appendix 3.

styles could balance out the asymmetry of warfare – pitting barbarians working for Romans against other barbarians who did not. Augustus' innovation was to recruit them in numbers not seen before (see Appendix 3.4). Earning less money than the legionary soldiers, the *auxilia* could be more cost-effectively deployed to augment the economy of force represented by the legions (table 10).

Regular pay motivated the majority of troops of Augustus' standing army to risk their lives, but public recognition could raise ordinary performance in ways financial compensation alone could not. Honour-bound to look out for the welfare of his comrades in battle, a soldier witnessed amazing acts of bravery and courage by men in his unit, reinforcing the sense of brotherhood and belonging. Military decorations (*dona*) rewarded exceptional performance or dedication beyond the call of duty among the lower ranks. Several types were awarded. When deserved, Augustus personally issued them to troops and encouraged his sons to do the same, as Tiberius did in Germania, Illyricum and Pannonia:

> As military prizes he [Augustus] was somewhat more ready to give *phalerae* or *torques*, valuable for their gold and silver, than *coronae* for scaling ramparts or walls, which conferred high honour; the latter he gave as sparingly as possible and without favouritism, often even to the common soldiers.[181]

(These distinctions were denied to the *legati Augusti*.)[182] To judge by the few recorded examples dating to the Augustan period that have come down to us, all grades in a legion participated (table 11). A *praefectus* and *primipilares* personally led their men in attacks on military installations, earning themselves *coronae*, and at least one centurion saved the life of a compatriot. The *primipilus* M. Vergilius Gallus Lusius received his two spears (*hastae*) without iron heads and a golden crown (*corona aurea*) in person from Augustus and Tiberius.[183] Many ordinary soldiers also engaged in acts of courage, earning themselves multiple decorations. L. Antonius Quadratus was decorated twice by Tiberius.[184]

While Roman troops fought gallantly to pacify unruly foreign lands, security for people living in the Italian homeland was often patchy in the first decades of Augustus' principate. The capital city was effectively a demilitarized zone where

Table 11. Military Awards Issued, 31 BCE–14 CE.

Rank and name	Award(s)	Source
Imperator:		
Imp. Caesar *Divi f.* Augustus	*Corona Civica*	Dio 53.16.4
Legati Augusti:		
M. Agrippa	*Corona Muralis, Vexillum*	Dio 51.21.3; Livy, *Peri.* 129.4
Praefecti:		
C. Fabricius Tuscus	*Corona Aurea, Hastae*	ZPE 13 (1974)
Primipilares:		
C. Allius Oriens	*Torques, Phalerae*	*CIL* XIII, 5206
L. Rufellius Severus	*Corona Vallaris*	*CIL* XI, 6224; V, 698
T. Statius Marrax	*Corona*	*ILS* 2368
M. Vergilius Gallus Lusius	*Corona Aurea, Hastae*	*CIL* X, 4862
Centuriones:		
L. Blattius Vetus	*Phalerae*	*NSA* 1893, p. 58
M. Caelius	*Torques, Phalerae, Corona Civica*	*CIL* XIII, 8648
M. Petronius Classicus		*CIL* III, 4060
L. Refidius Bassus		*CIL* XIII, 11837
Milites:		
M. Aemilius Soterias	*Torques, Phalerae*	*ILS* 2321
L. Antonius Quadratus	*Torques, Phalerae, Armillae*	*CIL* V, 4356 (2272)
L. Coelius	*Torques, Phalerae*	*CIL* V, 7495 (2337)
M. Fraxsanias	*Torques, Phalerae*	*CIL* III, 9885 (2322)
L. Gellius Varus	*Torques, Phalerae*	*CIL* V, 5586
M. Helvius Rufus	*Torques, Corona Civica*	*CIL* XIV, 3472 (2637)
C. Iulius [...]lus	*Torques*	*CIL* VIII, 5209
L. Leuconius Cilo	*Corona Aurea*	*CIL* V, 4902
Q. Sertorius Festus	*Torques, Corona Aurea*	*CIL* V, 3374
C. Vettius	*Torques, Phalerae*	*CIL* III, 4858 (2466)
M. Vireius	*Torques, Phalerae*	*CIL* III, 2718

Sources: Maxfield (1984), p. 161; Wardle (1990), p. 195. This list is not exhaustive.

armed soldiers did not patrol. Perhaps in part due to this, Rome remained a dangerous place for its inhabitants. In 47 BCE, fully three years before Iulius Caesar's assassination, the consuls were compelled to ban anyone from openly carrying weapons within the *pomerium*.[185] Yet there were still several attempts on Augustus' life, and he felt sufficiently at risk that he wore armour under his tunic while attending meetings of the Senate and took his bodyguard with him at other times and places. There were several conspiracies to assassinate him or Agrippa – plots are recorded in 31, 22 and 18 BCE, and one as late into his principate as 4 CE. His investigators (*speculatores*) seem to have been highly effective at foiling these attempts (see Appendix 3.1). Finally enacted under Augustus, the *Lex Iulia de Vi Publica* made it illegal to collect weapons in houses in the city and the country, except for those customarily used for wild game hunting or taken on trips by land and sea for personal safety.[186] Specifically to maintain peace and order in Rome, Augustus introduced the paramilitary *Cohortes Urbanae* or 'City

Cohorts' (see Appendix 3.7).[187] When he put on games in 2 CE, he deployed guards throughout the city to ensure thieves did not help themselves to people's property.[188] During the months following the 'Disaster of Varus' of 9 CE, the *urbaniciani* maintained patrols (*excubiae*) through the night.[189]

Augustus claimed to have rid the seas of pirates.[190] Dio, however, reports that in 6 CE pirates overran the coastal communities of the western Mediterranean, casting doubt on the *princeps'* assertion. Travellers going by road could still be assaulted, robbed, taken hostage for ransom or even murdered. Brigandage was a problem in several parts of the Roman world at the time of Augustus, notably in Cilicia, Gallia Cisalpina and Hispania Citerior. *Latrocinium* covered violent armed robbery committed by *latrones* or bandits; if caught, they could face a range of punishments up to execution.[191] Below them were the *grassatores*, footpads or muggers, who often operated in gangs (*factiones*); capture would entail time in the mines or exile, but not usually execution. Suetonius' report states:

> Many pernicious practices militating against public security had survived as a result of the lawless habits of the civil wars, or had even arisen in time of peace. Gangs of *grassatores* openly went about with swords by their sides, ostensibly to protect themselves, and travellers in the country, freemen and slaves alike, were seized and kept in confinement in the workhouses of the land owners; numerous leagues, too, were formed for the commission of crimes of every kind, assuming the title of some new guild.[192]

Their activities, if left unchecked, threatened the internal security of the armed Provinces of Caesar, the unarmed Provinces of the People and the homeland as well. Augustus' solution was to deploy the military and root out the sources of criminal behaviour:

> Therefore to put a stop to brigandage, he stationed guards of soldiers wherever it seemed advisable, inspected the workhouses, and disbanded all guilds, except such as were of long standing and formed for legitimate purposes.[193]

The stated mission of Nero Claudius Drusus' war in Raetia in 15 BCE was to eradicate bandits freely operating in Gallia Cisalpina and Italy.[194] (The offensive in the Alps was explicitly a 'Just War'.) In 5 BCE, Sulpicius Quirinius fought a hard war against the coalition of bandits called Homonadeis in Cilicia, taking 4,000 prisoners when he had completed his campaign. In the Iberian Peninsula, the measures taken by the robber named Corocotta to evade capture in 26 BCE succeeded in turning this ancient Robin Hood figure into a lovable old rogue who earned the clemency of Augustus and a cash reward. The outcome of this concerted action was to rid the world of brigandage, a fact lauded by Velleius Paterculus as *the* major achievement of the *Pax Augusta*.[195]

Riots threatened the peace of urban life from time to time (table 12). Then, as now, they were a way for the people to express their frustration with authority. In Rome in 21 BCE, Agrippa had to quell disturbances on two different occasions, once when Augustus refused to stand for consul and again over the election of a

Table 12. Incidents of Civil Protest and Riot, 31 BCE–14 CE.

Years	Region/City	Disturbance
28 BCE	Heroöpolis – Egypt	Riot
21	Rome	Riot
21	Athens	Peaceful protest
21	Kyzikos – Mysia	Riot
21	Tyre – Syria	Riot
21	Sidon – Syria	Riot
19	Rome	Riot
20	Alexandria	Riot
4	Hierosolyma – Iudaea	Riot
11 CE	Athens	Riot

Sources: Acts; Dio; Josephus; Orosius.

junior prefect who attended the Latin Festival. More serious, on his outbound journey to the East in the same year Augustus learned of violent clashes in the streets of several cities in Asia. He was informed that Roman citizens had been flogged and summarily executed in Mysia, Anatolia. Augustus' justice was swift, condemning the inhabitants of Mysia to slavery. Tyre and Sidon also received severe punishments for similar crimes. Following the removal of Archelaos and the annexation of Iudaea into the Province of Caesar in 6 CE, protests against the mandatory census in Hierosolyma rapidly spread to other parts of the country. When these vocal demonstrations became violent acts of sedition, they were suppressed with armed force by Coponius, the new *Praefectus Iudaeaorum*. Orosius informs us there was also a riot in Athens in 11 CE, a remarkable occurrence so late in Augustus' reign.[196]

Augustus as Victor
The term *Pax Augusta* was rarely used during the lifetime of the *princeps* and was not a motto he actively promoted.[197] It is known only from a few inscriptions erected by private individuals and officials in communities, such as the *decuriones* of *Colonia* Praeneste.[198] There was an altar to *Pax Augusta* at Narbo erected by one T. Domitius Romulus (fig. 13) and a *colonia* of that name in the Iberian Peninsula.[199] To prove he was effective at establishing peace, Augustus turned to ancient tradition. He secured votes in the Senate to close the doors of the Temple of Ianus Quirinus, 'which our ancestors ordered to be closed whenever there was peace, secured by victory, throughout the whole domain of the Roman People on land and sea'.[200] His boast was that while 'before my birth [it] is recorded to have been closed but twice in all since the foundation of the city, the Senate ordered [it] to be closed three times while I was *princeps*'.[201] The first two occasions occurred during his first ten-year period of *imperium*. The date of the third closing is not known with certainty, but was likely during the third *decennium*. There was a vote for closure in 13 BCE, but as Roman troops were actually fighting, legally it could not be permitted. Orosius states that it was in 1 BCE and

Figure 13. T. Domitius Romulus, a Roman citizen from Narbo, set up an altar to *Pax Augusta* in gratitude. The peace and prosperity of the Provinces of the People depended in part on the success of the army in the securing the Provinces of Caesar.

the doors remained shut for twelve years (but had to be opened again on account of the riot in Athens), but it seems a dubious claim as the Roman army was engaged in wars from Germania to Armenia – unless the Senate was willing to stretch the qualification.[202] It may be that Augustus simply counted the vote of 13 BCE in his total, even though the doors were kept open. There was no fourth occasion.

Commemorating Augustus' victories across the world were monuments of every type and style. In Epirus and Egypt stood cities dedicated to his victory. The Greek Nikopolis was a major attraction, drawing tourists to see the sights where the famous Battle of Actium had been fought, and touch the bronze beaks of Queen Kleopatra's captured ships. The Egyptian Nikopolis, with its modern buildings and amenities, threatened to take the trade away from Alexandria, the city founded by a great Macedonian king. Traffic on the road leaving Gallia Narbonnensis bound for Italy, passed a tower of tiered columns and sculptures that marked the end of wars in the Alps. On the Rhine, a similar monument celebrated the life of one of Rome's youngest and most successful commanders, Nero Claudius Drusus, at which the legions held annual races, while on the left bank of the Elbe, a trophy of decaying armour tied to a tree and rotting shields stacked beneath marked his northeastern-most march. In 9 BCE, the letter and decrees of the proconsul of Asia declared Augustus as 'the saviour who has brought war to an end', while the people of Hispania Ulterior Baetica paid for a gold statue dedicated to the *princeps* in the *Forum Augustum*, stating as their reason in the inscription beneath 'because by his beneficence and perpetual care the province has been pacified'.[203] There were many more inscriptions and altars paid for by grateful citizens or communities (such as the *Concilium Galiarum*) dedicated to the man who, they believed, had brought an end to war.

Rome too was decorated with tributes in brick and marble to Augustus' victories.[204] Arriving in Rome in 14 CE by way of the *Via Appia*, the visitor would pass through the *Porta Capena*. Close by was the Altar of Fortuna Redux, erected by a grateful nation for the return of Augustus in 19 BCE.[205] He would pass under the Arch of Nero Claudius Drusus *Imperator*, decorated with an equestrian statue of the commander caught in a dramatic attack pose, flanked by trophies of captured Germanic war spoils and bound warriors. On his way towards the city centre, he would pass temples erected by commanders of ages past, now repaired and made grander through Augustus' generosity. Approaching the *Forum Romanum* from the southeast along the *Via Sacra*, the visitor would pass through his arch with three gates, built to commemorate the return of *signa* and *aquilae* from Parthia. He would note the inscribed list of all the commanders who had ever been granted triumphs, ending with the name of Cornelius Balbus *ex Africa*.[206] It stood to the right of the Temple of *Divus Iulius* and the sacred spot before it where his body was burned. In front, the visitor would see the speakers' platform bearing the *rostra* of several ships captured at Actium, the arch for which likely stood on the left side. The tiled roofs of many buildings renovated by Augustus were decorated with terminals (*antefices*) stamped with the emblematic trophy erected after the sea battle. To his left, he would pass the Temple of Castor and Pollux restored by Tiberius and paid for from war spoils. It bore his and his brother's names on the entablature. (The attentive visitor would note the spelling as 'Claudianus' instead of 'Claudius' because of his adoption into the family of Augustus.) To retreat from the glare of the sun (or stay out of the rain), he would stroll within the wide two-storey arcade of the *Basilica Iulia* next door, built by Iulius Caesar from Gallic War spoils, but enlarged and completed by Augustus who renamed it the Basilica of Caius and Lucius.[207]

Once back in the *Forum*, he would pass the Temple of Saturn, whose repair was paid for by Munatius Plancus, and in the vaults of which were kept the strong boxes of the *Aerarium Saturni* and *Militare*. Upon the Capitolinus Hill, towering above our visitor to Rome, stood the Temple of Iupiter Optimus Maximus ('Jupiter the Best and Greatest') and the refurbished Temple of Iupiter Feretrius, where Augustus had placed laurels from his *fasces* upon his several returns from overseas. Beside it was the small but opulent Temple of Iupiter Tonans ('Jupiter the Thunderer'), erected in gratitude by Augustus for sparing him injury when a lightning bolt struck during the Cantabrian and Asturian War. At ground level, standing close by on the left, was the Temple of Concord dedicated by Tiberius on behalf of himself and his brother.

On the other side of the *Forum*, just to the right of his view, was the small Temple of Ianus, whose doors Augustus boasted he had caused to be closed three times. Behind it stood the *Curia Iulia*, where the Senate met and renewed Augustus' *imperium*. Upon its interior walls hung the silver shields of C. and L. Caesar and a statue of flying *Victoria* with the seats of the two consuls placed in front, and a third *sella curulis* set in between for Augustus when he attended meetings. Behind it he could still see the high wall enclosing the *Forum Augustum*. Just visible from here would be the roof of the grand Temple of Mars Ultor, built by Imp. Caesar to fulfill his solemn vow to the god for enabling his victory at the Battle of Phillipi. Supported by massive yet still elegant Corinthian columns, it was second only to the Temple of Iupiter Optimus Maximus in size.[208] With time allowing, the visitor could explore it, enjoy the rich marbles of its open and covered spaces, pay his respects to the image of Mars Ultor, gaze up at the gilt-bronze *quadriga* driven by Augustus, promenade its arcades lined with statues of the *viri triumphatores* and read their inspirational biographies – perhaps even catch a glimpse of the famous standards recovered from the Parthian king.

Returning to the *Forum Romanum*, turning right and sauntering along the *Via Flaminia* through the wide plain of the *Campus Martius*, the visitor would pass several buildings whose construction was paid from the proceeds of war booty – the Theatre of Pompeius Magnus (repaired by Augustus), Theatre of Cornelius Balbus, Amphitheatre of Statilius Taurus and a cluster of immense structures created by M. Agrippa. These include the Baths of Neptune, whose walls and ceilings were painted with naval battle scenes, and the Pantheon (which he had originally hoped to dedicate to his friend as the *Augusteum*). In the far distance he could admire the tree-covered, man-made mound of the Mausoleum of Augustus, in which were stored the ashes of three generations of the *Domus Augusti* who had borne arms in war – Marcellus, Drusus, Agrippa and the two young Caesars. After a pleasant walk he would reach the *Horologium* – also known as the *Solarium Augusti* – with an obelisk transported from Egypt in 30 BCE. It was precisely positioned so that its long shadow moved across a sun dial and reached its greatest extent on 23 September – Augustus' birthday.[209]

On that special day, the same shadow touched the adjacent *Ara Pacis Augustae*. Its exquisitely carved panels, picked out in colour, presented an image of Roman high society (priests, the friends and family of Augustus, with the *princeps* himself shown as *pontifex maximus*) processing to a dedication ceremony. Of the *Ara Pacis Augustae* in Rome, Augustus himself writes in *Res Gestae*:

> When I returned from Hispania and Gallia, in the consulship of Ti. Nero and P. Quinctilius [13 BCE], after successful operations in those provinces, the Senate voted in honour of my return the consecration of an altar to *Pax Augusta* in the *Campus Martius*, and on this altar it ordered the magistrates and priests and Vestal virgins to make annual sacrifice.[210]

A triumph of the sculptor's craft, many of the allegorical or divine figures on the *Ara Pacis* defy identification and interpretation today. Scholars have, for example, attempted to name the image of the central figure on the east front, outer face of the left-side segment wall. Venus, Tellus (Mother Earth), Italia and Ceres have variously been suggested, and a case has even been made that this is the avatar of *Pax Augusta*.[211] The argument goes that placed about her are shown many attributes of peace, and other details that strongly suggest this identification. In Greek mythology, the goddess of peace was one of the three *Horai* (*Horae* in Latin),

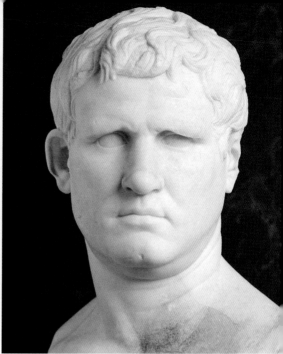

1. Imp. Caesar *Divi f.* (63 BCE–14CE) consciously promoted himself as a military commander and defined peace as 'secured by victory' (*Res Gestae* 13). In this bust he wears the oak crown (*corona civica*) decoration.

2. M. Agrippa (c. 64-12 BCE) was Imp. Caesar's friend since his teenage years and grew to become his indispensable right–hand man, winning the pivotal battle at Actium and quelling revolts in Cantabria, Crimea and Illyricum.

3. A fragment of an inscription from the *Forum Augustum* spells out the sponsor's full name. From 38 BCE the heir to Iulius Caesar's legacy brazenly used the acclamation 'commander' (*imperator*) as his first name.

4. Queen Kleopatra VII of Egypt (69–30 BCE) became M. Antonius' principal backer, providing him the means to field an army and navy against Imp. Caesar and Agrippa.

5. The ambitions and antics of *triumvir* M. Antonius (83-30 BCE) in the East brought him into conflict with Imp. Caesar. The ensuing civil war for supremacy engulfed the Roman world.

6. Originally an ally of Antonius, King Herodes (73–4 BCE) was denied his chance to fight in the Battle of Actium, depicted here in a wall painting from Herodium. He became a staunch supporter of Augustus and best friends with Agrippa.

7. With the death of Kleopatra in 30 BCE Imp. Caesar 'captured Egypt' and made it a Roman province. Its riches cleared the war debt and enabled him to reward his soldiers and political supporters with largesse.

8. Imp. Caesar enthusiastically promoted his victory at Actium. This trophy is assembled with naval equipment captured from the fleet of Antonius and Kleopatra.

9. On one side of this coin winged Victory stands on the prow of a Roman warship. The other side shows Imp. Caesar driving his four-horse chariot (*currus triumphalis*) at his triple triumph.

10. Imp. Caesar celebrated a triple triumph on 13-15 August 29 BCE. This coin shows the *toga picta*, *tunica palmata* and laurel crown worn by the triumphal commander along with the chariot he drove.

11. Imp. Caesar was voted triumphal arches for his victories. A single arch marked the Actian War. The Parthian Arch, erected on the *Via Sacra*, had three gates and statues.

12. By ending the Civil War Imp. Caesar 'saved the lives of Roman citizens'. On 16 January 27 BCE the Senate was awarded him the *corona civica* ('citizen's crown'). It was permanently displayed above the door of the *Palatium*.

13. Augustus was permitted the privilege of growing laurel trees beside the front doorposts of the *Palatium* (his home on the Palatinus Hill) as tokens of his devotion and honour.

14. In 27 BCE the Senate awarded Imp. Caesar the title *Augustus* and the Shield of Virtue (*clipeus virtutis*) in recognition of his leadership qualities and achievements. (It is shown alongside the military standards later received from the Parthians.)

15. Augustus sought to complete the conquest of the Iberian Peninsula. His deputy P. Carisius celebrated his defeat of the Astures in 26/25 BCE on a coin showing a trophy erected at the site of the last battle.

16. The mint at the newly established *colonia* for legionary veterans at Emerita Augusta produced coins showing war spoils seized by the army under the command of *Legatus Augusti Pro Praetore* P. Carisius.

17. A Parthian shown kneeling and surrendering a Roman standard would remind the beholder that in 20 BCE Augustus secured the return of the military ensigns lost by Crassus and Antonius.

18. Frahâta (Phraates) IV, 'King of Kings', ruled Parthia 37-2 BCE. He agreed to a negotiated pact with Augustus – perhaps brokered by Agrippa – in 20 BCE and sent five of his sons as hostages to Rome.

19. A re-enactor as a *legionarius* of the late first century BCE, wearing a bronze Montefortino-type helmet and chain mail shirt and carrying an oval shield, is shown in attack stance with unsheathed *gladius Hispaniensis*.

20. In 27 BCE Augustus effectively became commander-in-chief. In the legions under him the *centuria* of eighty infantrymen, led by a *centurio* and aided by his *optio*, was the basic combat unit. Other officers relayed commands by music and motions of a *signum* or *vexillum* standard. A legion comprised sixty centuries plus a hand-picked *legatus*, various senior officers and cavalry.

21. Technical innovation under Augustus led to the introduction of articulated, segmented plate armour and the Gallic-inspired iron helmet at the end of the first century BCE. The rectangular *scutum* gradually replaced the earlier oval design.

22. L. Calpurnius Piso (48 BCE–32 CE) was *Legatus Augusti Pro Praetore* of Galatia-Pamphylia. Over a three-year long campaign in Thracia he earned for himself the *ornamenta triumphalia*.

23. Ti. Claudius Nero (42 BCE–37 CE) was Augustus' eldest stepson. He proved an able commander and succeeded Agrippa as his right-hand man. Augustus later adopted him as Ti. Iulius Caesar.

24. 'REX IVBA', King Iuba II of Numidia (52/50 BCE–23 CE) was one of the most loyal allies of the Romans. A noted author and scholar, in 25 BCE he agreed to exchange his homeland for Mauretania, which flourished under his rule.

25. 'ΒΑΣΙΛΕΩΣ ΡΟΙΜΗΤΑΛΚΟΥ', King Roimetalkes I of Thracia, was a loyal ally of the Romans who actively supported Tiberius and Germanicus Caesar with troops during the Batonian War in Illyricum (6-9 CE).

26. Nero Claudius Drusus (38-9 BCE) was Augustus' youngest stepson. He proved his leadership abilities on campaigns in Raetia, Vindelicia, Noricum and Germania and was popular with the troops.

27. A coin celebrates the military successes of the Claudius brothers – Tiberius and Drusus – in Raetia, Noricum and Vindelicia in 15 BCE. The poet Horace also sang their praises.

28. In 12 BCE Nero Drusus launched a war of conquest against the Germanic nations. A naked German warrior is shown kneeling and surrendering a native flag standard.

29. For his victories in Germania Nero Drusus was posthumously awarded an arch and the war title *Germanicus*. Atop the arch trophies flank a statue of the commander (who craved *spolia opima*) charging the enemy.

30. Though already dead at the time of the inauguration of the *Ara Pacis Augustae* in 9 BCE the frieze nevertheless includes M. Agrippa. He is shown *velatus* (with his head covered). Augustus is on the extreme left.

31. Among the members of Augustus' family in this scene on the *Ara Pacis Augustae* are Tiberius (left), his brother Drusus (centre, wearing a *paludamentum*) and L. Domitius Ahenobarbus (right).

32. Inaugurated in 6 BCE, the *Tropaeum Alpium* commemorated the end of decades of campaigning by the Romans to subjugate the nations of the Alps. The full text of the inscription was preserved by Pliny the Elder in his *Naturalis Historia*.

33. This monument celebrated the final victory over forty-five Alpine nations achieved under Augustus' auspices. It features depictions of trophies of arms, armour and enchained men and women.

34. The Romans regarded themselves as a devout people. On this coin the moneyer L. Mescinius Rufus acknowledges the importance of war god Mars in religious observance.

35. Opened in 2 BCE, the Temple of Mars Avenger (*Templum Marti Ultori*) was the centrepiece of the *Forum Augustum* in Rome. The military ensigns recovered from Parthia were kept here.

36. Agrippa's eldest son was adopted by Augustus as C. Iulius Caesar (20 BCE-4 CE). Fêted by the Roman People Augustus had high hopes for him, but he ultimately proved a disappointment.

37. Upon reaching manhood and in preparation for a public career, brothers C. and L. Caesar were each in turn appointed *princeps iuventutis* and given spears and silvered shields in keeping with their status.

38. C. Caesar officially began his military career under the care of Tiberius on a punitive raid into Germania in 8 BCE. The troops were paid a bonus for ensuring the young man came to no harm during the campaign.

39. Officially surrendering to the Romans required that the defeated enemy hand over arms and hostages. Here a Germanic warrior presents a child to Augustus (shown as a magistrate) seated on a tribunal.

40. The lower segment of the *Gemma Augustea* – engraved after 10 CE – shows a group of Roman soldiers erecting a *tropaeum*. The captured arms and armour hang from an oak tree trunk in a tradition ascribed to the legendary Romulus.

41. The 'Blacas Cameo'
– engraved c. 20-50
CE – shows Augustus
wearing a sword-belt
(symbolising his military
authority) and the *aegis*
usually associated with
the goddess Minerva.

42. The 'Eagle Cameo'
– engraved after 27
BCE – shows a golden
eagle (the symbol of
Jupiter) clutching
a palm frond and a
corona civica, evoking
the victory honours
bestowed on Augustus.

43. This iconic statue (purportedly from the villa of Livia at Prima Porta) may represent in symbolic form the moment when Augustus was acclaimed by his soldiers for recovering the Roman military standards from the Parthian king in 20 BCE.

44. One of the three *aquilae* lost by P. Quinctilius Varus in 9 CE was retrieved seven years later by Germanicus Caesar. Augustus' grandson is shown on this coin in the same victory pose as the statue from Prima Porta and carrying an eagle standard.

divinities who brought justice and prosperity through the seasons of the year. *Pax* is attended by two goddesses who are also *Horae*. Allusions in the relief to wind, rain, stars, land and sea present her as a goddess for all seasons.[212] The panel on the east front, outer face of the right-side segment wall is generally agreed to show the tutelary warrior goddess Roma. She sits on a pile of arms, armour and shields.[213] On the west face, right-side of the outer wall, Aeneas – or alternatively Numa – sacrifices to the *Di* Penates, while on the left-side, Mars, father of twins Romulus and Remus, is shown.[214] The altar and its annual sacrifice were, perhaps, held in connection with the nearby *Horologium* or *Solarium Augusti*.[215] Mysteries remain about these important imperial structures.

Contemporary poets wrote of life and love, but hardly any, it appears, explicitly used the term *Pax Augusta*. Yet they sang of victory in all its forms. Vergil set the Battle of Actium to verse, describing how the oars of Imp. Caesar's and Agrippa's warships churned up the sea while burning missiles flew through the air.[216] Horace composed an ode in celebration of the commander-in-chief's victory at sea, the capture of Alexandria and the fall of Kleopatra; but in another he congratulated the soldier Plotius Numida upon his return from the war in Cantabria, and praised Augustus as a god on earth for subjugating the Britons and Parthians.[217] A poet could often say what a military man or a politician (especially one who was both) could not. After all, it took Vergil to articulate Rome's manifest destiny in just three words: *imperium sine fine*.

Nor did *Pax Augusta* appear on coins while Augustus was alive. Even the name of *Pax* or her avatar was rarely depicted (see Appendix 4). The Augustan doctrine was about projecting power and military strength (plate 42). Official messaging from the Rome mint – the nearest thing to propaganda in the modern sense – stressed aspects of *gloria* and *victoria*. The reverses of coins minted in the period 31–28 BCE showed the naval trophies of the Actian War, the triumphal arch, the god Mars the Avenger and Victory (plate 34). From 27–19 BCE, the trophy from Actium continued to be a motif, but now the honours granted Augustus – the Altar of Fortuna Redux, the *corona civica* – appeared, as well as a prolific series of different images celebrating the return of the standards from Parthia and the legend *SIGNIS RECEPTIS*. With the opening of the mints in Hispania Citerior, coins depicted spoils taken in the wars over the Astures and Cantabri, at the same time the mint in Pergamum announced *ARMENIA CAPTA*. From 18–9 BCE, the *tresviri monetales* in Rome approved a wide variety of images, including the gods Mars and Victory, the triple triumphal arch commemorating the Parthian Peace, two men holding up laurel branches to Augustus seated on a tribunal, and kneeling barbarians from Germania and Parthia in acts of surrender. The Spanish colonial mints showed Augustus driving a *triumphator*'s chariot and the embroidered *toga picta* or a laurel crown. From 8 BCE–2 CE and 3–12 CE, when the new mint at *Colonia* Copia Felix Munatia – now the source of gold and silver coins – came on stream, Augustus' adopted sons C. and L. Caesar appeared for the first time as *principes iuventutis* with their shields and spears. When the older boy went on his first mission, a coin design showed him on a horse galloping past military standards. Despite the premature deaths of the two boys, the coins showing C. and L. Caesar together continued to be minted. Thereafter, the martial imagery largely disappeared from new issues, the series abruptly ending with the image of Tiberius in his triumphal *quadriga*. The ongoing display of war-related themes on coins for so many years sustained the notion of military success, but also reminded Romans that they still had battles to win. The final clash of arms still lay ahead but, in the meantime, each victory secured *pax*.

On the obverse of every gold or silver coin was the bust of the man responsible for bringing victory: *CAESAR AVGVSTVS DIVI F.* He was not the first living Roman to place his likeness on the coinage (that pioneer was Iulius Caesar), but his heir took the concept to its logical extreme. Unlike his great uncle, whose portraits were brutally realistic, almost caricatures, Augustus' never betrayed his age.[218] His image was timeless. He was never shown with a furrow or wrinkle, and always without emotion. All busts of Augustus in bronze or marble were presented with this same eternally youthful and imperturbable countenance. His head of thick, tousled hair was variously shown bare, graced with a victor's wreath of laurel or the military distinction of a crown of a twisted leafy oak branch. The Blacas Cameo (plate 41) and the *gemma Augustea*, which may have been crafted as diplomatic gifts, project iconic depictions of military strength – and that of the Roman leader in particular. This carefully crafted image projected the ideal of the man leading the army to victory in the service of the Roman People, a man who just might defy Nature and live forever – unless he became a god first.

The meaning of the iconic (but enigmatic) statue of Augustus of Prima Porta now becomes clear. [219] The sculpture (perhaps a copy of one in bronze) blends a real occasion with a propaganda message. Augustus is shown frozen at the moment of receiving the acclamation of Roman troops following the recovery of the venerated legionary ensigns from the Parthians in 20 BCE (plate 43). The embossed decoration on his anatomical cuirass depicts the historical event along-side worldly emblems of victory (a trophy and figures from conquered barbarian nations) and mythological associations of a prosperous future; it is intended as a pictorial display to explain the statue to the casual viewer. The *paludamentum* (which would normally be attached at the shoulders) hangs around his waist as he would have worn it when he had disrobed after battle – this also explains why he carries no weapon. His outstretched right hand and fingers form a gesture used by Roman orators to convey wonder (*admiratio*), expressing the surprise mingled with admiration he feels at the spontaneous adulation of his fellow citizens.[220] The left hand, nowadays presumed to originally have held a sceptre or spear, likely once held a staff topped by an eagle (a copy of one of the rescued *aquilae* depicted on the cuirass) that he would proudly display to the assembled troops; this same pose was evoked on a later coin (plate 44) celebrating the retrieval by Augustus' own grandson of the standards Quinctilius Varus lost to the Germans.[221] Being careful to avoid appearing god-like, the then 43-year-old military leader is shown walking barefoot like a suppliant, both to indicate his humility and to demonstrate the complete absence of hubris. Amid the cheers of the soldiers Augustus is not only re-affirmed as *imperator* but as *pacificator* (the bringer of peace through victory) – specifically a victory made exceptional because he achieved it without bloodshed. It was a defining moment in the emerging legend of the restorer of the *Res Publica*, the son and avenger of the Divine Iulius, who had defeated a wayward queen and a haughty 'king of kings'.

Under the auspices of the man who had taken 'commander' as his first name, his team of deputies waged war against the People's enemies far beyond the borders of their realm. For those who could not accept defeat within them – and there were many – the process of pacification was brutal. So long as there was *bellum* there was the potential for *victoria*, and with it *pax*. Almost by design, war was being fought somewhere in virtually every one of the forty-five years that Augustus was commander-in-chief of the armed forces. The dirty little secret was that the mission could *never* be accomplished. This is how Augustus would retain the *imperium*. As Tacitus writes, looking back on this period, 'Peace there was, without a doubt, but a bloody one.'[222] An added benefit was that a general engaged in war was less likely than an idle one to turn against his supreme commander. In the event one was tempted, Augustus had the highest-paid soldiers stationed in Italy and kept his Germanic bodyguards close by.

Augustus did not enlarge the empire alone – much as he would like posterity to believe. Over four decades, his deputies operated semi-autonomously and the decisions they made while serving in the field contributed to expanding Rome's dominion just as much as his did. His privilege was to claim the victories and the glory as his own. It was an arrangement that worked because he deftly channelled the Romans' cultural trait of competitiveness for recognition and reward, and in doing so ensured their complaisance.

Picking the right men for the job was essential to his success. Every three years he had to appoint new *legati Augusti* for his regional commands. As frequently he had to pick legates for the twenty-eight legions (twenty-five after 9 CE), as well as the many *praefecti* who commanded the auxiliary units and *Cohortes Voluntariorum* (see Appendix 3.6). Additionally, he personally selected from the *Ordo Equester* the *praefectus Aegypti*, the *praefectus Iudaeorum*, the two *praefecti Praetorii*, the *praefectus Urbi*, the *praefectus Vigilum* and each *praefectus classis* of the several fleets. Every year, he chose which young men would fill the open positions for twenty-five or more tribunes with the broad stripe and 140 or so for legionary tribune with the narrow stripe. Augustus' skill at personnel selection was extraordinary, to judge by the results they delivered:

> For successful operations on land and sea, conducted either by myself or by my *legati* under my auspices, the Senate on fifty-five occasions decreed that thanks should be rendered to the immortal gods.[223]

These men together maintained Augustus' original *provincia* and augmented it with new territories in Galatia-Pamphylia, Germania (for a generation), Hispania Tarraconensis (formerly Citerior), Iudaea, Moesia, Noricum, Pannonia (by enlarging Illyricum) and Raetia. With the annexation of Egypt, they had helped Augustus nearly double the territory of the '*imperium* of the Roman People' compared to its extent in 44 BCE.[224] It was much more than either Pompeius Magnus or Iulius Caesar had accomplished in their lifetimes (compare maps 1 and 25).

After one of the most destructive civil wars in history, the near constant flow of news of victories over foreign enemies – all won in Augustus' name – assured the living generations of Romans of their rightful place among the ancestors, and bolstered their belief in the nation's exceptionalism. As well as restoring its polity, Augustus could claim that he had revived the greatness of the *Res Publica* as a military power and, as its commander-in-chief, implicitly justify his own primacy.

There *were* military setbacks, yet Augustus' organization proved remarkably resilient and was able to survive them. What made it possible were his formidable talents both for leadership and management. As a military leader Augustus: had a sense of personal mission and destiny; took the long view and consistently provided strategic direction; favoured fighting 'just wars' (wars of necessity) rather than executing a unified 'grand strategy' of imperialist expansion (wars of choice); and was prepared to explore diplomatic solutions over military actions, especially with Parthia. As a manager of war Augustus: established a professional standing army of citizen soldiers, augmented by non-Roman auxiliary troops; organized the means to finance the army's ongoing expenses; delegated operational and tactical decision making to trusted deputies; selected good candidates for field command positions and actively nurtured new talent to replace them; took a close personal interest in their performance; recognised and rewarded successful leaders for their achievements or acts of bravery; enforced discipline with punishments for offenders; assured the common soldiers of regular pay and a bonus at the end of their service; developed strong personal relationships with Rome's allies to retain their loyalty; assessed the risk of success or failure (the 'doctrine of the golden fish hook'), then scaled and resourced his military offensives for victory; communicated his accomplishments with the public and shared the spoils with them; and used political and religious protocols to secure his military power.

Under Augustus' auspices, the restored *Res Publica* endured and prospered. For four decades, *one* man determined the direction and shape of Roman military strategy. It was unprecedented and the achievement was exceptional. When Augustus died, the transition of power from him to his successor was virtually conflict-free. Roman did not fight Roman for the right to command.[225] That alone was a victory. The decades of struggle had been worth it. In the end there was peace – the *Pax Augusta*.

In His Own Words:
The Deeds of the Divine Augustus
(*Res Gestae Divi Augusti*)

Towards the end of his life, Augustus wrote an account of his achievements. Nowadays referred to as the *Res Gestae* (literally 'Things Done'), it was originally published on bronze tablets affixed to two columns, which stood in front of his Mausoleum in Rome. Intended for public display, copies were made and distributed across the Roman world and affixed on public buildings (see Güven, 1998). A near complete copy has survived as a marble inscription – written in the original Latin with a Greek translation – on a Temple of Augustus in Ancyra in Anatolia (the so-called *Monumentum Ancyranum* in Ankara, Turkey), but fragments have been found at Apollonia and Antioch, both in Pisidia (modern Antalya, Turkey). It might be considered Augustus' own attempt to write a first draft of history by establishing the official record of his legacy. Beginning with a short introduction, in thirty-five paragraphs – plus an addendum posthumously written by another author, perhaps a local magistrate of Ancyra – the inscription documents his political career, unparalleled generosity, his numerous diplomatic and military accomplishments, and the Roman People's approval of his deeds.

For explanatory notes on the inscription, see Brunt and Moore (1967) and Cooley (2009). For content relating to civil and foreign wars, see Lange (2008).

This translation is based on Frederick W. Shipley's, first published in 1924 in the Loeb Classical Library as *Velleius Paterculus and Res Gestae Divi Augusti*, which I have adapted and annotated with the kind help of Karl Galinsky.

Note: 'HS' is the Latin monetary symbol for *sestertius*, a large brass coin with a gold-like appearance, equivalent to one quarter of a silver *denarius* or one hundredth of a pure gold *aureus*.

* * *

THE DEEDS OF THE DIVINE AUGUSTUS, by which he placed the whole world under the sovereignty of the Roman People, and of the amounts he spent on the *Res Publica* and the Roman People; as engraved upon two bronze columns that have been placed in Rome, here below is a copy.

Tablet 1

1. At the age of 19 [44 BCE], on my own initiative and at my own expense, I raised an army by means of which I restored liberty to the Commonwealth

that had been oppressed by the tyranny of a faction. For this service the Senate, with complimentary resolutions, enrolled me in its order in the consulship of C. Pansa and A. Hirtius [43 BCE], giving me at the same time consular precedence in voting; it also gave me the *imperium*. It ordered me, as *pro praetor*, along with the consuls, 'to see that the Commonwealth suffered no harm'. In the same year, moreover, as both consuls had fallen in war, the People elected me Consul and a *Triumvir* for Re-establishing the Constitution.

2. Those who slew my father I drove into exile, punishing their deed by due process of law, and afterwards when they waged war upon the Commonwealth I twice defeated them in battle [at Philippi, 3 and 23 October 42 BCE].

3. Wars, both civil and foreign, I undertook throughout the world, on sea and land, and when victorious I spared all citizens who sued for pardon. The foreign nations which could, with safety, be pardoned I preferred to save rather than to destroy. The number of Roman citizens who bound themselves to me by military oath was about 500,000. Of these I settled in *coloniae* or sent back into their own *municpia*, after their term of service, something more than 300,000, and to all I assigned lands, or gave money as a reward for military service. I captured 600 ships [from Mylae, Naulochus and Actium], over and above those which were smaller than triremes.

4. Twice I triumphed with an ovation [40 and 36 BCE], three times I celebrated curule triumphs [on 13–15 August 29 BCE] and was saluted as *imperator* twenty-one times. Although the Senate decreed me additional triumphs I set them aside. When I had performed the vows which I had undertaken in each war I deposited upon the *Capitolium* the laurels which adorned my *fasces*. For successful operations on land and sea, conducted either by myself or by my *legati* under my auspices, the Senate on fifty-five occasions decreed that thanks should be rendered to the immortal gods. The days on which such thanks were rendered by Decree of the Senate numbered 890. In my triumphs there were led before my chariot nine kings or children of kings. At the time of writing these words I had been thirteen times consul and was in the thirty-seventh year of my tribunician power [14 CE].

5. The dictatorship offered me by the people and the Roman Senate, in my absence and later when present, in the consulship of M. Marcellus and L. Arruntius [22 BCE] I did not accept. I did not decline at a time of the greatest scarcity of grain the charge of the grain-supply, which I so administered that, within a few days, I freed the entire people, at my own expense, from the fear and danger in which they were. The consulship, either yearly or for life, then offered me I did not accept.

6. In the consulship of M. Vinicius and Q. Lucretius [19 BCE], and afterwards in that of P. Lentulus and Cn. Lentulus [18 BCE], and a third time in that of Paullus Fabius Maximus and Q. Tubero [11 BCE], when the Senate and the Roman People unanimously agreed that I should be elected overseer of laws and morals, without a colleague and with the fullest power, I refused to accept any power offered me which was contrary to the traditions of our

ancestors. Those things, which at that time the Senate wished me to administer, I carried out by virtue of my tribunician power; and even in this office I five times received from the Senate a colleague at my own request.

7. For ten years in succession I was one of the Triumvirs for Re-establishing the Constitution. To the day of writing this [I] have been *Princeps Senatus* for forty years [having commenced in 28 BCE]. I have been *Pontifex Maximus*, *augur*, a member of the Commission of Fifteen Men for Sacred Rites, one of the Seven Men for Sacred Feasts, an Arval Brother, a *sodalis Titius* and a fetial priest.

Tablet 2

8. As Consul for the fifth time [29 BCE], by order of the People and the Senate I increased the number of the patricians. Three times I revised the roll of the Senate. In my sixth consulship, with M. Agrippa as my colleague [28 BCE], I made a census of the people. I performed the *lustrum* after an interval of forty-one years. In this lustration 4,063,000 Roman citizens were entered on the census roll. A second time, in the consulship of C. Censorinus and C. Asinius [8 BCE], I again performed the *lustrum* alone, with the consular *imperium*. In this *lustrum* 4,233,000 Roman citizens were entered on the census roll. A third time with the consular *imperium* and with my son Ti. Caesar as my colleague I performed the *lustrum* in the consulship of Sex. Pompeius and Sex. Appuleius [14 CE]. In this *lustrum* 4,937,000 Roman citizens were entered on the census roll. By the passage of new laws I restored many traditions of our ancestors, which were then falling into disuse, and I myself set precedents in many things for posterity to imitate.

9. The Senate decreed that every fifth year vows should be undertaken for my health by the consuls and the priests. In fulfillment of these vows games were often held in my lifetime, sometimes by the four chief colleges of priests, sometimes by the consuls. In addition the entire body of citizens with one accord, both individually and by municipalities, performed continued sacrifices for my health at all the couches of the gods.

10. By Decree of the Senate [29 BCE] my name was included in the Hymn of the Salii, and it was enacted by law that my person should be sacred in perpetuity and that so long as I lived I should hold the tribunician power. I declined to be made *Pontifex Maximus* in succession to a colleague still living, when the People tendered me that priesthood which my father had held. Several years later [13 or early 12 BCE] I accepted that sacred office when he at last was dead who, taking advantage of a time of civil disturbance, had seized it for himself, such a multitude from all Italia assembling for my election, in the consulship of P. Sulpicius and C. Valgius [12 BCE], as is never recorded to have been in Rome before.

11. The Senate consecrated in honour of my return an altar to Fortuna Redux at the Porta Capena, near the Temple of Honour and Courage, on which it ordered the pontiffs and the Vestal Virgins to perform a yearly sacrifice on the anniversary of the day on which I returned to the city from Syria, in the

consulship of Q. Lucretius and M. Vinucius [12 October 19 BCE], and named the day, after my *cognomen*, the *Augustalia*.

12. At the same time, by Decree of the Senate, part of the praetors and of the tribunes of the People, together with the Consul Q. Lucretius and the leading men of the state, were sent to Campania to meet me, an honour which up to the present time has been decreed to no one except myself. When I returned from Hispania and Gallia, in the consulship of Ti. Nero and P. Quinctilius [13 BCE], after successful operations in those provinces, the Senate voted in honour of my return the consecration of an altar to *Pax Augusta* in the *Campus Martius*, and on this altar it ordered the magistrates and priests and Vestal virgins to make annual sacrifice.

13. Ianus Quirinus, which our ancestors ordered to be closed whenever there was peace, secured by victory, throughout the whole domain of the Roman People on land and sea, and which, before my birth is recorded to have been closed but twice in all since the foundation of the city, the Senate ordered to be closed three times while I was *princeps* [29, 25 and 1(?) BCE].

Tablet 3

14. My sons C. and L. Caesar, who Fortune snatched away from me in their youth, the Senate and the Roman People to do me honour made consuls designate, each in his fifteenth year [5 and 2 BCE respectively], providing that each should enter upon that office after a period of five years. The Senate decreed that from the day on which they were introduced to the Forum they should take part in the counsels of state. Moreover, the entire body of Roman knights gave each of them the title of *princeps iuventutis* and presented them with silver shields and spears.

15. To the Roman plebs I paid out HS300 per man in accordance with the will of my father, and in my own name in my fifth consulship [29 BCE] I gave HS400 apiece from the spoils of war; a second time, moreover, in my tenth consulship [24 BCE] I paid out of my own patrimony HS400 per man by way of bounty, and in my eleventh consulship [23 BCE] I made twelve distributions of food from grain bought at my own expense, and in the twelfth year of my tribunician power [12–11 BCE] I gave for the third time HS400 to each man. These largesses of mine reached a number of persons never less than 250,000. In the eighteenth year of my tribunician power, as consul for the twelfth time [5 BCE], I gave to 320,000 of the city plebs 60 *denarii* apiece. In the *coloniae* of my soldiers, as consul for the fifth time [29 BCE], I gave HS1,000 to each man from the spoils of war; about 120,000 men in the *coloniae* received this triumphal largesse. When consul for the thirteenth time [2 BCE] I gave 60 *denarii* apiece to the plebs who were then receiving public grain – these were a little more than 200,000 persons.

16. To the municipal towns I paid money for the lands, which I assigned to soldiers in my own fourth consulship [30 BCE], and afterwards in the consulship of M. Crassus and Cn. Lentulus the augur [14 BCE]. The sum which I paid for estates in Italia was about HS600,000,000, and the amount which

I paid for lands in the provinces was about HS260,000,000. I was the first and only one to do this of all those who up to my time settled colonies of soldiers in Italy or in the provinces; and later, in the consulship of Ti. Nero and Cn. Piso [7 BCE], likewise in the consulship of C. Antistius and Dec. Laelius [6 BCE], and of C. Calvisius and L. Pasienus [4 BCE], and of L. Lentulus and M. Messalla [3 BCE], and of L. Caninius and Q. Fabricius [2 BCE], I paid cash gratuities to the soldiers whom I settled in their own towns at the expiration of their service, and for this purpose I expended HS400,000,000 as an act of grace.

17. Four times I aided the Public Treasury with my own money, paying out in this manner to those in charge of the Treasury HS150,000,000; and in the consulship of M. Lepidus and L. Arruntius [6 CE] I contributed HS170,000,000 out of my own patrimony to the Military Treasury – which was established on my advice – that from it gratuities might be paid to soldiers who had seen twenty or more years of service.

18. Beginning with the year in which Cn. and P. Lentulus were consuls [18 BCE], whenever taxes were in arrears, I furnished from my own purse and my own patrimony tickets for grain and money, sometimes to 100,000 persons, sometimes to many more.

Tablet 4

19. I built the *Curia* and the *Chalcidicum* adjoining it, the Temple of Apollo on the Palatinus with its porticoes, the Temple of the Divine Iulius, the Lupercal, the Portico at the Circus Flaminius which I allowed to be called Octavia after the name of him who had constructed an earlier one on the same site, the state box at the Circus Maximus, the temples on the *Capitolium* of Iupiter Feretrius and Iupiter Tonans, the Temple of Quirinus, the temples of Minerva, of Iuno the Queen, and of Iupiter Libertas, on the Aventinus, the Temple of the Lares at the highest point of the *Via Sacra*, the Temple of the Di Penates on the Velia, the Temple of Youth, and the Temple of the Great Mother on the Palatinus.

20. The *Capitolium* and the Theatre of Pompeius – both works involving great expense – I rebuilt without any inscription of my own name. I restored the channels of the aqueducts, which in several places were falling into disrepair through age, and doubled the capacity of the aqueduct called the Marcia by turning a new spring into its channel. I completed the *Forum Iulium* and the basilica which was between the Temple of Castor and the Temple of Saturn – works begun and far advanced by my father – and when the same basilica was destroyed by fire I began its reconstruction on an enlarged site, to be inscribed with the names of my sons, and ordered that in case I should not live to complete it, it should be completed by my heirs. In my sixth consulship [28 BCE], in accordance with a Decree of the Senate, I rebuilt in the city 82 temples of the gods, omitting none which at that time stood in need of repair. As consul for the seventh time [27 BCE] I constructed the *Via*

Flaminia from the city to Ariminum, and all the bridges (except the Mulvian and the Minucian).

21. On my own ground I built the Temple of Mars Ultor and the *Forum Augustum* from the spoils of war [12 May 2 BCE]. On ground purchased for the most part from private owners I built the theatre near the Temple of Apollo which was to bear the name of my son-in-law M. Marcellus [dedicated 4 May 11 BCE]. From the spoils of war I consecrated offerings on the *Capitolium*, and in the Temple of the Divine Iulius, and in the Temple of Apollo, and in the Temple of Vesta, and in the Temple of Mars Ultor, which cost me about HS100,000,000. In my fifth consulship [29 BCE] I remitted 35,000 pounds weight of *aurum coronarium* contributed by the *municipia* and the *coloniae* of Italia, and thereafter, whenever I was addressed as *imperator*, I did not accept the *aurum coronarium*, although the *municipia* and *coloniae* voted it in the same kindly spirit as before.

22. Three times in my own name I gave a show of gladiators, and five times in the name of my sons or grandsons; in these shows there fought about 10,000 men. Twice in my own name I furnished for the people an exhibition of athletes gathered from all parts of the world, and a third time in the name of my grandson. Four times I gave games in my own name; as representing other magistrates twenty-three times. For the College of Fifteen Men, as master of that college and with M. Agrippa as my colleague, I conducted the *Ludi Saeculares* in the consulship of C. Furnius and M. Silanus [17 BCE]. In my thirteenth consulship [2 BCE] I gave, for the first time, the *Ludi Martiales*, which, since that time, the consuls by Decree of the Senate have given in successive years in conjunction with me. In my own name, or that of my sons or grandsons, on twenty-six occasions I gave to the people – in the circus, in the forum, or in the amphitheatre – hunts of African wild beasts, in which about 3,500 beasts were slain.

23. I gave the People the spectacle of a naval battle beyond the Tiber, at the place where the Grove of the Caesars now stands, the ground having been excavated for a length of 1,800 and a breadth of 1,200 feet. In this spectacle 30 beaked ships, triremes or biremes, and a large number of smaller vessels met in conflict. In these fleets there fought about 3,000 men exclusive of the rowers.

24. After my victory I replaced in the temples in all the cities of the province of Asia the ornaments which my antagonist [M. Antonius] in the war, when he despoiled the temples, had appropriated to his private use. Silver statues of me, on foot, on horseback, and in chariots were erected in the city to the number of about eighty; these I myself removed, and from the money thus obtained I placed in the Temple of Apollo golden offerings in my own name and in the name of those who had paid me the honour of a statue.

Tablet 5
25. I freed the sea from pirates. About 30,000 slaves, captured in that war, who had run away from their masters and had taken up arms against the

Commonwealth, I delivered to their masters for punishment. The whole of Italia voluntarily took oath of allegiance to me and demanded me as its leader in the war in which I was victorious at Actium [31 BCE]. The provinces of the Hispaniae, the Galliae, Africa, Sicilia and Sardinia took the same oath of allegiance. Those who served under my *signa* at that time included more than 700 senators, and among them 83 who had previously or have since been consuls up to the day on which these words were written, and about 170 have been priests.

26. I extended the boundaries of all the provinces, which were bordered by races not yet subject to our *imperium*. The provinces of the Galliae, the Hispaniae and Germania, bounded by the Ocean from Gades to the mouth of the Albis River, I reduced to a state of peace. The Alps, from the region which lies nearest to the Adriatic Sea as far as the Tuscan, I brought to a state of peace without waging on any tribe an unjust war. My fleet sailed from the mouth of the Rhenus River eastward as far as the lands of the Cimbri to which, up to that time, no Roman had ever penetrated either by land or by sea, and the Cimbri and Charydes and Semnones and other peoples of the Germans of that same region through their envoys sought my friendship and that of the Roman People. On my order and under my auspices two armies were led – at almost the same time – into Aethiopia and into Arabia (which is called the 'Happy') and very large forces of the enemy of both races were cut to pieces in battle and many towns were captured. Aethiopia was penetrated as far as the town of Nabata, which is next to Meroë. In Arabia the army advanced into the territories of the Sabaei to the town of Mariba.

27. Aegyptus I added to the empire of the Roman People. In the case of Armenia Maior, though I might have made it a province after the assassination of its King Artaxes, I preferred – following the precedent of our fathers – to hand that kingdom over to Tigranes, the son of King Artavasdes, and grandson of King Tigranes, through Ti. Nero who was then my stepson; and later, when the same people revolted and rebelled, and was subdued by my son Caius, I gave it over to King Ariobarzanes the son of Artabazus, King of the Medes, to rule, and after his death to his son Artavasdes. When he was murdered I sent into that kingdom Tigranes, who was sprung from the royal family of the Armenians. I recovered all the provinces extending eastward beyond the Adriatic Sea, and Cyrenae, which were then for the most part in possession of kings, and, at an earlier time, Sicilia and Sardinia, which had been seized in the Servile War [First 135–132 BCE, Second 104–100 BCE].

28. I settled colonies of soldiers in Africa, Sicilia, Macedonia, both Hispaniae, Achaea, Asia, Syria, Gallia Narbonensis, Pisidia. Moreover, Italia has 28 *coloniae* founded under my auspices, which have grown to be famous and populous during my lifetime.

29. From Hispania, Gallia and Dalmatia, I recovered, after conquering the enemy, many military *signa* which had been lost by other leaders. The Parthians I compelled to restore to me the spoils and *signa* of three Roman armies [of 53, 40 and 36 BCE], and to seek as suppliants the friendship of the

Roman People. These *signa* I deposited in the inner shrine, which is in the Temple of Mars Ultor [20 BCE].

30. The tribes of the Pannonii, to which no army of the Roman People had ever penetrated before my principate, having been subdued by Ti. Nero who was then my stepson and my *legatus*, I brought under the sovereignty of the Roman People, and I pushed forward the frontier of Illyricum as far as the bank of the Danuvius River. An army of Daci – which crossed to the south of that river – was, under my auspices, defeated and crushed, and afterwards my own army was led across the Danuvius and compelled the tribes of the Daci to submit to the orders of the Roman People.

31. Embassies were often sent to me from the kings of India, a thing never seen before in the camp of any leader of the Romans. Our friendship was sought, through ambassadors, by the Bastarnae and Scythae, and by the kings of the Sarmati who live on either side of the Tanais River, and by the king of the Albani, and of the Hiberi and of the Medes.

Tablet 6

32. Kings of the Parthians, Tiridates, and later Phrates, the son of King Phrates, took refuge with me as suppliants; of the Medes, Artavasdes; of the Adiabeni, Artaxares; of the Britons, Dumnobellaunus and Tin[comarus]; of the Sugambri, Maelo; of the Marcomanni and Suevi, [Segime]rus. Phrates, son of Orodes, king of the Parthians, sent all his sons and grandsons to me in Italia, not because he had been conquered in war, but rather seeking our friendship by means of his own children as pledges; and a large number of other nations experienced the good faith of the Roman People during my principate who never before had had any interchange of embassies or of friendship with the Roman People.

33. From me the peoples of the Parthians and of the Medes received the kings for whom they asked through ambassadors, the chief men of those peoples [5–4 BCE]; the Parthians Vonones, son of King Phrates, grandson of King Orodes; the Medes Ariobarzanes, the son of King Atavazdes, grandson of King Ariobarzanes.

34. In my sixth [28 BCE] and seventh [27 BCE] consulships, when I had extinguished the flames of the Civil War, after receiving by universal consent the absolute control of affairs, I transferred the Commonwealth from my own control to the will of the Senate and the Roman People. For this service on my part I was given the title of *Augustus* by Decree of the Senate [on 16 January 27 BCE], and the doorposts of my house were covered with laurels by public act, and a *corona civica* was fixed above my door, and a golden shield was placed in the *Curia Iulia* whose inscription testified that the Senate and the Roman People gave me this in recognition of my valour, my clemency, my justice, and my piety. After that time I took precedence of all in influence, but of power I possessed no more than those who were my colleagues in any magistracy.

35. While I was administering my thirteenth consulship [2 BCE] the Senate and the Equestrian Order and the entire Roman People gave me the title of 'Father of the Fatherland', and decreed that this title should be inscribed upon the vestibule of my house and in the *Curia Iulia* and in the *Forum Augustum* beneath the chariot pulled by four horses erected in my honour by Decree of the Senate. At the time of writing this I was in my seventy-sixth year [11 May–19 August? 14 CE].

App. 1. The sum total of the money, which he contributed to the treasury or to the Roman plebs or to discharged soldiers, was 600,000,000 *denarii*.

App. 2. The new works which he built were: the Temple of Mars, of Jupiter Tonans and Feretrius, of Apollo, of the Divine Iulius, of Quirinus, of Minerva, of Juno the queen, of Jupiter Libertas, of the Lares, of the Di Penates, of Youth, of the Mother of the gods, the Lupercal, the state box at the circus, the *Curia* with the *Chalcidicum*, the *Forum Augustum*, the *Basilica Iulia*, the Theatre of Marcellus, ... the Grove of the Caesars beyond the Tiber.

App. 3. He restored the *Capitolium* and sacred buildings to the number of 82, the Theatre of Pompeius, the aqueducts, the *Via Flaminia*.

App. 4. The expenditures provided for theatrical shows, gladiatorial sports, for exhibitions of athletes, for hunts of wild beasts, and the naval combat, and his gifts to *coloniae* in Italia, to cities in the provinces which had been destroyed by earthquake or conflagration, or to individual friends and senators, whose property he raised to the required rating, are too numerous to be reckoned.

*　　*　　*

Rerum Gestarum Divi Augusti, quibus orbem terra[rum] imperio populi Rom[ani] subiecit, et impensarum, quas in rem publicam populumque Romanum fecit, incisarum in duabus aheneis pilis, quae su[n]t Romae positae, exemplar sub[i]ectum.

Tabula I

1. *Annos undeviginti natus exercitum privato consilio et privata impensa comparavi. ~ per quem rem publicam a dominatione factionis oppressam in liberatatem vindicavi. Eo [nomi]ne senatus decretis honorif[i]cis in ordinem suum m[e adlegit C. Pansa et A. Hirti]o consulibus, con[sula]rem locum s[imul dan sententiae ferendae, et i]imperium mihi dedit. ~ Res Publica, n[e quid detrimenti caperet, a] me pro praetore simul cum consulibus pro[viden]dum [iussit. P]opulus autem eodem anno me consulem, cum [cos. uterqu]e in bel[lo ceci]disset, et triumvirum rei publicae costituend[ae creavit].*

2. *Qui parentem meum [interfecer]un[t eo]s in exilium expuli iudiciis legitimis ultus eorum [fa]cin[us, e]t postea bellum inferentis rei publicae vici b[is a]cie.*

3. *[B]ella terra et mari c[ivilia ex]ternaque toto in orbe terrarum s[aepe gessi] victorque omnibus v[eniam petentib]us civibus peperci. Exte[rnas] gentes, quibus tuto i[gnosci pot]ui[t, co]nservare quam excidere m[alui]. Millia civium Roma[no]rum [sub] sacramento meo fuerunt circiter [quingen]ta. Ex quibus dedu[xi in coloni]as aut remisi in municipia sua stipen[dis emeri]tis millia aliquant[o plura qu]am trecenta et iis omnibus agros a[dsignavi] aut pecuniam*

pro p[raemis mil]itiae dedi. Naves cepi sescen[tas praeter] eas, si quae minore[s quam trir]emes fuerunt.

4. *[Bis] ovans triumphavi et tri[s egi] curulis triumphos et appella[tus sum v]iciens et semel imperator. [decernente plu]ris triumphos mihi sena[t]u, qua[ter eis su]persedi. ~ L[aurum de f]asc[i]bus deposui in Capi[tolio votis, quae] quoque bello nuncupaveram, [sol]utis. Ob res a [me aut per legatos] meos auspicis meis terra ma[riqu]e pr[o]spere gestas qui[nquageniens et q]uinquiens decrevit senatus supp[lica]ndum esse dis immortalibus. Dies a[utem, pe]r quos ex senatus consulto [s]upplicatum est, fuere DC[CCLXXXX. In triumphis meis] ducti sunt ante currum meum reges aut r[eg]um lib[eri novem. Consul f]ueram terdeciens, cum [scribeb]a[m] haec, [et eram se]p[timum et] tricen[simu]m tribuniciae potestatis.*

5. *[Dic]tat[ura]m et apsent[i e]t praesent[i mihi delatam et a popul]o et a se[na]tu [M. Marce]llo e[t] L. Arruntio [cos.] non rec[epi. Non sum] depreca[tus] in s[umma f]rum[enti p]enuria curatio[n]em an[non]ae. [qu] am ita ad[min]ist[ravi, ut] in[tra] die[s] paucos metu et periclo p[r] aesenti civitatem univ[ersam liberarem impensa et] cura mea. Consul[atum] quoqu]e tum annum e[t perpetuum mihi] dela[tum non recepi.]*

6. *[Consulibus M. Vinicio et Q. Lucretio] et postea P. Lentulo et Cn. L[entulo et tertium Paullo Fabio Maximo] e[t Q. Tuberone senatu populoq]u[e Romano consentientibus] ut cu[rator legum et morum maxima potestate solus crearer nullum magistratum contra morem maiorem delatum recepi. Quae tum per me fieri senatus] v[o]luit, per trib[un]ici[a]m p[otestatem perfeci, cuius potes]tatis conlegam et [ips]e ultro [quinquiens mihi a sena]tu[de]poposci et accepi.*

7. *[Tri]umv[i]rum rei pu[blicae c]on[s]ti[tuendae fui per continuos an]nos [decem. P]rinceps s[enatus fui usque ad e]um d[iem, quo scrip]seram [haec, per annos] quadra[ginta. Pon]tifex [maximus, augur, XVvir]um sacris fac[iundis, VIIvirum ep]ulon[um, frater arvalis, sodalis Titius], fetialis fui.*

Tabula II

8. *Patriciorum numerum auxi consul quintum iussu populi et senatus. Senatum ter legi. Et in consulatu sexto censum populi conlega M. Agrippa egi. Lustrum post annum alterum et quadragensimum fec[i]. Quo lustro civium Romanorum censa sunt capita quadragiens centum millia et sexag[i]inta tria millia. ~ Tum [iteru]m consulari com imperio lustrum [s]olus feci C. Censorin[o et C.] Asinio cos. Quo lustro censa sunt civium Romanorum [capita] quadragiens centum millia et ducenta triginta tria mi[llia. Et tertiu]m consulari cum imperio lustrum conlega Tib. Cae[sare filio] m[eo feci,] Sex. Pompeio et Sex. Appuleio cos. Quo lustro ce[nsa sunt]civ[ium Ro]manorum capitum quadragiens centum mill[ia et n]onge[nta tr]iginta et septem millia. Legibus novi[s] m[e auctore l]atis m[ulta e]xempla maiorum exolescentia iam ex nostro [saecul]o red[uxi et ipse] multarum rer[um exe]mpla imitanda pos[teris tradidi].*

9. *Vota p[ro valetudine meo susc]ipi p[er cons]ules et sacerdotes qu[in]to qu[oque anno senatus decrevit. Ex iis] votis s[ae]pe fecerunt vivo m[e ludos aliquotiens sace]rdo[tu]m quattuor amplissima colle[gia, aliquotiens consules. Pr]iva[t]im*

etiam et municipatim univer[si cives unanimite]r con[tinente]r apud omnia pulvinaria pro vale[tu]din[e mea s]upp[licaverunt.]

10. *Nom[en me]um [sena]tus c[onsulto inc]lusum est in saliare carmen et sacrosanctu[s in perp]etum [ut essem et, q]uoad ivierem, tribunicia potestas mihi [esse, per lege]m sanc[tum est. Pontif]ex maximus ne fierem in vivi [c]onlegae l]ocum, [populo id sace]rdotium deferente mihi, quod pater meu[s habuer]at, r[ecusavi. Qu]od sacerdotium aliquod post annos, eo mor[t]uo q[ui civilis] m[otus o]ccasione occupaverat, ~ cuncta ex Italia [ad comitia mea] confluen[te mu]ltitudine, quanta Romae nun[q]uam [fertur ante i]d temp[us fuisse], recep[i] P. Sulpicio C. Valgio consulibu[s].*

11. *Aram [Fortunae] R[educis a]nte aedes Honoris et Virtutis ad portam Cap[enam pro] red[itu me]o senatus consacravit, in qua ponti[fices et] vir[gines Ve]stal[es anni]versarium sacrificium facere [decrevit eo] di[e quo co]nsul[ibus Q. Luc]retio et [M. Vi]nic[i]o in urbem ex [Syria redieram, et diem Augustali]a ex [c]o[gnomine] nos[t]ro appellavit.*

12. *[Senatus consulto ea occasion]e pars [praetorum e]t tribunorum [plebi cum consule Q.] Lu[cret]io et princi[pi] bus viris [ob]viam mihi mis[s]a e[st in Campan]iam, quo honos [ad ho]c tempus nemini praeter [m]e es[t decretus. Cu]m ex His[p]ania Gal[liaque, rebu]s in iis provincis prosp[e]re [gest]i[s], R[omam redi] Ti. Nerone P. Qui[nctilio c]o[n]s[ulibu]s, ~ aram [Pacis A]u[g]ust[ae senatus pro]redi[t]u meo consa[c]randam [censuit] ad campam [Martium, in qua ma]gistratus et sac[er]dotes [et v]irgines V[est]a[les ann]iversarium sacrific]ium facer[e decrevit.]*

13. *[Ianum] Quirin[um, quem cl]aussum ess[e maiores nostri voluer]unt, cum [p]er totum i[mperium po]puli Roma[ni terra marique es]set parta victoriis pax, cum pr[ius quam] nascerer, a co[ndita] u[rb]e bis omnino clausum [f]uisse prodatur m[emori]ae, ter me princi]pe senat]us claudendum esse censui[t].*

Tabula III

14. *[Fil]ios meos, quos iuv[enes] mihi eripuit for[tuna], Gaium et Lucium Caesares, honoris mei caussa senatus populusque Romanus annum quintum et decimum agentis consules designavit, ut [e]um magistratum inirent post quinquennium. Et ex eo die, quo deducti [s]unt in forum ut interessent consiliis publicis decrevit sena[t]us. Equites [a]utem Romani universi principem iuventutis utrumque eorum parm[is] et hastis argenteis donatum appellaverunt.*

15. *Plebei Romanae viritum HS trecenos numeravi ex testamento patris mei. et nomine meo HS quadringenos ex bellorum manibiis consul quintum dedi, iterum autem in consulatu decimo ex [p]atrimonio meo HS quadringenos congiari viritim pernumer[a]vi, et consul undecimum duodecim frumentationes frumento pr[i]vatim coempto emensus sum. ~ et tribunicia potestate duodecimum quadringenos nummos tertium viritim dedi. Quae mea congiaria p[e]rvenerunt ad [homi]num millia nunquam minus quinquaginta et ducenta. Tribuniciae potestatis duodevicensimum consul XII trecentis et viginti millibus plebis urbanae sexagenos denarios viritim dedi. Et colon[i]s militum meorum consul quintum ex manibiis viritim millia nummum singula dedi. acceperunt id triumphale*

congiarium in colonis hominum circiter centum et viginti millia. Consul tertium dec[i]mum sexagenos denarios plebei, quae tum frumentum publicum acciebat, dedi; ea millia hominum paullo plura quam ducenta fuerunt.

16. *Pecuniam [pr]o agris, quos in consulatu meo quarto et postea consulibus M. Cr[a]ssao et Cn. Lentulo augure adsignavi militibus, soliv municipis. Ea [s]u[mma s]estertium circiter sexsiens milliens fuit, quam [p]ro Italicis praedis numeravi. et ci[r]citer bis mill[ie]ns et sescentiens, quod pro agris provincialibus soliv. Id primus et [s]olus omnium, qui [d]eduxerunt colonias militum in Italia aut in provincis, ad memoriam aetatis meae feci. Et postea Ti. Nerone et Cn. Pisone consulibus, ~ et D. Laelio cos., et C. Calvisio et L. Pasieno consulibus, et L. Le[nt]ulo et M. Messalla consulibus, et L. Caninio ~ et Q. Fabricio co[s.], milit[i]bus, quos emeriteis stipendis in sua municpi[a dedux]i, praem[i]a numerato persolvi. ~ quam in rem sestertium q[uater m]illiens cir[cite]r impendi.*

17. *Quater [pe]cunia mea iuvi aerarium, ita ut sestertium milliens et quing[en]ties ad eos qui praerant aerario detulerim. Et M. Lepido et L. Ar[r]untio cos. in aerarium militare, quod ex consilio n[eo] co[ns]titutum est, ex [q]uo praemia darentur militibus, qui vicena [aut plu]ra sti[pendi]a emeruissent ~ HS milliens et septing[e]nti[ens ex pa]t[rim]onio [m]eo detuli.*

18. *[Ab eo anno q]uo Cn. et P. Lentuli c[ons]ules fuerunt, cum deficerent [vecti]g[alia, tum] centum millibus h[omi]num, tum pluribus multo frume[ntarios et n]umma[rio]s t[ributus ex horr]eo et patr[i]monio m[e]o edidi.*

Tabula IV

19. *Curiam et continens ei Chalcidicum templumque Apollinis in Palatio cum porticibus, aedem divi Iuli, Lupercal, porticum ad circum Flaminium, quam sum appellari passus ex nomine eius qui priorem eodem in solo fecerat Octaviam, pulvinar ad circum maximum, aedes in Capitolio Iovis Feretri et Iovis Tonantis, ~ aedem Quirini, aedes Minervae et Iunonis Reginae et Iovis Libertatis in Aventino, aedem Larum in summa sacra via, aedem deum Penatium in Velia, aedem Iuventatis, aedem Matris Magnae in Palatio feci.*

20. *Capitolium et Pompeium theatrum utrumque opus impensa grandi refeci sine ulla inscriptione nominis mei. Rovos aquarum compluribus locis vetustate labentes refeci, ~ et aquam quae Marcia appellatur duplicavi fonte novo in rivum eius inmisso. Forum Iulium et basilicam quae fuit inter aedem Castoris et aedem Saturni, ~ coepta profligataque poera a patre meo, perfeci, et eandem basilicam consumptam incendio ampliato eius solo sub titulo nominis filiorum m[eorum i]ncohavi, ~ et, si vivus non perfecissem, perfici ab heredibus [meis ius]si. Duo et octoginta templa deum in urbe consul sex[tu]m ex [auctori]tate senatus refeci, nullo praetermisso quod e[o] tempore [refici debeba]t. Consul septimum viam Flaminiam a[b urbe] Ari[minum refeci pontes]que omnes praeter Mulvium et Minucium.*

21. *In privato solo Martis Ultoris templum [f]orumque Augustum [ex ma]n[i]biis feci. Theatrum ad aede Apollinis in solo magna ex parte a p[r]i[v]atis empto feci, quod sub nomine M. Marcell[i] generi mei esset. Don[a e]x manibiis in Capitolio*

*et in aede divi Iu[l]i et in aede Apollinis de Vestae et in templo Martis Ultoris
consecravi, quae mihi constituerunt HS circiter milliens. Auri coronari pondo
triginta et quinque millia municipiis et colonis Italiae conferentibus ad
triumpho[s] meos quintum consul remisi, et postea, quotienscumque imperator
a[ppe]llatus sum, aurum coronarium non accepi, decernentibus municipii[s] et
colonis aequ[e] beni[g]ne adque antea decreverant.*

22. *Ter munus gladiatorium dedi meo nomine et quinquiens filiorum meorum aut
n[e]potum nomine; quibus muneribus depugnaverunt hominum ci[rc]iter decem
millia. ~ Bis athletarum undique accitorum spectaculu[m] p[o]pulo pra[ebui me]o
nomine et tertium nepo[tis] mei nomine. Ludos feci m[eo no]m[ine] quater, ~
aliorum autem m[agistr]atuum vicem ter et viciens. ~ [Pr]o conlegio XVvirorum
magis[ter con]legii collega M. Agrippa ~ lud[os s]aeclares, C. Furnio C. Silano
cos. [feci. C]onsul XIII ludos Mar[tia]les pr[imus fec]i, quos p[ost i]d tempus
deincep[s] ins[equen]ti[bus] annis [ex senatus consulto et lege fe]cerunt [co]n[su]les.
~ [Ven]ation[es] best[ia]rum Africanarum meo nomine aut filio[ru]m meorum et
nepotum in ci[r]co aut in foro aut in amphitheatris, popul[o d]edi sexiens et
viciens, quibus confecta sunt bestiarum circiter tria m[ill]ia et quingentae.*

23. *Navalis proeli spectaclum populo de[di tr]ans Tiberim, in quo loco nunc nemus
est Caesarum, cavato [s]olo in longitudinem mille et octingentos pedes ~ in
latudine[m mille] e[t] ducenti. In quo triginta rostratae naves triremes a[ut
birem]es ~ plures autem minores inter se conflixerunt. Q[uibu]s in classibus
pugnaverunt praeter remiges millia ho[minum tr]ia circiter.*

24. *In templis omnium civitatium prov[inci]ae Asiae victor ornamenta reposui, quae
spoliatis tem[plis i]s cum quo bellum gesseram privatim possederat. Satatuae
[mea]e pedestres et equestres et in quadrigeis argenteae steterunt in urbe XXC
circiter, quas ipse sustuli ~ exque ea pecunia dona aurea in aede Apollinis meo
nomine et illorum, qui mihi statuarum honorem habuerunt, posui.*

Tabula V

25. *Mare pacavi a praedonibus. Eo bello servorum, qui fugerant a dominis suis et
arma contra rem publicam ceperant, triginta fere millia capta dominis ad
supplicium sumendum tradidi. Iuravit in mea verba tota Italia sponte sual et me
be[lli] quo vici ad Actium ducem depoposcit. Iuraverunt in eadem ver[ba
provi]nciae Galliae, Hispaniae, Africa, Sicilia, Sardinia. Qui sub [signis meis
tum] militaverint, fuerunt senatores plures quam DCC, in ii[s qui vel antea vel
pos]tea consules facti sunt ad eum diem quo scripta su[nt haec LX]X[XIII,
sacerdo]tes ci[rc]iter CLXX.*

26. *Omnium prov[inciarum populi Romani], quibus finitimae fuerunt gentes quae
non p[arerent imperio nos]tro, fines auxi. Gallias et Hispanias provincias, i[tem
Germaniam qua inclu]dit Oceanus a Gadibus ad ostium Albis flumin[is pacavi.
Alpes a re]gione ea, quae proxima est Hadriano mari, [ad Tuscum pacari fec]i.
nulli genti bello per iniuriam inlato. Cla[ssis m]ea per Oceanum] ab ostio Rheni
ad solis orientis regionem usque ad fi[nes Cimbroru]m navigavit, ~ quo neque
terra neque mari quisquam Romanus ante id tempus adit, Cimbrique et
Charydes et Semnones et eiusdem tractus alli Germanorum popu[l]i per legatos*

amicitiam mean et populi Romani petierunt. Meo iussu et auspicio ducti sunt [duo] exercitus eodem fere tempore in Aethiopiam et in Ar[a]biam, quae appel[latur Eudaemon, [maxim]aeque hos[t]ium gentis utr[iu]sque cop[iae] caesae sunt in acie et [c]om[plur]a oppida capta. In Aethiopiam usque ad oppidum Nabata pervent[um]est, cui proxima est Meroe. In Arabiam usque in fines Sabaeorum pro[cess]it exercitus ad oppidum Mariba.

27. *Aegyptum imperio populi [Ro]mani adieci. Armeniam maiorum, interfecto rege eius Artaxe, c[u]m possem facere provinciam, malui maiorum nostrorum exemplo regn[u]m id Tigrani, regis Artavasdis filio, nepoti autem Tigranis regis, per T[i. Ne]ronem trad[er], qui tum mihi priv[ig]nus erat. Et eandem gentem postea d[e]sciscentem et rebellantem domit[a]m per Gaium filium meum regi Ariobarzani, regis Medorum Artaba[zi] filio, regendam tradidi ~ et post eius mortem filio eius Artavasdi. ~ Quo interfecto, Tig[ra]ne⟨m⟩ qui erat ex regio genere Armeniorum oriundus, in id regnum misi. Provincias omnis, quae trans Hadrianum mare vergunt ad orien[te]m, Cyrenasque, iam ex parte magna regibus eas possidentibus, et antea Siciliam et Sardiniam occupatas bello servili reciperavi.*

28. *Colonias in Africa Sicilia [M]acedonia utraque Hispania Achai[a] Asia S[y]ria Gallia Narbonensi Pi[si]dia militum deduxi. Italia autem XXVIII [colo]nias, quae vivo me celeberrimae et frequentissimae fuerunt, me [auctore] deductas habet.*

29. *Signa militaria complur[a per] alios d[u]ces ami[ssa] devicti[s hostibu]s re[cipe]ravi ex Hispania et [Gallia et a Dalm]ateis. Parthos trium exercitum Romanorum spolia et signa re[ddere] mihi supplicesque amicitiam populi Romani petere coegi. Ea autem si[gn]a in penetrali, quod e[s]t in templo Martis Ultoris, reposui.*

30. *Pannoniorum gentes, qua[s a]nte me principem populi Romani exercitus numquam ad[it], devictas per Ti. [Ne]ronem, qui tum erat privignus et legatus meus, imperio populi Romani s[ubie]ci protulique fines Illyrici ad r[ip]am fluminis Dan[uv]i. Citr[a] quod [D]a[cor]u[m tra]n[s]gressus exercitus meis a[u]sp[icis vict]us profligatusque [es]t, et pos[tea tran]s Dan[u]vium ductus ex[ercitus me]u[s] Da[cor]um gentis im[peri]a p[opuli] R[omani perferre coegit].*

31. *Ad me ex In[dia regum legationes saepe missae sunt nunquam visae ante id t]em[pus] apud qu[em]q[uam] R[omanorum du]cem. Nostram amic[itiam petie]run[t] per legat[os] B[a]starn[ae Scythae]que et Sarmatarum qui su[nt citra fl]umen Tanaim [et] ultra reg[es. Alba]norumque rex et Hiberorum e[t Medorum].*

Tabula VI

32. *Ad me supplices confug[erunt] reges Parthorum Tirida[te]s et post[ea] Phrat[es] regis Phrati[s] filiu[s]. ~ Medorum Ar[tavasdes, Adiabenorum] Artaxares, Britannorum Dumnobellaunus et Tin[comarus, Sugambr]orum Maelo, Marcomannorum Sueborum [Segime]rus. Ad [me re]x Parthorum Phrates, Orod[i]s filius, filios suos nepot[esque omnes] misit in Italiam, non bello superatu[s], sed amicitiam nostram per [libe]ror[um] suorum pignora petens.*

Plurimaeque aliae gentes exper[tae sunt p. R.] fidem me principe, quibus antea cum populo Roman[o nullum extitera]t legationum et amicitiae [c]ommercium.

33. *A me gentes Parthorum et Medoru[m per legatos] principes earum gentium reges pet[i]tos acceperunt: Par[thi Vononem, regis Phr]atis filium, regis Orodis nepotem. Medi Arioba[rzanem,] regis Artavazdis filium, regis Ariobarzanis nepotem.*

34. *In consulatu sexto et septimo, po[stquam b]ella [civil]ia oxstinxeram, perconsensum universorum [potens reru]m om[n]ium, rem publicam ex pea potestate ~ in senat[us populique Rom]ani [a]rbitrium transtuli. Quo pro merito meo senatu[s consulto Au]gust[us appe]llatus sum et laureis postes aedium mearum v[estiti] publ[ice coronaq]ue civica super ianuam meam fixa est ~ [et clu]peus [aureu]s in [c]uria Iulia positus, quem mihi senatum pop[ulumq]ue Rom[anu]m dare virtutis clement[iaequ]e iustitiae et pieta[tis caus]sa testatu[m] est pe[r e]ius clupei [inscription]em. Post id tem[pus a]uctoritate [omnibus praestiti, potest]atis au[tem n]ihilo ampliu[s habu]i quam cet[eri qui m]ihi quoque in ma[gis]tra[t]u conlegae f[uerunt].*

35. *Tertium dec[i]mum consulatu[m cum gereba]m, sena[tus et e]quester order populusq[ue] Romanus universus [appell]av[it me pat]re[m p]atriae idque in vestibu[lo a]edium mearum inscribendum et in c[u]ria [Iulia e]t in foro Aug. sub quadrig[i]s, quae mihi ex s.c. pos[it]ae [sunt, decrevit. Cum scri]psi haec, annus agebam septuagensu[mum sextum].*

App. 1. *Summa pecun[i]ae, quam ded[it vel in aera]rium [vel plebei Romanae vel di]missis militibus: denarium sexien[s milliens].*

App. 2. *Opera fecit nova aedem Martis, [Iovis] Ton[antis et Feretri, Apollinis], divi Iuli, Quirini, Minervae, [Iunonis Reginae, Iovis Libertatis], Larum, deum Penatium, ~ Iuv[entatis, Matris Magnae, Lupercal, pulvina]r ad circum, ~ curiam cum Ch[alcidico, forum Augustum, basilica]m Iuliam, theatrum Marcelli, ~ [p]or[ticum Octaviam, nemus trans T]iberim Caesarum.*

App. 3. *Refecit Capito[liam sacra]sque aedes [nu]m[ero octoginta] duas, thea[t]rum Pompei, aqu[aram r]iv[as, vi]am Flamin[iam].*

App. 4. *Impensa p[raestita in spec]tacul[a] sca[enica et munera] gladiatorum at[que athletas et venationes et] naumachi[am] et donata pe[c]unia [colonis municipiis oppidis] terrae motu incendioque consumpt[is] a[ut viritim] a[micis senat]oribusque, quorum census explevit, in[n]umera[bili]s.*

Appendix 2

Family and Friends:
The Men Who Served Augustus

Augustus managed the security of his *provincia* and order of battle through a formal organization comprising Roman officials with term-limited powers and the assistance of non-citizen allies bound by treaties. Short biographies (terminating at 14 CE) of those whose names have survived are presented here, listed in order of their family name (*nomen gentile*) or *cognomen* in the few cases the clan name is not known.

1. Romans

Many fellow citizens served Augustus as his hand-picked deputies or subordinates (*legati* and *praefecti*) and fought wars under his auspices during the period 31 BCE–14 CE. For in-depth discussions of these men's family and political connections with Augustus, see Atkinson (1958), Syme (1939a) and Syme (1986).

(a) Deputies (*Legati Augusti Pro Praetore*)

Augustus personally appointed his deputies from among both the patrician senatorial class, including the *nobiles* (high status men of families that had served as consuls) and the *novi homines* (men born outside the old aristocracy) who he promoted to prominent positions. Over a lifetime's career, a man might serve the *Res Publica* in a variety of official capacities with increasing responsibility. He could rise through the *cursus honorum* – the 'race for honour' or career ladder of public offices – undertaking civilian and military positions, located in Rome, Italy or overseas:

- *Vigintivir*: in his late teens he might be appointed to one of the twenty junior officials conducting administrative duties in Rome, such as the commission of three men (*triumviri monetales*) in charge of the Rome mint producing the copper and bronze coins.
- *Tribunus Militum*: in his twenties he could serve in the army on the staff of a *legatus legionis* as a military tribune; twenty-four such positions were filled annually.
- *Quaestor*: having reached age 25, he could be appointed as a finance officer on the staff of one of the proconsuls in a public province; there were openings for twenty posts annually.
- *Tribunus Plebis*: in his mid-twenties he could stand as one of the ten annually elected tribunes hearing appeals from citizens and defending their civil rights in legal cases.

- *Aedilis*: in his mid-twenties he could also stand for election as one of the six officials maintaining the city's public infrastructure and markets.
- *Praetor*: when he had reached 30, he could stand for election to one of the twelve magistracies (the most senior of which was the *praetor urbanus*) responsible for chairing the public courts and organizing public games.
- *Legatus Legionis*: appointed personally by Augustus, in this post he would be responsible for one of the twenty-two or so legions (excluding the units in Egypt which were the responsibility of the *Praefectus Aegypti*).
- *Consulis*: when he had reached 42 (but in the case of Augustus' family often at a much younger age through concessions), he could stand for one of the two annually elected consulships, responsible for chairing meetings of the Senate; the two consuls' names together were used to identify the year in Roman chronology.
- *Pro Consulis*: as an ex-consul he could be picked by lot to govern one of the twenty-two or so senatorial or public provinces.

At any point he could be picked by Augustus as a *legatus Augusti pro praetore* to govern one of the nine or more 'Provinces of Caesar' (Dio 53.12.1–2, 53.13.4–7, 53.14.1–4; Strabo *Geog.* 17.3.25; Suet., *Div. Aug* 47). With it came responsibility for pacification of the territory assigned to him, ensuring the security of his jurisdiction, and protecting of Roman citizens living within its borders. He had the necessary military power enshrined in law (*imperium*) to command all the army units stationed in his *provincia* (Dio 53.13.5–6) 'with Caesar's authority to exercise full powers, including capital punishment' (Joseph., *Bell. Iud.* 2.117). His tour of duty was as long as Augustus wished, but typically lasted three years (referred to as a *triennium*), though during the crises of 6 and 9 CE it was extended (Dio 55.28.1–2; Suet., *Div. Aug* 23.1). This compares to the term of the proconsul of a senatorial or public province of just one year's duration (Dio 53.13.2–3; *cf.* Dio 55.28.1–2). He was entitled to a complement of five *lictores* – one less than the number assigned to proconsuls, emphasizing his lesser status (Dio 53.13.2–4). A serving *legatus* wore military regalia on duty, in contrast to the proconsul who was expected to remain in civilian attire while managing his province (Dio 53.13.3).

A highly valued honour for a victorious commander was to be voted a full triumph, in which he drove a four-horse chariot (*currus triumphalis*) through the streets of Rome and along the *Via Sacra* (Suet., *Div. Aug.* 25.3). His face and arms would be daubed red and he would wear an elaborately embroidered toga (*toga picta*) and tunic (*tunica palmata*). He would be preceded in the military parade by captives and war spoils displayed on floats, whose contents were explained on signboards (*fercula*). His officers and troops would follow. The spectacle would conclude with a sacrifice at the *Capitolium*. A lower grade recognition was the *ovatio* with triumphal ornaments, in which the celebrating commander rode a horse. The honour might be accompanied by a honorary war title (*agnomen* or *cognomen*) and, in the case of Augustus and his family members, a victory arch of marble (*ianus*) surmounted by statues.

The ultimate distinction for a commander was to slay his enemy in battle and to strip his body of its armour and equipment. These rich spoils (*spolia opima*) would be taken by the victor and dedicated to Iupier Feretrius at his temple in Rome. Many tried, including M. Licinius Crassus and Nero Claudius Drusus, but neither was recognised during Augustus' time.

Many of these men were friends (*amici*), not just acquaintances, of Augustus. Some were bound to his family through marriage or adoption. Others were recognized through membership of a religious college (*collegia sacerdotum*), which carried with it great prestige. As important to Augustus as securing the *Pax Augusta* on Earth was safeguarding the *Pax Deorum* with the Roman pantheon. Himself *Pontifex Maximus* – the most important of the religious priesthoods – from 13 BCE, he held several other posts (*RG* 7; Dio 51.1.5). His *legati* could be active members of these *collegia*, which included:

- *Augures*, the second most important body of men, responsible for interpreting the will of the gods through the flight of birds;
- *Quindecemiri Sacris Faciundis*, the commission of fifteen men charged with consulting the Sybilline Books (*Libri Sybillini*) who oversaw the landmark *Ludi Saeculares* of 17 BCE;
- *Fratres Arvales*, the college of twelve 'Arval Brothers' responsible for the rites of the ancient cult of the Bona Dea and her sanctuary outside Rome;
- *Septemviri Epulones*, the college of seven men responsible for organizing banquets given in honour of the gods;
- *Fetiales*, responsible for negotiating treaties and reparations, and the ritual for declaring war at the Temple of Bellona – the ancient priesthood was re-established by Augustus in 31 BCE (Dio 50.4.5) and held by him alone until 6 CE, whence he shared it with two others.

For a discussion of the status and role of *legati Augusti pro praetore*, see Drogula (2015), pp. 345–73, and Hurlet (1997). For their priestly offices, see Röpke (2008). On triumphs see Beard (2007) and Lange (2015).

Sex. Aelius Catus (c. 45 BCE–After 4 CE). Little is known about the background of the son of Q. Aelius Catus. Conjecturally he was praetorian proconsul of Macedonia in c. 2–3 CE. Strabo writes 'in our own times, Aelius Catus transplanted from the country on the far side of the Ister into Thracia, 50,000 persons from among the Getae, a tribe with the same tongue as the Thraci, and they live there in Thracia now and are called "Moesi"' (Strabo, *Geog.* 7.3.10). He was elected ordinary consul for 4 CE.

L. Aelius Lamia (c. 64 BCE–After 22 BCE). A plebeian and a loyal friend of Cicero, Lamia is described by a contemporary as 'a man of the older type, who always tempered his old-fashioned dignity by a spirit of kindliness' (Vell. Pat. 2.116.3). At some point in his career, appointed as *praetor* (43 BCE), he served with distinction in the wars in Illyricum, Germania and Africa, but the lack of opportunities to display his courage denied him the triumphal insignia he might have deserved (Vell. Pat. 2.116.3). He was a *legatus Augusti pro praetore* in

Hispania Citerior for the period 25–22 BCE (Dio 53.29.1). His religious offices included the post of *quindecemir sacris faciundis* (*CIL* VI, 37058, 41034–41041) on the commission charged with consulting the Sybilline Books. He, or his son, served a single term as consul (3 CE).

M. Aemilius Lepidus (c. 45 BCE–After 9 CE). The son of patrician Paullus Aemilius Lepidus (consul 34 BCE) and Cornelia, a contemporary wrote floridly of Lepidus that he was 'a man who in name and in fortune approaches the Caesars, whom one admires and loves the more in proportion to his opportunities to know and understand him, and whom one regards as an ornament to the great names from whom he springs' (Vell. Pat. 2.114.5). He rose through the *cursus honorum* to become consul for 6 CE. During the Great Illyrian Revolt of 6–9 CE, Lepidus led one of the army groups with 'virtue and distinguished service' and 'vigilance and fidelity' (Vell. Pat. 2.125.5), in recognition for which Tiberius assigned him command of military operations at the mid-point of the campaign (Vell. Pat. 2.114.5, 2.115.2; Dio 56.12.2). At the end of the war he was granted triumphal ornaments (Vell. Pat. 2.115.3). He went on to govern Hispania Tarraconensis (formerly Hispania Citerior) and Lusitania, 'and the army in them were held in peace and tranquillity' (Vell. Pat. 2.125.5). His daughter Aemilia Lepida was betrothed to Germanicus' eldest son, Drusus, and his son Marcus to Germanicus' daughter, Iulia Drusilla (Tac., *Ann.* 6.40).

M. Agrippa (né M. Vipsanius Agrippa) (c. 64/63–March? 12 BCE). The son of L. Agrippa, Marcus was a *novus homo* descended from the obscure plebeian *gens Vipsania*. For reasons unknown, in his own lifetime he preferred to be called plain M. Agrippa. He was the life-long friend of Augustus and his right-hand man. Key military victories can be directly attributed to him which established Augustus as the supreme commander of the *imperium* of the Roman people. When and how they met is not recorded. Agrippa may have been with him when Iulius Caesar's great nephew went to Hispania to take part in the war against Pompeius Magnus in 45 BCE (Nic. 11). He was certainly with his friend in Apollonia, Illyricum in March 44 BCE when news of the dictator's murder arrived (Nic. 16; Suet., *Div. Aug.* 94). He was one of the small group advising him (Nic. 30) and a close and active supporter of Imp. Caesar – he helped him recruit troops in Campania (44 BCE), successfully prosecuted the conspirator C. Cassius Longinus in 43 BCE (Dio 46.49.3) and was at Philippi in 42 BCE nursing his friend back to health (Pliny, *Nat. Hist.* 7.148). His talent for military leadership and strategy emerged during the Perusine War, notably at Fulginiae (App., *Bell. Civ.* 5.35) in 40 BCE against L. Antonius, brother of *triumvir* M. Antonius. He was rewarded for his achievement and loyalty with the post of *praetor urbanus* (Dio 48.20.2). In that role he successfully saw off raids on Italian coastal towns and installations by marines operating under the command of Sex. Pompeius, the son of Pompeius Magnus. He went to Gallia Comata, where he quelled a rebellion of Aquitani in 38 BCE (App., *Bell. Civ.* 5.92), for which he was awarded a triumph, and the following year crossed the Rhine – only the second commander since Iulius Caesar to do so (Dio 48.49.3) – to assist the Ubii, for which he was rewarded with the consulship the following year. Agrippa served as consul for 37 BCE. In preparation for the full-blooded war against Sex. Pompeius the same year, Agrippa supervised operations to build a double harbour (*Portus Iulius*) beside the Bay of Pozzuoli for outfitting the hundreds of ships and training thousands of crewmen (Vell. Pat. 2.79.1; App., *Bell. Civ.* 5.96). His warships were equipped with several innovations to improve their chance of success against the enemy's agile vessels. With this fleet, in 36 BCE he won the crucial naval battles of Mylae (Dio 49.2.1–4; App., *Bell. Civ.* 5.106–108) and Naulochus (App., *Bell. Civ.* 5.119–121) off the coast of Sicily that eliminated the threat posed by the son of Pompeius Magnus, and for it he was rewarded with the *corona navalis*, a unique golden rostral crown (Dio 49.14.3; Livy, *Per.* 129;Ver., *Aen.* 8.683–684). In 35 and 34 BCE, he was in action again with Imp. Caesar in Illyricum to crush resistance to Roman occupation and to expand territory from the Sava River to the Danube (App., *Ill.* 16–22). In 34 BCE, Agrippa was elected aedile in Rome (Dio 49.42.2) and used his period in office to make substantial repairs to the decaying fabric of Rome's ancient infrastructure, including the *Aqua Marcia* and *Cloaca Maxima*. Appointed by Imp. Caesar to lead operations during the Actian War (Dio 50.9.2–3, 50.14.1–2) against M. Antonius and Kleopatra VII of Egypt, Agrippa commanded 'seek and destroy' missions along the western Greek coastline, culminating in his victory on 2 August 31 BCE at Actium (Dio 50.33–35; Florus 21.6; Plut., *Ant.* 65.2, 66.1–2). His reward was a blue *vexillum* pennant (Dio 51.21.3) to be flown on his flagship. In the aftermath of the war he returned to Italy and oversaw the demobilization of as many as half the extant civil war legions (Dio 51.3.5). Popular with the plebs, he was much disliked by the *nobiles*. Nevertheless, he was elected consul for both 28 and 27 BCE, a consequential period when the so-called 'constitutional settlements' were agreed that defined the division of provinces between Augustus and the Senate and command of the army in them (Dio 53 11–13). He was *censor* with Augustus and purged the Senate (Dio 52.42.1). In Rome from 29–23 BCE, Agrippa commissioned several public buildings (paid with his own funds) in the *Campus Martius*, including the *Diribitorium, Saepta Iulia*, a new aqueduct (*Aqua Virgo*), the city's first large-scale integrated baths, a park, artificial lake and the Pantheon (Dio 53.27). Receiving *imperium proconsulare* as governor *praepositus Orienti*, or governor general in the East (23–21 BCE), he drove efforts to reconcile with communities formerly supportive of M. Antonius, and befriended Herodes of Iudaea as well as other allies in the region (Joseph., *Ant. Iud.* 15.10.2 and Vell. Pat. 2.93.2; *cf.* Suet., *Div. Aug.* 66.3 and Pliny, *Nat. Hist.* 7.149). Speculatively, he may have laid the diplomatic groundwork which led to the return of *signa* and prisoners of war captured at the Battle of Carrhae in 53 BCE and since held by the Parthians. On his return to Rome, Agrippa married Iulia Caesaris (Dio 54.6.5), the only daughter of Augustus, in 20 BCE and she later bore him three sons – Caius, Lucius and Postumus – as well as two daughters – Vipsania Iulia (Iulia the Younger) and Vipsania Agrippina (Agrippina the Elder). In the West, he oversaw the repatriation of the Ubii to Roman territory (Strabo. *Geog.* 4.3.4; Suet., *Div. Aug.* 21.1).

In 19 BCE, after raising the morale of the despondent troops, he was instrumental in concluding the Cantabrian and Asturian War, ending the 200-year struggle to annex and pacify the entire Iberian Peninsula (Dio 54.11.2–6). For this achievement he was rewarded with a golden mural crown (*corona muralis*) and a second triumph, which he refused. He was in Rome in June to attend the *Ludi Saeculares*, presided over the events of the first day and later that month held chariot races (*CIL* VI, 32323.165). In the East again (17–13 BCE), he visited Herodes in his homeland (Joseph., *Ant Iud.* 16.14–16) and developed an empathy for the Jews, writing to the officials and magistrates to ensure they were treated according to law and that their legal priviliges were respected (Joseph., *Ant. Iud.* 16.165, 167–169). On the return, he detoured to Sinope to oversee operations to quell the Rebellion of Scribonius in the Cimerian Bosporus in 14 BCE, in which he was supported by Herodes of Iudaea and Polemon of Pontus (Dio 54.24.6; Orosius 21.28). Thereafter he no longer sent his war report to the Senate but to Augustus alone (Dio 54.24.8). In 13 BCE, Agrippa's *imperium* was extended as *maius* and, in addition, he received *tribunicias potestate*, making his powers equal to Augustus; only in his *auctoritas* was he the lesser figure. When the Pannonii rebelled in 11 CE, 50-year old Agrippa went to Illyricum to help M. Vinicius restore order (Dio 54.28.1–2). He achieved the result, but in doing so may have overexerted himself or contracted a fatal disease. He returned to Italy in 12 BCE and died in Campania (Dio 54.28.2–3). M. Agrippa received a state funeral in Rome, at which a bereft Augustus gave the eulogy, a Greek translation of which survives in part (*P. Köln* VI 249 or Inv. Nr. 4701 + 4722 Recto; *EJ* 366). His ashes were placed in the Mausoleum of Augustus (Dio 54.28.5). The sources agree on his loyalty (Dio 49.4.1–2, 54.29.3) and impatience (Suet., *Div. Aug.* 66.3). He was Augustus' 'good soldier and partner in victory' (Tac., *Ann.* 1.3), 'a man of distinguished character' (Vell. Pat. 2.96.1) and 'the noblest man of his day' (Dio 54.29.1), but another view portrays him as 'a cunning fox imitating a noble lion' (Hor., *Serm.* 2.3.186). The younger Seneca calls him a 'great souled man' (*Ep.*, 94.46) and records that he lived by the proverb 'harmony makes small things grow; lack of harmony makes great things decay' (*Ep.* 94.46). In later life he suffered intense pain in his leg, which may have been gout (Pliny, *Nat. Hist.* 23.58). His death led to the advancement of Tiberius as Augustus' right-hand man.

C. Antistius Vetus (c. 70 BCE–After 6 BCE). The *Antistii* were a plebeian branch of the *gens Antistia*. C. Vetus was likely the son of the proconsul of Hispania Ulterior (c. 60 BCE), who was the commander to whom reported the young *quaestor* C. Iulius Caesar (Vell. Pat. 2.43; Plut. *Caes.* 5.6; Suet. *Caes.* 7) early in his public career. In December 57 BCE, he was *tribunus plebis* supporting Cicero in his case against P. Clodius Pulcher, deeming it a priority (Cic., *Ad Q. Fr.* 2.1; *Ad Att.* 14.9.3). As a supporter of Caesar, Vetus' son went to Syria as *quaestor* (45 BCE), and a year later fought one of the sympathizers of the assassination, Q. Caecilius Bassus, proconsul of the province. Vetus besieged Bassus in his stronghold at Apameia, and only withdrew when the Parthians arrived; nevertheless, Vetus was acclaimed *imperator* by his troops. Encountering Brutus on his return to Rome at the end of 44 BCE, Vetus was persuaded to hand over the revenues he had withdrawn from the province, and also to join the side of the 'liberators'. After spending several months in Rome he rejoined Brutus, serving as his *legatus legionis*. He was at Philippi (October 42 BCE), but having been defeated, he surrendered and reconciled with the victors. In 35 BCE, Vetus was placed in charge – perhaps as proconsul of Gallia Transalpina – of prosecuting the Salassian War (Appian, *Ill.* 17); however, he failed to reduce the Salassi in the Alps. He was suffect consul (30 BCE) with Caesar's heir. Four years later, he went to Hispania Citerior as *legatus Augusti pro praetore*, prosecuting the Cantabrian War (26–25 BCE) with P. Carisius under Augustus, who was in the field in person (Vell. Pat. Pat. 2.90.4; Dio 53.25.1; Florus 2.33.51, 56; Orosius 6.21). When Augustus fell ill and had to retire to Tarraco, Vetus assumed command of combat operations and 'fought against them and accomplished a good deal, not because he was a better general than Augustus, but because the barbarians felt contempt for him and were defeated' (Dio 53.25.7–8). His, or his son's, name appears as *tresvir monetalis* on a low denomination coin minted in 16 BCE (e.g. *RIC* I 367; *RSC* 348). He, or his son, was elected consul for 6 BCE (Dio 55.9.1).

Sex. Appuleius (II) (c. 65 BCE–c. 5 CE). Plebeian-ranked Sextus was Augustus' nephew by virtue of being the son of *novus homo* Sex. Appuleius (I) and Octavia Maior, the *princeps'* elder half-sister. Sextus was consul with his half-uncle in 29 BCE (Dio 51.20.1). As proconsul, he went to Hispania Citerior and, having achieved victories there, was awarded a triumph held on 26 January 26 BCE (*Fast. Capitol.*). He then went as governor to Asia (23–22 BCE) and later served in Illyricum (8 BCE – Cassiodorus, *Chron. Min.* 2.135). Sextus was an *augur* (*ILS* 894 (Aesernia) dated to after 27 BCE) and perhaps also an *arvalis* by the time he was consul. He was married to Quinctilia, sister of P. Quinctilius Varus (*AE* 1966, 422).

L. Apronius (c. 45 BCE–After 28 CE). Apronius was a *novus homo* from one of the Italian *municipia*. He accompanied Vibius Postumus, perhaps as a *legatus legionis*, during the Great Illyrian Revolt (6–9 CE) and served with distinction, sharing in the triumphal ornaments granted by the Senate to the victorious commanders (Vell. Pat. 2.116.2–3). He is described by a contemporary as having 'earned by the distinguished valour which he displayed in this campaign also, the honours which he actually won shortly afterwards' (Vell. Pat. 2.116.3). He was suffect consul for 8 CE. Apronius was father-in-law of Plautius Silvanus.

L. Arruntius (L. Arruntius the Elder) (c. 60 BCE–c. 10 CE). Born a plebeian, Arruntius was one of the 'illustrious men' (Vell. Pat. 2.77.3) who was proscribed in 43 BCE, and then left Sex. Pompeius to join the heir of Iulius Caesar after the signing of the Treaty of Misenum (39 BCE). Under M. Agrippa, he commanded the central block of ships at the Battle of Actium (Plut., *Ant.* 65.1, 66.3); in 29 BCE, he was rewarded by being raised to patrician rank. He was consul for 22 BCE. He attended the *Ludi Saeculares* in 17 BCE as a *quindecemvir sacris faciundis* (*CIL* VI, 32323.151 = *ILS* 5050). He, or his son (consul 6 CE), is known to have written a history of the Punic Wars in the prose style of Sallust (Seneca, *Ep. Mor.* 114.17).

[?]. Articuleius Regulus (c. 35 BCE–After 14 CE). Regulus is known from an inscription (*ILS* 929) as the '*Leg. Imp. Caesaris Aug.*' of Lusitania, serving sometime between 2–14 CE.

C. Asinius Gallus (41 BCE–33 CE). Gallus was the son of C. Asinius Pollio, the senator and historian. Raised to patrician rank some time around 29 BCE, in 22 or 21 BCE he was appointed as a *tresvir monetalis*, one of the board of three commissioners supervizing the mint in Rome. He was known for his oratorical skill (Seneca, *Controv.* 4.4), some of it fierce (Tac., *Ann.* 1.12), and he wrote a book comparing his father to Cicero (Pliny the Younger, *Ep.* 7.4.3, 6). He attended the *Ludi Saeculares* in 17 BCE as a *quindecemvir sacris faciundis* (*CIL* VI, 32323.151 = *ILS* 5050). He was elected consul in 8 BCE with L. Marcius Censorinus – one of the two senators (or his son) who had tried to defend the dictator as he was struck down; there were allegations of bribery during his election, but Augustus refused to investigate them (Dio 55.5.3). During his term in office, repairs were carried out to the banks of the Tiber River (*CIL* VI, 1235). From 6 (or 5) BCE, he held the office of proconsul of Asia, and later (perhaps from 1 CE) he may have been governor of Hispania Tarraconensis. Upon the death of Augustus, C. Gallus was one of the leading senators alleged to have desire to rule (he is described as 'ambitious and incapable' in Tac., *Ann.* 1.13); but he was loathed by the new *princeps* Tiberius because, in 12 BCE, he had married his former – and beloved – wife, Agrippina Vipsania, daughter of M. Agrippa (Tac., *Ann.* 1.13).

L. Autronius Paetus (c. 70–After 28 BCE). The son of P. Autronius Paetus (the unsuccessful candidate for consul of 65 BCE), and a *novus homo*, L. Paetus was an early supporter of Caesar's heir and replaced him when elected suffect consul for 33 BCE. In 29/28 BCE, he was appointed proconsular governor of Africa (*CIL* I², 77); during his term in office there, he led his troops successfully in an unspecified military campaign and was acclaimed *imperator*, in recognition of which he celebrated a full triumph on 16 August 28 BCE (*Fast. Capitol.*).

Q. Caecilius Creticus Metellus Silanus (c. 35 BCE–After 17 CE). Son of patrician M. Iunius Silanus, Q. Silanus rose up the *cursus publicus* to become consul for 7 CE. He went to Syria in 13 CE and was succeeded by L. Calpurnius Piso in 17 CE (Tac. *Ann.* 2.43). His young daughter, Iunia, was betrothed to Germanicus Caesar's eldest son, Nero (Tac. *Ann.* 2.43; *ILS* 184 Rome).

A. Caecina Severus (c. 50 BCE–c. 25 CE). Severus was a *novus homo* descended from a prominent family of Volaterrae (Volterra) in Etruria. He rose through the *cursus honorum* to become suffect consul for 1 BCE. He was appointed to Moesia as its first *legatus Augusti pro praetore* when it was created around 5/6 CE (Dio 55.29.1; *AE* 1937, 62); he led his troops into neighbouring Illyricum in the Great Illyrian Revolt of 6–9 CE (Dio 55.29.3–30.5). After a major setback, he proved a competent commander (Vell. Pat. 2.112.4–6; Dio 55.32.3–4). He may have been proconsul of Africa for 8–13 CE (*AE* 1987, 992), but in 14 CE he was *Legatus Augusti Pro Praetore* of Germania Inferior in charge of *Legiones* I, V *Alaudae*, XX *Valeria Victrix* and XXI *Rapax* (Tac., *Ann.* 1.31, 1.37). In 15 CE, he reached his fortieth year of service with the army (Tac., *Ann.* 1.64). He had strong views on wives and the military, arguing that commanders should not be accompanied by their spouses on tours of duty (Tac. *Ann.* 3.33).

C. Caetronius (c. 30 BCE–After 14 CE). Caetronius was *Legatus* of *Legio* I (Tac. *Ann.* 1.44) stationed in Germania Inferior in 14 CE, reporting to A. Caecina Severus. He was instrumental in restoring order after the mutiny of the Rhine Legions.

Cn. Calpurnius Piso (c. 44/43 BCE–November? 20 CE). Descended from the old plebeian nobility of the *gens Calpurnii*, Cn. Piso was son of Cn. Calpurnius Piso (consul for 23 BCE) and brother of L. Piso (Piso the Augur). He was likely a *tribunus militum* in Hispania (inferred from Tac., *Ann.* 3.16.4), serving with Tiberius during the Cantabrian and Asturian War (26–25 BCE). In 23 or 22 BCE, he was appointed as *triumvir monetalis* to the commission supervizing the mint in Rome. He likely became *quaestor* in 19 or 18 BCE, which gave him a seat in the Senate. He may have gone to Achaea – where a legal wrangle caused him to bear an enduring grudge against the Athenians (Tac., *Ann.* 2.55) – or he may have accompanied Tiberius during the Alpine War (15 BCE) and/or his subsequent campaigns in Illyricum (11–9 BCE). He had an unpleasant temperament, being 'a man of violent temper, without an idea of obedience, with indeed a natural arrogance inherited from his father Piso' (Tac., *Ann.* 2.43). He was elected consul for 7 CE with Tiberius. Thereafter he went to Africa as proconsul (7/6 BCE, 4/3 CE or 6/5 CE), likely replacing Africanus Fabius Maximus; he told Strabo in person that the country was 'like a leopard's skin; for it is spotted with inhabited places that are surrounded by waterless and desert land' (Strabo, *Geog.* 2.5.33). He was in Hispania Tarraconensis in 5 or 6 CE. Appointed *pontifex* no later than 2 CE (*AE* 1949.9), on Augustus' death he replaced the *princeps* as *magister* in the college of the *Fratres Arvales* (*CIL* VI, 2023a) and may have joined the *Sodales Augustales*. He married Munatia Plancina (perhaps granddaughter of L. Munatius Plancus, consul 42 BCE, *censor* 22 BCE) and had two sons, Cnaeus (who changed his name to Lucius) and Marcus (Tac., *Ann.* 3.16). He would become infamous for his fraught relationship with Germanicus Caesar and allegations that he was implicated in his death (Tac., *Ann.* 2.55–58, 2.60, 2.69 (cf. Suet., *Calig.* 3), 2.70, 3.8–19; Sen. *Con. Cn. Piso patre*).

Cn. Calpurnius Piso (c. 70–After 23 BCE). Descended from the old plebeian nobility of the *gens Calpurnii*, Cn. Piso fought on the side of Pompeius Magnus in Africa (Caes., *Bell. Afr.* 3.1, 18.1) and then, after the assassination of Iulius Caesar, joined M. Brutus and Cassius Longinus before Philippi, before supporting Sex. Pompeius in Sicily (Tac., *Ann.* 43.3; Appian, *Bell. Civ.* 5.2.4ff). Despite his strongly anti-Caesarian politics, he was finally persuaded to stand for the consulship and was elected for 23 BCE – replacing A. Terentius Varro Murena, the consul designate, who died before taking office – with Augustus himself. When the *princeps* fell seriously ill that year, and later seemed to be actually facing death, Augustus resigned the consulship and passed over to Piso his official documents (including an account of the public finances and a roster of the army units in his provinces), inferring it was his intention that the co-consul should assume responsibility for the functioning of the state for the remainder of his consulship (Dio 53.30.1–2). However, Augustus passed his personal signet ring to M. Agrippa in a subtle, but clear, indication that the army was to actually obey Agrippa, not Piso (Dio 53.30.2). He was father of Cn. Piso (consul for 7 BCE) and L. Piso (Piso the Augur). His sons inherited from him his stubborn nature and irascible temperament (Tac., *Ann.* 2.43.3).

L. Calpurnius Piso (Piso the Pontifex) (48 BCE–32 CE). Descended from the old plebeian nobility of the *gens Calpurnii*, L. Piso was the son of L. Calpurnius Piso Caesoninus (consul 58 BCE) and brother of Calpurnia Pisonis, wife of the *dictator* C. Iulius Caesar. Promoted to patrician rank around 29 BCE, he was an independent-minded man whose virtue, tact and achievements were widely lauded: Horace dedicated his *Ars Poetica* to him (*Carm.* 2.12) and Antipater of Thessalonika dedicated several *Epigrams* to him; Tacitus remarks, 'never had he by choice proposed a servile motion, and, whenever necessity was too strong for him, he would suggest judicious compromises' (Tac., *Ann.* 6.10). He served as consul for 15 BCE and is recorded as having presided over a murder trial in Mediolanum (Milan) (Suet., *De Rhet.* 6). During the years 12–10 BCE, he was governor of Galatia-Pamphylia, and as *legatus Augusti pro praetore* led an army to Thrace in 11 or 10 to quell a rebellion of the Bessi and Sialetae, the former fleeing as soon as they heard of Piso's imminent arrival (Dio 54.34.5–6). After initial setbacks, over the three years of the *Bellum Thracicum* (13–11 BCE) he gradually overwhelmed those who stood against him (Livy, *Per.* 140) – Augustus is reported as having trusted him with *secreta mandata*, 'secret orders' (Seneca, *Epp.* 83.14), perhaps to supersede the *imperium* of the proconsul of Macedonia – and for his victories the Senate voted him triumphal ornaments and thanksgivings (Dio 54.34.7; Tac., *Ann.* 6.10). He may – but not with any certainty – have been proconsul of Asia, and then served as *legatus Augusti pro praetore* of Syria, replacing Quinctilius Varus (the alternative candidate being Piso the Augur). Piso was made a *pontifex* and in 14 CE he was a member of the priestly college of the *Fratres Arvales* (*CIL* VI, 2023a), perhaps joining as early as 15 BCE. He was author of several poems, short and epic (*Anth. Pal.* 9.428, 10.25). From 13 CE, as *praefectus urbi* he was invested with the powers necessary to maintain peace and order in the city of Rome; he proved so popular in the position that it was made a life-long appointment and it was said that 'his chief glory rested on the wonderful tact with which, as *praefectus urbi*, he handled an authority' (Tac., *Ann.* 6.10). Consul for a second time in 15 CE, Seneca confirms that 'he applied himself most diligently to his official duties'; however, he also observes that he 'was drunk from the very time of his appointment; he used to spend the greater part of the night at banquets, and would sleep until noon' (Sen., *Epp.* 83.15). For all his overindulgence in drinking, Tacitus remarks that he 'died a natural death, a rare incident in so high a rank' (Tac., *Ann.* 6.10).

L. Calpurnius Piso (Piso the Augur) (c. 50 BCE–24 CE). Descended from the old plebeian nobility of the *gens Calpurnii*, he was the son of Cn. Calpurnius Piso (consul for 23 BCE) and brother of Cn. Calpurnius Piso (consul for 7 BCE). Himself consul for 1 BCE with Cossus Cornelius Lentulus, Piso – others prefer Piso the Pontifex – went to Asia (*ILS* 8814 Mytilene). If the theory about Piso the Pontifex is wrong, then Piso the Augur may have been the L. Calpurnius Piso who assumed governorship as *legatus Augusti pro praetore* of Syria after Quinctilius Varus. Sharing the family trait, he is described as 'likewise an intractable fellow' (Tac., *Ann.* 2.43.3).

C. Calvisius Sabinus (c. 80–After 27 BCE). Sabinus was a *novus homo* who had served as an officer under Iulius Caesar, commanding five cohorts and some cavalry in Greece, where he 'was well received by the Aetolians, and having driven the enemy's garrisons from Calydon and Naupactum, possessed himself of the whole country' (Caesar, *Bell. Civ.* 3.34–35, 56). On the Ides of March 44 BCE, he was one of only two senators who tried to defend Iulius Caesar from his assassins (Nic. 96): an inscription (*ILS* 925 Spoletium) commemorates his *pietas* for his selfless action. He was elected consul along with L. Marcius Censorinus – the other senator who had tried to defend the dictator – for 39 BCE. He sided with Caesar's heir and was likely one of his admirals in Sicily during the war against Sex. Pompeius. As proconsul of Hispania Ulterior, Sabinus carried out military operations in the territory that were yet to be subjugated in the north of the Iberian Peninsula, for which he was granted a triumph, celebrated in Rome on 26 May 28 BCE (*Fast. Capitol.*). He later oversaw repairs to the *Via Latina* (*ILS* 889).

C. Calvisius Sabinus (c. 40 BCE–After 1 BCE). Son of C. Calvisius Sabinus who had fought in the Civil War (49–45 BCE) on the side of Iulius Caesar as a *legatus* and was consul of 39 BCE, he was himself elected consul for 4 BCE with L. Passienus Rufus. He may have served as governor of Hispania Tarraconnensis late in Augustus' principate. Among his religious appointments, Sabinus was *septemvir epulonum* and *curio maximus* (*ILS* 925 Spoletium).

L. Caninius Gallus (c. 45 BCE–After 8 CE). A member of the plebeian *gens Caninia* from Tusculum, his grandfather married a first cousin of M. Antonius (Val. Max. 4.2.6); his father was elected consul for 37 BCE with M. Agrippa. An L. Gallus is recorded as having 'conquered the Sarmati ... and driven them back across the Ister' (Dio 54.20.3) in 17/16 BCE. L. Gallus was a *tresvir monetalis* on the commission supervising at the mint in Rome in c. 12 BCE (e.g. *RIC* I 416 = *RSC* 383). He was elected suffect consul for 2 BCE, replacing M. Plautius Silvanus, and for part of his term served with Augustus himself. As proconsul, he went to Africa around 7/8 CE, perhaps directly after Cossus Cornelius Lentulus Gaetulicus. His priestly offices included *quindecemvir sacris faciundis*.

P. Carisius (c. 70–c. 10 BCE). Carisius was an early supporter of Iulius Caesar's young heir, taking an active command role in the war against Sex. Pompeius (App., *Bell. Civ.* 5.111.1). He was *legatus Augusti pro praetore* in Hispania Ulterior for 27–22 BCE (Dio 53.25.5, 8; Orosius 6.21), during which time he engaged the Astures who were rebelling against Roman rule (Florus 2.33); he subdued them at Lancia – reportedly with some assistance from C. Furnius (Dio 54.5.1–3) – but showed them clemency after having heard 'the plea that it would form a better monument of the Roman victory if it were left standing than if it were burnt' (Florus 2.33). He founded Emerita Augusta in 25 BCE for veterans of *Legiones* V *Alaudae* and X *Gemina*, and the mint there issued a series of coins proudly displaying his name and official title along with images of war spoils (e.g. *RIC* I 2, 4, 10, 15). He was considered cruel and given to indulging his taste for luxury, which was a causal factor in the uprising of the Astures and Cantabri in 20/19 (Dio 54.5.1).

C.[?] Carrinas (c. 45–After 28 BCE). The son of C. Carrinas, who had been executed on the orders of Sulla (Dio 51.21.6), his *gens* is not preserved. In 45 BCE, he was dispatched by Iulius Caesar to lead the war against the sons of Pompeius Magnus, a task in which he was unsuccessful (Appian, *Bell. Civ.* 4.83–84). He was suffect consul for 43 BCE (Dio 47.15.1) and two years later Caesar's heir sent him to Hispania Citerior to deal with Sex. Pompeius – whose supporters included Bocchus II (king of Mauretania) – but his performance fell below expectations and he was replaced by Asinius Pollio (App., *Bell. Civ.* 5.26). In 36 BCE, he went to Sicily in the ongoing war with Sex. Pompeius (App., *Bell. Civ.* 5.112). Carrinas was proconsular governor of Gallia Comata (31–28 BCE), during which time he quelled a rebellion of the Morini and their allies, and drove back over the Rhine a band of Suebi raiding from Germania, earning him a triumph, which he celebrated on 30 May 28 BCE (*Fast. Capitol.*): 'Not only did Carrinas, therefore, celebrate the triumph … but Caesar also celebrated it, since the credit of the victory properly belonged to his position as supreme commander' (Dio 51.21.6).

Nero Claudius Drusus (Nero Drusus, Drusus Germanicus, Drusus Maior, Drusus I, Drusus the Elder; posthumously Nero Claudius Drusus Germanicus) (13 January 38–? September 9 BCE). Born Decimus Claudius Drusus in Rome in 38 BCE, son of patricians Ti. Claudius Drusus and Livia Drusilla (Suet., *Claud.* 1.1, *Tib.* 3.1, 4.1, 4.3), he was younger brother of Ti. Claudius Nero (Suet., *Claud.* 1.5). Later in his youth, as his *praenomen* he took the name Nero (Suet., *Claud.* 1.1), a Sabine word meaning 'strong and valiant' (Suet., *Tib.* 1.2). He was popular and affable in nature, described effusively by a contemporary as 'a youth of as many and as great virtues as human nature can cherish, or industry acquire; and whose genius it is doubtful whether it was better adapted for the arts of war or of peace', while 'his sweet and engaging manners, his courteous and unassuming demeanour towards his friends, are said to have been inimitable' (Vell. Pat. 2.97.2–3). Displaying the Claudian trait for stubbornness, he was unwilling to give up easily when tested: in a letter to Tiberius describing a game of dice, Augustus writes, 'your brother made a great outcry about his luck, but after all did not come out far behind in the long run; for after losing heavily, he unexpectedly and little by little got back a good deal' (Suet., *Div. Aug.* 71.3). Nero Drusus was also willing to take great risks with his own life, recklessly seeking the *spolia opima* of his opponent on the battlefield (Suet., *Claud.* 1.4). He enjoyed a close relationship with Augustus, who 'loved him so dearly while he lived that he always named him joint-heir along with his sons, as he once declared in the Senate' (Suet., *Claud.* 1.5), though there were unproven rumours circulated at the time that – on account of him holding the view that the *princeps* should step down and restore the free elections of the *Res Publica* (Suet., *Tib.* 50.1) – Augustus sought his demise (Suet., *Claud.* 1.5). On account of his brother's success in the East, the reward was extended to Drusus, who was permitted to stand for public office five years before the stipulated qualification age (Dio 54.10.4): in 19 BCE, he became *quaestor* (Suet., *Claud.* 1.2) and, by decree, was promoted to *praetor* when Augustus left for the West in 16 BCE (Dio 54.19.6). In 15 BCE, at the age of 23, he led a campaign in Gallia Transalpina, first against the Carni and Taurisci (Strabo, *Geog.* 4.6.9), then prosecuted the Alpine War against the Raeti via the Reschen Pass (Strabo, *Geog.* 4.6.9; Dio 54.22.1–3), culminating in the siege of the main *oppidum* of the Genauni nation on 1 August (Horace, *Carm.* 4.14.34–38). Assisted by his older brother, he annexed the Kingdom of Noricum and defeated the Vindelici (Florus, 2.22; Dio 54.22.4–5; Horace, *Carm.* 4.4), establishing a new *colonia* at Augusta Vindelicorum. In 14 BCE, he became *Legatus Augusti Pro Praetore* of *Tres Galliae* (replacing Tiberius), based at *Colonia Copia Felix Munatia*, where he established the *Concilium Galliarum*, the council of all the nations of Gaul (Dio 54.32.1), and conducted a census (Cassiodorus, *Chron.* 385D). His primary mission, however, was to lead a war to conquer Germania (Dio 54.25.1; Eutropius, *Brev.* 7.9; Florus, 2.30), which was prompted by the invasion of tribes led by Maelo of the Sugambri while M. Lollius was governor (Strabo, *Geog.* 7.1.4; Dio 54.32.1, *cf.* Dio 54.20.5–6) in 17 BCE. In support of the coming campaign, Nero Drusus supervized a massive build-out of military infrastructure along the Rhine River, including a canal (*fossa Drusiana*) and a fleet (Suet., *Claud.* 1.2; Tac., *Ann.* 2.8). A unit of measurement – the *pes Drusianus*, the 'Drusus Foot' – was named after him (Hyginus, *Ag.* 11). In 12 BCE, he commenced the German War, which would last four years, beginning with an amphibious invasion from the Rhine, first devastating the lands of the Sugambri, then crossing Lacus Flevo (Dio 54.32.2; Pliny, *Nat. Hist.* 16.1–2) and sailing down the Ems River (Dio 54.32.2), during which the Bructeri launched an unsuccessful attack on the Roman ships (Strabo, *Geog.* 7.1.3) – though on the return his fleet ran aground on the Frisian coast and had to be rescued (Dio 54.32.2–3). For his victories he was made *praetor urbanus* for 11 BCE (Dio 54.33.2). During the campaign of that year, his army sailed up the Lupia and by land reached the Visurgis River (Dio 54.33.1–4), established a fort at Aliso, then on the return narrowly escaped disaster at the hands of the Cherusci at Arbalo (Pliny, *Nat. Hist.* 11.18). The army acclaimed him *imperator*, an honour promptly denied by Augustus, who granted him an *ovatio* instead (Suet., *Claud.* 1.3; Dio 54.33.5). In the spring of the following year, Drusus fought the Chatti

(Dio 54.36.3). He returned to *Colonia* Copia Felix Munatia in the summer to open the new federal sanctuary for the Gallic Council and altar dedicated to *Roma et Augustus*, an event attended on 1 August by both Augustus and Tiberius in person (Dio 54.36.3–4; Suet. *Claud.* 2.1). A fleet reached Jutland, home of the Cimbri (Pliny, *Nat. Hist.* 2.167) and was acclaimed as 'the first of Roman *duces* to sail the Northern Ocean, and beyond the Rhenus' (Suet. *Claud.* 1.2), an achievement of which Augustus was proud to include in his biography (*RG* 5.26). Drusus was elected consul in 9 BCE and, despite ominous portents, nevertheless returned to Germania to lead the campaign (Dio 55.1.1–2). That year, his army reached the Albis River and his men erected a *tropaeum* of captured arms and armour (Dio 55.1.3; Florus 2.30; Val. Max. 5.5.3; Ptolemy, *Geog.* 2.10). He was one of the commanders who fought to win the *spolia opima*, but the wording in the one extant account (Suet., *Claud.* 3.4) is ambiguous about whether he was successful. However, at the end of the season's campaign Drusus fell in a riding accident (Livy, *Peri.* 142); on Augustus' orders, his brother Tiberius raced to join him, but he arrived only just in time to hear his last words (Dio 55.2.1; Pliny, *Nat. Hist.* 7.20). He died, aged 29, at a place his men called *Castra Scelerata*, 'Accursed Fort', located between the 'Albis and Salas' Rivers (Suet., *Claud.* 1.3, 2.1; Strabo, *Geog.* 7.1.3). An altar dedicated to him, the *Ara Drusi*, was also erected (Tac., *Ann.* 2.7). Tiberius accompanied the body on foot from Germania to Rome (Suet., *Tib.* 7.3; Dio 55.2.1) in an act considered as supremely pious (Val. Max., *Factorum et Dictorum* 5.5.3), while crowds assembled along the road to pay their respects (Seneca, *Ad Marc.* 3.1–2). After being laid in state, the body was presented in the Forum Romanum and euloguized by Tiberius. Augustus then gave a eulogy at his funeral in the *Circus Flaminius*, describing him as 'a role model (*exemplum*) for the Caesars [himself, Caius and Lucius]' (Suet., *Claud.* 1.5). His ashes were placed in the Mausoleum of Augustus, where the *princeps* affixed beside the nîche a laudatory inscription he had himself composed, and later wrote a prose memoir of his stepson's life (Suet., *Claud.* 1.5). His reputation was forever after tied to his military exploits in Germania (Ovid, *Fasti* 1.597–598). Posthumously, the Senate granted Nero Drusus the hereditary battle title *Germanicus* – meaning 'The German' or 'of Germania' – as well as a triumphal arch on the *Via Appia* and statues (Suet., *Claud.* 1.4; *Tab. Heb.*; *Tab. Siar.*). In Mogontiacum, the Rhine Legions erected a cenotaph in his honour and held annual races there (Suet., *Claud.* 1.3). King Herodes named a tower in his harbour at Caesarea Maritima the *Druseion* in his honour (Joseph., *Bell. Iud.* 1.411–413). Several decades later, when serving as *praefectus equitum*, Pliny the Elder claimed that, while he slept in his room at army camp, he was visited by the ghost of Drusus; it implored Pliny to record his story and said that he feared his achievements might 'fade into oblivion', out of which came a twenty-two volume *Bella Germaniae*, 'History of the German Wars' (Pliny the Younger, *Ep.* 3.5; Tac., *Ann.* 2.69). His priestly offices included *augur*, probably from 19 BCE, and *arvalis* from 12 BCE (*AE* 1926.42, 1934.151; *CIL* IX, 2443). He married Antonia Minor (Plut., *Ant.* 87) in 18 BCE, to whom he remained faithful all his life (Val. Max., *Factorum et Dictorum* 4.3.3), and had several children by her, of whom only Germanicus, Livilla and Claudius survived (Suet., *Claud.* 1.6). After his death, his memory was cherished 'and it was believed that, had he succeeded, he would have restored the age of liberty' (Tac., *Ann.* 1.33).

C. Claudius Marcellus (42–23 BCE). Son of Octavia and C. Claudius Marcellus (*cos.* 50 BCE), the young man was much favoured by his uncle Augustus (Tac., *Ann.*1.3; Suet., *Div. Aug.* 66), with rumours circulating that he was marked out as his successor (Dio 53.30.2). He was betrothed to the daughter of Sex. Pompeius but married Augustus' only daughter, Iulia Caesaris (Suet., *Div. Aug.* 63). In 26 and 25 BCE, he accompanied Augustus and Tiberius to Hispania Citerior as *tribunus militum* (Suet., *Tib.* 9.1), where they arranged exhibitions – perhaps *decursiones* – for the troops at their camps (Dio 53.26.1). Pleased with his performance in the field, Augustus arranged for permission to be granted for Marcellus to stand as aedile ten years before the qualifying age (Dio 53.28.3) and to receive other honours (Dio 53.31.2). Aged 19, he commissioned a theatre in Rome, which was named after him (Suet., *Div. Aug.* 29; Dio 53.30.6), and he laid on lavish entertainments in the *Forum Romanum*, during which he 'sheltered the *Forum* during the whole summer by means of curtains stretched overhead and had exhibited on the stage a dancer who was a knight, and also a woman of high birth' (Dio 53.31.2–3). Despite treatment from Augustus' own physician, Musa, he died – perhaps from typhus – at Baiae (Baia); he was given a public funeral in Rome with eulogies and his ashes were placed in Augustus' own mausoleum (Dio 53.30.5). His memory was celebrated by Vergil in the *Aeneid*, during a private reading of which his mother Octavia fainted at hearing his name (Suet., *Verg.* 32).

L. Cornelius Balbus (Balbus the Younger) (c. 65–After 13 BCE). Nephew of L. Cornelius Balbus (Balbus the Elder, *suff. cos.* 40 BCE), the younger Balbus was a native of Gades in Hispania Ulterior, not a Roman citizen by birth (Vell. Pat. 2.51.3; Strabo, *Geog.* 3.5). He showed courage and daring from a young age: during the war between Caesar and Pompeius Magnus, at incredible risk to himself he entered the camp of the enemy at Dyrrhachium and held several conferences with the consul Lentulus, boasting 'his only doubt was what price to put upon himself' (Vell. Pat. 2.51.3). Through such acts of derring-do, he came to prominence. In 43 BCE, he was *quaestor* to C. Asinius Pollio (consul 40 BCE) in Hispania Ulterior, where he allegedly amassed a large fortune by despoiling the local population. That year he crossed over to Bogud, king of Mauretania. By 39 BCE, he was a *pontifex*. His whereabouts are not recorded again until 21 BCE, when he is found in Africa. During his term of office as proconsul he scored a noted victory over the Garamantes (Pliny, *Nat. Hist.* 5.5) for which he celebrated a triumph on 27 March 19 BCE (*Fast. Cap.*; Vell. Pat. 2.51.3) – it was the first given to a non-Roman by birth, and the last ever celebrated by a senator. Balbus fancied himself as a man of the arts. Cicero records (*Ad. Fam.* 10.32.5) that Cornelius Gallus had a dramatic poem of young Balbus in his possession. He wrote a play about his risky encounter with consul Lentulus and another dealing with the gods and their worship (Macrobius, *Saturnalia*, 3.6). He built a theatre in Rome (Suet., *Div. Aug.* 29.5) in 19 BCE in honour of his military victories –

funded by proceeds from the war (Tac., *Ann.* 3.72) – and dedicated it in 13 BCE (Pliny, *Nat. Hist.* 36.12.60), but which was inundated when the Tiber burst its banks (Dio 54.25.2). Dio notes, Balbus was so proud of the spectacles he laid on that he 'began to put on airs, as if it were he himself that was going to bring Augustus back [from Gaul]' (Dio 54.25.2; *RG* 2.12). One of his daughters was married to C. Norbanus Flaccus.

P. Cornelius Dolabella (c. 40 BCE–After 27 CE). A patrician, Dolabella is described as 'a man of noble-minded candour' (Vell. Pat. 2.125.5). As consul for 10 CE, he reconstructed the Arch of Dolabella (perhaps formerly the Porta Caelimontana) in Rome. Subsequently, he was a *septemvir epulonum* and a *soldalis Titii* (*CIL* III, 1741 (Ragusae) = *ILS* 938). In 14 CE, Dolabella was *Legatus Augusti Pro Praetore* of Dalmatia, displaying loyalty and vigilance in carrying out his duties, and is credited with building the road network which interconnected the province's cities.

Cn. Cornelius Lentulus (Augur) (c. 55 BCE–25 CE). Son of Cnaeus, Cornelius Lentulus was *consul ordinarius* for 14 BCE. He may have succeeded Calpurnius Piso in Thracia Macedioniaque and stopped incursions of the Daci and Sarmati who had crossed the Danube in 11 BCE (Florus 2.28; Dio 54.36.2). He was in Asia as proconsular governor in 2/1 BCE, and Illyricum in 1–4 CE. He may have received triumphal ornaments for a victory over the Getae (Tac., *Ann.* 4.44). When exactly he was appointed *augur* is not recorded (Tac., *Ann.* 3.59). He was *arvalis* in 14 CE. He was notorious for his immense wealth (estimated at HS400 million), stupidity and slowness of speech (Sen., *De Ben.* 2.27; Tac., *Ann.* 4.44).

Cossus Cornelius Lentulus Gaetulicus (c. 42 BCE–c. 25 CE). Born into the patrician *gens Cornelia*, Cossus advanced through the *cursus honorum* to become consul for 1 BCE with L. Calpurnius Piso (Piso the Augur). As proconsul of Africa (5–6 CE), Cossus came to the aid of King Iuba in fighting the Gaetuli (Flor., 2.31; Dio 53.26.2), earning for himself the honorific *agnomen Gaetulicus* and triumphal ornaments, which he celebrated with L. Passienus Rufus in 6 CE (Vell. Pat. 2.116.2; Orosius 6.21.18; Dio 55.28.3–4; *ILS* 120 El-Lehs; *IRT* 521, 301 Lepcis). Of the *agnomen*, Florus writes it was 'a title more extensive than his actual victory warranted' (Florus 2.31). Of his character, Tacitus writes he was a 'noble man' and 'it had been the glory of Lentulus, to say nothing of his consulship and his triumphal distinctions over the Gaetuli, to have borne poverty with a good grace, then to have attained great wealth, which had been blamelessly acquired and was modestly enjoyed' (Tac., *Ann.* 4.44). He was a member of the college of *quindecemviri sacris faciundis.* One extant source describes him as a great orator (Quint., *Inst.* 10.1.128).

L. Domitius Ahenobarbus (c. 55 BCE–25 CE). The *Ahenobarbi* (meaning 'red beards') formed a plebeian branch of the old and noble *gens Domitia*. Lucius was the only son of Cn. Domitius Ahenobarbus (Vell. Pat. Pat. 2.72.3), considered the best of his family (Suet., *Nero* 3). In his youth he was famed as an accomplished chariot-driver (Suet., *Nero* 4). He supported Sex. Pompeius, but then surrendered to M. Antonius, only to defect to Caesar's heir before the Battle of Actium in 31 BCE (Plut., *Ant.* 63; Tac., *Ann.* 4.44). At the treaty meeting in Tarentum (36 BCE), Lucius was betrothed to the younger Antonia (Tac., *Ann.* 4.44), the daughter of M. Antonius. He was elected aedile (22 BCE), *praetor* (c. 20/19 BCE), consul (16 BCE) and proconsul of Africa from (13/12 BCE). He was *Legatus Augusti* in Illyricum (before 1 BCE). He 'led an army across the Elbe [1 CE], penetrating further into Germania than any Roman before him' (Tac., *Ann.* 4.44), where he engaged the Hermunduri and settled them in the land formerly occupied by the Marcomanni (Dio 55.10a.2). Immediately after, he assumed command of all Roman forces in Germania (1 CE) and established provincial capital at Oppidum Ubiorum with a cult altar to Roma and Augustus (Dio 55.10a.2–3), for which reason it became known as Ara Ubiorum. In an undisclosed region between the Rhine and Ems Rivers, he constructed a plank roadway across marshland called the *Pontes Longi* (Tac., *Ann.* 1.63.3–4). For his exploits in Germania he received triumphal insignia (Suet., *Nero* 4; Tac., *Ann.* 4.44). As for his personality, 'he was haughty, extravagant and cruel', which extended to his taste for extreme blood sports, and the violence of his beast hunts and gladiatorial games displayed 'such inhuman cruelty that Augustus, after his private warning was disregarded, was forced to restrain him by an edict' (Suet., *Nero* 4). His disdain for social rank or good manners was exhibited when, as an aedile, he 'forced the *censor* L. Plancus to make way for him on the street', and later, when he held the offices of *praetor* and consul, he brought men of the equestrian order and matrons together on a public stage to act in a farce (Suet., *Nero* 4). In 14 CE, he was a member of the college of the *Fratres Arvales* (*CIL* VI, 2023a). He was the paternal grandfather of the future Emperor Nero and the maternal grandfather of Valeria Messalina, third wife of the future Emperor Claudius (Suet., *Nero* 5).

Paullus Fabius Maximus (c. 55 BCE–14 CE). Perhaps a distant relation of the famous general of the Second Punic War, P. Cornelius Scipio Africanus, he was the older son of Q. Fabius Maximus (*suff. cos.* 45 BCE) and brother of Africanus Fabius Maximus. He is described as a most noble man, a fine public speaker, as well as handsome and wealthy (Seneca, *Controv.* 2.4.11). Like Quinctilius Varus, his career began when he served as *quaestor* in the East, from 22–19 BCE (*IG* II². 4130 Athens). Likely *praetor* (but unattested) in c. 15 BCE, and *arvalis* thereafter, Paullus is next recorded as consul in 11 BCE and proconsul of Asia (10/9 BCE, 9/8 BCE or 6/5 BCE), where he is known for reforming the Roman calendar in that province (*SEG* 4.490). He was *Legatus Augusti Pro Praetore* ('*Legat. Caesaris*' on an inscription) of Hispania Taraconnensis in 3/2 BCE (*ILS* 8895 Bracara; *AE* 1974, 392 Bracara; *AE* 1993, 01030 Lucus Augusti; *CIL* II, 02581 Lucus Augusti). Paullus was a *pontifex* (*ILS* 919) and member of the *Fratres Arvales* (*CIL* VI, 2023a). An orator of modest talents (Seneca, *Controv.* 10), he was a patron of poets (Juvenal, *Saturae* 7.95): Horace mentions him by name in one of his works (Horace, *Odes* 4.1.10–11) and Ovid wrote to him while in exile (Ovid, *Ep. Ex Ponto* 1.2 and 3.1). Paullus married Marcia (*ILS* 8821 Paphos), daughter of L. Marcius Philippus (*suff. cos.* of 38 BCE) and Atia (a maternal aunt of Augustus)

– Marcia was, thus, a first cousin of the *princeps*. He was a confidant of Augustus in his later years and accompanied him as his only companion on his secret trip to Planasia to meet his adopted son Agrippa Postumus; the secret visit became known to Augustus' wife when Paullus told Marcia, who informed Livia (up to that point unaware of the trip), and the *princeps* allegedly felt betrayed by the breach of trust (Tac., *Ann.* 1.5.2). Maximus died – some at the time believed it was by suicide – in the summer of 14 CE, just before Augustus' own death (Tac., *Ann.* 1.5.2; Ovid, *Ep. Ex Ponto* 4.6 ff).

Africanus Fabius Maximus (c. 50 BCE–After 5 BCE). Perhaps a distant relation of the famous general of the Second Punic War, P. Cornelius Scipio Africanus, he was the younger son of Q. Fabius Maximus (*cos.* 45 BCE) and brother of Paullus Fabius Maximus (*cos.* 11 BCE). Maximus was consul in 10 BCE, proconsul of Africa in 6/5 BCE (*AE* 1953.40) and a *septemvir epulonum*.

C. Furnius (C. Furnius the Younger) (c. 60–After 17 BCE). Furnius is first mentioned as a man who had appealed to Augustus to save the life of his father, who had backed M. Antonius, reportedly saying 'one wrong alone I have received at your hands, Caesar; you have forced me to live and to die owing you a greater debt of gratitude than I can ever repay', an act which greatly endeared him to Augustus (Seneca, *De Ben.* 2.25.1 (Furnius)). He was rewarded with an enrollment in the ex-consuls (Dio 52.42.4). He had not long arrived in Hispania Citerior as *Legatus Augusti* in 22 BCE when the local Cantabri rose up in rebellion (Florus 2.33.51); but they had underestimated his resolve and were defeated by him, and Furnius was able to provide assistance to P. Carisius in the subjugation of the Astures at Lancia (Dio 54.5.1–3; Florus 2.33.56). Furnius was elected consul for 17 BCE (Dio 54.18.1).

C. Iulius Caesar (C. Caesar; C. Vipsanius Agrippa prior to 17 BCE) (14 August/ 13 September 20 BCE–21 February 4 CE). Born C. Vipsanius Agrippa to M. Agrippa and Iulia, Caius was adopted as a son of Augustus (14 June/15 July 17 BCE) – his maternal grandfather – and thereafter bore the name of Caesar (Suet, *Div. Aug.* 64.1; Dio 54.18.1). He was doted on by his adoptive father, who taught him reading, writing and swimming (Suet., *Div. Aug.* 641.1) and addressed him affectionately as 'my darling little donkey' in letters (A. Gellius, *Noc. Att.* 15.7.3). At just 14 years of age, he was taken with Tiberius and his troops on their exercises in Germania (Dio 55.6.4), and coins minted at the time – *RIC* 198 (*aureus*) and 199 (*denarius*) – show C. Caesar wearing a boy's *bulla* galloping right past an *aquila* standard beside two *signa*. In 5 BCE, he was made *princeps iuventutis* (*ILS* 134 Spoltore; *EJ* 63a = *CIL* V, 899 + 39207) and permitted to attend meetings of the Senate, despite his young age (Dio 55.9.9; Suet., *Div. Aug.* 26.2). The following year he was made *pontifex* (*ILS* 131 Rome), and in 2 BCE, with his brother, was permitted as *duumvir aedibus dedicandis* to consecrate a temple of Mars Ultor 'and all such buildings' (Dio 55.10.6). Augustus allowed him to sit in the meeting in Rome in which Herodes' sons Antipas and Antipater each argued that Iudaea should be give to him, not Archaelaus (Joseph., *Ant. Iud.* 17.9.5). With all the public adulation, Caius was growing up to be a spoiled brat, an unintended outcome which Augustus belatedly attempted to correct (Dio 55.9.1–2). His military service began with a posting to the Danube, but he refused to lead his men in person: 'indeed, he fought no war, not because no war broke out, but because he was learning to rule in quiet and safety, while the dangerous undertakings were regularly assigned to others' (Dio 55.10.17). Augustus decided to redeploy him following the inauguration of the *Forum Augustum* in 2 BCE. The following year he was appointed *praepositus Orienti* with *imperium proconsulare* and sent to the East (Dio 55.10.18–19). Before he departed, he married his relative, Livilla (Dio 55.10.18), daughter of Nero Claudius Drusus and Antonia Minor, sister of Germanicus. This command role seems to have better suited him as he 'was everywhere received with marks of distinction, as befitted one who was the emperor's grandson and was even looked upon as his son' (Dio 55.10.19). While on tour, he was made consul for 1 CE (*AE* 1967.458). On his mission, Augustus entrusted M. Lollius as Caius' *comes et rector*, 'companion and guide' (Suet., *Tib.*12.2). In the East, he conducted negotiations with King Phraates V of Parthia (Dio 55.10.20–21). When the Parthian informed him that Lollius had accepted bribes, the two Romans fell out when Caius accused him of extortion and treachery (Suet., *Tib.*12.2; Pliny, *Nat. Hist.* 9.58). His mission involved military action in Armenia. He besieged Artagira and, when it finally fell, was acclaimed *imperator* (Dio 55.10a.7), but on 9 September 3 CE, while close by the city's walls, Caius was wounded (*Fasti Gabini*; *RG* 27; Florus 2.31; Dio 55.10.19 says it occurred in Syria). With a weak physical constitution, he wrote to Augustus that year, resigned his commission and boarded a merchant vessel bound for Rome (Dio 55.10a.8–9); *en route*, Caius died on February 21, 4 CE, aged 23 – just eighteen months after his brother – at Lycia (*Fasti Gabini*; Suet., *Div. Aug.* 65.1; Dio 55.10a.9), where a cenotaph was erected to him (a fragment of which is now on display at the Archaeological Museum at Antalya). Caius' body was 'brought to Rome by the military tribunes and by the chief men of each city, and the golden shields and spears which he had received from the *equites* on entering the class of youths of military age were set up in the Senate House' (Dio 55.12.1). His ashes were laid in the Mausoleum of Augustus (Strabo, *Geog.* 5.3.8).

Drusus Iulius Caesar (Drusus Minor, Drusus II, Drusus the Younger; Nero Claudius Drusus prior to 4 CE) (7 October 16 or 15 BCE–14 September 23 CE). Born in Rome, Drusus was the son of Ti. Claudius Drusus (Tiberius) and Vispania Agrippina and was named after his famous uncle (Suet., *Tib.* 7.2). On account of his father's adoption by Augustus on 26 June 4 CE (Suet., *Tib.* 15.2), he joined *gens Iulia* and became a Caesar and brother of Germanicus, with whom he enjoyed good filial relations (Tac., *Ann.* 2.43). Possibly the following year, he married Livilla, youngest daughter of his uncle (Nero Claudius Drusus Germanicus) and aunt (Antonia Minor). A largely absent father, Tiberius appears to have been unloving towards his son, 'being exasperated at the former's vices; and, in fact, Drusus led a somewhat loose and dissolute life' (Suet., *Tib.* 52.1). He earned a reputation for licentiousness and cruelty – he was 'so cruel, in fact, that the sharpest swords were called "Drusian" after him' (Dio 57.13.1). When his father returned to Rome from self-imposed exile in 2 CE, Drusus was formally introduced to public life (Suet., *Tib.* 15). He was a *pontifex*, probably from 4 CE (*ILS* 107). Following the quelling of the Great Illyrian Revolt in 9 CE, though he had undertaken no active role in the war, Drusus 'was granted the privilege of attending the sittings of the Senate before becoming a member of that body and of voting ahead of the ex-praetors as soon as he should become *quaestor*' (Dio 56.17.3). He served as *quaestor* in 10 CE, and that year also became an *augur*. Three years later, Drusus was selected to join the *Fratres Arvales* (*CIL* VI, 2023a). Upon the death of Augustus, Drusus – then consul designate for 15 CE (Tac., *Ann.* 1.14) – read part of his father's speech to the Senate (Suet., *Tib.* 23) and became among the first men appointed as *sodales Augustales* (*ILS* 168 Rome). Also in 14 CE, now 30 years old, he was dispatched to join the legions in Germania Superior on his first military assignment (Tac., *Ann.* 1.24).

Germanicus Iulius Caesar (Germanicus Caesar; Nero Claudius Drusus before 9 BCE; Germanicus Claudius Drusus before 4 CE) (15 May 16 BCE–10 October 19 CE). Born Nero Claudius Drusus in Rome in 16 BCE, he was the son of Nero Claudius Drusus Germanicus and Antonia Minor (Suet., *Calig.* 1.1), and was the maternal grandson of M. Antonius (Plut., *Ant.* 87.3). Upon his father's death in 9 BCE, he adopted the honorific war title *Germanicus* as his *praenomen* (Suet., *Claud.* 1.3). He was educated by the *rhetor* Salanus, a teacher known to poet Ovid who credited him with developing the young man's talent for fiery public speaking (Ovid, *Ep. Ex Pont.* 2.5.5–8, 41–46). Like his father, he was affable and well liked: 'it is the general opinion that Germanicus possessed all the highest qualities of body and mind, to a degree never equalled by anyone; a handsome person, an unequalled valour ... and a remarkable desire and capacity for winning men's regard and inspiring their affection' (Suet., *Calig.* 3.1; cf. Dio 57.18.6–8 and comparison to Alexander the Great by Tac., *Ann.* 2.72–73). Also like Nero Drusus, he would engage in direct hand-to-hand combat (Suet., *Calig.* 3.2). Augustus was fond of the young man (Dio 56.25.2): indeed, one source states the *princeps* actively considered him to be his immediate successor (Suet., *Calig.* 4), though it seems Livia dissuaded him to formalise it. On account of his adoption by Tiberius at Augustus' request on 26 June 4 CE, he joined *gens Iulia* and became a Caesar, and the third in line of succession (Suet., *Tib.* 15.2). He enjoyed good filial relations with his adopted brother, Nero Claudius Drusus, Drusus the Younger (Tac., *Ann.* 2.43). He was appointed *quaestor* in 7 CE. After the premature deaths of Caius and Lucius Caesar, he was adopted by his uncle Tiberius, becoming a potential successor of Augustus. He was appointed *princeps iuventutis* ('the first of the youth') in 1 BCE or 1 CE (Ovid, *Ex Pont.* 2.5.41). During the emergency of the Great Illyrian Revolt, Germanicus was put in charge of *cohors voluntariorum*, which he recruited and trained in 6 CE, and took to the combat zone (Dio 55.30.1, cf. 55.32.1). At 23 years old, he led his contingent to success against the rebel Pannonian Mazaei nation in 7 CE (Dio 55.32.2–3). The following year, Germanicus was given command of an army group including legions, conducting operations in the Dinaric Alps, successfully besieging Splonum and Raetinum (Dio 56.11.1–7). In 8 BCE, he accepted joint command with Tiberius of one of the three army groups moving against Bato, the remaining rebel leader (Dio 56.12.2). In 9 CE, Germanicus was instrumental in concluding the counter-insurgency in central Illyricum, taking Arduba (Dio 56.15.1–3), and led the acclamation of Tiberius as *imperator*; he was granted triumphal ornaments with the other commanders (Dio 56.17.1; Vell. Pat. 2.116.1) and promoted to the rank of *praetor* (Dio 56.17.2). Following news of the disaster befalling P. Quinctilius Varus, he may have accompanied Tiberius on his trip to Rome or been placed in charge of operations on the Rhine while awaiting Tiberius' return with reinforcements (Suet., *Tib.* 17.2–18.1). When the feared German invasion did not transpire, he returned to civic life and performed advocacy in the courts, for which he earned great popularity (Dio 56.24.7). In 11 CE, he joined Tiberius on a low-risk raid across the Rhine into Germania (Dio 56.25.2), staying long enough to symbolically hold races on Augustus' birthday (23 September) on German soil (Dio 56.25.3). He was elected consul for 12 CE (Suet., *Calig.* 8.3), and in 13 BCE was appointed *legatus Augusti pro praetore* of *Tres Galliae* (Tac., *Ann.* 1.3) and initiated a census soon after arriving; he was at work in his province when news of Augustus' death arrived (Tac., *Ann.* 1.14; Suet., *Calig.* 1.1; Dio 57.3.1). His religious responsibilities included *augur* (*ILS* 173 Apamea in Bithynia; Tac., *Ann.* 2.17), perhaps dating from the same time he was appointed as *quaestor*, and *arvalis* perhaps as early as 4 CE. A multifaceted man, Germanicus was lauded for his oratory (Tac., *Ann.* 2.83.3) and skill as a writer of poems – including one composed in honour of Augustus' deceased horse (Pliny, *Nat. Hist.* 8.62) and possibly *Phaenomena*, a Latin translation of the original Greek work by Aratos – and comedies (Suet., *Claud.* 15.2). He is recorded as having had alektorophobia, a fear of chickens (Plut., *De Invid. et Od.*). He married M. Agrippa's daughter, Agrippina Maior, in 5 CE and had nine children by her, of whom his sons Drusus, Nero, Caius (also known as Caligula), and daughters Iulia Agrippina, Iulia Drusilla and Iulia Livilla survived (Suet., *Calig.* 7; *Tib.* 54.1).

L. Iulius Caesar (L. Caesar; Vipsanius Agrippa prior to 17 BCE) (14 June/15 July 17 BCE–20 August 2 CE). Born L. Vipsanius Agrippa to M. Agrippa and Iulia Caesaris, Lucius was adopted as a son of Augustus (14 June/15 July 17 BCE) – his maternal grandfather – and thereafter bore the name of Caesar (Suet, *Div. Aug.* 64.1; Dio 54.18.1). He was doted on by his adoptive father, who taught him reading, writing and swimming (Suet., *Div. Aug.* 641.1). Following the precedent established by his older brother, on coming of age in 2 BCE he was made *princeps iuventutis* and granted the same privileges (Dio 55.9.10; Suet., *Div. Aug.* 26.2): marking the event, Lucius and his brother are shown standing togate beside round shields and spears on widely circulated contemporary coins (e.g. *RIC* 206 (*aureus*), 207–212 (*denarius*)). Also in 3 or 2 BCE, Lucius was made *augur* (*ILS* 132 Rome) and the following year, with his brother, he was permitted to consecrate a temple of Mars Ultor 'and all such buildings' (Dio 55.10.6), likely as *duumvir aedibus dedicandis*. While his older brother was away on operations, 'it was his custom personally to read the letters of Caius in the Senate' (Dio 55.10a.9). For his first military assignment he was sent to *Tres Galliae*, where 'he, too, was being trained to rule by being dispatched on missions to many places' (Dio 55.10a.9). He died 'due to a sudden illness' (Dio 55.10a.10), aged 19 (*Fasti Gabini*), at Massilia (2 CE), where a cenotaph was erected to him (Suet., *Div. Aug.* 65.1; Dio 55.10a.9). Lucius' body was 'brought to Rome by the military tribunes and by the chief men of each city, and the golden shields and spears which he had received from the *equites* on entering the class of youths of military age were set up in the Senate House' (Dio 55.12.1). His ashes were laid in the Mausoleum of Augustus (Strabo, *Geog.* 5.3.8). Tiberius wrote a lyric poem in his honour (Suet., *Tib.* 70.2).

Ti. Iulius Caesar (Tiberius; Ti. Claudius Nero prior to 4 CE) (16 November 42 BCE–16 March 37 CE). Born in Rome, Tiberius was the son of Ti. Claudius Drusus and Livia Drusilla and older brother of Nero Claudius Drusus Germanicus (Suet., *Tib.* 4.1). His early years were traumatic, as his parents sought protection during the war against the murderers of C. Iulius Caesar (Suet., *Tib.* 6.2). His mother divorced the boy's father and married the man who would become Augustus; the two sons – Tiberius, 4, Drusus, just days old – went to live at the house of their father until he died five years later (Suet., *Tib.* 4.3). Tiberius delivered the eulogy at the funeral (Suet., *Tib.* 6.4). He also sponsored gladiatorial games in honour of his natural father and grandfather (Suet., *Tib.* 7.1). In 33 BCE, he was betrothed to Vipsania Agrippina, daughter of M. Agrippa, and later they were happily married (Suet., *Tib.* 7.2). During the Triple Triumph celebrating Actium, on 14 August 29 BCE, Tiberius rode the left horse pulling the triumphator's chariot (Suet., *Tib.* 6.4). He was educated by the *rhetor* Theodorus of Gadara, who apparently first detected his pupil's penchant for cruelty and often referred to him as 'mud kneaded with blood' (Suet., *Tib.* 57.1). Just a year after coming of age, in 26 BCE, now 16, he accompanied Augustus and C. Claudius Marcellus to Hispania Citerior as a *tribunus militum* during the Cantabrian and Asturian War (Suet., *Tib.* 9.1). There he arranged with Marcellus to put on exhibitions – perhaps *decursiones* – for the troops at their camps (Dio 53.26.1). In 23 BCE, he was appointed as *quaestor*, initially supervising the grain supply (*annona*), then later investigating slave-prisons across Italy whose owners had gained a reputation for also kidnapping unsuspecting travellers and concealing those seeking to avoid military service (Suet., *Tib.* 8). In 22 BCE, in the trial by jury of Fannius Caepio, the instigator of an assassination attempt on Augustus, Tiberius presented the prosecution case (Suet., *Tib.* 8.1; cf. 54.3.5–6; Vell. Pat. 2.91.4). In 20 BCE, he went with Augustus to Syria and Armenia, where he played a key role in restoring the kingdom to Tigranes (*RG* 5.27) and received back from Phraates of Parthia the *signa* lost by M. Crassus in 53 BCE (*RG* 5.29; Suet., *Tib.* 9.1). Following the Lollian Disaster (17 BCE), he went to Gallia Comata as *Legatus Augusti Pro Praetore* to replace M. Lollius in 16 BCE (Suet., *Tib.* 9.1), which soured relations between the two men. He was appointed *praetor* (16 BCE) and *consul ordinarius* (13 BCE) five years before the qualifying age

(Suet., *Tib.* 9.3; Dio 54.10.4). Mobilizing troops from Gallia Comata, he assisted his younger brother during the Alpine War of 15 BCE (Suet., *Tib.* 9.1–2), crossing Lake Geneva or Lake Constance with his troops (Dio 55.22.4), and then heading to Noricum before transferring to Illyricum (Suet., *Tib.* 9.1–2), where he commanded the Roman forces during the Pannonian War (12–9 BCE). Following the death of M. Agrippa in 12 BCE, Tiberius and his brother each took on the role of executor of Augustus' military policy. Augustus insisted Tiberius divorce Vipsania Agrippina and marry Iulia Caesaris, a request he protested against but reluctantly acceded to – it was a life-changing event which forever after haunted him (Suet., *Tib.* 7.2–3). While visiting Augustus in Ticinum in the summer of 9 BCE, he received news of his brother Drusus' accident and raced to be with him: despite insinuations that Tiberius was jealous of his younger brother (Suet., *Tib.* 50.1), he accompanied the body on foot from Germania to Rome (Suet., *Tib.* 7.3; Dio 55.2.1) in an act considered as supremely pious (Val. Max., *Factorum et Dictorum* 5.5.3) while crowds assembled along the road to pay their respects (Seneca, *Ad Marc.* 3.1–2). He took over the military operations in Germania to conclude the war in 8 and 7 BCE (Dio 55.8.3), during which 'he brought forty thousand prisoners [of the Sugambri nation] over into Gallia and assigned them homes near the bank of the Rhenus', for which he was granted triumphal ornaments (Suet., *Tib.* 9.2; *ILS* 95). In 7 BCE, he was elected consul for a second time and was given *tribunicia potestas* the following year. Over a decade, Tiberius had proved a highly competent commander, displaying *virtus* on numerous occasions. He was a strong disciplinarian, 'reviving bygone methods of punishment and ignominy, and even degrading the commander of a legion for sending a few soldiers across the river to accompany one of his freedmen on a hunting expedition' (Suet., *Tib.* 19), but displayed compassion when he made available his own horse-drawn cart or litter for use by wounded soldiers (Vell. Pat. 2.114.1–2). His weakness was wine: it is reported that 'even at the outset of his military career his excessive love of wine gave him the name of Biberius, instead of Tiberius, Caldius for Claudius, and Mero for Nero' (Suet., *Div. Aug.* 42.1). Yet his men respected him and he inspired deep loyalty (Vell. Pat. 2.104.4). He was physically fit and strongly built, yet his personality was intense, unsettling to many, not least Augustus: 'he strode along with his neck stiff and bent forward, usually with a stern countenance and for the most part in silence, never or very rarely conversing with his companions, and then speaking with great deliberation and with a kind of supple movement of his fingers. All of these mannerisms of his, which were disagreeable and signs of arrogance, were remarked by Augustus, who often tried to excuse them to the Senate and People by declaring that they were natural failings, and not intentional' (Suet., *Tib.* 68.3; *cf.* 21.2). Perhaps exhausted by his exploits, in protest at the favouritism shown C. and L. Caesar (the sons of M. Agrippa) as his heirs, or eager to escape a deteriorating marriage, he resigned all his powers and retired to Rhodes with his astrologer Thrasylus (Suet., *Tib.* 10.1–2). Later, while in exile, he negotiated to 'have the title of *legatus* of Augustus, so as to conceal his disgrace' (Suet., *Tib.* 12.1). His attempt to reconcile with C. Caesar while visiting Chios in 1 BCE was rebuffed (Dio 55.10.19) because the young man chose to believe certain slanders made by M. Lollius (Suet., *Tib.* 12.2). Eight years later, Tiberius returned from self-imposed exile to Rome as a private citizen in 2 BCE (Suet., *Tib.* 12.2). In 4 CE, he accepted the *tribunicia potestas* (Suet., Tib. 16.1), explaining he did so 'for the good of the *Res Publica*' (Vell. Pat. 2.104.1). After the deaths of C. and L. Caesar, Augustus adopted Tiberius as his son on 26 June 4 CE and he, in turn, adopted Germanicus (Suet., *Tib.* 15.2; Dio 55.13.2) – the indication was clear that Tiberius was now the intended heir apparent. Rebellion in Germania took Tiberius back across the Rhine in late 4 and again in 5 CE, ending in success for the Romans (Vell. Pat. 2.104.3, 5–7; Suet., *Tib.* 16.1; Dio 55.13.1a). A keen strategist, he masterminded a campaign against the Marcommanic king Marboduus beginning in 6 CE (Vell. Pat. 2.109.3–5), co-ordinating army groups approaching from three directions (one led by Sentius Saturninus, another by Tiberius in person), but the invasion had to be aborted, and a hasty treaty agreed with Marbouduus when the Breuci and Deasidiates rose up in Illyricum (Vell. Pat. 2.110.1–2; Dio 55.29.1–4). Tiberius 'was transferred to the charge of a new war, the most serious of all foreign wars since those with Carthage, which he carried on for three years with fifteen legions and a corresponding force of auxiliaries, amid great difficulties of every kind and the utmost scarcity of supplies' (Suet., *Tib.* 16.1; *cf.* Vell. Pat. 2.110–116). Under his command were Aemilius Lepidus, Caecina Severus, Plautius Silvanus, Valerius Messala Messallinus, Vibius Postumus and Germanicus Caesar, and the Thracians Raiskuporis and Roimetalkes (Dio 55.30.1–6). Though Dio alleges the *princeps* was frustrated by the slow rate of progress in quelling the insurgency (Dio 55.31.1), Suetonius quotes extracts of letters Augustus wrote to his adopted son on campaign with words of encouragement, addressing him as *vir fortissime et dux* νομιμώτατε, 'most charming and valiant of men and most conscientious of generals' (Suet., *Tib.* 21.4). After four brutal campaign seasons, the rebellion collapsed. 'He reaped an ample reward for his perseverance, for he completely subdued and reduced to submission the whole of Illyricum' (Suet., *Tib.* 16.2), and he and his generals were awarded triumphal ornaments. Receiving news of the Varian Disaster (end of summer of 9 CE), Tiberius sent troops ahead under Germanicus while himself making directly for Rome to receive instructions from Augustus (Vell. Pat. 2.117–122.2; Suet., *Tib.* 17.1), though he entered the city as a *triumphator* (Suet., Tib. 17.2). Subsequently, Tiberius led a low-risk raid across the Rhine into Germania in 11 CE (Dio 56.25.2), staying long enough to symbolically hold races on Augustus' birthday (23 September) on German soil (Dio 56.25.3). In 12 CE, he returned to Rome to celebrate his Illyrian triumph on 23 October (Suet., *Tib.* 20). When Germanicus set off for *Tres Galliae* in 13 BCE, Tiberius headed for Illyricum (Suet., *Tib.* 21.1; Vell. Pat. 2.123.1). He was recalled by his mother to be with Augustus just as he was entering Dalmatia, and was with the *princeps* when he died at Nola on 19 August 14 CE (Tac., *Ann.* 1.5). A contemporary wrote that Tiberius was 'the champion and the guardian of her empire' (Vell. Pat. 2.104.2) – titles he would be called upon to demonstrate as Augustus' successor.

Q. Iunius Blaesus (c. 35 BCE–31 CE). In 14 CE, Blaesus was *Legatus Augusti Pro Praetore* for Pannonia (Tac., *Ann.* 1.16) with three legions under his command (VIII *Augusta*, VIIII *Hispana*, XV *Apollinaris*). He is described as 'no ordinary helper, a man whom one does not know whether to consider more useful in the camp or better in the toga' (Vell. Pat. 2.125.5). Blaesus would be the last Roman citizen outside the imperial family to be permitted the acclamation *imperator* in 23 CE (Tac., *Ann.* 3.74; Vell. Pat. 2.125.5). He was the maternal uncle of L. Aelius Seianus, the notorious *Praefectus Praetorio* under Tiberius. His son was a *tribuus militum* at the time of the mutiny in 14 CE (Tac., *Ann.* 1.19). He is not to be confused with the suffect consul of 10 CE.

M. Licinius Crassus (Crassus the Younger) (c. 70–After 29 BCE). Grandson of the immensely wealthy *triumvir* M. Licinius Crassus, the younger Crassus fought on the side of Sex. Pompeius and later M. Antonius. Though he had not yet served as *praetor*, he was elected consul for 30 BCE with Iulius Caesar's heir. The following year, as proconsul, he went to Macedonia and Greece. From 29–27 BCE, Crassus waged a war against the Bastarnae, Moesi, Thraex and other *nationes* (Livy, *Peri.* 134–35), driving them back across the Danube (Dio 51.23–27). He was one of the commanders who fought to win the *spolia opima*: during the war he duelled with King Deldo of the Bastarnae, killing him and stripping him of his arms and armour (Dio 51.24.4). He would normally have expected to receive the public honour of taking the *spolia opima* to the Temple of Iupiter Feretrius on the *Capitolium* (Nepos, *Atticus* 20.3), but it was blocked by Augustus, who also assumed the acclamation of *imperator* (Dio 51.25.2). Instead, Crassus was granted a triumph, which took place in Rome on 2 July 27 BCE (*Fasti Triumphales*).

M. Lollius (c. 55 BCE–2 CE). The man who would come to be one of only two men under Augustus to lend their names to military disasters (Tac., *Ann.* 1.10) was a member of the plebeian *gens Lollia* and a *novus homo*. He may be the Marcus who Appian says was the *legatus* of M. Iunius Brutus at the Battle of Philippi (App. *Bell. Civ.* 4.6.49): after the battle, this Marcus, now a proscribed man, disguised himself as a slave to avoid capital punishment and was bought by a man named Barbula, before he was taken to Rome where his true identity was revealed by a friend who appealed to M. Agrippa, through whose intercession Marcus' name was removed from the proscription list. This Marcus became a friend of Iulius Caesar's heir and some time later served as his *legatus*, fighting against M. Antonius at the Battle of Actium (App. *Bell. Civ.* 4.6.49: the story continues that when Barbula – who was fighting on Antonius' side – was captured at Actium, he pretended to be a slave and was recognised by Marcus, who bought and freed him). Following the death of King Amyntas in 25 BCE, Lollius went to Galatia as first governor (Dio 53.26.3; Eutrop., 7.10.2) and began the process of its integration into the Roman Empire, including its army – *Legio* XXII *Deiotariana* (after Amyntas' father Deiotarus) – and the foundation of a new *colonia*. In 21 BCE, Lollius was elected to the consulship in a controversial year, during which only he served as consul, because Augustus declined to stand and the rival candidates squabbled in public; Agrippa was sent by Augustus to deal with the disorder (Dio 54.6.1–4). One of his deeds was to commission repairs to the *Pons Fabricius* (*CIL* VI, 1305, VI, 31549). During 19–18 BCE, Lollius was in Macedonia where he came to the aid of Roimetalkes of Thracia against the Bessi and won (Dio 54.20.3; an inscription places him in Philippi (*AE* 1933, 85)). He was at the *Ludi Saeculares* in 17 BCE as *quindecemir sacris faciundis* (*CIL* VI, 32323.151 = *ILS* 5050). His next assignment was a *Legatus Augusti* of Gallia Comata (17–16 BCE): it was here in 17 BCE that he fatefully encountered a band of marauders – comprising Sugambri, Tencteri and Usipetes – from across the Rhine River, and in the ensuing mêlée *Legio* V *Alaudae* lost its *aquila*, an event which came to be known as the *clades Lolliana*, 'Lollian Disaster' (Dio 54.20.4–5; Suet., *Div. Aug.* 23.1). The embarrassment prompted Augustus to go to the region in person in 16 BCE – despite Lollius having since recovered the legion's eagle standard (*RG* 5.29) – and replace him with his own stepson, Tiberius (Dio 54.20.6; Suet., *Div. Aug.* 21.1 and *Tib.* 9.1; *RG* 2.12 and 5.29). Lollius was given no other military commands after 16 BCE, yet – and despite the mishap in Gaul – Augustus still liked him well enough to entrust him as a 'companion and guide' (*comes et rector*) to C. Caesar on his mission in the East (Suet., *Tib.* 12.2) from 2 BCE alongside L. Aelius Seianus, P. Sulpicius Quirinius and M. Velleius Paterculus. The two men fell out when Phratakes V of Parthia accused him of accepting bribes from kings of the East, extortion and treachery (Vell. Pat., 2.102.1; Suet., *Tib.*12.2), and he was struck off the list of friends of Augustus (Pliny, *Nat. Hist.* 9.58). About his character, the account of a contemporary describes him as having 'a crafty and deceitful mind' (Vell. Pat. 2.102.1; *cf.* Pliny, *Nat. Hist.* 9.58), while another portrays him as model of reliability and a man above avarice (Horace, *Ode* 4.9, 34–44). He was generally disliked by the Roman people, who received news of his death – perhaps suicide by poison (Pliny, *Nat. Hist.* 9.58) – in 2 CE with 'joy' (Vell. Pat. 2.102.1). His granddaughter, Lollia Paulina, would marry Emperor Caius, better known as Caligula (Pliny, *Nat. Hist.* 9.58).

M. Lurius (c. 70–After 31 BCE). Lurius, perhaps originally from Illyricum, was proconsul of Sardinia during the war against Sex. Pompeius (37–36 BCE): he was attacked by Menas and, after an initial victory, was routed in a second engagement and forced to abandon the island (Dio 48.30.7). He is best known for his role in the Battle of Actium (2 September 31 BCE), where 'the command of the right wing of Caesar's fleet was entrusted to M. Lurius' (Vell. Pat. 2.82–87). He never served a term as consul.

C. Marcius Censorinus (c. 50 BCE–2/3 CE). The *Censorini* were a plebeian branch of *gens Marcia*. Caius was son of L. Marcius Censorinus, one of the friends of Q. Tullius Cicero when he was in Asia (Cic., *ad. Q. Fr.* 1.2.13), and perhaps the same man who was also the fierce supporter of M. Antonius, proconsul of Macedonia, and consul for 39 BCE. C. Censorinus served a term as *triumvir monetalis* on the commission supervising the mint in c. 18/17 BCE and appointed *augur* at about the same time (*RIC* I 85–86). It is possible he was a quaestorian legate under Agrippa and accompanied him in 14 BCE to Sinope at the time of the Rebellion of Scribonius in the Cimmerian Bosporus (Dio 54.24.6); when Agrippa departed, he may have remained there through 12 BCE, where an inscription hails him as 'protector of the city' and *Legatus Caesaris*, but not *pro praetore* (*AE* 1906.1) – though some historians argue this refers to a relative, perhaps an uncle. Censorinus was consul in 8 BCE (Dio 55.5.1; Pliny the Elder, *Nat. Hist.* 33.10.47) and apparently subsequently served as *Legatus Augusti Pro Praetore* of Syria (Joseph. *Ant. Iud.* 16.6.2), where he secured certain immunities for the Jewish population. He was wealthy: for a while he owned a house on the Palatinus Hill which had been once owned by M. Tullius Cicero (Vell. Pat. 2.14.2). Described as 'a man born to win the affections of men' (Vell. Pat. 2.102.1), he was immensely liked by the Roman people. When attending C. Caesar (Augustus' adopted son) in 2 or 3 CE on a visit somewhere in the East – possibly Galatia – he died; his loss was personally felt by Augustus and the Roman People, who received the news with deep sorrow (Vell. Pat. 2.102.1).

L. Munatius Plancus (c. 87–After 15 BCE). Son of C. Munatius Plancus, Lucius came to the attention of Iulius Caesar and served him as one of his *legati* during the Gallic War (e.g. Caes., *Bell. Gall.* 5.24, 5.25). Plancus subsequently fought on Caesar's side in the Civil War, where he successfully led attacks at Ilerda (Caes., *Bell. Civ.* 1.40) and in Africa (Caes., *Bell. Afr.* 4; he may have authored the *commentarius* of the *Bellum Africanum*). In 45 BCE he was *praetor*. He was governor of Gallia Comata in 44–43 BCE, where he founded a *colonia*, strategically situated on the Fourvière heights west of the confluence of the Rhône and Saône Rivers, and named it Copia Felix Munatia, later known as Lugdunum (Strabo, *Geog.* 4.3.1–2). He was elected consul for 42 BCE. A correspondent of M. Tullius Cicero (Cic., *Fam.* 10.1–24), Plancus was a fair-weather friend, switching sides whenever it suited him (Vell. Pat. 2.63.3). After Iulius Caesar's assassination, he joined Dec. Brutus, before betraying him (Vell. Pat. 2.64.1); had his own brother Plancus Plotius added to the list of proscribed men (Vell. Pat. 2.67.3); then joined M. Antonius in Egypt, where, having revealed the *triumvir*'s secrets to Imp. Caesar, he contributed to his downfall (Vell. Pat. 2.83.1–3). In 27 BCE, it was Plancus who proposed to the Senate that Imp. Caesar be granted the honorific title *Augustus* (Vell. Pat. 2.91.1). He was censor in 17 or 16 BCE, in which role he was largely ineffectual (Vell. Pat. 2.95.3). He was *epulo* in 40 BCE or earlier (inferred by the image of a *lituus* and pitcher on a *denarius* announcing Munatius as proconsul with M. Antonius: Sydenham 1190, Sear Imperators 253, Crawford 522/2) and initiated into the Mysteries of Eleusis at the end of the same decade (IG 2^2.4112). A statue with an inscription was erected in his honour by grateful Greek and Italian traders of Delos (*CIL* I^2 831 = *InsDelos* 1696 = *ILLRP* 360 = *ILS* 8961b). He restored the Temple of Saturn in the early 20s BCE (*CIL* VI, 1316; Suet., *Div. Aug.* 29.5). His grand mausoleum on top of Monte Orlando, which overlooks the city of Gaeta, is considered to be the most complete Roman tomb to have survived in all of Italy.

L. Nonius Asprenas Torquatus (c. 35 BCE–After 20 CE). Asprenas was the son of plebeian L. Nonius Asprenas and Quinctilia, sister of P. Quinctilius Varus.

While performing at the *lusus Troiae*, he injured himself but Augustus 'presented him with a golden necklace and allowed him and his descendants to bear the surname Torquatus' (Suet., *Div. Aug.* 43.2). He was suffect consul for 6 CE, and the following year was on the Rhine as *legatus* in charge of *Legiones* I and V *Alaudae* under the command of his uncle, Varus (Vell. Pat. 2.120.3). In the immediate aftermath of the massacre at Teutoburg in 9 CE, he received survivors and rendered assistance (Dio 56.22.4), earning praise from Velleius Paterculus, while reporting rumours that Asprenas had misappropriated the assets of many of the fallen (Vell. Pat. 2.120.3). From 12–15 or 13–16 CE, he was proconsul of Africa (*AE* 1952, 232; *CIL* VIII, 10023; Tac., *Ann.* 1.53). He was a *septemvir epulonum* by 15 CE, perhaps as early as 5 CE (*ILS* 151 Tacapen/Capsam). Asprenas was married to Calpurnia, daughter of L. Calpurnius Piso, the Pontifex (*ILS* 927).

M. Nonius Gallus (c. 65–After 29 BCE). From the town of Aesernia in Samnium (*CIL* IX, 2642), it was while serving his term as governor of Gallia Comata/Belgica in 29 BCE that Nonius Gallus subdued the Treveri (Dio 51.20.5) and was acclaimed *imperator* by his troops in 29 BCE (*ILS* 895).

C. Norbanus Flaccus (c. 85–After 17 BCE). A plebeian by birth from Etruria, Flaccus supported Iulius Caesar, and after his assassination transferred his allegiance to his heir. *Praetor* in 43 BCE, with Decidius Saxa and eight legions he intercepted the assassins at Philippi in 42 BCE and sent word to M. Antonius and Caesar's heir (Dio 47.35.2–36.2). Consul for 38 BCE, he was proconsul of Hispania (36–34 BCE) and, for unspecified victories there, was awarded a triumph which he celebrated in Rome on 12 October 34 BCE (*Fast. Capitol.*). He was at Actium (31 BCE) and after the battle went to Asia as proconsul (Joseph., *Bell. Iud.* 16.171). He was at the *Ludi Saeculares* in 17 BCE as *quindecemir sacris faciundis* (*CIL* VI, 32323.151 = *ILS* 5050). He was married to a daughter of L. Cornelius Balbus (the Younger).

L. Passienus Rufus (c. 45 BCE–c. 25 CE). A *novus homo*, Passienus rose through the *cursus publicus* to become consul in 4 BCE. Later, as proconsul of Africa, perhaps in 3 CE, Rufus fought the Gaetulici (Dio 55.28.4), was acclaimed *imperator* (*ILS* 120 El-Lehs) and in 6 CE shared triumphal ornaments with Cossus Cornelius Lentulus Gaetulicus (Vell. Pat. 2.116.2; *ILS* 140). His son, a *tribunus militum* with *Legio* XII *Fulminata* (*ILS* 8966), was adopted by, and his advancement was in part due to the influence of, C. Sallustius Crispus.

M. Plautius Silvanus (c. 45 BCE–After 9 CE). A member of the plebeian branch of *gens Plautia*, M. Silvanus was a *novus homo*. He was the son of Urgulania, a close friend of Tiberius' mother Livia, and rose up the *cursus honorum* in part through her influence. He was consul (2 BCE) with Augustus. He served as proconsul of Asia (4–5 CE) and then as a *Legatus Augusti Pro Praetore* in Galatia-Pamphylia (6 CE), where he may have taken on the Isauri in the Taurus Mountains (Dio 55.27.3). When the Great Illyrian Revolt (6–9 CE) erupted, he was called to assist and bring troops to assist Tiberius (Dio 55.34.6). In 7 CE, he marched east and joined up with A. Caecina Severus and Thracian King Roimetalkes in

Moesia. On reaching Illyricum, the commanders were immediately ambushed by the insurgents, taking significant casualties (Vell. Pat. 2.112.4). Silvanus went on to defeat Bato and his Breuci warriors, before turning his attention to the other rebels and brigands (Dio 55.34.7). Tiberius then assigned one of the three army groups to Silvanus (Dio 56.12.2). He remained in the region, leading mopping up operations, earning himself *ornamenta triumphalia* (*CIL* XIV, 3605–6 = *ILS* 921 near Tibur), and is mentioned on the same inscription on the family tomb as *septemvir epulonum*. He was son-in-law of L. Apronius.

C. Poppaeus Sabinus (c. 35 BCE–After 35 CE). Perhaps from Picenum (*ILS* 5671, 6562 Interamnia Praetuttianorum), Sabinus was a *novus homo* and 'a man of somewhat humble extraction' (Tac., *Ann.* 6.39) who became consul for 9 CE. Thereafter he went to govern Moesia (12–35 CE) – and Achaea and Macedonia as well (Tac., *Ann.* 1.80; Dio 58.25.4) – as *Legatus Augusti Pro Praetore*; he served in that office 'during twenty-four years he had the charge of the most important provinces, not for any remarkable ability, but because he was equal to business and was not too great for it' (Tac., *Ann.* 6.39). He enjoyed the friendship of both Augustus and Tiberius (Tac., *Ann.* 6.39) and, likely because of it, he died peacefully (Dio 58.25.4).

P. Quinctilius (or Quintilius) Varus (46 BCE–September? 9 CE). The man who would come to be one of only two men under Augustus to lend their names to military disasters (Tac., Ann. 1.10) was a member of the *gens Quinctilia* (or *Quintilia*), one of the oldest patrician families – but 'a famous rather than a high-born family' (Vell. Pat. 2.117.2) – and its members could trace their ancestry back to the legendary foundation of Rome. From Cremona, he was the son of Sex. Quinctilius Varus who was at the Battle of Philippi (October 42 BCE) on the side of Brutus and Cassius but, witnessing their defeat, arranged for his freedman to kill him rather than be captured alive. As *quaestor*, the impoverished young Publius accompanied Augustus and Tiberius to the East (22/20 BCE), where the citizens of Athens, Tenos (the Cycladic island of Tinos) and Pergamon erected statues and dedicated inscriptions to him for unknown acts of generosity or service. In c. 20 BCE, he married Agrippa's daughter Vipsania Marcella Agrippina. He went to Hispania Tarraconensis or *Tres Galliae* as *Legatus Legionis* of *Legio* XIX, and commanded it in the Alpine War (15 BCE) under Tiberius. He is described as 'a man of mild character and of a quiet disposition, somewhat slow in mind as he was in body, and more accustomed to the leisure of the camp than to actual service in war' (Vell. Pat. 2.117.2). He was consul with his brother-in-law Tiberius in 13 BCE (Dio 54.25), co-organizing *ludi votivi* that year (*CIL* VI, 386 = *ILS* 88 Rome), perhaps on the occasion of the return of Augustus from *Tres Galliae* and the Hispaniae. He went to Africa as proconsul (8–7 or 7–6 BCE) and succeeded C. Sentius Saturninus to Syria (6–4 BCE) as *Legatus Augusti Pro Praetore* (Joseph., *Ant. Iud.* 17.5.2), where it is noted 'that he was no despiser of money is demonstrated by his governorship of Syria: he entered the rich province a poor man, but left it a rich man and the province poor' (Vell. Pat. 2.117.2). While there, he quelled the violent Judaean Revolt (4 BCE) provoked by the mismanagement of *Procurator* Sabinus (Joseph., *Ant. Iud.* 17.9.3–5, 10.1–2). Varus forgave the mass of those who had rebelled, but punished Herodes' relations who had taken part and 2,000 were crucified for sedition (Joseph., *Ant. Iud.* 17.10.10). Back in Rome, he married Claudia Pulchra, a great-niece of Augustus (the fate of his first wife is not known). In 6 CE, he was appointed *Legatus Augusti* to Germania to drive the process of pacification and assimilation of the Germanic nations (Vell. Pat. 2.117.3). With *Legiones* XVII, XIIX and XIX he was ambushed at Teutoburg (9 CE) in an uprising planned and executed by Arminius and Segimerus of the Cherusci (Strabo, *Geog.* 7.1); he is reported to have taken his own life, and his adjutants attempted to burn the body (Vell. Pat. 2.117.3–119.3; Flor. 2.30.38; Dio 56.21). The Germans decapitated the charred corpse and Arminius sent the severed head to Marboduus, hoping to convince him to join the rebellion; instead, the Marcomannic king forwarded it to Augustus, who arranged for the dismembered body part to be buried in the family's tomb (Vell. Pat. 2.119.5).

L. Sempronius Atratinus (73 BCE–7 CE). A Calpurnius Bestia by birth, L. Atratinus was adopted into the patrician branch of *gens Sempronia*. In spring 56 BCE, he brought a charge of political violence (*vis*) against M. Caelius Rufus, who was defended in court by M. Tullius Cicero (his speech of 4 April, *Pro Caelio*, survives). Atratinus was elected *praetor suffectus* in 41 BCE because all the previously elected praetors had retired from office following the Treaty of Brundisium. In 40 BCE, he was co-opted as *augur* (*CIL* VI, 1976 = *ILS* 9338.3 Rome) and later in the year he and his colleague M. Valerius Messalla Corvinus convened the Senate to introduce Herodes, who received the title of King of Iudea (Joseph., *Ant. Iud.* 14.381, *Bell. Iud.* 1.282). A supporter of M. Antonius, Atratinus was *pro praetor* of Achaea in 39 BCE (*ILS* 9461 Thessaly) and commanded part of the fleet the *triumvir* had lent to Caesar's heir in his war against Sex. Pompeius in Sicily in 36 BCE (*BMCRR* II.501, 515). He was elected suffect consul for 34 BCE, taking up the position when M. Antonius resigned (Dio 49.39.1). During the Actian War, he switched his allegiance from Antonius to Caesar's heir. In 23 BCE, he was appointed proconsul of Africa, a public province under the accord of 28/27 BCE, with a legion; during his term he fought an unspecified war, for which he was awarded a full triumph, celebrated on 12 October 21 BCE (*Fast. Capitol.*). In 40 BCE, he was elected as one of the college of *augures*, a position he held until his death in 7 CE. The ruins of the burial mausoleum in which Atratinus' ashes were laid are located in Gaeta, Italy.

C. Sentius Saturninus (c. 45 BCE–After 4 CE). Son of C. Sentius Saturninus Vetulio, the early life of Caius is obscure. A *novus homo*, there is no evidence he completed any military service before 20 BCE. It appears he was sympathetic to the assassins of Iulius Caesar and was proscribed by the Triumvirs (43 BCE). He escaped Rome to join Sex. Pompeius in Sicily (Appian 4.45; Val. Max. 7.3.9.), and was one of several 'illustrious men' (Vell. Pat. 2.77.3; Appian, *Bell. Civ.* 5.139 cf. 5.52) who, after the signing of the Treaty of Misenum (39 BCE), left Sextus to join M. Antonius (Appian, *Bell. Civ.* 5.139, 579) and later defected to Caesar's heir. He was elected to the consulship in 19 BCE and served in that high office with distinction, respecting and applying the law firmly but fairly, notably exposing the corrupt practices of tax collectors. Of his year as consul, a contemporary writes, 'Caesar was absent from the city engaged in regulating the affairs of Asia and of the orient, and in bringing to the countries of the world by his personal presence the blessings of *Pax Augusta*. On this occasion Sentius, chancing thus to be sole consul with Caesar absent, adopting the rigorous regime of the older consuls, pursued a general policy of old-fashioned severity and great firmness, bringing to light the fraudulent tricks of the tax-collectors, punishing their avarice, and getting the public moneys into the treasury. But it was particularly in holding the elections that he played the consul. For in the case of candidates for the quaestorship whom he thought unworthy, he forbade them to offer their names, and when they insisted upon doing so, he threatened them with the exercise of his consular authority if they came down to the *Campus Martius*. Egnatius, who was now at the height of popular favour, and was expecting to have his consulship follow his praetorship as his praetorship had followed his aedileship, he forbade to become a candidate, and failing in this, he swore that, even if Egnatius were elected consul by the votes of the people, he would refuse to report his election. This conduct I consider as comparable with any of the celebrated acts of the consuls of the olden days' (Vell. Pat. 2.92.1–5). He was at the *Ludi Saeculares* in 17 BCE as *quindecemir sacris faciundis* (*CIL* VI, 32323.151 = *ILS* 5050). Saturninus later served as proconsul of Africa and, while visiting Carthago, performed certain religious rituals for the *colonia* (Tert., *Pall.* 2). Following in his father's footsteps, he was sent to Syria as *Legatus Augusti Pro Praetore* (9–6 BCE) and took his three sons with him as his *legati*; they were at the trial of Herodes' sons Alexander and Aristobulos in Berytus in 6 BCE (Joseph., *Ant. Iud.* 16.277–282, 344, 367–369, and 17.24, 89; *Bell. Iud.* 1.27). He then went to Germania as *Legatus Augusti*, either for 6–3 BCE following Tiberius, or from 3–5 CE following Domitius Ahenobarbus, but certainly before Varus. There he 'received triumphal honours, inasmuch as the Germans, through their fear of the Romans, made a truce, not merely once, but *twice*' (Dio 55.28.6; *cf.* Vell. Pat. Pat. 2.103, 105, 109). Saturninus is described by Paterculus as an 'excellent man' (Vell. Pat. 2.77.3, 2.92.1). Of his character, he writes that he was 'a man many-sided in his virtues, a man of energy and action, and of foresight, alike able to endure the duties of a soldier as he was well trained in them, but who, likewise, when his labours left room for leisure, made a liberal and elegant use of it, but with this reservation, that one would call him sumptuous and jovial rather than extravagant or indolent' (Vell. Pat. 2.105.2). His life after 4 CE is unknown from the extant accounts.

L. Sestius Quirinalis Albinianus (c. 70–c. 10 BCE). Suffect consul for 23 BCE, Sestius may have succeeded P. Carisius as *Legatus Augusti Pro Praetore* of Hispania Tarraconensis (22–19 BCE) or P. Silius Nerva (16–14 BCE). At the time of Augustus' visit to the region he may have set up the *Ara Sestianae* to the new cult of *Roma et Augustus* near Noeta in territory of the recently conquered Callaeci (Suet., *Div. Aug.* 52; Tac., *Ann.* 4.37).

C. Silius Aulus Caecina Largus (c. 30 BCE–24 CE). Born A. Caecina Largus and adopted by P. Silius Nerva (consul 20 BCE), C. Silius was consul for 13 CE. The following year, he took up the post of *Legatus Augusti Pro Praetore* of Germania Superior in Mogontiacum, in charge of *Legiones* II *Augusta*, XIII *Gemina*, XIV *Gemina* and XVI *Gallica* (Tac., *Ann.* 1.31). Remarkably, among a dinner service found buried at an Iron Age grave in Hoby on Lolland, Denmark, were two exquisite cups (made of silver by master craftsman Chirisophos), each bearing the graffito 'Silius'; one interpretation is that they may have been a diplomatic gift from the Roman commander to a tribal chief across the Rhine.

P. Silius Nerva (P. Silius the Younger) (c. 62–After 16 BCE). Son of P. Silius Nerva of the plebeian *gens Silia*, young Publius was a *novus homo* who rose to become consul (20 BCE) with M. Appuleius (Dio 54.7.4). He is recorded as *Legatus Pro Praetore* of Hispania Citerior in an inscription from Carthago Nova (*CIL* II.3414) dated to 19 BCE, and may have assisted M. Agrippa in Northern Spain when fighting the Astures and Cantabri (Dio 54.11.2–6). Later, he was proconsul of Illyricum. He commanded the Roman army in a successful campaign in 16 BCE in the Alps against the Cammunii and Venii (Venones) (Dio 54.20.1), the result of which was to break the will of the neighbouring Pannonii to fight and they sought terms with the Romans (Dio 54.20.2). His son was A. Licinius Nerva Silianus (Vell. Pat. 2.116.4).

P. Silius (c. 40 BCE–After 5 CE). Eldest son of *nobilis* P. Silius Nerva (consul 20 BCE), Publius was the brother of C. Silius (consul 13 CE). In 9 BCE, he was *Tresvir Monetalis* (*BMCRE* I 40). In 1/2 CE, he was *Legatus Augusti Pro Praetore* of Macedonia and Thrace, where Velleius Paterculus was serving as a *tribunus militum* (Vell. Pat. 2.101.3). He was suffect consul for 3 CE. Nothing is known of his life afterwards.

T. Statilius Taurus (c. 80–After 13 BCE). Taurus was descended from the *Statilii Tauri* of Lucania, the most accomplished branch of the plebeian *gens Statilia* to gain their success in Rome. A *novus homo*, he was an associate of Calvisius Sabinus (*cos.* 39 BCE) – a political duo Cicero described unflatteringly as a 'Minotaur' (Cic., *Ad Fam.* 12.25.1). Taurus was elected suffect consul in 37 BCE, replacing Caninius Gallus and serving with M. Agrippa as *consul ordinarius*. The following year, as a *legatus*, he commanded the fleet of ships loaned to Caesar's heir by M. Antonius for the war against Sex. Pompeius (Appian, *Bell. Civ.* 5.97–99, 103, 110). After Sextus fled from Sicily, Taurus took the fleet to Africa, using it to secure the province for Caesar as proconsul, for which he was awarded a triumph on 30 June 34 BCE. Thereafter he proved one of Augustus' most loyal and trusted *legati* alongside M. Agrippa (Vell. Pat. Pat. 2.127.1). Of him and Agrippa, Velleius Paterculus writes, 'in the case of these men their lack of lineage was no obstacle to their elevation to successive consulships, triumphs, and numerous priesthoods. For great tasks require great helpers, and it is important to the state that those who are necessary to her service should be given prominence in rank, and that their usefulness should be fortified by official authority' (Vell. Pat. 2.127.1–2). Taurus was an accomplished general: he was assigned to wind down military operations conducted by Augustus and Agrippa (35–34 BCE) in Illyricum (App., *Ill.* 5.27); at the Battle of Actium (31 BCE), he commanded the land army while M. Agrippa fought at sea (Plut., *Ant.* 65.2). He was acclaimed *imperator* three times during his career (*ILS* 893 Ilici = *CIL* II, 3556), once in Africa, perhaps also in Illyricum, and Hispania Tarraconensis (formerly Hispania Citerior). In 30 BCE, Taurus began constructing the first purpose-built stone amphitheatre in Rome to display gladiatorial and hunting combats – which up to that time had taken place in the Forum, with wooden stands temporarily erected for spectators – in the southern part of the Campus Martius, paid for from Actian War booty (Dio 51.23, 53.18; Suet. *Div. Aug.* 29.5; Strabo, *Geog.* 5.3.8; Tac., *Ann.* 3.72); 'because of this he was permitted by the people to choose one of the praetors each year' (Dio 51.23). He went to Hispania Citerior (29 BCE) – following after Calvisius Sabinus – and defeated the Astures, Cantabri and Vaccaei in the north of the peninsula (Dio 51.20.5). On his return to Rome, he was elected consul with Augustus for 26 BCE. While Augustus and Tiberius were away in *Tres Galliae* (16–13), Taurus was appointed *Praefectus Urbanus* in charge of affairs in Rome and Italy (Dio 54.19.6) and, 'though in advanced years, sustained it admirably' (Tac., *Ann.* 6.11). He may have been one of the *tresviri monetales* (8 BCE) with colleagues Regulus and Pulcher (e.g. *RIC* I 423, *C.* 421) supervising the mint in Rome. Among his religious appointments, he was *augur* (*CIL* X, 409 = *ILS* 893a) from the 30s BCE and *curio maximus* (*ILS* 925), likely following Calvisius Sabinus in that office. He continued to serve Augustus with distinction until his death (Tac., *Ann.* 6.11). His son Titus became consul in 11 CE.

P. Sulpicius Quirinius (c. 45 BCE–21 CE). Born into a wealthy plebeian family (not connected with the patrician *gens Sulpicia*), Quirinius was raised in Lanuvium in Latium (Tac., *Ann.* 3.48). Nothing is known of his early career, but after rising up the *cursus honorum*, in 15 BCE he went to Creta et Cyrenaica as proconsul; there he successfully subjugated the Nasamones (Strabo, *Geog.* 17.3.23). He is described as 'an indefatigable soldier' (Tac., *Ann.* 3.48). In Cyrenaica, Quirinius battled the Marmaridae and Garamantes, nations living in the Sahara desert; he '[like Cossus Cornelius Lentulus Gaetulicus] might have returned with the title of Marmaricus, had he not been too modest in estimating his victory' (Florus, 2.31). Having proved himself 'by his zealous services' (Tac., *Ann.* 3.48), he was elected consul for 12 BCE. Leaving Rome, he then went to Galatia-Pamphylia as *Legatus Augusti Pro Praetore* (5–3 BCE) and assumed command of *Legiones* V *Macedonica* and VII *Macedonica*; with them he engaged the coalition of bandits called Homonadeis operating in Cilicia (Strabo, *Geog.* 14.5.24), 'stormed some fortresses' (Tac., *Ann.* 3.48) and 'by famine and took 4,000 men prisoners, whom he settled as inhabitants in the neighbouring cities, but he left no person in the country in the prime of life' (Strabo, *Geog.* 12.6.5, 24; *CIL* XIV, 3613 'Lapis Tiburtinus' – some believe it refers to Quinctilius Varus). He received 'the honours of a triumph' (Tac., *Ann.* 3.48). He may have governed Asia, but certain proof is lacking. Trusted by Augustus, Quirinius was appointed *rector*, or personal 'guide', to his adopted son C. Caesar – along with M. Lollius (Suet., *Tib.* 12.2),

M. Velleius Paterculus and L. Aelius Seianus – on his mission in the East. He probably met the Parthian King Phraatakes in the diplomatic conference held on an island in the Euphrates River (Vell. Pat. 2.101.1–3). Following C. Caesar's untimely death in 4 CE, Quirinius was temporarily appointed *Legatus Augusti Pro Praetore* to Syria and with it command of *Legiones* III *Gallica*, VI *Ferrata*, X (*Fretensis*) and XII *Fulminata* until L. Volusius Saturninus arrived. At this time, following the dismissal of Herodes Archelaus, Iudaea became a district of Syria (Joseph., *Ant. Iud.*15.1.1). Quirinius organized a census of the new district (6–7 CE) to assess its tax base (Joseph., *Ant. Iud.* 18.1–2; *CIL* III, 6687; *EJ* 231 = *ILS* 2683; Luke, 2.1). The local population, led by Zadok and Theudas (*Acts* 5:36) and Iudas of Gamala in Galilee (*Acts* 5:37), rose up in protest, but Quirinius restored order quickly – although recorded in Jewish literature (Joseph., *Ant. Iud.* 18.6; *Acts* 5.37), it is not mentioned in surviving Roman accounts (Tac., *Hist.* 5.9).

L. Tarius Rufus (c. 57 BCE–After 14 CE). A *novus homo*, perhaps from Picenum (Pliny, *Nat. Hist.* 18.37; *CIL* V. 8112 (Este), *CIL* III.12010 (Zagreb)), Rufus was one of the naval commanders appointed by Agrippa during the Actian War in 31 BCE: he was ambushed in a dawn attack by Antonius' admiral C. Sosius before the main battle, but escaped capture (Dio 50.14.1–2). From 18–16 BCE, he may have had praetorian command of Illyricum (*CIL* III, 2877 f.) and Macedonia (an inscription from Amphipolis (*AE* 1936, 18) – commemorating a bridge built by *Legio* X *Fretensis* – refers to him as *pro praetor*). Returning to Rome, he was appointed as suffect consul from 1 July 16 BCE, when Augustus departed for the *Tres Galliae* following the *clades Lolliana*. He was an *amicus* of Augustus and Tiberius and became a wealthy man.

A. Terentius Varro Murena *or* **A. Licinius Varro Murena** (c. 60–After 23 BCE?). There are several references to Varro in the extant sources: they may be the same or different individuals. In 26/25 BCE, Terentius Varro was active in the Alps engaging the Salassi (Dio 53.25.3 Suet., *Div. Aug.* 21.1); following his complete victory over them, the *colonia* of Augusta Praetoria Salassorum (Aosta) was founded 'in the place where Varro had pitched his camp' (Strabo, *Geog.* 4.6.7). This – or another – Varro was *legatus* of Syria c. 24–23 BCE and waged war on bandits from Trachonitis who were harassing the Damascenes (Joseph., *Bell. Iud.* 1.398). A. Licinius Varro Murena was chosen as the consul for 23 BCE (Joseph., *Bell. Iud.* 1.398, *Ant. Iud.* 15.345; Fast. Capitol.). Licinius Varro (Dio 54.3.4) or Lucius Murena (Vell. Pat. 2.91.2, who states this individual 'might have passed as a man of good character') was related to Cilnius Maecenas as his brother-in-law and was implicated in a plot with Fannius Caepio (the instigator) to assassinate Augustus in 23 BCE, and summarily executed (Dio 54.3.5–6; Vell. Pat. 2.91.4).

M. Titius (c. 70–After 12 BCE). M. Titius, son of Lucius (*CIL* III, 7160 = *CIL* III, 455 = *ILS* 891), from plebeian *gens Titia*, was a nephew of L. Munatius Plancus (*cos.* 42 BCE). After the Ides of March assassination, he sided with the conspirators and was proscribed by the triumvirs. In 43 BCE, he joined

Sex. Pompeius, built a fleet and attacked installations on the coast of Etruria. In 40 BCE, he was captured, but following the Treaty of Misenum was permitted to return to Rome (Vell. Pat., 2.77.3). By 36 BCE, he was serving on M. Antonius' staff as *quaestor* in his Parthian War, where he demonstrated sounder judgment than some other more impulsive officers (Plut., *Ant*. 42.2–4). Sources implicate Titius in the execution of Sex. Pompeius in 35 BCE, though whether it was on the orders of Antonius or Plancus or his own decision is not clear (Appian, B*ell. Civ*. 5.140–144; Dio, 49.18.4–5; Vell. Pat., 2.79.5; Strabo, Geog. 3.2; Orosius 6.19.2; Livy, *Peri*. 131; Eutropius 7.6.1). He was a *pontifex*, perhaps in 34 BCE (*CIL* IX, 5853 (Auximum)). His betrayal of Pompeius was later remembered by the audience attending a performance held at the Theatre of Pompeius, who protested his presence, despite being *sponsor* of the games, and chased him out of the building (Vell. Pat., 2.79.5). Disillusioned with Antonius' and Kleopatra's leadership, and allegedly having been insulted by the queen (Plut., Ant. 58.3), in June/July 32 BCE he defected to Imp. Caesar's side; before the Battle of Actium, and with Statilius Taurus, he led a successful charge against M. Antonius' cavalry (Dio 50.13.5). He was appointed suffect consul for May–October 31 BCE after the resignation of M. Valerius Messalla Corvinus. From 13/12 BCE, he was *Legatus Augusti Pro Praetore* for Syria. In this role Titius received four children, four grandchildren and two daughters-in-law of Frahatak (Phraates) IV, king of Parthia, as hostages (Strabo, *Geog*. 16.1.28). King Herodes of Iudaea interceded to settle the quarrel between Titius and Archelaus, king of Cappadocia, when he accompanied Archelaus to Antiocheia (Josephus, *Ant. Iud*. 16.270). Titius married Fabia Paullina, the daughter of Quintus Fabius Maximus.

M. Valerius Messalla Corvinus (64 BCE–13 CE). Born into the *gens Valeria*, Messalla Corvinus was either the son of M. Valerius Messalla Niger (*cos*. 61 BCE), or alternatively of M. Valerius Corvus. 'A young man of distinction' (App., *Bell. Civ*. 4.38), he was among the proscribed men following Iulius Caesar's assassination (Dio 49.16.1, 50.10.1), having fled to Brutus, but his name was later scratched from the list (App., *Bell. Civ*. 5.113). He fought with Caesar's heir in the war against Sex. Pompeius (App., *Bell. Civ*. 5.102, 103, 105, 109, 110, 112), and on his return on 13 November 36 BCE was appointed as *augur* (Dio 49.16.1). He fought with Imp. Caesar during the Illyrian War in 36–35 BCE (App., *Ill*. 9.17). He was elected consul with him for 31 BCE (Dio 50.10.1). At the end of the Alexandrian War (30 BCE), he was responsible for quietly liquidating men being trained as gladiators for victory games Antonius had planned to stage for defeating his opponent (Dio 51.7.7). Messalla held commands in the East. In the West, he suppressed a revolt in Gallia Aquitania in 27 BCE (App., *Bell. Civ*. 4.38), for which he was awarded a triumph on 25 September 27 BCE (*Fast. Capit*.). Horace infers he was a most eloquent public speaker (Horace, *Ars Poetica* 3.21) and he was lauded for his skill by Cicero and others years later (Seneca the Younger, *Claudius* 10.2; Quin., *Inst*. 10.1.113) – in one speech he lauded the assassin Crassus as *imperator* and was not attacked by Augustus for doing so (Tac., *Ann*. 4.34). In 2 BCE, Messalla proposed, on behalf of the Senate, that Augustus accept the title

Pater Patriae, 'Father of the Fatherland' (Suet, *Div. Aug.* 58) – the honour of which Augustus was most proud. As an ex-consul, Messalla was later appointed *Praefectus Urbi* (Jerome, *Chron.* 26 BCE), whose role was 'to overawe the slaves and that part of the population which, unless it fears a strong hand, is disorderly and reckless' (Tac., *Ann.* 6.11); though the first to be appointed to the office, he quit within six days, saying 'the power of my office shames me' (Seneca the Younger, *Claudius* 10.2; cf. Tac., *Ann.* 6.11 and Jerome, *Chron.* 26 BCE). His son was M. Valerius Messala Messalinus, consul for 3 BCE; his daughter Valeria Messallina married T. Statilius Taurus; another daughter, also called Valeria, married M. Lollius.

M. Valerius Messalla Messallinus (43 BCE–c. 21 CE). Eldest son of M. Valerius Messalla Corvinus (consul 31 BCE), Messallinus was described by a contemporary as a man 'who was even more noble in heart than in birth, and thoroughly worthy of having had Corvinus as his father' (Vell. Pat. 2.112.1f.). In 21 BCE, he was appointed *quindecimvir sacris faciundis* (Tibullus, *Carm.* 2.5.17–18, 119–120), and attended the *Ludi Saeculares* in 17 BCE (*CIL* VI, 32323.151 = *ILS* 5050). He rose through the *cursus honorum* to be elected consul for 3 BCE, perhaps with his esteemed father's assistance. He was *Legatus Augusti Pro Praetore* of Illyricum and assigned leadership of the army group moving north/northwest in the war planned by Tiberius against Marboduus, which was aborted when the the Great Illyrian Revolt of 6–9 CE erupted in his own province (Dio 55.29.1–2). During the Revolt, he led the *Legio* XX from Siscia. After a shaky start in 6 CE – in which half of *Legio* XX found itself surrounded by the enemy before cutting its way out (Dio 55.30.1–2) – and with additional forces brought by Tiberius (Dio 55.30.4), Messallinus led his army to victory in the final year (Vell. Pat. 2.112.1–2), perhaps earning the legion the *agnomen Valeria Victrix*. He was one of the commanders honoured with triumphal ornaments in 9 CE (*Fast. Capitol.*; Dio 56.15.3). He is also one of the eminent men mentioned by Ovid in his works (Ovid, *Ep. Ex Pont.* 1.7, 2.2, *Tristia* 4.4). His brother was M. Aurelius Cotta Maximus Messallinus (Vell. Pat. 2.112.2).

C. Vibius Postumus (c. 45 CE–After 16 CE). A *novus homo* from an old family of Larinum in Samnium (*CIL* IX, 730; Cic., *Pro Cluentio* 25 and 165), Vibius Postumus rose to be suffect consul in 5 CE. As governor of Illyricum (c. 6–9 CE), he saw action during the Great Illyrian Revolt, leading one of the army groups and earning triumphal ornaments for his 'distinguished valour' (Vell. Pat. 2.116.2; cf. Dio 56.15.3). He was proconsul of Asia for a *triennium*, from 12–15 CE (Apollonides, *Anth. Pal.* 9.280, 791; *OGIS* 469 Samos). C. Vibius Postumus is mentioned on an inscription as *septemvir epulonum* of Colonia Romulensis (*AE* 1966.74 Romula).

M. Vinicius *or* **Vinucius** (c. 60 BCE–After 4 CE). Son of P. Vinicius (or Vinucius), Marcus was a *novus homo* described by a contemporary source as 'an illustrious man' (Vell. Pat. 2.104.2). In 25 BCE, Vinicius 'took vengeance upon some of the Germans (Κελτῶν) because they had arrested and slain Romans who entered their country to trade with them; and thus he, too, caused the title of *imperator* to be bestowed upon Augustus' (Dio 53.26.4). Suffect consul for 19 BCE, he was likely inducted into the college of *quindecemviri* at the same time if not before. From the following year, he may have served as proconsul in Achaea – where the *colonia* at Corinth named a voting tribe after him (*AE* 1919.2) – and was then appointed *Legatus Augusti* of Illyricum around 14 BCE (Flor. 2.24; *ILS* 8965). Seemingly unable to contain an insurrection there in 13 BCE during the *Bellum Pannonicum* (14–9 BCE), he appealed to Augustus, who sent M. Agrippa (Vell. Pat. 2.96.2; Dio 55.28.1–2), resulting in the suspension of hostilities. In 10 BCE, Vinicius moved north against an alliance of the Bastarnae and Daci and engaged them on the Hungarian Plain: an inscription (*AE* 1905.14 = *ILS* 8965 Frascati) records, '[M. Vinu]cius [patronymic], [consul], [septem]vir s[acris] f[aciundis], [legatus pro] praetore Augusti Caesaris* of [Illyricum, the first?] to advance across the Danuvius River, defeated in battle and routed an army (*exercitus*) of Daci and Basternae, and subjugated the Cotini, Osi, [name of tribe lost] and Anartii [to the power of the *Imperator* A]ugustus [and of the People of Rome]'. Between 2/3 and 4 CE, he was posted to Germania (following after Domitius Ahenobarbus) as *Legatus Augusti Pro Praetore*, where 'an extensive war had broken out' (Vell. Pat. 2.104.2). He proved up to the task and 'carried on this war with success in some quarters, and in others had made a successful defence, and on this account there had been decreed to him triumphal ornaments with an honorary inscription recording his deeds' (Vell. Pat. 2.104.2; perhaps *Not. Scav.* 1929, p. 31 (Cales)). Vinicius enjoyed good relations with Augustus, as a letter preserved by Suetonius records: 'I dined, dear Tiberius, with the same company; we had besides as guests Vinicius and the elder Silius. We gambled like old men during the meal both yesterday and today; for when the dice were thrown, who-ever turned up the "dog" or the six, put a *denarius* in the pool for each one of the dice, and the whole was taken by anyone who threw the "Venus"' (Suet., *Div. Aug.* 71.2). The *elogium* of Vinicius still survives (*Insc. It.* 13.2.91). The army commander turned historian Velleius Paterculus, whose father had served under M. Vinicius as *praefectus equitum*, dedicated his *Epitome of Roman History* to the grandson of the consul of 19 BCE (Vell. Pat. 2.104.3).

Sex. Vistilius (c. 40 BCE–32 CE). About his early life nothing survives. Vistilius was a *praetor* and close friend of Nero Claudius Drusus, who may have served with him in the Alpine and/or German Wars; after Drusus' death in 9 BCE, Vistilius 'transferred to his brother's cohort' (Tac., *Ann* 6.9). His sister Vistilia married Domitius Corbulo (Corbulo the Elder) around 4–1 BCE (Pliny, *Nat. Hist.* 7.39).

L. Volusius Saturninus (c. 60 BCE–20 CE). Son of Q. Volusius Saturninus, having served as suffect consul for 12 BCE. Lucius was selected as proconsul of Africa. He succeeded P. Sulpicius Quirinius as *Legatus Augusti Pro Praetore* in Syria in 4/5 CE. He was *epulo* at around the same time as his consulate. After the *princeps*' death in 14 CE, Volusius Saturninus and his son – the *augur* Lucius – erected a temple to *Divus Augustus*. In his obituary of him, the historian Tacitus writes, 'Volusius belonged to an old family which, nonetheless, had never advanced beyond the praetorship. He himself enriched it with the consulate, and, besides discharging the duties of the censorship in the selection of the equestrian decuries, became the first accumulator of the wealth which raised the family fortunes to such unmeasured heights' (Tac., *Ann.* 3.30).

(b) Prefects (*Praefaecti*)

The *praefecti* were recruited from among the *Ordo Equester* or 'Order of Knights' who ranked below the patrician aristocracy. Originally it comprised of men granted a horse at the public expense (*equites equo publico*) who served alongside the infantry. After the Social War (90–88 BCE), its members ceased to be a source of civilian cavalry (*turmae equitum*) when it was replaced by specialist non-citizen allies and auxiliaries and turned instead to commerce, banking and the law courts to make their fortunes. To gain entry into the *Ordo Equester* a man had own property or assets worth in excess of HS400,000, compared to a senator at HS1,000,000 (Dio 54.26.3). However, the *equites* provided Augustus with a pool of talent for recruiting military officers, such as the *tribuni laticlavii* and *praefecti alae* (Vell. Pat. 2.111.3):

> the emperor himself selects knights to be sent out as military tribunes (both those who are prospective senators and the others ...), dispatching some of them to take command of the garrisons of purely citizen-legions, and others of the foreign legions as well. In this matter he follows the custom then instituted by [Iulius] Caesar (Dio 53.15.2).

The *equites* were divided into six *turmae* of thirty men each. In 5 BCE, Augustus appointed C. Caesar as *princeps iuventutis* ('the first of the youth'), ranked a *sevir turmae* in charge of one of the six *turmae* of *iuniores*; he was followed by L. Caesar in 2 BCE (Dio 55.9.10) and Germanicus Caesar in around 1 BCE (Ovid, *Ex Pont.* 2.5.41). The *iuventus* included both *equites* and the young men who were destined to have careers as senators. Any who were appointed as *quaestor* automatically entered the Senate and left the *Ordo Equester*. *Equites* who had served as centurions in the army could also be promoted to the Senate (Dio 52.25.7). Those remaining in the *Ordo Equester* continued to serve as horsemen until they reached 35, at which age they became *seniores* and could retire (*cf.* Suet., *Div. Aug.* 38.3), but they retained their status as *equites* throughout their lives. Significantly, when the corpses of C. and L. Caesar were brought back to Rome, they were accompanied by military tribunes (Dio 55.12.1), recognizing they were bringing home one of their own, even though Caius had since become a senator because of his consulship in 1 CE (*ILS* 107 (7, 8) = *EJ* 61).

In the earlier days of the *Res Publica*, Livy explains the *principes iuventutis* formed a *seminarium Senatus*, a 'training school for the Senate' and that 'from it their consuls are chosen to be among the Fathers; from it they select their commanders (*imperatores*)' (Livy, *Ab Urbe Cond.* 42.61.5). Augustus employed them to fill the approximately 360 senior army officer positions, about half of which became open each year to equestrians, and in a variety of other confidential posts. The title *equites equo publico* became a necessary qualification for a young man's appointment as an officer in the legions or the *auxilia*. Having completed this preliminary military service, he could go on to become a *praefectus*, such as the two *Praefecti Praetorii* (e.g. Q. Ostorius Scapula and P. Salvius Aper); the *Praefectus Aegypti* (e.g. C. Aelius Gallus, succeeded by C. Petronius); and the *Praefectus Iudaeorum* (e.g. Coponius), reporting to the *Legatus Augusti Pro Praetore* of Syria (e.g. P. Sulpicius Quirinius) when Iudaea, Samaria, the Paralia and Galilee became a Roman province (Joseph. *Bell. Iud.* 2.117). The *procurator* who oversaw collection of tax revenues in a 'Province of Caesar' (e.g. Cyrenius in Iudaea, Sabinus in Syria) was also recruited from the *Ordo Equester*.

Augustus re-instituted the *transvectio equitum* – a parade having its origins in the fourth century BCE – as a ceremony held annually on 15 July (Suet, *Div. Aug.* 38.3). The *equites* paraded in full kit from the Porta Capena in the Servian Wall, through the *Forum Romanum*, past the Temple of Mars or of Honos et Virtus, and up to the Temple of Iupiter Optimus Maximus on the *Capitolium* (Livy, *AUC* 9.46.15; *Vir. Ill.* 32.2). Augustus 'would not allow an accuser to force anyone to dismount as he rode by, as was often done in the past', and indeed:

> permitted those who were conspicuous because of old age or any bodily infirmity to send on their horses in the review, and come on foot to answer to their names whenever they were summoned. Later he excused those who were over 35 years of age and did not wish to retain their horses from formally surrendering them (Suet, *Div. Aug.* 38.3).

At the end of the parade, religious observance was paid at their own Temple of Fortuna Equestris near the Theatre of Pompeius Magnus (Vitr., *De Arch.* 3.3.2) and their own gods, the Dioscuri twins Castor and Pollux, whose temple was restored in 6 CE by Tiberius in his and his younger brother's name; it was paid for with the war spoils of the campaign in Germania (Suet., *Tib.* 20). During the ensuing emergency of the Great Illyrian Revolt (6–9 CE), Augustus took the unusual step of suspending the *transvectio* (Dio 55.31.2).

For a discussion of the *equites*, see Brunt (1983), Hill (1930), McCall (2002) and Wiseman (1970).

C. Aelius Gallus (c. 55 BCE–After 24 BCE). Aelius Gallus was Augustus' second *Praefectus Aegypti* (26–24 BCE), replacing the disgraced C. Cornelius Gallus (Dio 53.23.5–7). Equestrian Aelius led an expedition to Arabia Felix (26/25 or 25/24 BCE) involving amphibious operations to transport troops, but which ended in disaster and the loss of much of his army to disease and hunger (*RG* 5.26; Pliny the Elder, *Nat. His.* 6. 32, 160–161; Joseph., *Ant. Iud.* 15.317; Dio 53.29.3–8). He may have been a personal friend of the geographer Strabo, who mentions accompanying him in Egypt down the Nile River to Syene (Strabo, *Geog.* 2.15.2). Aelius also failed to meet Augustus' expectations and was recalled after just two years to be replaced by C. Petronius.

[?]. Aemilius Rectus (c. 25 BCE–After 14 CE). Rectus was *Praefectus Aegypti* (14 or 15 CE). He is known from a consolatory oration (Seneca, *Ad Helvium* 19).

M. Ambibulus (c. 40 BCE–After 12 CE). Equestrian Ambibulus succeeded Coponius as *Praefectus Iudaeorum* in 9 CE (Joseph., *Ant. Iud.* 18.31). No civil unrest is recorded during his time in office. He was succeeded by Annius Rufus (Joseph., *Ant. Iud.* 18.31).

[?]. Annius Rufus (c. 35 BCE–After 14 CE). Equestrian Annius Rufus succeeded M. Ambibilus as *Praefectus Iudaeorum* in 12 CE (Joseph., *Ant. Iud.* 18.31). No civil unrest is recorded during his time in office. He was still prefect at the time of Augustus' death, 19 August 14 CE (Joseph. *Ant. Iud.* 18.2.2). He was succeeded by Valerius Gratus in 15 CE.

C. Cilnius Maecenas (29 January 70–? October 8 BCE). A wealthy equestrian from Etruria, Maecenas was an early ally of Augustus (Nic. 30); he may even have fought at Mutina, Perusia and Philippi on his side against the assassins of Iulius Caesar (Propertius 2.1, 25–30). If M. Agrippa is considered as Augustus' right-hand man, it could be said that Macecenas was his left-hand man. Maecenas was Augustus' point man, placed in 'charge of everything in Rome and Italy' (Tac., *Ann.* 6.11.1), working diligently behind the political scenes during the years of the Second Triumvirate and Civil War (Dio 49.16.2) and helping to broker the Treaty of Brundisium with M. Antonius in 40 BCE (Appian, *Bell. Civ.* 5.65). Maecenas uncovered a conspiracy to assassinate Caesar's heir in 31 BC, allegedly masterminded by M. Aemilius Lepidus' son (Vell. Pat. 2.88.3; Appian, *Bell. Civ.* 4.50; Dio 54.15.4; Livy, *Peri.* 133; Suet., *Div. Aug.* 19.1). Of him, Velleius Paterculus writes, 'he was not less loved by Caesar [Augustus] than Agrippa, though he had fewer honours heaped upon him, since he lived thoroughly content with the narrow stripe of the equestrian order' (Vell. Pat. 2.88.2). One source suggests he had an opinion about everything and could not refrain from speaking it (Suet., *Div. Aug.* 66.2). Nevertheless, 'he not only made himself liked by Augustus, in spite of resisting his impulsiveness, but also pleased everybody else, and though he had the greatest influence with the emperor, so that he bestowed offices and honours upon many men, yet he did not lose his poise, but was content to remain in the *Ordo Equester* to the end of his life' (Dio 53.7.4). There is an insinuation of impropriety involving his wife which caused Maeceanas to fall out of the *princeps'* favour in 16 BCE (Dio 54.19.5). He became patron of an informal group of poets – among them Q. Horatius Flaccus (Horace), Sex. Propertius, P. Vergilius Maro (Vergil) and L. Varius Rufus – who lauded the new era led by Augusta and sang the praises of his *legati*.

[?]. Coponius (c. 40 BCE–After 6 CE). Coponius enters recorded history as equestrian *Praefectus Iudaeorum* of the newly created province of Iudaea (Joseph., *Bell. Iud.* 2.117, *Ant. Iud.* 18.1–2), when Herod's son Archelaus was deposed in 6 CE. With his base in Caesarea Maritimae, Coponius reported to the *Legatus Augusti Pro Praetore* of Syria, P. Sulpicius Quirinius (Joseph., *Ant. Iud.* 18.2). During his term in office, the revolt led by Iudas of Gamala in Galilee broke out (Joseph., *Bell. Iud.* 2.117). The Temple featured a 'door of Coponius' (*Midrash* 1.3). He was succeeded in 9 CE by M. Ambibulus (Joseph., *Ant. Iud.* 18.31).

C. Cornelius Gallus (c. 70–26 BCE). Son of Cn. Cornelius Gallus from Forum Livii, the equestrian Gallus moved to Rome at a young age and was educated there by the same teacher who taught the poets P. Vergilius Maro (Vergil) and L. Varius Rufus. An early supporter of Caesar's heir, and the man who accepted the surrender of L. Pinarius Scarpus and his four legions in Africa (Dio 51.5.6, 51.9.1; Orosius 2.19), he was rewarded with the post of *Praefectus Aegypti* (Suet., *Div. Aug.* 66.1). An inscription (*EJ* 21 = *ILS* 8995 (Philae)) in Latin, Greek and Egyptian hieroglyphics from Aswan attests to fifteen days of battles in the Thebaid, during which Gallus claimed be retook five cities – Boresis, Koptos, Keramike, Diospolis Megali (Thebes) and Ophieon – from the Ethiopian Meroites, then led his men to the First Cataract, and received envoys of the king of Ethiopia at Philae. The Vatican Obelisk bears an inscription (*AE* 1964.255) from Gallus dedicating the ancient monument to Caesar and stresses his role in building the *Forum Iulium* on his orders. But Gallus harboured an 'ungrateful and envious spirit' (Suet., *Div. Aug.* 66.2). Bizarrely, 'he indulged in a great deal of disrespectful gossip about Augustus and was guilty of many reprehensible actions besides; for he not only set up images of himself practically everywhere in Egypt, but also inscribed upon the pyramids a list of his achievements' (Dio 53.23.5). Stripped of his portfolio by Augustus (Dio 53.23.6), the arrogant and determined Gallus left office in disgrace; when various indictments were brought against him and he was convicted by the Senate, he committed suicide in 26 BCE (*P. Oxy.* 37.2820; Dio 53.23.7; Suet., *Div. Aug.* 66.2; Suet., *Grammat.* 16). Fragments of an elegiac poem neatly penned by Gallus (or a scribe) on papyrus – the earliest known manuscript of literature written in Latin – have been found at Qasr Ibrim (Primis); it may have been left there by a member of the Roman garrison in the 20s BCE.

C. Iulius Aquila (c. 30 BCE–After 11 CE). Aquila was *Praefectus Aegypti* (10–11 CE). He is known from an inscription from Alexandria (*EE* VII, 448).

M. Magius Maximus *or* **M. Manius Maximus** (c. 30 BCE–After 13 CE). Maximus was *Praefectus Aegypti* (12–13 CE; *CIL* IX, 1125) and he may have been appointed to the position twice in his career (Philo of Alexandria, *Flaccus* 10.74).

P. Octavius (c. 40 BCE–After 3 CE). Octavius was *Praefectus Aegypti* (2–3 CE).

P. Ostorius Scapula (Before 35 BCE–After 10 CE). In 2 BCE, Scapula was appointed *Praefectus Praetorio*, one of the two senior equestrians commanding the *Cohortes Praetoriae*, with P. Salvius Aper (Dio 55.10.10). He was later appointed *Praefectus Aegypti* (3–10 CE).

C. (or P.) Petronius (c. 75–After 20 BCE). Petronius replaced Aelius Gallus as the third *Praefectus Aegypti* (25/24–20 BCE). He prosecuted a war against Kandake Amanirenas of the Meroitic kingdom of Kush (22 BCE), who had led an invasion of southern Egypt, and sacked several of their towns, including its capital, Napata (Dio 54.5; Strabo, *Geog.* 17.53–54; *RG* 26). He was a friend of Herodes, sending grain to Iudaea when the kingdom was suffering famine (Joseph., *Ant.* 15.9.2).

P. Rubrius Barbarus (c. 50 BCE–After 12 BCE). Barbarus was *Praefectus Aegypti* (?–12 BCE). He is known from an inscription from Casinum (*CIL* X, 5169).

P. Salvius Aper (Before c. 35 BCE–After 10 CE). In 2 BCE, Aper was appointed *Praefectus Praetorio*, one of the two senior equestrians commanding the *Cohortes Praetoriae*, the other being Q. Ostorius Scapula (Dio 55.10.10).

L. Seius Strabo (c. 46 BCE–After 15 CE). Born in Volsini, Etruria, Seius Strabo was a friend of Augustus (Macrobius, *Sat.* 2.4.18), which may help to explain his appointment at an unknown date to *Praefectus Praetorio*, the post he held at the time of Augustus' death (Tac., *Ann.* 1.7). Soon after, he became *Praefectus Aegypti*. He had one son by his first wife Aelia, L. Seius Tubero; after she died, he married Cosconia Lentuli Maligunensis Gallita, half-sister of Q. Iunius Blaesus, and by her had L. Aelius Seianus (who would become Tiberius' *Praefectus Praetorio* and right-hand man).

C. Turranius (c. 45–After 4 BCE). Turranius was *Praefectus Aegypti* (7–4 BCE).

[?]. Valerius Ligur *or* **P. Varius Ligur** (Before c. 25 BCE–After 14 CE). Some time in 14 CE or before, Valerius Ligur *may* have replaced Ostorius Scapula and Salvius Aper, perhaps as sole *Praefectus Praetorio*: our source records only that Augustus ordered that a seat should always be available for Valerius the Ligurian whenever the two of them went together to the Senate House (Dio 66.23.2), indicating he held him in high regard. Alternatively, he may be Varius Ligur (*CIL* V, 7598 = *PIR*[1] V 189, cf. 69; *ILS* 171 (Alba Pompeia)). Varius may have been the father of Varius Ligur (in Tac., *Ann.* 4.42 and 6.30).

2. Allies

Several nations, such as the tribal Batavi and Frisii or the kingdoms of Numidia, Pontus and Thracia, co-existed with the Roman Empire as allies (*socii, foederati*), not as subject peoples (Dio 54.9.1). Augustus 'never failed to treat them all with consideration as integral parts of the empire' (Suet., *Div. Aug* 48). Enjoying the favour of Augustus as their *patronus*, the allied leaders – kings in most cases, but also chiefs, potentates and magistrates (Strabo, *Geog.* 6.4.2 and 17.3.25) – promoted Roman interests in their realms as his *clientes* and were bound by treaty obligations to assist the Romans militarily with men and matériel when called upon to do so, and *vice versa*. As proxies, they might conduct campaigns without the Romans' direct involvement, but only with their prior consent. Many allies sent their children to Rome to be educated alongside Augustus' own, and he promoted marriages and friendships among them (Suet., *Div. Aug* 48). In return, Augustus would sponsor and represent each client king's interests – and, should they arise, grievances – in the Senate or courts in Rome.

For a detailed discussion of these so-called client kings, see Braund (1984b).

Amyntas (c. 70–25 BCE). Son of Brogitarix, king of Galatia, Amyntas was king of Lycaonia and Galatia and several adjacent territories (Strabo, *Geog,* 17.3.25). An astute and confident man, he was not above assassination to acquire new lands –

Antipater, a friend of Cicero (Cic., *Ad Fam.* 13.73; Strabo, *Geog.* 12.6.3, 14.5.24), was murdered to gain Derbe – or political machinations – Cappadocia and Isaura were awarded to him, 'where he built a palace for himself' (Strabo, *Geog.* 12.6.3), through courting Roman favour. He was an ally of M. Antonius and present at Actium (Plut., *Ant.* 61), likely with troops; however, in the days just before the battle began he switched to the side of Caesar's heir (Plut., *Ant.* 63). His alliance with Augustus flourished and he minted his own coins (e.g. BMC 9, 13 and 15 bear the inscription *ΒΑΣΙΛΕΟΣ ΑΜΥΝΤΟΥ*). On the death of Deiotarus II in c. 27 BCE, Galatia was given to Amyntas by Augustus (Strabo, *Geog,* 17.3.25). He was ambitious to extend his influence from his capital at Ancyra and to reduce threats to his power; to that end, he waged war against bandits from the Homonadeis nation living in the mountainous region of his kingdom (Strabo, *Geog.* 14.5.1): Amyntas 'made himself master of Cremna [later established as a Roman *colonia*] and passed into the country of the Homonadeis, who were supposed to be the most difficult to reduce of all the tribes. He had already got into his power most of their strongholds, and had killed the tyrant himself, when he was taken prisoner by an artifice of the wife of the tyrant, whom he had killed, and was put to death by the people' (Strabo, *Geog.* 12.6.5) in 25 BCE. In another version, 'he was killed by the Cilicians in an ambush, when invading the country of the Homonadeis' (Strabo, *Geog.* 12.6.3). After his death, Galatia was annexed as a Roman province under its first governor, M. Lollius (Dio 53.26.3; Eutrop., 7.10.2).

Deiotarus (II) (c. 65–c. 27 BCE). The only surviving son of tetrarch Deiotarus (I), who unswervingly supported the Romans during their wars in Asia (Plut. *De Stoic. Repugn.* 32), Deiotarus II succeeded his father upon his death in 40 BCE as king of Galatia. Cicero held both he and his father in high regard (Cic. *Phil.* 11.13). Deiotarus II was a trusted figure: in 51 BCE, while Cicero and his brother Quintus were campaigning in Cilicia, his own son and nephew remained in the care of the king (Cic., *Ad Att.* 5.17, 18; *Phil.* 11.12). After Iulius Caesar's assassination, he was an ally of M. Antonius and present at Actium (Plut., *Ant.* 61), likely with troops; however, just before the battle began, he switched to the side of Caesar's heir (Plut., *Ant.* 63). On the death of Deiotarus II in c. 27 BCE, Galatia was incorporated into the dominion of Amyntas (Strabo, *Geog,* 17.3.25).

Herodes *or* **Hordos** (Herod the Great) (74/73–4 BCE). Herodes came to prominence in 47 BCE when Iulius Caesar appointed his father, Antipater I the Idumaean (whose family were converts to Judaism), as *procurator* of Iudaea, and his 15-year old son became governor of Galilee. Herodes demonstrated his willingness to take tough decisions when he dealt with bandits in his jurisdiction and put their leader, Hezekiah, to death. His action led the sanhedrin to press charges for having executed Jews without trial and committing other violent acts (Joseph., *Ant. Iud.*, 14.159–60; *Bell. Iud.*, 1.204–05). The *Legatus* of Syria, Sex. Iulius Caesar, intervened, warning the high priest Hyrcanus II not to condemn Herodes (Joseph., *Iud. Ant.*, 14.170; Joseph., *Bell. Iud.*, 1.211). The warning was heeded, the charges were dismissed and Sextus appointed Herodes to be the governor of Samaria and Iudea in 46 BCE. He married Doris and by her had a son, Antipater. When the Roman governor was executed by Caecilius Bassus, Herodes and his brother Phasael rallied to the commander in Cilicia, C. Antistius Vetus, who was marching with his army against Bassus and blockaded him in Apameia. The siege dragged on until after Iulius Caesar's assassination and only ended with the arrival in Syria of C. Cassius Longinus as the new governor in 43 BCE. Longinus liked the young Herodes and retained him on the staff of the provincial administration. Meanwhile, Herodes' father was murdered by Malichus. With the departure of Longinus, Herodes arranged for the assassin to be killed. Malichus' allies – who included Antigonus, the son of Aristobulus of the rival Ashmonean lineage – unsuccessfully retaliated, but they sought to oust Herodes from Jerusalem. Antigonus sought the throne for himself, but Herodes had since secured the support of Hyrcanus – marrying his granddaughter Mariamne – and the backing of *triumvir* M. Antonius, who arrived in Syria in 41 BCE and appointed him and Phasael as tetarchs of Iudaea. The following year, taking advantage of the disruption in Syria, the Parthians under Pacorus, aided by Antigonus, seized parts of the territory and Asia. Faced with greater forces than their own, the Idumaean brothers evacuated Jerusalem and retreated to Baris. Phasael surrendered but Herodes escaped with his family to Masada. Failing to find support locally, in 40 BCE Herodes travelled to Rome and on his arrival there was welcomed by Imp. Caesar and Antonius. Presented as a friend and ally of the Romans, the Senate recognized him as the legitimate king of Iudaea (Joseph., *Ant. Iud.* 14.9.11–14; *Bell. Iud.* 1.10–14; Dio 48.26; Appian, *Bell. Civ.* 5.75). Returning to his kingdom, he assembled a large army: initial gains in Galilee, at Masada and Ressa, however, stalled at Jerusalem, where support for Antigonus remained strong. With help from Sosius, one of M. Antonius' legates, Jersualem finally fell, but popular feeling was against the victorous young king (Joseph,. *Ant. Iud.* 14.15–16; *Bell. Iud.* 1.15–18; Dio 49.22.2–6). Herodes ruthlessly established his authority with executions of his enemies, including prominent Jewish officials and the sanhedrin. In Egypt, Queen Kleopatra had designs of her own on his kingdom; only the intercession of Antonius prevented an invasion, and, when she travelled through Iudaea *en route* home, Herodes welcomed her, but resisted her famed charms (Joseph., *Ant. Iud.* 15.4). When the triumvirs fell out, Herodes initially stood by his mentor, Antonius, but his offer to bring ships and troops was declined and, instead, he was assigned a lesser mission to defeat Malchus, king of Arabia Felix, who had refused to pay tribute to Kleopatra (Joseph., *Ant. Iud.* 15.5.1–5). When Antonius was himself defeated at Actium, and ended his own life in Alexandria in 30 BCE, showing his usual willingness to take bold risks, Herodes had Hyrcanus executed on trumped-up charges (Joseph., *Ant. Iud.* 15.6.5) and presented himself to the victorious *triumvir*, offering to support him with the same loyalty he had shown Antonius (Joseph., *Ant. Iud.* 15.6.6–7). Imp. Caesar accepted, confirming Herodes' position as king of Iudaea, and further expanded his territory with the addition of Gadara and Samaria, as well as Gaza, Joppa and other coastal cities (Joseph., *Ant. Iud.* 15.6.7; *Bell. Iud.* 1.19,

20; cf. Plut., *Ant.* 72; Tac., *Hist.* 5.9); Herodes renamed Samaria Sebastia in honour of Augustus – in Greek σεβαστός (Strabo, *Geog.* 16.2.34). His relationship with his family then deteriorated. Accused of adultery, Herodes authorized his wife's execution, a decision which tormented him ever after, driving him to despair and depression and making him suspicious of anyone and everyone (Joseph., *Ant. Iud.* 15.3.5–9; *Bell. Iud.* 1.22.1–2). Herodes was a third generation Jew. He was disdained by the old Jewish families who could trace their faith back generations. He held deep fears of his people and paranoia of losing his throne to insurrection. Now established in power, Herodes embarked on an extensive programme, building a system of fortifications to protect himself from the Jewish population and constructing cities based on the Roman model, including the seaport of Caesarea Maritima, Sebastia and the fortress at Herodium, as well as Alexandrium and Hyrcania (Joseph., *Ant. Iud.* 16.2.1; *Bell Iud.* 1.21.2). He rebuilt the Temple at Jerusalem, graced the city with both a theatre and amphitheatre, and constructed the *Antonia* (after M. Antonius), a fortified palace for himself, naming one apartment *Caesareum* after Augustus and another *Agrippium* after M. Agrippa (Joseph., *Ant. Iud.* 15.11.1, 20.9.7; *Bell Iud.* 1.21.1). He also beautified Tripolis, Damascus, Berytus and other cities not under his direct rule with theatres, porticoes and other public amenities in the Roman style. On his way to Rome in 18 BCE, he presided in person at the games at Olympia, and made such a large donation to the event that he was honoured with the title of its perpetual president (Joseph., *Ant. Iud.* 16.2.2; *Bell. Iud.* 1.21.11–12). Arriving in Rome that year, he was received by Augustus and the Senate with the highest honour. He left his sons by Mariamne, Alexander and Aristobulus, in the city to be brought up at the court of Augustus. Herodes' loyalty to Augustus was rewarded in 20 BCE during a personal visit of the *princeps* with additional territories, the district of Paneas, as he previously had by those of Ituraea and Trachonitis (Joseph., *Ant. Iud.* 15.10.1–3; *Bell..* *Iud.* 1.21.4; Dio 54.9.3). He formed a close friendship with M. Agrippa, visiting him in Mitylene in 23 BCE and hosting him on a lavish state visit in Jerusalem in 15 BCE with great pomp and circumstance (Joseph., *Ant. Iud.* 16.13–16). Whenever called upon to assist, he responded: in 24 BCE, he provided Aelius Gallus with troops for his campaign in Arabia Felix; in 14 BCE, he provided M. Agrippa with ships for his campaign to quell the rebellion of Scribonius in the Cimmerian Bosporus (Joseph., *Ant. Iud.* 16.21). On the return, he accompanied Agrippa overland through Asia and Pamphylia in person. At home he remained unpopular and there were plots to assassinate him. Nevertheless, when a great famine afflicted his kingdom and the adjacent countries, he distributed vast quantities of grain he had specially imported from Egypt, and not only fed the population of Iudaea at his own cost, but supplied many of the neighbouring provinces with seed to plant for the next year's harvest (Joseph., *Ant. Iud.* 15.9; Dio 54.24.6). Herodes' son Alexander married the daughter of Archelaus, king of Cappadocia, and Aristobulus was wedded to Berenice, the daughter of his own sister Salome; the brother and sister of the king of Iudaea, Pheroras and Salome, conspired with Antipater to turn the regent against his other sons. Now suspicious of plots against him, no one around him was safe. He accused his two sons by Mariamne before Augustus while at Aquileia in 11 BCE, but the *princeps* interceded to reconcile them; three years later, Herodes received new allegations of an attempt by Alexander to poison him and, when Augustus consented, he arranged for his and his brother's execution, along with many of his friends, in 6 BCE (cf. Macrobius, *Sat.* 2.4.11). Antipater, too, was accused of conspiracy and tried before Quinctilius Varus (Joseph., *Ant. Iud.* 15.10.1, 16.1, 3, 4, 7, 8, 10, 11, 17.1–5; *Bell. Iud.* 1.23–32). In 4 BCE, Herodes finally ordered the execution of Antipater. By then Herodes' health had weakened and he suffered terrible pains in his stomach and intestines, and he likely died in Jericho that year. After a spectacular state funeral, which included units of Thracian, German and Galatian troops, he was buried at Herodium (Joseph., *Ant. Iud.* 17.8.3; *Bell. Iud.* 1.33). Herodes bequeathed his vast wealth in cash – 10 million *drachmai* – and precious goods to Augustus (Joseph., *Ant. Iud.* 17.8.1), who returned and distributed it among the surviving children (Joseph., *Ant. Iud.* 17.11.5). By the time of his death, he had married ten times; with Augustus' consent, his kingdom was divided between Herodes Archelaus as *ethnarch* (Joseph., *Ant. Iud.* 17.11.4, 17.13.1; Matthew 2:22), his son by his sixth wife, Malthace from Samaria, and Philip and Herodes Antipas (Joseph., *Ant. Iud.* 17.11.4–5).

Iuba *or* **Iobas** (Iobas, Juba II) (52/50 BCE–c. 20 CE). Son of the Berber king Iuba I of Numidia (Strabo, *Geog.* 17.3.7), Iuba II was a young boy when his father died in 46 BCE. He was transported by Iulius Caesar as a prisoner to Rome and displayed as a trophy in his triumph (App., *Bell. Civ.* 2.101; Plut., *Caes.* 55). Raised and educated in Italy, he became a friend of Caesar's heir, accompanying him on campaign in the East (Dio 51.15.6); subsequently, he benefitted from the death of M. Antonius in 30 BCE and received back his father's kingdom (Dio 51.15.6; Plut., *Ant.* 87; Strabo, *Geog.* 17.3.7). Around 25 BCE, Augustus exchanged Numidia with him for Mauretania and the possessions of Bokchus and Bogud, bringing the Gaetuli under his rule (Dio 53.26.2; Strabo, *Geog.* 17.3.9). Some rose up in revolt; the forces Iuba sent against them were unsuccessful in quelling the rebels, and he had to approach Cossus Cornelius Lentulus, proconsul of Africa (5–6 CE), to assist him (Flor., 2.31). His rule was characterized by a long period of peace and prosperity. His coins bear his portrait and proudly declare him *REX IUBA* (e.g. MAA 94 = SNG Copenhagen 593; MAA 97 = SNG Copenhagen 56; MAA 208 = SNG Copenhagen 618). He used his position to modernize his kingdom, beautifying the coastal town of Iol in the Graeco-Roman style to become its new capital city Caesareia (Strabo, *Geog.* 17.3.12; Eutrop., 7.10). He also used his time to write histories (including volumes on Africa, Arabia, early Rome and the lives of eminent painters), various treaties (including one on the natural world and another on grammar) and epigrams (including one about a bad actor named Leonteus); his works were highly regarded and often cited by later Roman writers (e.g. Pliny, *Nat. Hist.* 5.1, 6.26, 66.28, 6.30, 12.31, 25.38). In 25 BCE, he married Kleopatra Selene, daughter of Antonius and Kleopatra VII of Egypt, and had a son, Ptolemaeus (Strabo, *Geog.* 17.3.7). He may have married a second time after the death of Selene to Glaphyra, daughter of Archelaus, king of Cappadocia, and widow of Alexander, son of Herodes of Iudaea. He died while Strabo was writing his *magnum opus* (Strabo, *Geog.* 17.3.7) and was deified (Lactant. *De Fals. Relig.* 1.11; Minucius Felix, 23). His kingdom passed to his son, Ptolemaeus (Strabo, *Geog.* 17.3.25).

M. Iulius Cottius (Cottius I) (c. 50 BCE–c. 20 CE). A nobleman of the Ligures nation living in the vicinity of Mont Cenis in the western Alps (Strabo, *Geog.* 4.1.5, 4.1.9, 4.6.6), Cottius was son of King Donnus (*CIL* V, 7232), who may have sided with C. Iulius Caesar during his Gallic War. Though the Gallic nations succumbed to direct Roman rule, Cottius secured the independence of his people (Amm. Marc., 15.10.1), 'because he had ruled his subjects with a just government, and when admitted to alliance with the Roman state, procured eternal peace for his nation' (Amm. Marc., 15.10.7). An inscription (*AE* 1904, 00173 = *AE* 1905, 00048 = *AE* 1996, 00971) connects M. Agrippa and Cottius, perhaps commemorating an official visit by Augustus' *legatus pro praetore* (18–13 BCE) while he was travelling to or from *Tres Galliae*. Cottius became a Roman citizen with a Julian *nomen genticulum* and the office of *praefectus*, possibly renouncing his status as a king (*rex*), allowing him to continue to rule his mountain domain independently (Amm. Marc., 15.10.2) – the triumphal arch he completed in 9 BCE, bearing an inscription in honour of Augustus and listing his fourteen *civitates* (*CIL* V, 7231; cf. Pliny, *Nat. Hist.* 3.24.4 mentions twelve which 'had shown no hostility' down to his day, and Dio 53.26.5), still stands at Susa. He constructed and maintained a highway as a short cut through the western Alps (Amm. Marc., 15.10.1–2, 8; Strabo, *Geog.* 4.1.3) – nowadays called the Cottian Alps – connecting Augusta Taurinorum in Italy to Brigantium, Gallia Narbonensis, via his capital at Segusio (Amm. Marc., 15.10.3); to raise revenue, he probably collected tolls from travellers, just as the Salassi did (Strabo, *Geog.* 4.6.7). He was succeeded by his son, M. Iulius Cottius (II).

Marboduus (Marbod) (c. 30 BCE–37 CE). The king of the Marcomanni lived his early life as a private citizen in Rome and 'enjoyed the favour of Augustus' (Strabo, *Geog.* 7.1.3). He was 'a man of noble family, strong in body and courageous in mind, a barbarian by birth but not in intelligence, he achieved among his countrymen no mere chief's position gained as the result of internal disorders or chance or liable to change and dependent upon the caprice of his subjects, but, conceiving in his mind the idea of a definite empire and royal power' (Vell. Pat. 2.108.2). Around 10 BCE, Marboduus returned to his people, who were living close by the Main River; he 'was placed in charge of the affairs of state' and 'took the rulership' (Strabo, *Geog.* 7.1.3). He built a coalition of nations and 'resolved to remove his own race far away from the Romans and to migrate to a place where, inasmuch as he had fled before the strength of more powerful arms, he might make his own all powerful' (Vell. Pat. 2.108.2). He settled them further east in the region of Bohaemium (Vell. Pat. 2.109.5; Tac., *Ann.* 2.63). At the same time, Marboduus built up his army (70,000 infantry and 4,000 cavalry), claiming it was a defensive force: 'his policy toward Rome was to avoid provoking us by war, but at the same time to let us understand that, if he were provoked by us he had in reserve the power and the will to resist' (Vell. Pat. 2.109.1–2). Perceived as a threat to Roman ambitions in Germania, Tiberius planned a massive multi-pronged invasion of his territory in 6 CE and assembled the men and matériel to do so (Vell. Pat. 2.108.1, 109.5). When the Great Illyrian Revolt unexpectedly broke out that year – in large part provoked by troop levies for the Marcomannic War imposed on the Breuci and Daesitiates by M. Valerius Messala Messallinus – Tiberius had to hastily negotiate a treaty with Marboduus (who refrained from joining the rebels) and withdraw (Vell. Pat. 2.110.3). Augustus later claimed the king 'of the Marcomanni and Suebi' was among the 'kings who sought refuge with me as suppliants' (*RG* 32.1). Hoping to sway him to his cause in uniting against the Romans after Teutoburg in 9CE, Arminius sent the head of P. Quinctilius Varus to him, but Marboduus stood by his treaty obligations and sent the body part to Augustus (Vell. Pat. 2.119.5). He remained neutral for the rest of Augustus' principate.

Polemon Pythodoros (Polemon I) (c. 60 BCE–After 2 BCE). Polemon was son of Zenon (Zeno), the orator and a prominent aristocrat from Laodikeia (Laodicea) on the Lycus Anatolia. On account of his father's loyalty to M. Antonius during the Parthian War (40 BCE), young Polemon was appointed king of Cilicia in 39 BCE (App., *Bell. Civ.* 5.75). He joined Antonius in the campaign of 36 BCE, but was taken prisoner and only gained his freedom after a ransom was paid (Dio 49.25.1–2; Plut., *Ant.* 38). The following year, Polemon helped Antonius to form an alliance of Artavasdes I of Media Atropatene (an ally of Parthia) with Rome, for which he was rewarded by the *triumvir* with the addition of Armenia Minor to his dominion (Dio 49.33.1–2, 44.3). In 31 BCE, he provided troops to Antonius for the Actian War (Plut., *Ant.* 61), but had also secretly established relations with the then *triumvir*, C. Octavius, thereafter becoming his ally. In 27 BCE, Polemon 'was enrolled among the friends and allies of the Roman people' (Plut., *Ant.* 61; Dio 53.25.1), and 'because of his bravery and honesty, was thought worthy even of a kingdom, at first by Antonius and later by Augustus' (Strabo, *Geog.* 12.8.16). Under Augustus, Polemon proved a loyal client king and prospered, expanding his kingdom to encompass the Bosporan Kingdom, Cilicia, Colchis and Pontus. In 16 BCE, M. Agrippa called upon his assistance during the revolt in the Cimerian Bosporus in which the usurper Scribonius claimed to be the legitimate successor to King Asander. Polemon arrived on the promontory but mishandled the counter-insurgency, becoming part of the problem himself and the target of public discontent (Dio 54.24.5). The rebellion was eventually quelled and that year he married Dynamis, widow of Asander, establishing himself as the sovereign of the country (Dio 54.24.6). When she died two years later, Polemon married Pythodorida of Pontus (Strabo, *Geog.* 12.3.29). Their children included Zenon (Zeno-Artaxias or Artaxias III, who became King of Armenia, crowned by Germanicus), M. Antonius Polemon Pythodoros – also known as Polemon II of Pontus – (Strabo, *Geog.* 12.3.29) and Antonia Tryphaena (who married Kotys VIII of Thrace). An inscription from 2 BCE shows he was still alive at that time (*CIL* II, 3524). At an unknown date, Polemon fought the nomadic Aspurgiani in the mountains of Phanagoria, only to be defeated, taken prisoner and executed

284 Augustus at War

(Strabo, *Geog.* 12.3.29). He was succeeded by his wife; she was assisted by her son, Polemon (II), who became regent over Armenia Maior (Strabo, *Geog.* 12.3.29).

Raiskuporis (Rhescuporis II) (c. 28 BCE–19 CE). A son of Kotys (Cotys) II, Tacitus describes Raiskuporis (Rhescuporis) II as having 'a fierce and ambitious spirit, which could brook no partner' (Tac., *Ann.* 2.64). During the Great Illyrian Revolt (a.k.a. Batonian War), Raiskuporis joined Roimetalkes (Rhoemetalces) I in coming to the aid of Tiberius and Germanicus in 7 CE (Dio 55.30.5–6) and served with some distinction. Upon the death of Roimetalkes in 12 CE, Augustus assigned the wilder western half of the Sapaean kingdom of Thrace to Raiskuporis (Tac., *Ann.* 2.64). Initially tolerant of Kotys, he soon began to plot to oust him and forcibly annex his realm; only the threat of punishment from Augustus crimped his ambition (Tac., *Ann.* 2.64). As soon as news reached him of Augustus' death, he gave full vent to it.

Roimetalkes (Rhoemetalces I) (c. 31 BCE–12 CE). Son of Kotys (Cotys) II, Roimetalkes became regent of the Sapaean kingdom of Thrace in 11 BCE when his uncle Raiskuporis (Rhescuporis) I, aided by M. Lollius (Dio 54.20.2), died in battle fighting the rebellious Thracian Bessi nation led by their warchief Vologases, a man claiming to have supernatural powers (Dio 54.34.5). He left no heir. Roimetalkes and his family had fled during the uprising and only returned to the kingdom when Augustus granted him rule of it; a subsequent rebellion in his realm (*Bellum Thracicum*) was put down with the assistance of L. Calpurnius Piso Caesonius and troops mobilized from Galatia-Pamphylia (Flor. 2.27; Dio 54.34.6). Roimetalkes came to the aid of Tiberius and Germanicus during the Great Illyrian Revolt (a.k.a. Batonian War) in 6 and 7 CE (Dio 55.30.5–6). His queen was Pythodoris and they had a son, Kotys VIII; his older brother was Kotys VII, and his younger brother Raiskuporis II. After his death, Augustus assigned the western half of the kingdom to Raiskuporis II, and the more prosperous eastern half to his son, Kotys VIII (Tac., *Ann.* 2.64).

Rolis (Roles) (late first century BCE–early first century CE). Rolis was king of the Getae nation. He helped M. Licinius Crassus capture Bastarnae at their last stand in 30 BCE in Moesia (Dio 51.24.7). Crassus came to his assistance against a rival king, Dapyx (51.26.1–2). When he visited Imp. Caesar, presumably on the occasion of Crassus' triumph (13 August 29 BCE), he was treated as his friend and ally because of his service.

Segimerus (Segimer, Sigimer) (late first century BCE–early first century CE). Segimerus (or Segimer, or Sigimer) was a noble of the Cherusci, a Germanic nation living between the Weser and Ems Rivers, which Iulius Caesar associated with 'outrages and raids' (Caes., *Bell. Gall.* 6.10). As a young warrior, Segimerus may have been in the war band made up of alliance members raiding across the Rhine into Roman-held Belgica in 17 BCE (Flor., 2.30.24), and/or he might have fought at the ambush of Nero Claudius Drusus at Arbalo in 11 BCE (Pliny, *Nat. Hist.* 11.18). Probably, at the time of Tiberius' expeditions in 8 and 7 BCE

(Dio 55.8.3), the Cherusci made a treaty with the Romans. In keeping with established practice between allies (Strabo, *Geog.* 7.1.4), he handed over his sons, Arminius (Vell. Pat. 2.118.2) and Flavus, to the Romans as a hostages; his other son, Sesithacus (Strabo, *Geog.* 7.1.4), may not have been born or old enough at the time. The boys were educated in Rome and raised as members of the *Ordo Equester* (Vell. Pat. 2.118.2). Segimerus likely remained in Germania, while men of the Cherusci served with the Roman army 'on private campaigns' under Arminius (Vell. Pat. 2.118.2) and Flavus (Tac., *Ann.* 2.9), perhaps seeing action in Illyricum (6–9 CE. For reasons that are still not well understood, Arminius convinced his father to join him in a plot to oust the army of occupation in Germania, exploiting the trust they had earned with Quinctilius Varus (Dio 56.19.2), and to lead him and his troops to destruction at *saltus Teutoburgiensis* in the summer of 9 CE. The conspirators invested time in building trust with Varus. It worked. When informed by Segestes (Vell. Pat. 2.118.4) that his brother-in-law Segimerus was involved in a plot, Varus did not believe him (Dio 55.8.3). Segimerus had a brother, Inguiomerus, whose 'influence with the Romans was longstanding' (Tac., *Ann.* 1.60.1).

Sitas (late first century BCE–early first century CE). Sitas was king of the Dentheleti nation in Thracia. The blind regent was an ally of the Romans, who were obliged to assist him when he was attacked by the Bastarnae in 30 BCE (Dio 51.23.4).

Order of Battle:
The Army of Augustus

The nationalized army of Augustus comprised legions, auxiliary units, volunteer corps and several fleets, as well as personal bodyguards, an urban paramilitary police force and firefighters, altogether representing 225,000–300,000 men.

1. Personal Bodyguard (*Germani Corporis Custodes*)

There were several attempts to assassinate Augustus during his lifetime. To foil them, Augustus employed investigators (*speculatores*). He appreciated their service: 'Augustus himself writes that he once entertained a man at whose villa he used to stop, who had been his *speculator*' (Suet., *Div. Aug.* 74).

He also employed armed guards. Hired non-Roman troops were highly valued as bodyguards by affluent individuals during the late first century BCE. The Statilii family had as many as 130 Germans in their employ (*ILS* 7448 f.). Iulius Caesar had a unit of 900 Gallic cavalry (Caes., *Bell. Civ.* 1.41), as well as Germanic (perhaps Suebic) cavalry (Caes., *Bell. Gall.* 7.13.1, 67.5, 70.2–7, 80.6) while on campaign. Augustus kept a personal armed troop of foreign mercenaries (e.g. Pliny the Elder, *Nat. Hist.* 7.46, Dio 54.3.4). Initially he employed a unit recruited from the Calagurritani of Hispania Taraconnensis until the time M. Antonius was overthrown (Suet., *Div. Iul.* 86.1, *Div. Aug.* 49.1; *cf.* Appian, *Bell. Civ.* 2.109). It was then replaced by the *Germani Corporis Custodes*. Comprised of Germanic horsemen, they were recruited among the Batavi (Dio 55.24.7) – considered the finest horsemen of their day – and the Ubii. Augustus retained the *Custodes* until the defeat of Varus (Suet. *Div. Aug.* 49.1), temporarily removing them from Rome until the emergency ended (Dio 56.23.4). They returned to service in 14 CE (Tac., *Ann.* 1.24.2, *cf.* Suet., *Galba* 12.2). They were later reconstituted as an élite unit of imperial household cavalry, known as *Equites Singulares Augusti*.

For a discussion, see Speidel (1994).

2. Praetorian Guard (*Cohortes Praetoriae*)

From the earliest times, a unit of élite troops accompanied the *praetor* or commander of the Roman army on campaign (Sallust, *Cat.* 60; Cic., *Cat.* 11; Caes. *Bell. Gall.* 1.40; Livy, 2.20; Appian, *Bell. Civ.* 3.67, 5.3). In 49 BCE, Iulius Caesar had a *cohors praetoria caetratorum*, a bodyguard of Spanish shield-men (Caes., *Bell. Civ.* 1.75) in his service. After Actium (31 BCE), Caesar's heir had five *Cohortes Praetoriae*, which he had recruited from *evocati*, legionaries recalled to the standards (Orosius 6.19.8; App., *Bell. Civ.* 3.66, 69), who marched under a single ensign (App., *Bell Civ.* 3.40). He combined them with M. Antonius' three Praetorian Cohorts (App., *Bell. Civ.* 3.45, 3.67), increasing the total number to nine – numbered I through to VIIII – by the close of his principate, and established them as a separate force (Tac., *Ann.* 4.5.3). Augustus allowed no more than three (each of perhaps up to 1,000 men) to be billeted in Rome at any one time (Suet., *Div. Aug.* 49; *cf. Tib.* 37). They were scattered throughout the city (Tac., *Ann.* 4.2.1), the rest being located around Italy (Suet. *Div. Aug.* 49; Paullus *Dig.* 1.15.3 pr) – perhaps at Aquileia, Ariminum, Brundisium, Ravenna and Ticinum, where Augustus was a regular visitor – eventually becoming a force 10,000-strong (Dio 55.24.6). *Praetoriani* were recruited from men of Etruria, Latium, Umbria and the old Italian *coloniae* (Tac., *Ann.* 4.5). Each cohort had its own *tribunus*, but in 2 BCE they were brought under the overall command of two senior equestrian *praefecti praetorio*, known by name as Q. Ostorius Scapula and P. Salvius Aper (Dio 55.10.10); they were succeeded sometime in or before 14 CE by P. Valerius Ligur (Dio 60.23.2) alone or jointly with L. Seius Strabo.

The primary function of the Praetorian Cohorts was to provide the *princeps* with a guard detail while in the city – Augustus personally gave the daily watch-word to the contingent on duty at his home on the Palatinus (Tac., *Ann.* 1.7.5) – and when he was on campaign. They also accompanied him on trips, which he often did in a litter by night or by sea (Suet., *Div. Aug.* 53.2, 82.1), as well as members of his family on missions when two cohorts were usually despatched (Tac., *Ann.* 1.24.2 and 2.20). They may also have been assigned to other duties *ad hoc*. There is evidence that *Praetoriani* of *Cohors* VI were despatched to fight a fire at Ostia – perhaps to supplement the beleaguered civilians in the port city – since one soldier is recorded as having perished in the attempt and was buried with a public funeral in the Augustan period (*CIL* XIV, 4494 = *ILS* 9494 = *EJ* 252). In addition to infantry there was Praetorian cavalry, which rode with the *militia equestris* at a *decursio* during Augustus' funeral in 14 CE (Dio 56.42.2; Tac., *Ann.* 1.24.2).

Keen to secure the loyalty of the men, Augustus' first act of 28 BCE was to raise their pay to double that of regular legionaries 'so that he might be strictly guarded' (Dio 53.11.5). A guardsman received 2 *denarii* per day, or HS3,000 annually (Tac., *Ann.* 1.17). His term of service was originally sixteen years, then reduced to twelve in 14 BCE (Dio 54.25.6), but raised to sixteen again under Augustus' military reforms in 5 CE (Dio 55.23.1). Upon honourable discharge, each retiree received a cash bonus (*praemia*) of HS20,000 (or nearly seven years' pay) – HS8,000 more than regular legionaries (Dio 55.23.1; Tac., *Ann.* 1.17). The men of the Praetorian Cohorts each received HS1,000 from the estate of the deceased *princeps* – more than three times that paid to regular legionaries (Suet., *Div. Aug.* 101.2). Forty *Praetoriani* had the honour of carrying the body of Augustus to lay it in state (Suet., *Div. Aug.* 99.2).

For detailed discussions, see Allen (1908), Bingham (1997), Daugherty (1992), Durry (1938) and Rankov (1994).

3. Citizen Army (*Legiones*)

After the Civil War (31–30 BCE), some fifty to sixty legions of varying strengths were in existence. Three years later, Augustus had dissolved almost half of the legions and demobbed around 120,000 men (*RG*, 15; Dio 55.23.7). Before the Varian Disaster (9 CE), there were twenty-eight legions, after it twenty-five, each nominally 6,200 men strong (Festus 453 L), though in practice likely fewer – perhaps 5,280 soldiers per legion – so the available army at full strength including officers was between 140,000 and 174,000 men.

Every legion had an index number to identify it, though as a result of the rationalization and consolidation of units some numbers appeared twice. Many legions had a title (*agnomen*), awarded either for victory in battle denoting where it was won (e.g. XI *Actiaca*, VIIII *Hispana*), or indicating its origin (e.g. X *Gemina*, 'twin' from merging two legions into one: Caes., *Bell. Civ.* 3.4.), or recognizing an honour personally awarded by Augustus (e.g. II *Augusta*, 'Second Augustus' Own': Dio 54.11.5).

Commanding the legion (from *legere*, meaning 'to choose') was the *legatus legionis*, a man appointed by Augustus from the patrician class, *nobiles* or *novi homines* (e.g. P. Quinctilius Varus of *Legio* XIX in 15 BCE; Sex. Vistilius: Tac., *Ann.* 6.9; Numonius Vala in 9 CE: Vell. Pat. 2.119.4). He was usually an ex-praetor, but he could be an ex-quaestor, ex-aedile or ex-plebeian tribune. A man in his forties, he would typically serve for one to three years. A unit (*ala*) of 120 mounted legionaries (*equites legionis*) provided an escort for the *legatus* as well as a messenger service for him and his staff.

Assisting the legate was a military tribune (*tribunus militum*) 'with the broad stripe' (*tribunus laticlavius*) and five junior tribunes with 'narrow stripe' (*tribuni angusticlavi*), who were appointed from the *ordo equester*. Iulius Caesar was generally disappointed by the quality of these officers (Caes., *Bell. Gall.* 1.39); Augustus tried to improve their calibre and, like Caesar, hand-picked them before deployment (Dio 53.15.2). Typically men in their late teens, they served a term of one year: at age 17, Tiberius was a *tribunus militum* in Hispania Citerior in 25 BCE (Suet., *Tib.* 9.1), and similarly Velleius Paterculus (Vell. Pat. 2.104.3). The detachments (*vexillarii* or *vexillationes*) of *Legiones* I, V, XX and XXI involved in the punitive raid into Germania in 14 CE were led by a military tribune named Novellius Torquatus Atticus (*CIL* XIV, 3602 (Tibur) = *ILS* 950).

Third in the command structure was the camp prefect (*praefectus castrorum*), a new career position introduced under Augustus, one based on the *praefactus fabrum* of earlier times. He was responsible for provisioning the legion, managing the camp's facilities and their security, as well as soldiers' training and the artillery (e.g. Hostilius Rufus: Obsequens 72; L. Eggius: Vell. Pat, 2.119.4; L. Caecidius: Vell. Pat. 2.120.3). He was recruited from the *Ordo Equester*.

An *aquilifer* (e.g. Arrius: Crinagoras, *Pal. Ant.* 7.741.) carried the most important ensign of the legion – the eagle (*aquila*) clutching lightning bolts in its talons, the symbol of Jupiter – on a pole. To lose it was a shameful act (*infamia*), and for this reason the *Clades Lolliana* of 17 BCE and *Clades Variana* of 9 CE caused Augustus great embarrassment (Suet., *Div. Aug.* 23.1).

The basic tactical unit of the legion was the cohort (*cohors*); ten *cohortes* (numbered I through to X), representing some 480 men each, formed a legion, the first being of double size (960) – thus the legion at full strength would field 5,280 soldiers. A cohort comprised six centuries (*centuriae*) of up to 80 men under the command of a *centurio* (e.g. M. Caelius, *Legio* XIX: *CIL* XIII, 8648; Canidius: Florus 2.26). The century consisted of ten *contubernia* of eight men messing together.

A centurion could be appointed from the *Ordo Equester* or promoted from the ranks of the ordinary men after having proved his leadership skills and courage. Aufidienus Rufus began his career as an ordinary soldier, serving in that capacity for several years, followed by promotion to centurion, culminating in his appointment as *praefectus castrorum* of one of the Danube legions, where he is recorded in 14 CE (Tac., *Ann*.1.20). The *centurio* was distinguished from the rank and file by the transverse crest on his helmet. He carried a vine staff (*vitis*), which he used for casual corporal punishment, such as used by Lucilius – targeted by the mutineers of AD 14 – 'to whom, with soldiers' humour, they had given the name "Bring Another" [*cedo alteram*], because when he had broken one vine-stick on a man's back, he would call in a loud voice for another and another' (Tac., *Ann*. 1.23). The mental toughness of centurions is frequently described in the ancient sources (e.g. Maevius' defiance before M. Antonius in 30 BCE, Val. Max. 3.8.8).

Assisting the centurion was his personally appointed deputy (*optio*) and a man (*tesserarius*) designated for issuing the writing tablets containing the watchword; a standard bearer (*signifer*, e.g. Q. Coelius Actiacus of *Legio* XI: *CIL* V, 2503 (Ateste)) and a horn player (*cornicen*), who together relayed orders on the battle-field. The centurion of the First Cohort was the *Primuspilus* and, by rank, the most senior centurion of the entire legion. The career of M. Vergilius Gallus Lusius included a stint as *primuspilus* with *Legio* XI before a promotion to *Praefectus Cohortis* with *Cohors* I *Ubiorum peditum et equitum* (*CIL* X, 4862 (Ven-afrum)) = *ILS* 2690). In general, the men advancing beyond the rank of *primuspilus* were officers who *began* their career as centurions, and in exceptional cases were soldiers of the Praetorian Cohorts who had been promoted to the centurionate.

A free-born, healthy man of minimum age of 16 or 17 was eligible to enlist as a legionary soldier (*miles gregarius*), nicknamed a *caligatus*. The names of many survive, and occasionally details of their careers: e.g. M. Billienus Actiacus of *Legio* XI who fought at Actium (*ILS* 2443); L. Plinius of *Legio* XX (*ILS* 2270); Caelius Caldus (Vell. Pat. 2.120.6); M. Aius, serving in the *centuria* of Fabricius (Kalkriese); and T. Vibus, *centuria* of Tadius (Kalkriese). In Augustus' time, most came from the *coloniae* and *municipia* of Italia and Gallia Cisalpinia. Increasingly, the ranks of *caligati* were supplemented by provincial recruits from Narbonensis, the *Tres Galliae* and the Hispaniae. A legionary was contracted to serve for sixteen years (Tac. *Ann*. 1.19), but the term of service was raised to twenty years after 5 CE (Dio 55.23.1, 57.6.5). Training was intense, physical and comprehensive. A team of specialists covered drill, formation fighting, swordsmanship, archery, horse riding, swimming, route marches, camp building and leaping over ditches in full kit (Veg., 1.9–28). He was expected to march 20 miles in five hours on a day in summer at normal 'military step' (*militaris gradus*), but in wartime a forced march (*magna itinera*) at the swifter 'full step' (*plenus gradus*) could increase this to 24 miles (Veg. 1.9).

A legionary was equipped with a full array of protective kit (*armatura*). Archaeological finds attest to there being a continuous process of innovation in design of equipment during the Augustan period, perhaps driven by the exigencies of local warfare. A large oval shield (*scutum*), made from thin sheets of wood laminated into a kind of plywood, curved to protect the body and held by a central hand grip (*umbo*), evolved into a wider, squarer shape. On the march, the shield was usually protected by a cover of stitched leather or goatskin. The head protection (*casis*, *galea*) featured an integral neck guard and articulated cheek plates (*bucculae*) tied at the chin. Its design changed from the conical – so-called Montefortino – helmet made of bronze in widespread use in 31 BCE; to the 'jockey-cap' style – or Coolus – helmet with a separate eye/brow guard to deflect blows to the face, and a wider neck guard; and finally into the so-called Weisenau (or 'Imperial Gallic A' type according to Robinson's (1975) classification), made of iron with detailing at the front and back to strengthen the dome. Body armour of a shirt of riveted links (*lorica hamata*) or scales (*lorica squamata*) may have been worn over an arming doublet of linen or leather with a decorative fringe (*pteryges*) to allow for greater movement. From c. 15 BCE, a new form of articulated, segmented plate armour (the so-called *lorica segmentata*) was introduced; finds from Dangstettten and Kalkriese show conclusively it was worn by some troops in the Alpine and German Wars. A heavy leather belt, with a sporran (*cingulum*) covered with bronze discs or plates to protect the genitals, completed the panoply.

His weaponry consisted of two javelins (*pila*), each made with an iron shank attached with a pin to a wooden shaft designed to break on impact so that it could not be thrown back (Plut., *Mar.* 25.1–2; Caes., *Bell. Gall.* 1.25); a short, double-edged sword tapering to a sharp point (*gladius*) for cutting and thrusting; and a short dagger (*pugio*) as a sidearm of last resort. Finds from Haltern, Hedemünden, Kalkriese, Mainz, Mannheim, Nauportus, Nijmegen and Oberaden reveal variations in design in the same type of equipment. Soldiers often paid to have their kit – belts, daggers and scabbards in particular – decorated with engravings and coloured inlays to very high standards of workmanship to make them unique, personal pieces. Thus there was little uniformity in the appearance of troops in combat gear, even in an individual *centuria*.

Additionally, soldiers carried an entrenching tool (*dolabra*) – combining a pick on one side and a spade on the other – for digging ditches, a saw, a pan (*trulla*), a length of chain and rope, personal clothing in a bag, all carried on a pole over the left shoulder, and two palisade stakes (*sudes*) over the right. At the end of a day's route march, legionaries dug a temporary camp with a ditch and earthen bank (e.g. Dio 56.21.1); those not on watch duty slept in their *contubernia* in tents (*sub pellibus* or *sub tentoriis*) made of goatskin which, when collapsed and packed, were usually transported by a mule or on a wagon; because of its appearance, and the fact it emerged from a rolled-up form, a tent was nicknamed a *papilio*, 'butterfly'. A semi-permanent summer camp (*castra aestiva*) could be erected for campaigning in theatre, such as at Minden. The army might return to a permanent winter base (*castra hiberna*) with barracks constructed of wood, like Haltern, at the end of the season. At this time, the fort or fortress might be shared – such as at Carnuntum, Nijmegen-Hunerberg and Oberaden, which each likely housed two legions plus auxiliary troops. Great attention was paid to the position and design of defensive fortifications and stockades (e.g. Caes., *Bell. Civ.* 3.63, 3.66), the erection of which was overseen by the *praefectus castrorum*.

A legionary could not marry while in service, and if he was already married the act of enlistment was an automatic form of divorce. Centurions and higher-ranking officers were, however, permitted wives, though their presence in camp was frowned upon except during winter (Suet., *Div. Aug.* 24.1). All ranks could have slaves or freedmen to assist with handling baggage (*impedimenta*), minding pack animals, attending to general chores and, on occasions, fighting (Dio 56.20.2, *cf.* 78.26.5–6; Tac. *Ann.* 1.23). An inscribed lead disc with a hole in the centre – which may have been a luggage tag – found at Dangstetten reveals that when Quinctilius Varus was legate of *Legio* XIX there was a *lumentarius* (a slave for handling baggage) assigned to the First Cohort named Privatus. On the tombstone of *centurio* M. Caelius, on either side of his image, are the heads of his *liberti* Privatus and Thiaminus.

On the battlefield, the legion typically deployed in cohorts, formed up in blocks with space in between, arrayed as two (*duplex acies*) or three rows (*triplex duplex*) (e.g. Caes., *Bell. Civ.* 1.83), with cavalry placed on the flanks. To break the enemy line or receive a massed oncoming opponent, the front line would launch volleys of *pila*, then assume a wedge formation (*cuneus*) and charge with swords drawn (e.g. Caes., *Bell. Gall.* 6.40). After engagement, the lines could be rotated, so that fresh troops would move forward to replace tired ones retiring to the rear. If surrounded, the unit could form a defensive square (*quadratus*) or the so-called 'tortoise' (*testudo*).

Honours were awarded for conspicuous acts of valour (Suet., *Div. Aug.* 25.3). The centurion *primipilus* Gallus Lusius cited above received *dona militaria* of two spears (*hastae*) without iron heads and a golden crown (*corona aurea*) in person from Augustus and Tiberius (*CIL* X, 4862 (Venafrum) = *ILS* 2690). The *corona muralis* was awarded to the first man to scale a wall, the *corona vallaris* for a rampart; both were crowns worn on the head and decorated to simulate the exterior of a defensive fortification. Augustus was himself awarded the *corona civica* – a wreath of leafy oak twigs for saving the lives of Roman citizens – by the Senate and permitted to display outside his home, the *Palatium* (Dio 53.16.4; Suet., *Calig.* 19). L. Antonius Quadratus (*CIL* V, 4365) was decorated twice by Ti. Caesar; during his career with *Legio* XX he garnered bangles (*armillae*), as well as collars (*torques*) modelled after those worn around the neck by Iron Age 'Celtic' warriors, and medals (*phalerae*), which he proudly wore mounted on a leather harness upon his torso.

At this time, a legionary received 10 *asses* per day (Tac., *Ann.* 1.17) – a cup of cheap wine at a bar cost 1 *as*, a fine quality Falernian 4 *asses*, a loaf of bread 2 *asses* (*CIL* IV, 1679, graffito at the Bar of Hedone or Colepius, Pompeii) – or HS900 annually paid in three lump sums; but there were deductions for the cost of food, clothing and armour, and a contribution to a compulsory savings scheme, leaving the legionary around half his pay to spend in hard cash.

A retiring soldier, or *veteranus*, received a *praemia* of HS12,000 (or just over thirteen years' pay) upon discharge – a full HS8,000 less than the soldier in the Praetorian Cohorts (Dio 55.23.1). *Veterani* could move to one of the many *coloniae* founded by Augustus (e.g. twenty-eight alone in Italy: *RG* 28), as C. Valerius Arsaces of *Legio* V *Alaudae* did (*CIL* IX,1460). Antonius Quadratus mentioned above settled as a *veteranus* at Brixia (Brescia).

With an honourable discharge (*honesta missio*), a man could still be recalled by Augustus to the eagles as a reservist (*evocatus*, meaning 'invited') for up to five years:

> Augustus began to make a practice of employing from the time when he called again into service against Antonius the troops who had served with his father, and he maintained them afterwards; they constitute even now a special corps, and carry rods, like the centurions (Dio 55.24.8).

Evocati ranked above the serving legionaries, but were excused ordinary fatigue duties and allowed to ride horses on the march (Caes., *Bell Gall.* 7.65). During the *Bellum Batonianum*, a large *vexillarius* of veterans located near Sirmium was wiped out by the Breuci (Vell. Pat., 2.110. 6, *cf.* Dio 55.32.3–4).

Upon the death of Augustus, the men of the legions each received HS300 from the estate of the deceased *princeps* (Suet., *Div. Aug.* 101.2). The mutinies of the legions on the Danube and Rhine rivers in the weeks immediately following the death of Augustus in September 14 CE (Tac., *Ann.* 1.31–49; Dio 57.3.1–6.5), however, suggest that the retirement process was flawed and open to abuse: afterwards, the disgruntled *veterani* who had fomented mutiny were redeployed to Raetia on the pretence that the Suebi were planning a raid (Tac., *Ann.* 1.44).

For detailed – and sometimes contentious – discussions of the evidence for the organization and deployments of legions under Augustus, see Allen (1908); Gilliver (2007); Goldsworthy (1996); Hardy (1887, 1889 and 1920); Keppie (1984 and 1996); Le Bohec (1994); Parker (1928), pp. 72–92; Speidel (1982 and 1992a); Syme (1933); Swan (2004), pp. 158–68; and Tarn (1932). For Augustan/early Imperial legionary arms and armour, see Bishop (2002); Bishop and Coulston (2006), pp. 73–127; D'Amato and Sumner (2009), pp. 63–190; Robinson (1975); and Strassmeir and Gagelman (2011 and 2012). For military bases and fortresses, see Bishop (2012) and von Schnurbein (2000). For military awards, see Maxfield (1981).

The legions known to be in operation under Augustus were:

I *Germanica* (formerly *Augusta*?). Likely raised by Iulius Caesar in 48 BCE to fight in his war against rival *triumvir* Cn. Pompeius Magnus, *Legio* I is first recorded in action at Dyrrhachium (Durrës) on 10 July of that year (Caes., *Bell. Civ* 1.27). After the assassination, his heir took command of it, fielding it in his campaign against Sex. Pompeius (App., *Bell. Civ.* 5.112). It also saw action in the protracted Cantabrian and Asturian War of 29–19 BCE (Dio 53.25.5–8), where it may be the legion recorded as having its *agnomen Augustus* stripped for indiscipline by M. Agrippa (Dio 54.11.5). Some modern historians interpret this act to mean the legion ceased to be a *iusta legio* and was disbanded, while others dispute this. In the ensuing drawdown it – or a reconstituted *Legio* I – may have moved to Aquitania or Celtica, and then served with Tiberius. It received its *signa* from Tiberius (Tac. *Ann.* 1.42), perhaps on the occasion of the Alpine War (15 BCE) against the Vindelici. It was then transferred to Gallia Belgica – perhaps stationed at Batavodurum (Nijmegen) in the country of the Batavi nation if a single graffito is authentic – and fought in the German War (12–9 BCE) under Nero Claudius Drusus Germanicus; it may have earned the *agnomen Germanica* there (*AE* 1976, 515; *CIL* XII, 2234; Tac. *Ann.* 1.42). His brother Tiberius included *Legio* I in the mobilization for the Marcomannic War against Marboduus (6 CE), where it was to march along the Main and Elbe, but after news of the Great Illyrian Revolt arrived, the advance was abandoned and the unit returned to its base on the Rhine. After the Varian Disaster (9 CE), it was based at a winter camp shared with *Legio* XX in the vicinity of Ara Ubiorum (Cologne), whose *Legatus Legionis* C. Caetronius in 14 CE reported to *Legatus Augusti Pro Praetore* A. Caecina Severus of the new military district of Germania Inferior (Tac. *Ann.* 1.37.3, 1.44), which had been created in the wake of the *clades Variana*.

II *Augusta*. Possibly founded as the *Legio* II *Sabina* by consul Vibius Pansa from recruits in Italy in 43 BCE (App., *Bell. Civ.* 3.65), it fought at Philippi (October 42) on the side of the conspirators. It was acquired by the victors of the battle and went to see action under the heir of Iulius Caesar's heir at Perusia (41 BCE) against L. Antonius. It may have subsequently transferred to Gallia Belgica (where it likely received the title *Gallica*) and its veterans settled at Arausio (Orange). The legion relocated to Hispania Citerior, where it took part in the Cantabrian and Asturian War (29–19 BCE). The veterans of that campaign helped construct *Colonia* Iulia Gemella Acci in Hispania Tarraconnensis, though its own veterans settled in Barcino (Barcelona) and Cartenna (Mostaganem) – also called *Colonia* Augusta Legio Secunda (Pliny the Elder, *Nat. Hist.* 5.20) – in Mauretania. After the Varian Disaster, it transferred to Mogontiacum (Mainz) in Germania Superior, perhaps in 10 CE (*CIL* XIII, 7234). For a detailed discussion, see Keppie (2002).

III *Augusta*. Though it is not documented before 5 CE, *Legio* III was likely founded by Vibius Pansa in 43 BCE and fought for the conspirators at Philippi in October the following year (App., *Bell. Civ.* 5.3). After its defeat, it was co-opted and saw action in the war against Sex. Pompeius. From 30 BCE, it was stationed in Africa, though the location of its winter camp within the province often changed. As the local permanent garrison, it may have participated in the Gaetulician War (6–8 CE) under Cossus Cornelius Lentulus (Dio 28.3–4). An inscription on a milestone (*ILS* 151 = *EJ* 290) confirms it built the road from Tacapes to its winter camp, possibly at Theveste, in 14 CE.

III Cyrenaica. This legion may have been founded by Aemilius Lepidus, who was *triumvir* with jurisdiction of Cyrenaica in 36 BCE, or by M. Antonius, who assumed responsibility that same year. It was variously located at Thebes, Bernike in the Thebaïd and Alexandria from 35 BCE, where it shared a winter camp with *Legio* XXII *Deiotariana* (Strabo, *Geog.* 17.12, writing around 21 BCE, mentions one legion 'is stationed in the city and the others [two] in the country'). It may have been active in the attack on Arabia Felix (Yemen) under equestrian *Praefectus Aegypti* Aelius Gallus (26–25 BCE); and against Nubia under C. Petronius (24 BCE) and the sack of its capital city, Napata (22 BCE). It is attested by an inscription (*EJ* 232, *AE* 1910, 207) at Mons Claudianus (dated to 10 CE). The names of thirty-six legionaries – nine born in Galatia, six in Ancyra, four in Alexandria, and one each in Cyrene, Cyprus and Syria, and one (perhaps from Vercellae) in Italy – recorded as serving with *Legio* III are found on an inscription at Koptos (Qift in Egypt, *CIL* III, 6627), dated to Augustus', or latest Tiberius', principate. For a detailed discussion, see Sanders (1941).

III Gallica. Iulius Caesar may have raised this legion from veterans in Gallia Comata who had missed Pharsalus on account of sickness (Caes., *Bell. Alex.* 44.4) and others of the old *Legio* XV returning to Italy. A *Legio* III is recorded as having fought at Munda on 17 March 45 BCE (Caes., *Bell. Hisp.* 30). M. Antonius took this legion to Parthia in 36 BCE (Tac., *Hist.* 3.24.2). It may have been part of the army accompanying Augustus and Tiberius to Armenia and Parthia in 20 BCE before settling in Syria. In the year Herodes died (4 BCE), under the provincial legate P. Quinctilius Varus, the legion was likely one of the three involved in quelling rebellions of the Jewish messianic claimants Iudas, Simon and Athronges (Joseph., *Ant. Iud.* 17.10.9). An inscription in Cyprus confirms its *agnomen* as *Gallica* (*CIL* III, 217).

IIII Macedonica. *Legio* IIII was likely originally raised by Iulius Caesar in 48 BCE to fight in his war against Pompeius Magnus and may have been in action (Caes., *Bell. Civ.* 3.29.) at Dyrrhachium (Durrës) in the spring of that year. Based in Macedonia, it was to be part of the army group assembling for a major campaign against Parthia, but the operation was cancelled when the dictator was murdered. Transferred to Italy by M. Antonius, the men of the legion switched their allegiance with another legion called *Martia* to the heir of Iulius Caesar (App., *Bell. Civ.* 3.45; Cic., *Phil.* 14.27). It fought at Mutina (Modena) in April 43 BCE, where it was defeated by a *Legio* V and *Martia* was destroyed (Cic., *Ad Fam.* 10.33.4). It saw action at Philippi, and on returning to Italy fought against L. Antonius at Perusia (Perugia), evidence for which are sling bullets (*glandes*) found at the town. It fought at Actium (31 BCE) and veterans were settled at Firmum Picenum (Fermo), attested by an inscription (Dessau 2340). Two years later it was in Hispania Tarraconnensis (Dessau 2454) as part of the grand army fighting in the Cantabrian and Asturian War (29–19 BCE). Its winter camp from 20–15 BCE was Palencia (Herrera de Pisuerga) and its veterans may have settled at Cuartango. It remained in the Iberian Peninsula for the duration of Augustus' principate (e.g. *RPC* 1.319, 1.325). The tombstone of M. Percennius from

Philippi, '*miles*' of '*Legio* IV' – possibly related to one of the known ringleaders of the 14 CE mutiny – was found at Tilurium (Gardun near Trilj, Croatia; *CIL* III, 14933).

IIII *Scythica*. Formed after 42 BCE by M. Antonius, the legion may have taken part in the failed Parthian War (39–36 BCE). It was in Macedonia and Moesia and may have earned its *agnomen* under the command of M. Licinius Crassus, grandson of the infamous *triumvir* (Dio 51.23.2–27.3) in the Balkans (29–27 BCE). It saw action in the war to quell the Great Illyrian Revolt (6–9 CE) under A. Caecina Severus' leadership (Dio 55.32.3–4n., cf. 29.3n, 30.3–4n). It was likely based at Viminacium (Stari Kostolac in eastern Serbia) on the Danube River.

V *Alaudae*. Recruited from local non-citizens by Iulius Caesar in Gallia Transalpina in 52 BCE (Caes., *Bell. Gall.* 5.24), paid for by the commander out of his own funds, it became a *iusta legio* sometime between 51 and 47 BCE, and its soldiers were later enfranchised (Suet. *Caes.* 24.2). (The *agnomen* referred to the pointed helmet or the crest the Gallic warriors wore on their helmets, resembling the tuft of the lark, *Alauda cristata* (Pliny, *Nat. Hist.* 11.44).) It may have been at the Siege of Alesia (42 BCE); the legion crossed the Rubicon River with its commander in January 49 BCE and was likely quartered in Apulia (Caes, *Bell. Civ.* 1.14, 1.18). It saw action at Dyrrhachium (48 BCE), Africa (47 BCE; Caes. *Bell. Afr.* 1), Thapsus (46 BCE) – where it stood against charging elephants deployed by Caesar's enemies (Caes. *Bell. Afr.* 81, 84) – and at Munda (17 March 45 BCE; Caes., *Bell. Hisp.* 30). After the dictator's murder, the legion sided with M. Antonius (Cic., *Epist.* 89) and fought for him at Mutina (43 BCE) against Caesar's legal heir. When both men reconciled, the legion went on with seven others to Philippi (42 BCE) to exact revenge on the murderers of its founder (App., *Bell. Civ.* 5.3). It went east with Antonius and may have participated in the failed Parthian War (39–36 BCE; *CIL* IX, 1460 citing the *cognomen* of one of its soldiers as *Arsaces*) and fought on his side at Actium (31 BCE). The victor of the battle removed the legion to join the massed forces battling the Cantabri and Astures (29–19 BCE). Its veterans settled in *colonia* Augusta Emerita (Mérida) in Lusitania (Dio 53.26.1), founded in 25 BCE. In the ensuing drawdown, the legion transferred to Gallia Belgica. In 17 BCE, under its *legatus* M. Lollius, *Legio* V was ambushed by a raiding party of Germans from across the Rhine, who wrenched away its *aquila* – an event which came to be called the *clades Lolliana*, 'Lollian Disaster' (Vell. Pat. 2.97.1; Dio 54.20.4–6). The eagle was subsequently retrieved (Crin., *Anth. Pal.* 7.741). After the subsequent *clades Variana*, the 'Varian Disaster' of 9 CE, it was quartered at Vetera (Xanten) – meaning 'The Old One' – which it shared with *Legio* XXI (Tac. *Ann.* 1.31.3, 1.45.1), and at the time of Augustus' death in 14 CE reported to A. Caecina Severus, the *legatus Augusti pro praetore* of the military district of Germania Inferior.

V *Macedonica*. Likely formed at the time of the Second Triumvirate, the earliest mention of the legion is the foundation of a *colonia* for it at Berytus (Beirut) in Syria by M. Agrippa in 15 or 14 BCE (Strabo, *Geog.* 16.2.19). Its history before that event is obscure. It may have been founded by Iulius Caesar – perhaps as *Legio* V *Gallica*, whose veterans settled in Antiocheia-in-Pisidia (Dessau 2237, 2238), or as V *Urbana*, known from Ateste (modern Este, Dessau 2236). *Legio* V likely fought in the Thracian War (c. 13–11 BCE) under L. Calpurnius Piso, where it may have won its *agnomen Macedonica* (Dessau 2695) and then returned to Galatia. It was transferred to Oescus (Gigen) in Moesia in 6 CE.

VI *Ferrata*. Iulius Caesar created the legion in 52 BCE in Gallia Cisalpina for his Gallic War of 58–50 BCE (Caes., *Bell. Gall.* 8.4). How it earned the *agnomen Ferrata* ('ironclad') is not known. It saw action in the war against Pompeius Magnus, fighting at the battles of Ilerda (summer 49 BCE), Dyrrhachium (early 48 BCE) and Pharsalus (9 August 48 BCE). The legion followed Iulius Caesar to Alexandria (48/47 BCE), turned the odds in his favour at the battle of Zela (2 August 47 BCE) in Pontus and was present at Munda (17 March 45 BCE). Its veterans built *Colonia* Iulia Paterna Arelatensium Sextanorum (Arles) for their retirement in Gallia Narbonensis. Reconstituted by M. Aemilius Lepidus, who gave it to M. Antonius (43 BCE), *Legio* VI took part at the Battle of Philippi in October of the following year as one of his eight veteran legions (App., *Bell. Civ.* 5.3). At the end of the civil war, its veterans were given lands in the *colonia* of Beneventum (Benevento). M. Antonius transferred the legion to Iudaea, where it assisted Herodes in asserting his claim to the throne (37 BCE), and participated in the failed Parthian War (39–36 BCE). It fought on the losing side during the Actian War (31 BCE). The victor sent it back to Syria, where it would remain until the end of the Empire. In 20 BCE, it accompanied Augustus and Tiberius to Armenia. In the year Herodes died (4 BCE), under the provincial legate P. Quinctilius Varus, the legion was involved in quelling rebellions of the Jewish messianic claimants Iudas, Simon and Athronges (Joseph., *Ant. Iud.* 17.10.9). The location of its winter camp is uncertain, but may have been in Galilee (*RE* 12.1591, Tac. *Ann.* 2.79.2), Raphanaea (Rafniye) or Cyrrhus (Khoros). Veterans were later settled at Ptolemais (Acre).

VI *Victrix*. When Iulius Caesar's *Legio* VI swore its allegiance to M. Antonius following its founder's assassination, the dictator's legal heir established his own (41 BCE), perhaps with veterans defecting from the original. The following year it was at the siege of Perusia (40 BCE) fighting for Iulius Caesar's heir, as attested to finds of sling stones (*glandes*, *CIL* XI, 6721, nos. 20–23). In the war against Sex. Pompeius it saw action in Sicily, and in the Actian War it fought against Antonius. The legion was one of the eight taking part in the protracted Cantabrian and Asturian War (29–19 BCE) in the Iberian Peninsula. It remained there for the rest of Augustus' principate. Veterans of the legion were among the first settlers of the *coloniae* at Augusta Emerita (Mérida; Dio 53.26.1), Caesaraugusta (Zaragoza) and Corduba (Cordoba). For a detailed discussion, see Grapin (2003).

VII *Macedonica*. One of the oldest legions of Augustus' army, it is recorded as serving with Iulius Caesar in the Gallic War (58–50 BCE), during which it played an active role (e.g. Plut. *Caes.* 2.23, 2.26, 3.7, 4.32, 5.9, 7.62, 8.8). It also fought for him in the war against Pompeius Magnus, fighting at the battles of Ilerda (summer 49 BCE), Dyrrhachium (early 48 BCE) and Pharsalus (9 August 48 BCE). Veterans settling in Italy were recalled to join in Iulius Caesar's African War (46 BCE), where they fought at Thapsus (Caes. *Bell. Afr.* 81), before retiring the following year to Capua (Dessau 2225) and Lucca. After the dictator's murder, many retirees flocked to Iulius Caesar's heir in the autumn of 44 BCE (Cic., *Phil.* 11.37), forming a reconstituted *Legio* VII under the *agnomen Paterna* (meaning 'ancestral'). It fought at Mutina (Modena, Cic., *Phil.* 1.c) in April 43 BCE, saw action at Philippi and on returning to Italy fought against L. Antonius at Perusia (Perugia) in 41 BCE. In 36 BCE, veterans settled in Gallia Narbonnensis, though serving troops likely took part in the war against Sex. Pompeius. It may have played a role in the Actian War (31 BCE). It may have remained in the Balkans before transferring to the province of Galatia-Pamphylia with its creation in c. 25 BCE. *Legio* VII fought in the Thracian War (c. 13–11 BCE) under L. Calpurnius Piso, where it may have won its *agnomen Macedonica* (Dessau 2695), and then returned to Galatia. From 7 CE, it returned to the Balkans and took part in the Batonian War (Dio 55.32.3–4n) under Tiberius. After 9 CE, Tilurium (Gardun near Trilj) in Dalmatia became its base (cf. *ILS* 2280 = *EJ* 265) – though it possibly shared the fortress at Burnum (Kistanje) with *Legio* XI – for the duration of Augustus' principate. Veterans – at least fifteen are known from tombstones – settled at the old Caesarian *colonia* at Narona (between present day Metković and Vid, Croatia) beside the Neretva River; also at a locality northwest of it known as *vicus Scunasticus* (where two dedication slabs offering prayers to *Divus Augustus* and Tiberius have been found: see *AE* 1950, 44; *AIJ* 113–14 found between Humac and Ljubuški), Rusazu (AE 1921, 16), Tupusuctu (*CIL* VIII, 8837) and Saldae (Béjaïa) in Mauretania (*CIL* VIII, 8931). For a detailed discussion, see Mitchell (1976).

VIII *Augusta or Gallica.* *Legio* VIII was one of the oldest legions of Augustus' army, formed of veterans from Iulius Caesar's old legion (Cic., *Phil.* 11.37; App., *Bell. Civ.* 3.47). Caesar mentions it serving with him in the Gallic War (58–50 BCE) and playing an active role (Caes., *Bell. Gall.* 2.23, 7.47, 8.8). Initially, its honorary title was *Gallica*. It fought for him in the war against Pompeius Magnus (Caes., *BC* 1.18), fighting at the battles of Corfinium (Corfinio) and Brundisium (Brindisi) in 49 BCE, and was based in Apulia. It also saw action at Dyrrhachium (early 48 BCE) and Pharsalus (9 August 48 BCE). Veterans settling in Campania were recalled to join in Iulius Caesar's African War (46 BCE), seeing action at Thapsus (Caes. *Bell. Afr.* 81), before retiring the following year to Casilinum near Capua. Rallying to the heir of Iulius Caesar, retirees followed him to Mutina (Modena) in 43 BCE to stand against M. Antonius, for which it earned the *agnomen Mutinensis* (Dessau 2239), and to Philippi the following year. *Legio* VIII fought at Perusia (Perugia) against L. Antonius, as sling shot from the site attests. Men of the legion likely fought in the Actian War (31 BCE). Veterans settled at Forum Iulii (Fréjus), which was sometimes called by the alternative name *Colonia* Octavorum (*CIL* XII, 38). After 27 BCE, Augustus moved

Legio VIII to Africa. A detachment saw service in the Cantabrian and Asturian War (29–19 BCE) and another in the Balkans, where it may have distinguished itself and garnered the honour *Augusta* ('Augustus' Own'). Veterans settled in the renewed *Colonia* Iulia Augusta Felix Berytus (Beirut) in Phoenicia (*CIL* III, 14165–6, which calls it *Gallica*), and were visited by M. Agrippa in 15 BCE (Strabo, *Geog.* 16.2.19). From Moesia, *Legio* VIII was picked to take part in the Marcomannic Campaign of 6 CE under Tiberius, which was aborted, and was redirected to Illyricum to support the effort to quell the Great Illyrian Revolt (Dio 55.32.3–4n, cf. 55.29.3n, 55.30.3–4n). After 9 CE, the troops were stationed near Poetovio (Ptuj) in the new province of Pannonia. Thereafter, veterans settled in Emona and Scarbantia (Sopron; Pliny, *Nat. Hist.* 3.146).

VIIII *Hispana* or *Hispaniensis*. *Legio* VIIII was one of the oldest legions of Augustus' army, reconstituted by him from the old legion of Iulius Caesar. It is recorded as serving with Caesar in the Gallic War (58–50 BCE), during which it played an active role (Caes., *Bell. Gall.* 2.23, 7.47, 8.8). It also fought for him in the war against Pompeius Magnus, fighting at the battles of Ilerda (summer 49 BCE), Dyrrhachium (early 48 BCE) and Pharsalus (9 August 48 BCE). Veterans settling in Italy were recalled to join in Iulius Caesar's African War (46 BCE), taking part at the Battle of Thapsus (Caes. *Bell. Afr.* 81) before retiring the following year to Picenum and Histria. Men of *Legio* VIIII fought under the command of his legal heir in the war against Sex. Pompeius, for which it may have been called *Triumphalis* (Dessau 2240), and then transferred to Illyricum, where distinguished service may have won it the battle honour *Macedonica* (Dessau 928). It fought in the Actian War (31 BCE) and then relocated to Hispania Tarraconensis to take part in the War of the Cantabri and Astures (29–19 BCE), during which it likely won its distinctive *agnomen Hispana* (or *Hispaniensis*). At the end of the conflict, it may have been drawn down and accompanied M. Agrippa to Gallia Belgica. It may have been part of the force invading Germania under Nero Claudius Drusus in the German War (12–9 BCE) before being re-assigned to Illyricum (*CIL* 5, 911 from Aquileia; *cf.* Dio 55.29.1n, 55.32.3n) or Sirmium on the Danube. From 9 through to 14 CE, the legion was in Pannonia in the city of Siscia (Sisak).

X (*Fretensis*). Needing to bolster his army to wage war against Sex. Pompeius, the heir of Iulius Caesar founded *Legio* X in 41 or 40 BCE. Theodor Mommsen proposed that the legion won its honorary title *Fretensis* ('ironclad') for guarding the Strait of Misenum and taking part in Mylae and Naulochus (both 36 BCE) under M. Agrippa. It was on the winning side at Actium (31 BCE). Some veterans of *Legio* X settled in *Colonia* Veneria (Cremona), while others went to Brixia (Brescia; Dessau 2241, which calls it *Veneria*), Capua and *Colonia* Augusta Aroe Patrensis (Patras). The legion was moved about to several different theatres of operation, including Cyrrhus – where it guarded the route from the Euphrates River to Alexandria near Issus, perhaps being present in Armenia when the Parthians handed over the *aquilae* lost at Carrhae in 53 BCE to Tiberius in 20 BCE – and Macedonia, where an inscription commemorates a bridge constructed by

Legio X *Fretensis* under '*Pro Praetore Legatus*' L. Tarius Rufus in c. 17 BCE (*AE* 1936, 18 (Amphipolis) = *EJ* 268 from Strymon Valley; Dio 54.20.3n). The legion may possibly have been one of the three involved in quelling rebellions of the Jewish messianic claimants Iudas, Simon and Athronges under the provincial legate P. Quinctilius Varus (Joseph., *Ant. Iud.* 17.10.9) in 4 BCE, thereafter remaining at Jerusalem (Joseph., *Ant. Iud.* 17.11.1), though the earliest reference to it being in Syria is 17 CE (Tacitus, *Ann.* 2.57.2), well after Augustus' principate. Some veterans settled in the *colonia of* Ptolemais (Acre).

X *Gemina*. *Legio* X was one of the oldest legions in Augustus' army. It served with Iulius Caesar in the Gallic War (58–50 BCE), during which it played an active role, and he regarded it as his favourite legion (e.g. Caes., *Bell. Gall.* 1.40–42, 2.23, 2.25–26, 7.47, 7.51; Plut. *Caes.* 19.4–5). It also fought for him in the war against *triumvir* Pompeius Magnus, fighting at the battles of Ilerda (summer 49 BCE), Dyrrhachium (early 48 BCE) and Pharsalus (9 August 48 BCE). Veterans settling in Italy were recalled to join in Iulius Caesar's African War, fighting at Thapsus (46 BCE; Caes. *Bell. Afr.* 81) and Munda (17 March 45 BCE; Caes., *Bell. Hisp.* 30, 31) before retiring the following year to Narbo Martius (Narbonne), which was renamed *Colonia* Iulia Paterna Decumanorum ('the ancestral Julian *colonia* of the Tenth') in their honour. In the civil war following the assassination of Iulius Caesar, *triumvir* M. Aemilius Lepidus reconstituted the unit as *Legio* X *Equestris* in 44/43 BCE; it was transferred to M. Antonius and fought at Philippi (October 42 BCE). Antonius took the legion on his unsuccessful campaign to Armenia (36–34 BCE). He then fielded it at Actium (31 BCE), where it surrendered to the victor, but despite settling its veterans at *Colonia* Augusta Aroe Patrensis (Patras), the serving men mutinied and Caesar's heir stripped it of its *agnomen*. Other troops from disbanded units were assigned to the legion and it gained the name *Gemina* ('twin'). It was sent to Petavonium (Rosinos de Vidriales) in Hispania Tarraconnensis to take part in the Cantabrian and Asturian War (29–19 BCE), and its presence in the region is attested by inscriptions (e.g. Dessau 2256, 2644). It remained there for the duration of Augustus' principate. However, for insubordination – specifically 'demanding their discharge in insolent fashion' – Augustus 'disbanded the entire *Legio* X in disgrace without the rewards which would have been due for faithful service' (Suet., *Div. Aug.* 24), though when is not disclosed; and other units, also not disclosed, were similarly punished. Veterans were settled at *coloniae* Augusta Emerita (Mérida; Dio 53.26.1), Caesaraugusta (Zaragoza) and Corduba (Cordoba), as attested by coins (e.g. *RPC* 1.16 and 1.325; *EJ* 342, 343; *ILS* 2707; cf. Dio 53.26.1).

XI *Actiaca* (later *Claudia*). Iulius Caesar founded *Legio* XI in 58 BCE in readiness for his Gallic War (58–50 BCE), in which it played an active role (Caes., *Bell. Gall.* 2.23, 8.6, 8.8, 8.24). In January 49 BCE, the legion crossed the Rubicon River with its commander and was billetted in Apulia. It saw action at Dyrrhachium (48 BCE), Pharsalus (9 August 48 BCE) and Munda (17 March 45 BCE), after which it was disbanded and veterans settled at Bovianum (Boiano). Caesar's heir resurrected the unit and it fought at Philippi (October 42 BCE), and it was in action quelling a rebellion at Perusia (Perugia) that year (*CIL* XI, 6721, 25–27). It may have taken part in the war against Sex. Pompeius (37–36 BCE) in Sicily. It fought on the winning side at Actium (31 BCE), gaining the legion the *agnomen Actiaca* (Dessau 2243, 2336) as well as some of its troops – like M. Billiacus, whose tombstone was found at Vicenza (*ILS* 2243 = *EJ* 254). While it was stationed at Poetovio (Ptuj), on the eve of the Great Illyrian Revolt (6–9 CE) it arrived to assist Tiberius with *legiones* IIII *Scythica* and VIII *Augusta* under the command of A. Caecina Severus (Dio 55.32.3–4n; cf. 55.29.3n, 55.30.3–4n). After the war, it remained in the region in the new province of Dalmatia, based at the winter camp at Burnum (Kistanje), which it shared with *Legio* VII. Detachments likely operated across the province, such as at its capital Salonae (Split) and at Gardun, and engaged in road construction. For a discussion of the title *Actiaca*, see Keppie (1971).

XII *Fulminata*. Iulius Caesar founded *Legio* XII (Dessau 2242, *CIL* XI, 6721, 20–30) in 58 BCE in readiness for his Gallic War (58–50 BCE), in which it took an active part (e.g. Caes., *Bell. Gall.* 2.23, 2.25, 3.1, 7.62, 8.24; Plut., *Caes.* 20.7). It was one of the legions which crossed the Rubicon River with its commander in January 49 BCE (Caes., *Bell. Civ.* 1.15) and fought in the Civil War (e.g. Scaeva, the legion's eighth-ranking *centurio*, was rewarded for gallantry with promotion to *primus pilus*, as cited in Caes, *Bell. Civ.* 3.53.5) and at Pharsalus (9 August 48 BCE). It was disbanded and its veterans granted land in Parma (45 BCE). Following the assassination of Iulius Caesar, *triumvir* M. Aemilius Lepidus reconstituted the unit in 44/43 BCE, and gave it to M. Antonius. It may have fought with Antonius against Caesar's heir at Mutina (Modena) in 42 BCE. It may have been at Philippi (October 42 BCE) and is known from inscriptions on sling bullets (*glandes*) to have been at Perusia (Perugia). It relocated to Syria and took part in Antonius' failed Parthian War (39–36 BCE), and, remaining loyal to him (coin Dessau 2241, 1), later fought on his side at Actium (31 BCE). Together with *Legio* X *Gemina*, many veterans were settled by Agrippa at *Colonia* Augusta Aroe Patrensis (Patras, *CIL* III, 7261 and X, 7371, which uses the *agnomen Fulminata*) in 16–14 BCE, and Venusia (Venosa, *CIL* IX, 435). The active men of XII *Fulminata* were deployed to occupy Aegyptus – probably based at Babylon (Cairo) – perhaps moving to Africa as late as 6 CE, but returned to Syria (*CIL* III, 6097). In 20 BCE, the legion may have accompanied Augustus and Tiberius to Armenia. In the year Herodes died (4 BCE), under the provincial legate P. Quinctilius Varus, the legion was likely involved in quelling rebellions of the Jewish messianic claimants Iudas, Simon and Athronges. How and where it earned its *agnomen* – *fulminata* means 'lightning strike' – is unknown. In 14 CE, it was quartered in Syria at Melitene (Malatya) or Raphanaea (Rafniye).

XIII *Gemina*. *Legio* XIII was established in 57 BCE by Iulius Caesar from men in Gallia Cisalpina, and saw action (Caes. *Bell. Gall.* 2.2, 5.53, 6.1, 7.51, 8.2, 8.11, 8.54) during the Gallic War (58–50 BCE). It crossed the Rubicon River with its commander in January 49 BCE (Caes., *Bell. Civ.* 1.7, 1.12) and was stationed at Apulia while events unfolded. It saw action at Dyrrhachium (48 BCE) and

Pharsalus (9 August 48 BCE), after which it was disbanded (autumn 48 BCE). Veterans settling in Italy were recalled to join in Iulius Caesar's African War (46 BCE) and probably fought with him at Munda (17 March 45 BCE). The legion was then disbanded and its veterans found homes at Hispellum (Spello). Caesar's heir resurrected the unit to take part in the war against Sex. Pompeius (37–36 BCE) in Sicily (App. *BC* 5.87). After Actium (31 BCE), it was supplemented with troops from other disbanded legions – on account of which it was called *Gemina* ('twin') – and sent to Illyricum or Gallia Transpadana. Based in Iulia Aemona (Ljubljana), it went on to play an active role in the Alpine War (15 BCE) under the command of Nero Claudius Drusus Germanicus. Graffiti on a pottery sherd and a helmet indicate that the legion – or detachments of it – were stationed in Batavodurum (Nijmegen) as part of the invasion force for the German War (12–9 BCE) under the same commander. It was a member of Tiberius' army group in the Marcomannic Campaign of 6 CE, but when the Great Illyrian Revolt erupted it was dispatched to assist in the effort to quell the insurgency (Dio 55.29.1n, 55.32.3n; Dessau 2638 from Aquileia). After the military disaster at Teutoburg (9 CE), it stayed briefly at Augusta Vindelicorum (Augsburg) in Raetia before relocating to the military district of Germania Superior and sharing the winter camp of Mogontiacum (Mainz) with *Legio* XIV *Gemina*, under *Legatus Augusti Pro Praetore* C. Silius (Tac. *Ann.* 1.31); it stayed there for the remainder of Augustus' principate. Veterans settled in Hispellum (Spello; *CIL* XI, 1933) and at Uthina in Africa (Dessau 6784).

XIV *Gemina*. *Legio* XIV was established in 57 BCE by Iulius Caesar from men in Gallia Cisalpina (Caes. *Bell. Gall.* 2.2, 6.1, 8.4) during the Gallic War (58–50 BCE). It fought for him in the war against Pompeius Magnus, fighting at the battles of Ilerda (summer 49 BCE), Dyrrhachium (early 48 BCE) and very likely at Pharsalus (9 August 48 BCE). Veterans settling in Italy were recalled to join in Iulius Caesar's African War (46 BCE) before it was disbanded. After 41 BCE, Caesar's heir resurrected the unit and it took part in the war against Sex. Pompeius (37–36 BCE) in Sicily. After Actium (31 BCE), its veterans were settled in Ateste (Este). The legion was supplemented with troops from other disbanded legions – on account of which it was called *Gemina* ('twin') – and sent to Illyricum, and possibly Gallia Transpadana or Aquitania. It was picked to participate in the Marcomannic Campaign of 6 CE, but when the Great Illyrian Revolt erupted that year it was dispatched to assist in the effort to quell the insurgency (Dio 55.29.1n, 55.32.3n; cf. *ILS* 2649, *CIL* 5.8272 from Aquileia). After the Varian Disaster (9 CE), it likely relocated to Vetera (Xanten), under the command of L. Asprenas (Vell. Pat. 2.120.1). It later moved to the military district of Germania Superior (Tac. *Ann.* 1.37.3), sharing the winter camp of Mogontiacum (Mainz) with *Legio* XIII *Gemina* in the military district of Germania Superior under *Legatus Augusti Pro Praetore* C. Silius (Tac. *Ann.* 1.31), where it stayed for the remainder of Augustus' principate.

XV *Apollinaris*. Faced with the challenge of bolstering his army to wage war against Sex. Pompeius, the heir of Iulius Caesar founded *Legio* XV in 41 or

40 BCE. After seeing action in Sicily, it likely transferred to campaign in Illyricum (36–35 BCE). It was on the winning side at Actium (31 BCE); perhaps for valour during the battle it earned the honorary title which signifies a sacred association with Augustus' favourite god, Apollo (Suet., *Div. Aug.* 18.2). Thereafter, its veterans were settled in Ateste (Este; *CIL* V, 2516). It was picked to participate in the Marcomannic Campaign of 6 CE, but when the Great Illyrian Revolt erupted that year it was dispatched to assist in the effort to quell the insurgency (Dio 55.29.1n, 55.32.3n; *CIL* V, 891, 917, 928 from Aquileia), perhaps stationed at Siscia (Sisak). Following the Varian Disaster (9 CE), *Legio* XV may have relocated temporarily to Iulia Aemona/Emona (Ljubljana; *CIL* III, 10769; Dessau 2264) or Vindobona (Vienna) in Pannonia. By the time of Augustus' death in 14 CE, it was probably already installed at Carnuntum (located east of Vienna) on the Danube River. After the mutiny of 14 CE, *veterani* settled in Emona (*CIL* III, 3845 = *ILS* 2264) and Scarbantia (modern Sopron; *CIL* III, 4229, 4235, 4247, 14355/14; Pliny, *Nat. Hist.* 3.146). For a detailed discussion, see Šašel Kos (1995).

XVI *Gallica*. Needing to bolster his army to wage war against Sex. Pompeius, the heir of Iulius Caesar founded *Legio* XVI in 41 or 40 BCE, giving it the honorary title which signifies Apollo. After seeing action in Sicily, it transferred to Africa. After Actium (31 BCE), it saw service in Raetia under Nero Claudius Drusus Germanicus. It is called *Gallica* on a few inscriptions (e.g. Dessau 2034). From its base at Mogontiacum (Mainz), it took part in the German War (12–9 BCE). It was one of the units chosen to participate in the Marcomannic Campaign of 6 CE, but when the Great Illyrian Revolt broke out that year it was dispatched to assist in the effort to quell the insurgency. Following the Varian Disaster (9 CE), *Legio* XVI relocated to Germania (Dessau 2265, 2266), temporarily to Ara Ubiorum (Cologne). It returned to Mogontiacum (Tac. *Ann.* 1.37.3), the winter camp it shared with *Legio* XIV in the new military district of Germania Superior under *Legatus Augusti Pro Praetore* C. Silius (Tac. *Ann.* 1.31), where it remained well after Augustus' death in 14 CE.

XVII. Absent of proof, its existence is inferred because there was a *Legio* XIIX and a XIX. Nothing is known about the origins of *Legio* XVII. It may have been founded by Iulius Caesar's heir in 41 or 40 BCE for the war against Sex. Pompeius. After Actium (31 BCE), it may have seen service in Gallia Aquitania under command of M. Agrippa, sent there to put down a rebellion in 39 BCE. It may have taken part in the Alpine War (15 BCE) under Tiberius, before relocating to the Rhine. During the preparations for the German War (12–9 BCE) under Nero Claudius Drusus Germanicus, it may have been quartered at Vetera (Xanten), meaning 'The Old One' – before moving to Oberaden, Holsterhausen or Haltern as the army group advanced into Germania along the Lippe River and began the work of pacification under Tiberius (8 BCE and 4–5 CE). Under *Legatus Augusti Pro Praetore* P. Quinctilius Varus, it was annihilated in 9 CE and never reconstituted.

XIIX. Nothing is known about the origins of *Legio* XIIX (not 'XVIII'). It may have been founded by Iulius Caesar's heir in 41 or 40 BCE for the war against Sex. Pompeius. After Actium (31 BCE), it may have seen service in Gallia Aquitania under command of M. Agrippa, sent there to put down a local rebellion in 39 BCE. It may have taken part in the Alpine War (15 BCE) under Tiberius, before relocating to the Rhine. During the preparations for the German War (12–9 BCE) under Nero Claudius Drusus Germanicus, it may have been quartered at Ara Ubiorum (Cologne) or Novaesium (Neuss), before moving to Oberaden, Holsterhausen or Haltern as the army group advanced into Germania along the Lippe River and began pacification operations under Tiberius (8–7 BCE and 4–5 CE). Under *Legatus Augusti Pro Praetore* P. Quinctilius Varus, it was annihilated in 9 CE. It was never reconstituted. A monument was erected to centurion M. Caelius, who fell 'in the Varian War', by his son and brother (*CIL* XIII, 8648 = *AE* 1952).

XIX. Nothing is known about the origins of *Legio* XIX. It may have been founded by Iulius Caesar's heir in 41 or 40 BCE for the war against Sex. Pompeius. After Actium (31 BCE), it may have seen service in Gallia Aquitania under command of M. Agrippa, sent there to put down a rebellion in 39 BCE. It likely took part in the Alpine War (15 BCE) under Tiberius – attested by the find of an iron catapult bolt (fig. 6) embossed with the signature 'LEG XIX' found at Döttenbichl (near Oberammergau in Bavaria). During the preparations for the German War (12–9 BCE) under Nero Claudius Drusus Germanicus, it may have been stationed at Vetera (Xanten) – meaning 'The Old One' – before moving to Oberaden, Holsterhausen or Haltern as the army group advanced into Germania along the Lippe River and began pacification operations under Tiberius (8 BCE and 4–5 CE). Under *Legatus Augusti Pro Praetore* P. Quinctilius Varus, it was annihilated in 9 CE and its *aquila* was taken as a trophy by the rebels. Although the legion's eagle standard was recovered from the Bructeri in 15 CE by L. Stertinius for Germanicus Caesar (Tac., *Ann.* 1.60.4), it was never reconstituted.

XX *Valeria Victrix*. *Legio* XX may have been founded after Actium (31 BCE), when units from opposing sides were combined. It went to Hispania Taraconnesis as part of the grand army in the Cantabrian and Asturian War (29–19 BCE), after which veterans were settled at *coloniae* Augusta Emerita (Mérida; Dio 53.26.1; *CIL* II, 32 of *miles* C. Axonius), founded in 25 BCE. Detachments appear to have gone to the Balkans in 20 BCE (Dessau 2651) or northern Italy (*CIL* V, 939, 948). It received its *signa* from Tiberius (Tac. *Ann.* 1.42), perhaps on the occasion of the Alpine War (15 BCE). Stationed at Burnum (Kistanje; Dessau 2651), it was to participate in the Marcomannic Campaign of 6 CE (Dessau 2270), but when the Great Illyrian Revolt (6–9 CE) erupted that year, it was dispatched to assist in the effort to quell the insurgency. Under *Legatus Augusti Pro Praetore* of Illyricum M. Valerius Messalla Messallinus, it found itself surrounded by the Pannonii and had to cut its way through (Vell. Pat. 2.112.2, cf. Dio 55.30.1n). The honorific title *Valeria Victrix* was likely awarded during Augustus' principate (Dio 55.23.6) and may indicate its close connection with the

Legatus Augusti. After the Varian Disaster (9 CE), it was based at a winter camp shared with *Legio* I located in the vicinity of Ara Ubiorum (Cologne); in 14 CE, it reported to *Legatus Augusti Pro Praetore* A. Caecina Severus of the new military district of Germania Inferior (Tac. *Ann.* 1.37, 1.44).

XXI *Rapax*. The origins of the legion are obscure. *Legio* XXI may have been founded by Iulius Caesar's heir in 41 or 40 BCE to bolster his forces for the war against Sex. Pompeius. It may, however, have been established to take part in the Alpine War (15 BCE) by Nero Claudius Drusus Germanicus, as inscriptions of soldiers (*CIL* V, 4858, 5033) show their places of birth to have been in the foothills of the Alps, e.g. Brixia (Brescia) and Tridentum (Trento). It was stationed in Vindelicia down to 6 CE (Dessau 847), but when the Great Illyrian Revolt erupted it assisted in the effort to quell the insurgency (Dio 55.29.1n, 55.32.3n). After the Varian Disaster of 9 CE, the legion was quartered at Vetera (Xanten), which it shared with *Legio* V (Tac. *Ann.* 1.31, 1.45). In 14 CE, its legate reported to the *Legatus Augusti Pro Praetore* of the military district of Germania Inferior, A. Caecina Severus. The circumstances leading to its *agnomen Rapax* – meaning 'grasping' or 'rapacious' – are not recorded.

XXII *Deiotariana*. When the client kingdom of Galatia was bequeathed by Amyntas to Augustus in 25 BCE (Dio 55.26.3), its army was absorbed as a *iusta legio* into the Romans' as *Legio* XXII (Dessau 2274). Its *agnomen* paid homage to Deiotarus (c. 105–40 BCE), leader of the Tolistobogii, who had been loyal to Rome during the Mithradatic Wars (89–63 BCE) and stood with Iulius Caesar against Pharnakes (Pharnaces) II, king of Pontus. Relocated to Aegyptus, from 35 BCE it shared a winter camp at Alexandria with *Legio* III *Cyrenaica*. It may have been active in the attack on Arabia Felix (Yemen) under equestrian *Praefectus Aegypti* Aelius Gallus (26–25 BCE); and against Nubia under C. Petronius (24 BCE), culminating in the sacking of its capital city, Napata (22 BCE).

4. Non-citizen Army (*Auxilia*)

The many long-serving, professional auxiliary units in Augustus' army comprised of *alae* of cavalry and *cohortes* of infantry from *ad hoc* drafts of subject peoples and treaty allies (*socii, foederati*). In total, these units likely matched the legions for headcount (Tac., *Ann.* 4.5) – but Tacitus remarked that 'any detailed account of them would be misleading, since they moved from place to place as circumstances required, and had their numbers increased and sometimes diminished' (Tac., *Ann.* 4.5); and Cassius Dio did not know how many there were either (Dio 55.24.5 and 55.24.8).

Their precise organization is not entirely clear. From the treatise *De Munitionibus Castrorum*, written by an unknown author commonly referred to as 'Pseudo-Hyginus' who lived well after Augustus' time, there appear to have been:

- *Ala quingenaria*: 'Wing of 500', a cavalry unit comprising sixteen *turmae* of thirty to thirty-two men, each commanded by a *decurio*, for a total of 512.
- *Ala milliaria*: 'Wing of 1,000', a cavalry unit comprising twenty-four *turmae* of thirty to thirty-two, each commanded by a *decurio*, for a total of 768; or by

other reckoning twenty-four *turmae* of forty men, for a total of 960, plus officers.

- *Cohors peditata quingenaria*: 'Cohort of 500 Foot', a combat unit of six *centuriae* of eighty infantrymen, each commanded by a *centurio*, for a total of 480 plus officers.
- *Cohors peditata milliaria*: 'Cohort of 1,000 Foot', a combat unit of ten *centuriae* of eighty infantrymen, each commanded by a *centurio*, for a total of 800 plus officers.
- *Cohors quingenaria equitata*: 'Cohort of 500 Horse', a part-mounted mixed unit of eight or ten *turmae* of thirty-two cavalrymen each plus six *centuriae* of sixty-four or eighty infantrymen for a total of 512–608 plus officers.
- *Cohors milliaria equitata*: 'Cohort of 1,000 Horse', a part-mounted mixed unit of eight or ten *turmae* of thirty-two cavalrymen each plus ten *centuriae* of sixty-four or eighty infantrymen for a total of 1,040 plus officers.

Examples include the *Cohors* I *Batavorum C.R.* a *milliaria equitata*, formed of Batavi cavalry and infantry from the Netherlands; *Cohors* I *Ubiorum peditum et equitum*, a unit of Germanic infantry and cavalry from the Rhineland (*CIL* X, 4862 = *ILS* 2690); *Cohors* II *Ituraerorum* (*ILS* 8899), a mounted unit of Syrian-Arabic people living in the region of modern Lebanon (*sagitarii Ituraei* were part of Iulius Caesar's army in 46 BCE (Caes., *Bell. Afr.* 20.1); and *Cohors Trumplinorum* (*CIL* V, 4910 Raetia; *ILS* 847), an infantry unit comprised of Trumplini recruited from around Brixia (Brescia) in the foothills of the Italian Alps. They fought with their own weapons, using their preferred fighting techniques that made them distinct.

A *cohors* was usually commanded by *praefectus* (e.g. Ti. Flavius Miccalus: Istanbul, Arkeoloji Müzesi Inv. 73.7 T) recruited from the *Ordo Equester*. Augustus also experimented by permitting the sons of senators 'the command [as *praefecti*] of an *ala* of cavalry as well and, to afford all of them the opportunity to experience life in camp (*expers castrorum*), he usually appointed two senators' sons to command each *ala*' (Suet., *Div. Aug.* 38.2; *CIL* XIV, 2105).

In addition, there were units under the command of local leaders (*duces*), such as the *Ala Atectorigiana*, presumably led by a Gallic *dux* named Atectorix (*CIL* XIII, 1041 = *ILS* 2531). Avectius and Chumstinctus came from the Belgic nation of the Nervii (Livy, *Peri.* 141), and as *tribuni* were presumably in command of units of their countrymen, fighting on the side of Nero Claudius Drusus in Germania in 10 BCE. Romans could be involved in training the troops of these allies, as in the case of the cavalry and infantry of Thracian king Roimetalkes (Florus 2.27). They too fought with their own weapons, using their preferred fighting techniques. Their local knowledge could be useful when trekking through unfamiliar territory. The Frisii were able to assist Nero Drusus on his expedition to and from Germania in 12 BCE (Dio 54.32.2–3; Tac., *Ann.* 4.72). Tiberius picked Namantabagius, 'a conquered barbarian' (a man from Germania, Raetia or Noricum) to accompany him on the journey to meet his dying brother (Val. Max. 5.3.3). Iulius Caesar used trusted Romanised Gallic nobles as interpreters (Caes., *Bell. Gall.* 1.47 and 1.53).

The regular men of a *cohors* were recruited from non-Romans of the same nationality. It is not clear if their service at this period was stipulated at sixteen or twenty years, or if it ceased when the leader died, after which they may have continued to serve under another commander, or if disbanded, perhaps they transferred to a different active contingent.

For detailed discussions of the evidence for *auxilia*, see Cheesman (1914), Haynes (2013), Holder (1980), Kennedy (1983), Keppie (1996), Knight (1991), Matei-Popescu (2013), Meyer (2013), Roxan (1973), Saddington (1985) and Spaul (2000). This list of auxiliary units is not exhaustive, but is indicative of the variety of national *alae* and *cohortes* likely in the service of Augustus.

Natio	*Ala*	*Cohors*
Alpes		I *Alpinorum*
		I *Alpinorum* E.
		II *Alpinorum* E.
		III *Alpinorum* E.
Aquitani		I *Aquitanorum*
		I *Aquitanorum* V.E.
		II *Aquitanorum* E.
		III *Aquitanorum* E.C.R.
		IV *Aquitanorum* E.C.R.
Astures	I *Asturum*	I *Asturum et Callaecorum*
	II *Asturum*	II *Asturum et Callaecorum*
	III *Asturum*	
Batavi	*Batavorum*	I *Batavorum* C.R.
		I *Batavorum* M.
		II *Batavorum* M.
		III *Batavorum* M.
		IV *Batavorum* M.
		V *Batavorum* M.
		VI *Batavorum* M.
		VII *Batavorum* M.
		VIII *Batavorum* M.
		IX *Batavorum* M.E.
Belgae		I *Belgarum* E.
		I *Belgica*
Biturgi		I *Biturigum*
		II *Biturigum*
Bosporani	*Bosporanorum*	*Bosporanorum* M.
		I *Bosporiana*
		II *Bosporanorum*

Breuci		I *Breucorum*
		II *Breucorum*
		III *Breucorum*
		IV *Breucorum*
		V *Breucorum*
		VI *Breucorum*
		VII *Breucorum*
		VIII *Breucorum*
Callaeci		[see: Astures and Lucus]
Cananefates	I *Canninefatium C.R.*	*Canninefatium*
Cantabri		I *Cantabrorum*
		II *Cantabrorum*
Celtiberi	I *Hispanorum*	I *Celtiberorum*
	I *Hispanorum Auriana*	II *Celtiberorum*
	I *Hispanorum Campagonum*	III *Celtiberorum*
	I *Hispanorum Vettonum C.R.*	I *Hispanorum*
		I *Hispanorum E.*
		I *Hispanorum V.E.*
		II *Hispanorum*
		II *Hispanorum E.*
		II *Hispanorum Scutata Cyrenaica*
		III *Hispanorum*
		IV *Hispanorum*
		V *Hispanorum*
		VI *Hispanorum*
Cilici		I *Cilicum*
		II *Cilicum*
		III *Cilicum*
Corsici	I *Corsorum C.R.*	[see: Ligures]
	I *Corsorum*	
Creti	I *Cretum*	
Cyprii		I *Cypria*
		II *Cypria*
		III *Cypria*
		IV *Cypria*
Cyrenaici	I *Cyrenaica*	
	II *Augusta Cyrenaica*	
	III *Cyrenaica S.*	
	III *Augusta Cyrenaica*	
Cyrrhestici		I *Cyrrhestarum*
		II *Cyrrhestarum*

Frisii		I *Frisiavonum*
Gaetulici	*Gaetulorum V.*	
Galli	*Gallorum Indiana*	I *Gallica C.R.E.*
	Augusta Gallorum Petriana	II *Gallica*
	Augusta Gallorum	I *Gallorum*
	Augusta Gallorum Proculeiana	II *Gallorum*
	Gallorum V.	II *Gallorum Macedonica E.*
		II *Gallorum E.*
		III *Gallorum*
		IV *Gallorum*
		V *Gallorum*
		VI *Gallorum*
		VII *Gallorum*
		VIII *Gallorum*
		IX *Gallorum*
		X *Gallorum*
		XI *Gallorum*
Germani		I *Germanorum C.R.*
		I *Germanorum M.E.*
Helvetii		I *Helvetiorum*
Ituraei		II *Ituraerorum E.*
Ligures		I *Ligurum*
		II *Gemina Ligurum et Corsorum*
Lingones		I *Lingonum E.*
		II *Lingonum E.*
		III *Lingonum E.*
		IV *Lingonum E.*
		V *Lingonum*
Lucus		*Lucensium*
		I *Lucensium E.*
		I *Lucensium Hispaonorum p.f.*
		II *Lucensium E.*
		III *Lucensium*
		IIII *Callaecorum Lucensium E.*
		V *Callaecorum Lucensium E.*
Lusitani		I *Augusta Praetoria Lusitanorum E.*
		I *Lusitanorum*
		I *Lusitanorum Cyrenaica*
		II *Lusitanorum E.*
		III *Lusitanorum E.*
		IV *Lusitanorum*

		V *Lusitanorum*
		VI *Lusitanorum*
		VII *Lusitanorum E.*
Macedonii		*Macedonum E.*
Menapii		I *Menapiorum*
Montani		I *Montanorum*
		I *Montanorum C.R.*
Morinii		I *Morinorum*
Nemetes		*Nemetum*
Nervii		I *Nerviorum*
		II *Nerviorum*
		III *Nerviorum C.R.*
		IV *Nerviorum C.R.*
		V *Nerviorum C.R.*
		VI *Nerviorum C.R.*
Norici	*Noricorum*	I *Noricorum*
Parthia	*Parthorum*	
Phrygi	VII *Phrygum*	
Raeti		I *Raetorum*
		I *Raetorum E.*
		II *Raetorum*
		II *Raetorum C.R.*
		III *Raetorum*
		IV *Raetorum*
		IV *Raetorum E.*
		V *Raetorum*
		VI *Raetorum*
		VII *Raetorum E.*
		VIII *Raetorum C.R.*
		Raetorum et Vindelicorum
Raurici (Rauraci)		[see: Sequani]
Sardi	I *Sardorum*	
	II *Sardorum E.*	
Sequani		I *Sequanorum et Rauracorum E.*
Sugambri		I *Sugambrorum V.E.*
		I *Claudia Sugambrorum*
		II *Sugambrorum*

		III *Sugambrorum*
		IV *Sugambrorum*
Sunucori		I *Sunucorum*
Treveri	*Treverorum*	
Trumplinii		*Trumplinorum*
Tungri	*Tungrorum Frontoniana*	I *Tungrorum M.*
	I *Tungrorum*	II *Tungrorum M.E.C.L.*
Ubii		I *Ubiorum*
Usipetes (Usipi)		*Usiporum*
Vallensi	*Vallensium*	
Vangiones		I *Vangionum M.E.*
Varciani		I *Varcianorum*
		II *Varcianorum*
Vindelici		I *Vindelicorum M.*
		II *Vindelicorum*
		III *Vindelicorum*
		IV *Vindelicorum*
Voconti	*Augusta Vocontiorum*	
	Vocontiorum	

Abbreviations used: *E.* = *equitata*; *C.R.* = *civium Romanorum*; *M.* = *milliaria*; *S.* = *sagittariorum*; *V.* = *veteranorum*.

5. Navy (*Classes*)

Augustus had some 900 warships (*naves longas*), 300 of which had been captured from Sex. Pompeius in 36 BCE (App., *Bell. Civ.* 5.108, 5.118) and 300 from M Antonius at Actium in 31 BCE (*RG* 3.4, Plut. *Ant.* 68). Navies were distributed around the Roman Empire – attached to provincial commands, or flotillas of vessels belonging to particular legions located on rivers. Each was commanded by an equestrian rank *praefectus classis* reporting directly to Augustus (*cf.* Caes., *Bell. Civ.* 1.36). After Actium, ships were generally either triremes (three banks of oars) or biremes (two banks), with a large single mainsail, steered by two large oars mounted at the stern. The crew of each ship was commanded by a centurion as captain (*navarchus*), with his *optio*, standard bearers and trumpeters, a helmsman (*gubernator*), marines (*milites classiarii*), armed sailors (*nautae*) and oarsmen (*remigae*) supplemented by an artillery crew (*balistarii*) and archers (*sagittarii*). The shipyards contained the workshops of the carpenters (*fabri navales*), specialist workmen (*artifices*), sail and rigging makers (*velarii*) and offices of the administrative staff.

For detailed discussions of marines, their organization and types of warships, see D'Amato (2009); Keppie (1996); Kienast (1966); Pitassi (2011); Saddington (1990); and Starr (1941).

The fleets known to have been in operation under Augustus were:

Alexandrina. Founded by Imp. Caesar around 30 BC, the *Classis Alexandrina* likely initially comprised of ships that fought at the Battle of Actium. Its vessels patrolled the eastern Mediterranean, Nile River and Red Sea. For his campaign in Arabia Felix Aelius Gallus commissioned eighty new vessels (biremes, triremes and galleys) from the shipyard at Kleopatris (Strabo, *Geog.* 16.4.23).

Foroiuliense. Ships captured at the Battle of Actium (31 BCE) were sent by Augustus to Forum Iulii (Fréjus), where they patrolled the contiguous coastline of Gallia Narbonnensis for the remainder of his principate (Tac., *Ann.* 4.5).

Germanica. Nero Claudius Drusus Germanicus constructed a fleet of ships to transport his army via a specially constructed canal (*fossa Drusiana* or *fossae Drusinae*) deep into Germania during the war (12–9 BCE). It may have been based at Bonna (Bonn) or distributed among the winter camps along the lower Rhine River (Florus, 2.30.26). It was the first Roman fleet to reach Jutland (Augustus, *RG* 26.4; Pliny the Elder, *Nat. Hist.* 2.67. 167; Suet., *Claud.* 2.1.), but was shipwrecked on the Frisian coast when returning to the Rhine from the Ems (12 BCE). Tiberius may have used many of the same vessels during his punitive expedition of Germania, which reached the Elbe River in 5 CE (Vell. Pat., 2.106, 2f.; cf. 2.121.1).

Misenensis. When ships carrying grain and oil sailing from North Africa and Sicily to Rome were attacked by Sex. Pompeius, M. Agrippa was commissioned in 37 BCE to build a fleet of ships to wage war against him. The hulls of the *triremes* and *quinqueremes* [three banks of oars] were provided by the coastal cities of Italy and brought to a harbour – the *Portus Iulius*, which he specially constructed at great speed at Cumae on the Bay of Naples – to be outfitted and receive their crews (Dio, 48.49.4–50.1–3; App., *Bell. Civ.* 5.11; Pliny the Elder, *Nat. Hist.* 36.125; Suet., *Div. Aug.* 16.1; Vell. Pat., 2.79.1–2; Vergil, *Georg.* 2.161–64). After the war, the fleet was moved to Misenum, from which it continued to patrol the shipping lanes between Africa and Rome.

Ravennas. The fleet at Ravenna was constructed to guard the Adriatic coast of Italy from raids by forces of Sex. Pompeius in Illyricum (App. *BC* 5.80). After the war, it continued to patrol the region for the remainder of his principate (Tac., *Ann.* 4.5). The port was connected to the southern branch of the Po River by a canal (*Fossa Augusta*).

Sociae Triremes. An unknown number of other fleets or flotillas were stationed with the legions or *auxilia* (Tac., *Ann.* 1.11), and also operated by client kings around the empire (e.g. Herodes, whose Royal Harbour at Caesarea Martimae – possibly equipped with ship sheds – was begun around 20 BCE (Joseph., *Ant. Iud.* 16.21).

6. Conscript and Volunteer Corps (*Cohortes Ingenuorum* and *Cohortes Voluntariorum*)

Under Augustus, there were up to forty-six units of conscripts and volunteers representing some 23,000 men (equivalent to four legions).

Some cohorts were comprised of centuries of non-volunteer citizens, which may have been created for special duties or missions (e.g. *Cohors Augusta* I (*CIL* X, 4862), *Cohors* II *Classica* (*CIL* III, 6687)). The *praefectus* C. Fabricius Tuscus commanded one such unit known as *Cohors Apulae Civium Romanorum* (*AE* 1973, 501), recruited from the men of Apulia before 6 CE, which was at some point transferred to province Asia with its garrison in or near Alexandria Troas. *Cohors* I *Aquitanorum Veterana* (*CIL* XIII, 7399a) was formed from the men of the fleet at Forum Iulii for service in Aquitania to support the *Bellum Cantabricum* in 26 BCE.

In times of emergency, a levy of freeborn citizens (*dilectus ingenuorum*) could raise men for new units to serve in the nation's defence. By an ancient law, men from 17 to 46 were eligible for the draft (Polybius 6.19.2; Aulus Gellius 10.28.1), though men under 35 were most sought-after (*cf.* Livy, *AUC* 22.11.9; Veg. 1.4). Men were selected by lot and the chosen ones took the military oath (Dio 38.35.4). They were commanded by tribunes (e.g. *CIL* III, 14216, 8 Dolbreta). Two or six units were created from enforced levies held during the Great Illyrian Revolt (a.k.a. The Batonian War) of 6–9 CE, which also included freedmen (*liberti*), both under the command of Germanicus Caesar (Dio 55.31.1, Suet., *Div. Aug.* 25.2); but in the aftermath of the Varian Disaster of 9 CE, Roman citizens (many from among the city's disgruntled poor), freedman and slaves – quickly manumitted and made freedmen to make up the numbers – were recruited (e.g. Dio 56.23.3; Vell. Pat. 2.111.1; Tac. *Ann.* 1.31; Macrobius, *Sat.* 1.11.32) and accompanied Tiberius back to Germania (Dio 56.23.3). Freed slaves serving with levied cohorts were among those encouraging the legionaries at Ara Ubiorum in Germania Inferior to mutiny in 14 CE (Tac., *Ann.* 1.31).

Units of the free born – *Cohortes Voluntariorum* – were kept separate from those of the freedmen and they were issued different arms and equipment (Suet., *Div. Aug.* 25.2). One such was *Cohors* I *Campana*, recruited from men of Campania (*CIL* III, 8438 Narona/Dalmatia = *ILS* 2597). An inscription from Illyricum (*CIL* III, 10854 Siscia) records a *Cohors* XXXII *Voluntariorum Civium Romanorum*, suggesting there were up to thirty-two of these in active service under Augustus.

For a detailed discussion, see Brunt (1974); Orth (1978); Speidel (1976); and Spaul (2000).

7. Paramilitary Urban or City Police (*Cohortes Urbanae*)

The *Cohortes Urbanae* were instituted by Augustus to maintain peace and order in the City of Rome (Dio 52.21.1–2; Suet., *Div. Aug.* 37), perhaps as early as 27 BCE. Commanded by the *Praefectus Urbi* (a former consul, whose jurisdiction covered the city and up to 100 miles around (Dio 52.33.1) – most famously L. Calpurnius Piso Caesonius (Tac., *Ann.* 6.10)), the corps complemented the *Cohortes Praetoriae* and comprised three cohorts, numbered X through to XII, to continue the sequence – and each comprised six centuries. As paramilitary police, the *urbaniciani* were employed to enforce public order and deal with riots. During the months following the *Clades Variana* of 9 CE, they maintained patrols (*excubiae*) throughout the city during the night time (Suet., *Div. Aug.* 23.1). A fourth unit of the *Cohortes Urbanae* was also stationed in *Colonia* Copia Felix Munatia (Lugdunum, Lyon) to guard the mint, which produced silver and coins from 15 BCE onwards. An *optio carceris*, a deputy to a centurion in charge of a prison, is recorded both in Rome and Lugdunum (*CIL* IX, 1617 = *ILS* 2117; *CIL* XIII, 1833 = *ILS* 2116; and *CIL* VI, 531 = *ILS* 3729 (238–244)). The men of the Urban Cohorts each received 500 *sestertii* from the estate of the deceased *princeps*, HS200 more than the regular legionaries (Suet., *Div. Aug.* 101.2).

For a detailed discussion, see Echols (1958); Freis (1967); and Nippel (1995).

8. Firefighters (*Vigiles Urbani, Cohortes Vigilum*)
During the Late Republic, powerful Roman families owned troops of slaves to guard their properties and fight the fires which frequently broke out and devastated regions of the city. The most notorious of them belonged to M. Licinius Crassus: if fire threatened a building, his men would arrive, demand payment from the owner to extinguish the fire or else watch the property go up in flames (Plut. *Crass.* 2). C. Cilnius Maecenas urged Augustus to establish a corps under an equestrian *praefectus* (Dio 52.24.4). In 26 BCE, Augustus assigned fire-fighting to the aediles; in 22 BCE, Augustus entrusted the curule aediles with the responsibility for putting out fires in Rome, for which purpose he granted them 600 slaves as assistants (Dio 53.24.6, 54.2.4n, cf. *Dig.* 1.15.1). In 7 BCE, when the city of Rome was organized into fourteen regions (comprising over 200 *vici*, or wards), this function was transferred to the colleges of *vicomagistri* (Dio 55.8.7n).

In 6 CE, a year during which Romans living in the city suffered a wretched combination of severe famine and devastating fires, Augustus founded the *Vigiles Urbani*, the 'Urban Watch' (or *Cohortes Vigilum*), specifically as a firefighting force (Suet. *Div. Aug.* 25.2, 30.1; Dio 55.26.1, 4–5; Tac. *Ann.* 13.27.1). Commanded by an equestrian *Praefectus Vigilum* appointed by Augustus himself (Dio 52.33.1, 58.9.3; *Dig.* 1.2.2.33), the 6,000 men were organized into four *cohortes* (Dio 55.24.6), each of seven *centuriae*, recruited from among *liberti*, freedmen (Suet. *Div. Aug.* 25.2; Dio 55.26.4). Equipped with axes, buckets, rope, chain and cart-mounted water pumps (*siphones*), they also served as the city's night watch and assisted the *Cohortes Urbanae* in enforcing public order, arresting thieves and capturing runaway slaves (cf. Dio 55.26.4 on the *praefectus*' duties). Funded by a 2 per cent tax on the sale of slaves (Dio 55.33.4), the *Vigiles* had barracks located in the city and proved very popular with the public (Dio 55.26.5). An *optio carceris* in charge of the prison is recorded with the *vigiles* (*CIL* VI, 32748; VI, 1057, 2, 10 (205)).

For a detailed discussion, see Daugherty (1992).

Propaganda Wars: The Coins of Augustus

Augustus used coins to propagate news of his military successes. They celebrated the victory at the Battle of Actium, the return of the legionary *aquilae* and *signa* from Parthia, the capture of new territories, his return from successful ventures abroad and other related themes. Coins remained in circulation for decades. The cumulative effect of years of such messaging reinforced the primacy of Augustus and of his crucial role in managing the security of the *imperium* of the Roman People. For discussions of coins in imperial policy and their often vague meanings, see Levick (1999), Romer (1978), Sutherland (1978) and Wallace-Hadrill (1986).

The mint at the Temple of Iuno Moneta in Rome produced coins under the official board of four moneyers until 40 BCE. Thereafter, various officials produced coins for Imp. Caesar/Augustus. In the 20s BCE, production was augmented by other mints in *Colonia* Caesaraugusta, *Colonia* Augusta Emerita, *Colonia* Patricia and Pergamon, which were closer both to the source of the precious metals and the army camps where coins were distributed as pay for the soldiers. From 18 BCE, *tresviri aere argento auro flando feriundo* – literally 'three men for striking (and) casting bronze, silver, gold (coins)' – again oversaw production in Rome. After 15 BCE, production of gold (*aurei, quinarii*) and silver (*denarii, quinarii*) coins moved entirely from Rome to *Colonia* Copia Felix Munatia (Lugdunum), guarded by one of the *Cohortes Urbanae*. These Gallic issues were often marked '*IMP*' with the cumulative number of his imperatorial acclamations at the date of issue. From then on, the Rome mint struck only the low denomination bronze, brass and copper coins (*sestertii, dupondii, asses, semis, quadrans*), stamped 'SC' as having been issued under *senatus consultum*, a lawful decree of the Senate.

Coins often appeared with slight variations owing to the skills of individual die-makers, and dies could be replaced when one or both halves wore out, so that several versions of the same type might be struck. The same dies were often used to strike both the gold and silver coins of a particular issue. This catalogue is selective, including only the important types produced during the period 31 BCE–14 CE.

Abbreviations used: AV = *aurum* (gold); AR = *argentum* (silver); AE = *aes* (brass, bronze or copper); *BMC* = Mattingly, H., *Coins of the Roman Empire in the British Museum. Volume 1*; *CBN* = Giard, J.-B., *Catalogue des Monnaies de l'Empire*

Romain; Cohen = Cohen, H., *Description Historique des Monnaies frappées sous l'Empire Romain*; RCV = Sear, D., *Roman Coins and Their Values. Volume 1*; RIC = Sutherland, C.H.V., *Roman Imperial Coinage. Volume 1*; RSC = Seaby, H.A., *Roman Silver Coins, Volume I.*

1. AR *denarius*. Rome mint. Struck c. 32–31 BCE. Obverse: Bare head of Imp. Caesar facing left, without legend. Reverse: CAESAR – DIVI F across field. Winged Victory alighting left on globe, holding wreath and palm. (Numismatic references: *BMC* 603; Cohen 64; Paris 37; *RIC* 254b.) *The coin anticipates Imp. Caesar's victory over Queen Kleopatra and her partner M. Antonius in the coming war.*

2. AR *denarius*. Rome mint. Struck c. 32–31 BCE. Obverse: Head of Venus or Pax right, wearing stephane and necklace, without legend. Reverse: CAESAR – DIVI F across field. Imp. Caesar in military dress rushing left, extending right hand and holding transverse spear in left. (Numismatic references: *BMC* 609; Cohen 70; Paris 1; *RCV* 397; *RIC* 251.) *The coin anticipates the victory of Imp. Caesar over Queen Kleopatra and her partner M. Antonius in the coming war.*

3. AR *denarius*. Italian (Brundisium or Rome?) mint. Struck 30–29 BCE. Obverse: Bare head of Imp. Caesar facing right, without legend. Reverse: Actian War Arch, showing a single span surmounted by Imp. Caesar in facing triumphal *quadriga*; IMP CAESAR on the architrave, without legend. (Numismatic references: *BMC* 624; *RIC* 267; *RSC* 123.) *The coin commemorates victory over Queen Kleopatra and her partner M. Antonius during the Actian War of 31 BCE.*

4. AR *denarius* (plate 9). Italian (Brundisium or Rome?) mint. Struck 30 BCE. Obverse: Victory, draped, standing right on prow, holding palm frond over left shoulder in left hand and wreath in extended right hand. Reverse: IMP CAESAR in exergue. Imp. Caesar driving triumphal *quadriga* right, the car ornamented with figures on its front and side panels, holding reins in left hand and branch in right. (Numismatic references: *BMC* 617–9 = *BMCRR* Rome 4343–5; *BN* 98–104; *CRI* 416; *RIC* 264; *RSC* 115.) *The coin commemorates Imp. Caesar's victory over Queen Kleopatra and her partner M. Antonius at the Battle of Actium of 2 September 31 BCE.*

5. AR *denarius* (plate 8). Italian (Brundisium or Rome?) mint. Struck 29–27 BCE. Obverse: Bare head of Imp. Caesar facing right, without legend. Reverse: IMP CAESAR. *Tropaeum* decorated with captured body armour, its base crossed with rudder and anchor and set on a ship's prow to right. (Numismatic references: *BMC* 625; *RIC* 265a; *RSC* 119; Sear 1556.) *The coin commemorates Imp. Caesar's victory over Queen Kleopatra and her partner at the Battle of Actium of 2 September 31 BCE.*

6. AR *denarius*. Italian (Brundisium or Rome?) mint. Struck 29–27 BCE. Obverse: Laureate head of Imp. Caesar facing right, as Terminus, with thunderbolt behind. Reverse: IMP CAESAR legend to the left and right of Imp. Caesar, togate, seated left on curule chair, holding Victoriola right. (Numismatic references: *BMC* 637; *RIC* 270.) *The coin commemorates Imp. Caesar's victory over Queen Kleopatra and her partner at the battles of Actium and Alexandria.*

7. AR *quinarius*. Italian (Brundisium or Rome?) mint. Struck 28 BCE. Obverse: CAESAR IMP VII. Bare head of Imp. Caesar facing right. Reverse: ASIA RECEPTA. Winged Victory standing left on *cista mystica* flanked by two snakes. (Numismatic references: *BMC* 647; Cohen 14; *RIC* 276; *RSC* 14.) *This coin celebrates the reconquest of Asia Minor from Kleopatra and her partner M. Antonius in 30 BCE.*

8. AV *aureus*. Uncertain (Pergamon?) mint. Struck 28 BCE. Obverse: CAESAR DIVI F COS VI. Bare head of Imp. Caesar facing right. Reverse: AEGVPTO / CAPTA in two lines. Crocodile standing right, closed mouth. (Numismatic references: *BMC* 655; *RIC* 544.) *The coin celebrates the capture of Egypt after the surrender of Queen Kleopatra's army in August 30 BCE.*

9. AR *denarius*. Uncertain (Pergamon?) mint. Struck 28 BCE. Obverse: CAESAR DIVI F COS VI. Bare head of Imp. Caesar facing right. Reverse: AEGVPTO / CAPTA in two lines. Crocodile standing right, closed mouth. (Numismatic references: *BMC* 653; Cohen 4; Paris 928; *RIC* 545.) *The coin celebrates the capture of Egypt after the surrender of Queen Kleopatra's army in August 30 BCE. (Other versions show the crocodile with an open mouth or a hippopotamus.) Forgeries of this type made in ancient times have been found.*

10. AE *as*. Philippi mint. Struck 27–10 BCE. Obverse: VIC – AVG across field. Winged Victory standing left. Reverse: COHOR PRAE. PHIL in exergue. Three army *signa*. (Numismatic references: *BMC* 23; *RPC* I 1651; Sear 32; *SNG ANS* 674.) *The coin was minted at Augusta Iulia Philippensis, a* colonia *of veterans of* Cohortes Praetoriae *who settled in Macedonia.*

11. AR *denarius*. *Colonia* Emerita Augusta mint. Struck c. 25–23 BCE by legate P. Carisius. Obverse: CAESAR AVGVS TRIBVN POTEST. Head of Augustus right. Reverse: P CARISIVS / LEG / AVGVSTI in three lines. (Numismatic references: Cohen 392; *RIC* 22.) *This coin asserts the authority of* Legatus Augusti Pro Praetore *P. Carisius in his province.*

12. AR *denarius*. *Colonia* Emerita Augusta mint. Struck c. 25–23 BCE by legate P. Carisius. Obverse: IMP CAESAR AVGVST. Bare head of Augustus facing right. Reverse: P CARISIVS LEG PRO PR. View of a gate looking back into the city of Emerita Augusta. (Numismatic reference: *RIC* 9a.) *This coin was minted in the* colonia *founded by P. Carisius for veterans after the* Bellum Cantabricum et Asturicum, *26–25 BCE.*

13. AR *quinarius*. *Colonia* Emerita Augusta mint. Struck c. 25–23 BCE by legate P. Carisius. Obverse: AVGVST. Bare head of Augustus right. Reverse: P CARISI LEG. Victory standing right, placing wreath on a trophy. (Numismatic reference: *RIC* 1a.) *The coin celebrates Carisius' victory in the war against the Astures in 26–25 BCE.*

14. AR *denarius*. *Colonia* Emerita Augusta mint. Struck c. 25–23 BCE by legate P. Carisius. Obverse: IMP CAESAR AVGVST. Bare head of Augustus right.

Reverse: P CARISIVS LEG PRO PR. Crested helmet between *gladius hispanienis* and *bipennis*. (Numismatic references: *BMC* 281; Cohen 406; Paris 1046 pl. XLII; *RIC* 7a; *RSC* 405.) *The coin shows war spoils gathered by Carisius after his successful war against the Astures in 26–25 BCE.*

15. AR *denarius* (plate 16). *Colonia* Emerita Augusta mint. Struck c. 25–23 BCE by legate P. Carisius. Obverse: IMP CAESAR AVGVST. Bare head of Augustus facing right. Reverse: P CARISIVS LEG PRO PR. *Tropaeum* from which hang captured body armour, erected on a hill covered with shields, swords, *bipennes* and spears. (Numismatic references: *BMC* 284; *RIC* 4b.) *The coin shows the trophy decorated with war spoils gathered by Carisius after his successful war against the Astures in 26–25 BCE.*

16. AR *denarius* (fig. 4). Rome mint. Struck c. 19 BCE. Obverse: Q RVSTIVS FORTVNAE. Jugate busts facing right of Fortuna Victrix wearing round helmet, holding *patera*, and Fortuna Felix, diademed above bar with ram's head finials. ANTIAT in exergue. Reverse: CAESAR AVGVSTO, ornamented rectangular altar inscribed FOR RE, EX SC in exergue. (Numismatic references: *BMC* 4; *RIC* 322.) *The coin commemorates the Senate's vote to erect an altar to the goddess Fortuna upon the safe return of Augustus from the East on 12 October 19 BCE. The altar was dedicated on 15 December that year.*

17. AR *denarius*. Spanish (*Colonia* Caesaraugusta?) mint. Struck 19 BCE. Obverse: CAESAR AVGVSTVS, bare head facing right. Reverse: Oak wreath; OB CIVIS above; SERVATOS below. (Numismatic references: *BMC* 330; *RIC* 40a.) *The inscription on the reverse commemorates the decree of the Senate on 13 January 27 BCE bestowing the* corona civica *on Augustus – and the right to display it in perpetuity on the facade of his house on the Palatinus Hill – for having 'saved the lives of citizens'.*

18. AR *denarius*. Spanish (*Colonia* Patricia?) mint. Struck 19–18 BCE. Obverse: CAESAR AVGVSTVS, bare head facing right. Reverse: OB CIVIS SERVATOS in three lines within oak wreath, with wreath ties drawn upward. (Numismatic references: *RIC* 77a; *RSC* 208.) *The inscription on the reverse commemorates the decree of the Senate on 13 January 27 BCE bestowing the* corona civica *on Augustus – and the right to display it in perpetuity on the facade of his house on the Palatinus Hill – for having 'saved the lives of citizens'.*

19. AR *denarius*. Spanish (*Colonia* Patricia?) mint. 19–18 BCE. Obverse: Laureate head of Augustus facing right. Reverse: FORTVN REDVC CAESARI AVG S P Q R, inscribed in three lines on rectangular altar. (Numismatic references: *CBN* 54d; *RIC* 56a.) *The coin produced at a provincial mint commemorates the Senate's vote to erect an altar to the goddess Fortuna upon the safe return of Augustus to Rome on 12 October 19 BCE. The altar was dedicated on 15 December that year.*

20. AR *denarius*. *Colonia* Caesaraugusta mint. Struck 19–18 BCE. Obverse: CAESAR AVGVSTVS. Oak-wreathed head facing right. Reverse: Winged Victory flying right holding wreath in both hands over shield inscribed CL V, and resting against column. (Numismatic reference: *BMC* 341; Cohen 289 var.

(bare head); *RIC* 46 var. (head left).) *This coin was issued after the successful conclusion of the* Bellum Cantabricum *by M. Agrippa operating under the auspices of Augustus.*

21. AR *denarius*. Rome mint. Struck c. 19 BCE by moneyer L. Aquillius Florus. Obverse: L AQVILLIVS FLORVS IIIVIR. Draped bust of Virtus facing right, wearing helmet with a long crest and a feather on the side. Reverse: AVGVSTVS CAESAR. Augustus, driving *biga* of elephants to left, holding laurel branch over the backs of the elephants. (Numismatic references: *BMC* 36; *BMCRR* 4545; Cohen 354; *RIC* 301.) *There is no report in the extant historical accounts of Augustus celebrating a triumph with a biga pulled by elephants.*

22. AR *denarius* (plate 14). *Colonia* Patricia mint. Struck c. 19 BCE. Obverse: CAESAR AVGVSTVS. Bare head of Augustus facing right. Reverse: SIGNIS RECEPTIS. *Aquila* on left and army *signum* standard on right flanking S P Q R arranged around shield inscribed CL V. (Numismatic references: *BMC* 418; Cohen 265; *RIC* 86a.) *The coin celebrates the return of the army insignia from the Parthians in 20 BCE. This event was memorialized on the coinage more than any other imperial achievement of Augustus.*

23. AR *denarius*. Uncertain (*Colonia* Caesaraugusta?) mint. Struck c. 19 BCE. Obverse: CAESAR AVGVSTVS. Bare head of Augustus facing right. Reverse: SIGNIS RECEPTIS. Mars, helmeted and cloaked, standing facing head right, right hand holding *aquila*, left hand holding army *signum* over shoulder. (Numismatic references: *BMC* 332; *CBN* 1310; Cohen 259; *RIC* 41.) *The coin celebrates the return of the army insignia from the Parthians in 20 BCE.*

24. AR *denarius*. Spanish (Tarraco?) mint. Struck 19–18 BCE. Obverse: CAESARI / AVGVSTO. Laureate head of Augustus facing right. Reverse: Round domed tetrastyle temple of Mars Ultor set on three steps, containing triumphal *currus* carrying *aquila* and miniature *quadriga*. S P Q R in exergue. (Numismatic references: *RIC* 120.) *The coin celebrates the return of the army insignia from the Parthians in 20 BCE.*

25. AR *denarius*. Spanish mint (*Colonia* Caesaraugusta?). Struck c. 19–18 BCE. Obverse: CAESAR AVGVSTVS. Bare head of Augustus facing left. Reverse: MARTIS VLTORIS. Statue of Mars Ultor holding *aquila* and *tropaeum*, standing left within tetrastyle temple with ornate domed roof. (Numismatic references: *BMC* 329; *RIC* 39b.) *The coin celebrates the return of the army insignia from the Parthians in 20 BCE.*

26. AR Cistophoric *tetradrachma*. Asia Minor (uncertain) mint. Struck 19/18 BCE. Obverse: IMP IX TR PO V. Bare head of Augustus facing right. Reverse: MART – VLTO across field. Circular temple showing four columns on podium of five steps, military standard within. (Numismatic references: *BMC* 704; Cohen 202 (25 Fr.); Paris 989; *RIC* 507; *RPC* 2220.) *The coin celebrates the return of the army insignia from the Parthians in 20 BCE.*

27. AR *denarius* (plate 12). Spanish (*Colonia* Patricia?) mint. Struck c. 19 BCE. Obverse: Bare head of Augustus facing right. Reverse: OB / CIVIS / SERVATOS

in three lines; all within oak wreath. (Numismatic references: *BMC* 378–80; *RIC* 77a; *RSC* 208.) *The inscription on the reverse commemorates the decree of the Senate on 13 January 27 BCE bestowing the* corona civica *on Augustus – and the right to display it in perpetuity on the facade of his house on the Palatinus Hill – for having 'saved the lives of citizens'.*

28. AR *denarius* (plate 13). Spanish (*Colonia* Caesaraugusta?) mint. Struck 19–18 BCE. Obverse: Oak-wreathed bust of Augustus facing right. Reverse. CAESAR AVGVSTVS. Two laurel branches flanking S P / Q R in two lines arranged around shield inscribed CL V. (Numismatic references: *BMC* 354 (*Colonia* Patricia); *CBN* 1335 (Nimes); Cohen 51; *RIC* 36a.) *The inscription on the reverse commemorates the bestowing by the Senate on Augustus of two laurel crowns and the* Clipeus Virtutis *– and the right to display them, in perpetuity, on the facade of his house on the Palatinus Hill – on 16 January 27 BCE.*

29. AR *denarius*. Rome or Pergamum mint. Stuck c. 19–18 BCE. Obverse: Bare head of Augustus facing right. Reverse. CAESAR – DIVI F / ARMEN – RECEPT / IMP – VIII in three lines. Armenian warrior in national costume and head dress standing facing front, holding spear in right hand and resting left hand on bow set on ground. (Numismatic references: *BMC* 678; Cohen 59; *RIC* 519.) *The coin celebrates the capture of Armenia from the Parthians in 20 BCE.*

30. AR *denarius* (fig. 3). Pergamon mint. Stuck c. 19–18 BCE. Obverse: AVGVSTVS. Bare head of Augustus facing right. Reverse. ARMENIA – CAPTA across field. Armenia tiara and bow case with quiver. (Numismatic references: *BMC* 672; *BN* 995; Cohen 11; *RIC* 516.) *The coin celebrates the capture of Armenia from the Parthians in 20 BCE.*

31. AR *denarius* (plate 17). Rome mint. Struck 19 BCE by moneyer P. Petronius Turpilianus. Obverse: TVRPILIANVS / III VIR FERON. Diademed and draped bust of Feronia with bead necklace facing right. Reverse: CAESAR AVGVSTVS SIGN RECE. Parthian wearing trousers, kneeling right, presenting standard inscribed X. (Numismatic references: *RCV* 1603; Seaby 484.) *The coin celebrates the return of the army insignia from the Parthians in 20 BCE.*

32. AR *cistophorus*. Pergamum mint. Struck 19–18 BCE. Obverse: IMP IX TR PO V. Bare head of Augustus facing right. Reverse: S P R / SIGNIS / RECEPTIS in three lines in the opening of a single-span triumphal arch surmounted by large statue of Augustus in facing triumphal *quadriga*, IMP IX TR POT V on architrave. (Numismatic references: *BMC* 703 (= *BMCRR* East 310); *CBN* 982; *RPC* 2218; *RIC* 510; *RSC* 298.) *The coin shows the arch to be raised to celebrate the return of the army insignia from the Parthians in 20 BCE. A* cistophorus *was equivalent to 3 denarii.*

33. AR *denarius*. *Colonia* Emerita Augusta mint. Struck 19–18 BCE. Obverse: Head of Augustus facing left, wearing oak wreath. Reverse: CAESAR / AVGVSTVS in two lines. Two laurel branches (or trees) upright. (Numismatic references: *BMC* 318–20 = *BMCRR* Gaul 144–46; *BN* 1285–86; *RIC* 33b;

RSC 48.) *The Senate bestowed on Augustus the award of two laurel crowns and the* Clipeus Virtutis – *and the right to display them, in perpetuity, on the facade of his house on the Palatinus Hill – on 16 January 27 BCE.*

34. AR *denarius* (fig. 5). *Colonia* Patricia mint. Struck 18 BCE. Obverse: CAESARI AVGVSTO. Laureate head of Augustus facing right. Reverse: MAR VLT. Domed, hexastyle temple of Mars Ultor, *aquila* flanked by two standards within. (Numismatic references: *BMC* 373; *RCV* 1623; *RIC* 105a; *RSC* 190.) *The coin celebrates the return of the army insignia from the Parthians in 20 BCE.*

35. AR *denarius* (plate 10). *Colonia* Patricia mint. Struck 18 BCE or later. Obverse: SPQR PARENT CONS SVO. *Triumphator's toga picta* over *tunica palmata* flanked on left by eagle-tipped rod of *imperium* and on right by wreath. Reverse: CAESARI / AVGVSTO in exergue. Triumphal *quadriga* advancing right, ornamented with one Victory and surmounted by a small galloping *quadriga*. (Numismatic references: *BMC* 399; *RIC* 99; *RSC* 78b.) *The coin's legend appears to bestow an honour by the Senate and Roman People on an absent Augustus. (On the ambiguity of the legend, see Wallace-Hadrill (1986).) Forgeries of this type made in ancient times have been found.*

36. AV *aureus*. *Colonia* Patricia mint. Struck 18–17 BCE. Obverse: S P Q R CAESARI AVGVSTO. Bare head of Augustus facing right. Reverse: VOT P SVSC PRO SAL ET RED I O M SACR. Mars, helmeted and cloaked, standing left, holding a *vexillum* in right hand and *parazonium* over left shoulder. (Numismatic references: *BMC* 437; *RIC* 149a.) *The inscription on the reverse translates as 'public vows have been undertaken, holy to Jupiter the Best and Greatest, for the well-being and the return [of the emperor]'.*

37. AR *denarius*. *Colonia* Patricia mint. Struck 18–17 BCE. Obverse: S P Q R CAESARI AVGVSTO. Bare head of Augustus facing right. Reverse: VOT P SVSC PRO SAL ET RED I O M SACR. Mars, helmeted and cloaked, standing left, holding a *vexillum* in right hand and *parazonium* over left shoulder. (Numismatic references: *BMC* 441; *RIC* 148.) *The inscription on the reverse translates as 'public vows have been undertaken, holy to Jupiter the Best and Greatest, for the well-being and the return [of the emperor]'. (Silver version of 36.)*

38. AV *quinarius*. Spanish (*Colonia* Patricia?) mint. Struck c. 18–16 BCE. Obverse: AVG – VST. Bare head of Augustus facing right. Reverse: Victory standing on globe right, holding *aquila* up while holding branch down. (Numismatic references: *BMC* 424; *RIC* 121 (same reverse die).) *This coin was minted after M. Agrippa concluded the* Bellum Cantabricum *in 19 BCE and may celebrate his victory under the auspices of Augustus.*

39. AV *aureus*. *Colonia* Patricia mint. Struck 18–16 BCE. Obverse: SPQR IMP CAESARI AVG COS XI TR POT VI. Bare head of Augustus facing right. Reverse: CIVIB ET SIGN MILIT A PART RECVPER. Triumphal arch with three portals, Augustus in *quadriga* between two Parthians on top. (Numismatic

references: *BMC* 427; Cohen 82; *RIC* 131.) *The reverse depicts the Parthian War Arch. Straddling the* Via Sacra, *the central gate supports a chariot driven by Augustus as* triumphator, *while the two flanking portals bear statues of Parthian archers. In this depiction, all the arches are shown the same size. The inscription on the reverse translates as 'because of the citizens and of the militia, recovered from the Parthians'.*

40. AR *denarius* (plate 11). *Colonia* Patricia mint. Struck 18–16 BCE. Obverse: SPQR IMP CAESARI AVG COS XI TR POT VI. Bare head of Augustus facing right. Reverse: CIVIB ET SIGN MILIT A PART RECVPER. Triumphal arch with three portals, Augustus in *quadriga* between two Parthians on top. (Numismatic references: *BMC* 428; Cohen 83; *RIC* 134a; *RSC* 84.) *The reverse depicts the Parthian War Arch. Straddling the* Via Sacra, *the central gate supports a chariot driven by Augustus as* triumphator, *while the two flanking portals bear statues of Parthian archers. In this depiction, all the arches are shown the same size. The inscription on the reverse translates as 'because of the citizens and of the militia, recovered from the Parthians'.*

41. AR *denarius*. Rome mint. Struck 16 BC by moneyer L. Mescinius Rufus. Obverse: S COB R P CVM SALVT IMP CAESAR AVGVS CONS. Young man's head facing front, slightly turned to right on roundel within *imago clipeata*. Reverse: L MESCINIVS RVFVS III VIR. Mars, naked but for helmet, holding spear and *parazonium*, standing on pedestal inscribed S P Q R V P / S PR S ET / RED AVG. (Numismatic references: *BMC* 90; *CBN* 341; Cohen 465. *RIC* 356.) *This coin is exceptional for the front-facing portrait of the man whose identity is unclear.*

42. AR *denarius* (plate 34). Rome mint. Struck 16 BCE by moneyer L. Mescinius Rufus. Obverse: Laureate head of Augustus facing right. Reverse: L MESCINIVS RVFVS, Mars, helmeted and cloaked, holding transverse spear and *parazonium*, standing left on pedestal inscribed S P Q R / V PR RE / CAES in three lines. (Numismatic references: *BMC* 86; *RIC* 351; *RSC* 463a.) *Among the pantheon Mars Ultor was an important god for Augustus, to whom he dedicated his* Forum Augustum *on 12 May 2 BCE.*

43. AR *denarius*. Rome mint. Struck 16 BCE. Obverse: Bare head of Augustus facing right. Reverse: Triumphal arch inscribed S P Q R / IMP CAE in two lines surmounted by *quadriga*, Augustus driving chariot, holding branch and sceptre; smaller arches on either side surmounted by archer and slinger. L VINICIVS in exergue. (Numismatic references: *BMC* 77–78 = *BMCRR* Rome 4477–78; *BN* 348–51; *RIC* 359; *RSC* 544.) *The reverse depicts the Parthian War Arch. Straddling the* Via Sacra, *the central gate supports a chariot driven by Augustus as* triumphator, *while the two flanking portals bear statues of Parthian archers. (Compare to no. 3.)*

44. AV *aureus. Colonia* Copia Felix Munatia (Lugdunum) mint. Struck 15–13 BCE. Obverse: AVGVSTVS DIVI F. Bare head of Augustus facing right. Reverse: IMP – X across field. ACT in exergue. Apollo Citharoedus standing left, holding plectrum and lyre. (Numismatic references: *BMC* 459; Calicó

215; Lyon 27; *RIC* 170.) *This coin celebrates the Actian Games at Nikopolis, the city founded upon the site of Imp. Caesar's camp at Actium.*

45. AV *aureus*. *Colonia* Copia Felix Munatia (Lugdunum) mint. Struck 15–13 BCE. Obverse: AVGVSTVS DIVI F. Bare head of Augustus facing right. Reverse: IMP X in exergue. Togate Augustus seated left on curule chair set on low dais, receiving branches from two men each wearing a cloak and bearing a *parazonium*. (Numismatic references: *BMC* 447; *RIC* 164a.) *The coin celebrates the victory of Augustus' stepsons, Nero Claudius Drusus and Ti. Claudius Nero, over the Raeti, Vindelici and Norici in 15 BCE.*

46. AR *denarius* (plate 27). *Colonia* Copia Felix Munatia (Lugdunum) mint. Struck 15–13 BCE. Obverse: AVGVSTVS DIVI F. Bare head of Augustus facing right. Reverse: IMP X in exergue. Togate Augustus seated left on curule chair set on low dais, receiving branches from two men each wearing a cloak and bearing a *parazonium*. (Numismatic references: *BMC* 446; *CBN* 1366; Cohen 133; Lyon 13; *RSC* 135; *RIC* 165a.) *The coin celebrates the victory of Augustus' stepsons, Nero Claudius Drusus and Ti. Claudius Nero, over the Raeti, Vindelici and Norici in 15 BCE. (Silver version of 45.)*

47. AR *denarius* (plate 28). Rome mint. Struck 12 BCE by moneyer L. Caninius Gallus. Obverse: AVGVSTVS. Bare head of Augustus facing right. Reverse: L CANINIVS GALLVS III VIR. Long-haired, bearded and naked barbarian wearing only a cloak, kneeling right, offering *vexillum* to right. (Numismatic references: *BMC* 128; *RIC* 416.) *The coin celebrates the victory of Augustus' stepson, Nero Claudius Drusus, over the Germans in 12 BCE.*

48. AR *denarius*. *Colonia* Copia Felix Munatia (Lugdunum) mint. Struck 15–12 BCE. Obverse: AVGVSTVS DIVI F. Bare head of Augustus facing right. Reverse: IMP – X across field. SICIL in exergue. Diana standing left, head right holding spear and bow, dog standing at feet. (Numismatic references: *BMC* 463; Cohen 146 (6 Fr.); Paris 1393 pl. LVI (same dies); *RIC* 173a.) *This type of Diana of Sicily may refer back to Augustus' defeat of the renegade Sex. Pompeius twenty-four years earlier at the Battle of Naulochus off the coast of Sicily in 36 BCE.*

49. AE *as*. *Colonia* Copia Felix Munatia (Lugdunum) mint. Struck 10 BCE–14 CE. Obverse: PONTIF MAX CAESAR. Laureate head of Augustus facing right. Reverse: Front elevation of the Altar of *Roma et Augustus* at Condate, decorated with the *corona civica* between laurels, flanked by nude male figures; to left and right, winged Victories on columns, facing one another. ROM ET AVG below. (Numismatic references: *BMC* 550; *RIC* 230.) *The sacred precinct at Condate was opened on 1 August 10 BCE and was the site of annual sacrifices by the* Concilium Galliarum. *This coin type was minted to the end of Augustus' reign.*

50. AV *aureus*. *Colonia* Copia Felix Munatia (Lugdunum) mint. Struck 8 BCE. Obverse: AVGVSTVS DIVI F. Laureate head of Augustus facing right. Reverse: IMP XIIII in exergue. Togate Augustus seated left on curule chair set on low

dais, receiving a child from a bearded barbarian man wearing a cloak. (Numismatic references: *BMC* 492; Calicò 235; *CBN* 1451; Cohen 174; *RIC* 200.) *The coin was minted after Tiberius concluded the* Bellum Germanicum *begun by his younger brother. He made treaties with several nations, including the Cherusci, which involved handing over hostages, among whom might have been Arminius and Flavus.*

51. AR *denarius* (plate 39). *Colonia* Copia Felix Munatia (Lugdunum) mint. Struck 8 BCE. Obverse: AVGVSTVS DIVI F. Laureate head of Augustus facing right. Reverse: IMP XIIII in exergue. Togate Augustus seated left on curule chair set on low dais, receiving a child from a bearded barbarian man wearing a cloak. (Numismatic references: *BMC* 493–95 = *BMCRR* Gaul 216–18; *BN* 1453–55; *RIC* 201a; Lyon 65; *RSC* 175.) *The coin was minted after Tiberius concluded the* Bellum Germanicum *begun by his younger brother. He made treaties with several nations, including the Cherusci, which involved handing over hostages, among whom might have been Arminius and Flavus. (This is the silver version of no. 50.)*

52. AV *aureus*. *Colonia* Copia Felix Munatia (Lugdunum) mint. Struck 8 (or 2) BCE. Obverse: AVGVSTVS DIVI F. Laureate head of Augustus facing right. Reverse: C CAES above, AVGVS F in exergue. C. Caesar holding reins in right hand, sword and shield in left, on horse galloping to right with a *bulla* around his neck. To left, an *aquila* between two army *signa*. (Numismatic references: Biaggi 90–91; *BMC* 498–99; *BN* 1457–60; Calicó 174; Lyon 68 (D287/R310); *RIC* 198.) *The coin may mark the occasion in 8 BCE when the 14-year-old C. Caesar accompanied Tiberius to* Tres Galliae *and* Germania *to take part in military exercises; or the ceremony to inaugurate the* Forum Augustum *on 12 May 2 BCE.*

53. AR *denarius* (plate 38). *Colonia* Copia Felix Munatia (Lugdunum) mint. Struck 8 (or 2) BCE. Obverse: AVGVSTVS DIVI F. Laureate head of Augustus facing right. Reverse: C CAES above, AVGVS F in exergue. C. Caesar holding reins in right hand, sword and shield in left, on horse galloping to right with a *bulla* around his neck. To left, an *aquila* between two army *signa*. (Numismatic references: *BMC* 500; Lyon 69; *RIC* 199; *RSC* 40.) *The coin may mark the occasion in 8 BCE when the 14-year-old C. Caesar accompanied Tiberius to* Tres Galliae *and* Germania *to take part in military exercises; or the ceremony to inaugurate the* Forum Augustum *on 12 May 2 BCE. (This is the silver version of no. 52.)*

54. AE *as*. Phoenicia (*Colonia* Iulia Augusta Felix Berytus) mint. Struck 6–4 BCE by P. Quinctilius Varus as *legatus*. Obverse: IMP CAESA[R] AVGVSTVS. Bare head of Augustus facing right. Reverse: P QVINTILLVS VARVS. Two *aquilae*. (Numismatic references: *AUB* 35–36; *BMC* 55; Rouvier 493; *RPC* 4535.) *A low denomination coin issued by a* colonia *of veterans with the approval of the* legatus Augusti pro praetore.

55. AV *aureus*. *Colonia* Copia Felix Munatia (Lugdunum) mint. Struck 2 BCE–4 CE. Obverse: CAESAR AVGVSTVS DIVI F PATER PATRIAE. Laureate head of Augustus facing right. Reverse: AVGVSTI F COS DESIG PRINC IVVENT. Caius and Lucius Caesar standing front, each resting on shield and

behind each shield, a spear. Above on right *lituus* and on left a *simpulum*. In exergue C L CAESARES. (Numismatic references: *BMC* 515; Calicò 176; Cohen 42; *RIC* 206.) *When the two Caesar brothers took turns to serve as* princeps iuventitis *they each received a silver shield and a spear from the* Equester Ordo. *This is the most common* denarius *type minted under Augustus, which continued to be struck even after the death of both young men.*

56. AR *denarius* (plate 37). *Colonia* Copia Felix Munatia (Lugdunum) mint. Struck 2 BCE–4 CE. Obverse: CAESAR AVGVSTVS DIVI F PATER PATRIAE. Laureate head of Augustus facing right. Reverse: AVGVSTI F COS DESIG PRINC IVVENT. C. and L. Caesar standing front, each resting on shield and behind each shield, a spear. Above on right *lituus* and on left a *simpulum*. In exergue C L CAESARES. (Numismatic references: *BMC* 533; *RCV* 1597; *RIC* 207; *RSC* 43.) *When the two Caesar brothers took turns to serve as* princeps iuventitis *they each received a silver shield and a spear from the* Ordo Equester. *(This is the silver version of no. 55.)*

57. AE *as*. Phoenicia (*Colonia* Iulia Augusta Felix Berytus) mint. Struck 12–14 CE by Q. Caecilius Metellus Creticus Silanus as *legatus*. Obverse: IMP AVG. Bare of Augustus facing right. Reverse: PERMISSV SILANI. Two *aquila* and military standards. (Numismatic references: *RPC* 4541; Rouvier 495–96.) *A low denomination coin issued by the* colonia *of veterans with the approval of the* legatus Augusti pro praetore.

58. AR *denarius* (fig. 12). *Colonia* Copia Felix Munatia (Lugdunum) mint. Struck 13–14 CE. Obverse: CAESAR AVGVSTVS DIVI F PATER PATRIAE. Laureate head of Augustus facing right. Reverse: TI CAESAR AVG F TR POT XV. Tiberius, laureate, standing togate to right in triumphal *quadriga*, holding laurel and eagle-tipped sceptre; the horses' heads all face right. (Numismatic references: *BMC* 512; *RIC* 222.) *The coin celebrates Tiberius' triumph of 23 October 12 CE for his victory in Illyricum during the* Bellum Batonianum.

Glossary

Acies – Battle order: e.g. in *triplex acies* a legion was deployed as four cohorts at the front, three in the second row and three in the third row.

Ad locutio – Address by a commander to his assembled troops.

Aedilis – Aedile, magistrate in charge of public works, regulating state festivals and enforcing public order.

Aes – 'Copper', a coin worth one half *dupondius* (*asses* pl.).

Agmen – Column of troops.

Ala – 'Wing', legionary cavalry on wings of battle formation (*alae* pl.).

Amphora – Tall jar in which olive oil, fish sauce, wine and other products were carried and stacked in the holds of ships.

Annona – Personification of the grain supply of Rome.

Apex – Spiked cap worn by a *flamen*.

Aquila – 'Eagle', the eagle standard of a legion.

Aquilifer – Standard bearer carrying the *aquila*.

Ara – Altar.

As – 'Copper', Roman coin worth half one *dupondius* (*aes, asses* pl.).

Auctoritas – Influence from having prestige, personal authority.

Augur – Soothsayer specializing in interpretation of bird flight.

Augustus – 'Revered One', honourific title voted to Imp. *Divi f.* in 27 BCE.

Aureus – 'Gold', highest denomination gold coin worth twenty-five *denarii* (*aurei* pl.).

Auspex – Soothsayer specializing in interpreting flight of birds.

Auspicia – Auspices.

Auxilia – 'Helpers', support troops of allied or non-Roman citizens.

Ballista – Artillery weapon throwing bolts or stones.

Bellator – 'Warrior', Roman war-fighter (*bellatores* pl.).

Caligatus – 'Boot wearer', ordinary soldier of a legion (*caligati* pl.).

Campus Martius – 'Field of Mars', a large park and recreation ground in northwest Rome.

Capitolinus – Hill in Rome on which was built the Temple of Iupiter Optimus Maximus.

Carru triumphali – Decorated chariot used in a triumph.

Catapulta – Artillery weapon throwing bolts.

Censor – Magistrate in charge of the *census*.

Census – Assessment of taxable assets carried out every five years (*lustum*).

Centuria – 'Century', unit of eight *contubernia* eighty men; sixty centuries formed a *legio*.

Centurio – 'Centurion', officer in charge of a *centuria*.

Clementia – 'Clemency', the Roman virtue of showing mercy.

Cohors – 'Cohort', unit of six centuries, or twelve in a First Cohort (*cohortes* pl.).

Cohors Praetoria – 'Praetorian Cohort', Praetorian Guard (*Cohortes Praetoriae* pl.).

Cohorts Voluntariorum – Levy of citizens serving in cohort of volunteers (*cohortes voluntariorum* pl.).

Colonia – 'Colony', city founded for retired legionaries.

Commilitio – 'Fellow soldier', a form of address to legionaries usually by a senior officer (*commilitiones* pl.).

Confarreatio – Traditional form of wedding.

Concilium – Advisory committee of the senior commanding officer formed of his immediate reports.

Consulis – One of the two highest magistrates of the *res publica*, elected annually.

Contio – 'Meeting', an address by a magistrate to the people or the commander to his troops to present a proposal.

Cuneus – 'Wedge', attack formation used by Roman army.

Curator viarum – Manager of roads (*curatores* pl.).

Curia Iulia – Senate House.

Currus – two-wheeled chariot used during triumphal parades.

Cursus honorum – 'Race of honour', the career ladder leading to the consulship.

Decursio – Military exercise performed as a pageant on special occasions.

Denarius – Silver coin, worth four *sestertii* (*denarii* pl.).

Dilectus ingenuorum – Levy of civilians into *cohortes voluntariorum*.

Dupondius – Bronze coin, worth two *asses* or one half a *sestertius* (*dupondii* pl.).

Editor – Sponsor of the *ludi* or *munera*.

Equites – 'Knights', the middle or business class of Roman society.

Evocatus – 'Summoned one', reservist, an honourably discharged *miles gregarius* available for recall on the orders of a consul or military commander (*evocati* pl.)

Exercitus – Army.

Fasces – The tied bundle of rods around an axe carried by *lictores* as a symbol of the consul's or *praetor*'s high office.

Fercula – Placard carried on a pole with painted words to explain the exhibit in a triumph.

Feria – Public holiday and festival day (*feriae* pl.).

Flamen – Priest (*flamines* pl.).

Framea – Germanic spear or javelin (*frameae* pl.).

Frater – 'Brother', a form of address used by soldiers (*fratres* pl.).

Forum Romanum – Roman Forum in central Rome.

Gladius – Short stabbing and thrusting weapon used by legionaries (*gladii* pl.).

Haruspex – Soothsayer specializing in interpreting animal entrails.

Hasta – Javelin used by Roman *auxilia* and cavalry.

Honesta – 'Honesty', the Roman virtue of respectability.

Hostis publicus – 'Public enemy', enemy of the state.

Humanitas – 'Humanity', the Roman virtue associated with being cultured from having a good education.

Ianus – 'Arch', portal or triumphal arch.

Imago – Mask of wax made during the lifetime of a Roman citizen; military standard bearing a small statue bust of the *princeps*.

Impedimenta – Baggage train.

Imperator – 'Commander', a title shouted by troops to a victorious leader after a victory.

Imperium – Legal power vested in certain Roman magistrates to give absolute orders and enforce obedience.

Imperium proconsulare – Legal power to govern territories beyond Italy, including the right to wage war.

Imperium proconsuare maius – 'Supreme power' to govern territories beyond Italy, which was superior to that of all other consuls and proconsuls.

Industria – Roman virtue of working hard.

Kalendae – 'Calends', first day of the month.

Laudatio – Eulogy.

Legatus Augusti Pro Praetore – Governor of one of the Provinces of Caesar (propraetorian provinces), 'delegated' the *imperium* by Augustus.

Legatus Legionis – Commander of a *legio*, 'delegated' the *imperium* by Augustus.

Legio – Unit of ten *cohortes*, approximately 6,000 men (*legiones* pl.).

Libertas – Roman virtue of independence, freedom of speech.

Liburna – 'Liburnian', type of ship, usually with two rows of oarsmen.

Lictor – Bodyguard of a senior magistrate: a *consul* had twelve, a *praetor* six, a *pro praetor* five and an *aedile* two (*lictores* pl.).

Lituus – Crooked staff used by an augur when interpreting bird flight.

Lorica hamata – Body armour made of chain or ring mail.

Lorica squamata – Body armour made of scales attached to a backing of cloth or leather.

Lorica segmentata – Body armour made of articulated metal plates (a non-Roman term coined in the sixteenth century).

Ludi – Roman blood games, held for religious observance and increasingly used to further political ends.

Lustrum – Period of five years.

Medicus – 'Medic', doctor.

Miles – Common soldier, *miles gregarius* (*milites* pl.).

Moderatio – 'Moderation', Roman virtue of restraint from excess, self-control.

Modius – Measure of grain equivalent to a third of an *amphora*.

Mos maiorum – 'The ways of the elders', traditional values and forms of worship.

Munera – Roman blood games held for political and entertainment purposes.

Municipium – Chartered provincial Roman city.

Navis longa – 'Long ship', warship.

Nobiles – Group of men who had served as consul or came from a consular family, a status not an official class.

Novus homo – 'New man', a man not of the *nobiles*.

Officium – 'Service', the staff – office – responsible for record keeping.

Oppidum – Town or defensible settlement, often on a hill.

Onager – 'Wild ass', artillery weapon throwing stones.

Optimates – Conservative bloc of the Roman senators seeking to preserve the *status quo*.

Ornamenta – Ceremonial trappings of a lower grade triumph.

Ovatio – Lower form of triumph awarded to a victorious commander who was permitted to ride on a horse or walk through the streets of Rome.

Palatinus – Hill in Rome, location of homes originally of the Roman élite.

Palatium – Augustus' house on the Palatinus Hill.

Paludamentum – Cloak worn by a high-ranking officer.

Parazonium – Weapon with a leaf shaped blade (approximately 15″–19″ long) carried by a high-ranking officer.

Paterfamilias – Legal master of the household.

Pietas – Roman virtue of respect for the natural order of things.

Pilum – Roman javelin used by legionaries (*pila* pl.).

Pompa – Procession in a religious rite or funeral.

Pompa triumphalis – Full triumph in which the *triumphator* rode in a chariot followed by floats displaying the captive and spoils of war.

Pontifex Maximus – 'Chief road builder' (from *pont*, Etruscan for 'road'?), chief priest.

Populares – Progressive bloc of Roman senators seeking to change the *status quo*.

Praefectus – 'Prefect', senior officer or magistrate.

Praefectus Aegypti – 'Prefect of Egypt', the governor of province Aegyptus.

Praefectus Castrorum – 'Camp Prefect', third in command of a *legio*.

Praefectus Equitum – 'Prefect of Horse', senior officer in command of a *turma*.

Praefectus Praetorio – Commander of the *Cohors Praetoria*.

Praemia – Cash lump-sum paid to a soldier upon honourable discharge from the army.

Praeda – Booty captured from a defeated enemy in war.

Praepositus – 'Overseer', special envoy or governor general.

Praetor – Senior magistrate responsible for administering law, the *ludi* and *feriae*.

Praetor Urbanus – Chief *praetor* in charge of administration of law in Rome.

Praetorianus – Soldier in the Praetorian Cohorts (*praetoriani* pl.).

Praetorium – 'Praetor's building', house of the senior officer of a *legio*.

Pridianum – Report of troop numbers as at 31 December, prepared annually by a legate's *officium* (*pridiana* pl.).

Primus Pilus – 'First javelin', the most senior *centurio* of a *legio*.

Princeps – 'The First One', the title adopted by Augustus to describe his leadership position.

Princeps Praetorii – Officer in charge of the army unit's *officium*.

Principalis – Non-commissioned officer of a *centuria*, e.g. *cornicen*, *signifer* (*principales* pl.).

Principia – 'Front line', headquarters building in a Roman fort.

Proconsulis – 'Former consul', governor of a senatorial province.

Propraetor – 'Former praetor', governor of an imperial province.

Quaestor – Junior magistrate in charge of law courts and public financial accounting.

Res Gestae – 'Things Done', the title of Augustus' autobiography.

Res Publica – 'Public Thing', the commonwealth of the Roman state.

Rostra – Tribunal, speaker's platform in *Forum Romanum*.

Rostrum – Bronze ram fitted to the front of a warship.

Sacerdos – Priest (*sacerdotes* pl.).

Saeculum – A period estimated to be the lifetime of a man, approximately 100 years.

Salutatio – Morning visit by clients to the patron.

Sarcina – Backpack of clothing, equipment, rations and supplies carried by a legionary on the march (*sarcinae* pl.).

Scutum – Roman shield (*scuta* pl.).

Semis – Roman coin worth half one *as*.

Senatus Consultum – Decree of the Senate.

Sestertius – Brass coin, equal in value to one-quarter *denarius* (*sestertii* pl.).

Signifer – Standard bearer carrying the centurial *signum*.

Signum – Unit standard (*signa* pl.).

Socius – Ally, associate (*socii* pl.)

Spolia opima – Prized spoils taken from a deceased commander after armed one-to-one combat, usually by a senior Roman officer.

Suffectus – A consul replacing another who had resigned during his term in office.

Suovetaurilia – Religious rite to Mars involving the sacrifice of a pig, sheep and bull.

Summum imperium auspiciumque – Military power permitting the holder to primacy over another when two commanders held the same rank.

Testudo – 'Tortoise', battle formation using shields raised over the heads.

Toga praetexta – White toga with a broad purple stripe along the curved edge.

Toga pura – 'Manly gown', the all-white toga worn by Roman adult men.

Toga virilis – 'Manly gown', the all-white toga worn by Roman adult men.

Tresvir – 'Three Man', a member of a board responsible for a state function, e.g. *tresviri monetales* who were responsible for managing the coin supply.

Tribunus – Tribune: *tribunus plebis*, a representative of the people elected annually; *tribunus laticlavius*, the second in command of a *legio*, was accompanied by five junior *tribuni angusticlavii*.

Tribunicia potestas – Legal power and personal immunity of a plebeian tribune.

Triennium – Period of three years.

Triumphator – The military commander awarded an *ovatio* or *pompa triumphalis*.

Triumvir, IIIvir – Member of a commission of three political leaders (*triumviri* pl.).

Tropaeum – 'Trophy' made of captured weapons (*tropaea* pl.).

Tumulus – Cenotaph shaped like a raised circular dome (*tumuli* pl.).

Veteranus – 'Veteran', honourably discharged soldier having served his full term.

Vexillum – Flag standard.
Vexillarius – Detachment.
Via Praetoria – Cross road in a Roman camp leading to *principia*.
Via Principalis – Main street of a Roman camp.
Via Sacra – 'Sacred Way', the main road running through the Forum Romanum.
Virtus – 'Manliness', Roman virtue of courage.

Place Names

Cities and Towns

Actium	Aktion
Alexandria	Alexandria
Aliso	*Anreppen* or *Haltern-am-See?*
Amisos	Samsun
Andetrium	Muč
Antiocheia	Antakya
Apollonia	Pojani
Aquileia	Aquilea
Ara Ubiorum	(after 1CE) Cologne, Köln
Aracillum	Aradillos or Espina del Gallego?
Arausio	Orange
Arelate	Arles
Ariminum	Rimini
Artaxata	Artashat
Assos	Behramkale
Athenae	Athens, Athenai
Atuatuca	*Tongres, Tongeren?*
Augusta Emerita	Mérida
Augusta Paetoria Salassorum	Aosta
Augusta Taurinorum	Turin
Augusta Treverorum	Trier
Augusta Vindelicorum	Augsburg
Autricum	Chartres
Axima	Aime
Baiae	Baia
Barcino	Barcelona
Batavodurum	Hunerberg, Kops Plateau, Nijmegen
Beneventum	Benevento
Brixia	Brescia
Brigantium	Briançon
Brundisium	Brindisi
Burdigala	Bordeaux
Burnum	Roman camp near modern Kistanje, Croatia
Byzantium	Istanbul, Constantinople
Caesaraugusta	Zaragoza

Caesarea Maritima	Caesarea
Carnuntum	Roman fortress located east of Vienna
Cartenna	Mostaganem
Carthago Nova	Cartagena
Cenabum	Orléans
Chersonesus	Sevastopol
Cibalae	Vinkovici
Colonia Alexandria Augusta Troadis	Eski Stambul
Colonia Augusta Buthrotum	Butrint
Colonia Copia Felix Munatia	Lyon (Fourvière)
Colonia Iulia Augusta Felix Berytus	Beirut
Colonia Laus Iulia Corinthiensis	Corinth, Korinthos
Colonia Obsequens Iulia Pisana	Pisa
Corduba	Cordoba
Cyrrhus	Khoros
Dyrrhacium	Durrës
Emona	Ljubljana
Ephesus	Roman city near Selçuk, Izmir
Epidaurum	Cavtat
Fectio	Vechten
Forum Iulii	Fréjus
Fulginiae	Foligno
Gabii	Roman town near modern Osteria dell'Osa
Gadara	Umm Qais
Glanum	St-Rémy-de-Provence
Hierosylima	Jerusalem
Illium (Illion)	Hisarlik, Troy
Koptos	Qift, Egypt
Lampasakos	Lapeski
Laodikeia	Loadikya
Legio	León
Lugdunum	(after mid-first century CE) Lyon
Massalia	Marseille
Mediolanum Santonum	Saintes
Melitene	Malatya
Messana	Messina
Methone	Methoni
Mogontiacum	Mainz
Mutina	Modena
Mytilene	Mytilini
Nemausus	Nîmes
Napata	Karima
Narbo	Narbonne
Nikopolis	'Victory City', Preveza, Greece
Nikopolis	'Victory City' east of Alexandria, Egypt

Nissus	Niš
Novaesium	Neuss
Oescus	Gigen
Oppidum Ubiorum	(prior to 1CE) Cologne, Köln
Palencia	Herrera de Pisuerga
Perusia	Perugia
Pola	Pula
Portus Iulius	Roman port at Lake Lucrino, Gulf of Baia
Ptolemais	Acre
Puteoli	Pozzuoli
Racilium	see Aracillum
Raphanaea	Rafniye
Ravenna	Ravenna
Rhegium	Reggio di Calabria
Roma	Rome, Roma
Salona	Solin
Samosata	Samsat
Scarbantia	Sopron
Segisama	Sasamón
Segusio	Susa
Scupi	Skopje
Sinope	Sinop
Sirmium	Mitrovica
Siscia	Sisak
Sutrium	Sutri
Syene	Aswan
Tarsus	Tarsus
Tarraco	Tarragona
Tergestum	Trieste, Triest
Tibur	Tivoli
Ticinum	Pavia
Tilurium	Gardun near Trilj, Croatia
Tridentum	Trento
Tyndaris	Tindari
Venusia	Venosa
Vienna	Vienne on the Rhône
Viminacium	Stari Kostolac, Serbia
Vindobona	Vienna
Vorgium	Carhaix

Islands

Capreae	Capri
Kerkyra, Corcyra	Corfu
Pandateria	Ventotene
Planasia	Pianosa

Rhodos — Rhodes
Siciliae — Sicily
Strongyle — Stromboli
Trimerus — Isole Tremiti

Mountains

Mons Alma — Fruska Gora
Mons Claudius — Papuk Hills
Mons Medullus — *Peña Sagra?*
Mons Vindius — *Peña Santa?*
Matrona Mons — Mount Genèvre

Rivers

Albis — Elbe
Amisia — Ems
Aous — Vjosë
Arar — Saône
Danuvius — Danube, Donau
Dravus — Drava, Drave
Drinus — Drina
Garonna — Garonne
Ister — Danube, Donau
Liger — Loire
Mosa — Meuse
Mosella — Moselle, Mosel
Minius — Miño, Minho
Nilus — Nile
Padus — Po
Pyramus — Ceyhan
Rhenus — Rhine, Rhein
Rhodanus — Rhône
Savus — Sava, Save, Száva

Seas

Mare Aegaeum — Aegean Sea
Mare Germanicum — North Sea
Mare Internum — Mediterranean Sea
Oceanus Atlanticus — Atlantic Ocean
Pontus Euxinus — Black Sea
Sinus Ambracius — Ambracian Gulf
Sinus Arabicus — Red Sea
Sinus Hadriaticus — Adriatic Sea

Notes

Abbreviations
(a) *Modern*

AE	*L'Année Epigraphique.*
BMCRE	H.B. Mattingly *et al.*, *Coins of the Roman Empire in the British Museum* (London, 1923–62).
BMCRR	H.A. Grueber, *Coins of the Roman Republic in the British Museum* (London, 1910).
C	H. Cohen, *Description historique des monnaies frappées sous l'Empire Romain* (Paris, 1880–92).
CAH	A.K. Bowman *et al.*, *The Cambridge Ancient History, Volume X: The Augustan Empire, 43BC–AD69* (Cambridge, 1996).
Calicó	X. and F. Calicó, *Catálogo de Monedas Antiguas de Hispania* (Barcelona, 1979).
CBN	*Catalogue des monnaies de l'empire romaine, Bibliothèque nationale* (Paris, 1976–88).
CIG	*Corpus Inscriptionum Graecarum* (Berlin, 1828–77).
CIL	T. Mommsen *et al.*, *Corpus Inscriptionem Latinarum* (Berlin, 1863–).
CRA	P. Erdkamp, *A Companion to the Roman Army* (Oxford, 2007).
EJ	V. Ehrenberg and A.H.M. Jones, *Documents Illustrating the Reigns of Augustus and Tiberius* (Oxford, 1949; Second revised edition, 1955).
Eph. Epig.	*Ephemeris Epigraphica.*
IGR	*Inscriptiones Graecae et res Romanas pertinentes.*
ILS	*Inscriptiones Latinae Selectae.*
ILTG	P. Wuilleumier, *Inscriptions Latines des Trois Gaules* (Paris, 1963).
JbSGU	*Jahrbuch (Jahresbericht) der Schweizerischen Gesellschaft für Urgeschichte.*
JRA	*Journal of Roman Archaeology.*
JRMES	*Journal of Roman Military Equipment Studies.*
JRS	*Journal of Roman Studies.*
Klose	D.O.A. Klose, *Die Münzprägung von Smyrna in der römischen Kaiserzeit* (Berlin, 1987).
MDAI(I)	*Mitteilungen des Deutschen Archäologischen Instituts (Abteiling Instanbul).*
RIC	H.B. Mattingly and E.A. Sydenham, *Roman Imperial Coinage* (London, 1913–56).
RIL	*Rendiconti del Instituto Lombardo di scienza e lettere, Classe di Lettere.*
RPC	A. Burnett *et al.*, *Roman Provincial Coinage, Vol. I* (London, 1992).
RSC	H.A. Seaby *et al.*, *Roman Silver Coins, Volume 1*, (London, 1978–87).
S	D.R. Sear, *Roman Coins and Their Values* (Fifth revised edition, London, 2000).
SIG³	W. Dittenberger, *Sylloge Inscriptionum Graecarum* (Third revised edition, Leipzig, 1883).
SNG Aulock	H. von Aulock, *Sylloge Nummorum Graecorum, Deutschland, Cilicia* (Berlin, 1981).
SNG Copenhagen	*Sylloge Nummorum Graecorum, Danish National Museum* (Copenhagen, 1942–79).
SNG Levante	E. Levante, *Sylloge Nummorum Graecorum, Switzerland 1: Cilicia* (Bern, 1986).
Svoronos	J. Svoronos, *Ta Nomismata tou Kratous ton Ptolemaion* (Athens, 1904–08).

(b) *Ancient Authors*

Amm. Marc.	Ammianus Marcellinus, *Rerum Gestarum*.
App., *Bell. Civ.*	Appian, *Bellum Civile*.
App., *Ill.*	Appian, *Illyrike*.
Athen., *Deipn.*	Athenaeus, *Deipnosophistai*.
Aul. Gell., *Noct. Att.*	Aulus Gellius, *Noctes Atticae*.
Caes., *Bell. Alex.*	Caesar, *Bellum Alexandrinum*.
Caes., *Bell. Gall.*	Caesar, *Bellum Gallicum*.
Caes., *Bell. Hisp.*	Caesar, *Bellum Hispanicum*
Cato, *Agr.*	Cato the Elder, *De Agricultura*.
Cic., *Amic.*	Cicero, *De Amicitia*.
Cic., *Att.*	Cicero, *Ad Atticum*.
Cic., *Brut.*	Cicero, *Brutus*.
Cic., *Div.*	Cicero, *De Divinatione*.
Cic., *Font.*	Cicero, *Pro Fonteio*.
Cic., *Leg.*	Cicero, *De Legibus*.
Cic., *Ora.*	Cicero, *De Oratore*.
Cic., *Prov. Cons.*	Cicero, *De Provinciis Consularibus*.
Cic., *Tusc. Disp.*	Cicero, *Tusculanae Disputationes*.
Dio	Cassius Dio, *Romaiki Historia*.
Diog. Laert.	Diogenes Laertius, *Bion kai Gnomon ton en Philosophiai*.
Diod. Sic.	Diodorus Siculus, *Bibliotheka Historika*.
Ennius, *Ann.*	Ennius, *Annales*.
Eutrop., *Brev.*	Eutropius, *Breviarium*.
Frontin., *Aq.*	Frontinus, *De Aquis*.
Hdt.	Herodotus, *Istorion*.
Hor., *Carm.*	Horace, *Carmina*.
Joseph., *Ant. Iud.*	Josephus, *Antiquitatae Iudaicae*.
Joseph., *Bell. Iud.*	Josephus, *Bellum Iudaicum*.
Livy, *AUC*	Livy, *Ab Urbe Condita*.
Livy, *Peri.*	Livy, *Periochae*.
Nic.	Nikolaos of Damaskos, *Bios Kaisaros*.
Ov., *Fast.*	Ovid, *Fasti*.
Ov., *Pont.*	Ovid, *Epistulae Ex Ponto*.
Ov., *Tr.*	Ovid, *Tristia*.
Paus.	Pausanias, *Ellados Periegisis*.
Pliny, *Ep.*	Pliny the Younger, *Epistulae*.
Pliny, *Nat. Hist.*	Pliny the Elder, *Naturalis Historia*.
Plut., *Ant.*	Plutarch, *Antonios*.
Plut., *Brut.*	Plutarch, *Broutos*.
Plut., *Caes.*	Plutarch, *Kaisar*.
Plut., *Cass.*	Plutarch, *Kassios*.
Plut., *De Invid. et Od.*	Plutarch, *De Invidiam et Odium*.
Plut., *Mar.*	Plutarch, *Marios*.
Plut. *Pomp.*	Plutarch, *Pompeios*.
Polyb.	Polybius, *Istoria*.
Ptol., *Geog.*	Ptolemy, *Geography*.
RG	Augustus, *Res Gestae*.
Sen., *Constant.*	Seneca the Younger, *De Constantia Sapientis*.
Sen., *Ep.*	Seneca the Younger, *Epistulae Morales*.
Sen., *Nat. Qu.*	Seneca the Younger, *Quaestiones Naturales*.
Sen., *Ira*	Seneca the Younger, *De Ira*.
Sen., *Polyb.*	Seneca the Younger, *De Consolatione ad Polybium*.
Sen., *Suas.*	Seneca the Elder, *Suasoriae*.

Strab., *Geog.*	Strabo, *Geographika.*
Suet., *Calig.*	Suetonius, *Caius.*
Suet., *Div. Aug.*	Suetonius, *Divus Augustus.*
Suet., *Div. Claud.*	Suetonius, *Divus Claudius.*
Suet., *Div. Iul.*	Suetonius, *Divus Iulius.*
Suet., *Div. Vesp.*	Suetonius, *Divus Vespasianus.*
Suet., *Grammat.*	Suetonius, *De Grammaticis.*
Suet., *Ner.*	Suetonius, *Nero.*
Suet., *Tib.*	Suetonius, *Tiberius.*
Suet., *Verg.*	Suetonius, *Vita Vergili.*
Tac., *Agr.*	Tacitus, *Agricola.*
Tac., *Ann.*	Tacitus, *Annales.*
Tac., *Germ.*	Tacitus, *Germania.*
Tac., *Hist.*	Tacitus, *Historiae.*
Val. Max.	Valerius Maximus, *Facta et Dicta Memorabilia.*
Vell. Pat.	Velleius Paterculus, *Historiae Romanae.*
Xen., *Anab.*	Xenophon, *Anabasis.*
Zonar.	Zonaras, *Epitome Istorion.*

Chapter 1: Seek and Destroy

1. Dio 50.10.1.
2. The *tresviri rei publicae constituendae*, which modern historians call the Second Triumvirate to distinguish it from the First (comprising C. Iulius Caesar, Cn. Pompeius Magnus and M. Licinius Crassus): Dio 46.55.1–4; Plut., *Ant.* 30.4; Suet., *Div. Aug.* 8.3, 12.1. On the legal basis of the Second Triumvirate, see Millar (1973).
3. Dio 50.1–10.
4. Dio 47.1.1; Plut., *Ant.* 55.2; Suet., *Div. Aug.* 13.1.
5. Plut., *Ant.* 31.1–3, 53.5, 56.2, 57.2.
6. Plut., *Ant.* 54.1.
7. Plut., *Ant.* 37–53.
8. Plut., *Ant.* 54.3–4.
9. Plut., *Ant.* 55.1–2.
10. *RG* 25.2. For the text of a *sacramentum* see *ILS* 8781 (Gangra in Paphlagonia) dated to 3 BCE.
11. Florus 2.21.2.
12. Dio 50.4.5: 'ἅπερ που λόγῳ μὲν πρὸς τὴν Κλεοπάτραν, ἔργῳ δὲ καὶ πρὸς τὸν Ἀντώνιον ἔτεινεν'; 50.6.1.
13. Dio 50.4.2–3.
14. For examples of pre-war propaganda see Finley (1985). For examples of *Divi filius* on coins see Appendix 4.
15. Dio 50.4.4–5. Having the ceremony in Rome spared him the customary burden of delivering the message in person to the offender on foreign soil.
16. Dio 50.2.2–3.
17. Dio 50.2.5.
18. Vell. Pat. 2.84.2.
19. Nic. 11.
20. App., *Bell. Civ.* 3.9; Dio 45.1.7–8; Vell. Pat. 2.59.4.
21. Suet., *Div. Aug.* 10.3.
22. Perusine War: App., *Bell. Civ.* 5.32–35. War Against Sex. Pompeius: App., *Bell. Civ.* 5.93–128. L. Antonius was the younger brother and a supporter of M. Antonius.
23. App., *Ill.* 20; Pliny, *Nat. Hist.* 7.148; Dio 49.35.2, 38.4; Suet., *Div. Aug.* 20: *He was wounded, too, in Dalmatia, being struck on the right knee with a stone in one battle, and in another having a leg and both arms severely injured by the collapse of a bridge | Delmatico etiam vulnera excepit, una acie dextrum genu lapide ictus, altera et crus et utrumque brachium ruina pontis consauciatus.*
24. Suet., *Div. Aug.* 68.

25. Imp. Caesar's comportment: Suet., *Div. Aug.* 79.1; height, eyes: Suet., *Div. Aug.* 79.2 citing Iulius Marathus. Hair: Suet., *Div. Aug.* 79.1.
26. Caesar's limp: Suet., *Div. Aug.* 80 – perhaps related to the injury at Metulus: see note 23.
27. Suet., Div. Aug. 81.1: *Graves et periculosas valitudines per omnem vitam aliquot expertus est.*
28. Pre-battle sickness: e.g. Suet., *Div. Aug.* 8.1, 13.1 and 81.1; Dio 53.25.7.
29. Nic. 11.
30. Alföldi (1976), pp. 25–30. Balbus: Suet., *Div. Iul.* 81.2; Dio 54.25.2. Oppius: Suet., *Div. Iul.* 52.2, 53, 56.1, 72.
31. Suet., *Div. Aug.* 66.1. Q. Salvidienus Rufus, one of the select group of friends present with Caesar at Apollonia in the days following the Ides of March, had been executed in 40 BCE when it was discovered he had sought to switch allegiance to Antonius.
32. Dio 50.9.2–3, 50.14.1.
33. Suet., *Div. Aug.* 94.12; Vell. Pat. 2.59.5.
34. For an assessment of Agrippa's origins see Powell (2015), pp. 200–02.
35. For an assessment of Agrippa's abilities see Powell (2015), pp. 203–06.
36. Agrippa was 25 when he led his men across the Rhine, Iulius Caesar 45.
37. Agrippa's naval crown – source.
38. Dio 50.9.2.
39. Dio 50.9.2–3.
40. Orosius 6.19.7: *inde Corcyram cepit; fugientes navali proelio persecutus profligauit multisque rebus cruentissime gestis ad Caesarem venit.*
41. Dio 50.12.1.
42. Orosius 6.19.6.
43. Dio 50.11.3; Orosius 6.19.6.
44. Dio 50.11.3 = Zonar. 10.29.
45. Plut., *Ant.* 34.6; Dio 50.14.2.
46. Dio 50.11.5, 50.88.2.
47. Dio 50.11.1; Plut., *Ant.* 62.2.
48. Dio 50.11.2–6.
49. Dio 50.12.7.
50. Dio 50.12.1.
51. Dio 50.12.8.
52. Dio 50.12.8: ταῦτ᾿ οὖν προκατασχόντες οἱ Ἀντωνίειοι ἐπί τε τοῦ στόματος πύργους ἑκατέρωθεν ἐπῳκοδόμησαν καὶ τὸ μέσον ναυσὶ διέλαβον, ὥστε σφίσι καὶ τοὺς ἔκπλους καὶ τὰς ἀναχωρήσεις ἀσφαλεῖς εἶναι· αὐτοί τε ἐπὶ θάτερα τοῦ 1 πορθμοῦ κατὰ τὸ ἔρόν, ἐν χωρίῳ ὁμαλῷ μὲν καὶ πλατεῖ, ἐμμαχέσασθαι δὲ ἢ ἐνστρατοπεδεύσασθαι ἐπιτηδειοτέρῳ, ἐνηυλίζοντο· ἐξ οὗπερ οὐχ ἥκιστα τῇ νόσῳ καὶ ἐν τῷ χειμῶνι, καὶ ἐν τῷ θέρει πολὺ μᾶλλον, ἐπιέσθησαν; *cf.* 50.15.3.
53. Vell. Pat. 2.84.1.
54. Plut., *Ant.* 67.7 and 68.4–5.
55. Plut., *Ant.* 56.4; Dio 50.6.5.
56. Dio 50.12.4: καὶ ἐν αὐτῷ ἐπὶ μετεώρου, ὅθεν ἐπὶ πάντα ὁμοίως τῆς τε ἔξω τῆς πρὸς Πάξοις θαλάσσης καὶ τῆς εἴσω 1 τῆς Ἀμπρακικῆς τῆς τε ἐν τῷ μέσῳ αὐτῶν, ἐν ᾧ οἱ λιμένες οἱ πρὸς τῇ Νικοπόλει εἰσίν, ἄποπτόν ἐστιν, ἱδρύθη – the islands he refers to are Paxos and Antipaxos. *Cf.* Florus 2.21.11.4; Livy, *Peri.* 132.2.
57. Vell. Pat., 2.84.1.
58. Dio 50.12.4.
59. Dio 50.12.4: κἀκ τούτου καὶ ἐφήδρευε καὶ ἐφώρμει τῷ Ἀκτίῳ καὶ κατὰ γῆν καὶ κατὰ θάλασσαν. ἤδη μὲν γὰρ ἤκουσα ὅτι καὶ τριήρεις ἐκ τῆς ἔξω θαλάσσης ἐς τὸν κόλπον διὰ τοῦ τειχίσματος ὑπερήνεγκε, βύρσαις νεοδάρτοις ἀντὶ ὁλκῶν ἐλαίῳ ἐπαληλιμμέναις. *cf.* with Caesar's later use of the *diolkos*.
60. Plut., *Ant.* 61.1–2; Vell. Pat. 2.84.1–2. Imp. Caesar's army was drawn from the western half of the empire, Antonius' from the east – Dio 50.6.3–6. Dio 50.16.2 mentions Antonius' army comprised of hoplites, cavalry, slingers, peltasts, archers and mounted archers. Plut., *Ant.* 61.1–2 also lists the client kingdoms arrayed with him: *Of subject kings who fought with him, there were Bocchus the king of Libya, Tarcondemus the king of Upper Cilicia, Archelaüs of Cappadocia, Philadelphus of Paphlagonia,*

Mithridates of Commagene, and Sadalas of Thrace. These were with him, while from Pontus Polemon sent an army, and Malchus from Arabia, and Herod the Jew, besides Amyntas the king of Lycaonia and Galatia; the king of the Medes also sent an auxiliary force | ἐν αἷς ὀκτήρεις πολλαὶ καὶ δεκήρεις κεκοσμημέναι σοβαρῶς καὶ πανηγυρικῶς, στρατοῦ δὲ μυριάδες δέκα, δισχίλιοι δ' ἱππεῖς ἐπὶ μυρίοις. βασιλεῖς δὲ ὑπήκοοι συνεμάχουν Βόκχος ὁ Λιβύων καὶ Ταρκόνδημος ὁ τῆς ἄνω Κιλικίας, καὶ Καππαδοκίας μὲν Ἀρχέλαος, Παφλαγονίας δὲ Φιλάδελφος, Κομμαγηνῆς δὲ Μιθριδάτης, Σαδάλας δὲ Θράκης. οὗτοι μὲν αὐτοὶ παρῆσαν, ἐκ δὲ Πόντου Πολέμων στρατὸν ἔπεμπε, καὶ Μάλχος ἐξ Ἀραβίας καὶ Ἡρώδης ὁ Ἰουδαῖος, ἔτι δὲ Ἀμύντας ὁ Λυκαόνων καὶ Γαλατῶν βασιλεύς· ἦν δὲ καὶ παρὰ τοῦ Μήδων βασιλέως ἀπεσταλμένη βοήθεια.

61. Plut., *Ant.* 42.4; Career: Plut. *Ant* 34.6.
62. Vell. Pat. 2.87.3.
63. Dio 50.13.4.
64. Plut., *Ant.* 63.2.
65. Dio 50.13.4.
66. Dio 50.13.5.
67. Dio 50.13.5: Ἀγρίππας δὲ τότε μὲν τήν τε Λευκάδα καὶ τὰ ἐν αὐτῇ σκάφη αἰφνιδίως ἐπεσπλεύσας ἔλαβε.
68. Vell. Pat. 2.84.2: *Denique in ore atque oculis Antonianae classis per M. Agrippam Leucas expugnata, Patrae captae, Corinthus occupata, bis ante ultimum discrimen classis hostium superata*; Dio 50.13.5.
69. Dio 50.13.2–3: καὶ ἦλθε μὲν οὐ πολλῷ ὕστερον, οὐ μέντοι καὶ ἐς ἀγῶνα εὐθὺς κατέστη, καίτοι ἐκείνου τόν τε πεζὸν πρὸ τοῦ στρατοπέδου σφῶν συνεχῶς προπαρατάσσοντος καὶ ταῖς ναυσὶ πολλάκις σφίσιν ἐπιπλέοντος, τάς τε ὁλκάδας αὐτῶν κατάγοντος, ὅπως πρὶν πᾶσαν τὴν δύναμιν αὐτῷ συνελθεῖν, μόνοις τοῖς τότε παροῦσίν οἱ συμμίξῃ.
70. Orosius 6.19.7: *Antonius defectu et fame militum suorum permotus bellum maturare instituit ac repente instructis copiis ad Caesaris castra processit et uictus est.*
71. Orosius 6.19.8; Dio 50.14.3.
72. Dio 50.15.1.
73. Dio 51.15.2.
74. Dio 50.13.6 and 8; Plut., *Ant.* 63.2; Vell. Pat. 2.84.2.
75. Plut., *Ant.* 40.5.
76. Dio 50.11.1: τοιούτων δὴ σημείων προφανέντων σφίσιν οὔτε ἐφοβήθησαν οὔθ' ἧττόν τι ἐπολέμησαν, ἀλλὰ τὸν μὲν χειμῶνα κατασκοπαῖς τε χρώμενοι καὶ παραλυποῦντες ἀλλήλους διετέλεσαν.
77. Dio 50.31.1.
78. Dio 51.14.6; Suet., *Div. Aug.* 17.4.
79. Dio 50.31.2.
80. Lange (2011), p. 608 n. 1, p. 609 n. 5 and 6 puts Velleius Paterculus, Plutarch, Florus, Ostorius, Ferrabino (1924), Tarn (1938) and Syme (1939) in this camp.
81. Lange (2011) p. 608 n. 3 puts Dio, Kromayer (1899), Gilles, Leake (1835), Merivale and Gravière (1885), Richardson (1937), Carter (1970), Grant (1972) and Kienast (1999) in this camp.
82. Lange (2011) p. 610 n. 14 cites Pelling (1988) – or as a modern day general has articulated, 'the best plan is the one that gives the most options at the last possible minute' (Lt Gen. Mike Flynn interviewed on Charlie Rose 2 February 2015, http://www.charlierose.com/watch/60510282 – accessed 29 February 2016).
83. Dio 50.15.1.
84. Plut., *Ant.* 63.3–5 *cf.* 56.2.
85. Dio 50.31.2; Plut., *Ant.* 65.1.
86. Vell. Pat. 2.85.1: *Advenit deinde maximi discriminis dies, quo Caesar Antoniusque productis classibus pro salute alter, in ruinam alter terrarum orbis dimicavere.*
87. Dio 51.1.1–2.
88. Plut., *Ant.* 61.1–2.
89. Florus 2.21.5.
90. Orosius 6.19.8.

91. Florus 2.21.6: *Caesaris naves a bini remigum in senos nec amplius ordines creverant; itaque habites in omnia quae usus posceret, ad impetus et recursus flexusque capiendos, illas gravis et ad omnia praepeditas singulas plures adortae missilibus, simul rostris, ad hoc ignibus iactis ad arbitrium dissipavere.*
92. Pitassi (2011), pp. 125–26; Rogers (2008), pp. 199–226.
93. Dio 50.23.2, 50.18.4 inferred.
94. Orosius 6.19.8; Plut., *Ant.* 65.1; Dio 50.31.3.
95. Plut., *Ant.* 61.1.
96. Florus 2.21.5: *ducentae non minus hostium*; Orosius 6.19.9: *classis Antonii centum septuaginta navium fuit.*
97. Plut., *Ant.* 64.1; Orosius 6.19.6–9; Dio 50.15.4, 50.12.1.
98. Dio 50.14.1–2, 50.31.2.
99. Plut., *Ant.* 61.1: *ἐν αἷς ὀκτήρεις πολλαὶ καὶ δεκήρεις κεκοσμημέναι σοβαρῶς καὶ πανηγυρικῶς.*
100. Dio 50.23.2.
101. Dio 50.18.4–6 has Antonius dismissing Agrippa's fleet, putting into his mouth the words: *so great is the difference between us two; but, as a rule, it is those who have the better equipment that secure the victories* | *τοσοῦτον μὲν ἀλλήλων διαφέρομεν, τὰ δὲ δὴ πολλὰ τῶν ἄμεινον παρεσκευασμένων καὶ αἱ νῖκαι γίγνονται.*
102. Florus 2.21.5–6: *sed numerum magnitudo pensabat. Quippe a sensis novenos remorum ordines, ad hoc turribus atque tabulatis adlevatae castellorum vel urbium specie, non sine gemitu maris et labore ventorum ferebatur; quae quidem ipsa moles exitio fuit.*
103. Dio 50.23.3: *καὶ ἐπ᾿ αὐτὰ πύργους τε ὑψηλοὺς ἐπικατεσκεύασε καὶ πλῆθος ἀνθρώπων ἐπανεβίβασεν, ὥστε καθάπερ ἀπὸ τειχῶν αὐτοὺς μάχεσθαι.*
104. Plut., *Ant.* 64.2: *λέγων ὅτι δεῖ μηδένα φεύγοντα τῶν πολεμίων διαφυγεῖν.*
105. See the careful analysis of Lange (2011) pp. 612–15.
106. Dio 50.31.4; Plut., *Ant.* 65.4.
107. Vell. Pat. 2.85.2; Dio 15.19.1.
108. Vell. Pat. 2.77.3.
109. Plut., *Ant.* 65.3.
110. Dio 50.31.4.
111. On *gens Luria* see Syme (1984b), p. 169.
112. Dio 50.31.4.
113. Plut., *Ant.* 65.3; Dio 50.31.4.
114. (MA 4–135 Florus 2.21.3: *Aureum in manu baculum, ad latus acinaces, purpurea vestis ingentibus obstricta gemmis.*
115. Dio 47.24.3; Livy, *Peri.* 122; he is described as 'Q[uaestor] P[ropraetore]' on a silver *denarius* minted 41 BCE: Sydenham 1188, Sear *Imperators* 250, RBW 1800, Crawford 517–18.
116. Plut., *Ant.* 65.1. M Insteius: see Pandélis M. Nigdélis (1994). M. Octavius: Cic. *Ad Fam.* 8.2.2; Caes., *Bell. Civ.* 3.5; Dio, 41.40, 42.11; Oros. 6.15; Plut., *Cat.* 65.2, *Ant.* 65.1.
117. Plut., *Ant.* 60.3.
118. Vell. Pat. 2.85.2.
119. Dio 50.31.4.
120. Plut., *Ant.* 65.4.
121. Dio 50.31.4.
122. Plut., *Ant.* 65.5; *cf.* Dio 50.31.4.
123. Dio 50.31.5.
124. Dio 50.31.6. Carter (1970) pp. 217–18 argues Antonius arrayed his fleet in two lines.
125. Plut., *Ant.* 65.4. Romans measured time as hours after sunrise. Sunrise in Athens on 2 September is 6.56am.
126. Carter (1970) p. 218.
127. Iapyx: Vergil, *Aen.* 8.710: *fecerat ignipotens undis et Iapyge ferri.*
128. Orosius 6.19.10.
129. Plut., *Ant.* 66.1–2: *ἀρχομένου δὲ τοῦ ἀγῶνος ἐν χερσὶν εἶναι, ἐμβολαὶ μὲν οὐκ ἦσαν οὐδὲ ἀναρρήξεις νεῶν, τῶν μὲν Ἀντωνίου διὰ βάρος ῥύμην οὐκ ἐχουσῶν, ἢ μάλιστα ποιεῖ τὰς τῶν ἐμβόλων πληγὰς ἐνεργούς, τῶν δὲ Καίσαρος οὐ μόνον ἀντιπρώρων συμφέρεσθαι πρὸς χαλκώματα στερεὰ καὶ τραχέα*

φυλασσομένων, ἀλλὰ μηδὲ κατὰ πλευρὰν ἐμβολὰς διδόναι θαρρουσῶν. ἀπεθραύοντο γὰρ τὰ ἔμβολα ῥᾳδίως ἢ προσπέσοιε σκάφεσι τετραγώνων ξύλων μεγάλων σιδήρῳ συνηρμοσμένων πρὸς ἄλληλα δεδεμένοις. ἦν οὖν πεζομαχίᾳ προσφερὴς ὁ ἀγών· τὸ δὲ ἀληθέστερον εἰπεῖν, τειχομαχία. τρεῖς γὰρ ἅμα καὶ τέσσαρες περὶ μίαν τῶν Ἀντωνίου συνείχοντο, γέρροις καὶ δόρασι καὶ κοντοῖς χρωμένων καὶ πυροβόλοις· οἱ δὲ Ἀντωνίου καὶ καταπέλτας ἀπὸ ξυλίνων πυργων ἔβαλλον.

130. Dio 50.32.1–8.
131. Dio 50.32.7: *ἐδύναντο, αἱ δὲ ἔπασχον. ἐπονοῦντο δὲ καὶ ἔκαμνον τοῖς μὲν οἵ τε κυβερνῆται καὶ οἱ ἐρέται μάλιστα, τοῖς δὲ οἱ ἐπιβάται· καὶ ἐφ́κεσαν οἱ μὲν ἱππεῦσι τοτὲ μὲν ἐπελαύνουσι τοτὲ δὲ ἐξαναχωροῦσι διὰ τὸ τούς τε ἐπίπλους καὶ τὰς ἀνακρούσεις ἐπ' αὐτοῖς εἶναι, οἱ δὲ ὁπλίταις τούς τε πλησιάζοντάς σφισι φυλασσομένοις καὶ κατέχειν αὐτούς.*
132. Plut., *Ant.* 66.3.
133. Carter (1970) pp. 222–23 argues breaking a hole in Agrippa's line was Antonius' battle plan from the start.
134. Dio 50.33.1–3; Plut., *Ant.* 66.3–4. The sixty ships, which escaped, represented 35 per cent of his fleet – no mean achievement under the circumstances.
135. Dio 50.33.3; Plut., *Ant.* 66.5; Vell. Pat. 2.85.3; Florus 2.21.9.
136. Plut., *Ant.* 67.1.
137. Plut., *Ant.* 67.2: *ἐν τούτῳ δὲ λιβυρνίδες ὤφθησαν διώκουσαι παρὰ Καίσαρος· ὁ δὲ ἀντίπρωρον ἐπιστρέφειν τὴν ναῦν κελεύσας τὰς μὲν ἄλλας ἀνέστειλεν.*
138. 'No battle plan ever survives contact with the enemy', attributed to Helmuth Karl Bernhard Graf von Moltke.
139. Dio 50.33.4.
140. Dio 50.33.6–8: *οἱ μὲν γὰρ τά τε κάτω τῶν νεῶν πάντα πέριξ ἐκακούργουν καὶ τὰς κώπας συνέθραυον τά τε πηδάλια ἀπήραττον, καὶ ἐπαναβαίνοντες ἐπὶ τὰ καταστρώματα τοὺς μὲν κατέσπων ἀντιλαμβανόμενοι τοὺς δὲ ἐώθουν, τοῖς δὲ ἐμάχοντο ἅτε καὶ ἰσοπληθεῖς αὐτοῖς ἤδη ὄντες· οἱ δὲ τοῖς τε κοντοῖς σφᾶς διεωθοῦντο καὶ ταῖς ἀξίναις ἔκοπτον, πέτρους τε καὶ ἄλλους τινὰς ὄγκους ἐπ' αὐτὸ τοῦτο παρεσκευασμένους ἐπικατέβαλλον, καὶ τούς τε ἀναβαίνοντας ἀπεκρούοντο καὶ τοῖς ἐς χεῖρας ἰοῦσι συνεφέροντο. εἴκασεν ἄν τις ἰδὼν τὰ γιγνόμενα, ὡς μικρὰ μεγάλοις ὁμοιῶσαι, τείχεσί τισιν ἢ καὶ νήσοις πολλαῖς καὶ πυκναῖς ἐκ θαλάσσης πολιορκουμέναις. οὕτως οἱ μὲν ἐπιβῆναί τε τῶν σκαφῶν ὥσπερ ἠπείρου καὶ ἐρύματός τινος ἐπειρῶντο, καὶ πάντα τὰ ἐς τοῦτο φέροντα σπουδῇ προσῆγον· οἱ δὲ ἀπεωθοῦντο αὐτούς, ὅ τι ποτὲ ἐν τῷ τοιούτῳ φιλεῖ δρᾶσθαι μηχανώμενοι.*
141. Florus 21.6: *itaque habitis in omnia quae usus posceret, ad impetus et recursus flexusque capiendos, illas gravis et ad omnia praepeditas singulas plures adortae missilibus, simul rostris, ad hoc ignibus iactis ad arbitrium dissipavere.*
142. Dio 50.34.1; Vell. Pat. 2.85.4.
143. Dio 50.34.2–7: *κἀνταῦθα ἄλλο αὖ εἶδος μάχης συνηνέχθη. οἱ μὲν γὰρ πολλαχῇ ἅμα προσπλέοντές τισι βέλη τε πυρφόρα ἐπ' αὐτοὺς ἐξετόξευον καὶ λαμπάδας ἐκ χειρὸς ἐπηκόντιζον καί τινας καὶ χυτρίδας ἀνθράκων καὶ πίττης πλήρεις πόρρωθεν μηχαναῖς ἐπερρίπτουν· οἱ δὲ ταῦτά τε ὡς ἕκαστα διεκρούοντο, καὶ ἐπειδή τινα αὐτῶν διεκπίπτοντα τῶν τε ξύλων ἥπτετο καὶ φλόγα αὐτίκα πολλήν, ἅτε ἐν νηί, ἤγειρε, τὸ μὲν πρῶτον τῷ ποτίμῳ ὕδατι ᾧ ἐπεφέροντο ἐχρῶντο, καί τινα κατέσβεσαν, ἐπεὶ δὲ ἐκεῖνο καταναλώθη, ἤντλουν τὸ θαλάττιον. καὶ εἰ μὲν πολλῷ τε καὶ ἀθρόῳ αὐτῷ ἐχρῶντο, ἐπεῖχόν πως τῇ βίᾳ τὸ πῦρ· ἀδύνατοι δὲ δὴ πανταχῇ τοῦτο ποιεῖν ὄντες 'οὔτε γὰρ πολλὰ ἢ καὶ μεγάλα τὰ ἀντλητήρια εἶχον, καὶ ἡμιδεᾶ αὐτὰ ἅτε ταραττόμενοι ἀνέφερον' οὐχ ὅσον οὐκ ὠφελοῦντί τι, ἀλλὰ καὶ προσπαρώξυνον αὐτό· ἡ γὰρ ἅλμη ἡ θαλαττία ἂν κατ' ὀλίγον ἐπιχέηται φλογί, ἰσχυρῶς αὐτὴν ἐκκαίει. ὡς οὖν καὶ ἐν τούτῳ ἥττους ἐγίγνοντο, τά τε ἱμάτια αὐτῶν τὰ παχέα καὶ τοὺς νεκροὺς ἐπέβαλλον· καὶ χρόνον μέν τινα ἐκολούσθη τε ὑπ' αὐτῶν τὸ πῦρ καὶ ἔδοξέ πῃ λωφᾶν, ἔπειτα δὲ ἄλλως τε καὶ τοῦ ἀνέμου σφοδρῶς ἐπισπέρξαντος ἐπὶ πλεῖον ἐξέλαμψεν, ἅτε καὶ ὑπ' αὐτῶν ἐκείνων αὐξανόμενον. καὶ μέχρι μὲν μέρος τι νεὼς ἐκαίετο, προσίσταντό τέ τινες αὐτῷ καὶ ἐς αὐτὸ ἐσεπήδων, καὶ τὰ μὲν ἀπέκοπτον τὰ δὲ διεφόρουν· καὶ αὐτὰ οἱ μὲν ἐς τὴν θάλασσαν οἱ δὲ καὶ ἐπὶ τοὺς ἐναντίους ἐρρίπτουν, εἴ πως καὶ ἐκείνους τι λυμήναιντο. καὶ ἕτεροι πρὸς τὸ ἀεὶ ὑγιὲς αὐτῆς μεθιστάμενοι ταῖς τε χερσὶ ταῖς σιδηραῖς καὶ τοῖς δόρασι τοῖς μακροῖς τότε δὴ καὶ τὰ μάλιστα ἐχρῶντο, ὅπως τινὰ ἀντίπαλον ναῦν προσαρτήσαντές σφισι μάλιστα μὲν μετεκβῶσιν ἐς αὐτήν, εἰ δὲ μή, καὶ ἐκείνην συγκαταφλέξωσιν.* During explorations of the sea floor off the coast of Preveza in 1993 and 1994, divers of The University of South Florida and The Greek Ministry of Culture found what are believed to be

stone balls (12cm, 4.7ins, in maximum diameter) fired by ballistas or catapults, presumably during the Battle of Actium (online at http://luna.cas.usf.edu/~murray/actium/brochure.html – accessed 29 February 2016).

144. Dio 50.35.1–4.
145. Orosius 6.19.10: *ab hora quinta usque in horam septimam incerta uincendi spe grauissimae utrimque caedes actae; reliquum diei cum subsequente nocte in uictoriam Caesaris declinauit.*
146. Suet., *Div. Aug.* 17.2: *Nec multo post navali proelio apud Actium vicit, in serum dimicatione protracta, ut in nave victor pernoctaverit.*
147. Plut., *Ant.* 68.1.
148. Orosius 6.19.10.
149. Dio 51.1.1–2, 56.30.5.
150. Florus 2.21.7: *Quippe inmensae classis naufragium bello factum toto mari ferebatur, Arabumque et Sabaeorum et mille aliarum Asiae gentium spolia purpura auroque inlita adsidue mote ventis maria revomebant.*
151. Plut., *Ant.* 68.1.
152. Plut., *Ant.* 68.1; Orosius 6.19.12.
153. Plut., *Ant.* 68.3.
154. Plut., *Ant.* 68.3; Vell. Pat. 2.85.5–6.
155. Lobur (2008) p. 123 highlights the error in Vell. Pat. 2.87.3, which lists Crassus among those who committed suicide.
156. Suet., *Div. Aug.* 17.2; Appian, *Bell. Civ.* 5.73; Dio 51.1.4.
157. Vell. Pat. 2.86.
158. Dio 51.2.1–5.
159. Dio 51.1.4.
160. Dio 51.3.2.
161. Vell. Pat. 2.84.2; Dio 50.13.5.
162. Plut., *Ant.* 68.4; Dio 51.4.1. The rejection of Paul Graindor's argument that there were riots in Athens during his visit in 31/30 BCE by Hoff (1989) p. 268 – citing Bowersock (1964) who places the civil unrest in 22/21 BCE – is accepted here.
163. Dio 51.15.2.
164. Plut., *Ant.* 68.4–5.
165. Strabo 7.7.6.
166. Dio 51.1.2–3: the foundations with the sockets for the captured ships' *rostra* can still be seen at the site.
167. Dio 51.3.1.
168. Dio 51.3.1, 51.3.4.
169. Dio 51.3.5.
170. Vell. Pat. 2.88.2.
171. Dio 51.3.5–6. Whenever Caesar wrote a letter to Agrippa and Maecenas or any of his other close friends containing confidential information, he would use a monoalphabetic substitution cipher, a coding system which shifted each letter of a word a single place in the alphabet, according to Dio 51.3.7 and Suet., *Div. Aug.* 88.
172. Plut., *Ant.* 73.3.
173. Vell. Pat. 2.88.3; Appian 4.50; Dio 54.15.4; Livy, *Peri.* 133; Suet., *Div. Aug.* 19.1.
174. Dio 51.4.3.
175. Dio 51.1, 51.4.3.
176. Dio 51.4.3 infers the search party included veterans.
177. Dio 51.4.4–5: Dio notes all senior officials went except the tribunes and two praetors, who remained in Rome in pursuance of a decree.
178. Orosius 6.19.14: *Brundisium uenit; ibi orbis terrarum praesidia diuisis legionibus conposuit.*
179. Dio 51.4.2–8; Orosius 6.19.14; Suet., *Div. Aug.* 17.3.
180. Dio 51.4.6.
181. Dio 51.4.7–8: it was an ironic reversal of the proscriptions of 43 and 42 BCE.
182. Dio 51.5.1.

183. Suet., *Div. Aug.* 17.5 says twenty-seven days; Dio 51.5.1 says thirty days.
184. Suet., *Div. Aug.* 17.3; Orosius 6.19.14.
185. Dio 51.5.6, 9.1; Orosius 6.19.15.
186. Orosius 6.19.15; Dio 51.9.1. Dio 51.5.6 reports that after Actium, Antonius had tried to land in Africa but he was denied entry by Scarpus – it was a bitter exchange because Antonius had appointed Scarpus to the command against encroachment from Caesar. Scarpus minted a silver *denarius*, among the very first struck immediately after Actium, showing an open hand on the obverse signalling a gesture of friendship toward Caesar with the legend IMP CAESARI SCARPVS IMP, and a winged Victory standing right on globe, holding palm-branch and wreath on the reverse with DIVI F AVG PONT: Crawford 546/6; CRI 413; RIC I 534; Sydenham 1282; RSC 500.
187. Dio 51.6.1.
188. Dio 51.6.1: ἵν᾽ οἵ τε Αἰγύπτιοι ὡς καὶ ἀνδρός τινος ἤδη βασιλεύοντός σφων προθυμηθῶσι, καὶ οἱ ἄλλοι προστάτας ἐκείνους, ἄν γέ τι δεινόν σφισι συμβῇ, ἔχοντες καρτερήσωσι.
189. Dio 51.6.4.
190. Dio 51.6.5.
191. Dio 51.6.6: ὁ δὲ τὰ μὲν δῶρα ἔλαβεν οἰωνὸν ποιούμενος, ἀπεκρίνατο δὲ τῷ μὲν Ἀντωνίῳ οὐδέν, τῇ δὲ Κλεοπάτρᾳ φανερῶς μὲν ἄλλα τε ἀπειλητικὰ καὶ ὅτι, ἂν τῶν τε ὅπλων καὶ τῆς βασιλείας ἀποστῇ, βουλεύσεται περὶ αὐτῆς ὅσα χρὴ πρᾶξαι, λάθρα δὲ ὅτι, ἐὰν τὸν Ἀντώνιον ἀποκτείνῃ, καὶ τὴν ἄδειαν αὐτῇ καὶ τὴν ἀρχὴν ἀκέραιον δώσει.
192. Dio 51.8.1–4.
193. Dio 51.8.5. Orosius 6.19.13 states Antonius and Kleopatra had a fleet stationed at Paraetonium and Pelusium ready to take them to renew the war effort elsewhere.
194. Dio 51.8.6.
195. Dio 51.8.5; Orosius 6.19.14. Pelusium lay 30km (20 miles) to the southeast of the modern Port Said. Dio, 51.9.5 suggests Kleopatra secretly allowed it to be taken by Imp. Caesar in the hope of receiving his clemency, being allowed to keep her kingdom and a later chance at fulfilling her imperial ambition.
196. Dio 51.10.1; Suet., *Div. Aug.* 17.3.
197. Val. Max. 3.8.8; *cf.* Plut., *Ant.* 64.2 for the story of a centurion on Antonius' side.
198. Val. Max. 3.8.8: *Idem constantiae propositum secutus Maeuius centurio diui Augusti, cum Antoniano bello saepe numero excellentes pugnas edidisset, inprouisis hostium insidiis circumuentus et ad Antonium Alexandriam perductus interrogatusque quidnam de eo statui deberet, 'iugulari me' inquit 'iube, quia non salutis beneficio neque mortis supplicio adduci possum ut aut Caesaris miles ⟨esse⟩ desinam aut tuus incipiam. ceterum quo constantius uitam contempsit, eo facilius impetrauit: Antonius enim uirtuti eius incolumitatem tribuit.*
199. Dio 51.10.2.
200. Dio 51.10.3.
201. Dio 51.19.6: τήν τε ἡμέραν ἐν ᾗ ἡ Ἀλεξάνδρεια ἑάλω, ἀγαθήν τε εἶναι καὶ ἐς τὰ ἔπειτα ἔτη ἀρχὴν τῆς ἀπαριθμήσεως αὐτῶν νομίζεσθαι. The date was thereafter considered auspicious: see Ch. 3, n. 88–89.
202. Dio 51.10.4.
203. Dio 51.10.5.
204. Dio 51.10.5–6.
205. Dio 51.10.7–14.6; Livy, *Peri.* 133.2; Eutropius 7.7; Suet., *Div. Aug.* 17.4; Strabo, *Geog.* 17.10.
206. Dio 51.10.7; Suet., *Div. Aug.* 17.4.
207. Caesarion: Dio 51.15.5; Plut., *Ant.* 81.2. Antyllus: Plut., *Ant.* 81.1 and 87.1.
208. Suet., *Div. Aug.* 18.2; Livy, *Peri.* 133.2; Orosius 6.19.16, 19.
209. Eutropius 7.7.
210. Dio 51.17.1.
211. Strabo, *Geog.* 17.8. Iulius Caesar had seen it too, seventeen years before.
212. Suet., *Div. Aug.* 18.1: *Per idem tempus conditorium et corpus Magni Alexandri, cum prolatum e penetrali subiecisset oculis, corona aurea imposita ac floribus aspersis ueneratus est, consultusque, num et Ptolemaeum inspicere uellet, 'regem se uoluisse ait uidere, non mortuos'.* The memory of Alexander

exerted a great power over the two Caesars. Thirty-eight years before, when his great uncle had been a *quaestor*, a junior administrator, serving in Hispania Ulterior he had noticed a statue of Alexander the Great in the Temple of Hercules at Gades (modern Cadiz), *cf.* Suet., *Div. Iul.* 7.1: *he heaved a sigh, and as if out of patience with his own incapacity in having as yet done nothing noteworthy at a time of life when Alexander had already brought the world to his feet, he straightway asked for his discharge, to grasp the first opportunity for greater enterprises at Rome.* | *ubi cum mandatu praetoris iure dicundo conventus circumiret Gadisque venisset, animadversa apud Herculis templum Magni Alexandri imagine ingemuit et quasi pertaesus ignaviam suam, quod nihil dum a se memorabile actum esset in aetate, qua iam Alexander orbem terrarum subegisset, missionem continuo efflagitavit ad captandas quam primum maiorum rerum occasiones in urbe.*

213. Dio 51.16.5.
214. Suet., *Div. Aug.* 18.2: *Aegyptum in provinciae formam redactam ut feraciorem habilioremque annonae urbicae redderet, fossas omnis, in quas Nilus exaestuat, oblimatas longa vetustate militari opere detersit.*
215. Dio 51.18.1: ὁ δ᾽ οὖν Καῖσαρ ὥς τά τε προειρημένα ἔπραξε, καὶ πόλιν καὶ ἐκεῖ ἐν τῷ τῆς μάχης χωρίῳ συνῴκισε.
216. Strabo, *Geog.* 17.10.
217. Dio 51.17.6–7: χρήματα δὲ πολλὰ μὲν ἐν τῷ βασιλικῷ εὑρέθη ᾽πάντα γὰρ ὡς εἰπεῖν καὶ τὰ ἐκ τῶν ἁγιωτάτων ἱερῶν ἀναθήματα ἡ Κλεοπάτρα ἀνελομένη συνεπλήθυσε τὰ λάφυρα τοῖς Ῥωμαίοις ἄνευ τινὸς οἰκείου αὐτῶν μιάσματος, πολλὰ δὲ καὶ παρ᾽ ἑκάστου τῶν αἰτιαθέντων τι ἠθροίσθη. καὶ χωρὶς οἱ λοιποὶ πάντες, ὅσοι μηδὲν ἴδιον ἔγκλημα λαβεῖν ἐδύναντο, τὰ δύο μέρη τῶν οὐσιῶν ᾐτήθησαν. καὶ ἀπ᾽ αὐτῶν πάντες μὲν οἱ στρατιῶται τὰ ἐποφειλόμενά σφισιν ἐκομίσαντο, οἱ δὲ δὴ καὶ τότε τῷ Καίσαρι συγγενόμενοι πεντήκοντα καὶ διακοσίας δραχμάς, ὥστε μὴ διαρπάσαι τὴν πόλιν, προσεπέλαβον.
218. Dio 51.17.8.
219. Dio 51.25.2.
220. Dio 50.6.3–6.
221. Dio 51.21.6.
222. *Fast. Capitol.*
223. The campaign of M. Crassus is described by Dio in remarkable detail. In 51.27.2 he writes: *All these operations took a long time; but the facts I record, as well as the names, are in accordance with the tradition which has been handed down.* | ταῦτα μὲν ἐν χρόνῳ ἐγένετο, γράφω δὲ τά τε ἄλλα ὥς που παραδέδοται, καὶ αὐτὰ τὰ ὀνόματα (*Cf.* 51.25.2). He may have consulted chronicles, official histories or even the biography of Crassus in preparing his account.
224. Dio 51.22.1.
225. Dio 51.22.3, 51.22.6, 51.23.3–4.
226. Dio 51.23.3.
227. Dio 51.23.4.
228. Dio 51.23.4: τὸ δὲ δὴ πλεῖστον περὶ τῇ Μακεδονίᾳ φοβηθεὶς ἀντεπῆλθέ σφισι.
229. Dio 51.23.4: καὶ αὐτοὺς ἐκ τῆς προσόδου μόνης καταπλήξας ἐξέωσεν ἀμαχεὶ ἐκ τῆς χώρας.
230. Dio 51.23.5.
231. Florus, 2.26: *Vnus ducum ante aciem postulato silentio: 'Qui vos estis?', inquit, responsum invicem: 'Romani gentium domini'. Et ille 'ita' inquit 'fiet, si nos viceritis'. Accepit omen Marcus Crassus.*
232. Dio 51.24.1.
233. Dio 51.24.2.
234. Dio 51.24.3: Κράσσος δὲ ἐν τούτῳ τῆς νυκτὸς ἐς ὕλην τινὰ προχωρήσας, καὶ προσκόπους πρὸ αὐτῆς καταστήσας, ἀνέπαυσέ τε τὸ στράτευμα, καὶ μετὰ τοῦτο τῶν Βαστάρνων μόνους τε ἐκείνους εἶναι νομισάντων καὶ ἐπιδραμόντων σφίσιν, ἔς τε τὰ λάσια ἀναχωροῦσιν ἐπακολουθησάντων, πολλοὺς μὲν ἐνταῦθα πολλοὺς δὲ καὶ.
235. The theme of women and children trapped by wagons occurs frequently in accounts of battles: Compare to Marius' attack on the Cimbri, Suetonius on Boudicca.
236. Dio 51.24.4.
237. Dio 51.24.5.
238. For *spolia opima* see Harrison (1989) and Rich (1999).

239. Florus 2.26: *Non minimum terroris incussit barbaris Comicius centurio satis barbarae, efficacis tamen apud tales homines stoliditatis, qui foculum gerens super cassidem, agitatum motu corporis, flamman velut ardenti capite funditabat.*
240. Dio 51.24.5.
241. Dio 51.24.6.
242. Dio 51.24.7. On the policies determining distribution of war booty see Shatzman (1972).
243. Dio 51.25.2.
244. Dio 51.25.1: πράξας δὲ ταῦτα ὁ Κράσσος ἐπὶ τοὺς Μυσοὺς ἐτράπετο, καὶ τὰ μὲν πείθων τινὰς τὰ δὲ ἐκφοβῶν τὰ δὲ καὶ βιαζόμενος, πάντας μὲν πλὴν πάνυ ὀλίγων, ἐπιπόνως δὲ δὴ καὶ ἐπικινδύνως κατεστρέψατο.
245. Dio 51.25.2.
246. Dio 51.25.2.
247. Dio 51.18.2.
248. Dio 51.18.2: πρόφασιν μὲν ὡς καὶ περὶ τὴν Αἴγυπτον ἀσχολίαν ἔχων, ἔργῳ δὲ ἵν᾽ ἐκτρυχωθεῖεν ἐν τούτῳ μαχόμενοι πρὸς ἀλλήλους.
249. Dio 51.18.3: papers on hostages?
250. *RG* 8; Dio 52.42.5; Tac., *Ann.* 11.25.3.
251. The *Lex Saenia de plebeiis in patricios adlegendis*: Tac., *Ann.* 11.25; Dio 52.42.5; *RG* 8.1. For a full discussion see Botsford (1908) and Nicholls (1967).
252. Dio 51.23.1, 53.18; Suet. *Div. Aug.* 29.5; Strabo, *Geog.* 5.3.8; Tac., *Ann.* 3.72.
253. Dio 51.23.1: καὶ διὰ τοῦτο στρατηγὸν ἕνα παρὰ τοῦ δήμου κατ᾽ ἔτος αἱρεῖσθαι ἐλάμβανε.
254. Dio 51.25.3.
255. Dio 51.25.3: οὕτω καὶ ἄκων ἐξανέστη, καὶ σπουδῇ χωρήσας ἀνέλπιστός τε αὐτοῖς ἐπέπεσε, καὶ κρατήσας σπονδὰς ὁποίας ἠθέλησεν ἔδωκεν.
256. Dio 51.25.4.
257. Dio 51.25.5.
258. Dio 51.26.1–2: καὶ ὃς ἐπικουρήσας οἱ τήν τε ἵππον τῶν ἐναντίων ἐς τοὺς πεζοὺς ἐσήραξε, καὶ συμφοβήσας ἐκ τούτου καὶ ἐκείνους μάχην μὲν οὐδεμίαν ἔτ᾽ ἐποιήσατο, φόνον δὲ δὴ φευγόντων ἑκατέρων πολὺν εἰργάσατο. καὶ μετὰ τοῦτο τὸν Δάπυγα πρὸς φρούριόν τι καταφυγόντα ἀπολαβὼν ἐπολιόρκει· κἂν τῇ προσεδρείᾳ ἑλληνιστί τις αὐτὸν ἀπὸ τοῦ τείχους ἀσπασάμενος ἔς τε λόγους οἱ ἦλθε καὶ προδοσίαν συνέθετο. ἁλισκόμενοι οὖν οὕτως οἱ βάρβαροι ἐπ᾽ ἀλλήλους ὥρμησαν, καὶ ὅ τε Δάπυξ ἀπέθανε καὶ ἄλλοι πολλοί. τὸν μέντοι ἀδελφὸν αὐτοῦ ζωγρήσας ὁ Κράσσος οὐχ ὅτι τι κακὸν ἔδρασεν, ἀλλὰ καὶ ἀφῆκε.
259. Dio 51.26.3–4.
260. Dio 51.26.5. Cf. Dio 38.10.1–3.
261. Dio 51.26.6.
262. Dio 51.27.1: ἐπὶ δὲ Ἀρτακίους ἄλλους τε τινας οὔθ᾽ ἁλόντας ποτὲ οὔτ᾽ αὖ προσχωρῆσαί οἱ ἐθέλοντας, καὶ αὐτούς τε μέγιστον ἐπὶ τούτῳ φρονοῦντας καὶ τοῖς ἄλλοις ὀργήν τε ἅμα καὶ νεωτερισμὸν ἐμποιοῦντας, αὐτός τ᾽ ἐπεστράτευσε, καί σφας τὰ μὲν βίᾳ, δράσαντας οὐκ ὀλίγα, τὰ δὲ καὶ φόβῳ τῶν ἁλισκομένων προσηγάγετο.
263. On *spolia opima* see Drogula (2015), pp. 352–53 and McPherson (2009).
264. Suet., *Div. Aug.* 30.2; Livy, *AUC* 4.20.7; Dio 44.4.3. It was a modest building regarded by many Romans as the city's first temple dating back to the time of its founder Romulus, to commemorate his winning of the *spolia opima* from Acron, king of the Caeninenses, and to serve as a sacred repository for them.
265. Livy, *AUC* 4.20.7.
266. *RG* 19. Cf. Nepos, *Atticus* 20.3: Atticus suggested that it be restored; cf. *RG* 19.
267. Dio 44.4.3: σκῦλά τέ τινα ὁπῖμα ἐς τὸν τοῦ Διὸς τοῦ Φερετρίου νεὼν ἀναθεῖναί οἱ ὥσπερ τινὰ πολέμιον αὐτοστράτηγον αὐτοχειρίᾳ πεφονευκότι, καὶ τοῖς ῥαβδούχοις δαφνηφορῶσιν ἀεὶ χρῆσθαι, μετά τε τὰς ἀνοχὰς τὰς Λατίνας ἐπὶ κέλητος ἐς τὴν πόλιν ἐκ τοῦ Ἀλβανοῦ ἐσελαύνειν ἔδοσαν.
268. Dio 51.25.2. Dio states: *he did not receive the title of* imperator, *as some report* | οὐ μέντοι καὶ τὸ τοῦ αὐτοκράτορος ὄνομα, ὥς γέ τινές φασιν, ἔλαβεν. For a discussion see Cartledge (1975), p. 36, who notes Crassus was 'lucky to escape with his life'. See Ch. 4, n. 90 on the refusal of Nero Claudius Drusus' imperatorial acclamation in 11 BCE.

269. Dio 51.25.2. Theodor Momsen placed this event in the autumn of the year: see Schumacher (1985), pp. 209–10.
270. Dio 51.25.2.
271. Dio 51.21.5.
272. *ILS* 895: unlike Crassus, based on the inscription that shows Gallus *was* permitted to retain the title.
273. On the history of the Roman conquest of the Iberian Peninsula see Keay (1988), pp. 8–44, and Curchin (1995), pp. 7–52.
274. Dio 51.20.5. Taurus may have won one of his three imperatorial acclamations here, but it is nowhere recorded.
275. Dio 51.20.5: ἄλλα τε ὡς καθ' ἑκάστους ταραχώδη συχνὰ ἐγίγνετο· ἀλλ' ἐπειδὴ μηδὲν μέγα ἀπ' αὐτῶν συνηνέχθη, οὔτε ἐκεῖνοι τότε πολεμεῖσθαι ἐνόμιζον οὔτε ἐγὼ ἐπιφανές τι περὶ αὐτῶν γράψαι ἔχω.
276. Lange (2009a), p. 93, convincingly shows that Augustus was acknowledged to have won both a civil war – the Actian War – *as well as* an external or foreign war – viz. the Alexandrian War.
277. Dio 51.20.2; *cf.* Aul. Gell., *Noct. Att.* 5.6.1–7: the crown of laurels on Imp. Caesar's profile begins to appear more frequently on coins from this time. The privilege had been accorded to Pompeius Magnus in 61 (Cic., *Att.* 1.18.6, Dio 37.21.4, Vell. Pat. 2.40.4) and Iulius Caesar in 45/44 BCE (Suet., *Div. Iul.* 45.2).
278. Dio 51.19.1, 51.19.5.
279. Dio 51.19.2.
280. Dio 51.19.3, 51.19.5.
281. Dio 51.19.7.
282. Suet., *Div. Aug.* 53.2; *cf.* Dio 54.10.4: Caesar generally preferred to arrive at night to avoid sycophantic crowds.
283. Dio 51.1.5; Suet., *Div. Aug.* 22; *RG* 13.
284. Dio 51.1.5, 24.37.1–2. The *augurium salutis* was an augural inquiry of the gods for the well-being of the Roman People (*salus populi Romani*). It had last been performed in 63 BCE (Dio 37.24.1–3). Revived by Augustus (Dio 51.20.4), performing this annual rite in combination with the closure of the doors of the Temple of Ianus publicly marked the phases of war making and its ending. See Lange (2009a) pp. 140–1.
285. E.g. *RIC*² 263, 264, 265. Gurval (1998), pp. 47–50, but *cf.* Zanker (1990), pp. 53–57.
286. Dio 51.21.3: καὶ ἐτίμησεν ὥσπερ εἴθιστο, καὶ τόν τε Ἀγρίππαν ἄλλοις τέ τισι καὶ σημείῳ κυανοειδεῖ ναυκρατητικῷ προσεπεσέμνυνε.
287. Livy, *Peri.* 129.4. Reinhard (1933), p. 60, notes that the award was unique in the recorded history of antiquity.
288. Dio 51.21.3.
289. See *Aegyptische Urkunden aus den Koeniglichen Museen zu Berlin, Griechische Urkunden,* 4.1047, II, 13–14 (Berlin 1912). Maecenas also had an estate in Egypt.
290. Dio 53.27.5. Probably the *Domus Rostrata*, the house grotesquely decorated with beaks captured from pirates' ships in 67 BCE, which he had taken from Pompeius Magnus.
291. Servius, *Ad Georg.* 3.29. They would stand near the *columna rostrata* commemorating the victory of C. Duilius over the Carthaginians at Mylae in 260 BCE.
292. Keppie (1971) cites *CIL*, V 890 (Aquileia), 2389 (Ferrara), 2501 (Ateste), 2503 (Ateste) and 2339 (Patavium). Each man had the simple form *praenomen* and *nomen gentile*, and adopted *Actiacus* as his *cognomen*.
293. The battle honour appears on tombstones from several, but not all, veterans at Ateste: e.g. *CIL* V, 2495, 2497(?), 2399, 2501–2503, 2507, 2508, 2514–2516, 2518–2520.
294. *RG* 4; Livy, *Peri.* 113; Dio 51.21.5–9; Strabo, *Geog.* 12.3.6, 12.3.25; Vell. Pater. 2.89.1; Suet., *Div. Aug.* 22, 41.1, *Tib.* 6; Florus 2.21.10; Servius, *ad Aen.* 8.714; Orosius 6.20.1.
295. Beard (2007), p. 81–82.
296. Suet., *Tib.* 6.4. An inscription at Nikopolis depicts Augustus in the *triumphator*'s chariot with the members of his familty: see Beard (2007), p. 224.
297. Dio 51.21.5–6.
298. Dio 51.21.7.

299. Dio 51.21.8. After the triumph the children were taken into the care of Caesar's sister, Octavia, and raised in her household – Plut., *Ant.* 87.1.
300. Dio 51.20.2, 51.21.9.
301. Dio 51.2.2. The execution was likely by strangulation or beheading, as had been the fate of Vercingetorix, the Gallic war chief under Iulius Caesar.
302. Dio 51.24.7.
303. Dio 51.22.1.
304. For a discussion of Augustus' promotion of the Caesar cult as a precursor to a cult of his own after his death, see White (1988).
305. Dio 51.22.1: ἐνέστησε δὲ ἐς αὐτὸ τὸ ἄγαλμα τὸ τῆς Νίκης τὸ καὶ νῦν ὄν, δηλῶν, ὡς ἔοικεν, ὅτι παρ᾽ αὐτῆς τὴν ἀρχὴν ἐκτήσατο. Dio remarks that the statue was still in existence at the time he was writing his book.
306. Dio 53.2.3. The wealth of Egypt was immense – see Maddison (2007), p. 27. The Visual Capitalist suggests that the wealth of Egypt represented 'at least 25% of global gross domestic product (GDP) at the time'; it contributed very significantly to Augustus' estimated $4.6 trillion net worth (http://www.visualcapitalist.com/richest-people-human-history).
307. Dio 51.21.3.
308. Suet., *Div. Aug.* 41.1: *the rate of interest fell, and the value of real estate rose greatly | ut faenore deminuto plurimum agrorum pretiis accesserit.* Cf. Dio 51.21.5 writes the interest charged on loans rose to 12 per cent.
309. Dio 51.21.4: τῶν τε δυσχερῶν πάντων οἱ Ῥωμαῖοι ἐπελάθοντο, καὶ τὰ ἐπινίκια αὐτοῦ ἡδέως ὡς καὶ ἀλλοφύλων ἁπάντων τῶν ἡττηθέντων.
310. For a full discussion of *damnatio memoriae see* Flower (2006), pp. 116–21. On the *damnatio memoriae* of Antonius see Lange (2009a), pp. 136–40. Lange notes that Antonius' name was scratched from the *Fasti Consulares* in 30 BCE, but restored after Imp. Caesar's return to Rome in 29 BCE. Augustus conspicuously and purposely omitted the dishonored *triumvir's* name from his own monumental record of achievements (e.g. see *RG* 24.1).
311. Dio 51.19.3; Plut., *Ant.* 86.5.
312. The colossal statue now stands in the Venice Archaeological Museum; see plate 24 in Powell (2015).
313. Dio 51.21.3.
314. Dio 53.1.2: τὸν γὰρ Ἀγρίππαν ἐς ὑπερβολὴν ἐτίμα.
315. Dio 53.1.1.
316. Dio 53.1.6.
317. Dio 53.17.2–3.
318. On the meaning of *Res Publica Restituta* see Judge and Harrison (2008), pp. 140–66 and 314–46, for excellent reviews of current academic thought; Syme (1959), p. 36; Bay (1972), p. 120; Cartledge (1975), p. 37, who notes the opinion of Millar (1973) that after Actium Imp. Caesar was 'ever a monarch'; and Galinsky (1996), pp. 64–67, proposes the restoration also had a moral dimension, invoking old Roman values and virtues.
319. *Aureus*: obverse – LEGES ET IURA P R RESTITUIT, Imp. Caesar, togate, sitting on curule chair, holding scroll, facing left; reverse – IMP CAES DIVI F COS VI, laureate head of Imp. Caesar facing right. (*Cf. RG* 34). For a discussion see Abday and Harling (2005). The coin, discovered in England, is now in the British Museum.
320. Dio 53.2.1 records that Imp. Caesar provided funds for the grain dole, ordering two ex-praetors to supervise the budget, and Dio 53.2.3 that he appointed the *praetor urbanus. Cf. RG* 15.
321. Dio 53.1.3. The formal title was *Princeps Senatus*.
322. Dio 53.17.6.
323. Suet., *Div. Aug.* 35; *cf.* 300 at the time of the founding of the Republic reported in Livy, *Peri.* 60, and how numbers were augmented by Iulius Caesar to 900 members as reported in Dio 43.47 and Suet., *Div. Caes.* 80, but restated as 1,000 in *Div. Aug.* 35.1 and Dio 52.42.1.
324. Dio 52.42.4–5. See Ch. 1, n. 250.
325. Dio 52.42.6–7.
326. Dio 52.42.8.

327. *RG* 20.
328. *RG* 19; Dio 53.1.3.
329. Dio 51.19.2.
330. Dio 53.1.4–5.
331. Beacham (1999), p. 24.
332. Dio 53.1.4–5.
333. *Fast. Capitol.*
334. Strabo, *Geog.* 17.1.53.
335. *EJ* 21 = *ILS* 8995 (Philae); Strabo, *Geog.* 17.1.54.
336. *RG* 26; Ptol. 4.7.32. The 30 miles refers to the distance heading south from Philae. The text on the stele, in Latin, Greek and Egyptian hieroglyphs, refers to the king being 'taken under protection' of Gallus. For a full discussion and reconstructions of the text see Hoffman, Minas-Nerpel and Pfeiffer (2009), and Judge and Harrison (2008), pp. 72–75.

Chapter 2: Command and Conquer

1. Dio 53 Index; *Fasti Praenestini: CIL* I.1² (Rome) (a) p. 231, (b) p. 236 = Dessau 2.2.8844 (*Fasti Praenestini CIL* I.1² 236 (Rome) – Agrippa's consulate is mentioned for 16 January and for 24 April = Dessau 2.2.8844 indicates 23 April; Tacitus, *Annales* 1.3.1 uses the phrase *geminatis consulatibus*.
2. Drogula (2015), pp. 354–55, refers to the *Lex Titia* or the statement 'all of Italy' in the law permitting Caesar to command the army in prosecution of the war against Antonius and Kleopatra.
3. Caesar was meticulous about carefully preparing what he wanted to say. Rather than commit his speech to memory and risk forgetting any points, he wrote his thoughts down: Suet., *Div. Aug.* 84.2; Dio 54.25.5.
4. Dio 53.3–11.4. For a full discussion of the account presented by Dio and Augustus' version of events in *Res Gestae* see Turpin (1994), pp. 427–37.
5. Dio 53.2.7, 50.11.1.
6. Dio 50.11.2.
7. Dio 50.11.4, 50.12.1–3. On the *imperium* of Augustus see Jones (1951).
8. Dio 50.12.1.
9. Dio 53.11.5.
10. *RG* Introduction: *orbem terrarum imperio populi Romani subiecit*.
11. Dio 53.12.1–2, 53.13.4–7, 53.14.1–4; Strabo, *Geog.* 17.3.25.
12. Strabo, *Geog.* 17.3.25: ἐπειδὴ γὰρ ἡ πατρὶς ἐπέτρεψεν αὐτῷ τὴν προστασίαν τῆς ἡγεμονίας, καὶ πολέμου καὶ εἰρήνης κατέστη κύριος διὰ βίου, δίχα διεῖλε πᾶσαν τὴν χώραν καὶ τὴν μὲν ἀπέδειξεν ἑαυτῷ τὴν δὲ τῷ δήμῳ, ἑαυτῷ μὲν ὅση στρατιωτικῆς φρουρᾶς ἔχει χρείαν· αὕτη δ' ἐστὶν ἡ βάρβαρος καὶ πλησιόχωρος τοῖς μήπω κεχειρωμένοις ἔθνεσιν ἢ λυπρὰ καὶ δυσγεώργητος, ὥσθ' ὑπὸ ἀπορίας τῶν ἄλλων ἐρυμάτων δ' εὐπορίας ἀφηνιάζειν καὶ ἀπειθεῖν, τῷ δήμῳ δὲ τὴν ἄλλην ὅση εἰρηνικὴ καὶ χωρὶς ὅπλων ἄρχεσθαι ῥᾳδία. Cf. Suet., *Div. Aug.* 47.1.
13. Dio 53.12.4; Strabo, *Geog.* 17.3.25.
14. Dio 53.12.4, 53.13.1; Strabo, *Geog.* 17.3.25; Suet., *Div. Aug.* 47.1.
15. Dio 53.12.5–7: Dio notes Augustus soon swapped Cyprus and Narbonensis for Illyricum/Dalmatia; Strabo, *Geog.* 17.3.25.
16. Dio 53.12.3. See Crook (1996), pp. 78–79; Parker (1928), pp. 72–92; Drogula (2015), pp. 354–55.
17. Orosius 6.19.14. The English word delegate finds its root in the Latin *delegatus*, meaning 'sent on a commission', from the verb *delegare*.
18. Joseph., *Bell. Iud.* 2.117. On the responsibilities of a legate and his commander see Caes., *Bell. Civ.* 3.51: 'The duties of a legate and of a commander are different: the one ought to do everything under direction, the other should take measures freely in the general interest.' | *Aliae enim sunt legati partes atque imperatoris: alter omnia agere ad praescriptum, alter libere ad summam rerum consulere debet.*
19. Dio 53.15.1.
20. See Drogula (2015), pp. 355–56.

21. Dio 53.15.6: ἐκεῖνα δὲ ἐπὶ πᾶσιν ὁμοίως ἐνομοθετήθη, μήτε καταλόγους σφᾶς ποιεῖσθαι, μήτ᾽ ἀργύριον ἔξω τοῦ τεταγμένου ἐσπράσσειν, εἰ μὴ ἤτοι ἡ βουλὴ ψηφίσαιτο ἢ ὁ αὐτοκράτωρ κελεύσειεν· ὅταν τέ τῳ ὁ διάδοχος ἔλθῃ, ἔκ τε τοῦ ἔθνους αὐτίκα αὐτὸν ἐξορμᾶσθαι καὶ ἐν τῇ ἀνακομιδῇ μὴ ἐγχρονίζειν, ἀλλ᾽ ἐντὸς τριῶν μηνῶν ἐπανιέναι.

22. Dio, 53.13.3.

23. Dio, 53.13–2-4.

24. Dio 53.16.7–8.

25. Dio 53.16.6, 8; Vell. Pat. 2.91.1. See Turpin (1994), p. 437.

26. Dio 53.16.7–8; Suet., *Div. Aug.* 7; Vell. Pat. 2.91; Florus 4.12; Orosius 6.20; Censorinus 22; Ovid, *Fasti* 1.607.

27. For an example of usage of the full name see *CIL* III, 6070.749/5.

28. Dio 53.16.4–5; Aul. Gell., *Noct. Att.* 5.6.11–12. Coins: examples include *BMCRE* 317 (Rome), *RIC* I 36a (Caesareaugusta), *RIC* I 77a (Caesareaugusta), *RIC* I 79a (*Colonia* Patricia). The 'civic crown' (*corona civica*) was a military award of a wreath made of oak leaves tied with a fillet (also called the *corona querceis*) and was worn on the head.

29. The cardinal virtues were *Virtus, clementia, iustitia* and *pietas*. On these see Galinsky (1996), pp. 80–88.

30. Dio 51.22.1.

31. Dio 53.22.5: τότε μὲν δὴ ταῦτα ὁ Αὔγουστος ἔπραξε, καὶ ἐξώρμησε μὲν ὡς καὶ ἐς τὴν Βρεττανίαν στρατεύσων, ἐς δὲ δὴ τὰς Γαλατίας ἐλθὼν ἐνταῦθα ἐνδιέτριψεν· ἐκεῖνοί τε γὰρ ἐπικηρυκεύσεσθαί οἱ ἐδόκουν.

32. Caes., *Bell. Gall.* 4.20–36 and 5.1–23.

33. See Mommsen (1954) on a purported fragment of Livy, *AUC* concerning Augustus and Britain.

34. Dio 53.22.5: καὶ τὰ τούτων ἀκατάστατα ἔτι, ἅτε τῶν ἐμφυλίων πολέμων εὐθὺς ἐπὶ τῇ ἁλώσει σφῶν ἐπιγενομένων, ἦν.

35. App., *Bell. Civ.* 5.92.

36. Tib. 1.7.3–8; Eutrop. 7.9; Suet., *Tibullus: cuius etiam contubernalis Aquitanico bello militaribus donis donatus est.* App., *Bell. Civ.* 4.38. Tibullus would be better known in later ages for his Latin poetry.

37. *Fast. Capitol.*

38. Dio 51.21.6; see Ch. 1, n. 221.

39. For the transformation of Gallic communities into Roman provinces see the excellent survey by Woolf (1998).

40. Roth (1999), p. 237.

41. Powell (2015), pp. 140–42.

42. Dio 53.25.1; Plut., *Ant.* 61.

43. Dio 53.21.1.

44. *Fast. Capitol.*

45. *RG* 32: Dumnobellaunus may have ruled the Cantiaci whose territory covered Kent or Trinovantes of Essex; Tin[comarus] likely ruled the Atrebates located in Berkshire and Hampshire.

46. Dio 53.25.2.

47. Dio 53.22.1. Strabo, *Geog.* 2.5.8 speculated about the cost benefit of annexation of the island in the last decade of the First Century BCE: *For although they could have held even Britannia, the Romans scorned to do so, because they saw that there was nothing at all to fear from the Britons (for they are not strong enough to cross over and attack us), and that no corresponding advantage was to be gained by taking and holding their country. For it seems that at present more revenue is derived from the duty on their commerce than the tribute could bring in, if we deduct the expense involved in the maintenance of an army for the purpose of guarding the island and collecting the tribute; and the unprofitableness of an occupation would be still greater in the case of the other islands about Britannia.* | τὸ δ᾽ ἐκεῖθεν ἐπὶ τὴν Βρεττανικὴν δύναται συμφωνεῖν τῷ ἀπὸ Βυζαντίου ἐπὶ Βορυσθένη· τὸ δ᾽ ἐκεῖθεν ἐπὶ τὴν Ἰέρνην οὐκέτι γνώριμον πόσον ἄν τις θείη, οὐδ᾽ εἰ περαιτέρω ἔτι οἰκήσιμά ἐστιν, οὐδὲ δεῖ φροντίζειν τοῖς ἐπάνω λεχθεῖσι προσέχοντας· πρός τε γὰρ ἐπιστήμην ἀρκεῖ τὸ λαβεῖν, καθάπερ ἐπὶ τῶν νοτίων μερῶν, ὅτι ὑπὲρ Μερόης μέχρι τρισχιλίων σταδίων προελθόντι τῆς οἰκησίμου τίθεσθαι πέρας προσῆκεν (οὐχ ὡς ἂν τούτου ἀκριβεστάτου πέρατος ὄντος, ἀλλ᾽ ἐγγύς γε τἀκριβοῦς), οὕτω κἀκεῖ τοὺς ὑπὲρ τῆς Βρεττανικῆς οὐ πλείους τούτων θετέον ἢ μικρῷ πλείους, οἷον τετρακισχιλίους. πρός τε τὰς ἡγεμονικὰς χρείας οὐδὲν

ἂν εἴη πλεονέκτημα τὰς τοιαύτας γνωρίζειν χώρας καὶ τοὺς ἐνοικοῦντας, καὶ μάλιστα εἰ νήσους οἰκοῖεν τοιαύτας, αἳ μήτε λυπεῖν μήτ᾽ ὠφελεῖν ἡμᾶς δύνανται μηδὲν διὰ τὸ ἀνεπίπλεκτον· καὶ γὰρ τὴν Βρεττανικὴν ἔχειν δυνάμενοι Ῥωμαῖοι κατεφρόνησαν, ὁρῶντες ὅτι οὔτε φόβος ἐξ αὐτῶν οὐδὲ εἷς ἐστιν (οὐ γὰρ ἰσχύουσι τοσοῦτον ὥστ᾽ ἐπιδιαβαίνειν ἡμῖν) οὔτ᾽ ὠφέλεια τοσαύτη τις, εἰ κατάσχοιεν. πλέον γὰρ ἐκ τῶν τελῶν δοκεῖ προσφέρεσθαι νῦν ἢ ὁ φόρος δύναται συντελεῖν, ἀφαιρουμένης τῆς εἰς τὸ στρατιωτικὸν δαπάνης τὸ φρουρῆσον καὶ φορολογῆσον τὴν νῆσον· πολὺ δ᾽ ἂν ἐπιγένοιτο τὸ ἄχρηστον ἐπὶ τῶν ἄλλων τῶν περὶ ταύτην νήσων.

48. Dio 53.22.5: κἀντεῦθεν ἔς τε τὴν Ἰβηρίαν ἀφίκετο, καὶ κατεστήσατο καὶ ἐκείνην. For a summary of the wars before Augustus see Van Nostrand (1915), pp. 84–91.

49. Florus 2.33; Orosius 6.21.4. For surveys of archeological evidence see Morillo and García-Marcos (2002), pp. 779–89, and Rodà de Llanza (2003), pp. 53–63.

50. The military settlement in Álava was active between 40–30 BCE: see Morillo (2011), pp. 12–13. On Celt-Iberian war and society see Almagro-Gorbea and Lorrio (2004).

51. Dio 51.20.5, 53.25.2.

52. Florus 2.33: *qui non contenti libertatem suam defendere proximis etiam imperitare temptabant Vaccaeosque et Turmogidos et Autrigonas crebris incursionibus fatigabant. Cf.* Strabo, *Geog.* 3.3.8.

53. Dio 56.43.3: Κοροκότταν γοῦν τινα λῃστὴν ἐν Ἰβηρίᾳ ἀκμάσαντα τὸ μὲν πρῶτον οὕτω δι᾽ ὀργῆς ἔσχεν ὥστε τῷ ζωγρήσαντι αὐτὸν πέντε καὶ εἴκοσι μυριάδας ἐπικηρῦξαι, ἔπειτ᾽ ἐπειδὴ ἑκὼν οἱ προσῆλθεν, οὔτε τι κακὸν εἰργάσατο καὶ προσέτι καὶ τῷ ἀργυρίῳ ἐκείνῳ ἐπλούτισε. For an in-depth discussion of brigandage in the Roman world see Grünewald (2004).

54. Strabo 3.4.5; Dio 53.25.5; Florus 2.33; Suet., *Div. Aug.* 20 and 21. For a discussion of the *Bellum Cantabricum et Asturicum* see Morillo (2011), pp. 13–15.

55. For a discussion of the number and whereabouts of units present see Syme (1934a), pp. 298–301. Curchin (1995), p. 69.

56. Curchin (1995), pp. 71–72, casts doubt on the presence of *Cohors Thracum*.

57. For a discussion of the legates with Augustus see Syme (1934a), pp. 301–02. Florus 2.33 mentions M. Agrippa was involved, which is problematic since he was certainly in Rome at this time. Magie (1920), p. 335, suggests Florus may have compressed three different campaigns into a single statement.

58. Florus 2.33; Orosius 6.21.6–7; Dio 53.25.7–8; Velleius 2.90.4.

59. See Syme (1934a), p. 315.

60. App., *Bell. Civ.* 5.111.1; Florus 2.33; Orosius 6.21.10; Dio 53.25.8, 54.5.1–2. See Syme (1934a), pp. 315–16.

61. Suet., *Tib.* 9.1.

62. Dio 53.25.6.

63. Strabo, *Geog.* 3.3.6; Lucan, *Pharsalia* 6.259; Silius Italicus, *Punica* 5.195–97. For a discussion of evidence for arms of the Cantabri see Illarregui (2005).

64. The weapon is depicted on the *denarius* of Carisius (*BMC* 281; Cohen 406; Paris 1046 pl. XLII; *RIC* 7a; *RSC* 405.).

65. Strabo, *Geog.* 3.4.15; Arrian, *Techne Taktike* 40.

66. Strabo, *Geog.* 3.4.18.

67. Dio 53.25.5–6: αὐτὸς δὲ ὁ Αὔγουστος πρός τε τοὺς Ἀστυρας καὶ πρὸς τοὺς Καντάβρους ἅμα ἐπολέμησε. For an interpretation of the confused chronology see Syme (1934a), pp. 295–301.

68. Florus 2.33. Two Roman camps have been identified in the locality of La Poza in Peña Cutral (Enmedio, Prov. Cantabria) near the native hillfort of Las Rabas: see Torres-Martínez, Martínez Velasco and Pérez Farraces (2012), p. 527.

69. Attica/Velica: Dio 53.25.6, Orosius 6.2.5 – on its modern identity see Syme (1934a), p. 310; Bergida: Florus 2.33.

70. Dio 53.25.7. Florus 2.33; Orosius 6.21.4: *Vinnium montem natura tutissimum confugerunt. Mons Vinnius* may have been one of the mountain peaks in the Cordillera Cantábrica.

71. Dio 53.25.5–6: καὶ ἐπειδὴ μήτε προσεχώρουν οἵ τε ἐπὶ τοῖς ἐρυμνοῖς ἐπαιρόμενοι, μήτε ἐς χεῖρας διά τε τὸ τῷ πλήθει ἐλαττοῦσθαι καὶ διὰ τὸ ἀκοντιστὰς τὸ πλεῖστον εἶναι ᾖσαν, καὶ προσέτι καὶ πράγματα αὐτῷ πολλά, εἴ που κινηθείη, τά τε ὑπερδέξια ἀεὶ προκαταλαμβάνοντες καὶ ἐν τοῖς κοίλοις τοῖς τε

ὑλώδεσιν ἐνεδρεύοντες παρεῖχον, ἐν ἀπόρῳ παντάπασιν ἐγένετο. *Cf.* Orosius 6.21.6. See Syme (1934a), pp. 302–05.

72. Orosius 6.21.5.

73. Florus 2.33; Orosius 6.21.4: *hostibus admoueri classem atque exponi copias iubet*; Strabo, *Geog.* 3.3.8. *Cohors* I *Aquitanorum Veterana* e.g. *CIL* XIII, 7399a.

74. Dio 53.27.3, 53.28.1; Florus 2.33.49–50; Orosius 6.21.11. Florus 2.33 mentions Aracillum, but Orosius 6.21 mentions Racilium. For a discussion see Martino (1982), pp. 32–33, 94–98 and 142. Illarregui (2005), p. 84, notes evidence of burning at several archaeological sites including Castro de Fontibre, Argüeso, and Castro de San Julián.

75. Florus 2.33: *quasi quadam cogebat indagine*.

76. For a full discussion of the site and finds of catapult bolt points and ballista stones see Torres-Martínez, Martínez Velasco and Pérez Farraces (2012).

77. Avery (1957), pp. 225 and 227.

78. Suet., *Verg.* 106–09: *Augustus vero – nam forte expeditione Cantabrica aberat – supplicibus atque etiam minacibus per iocum litteris efflagitarat, ut 'sibi de* Aeneide,*' ut ipsius verba sunt, 'vel prima carminis hupographe vel quodlibet kolon mitteretur'.*

79. Dio 53.23.5: πολλὰ μὲν γὰρ καὶ μάταια ἐς τὸν Αὔγουστον ἀπελήρει, πολλὰ δὲ καὶ ἐπαίτια παρέπραττε· καὶ γὰρ καὶ εἰκόνας ἑαυτοῦ ἐν ὅλῃ ὡς εἰπεῖν τῇ Αἰγύπτῳ ἔστησε, καὶ τὰ ἔργα ὅσα ἐπεποιήκει ἐς τὰς πυραμίδας ἐσέγραψε.

80. Dio 53.23.6, Rutledge (2001), Case 99, characterises Largus as a *delator*, an accuser or informer.

81. Dio 53.23.7.

82. Dio 53.23.7; Suet., *Div. Aug.* 66.2; Suet., *Grammat.* 16.

83. Dio 53.24.1.

84. Dio 53.24.2: ὁ μέντοι Προκουλείος οὕτω πρὸς αὐτὸν ἔσχεν ὥστ᾽ ἀπαντήσας ποτὲ αὐτῷ τήν τε ῥῖνα καὶ τὸ στόμα τὸ ἑαυτοῦ τῇ χειρὶ ἐπισχεῖν, ἐνδεικνύμενος τοῖς συνοῦσιν ὅτι μηδ᾽ ἀναπνεῦσαί τινι παρόντος αὐτοῦ ἀσφάλεια εἴη.

85. Strabo, *Geog.* 2.5.12: he acknowledges his friendship with Gallus and accompanied him on a trip down the Nile to Syene and the border with Ethiopia.

86. Strabo, *Geog.* 4.6.7.

87. App., *Ill.* 17.

88. Dio 53.25.3; Suet., *Div. Aug.* 21.1.

89. Strabo, *Geog.* 4.6.7.

90. Dio 53.25.3.

91. Livy, *Peri.* 135: *Salassi, gens Alpina, perdomiti.* Eutrop., 7.9.

92. Suet., *Div. Aug.* 21.

93. Dio 53.25.4: καὶ συμβῆναι καταναγκάσας ἀργύριόν τέ τι ῥητόν, ὡς καὶ μηδὲν δεινὸν ἄλλο δράσων, ᾔτησε, κἀκ τούτου πανταχῇ πρὸς τὴν ἔσπραξιν δῆθεν αὐτοῦ στρατιώτας διαπέμψας συνέλαβέ τε τοὺς ἐν τῇ ἡλικίᾳ καὶ ἀπέδοτο, ἐφ᾽ ᾧ μηδείς σφων ἐντὸς εἴκοσιν ἐτῶν ἐλευθερωθείη.

94. Strabo, *Geog.* 4.6.7.

95. Strabo, *Geog.* 4.6.7; Dio 53.25.5.

96. Dio 51.21.6, 53.25.4.

97. Dio 53.25.7; Suet., *Div. Aug.* 81.1: *cum etiam destillationibus iocinere vitiato ad desperationem redactus contrariam.*

98. Suet., *Div. Aug.* 81.1; Dio 53.25.7; Florus 2.33.

99. Dio 53.25.8: Γάιος δὲ Ἀντίστιος προσεπολέμησέ τε αὐτοῖς ἐν τούτῳ καὶ συχνὰ κατειργάσατο, οὐχ ὅτι καὶ ἀμείνων τοῦ Αὐγούστου στρατηγὸς ἦν, ἀλλ᾽ ὅτι καταφρονήσαντες αὐτοῦ οἱ βάρβαροι ὁμόσε τε τοῖς Ῥωμαίοις ἐχώρησαν καὶ ἐνικήθησαν. καὶ οὕτως ἐκεῖνός τέ τινα ἔλαβε, καὶ Τίτος μετὰ ταῦτα Καρίσιος τήν τε Λαγκίαν τὸ μέγιστον τῶν Ἀστύρων πόλισμα ἐκλειφθὲν εἷλε καὶ ἄλλα πολλὰ παρεστήσατο. Dio has Carisius' *praenomen* as Titus whereas coins show P. for Publius. *Cf.* Florus 2.33.

100. Such a camp with *agger* and *fossae duplex* has been identified at El Castichu de la Carisa, Lena in prov. Asturias and dated to 25 BCE: Morillo (2011), p. 14.

101. Florus 2.33: the Roman historian specifically states *montibus niveis*, which would date this event to the end of the winter of 26/25 BCE or the spring of 25. *Cf.* Orosius 6.21.10. For a discussion of the tangled sources see Syme (1934a), p. 307.

102. Florus 2.33: *Reliquias fusi exercitus validissima civitas Lancia excepti, ubi cum locis adeo certatum est, ut cum in captam urbem faces poscerentur, aegre dux impetraverit veniam, ut victoriae Romanae stans potius esset quem incensa monumentum.*

103. Orosius 6.2.7: *nam et Medullium montem Minio flumini inminentem; cf.* Florus 2.33. The Miño is the longest river in Galicia, Spain, with a length of 340km. For a discussion of the whereabouts of Mons Medullus see Magie (1920), pp. 334–45, and Syme (1934a), p. 296 and 302–03.

104. Florus: 2.33 says 18 miles; Orosius 6.21.7 says 15 miles.

105. For a discussion of this and other *tropaea* see Powell (2016).

106. *RIC* I 1, a silver *quinarius* shows Victory crowning a trophy while *RIC* I 4, a *denarius*, shows the trophy itself. Both, minted at Emerita Augusta, bear the legend P CARISIVS LEG AVGVSTI PRO P.

107. Dio 53.26.1. See Syme (1934a), p. 307.

108. Dio 53.26.2; Strabo, *Geog.* 17.3.9.

109. Strabo, *Geog.* 12.6.3, 5.

110. Dio 53.26.3; Eutrop. 7.10.2.

111. Ramsay (1916 and 1924).

112. Dio 53.26.5: καὶ ἐψηφίσθη μέν που καὶ τὰ ἐπινίκια αὐτῷ καὶ ἐπὶ τούτοις καὶ ἐπὶ τοῖς ἄλλοις τοῖς τότε γενομένοις· ἐπεὶ δ᾽ οὐκ ἠθέλησεν αὐτὰ πέμψαι, ἁψίς τε ἐν ταῖς Ἄλπεσι τροπαιοφόρος οἱ ᾠκοδομήθη, καὶ ἐξουσία ἐδόθη τοῦ τῇ πρώτῃ τοῦ ἔτους ἡμέρᾳ καὶ τῷ στεφάνῳ καὶ τῇ ἐσθῆτι τῇ νικητηρίᾳ ἀεὶ χρῆσθαι. Florus 2.33 also mentions *digna res lauro*, a laurel crown.

113. Dio 53.26.5; Suet., *Div. Aug.* 22; *RG* 13.

114. Dio 53.29.1.

115. Dio 53.28.3: ταῦτα μὲν ἀποδημοῦντι ἔτ᾽ αὐτῷ ἐψηφίσθη, ἀφικομένῳ δὲ ἐς τὴν Ῥώμην ἄλλα τινὰ ἐπί τε τῇ σωτηρίᾳ καὶ ἐπὶ τῇ ἀνακομιδῇ αὐτοῦ ἐγένετο. τῷ τε Μαρκέλλῳ βουλεύειν τε ἐν τοῖς ἐστρατηγηκόσι καὶ τὴν ὑπατείαν δέκα θᾶττον ἔτεσιν ἤπερ ἐνενόμιστο αἰτῆσαι, καὶ τῷ Τιβερίῳ πέντε πρὸ ἑκάστης ἀρχῆς ἔτεσι τὸ αὐτὸ τοῦτο ποιῆσαι ἐδόθη.

116. L. (Aelius) Lamia: Cassiodorus *Chron.* Ann. 730; *cf.* L. (Aemilius Paullus) Lepidus: Dio 53.29.1. On the identity of the governor see Syme (1934a), pp. 315–16.

117. Vell. Pat. 2.116.3: *vir antiquissimi moris et priscam gravitatem semper humanitate temperans*

118. Dio 53.29.1–2: ἀπηλλάγη, ἐπανέστησαν, καὶ πέμψαντες πρὸς τὸν Αἰμίλιον, πρὶν καὶ ὁτιοῦν ἐκφῆναί οἱ, σῖτόν τε καὶ ἄλλα τινὰ χαρίσασθαι τῷ στρατεύματι βούλεσθαι ἔφασαν, κἀκ τούτου στρατιώτας συχνοὺς ὡς καὶ κομιοῦντας αὐτὰ λαβόντες ἔς τε χωρία αὐτοὺς ἐπιτήδειά σφισιν ἐσήγαγον καὶ κατεφόνευσαν.

119. Dio 53.29.2; Vell. Pat. 2.90.1.

120. Dio 53.29.3.

121. Strabo, *Geog.* 16.4.22: τοῦτον δ᾽ ἔπεμψεν ὁ Σεβαστὸς Καῖσαρ διαπειρασόμενον τῶν ἐθνῶν καὶ τῶν τόπων τούτων τε καὶ τῶν Αἰθιοπικῶν, ὁρῶν τήν τε Τρωγλοδυτικὴν τὴν προσεχῆ τῇ Αἰγύπτῳ γειτονεύουσαν τούτοις, καὶ τὸν Ἀράβιον κόλπον στενὸν ὄντα τελέως τὸν διείργοντα ἀπὸ τῶν Τρωγλοδυτῶν τοὺς Ἄραβας· προσοικειοῦσθαι δὴ διενοήθη τούτους ἢ καταστρέφεσθαι. Confirmed by *RG* 26. Strabo accompanied Gallus on a trip down the Nile River – *Geog.*, 2.5.12.

122. Strabo, *Geog.* 16.4.22, 24. Other?

123. Strabo, *Geog.* 16.4.23, 17.1.53; Joseph., *Ant. Iud.* 15.317.

124. The Red Sea?

125. Dio 53.29.4.

126. Strabo, *Geog.* 16.4.22.

127. This example of trust betrayed anticipates the story of Arminius and Varus in 9 CE.

128. Strabo, *Geog.* 16.4.24.

129. Dio 53.29.4.

130. Dio 53.29.5: τὸ δὲ δὴ νόσημα οὐδενὶ τῶν συνήθων ὅμοιον ἐγίγνετο, ἀλλ᾽ ἐς τὴν κεφαλὴν ἐνσκῆψαν ἐξήραινεν αὐτήν, καὶ τοὺς μὲν πολλοὺς αὐτίκα ἀπώλλυε, τῶν δὲ δὴ περιγιγνομένων ἔς τε τὰ σκέλη κατήει, πᾶν τὸ μεταξὺ τοῦ σώματος ὑπερβάν.

131. Strabo, *Geog.* 16.4.24. It may have been scurvy.
132. Strabo, *Geog.* 16.4.24.
133. Strabo, *Geog.* 16.4.24; *cf.* Dio 53.29.6–7.
134. Strabo, *Geog.* 17.1.53: Γάλλος τε Αἴλιος μέρει τῆς ἐν Αἰγύπτῳ φρουρᾶς εἰς τὴν Ἀραβίαν ἐμβαλὼν εἴρηται τίνα τρόπον ἐξήλεγξε τοὺς ἀνθρώπους ἀπολέμους ὄντας: εἰ δὴ μὴ ὁ Συλλαῖος αὐτὸν προὐδίδου, κἂν κατεστρέψατο τὴν εὐδαίμονα πᾶσαν.
135. Strabo, *Geog.* 16.4.24: δι᾽ ἃς αἰτίας οὐδ᾽ ἐπὶ πολὺ πρὸς τὴν γνῶσιν τῶν τόπων ὤνησεν ἡ στρατεία αὕτη: μικρὰ δ᾽ ὅμως συνήργησεν. Pliny, *Nat. Hist.* 6.32 attributes to the expedition several natural history discoveries and states that: *in his expedition, Gallus destroyed the following towns, the names of which are not given by the authors who had written before his time, Negrana, Nestum, Nesca, Masugum, Caminacum, Labecia, and Mariva above-mentioned, 6 miles in circumference, as also Caripeta, the furthest point of his expedition.* | *Gallus oppida diruit, non nominata auctoribus qui ante scripserunt, Negranam, Nestum, Nescam, Magusum, Caminacum, Labaetiam et supra dictam Maribam circuitu VI, item Caripetam, quo longissime processit.*
136. Dio 53.29.8: πρῶτοι μὲν δὴ Ῥωμαίων οὗτοι, νομίζω δ᾽ ὅτι καὶ μόνοι, τοσοῦτον ἐπὶ πολέμῳ τῆς Ἀραβίας ταύτης ἐπῆλθον: μέχρι γὰρ τῶν Ἀθλούλων καλουμένων, χωρίου τινὸς ἐπιφανοῦς, ἐχώρησαν.
137. *RG* 26.
138. Dio 53.29.8; Strabo, *Geog.* 17.1.54. On Ethiopians see Pliny, *Nat. Hist.* 5.8. Opper (2014), p. 23.
139. The bronze head is now in the British Museum, accession number GR 1911.9–1.1. For a discussion of the artefact see Opper (2014), pp. 8–17.
140. Strabo, *Geog.* 17.1.
141. Strabo, *Geog.* 16.4.24.
142. Dio 53.30.1.
143. Dio 53.30.2: διαλεχθεὶς δέ τινα αὐτοῖς περὶ τῶν δημοσίων πραγμάτων τῷ μὲν Πίσωνι τάς τε δυνάμεις καὶ τὰς προσόδους τὰς κοινὰς ἐς βιβλίον ἐσγράψας ἔδωκε, τῷ δ᾽ Ἀγρίππᾳ τὸν δακτύλιον ἐνεχείρισε. The significance was two-fold. The *imperium proconsulare maius* gave him power that was superior to all other consuls and proconsuls in all provinces, not just his own. The power of a plebeian tribune gave him the right to veto decrees of the Senate and personal immunity, without having to hold the office of the tribunate itself – though in practice he used it on behalf of the Senate to advance its wishes (*RG* 6). On the transfer of powers (the so-called Second Constitutional Settlement), see Grant (1949); Jameson and Jameson (1969); and Salmon (1956). *Cf.* Ch. 7, n. 35.
144. Suet., *Div. Aug.* 59; Dio 53.30.3.
145. Dio 53.30.4. On the rumours of Livia's hand in Marcellus' death see Dio 53.33.4.
146. Dio 53.30.5.
147. Suet., *Verg.* 110–14; Marcellus' name is mentioned in *Aen.*, 6.883.
148. Dio 53.30.2 and 4–6; 53.30.1–3. In the 30s BCE, by popular consent, Imp. Caesar had been granted use of the appellation *Princeps Civitatis* ('First Man of the State') or *Princeps Civium* ('First Citizen'). It was an unofficial, courtesy title and did not confer upon him any formal social or political rank (Tac. *Ann.* 3.53). It is the origin of the word principate. Modern historians refer to the period of imperial autocracy established by him and his immediate successors as the Principate to distinguish it from the preceding epoch known as the Republic.
149. Vell. Pat. 2.93.2; Suet., *Div. Aug.* 66.3, *Tib.* 10.1; Pliny, *Nat. Hist.* 7.149; Tac., *Ann.* 14.53.3, 55.2–3; Dio 53.32.1; Joseph., *Ant. Iud.* 15.10.2 For a novel interpretation of Agrippa's mission see Magie (1908), pp. 145–52.
150. Dio 53.32.1.
151. Dio 54.8.1.
152. Vell. Pat. 2.91.1.
153. Suet., *Div. Aug.* 23.1.
154. For example *RIC* I 1 and 2, 4, 7, 10, 15 and 19 bear the legend P CARISIVS LEG AVGVSTI PRO P. See Powell (2016).
155. Vell. Pat. 2.94.1.

156. Suet., *Tib.* 8.1: *et repurgandorum tota Italia ergastulorum, quorum domini in invidiam venerant quasi exceptos supprimerent non solum viatores sed et quos sacramenti metus ad eius modi latebras compulisset.* The *ergastula* were prisons for slaves, who were made to work in chains in the fields.
157. Suet., *Div. Aug.* 24.1.
158. Dio 54.1.1–2.
159. Dio 54.1.3.
160. Dio 54.1.3–4.
161. Dio 54.3.2. Proconsul Primus likely followed M. Licinius Crassus – see Ch. 1, n. 223.
162. Dio 54.3.4: τοῦ τε συναγορεύοντος τῷ Πρίμῳ Λικινίου Μουρήνου ἄλλα τε ἐς αὐτὸν οὐκ ἐπιτήδεια ἀπορρίψαντος, καὶ πυθομένου 'τί δὴ ἐνταῦθα ποιεῖς, καὶ τίς σε ἐκάλεσεν;' τοσοῦτον μόνον ἀπεκρίνατο ὅτι 'τὸ δημόσιον.
163. Dio 54.3.5; Vell. Pat. 2.91.2.
164. Vell. Pat. 2.91.2–4. and 2.93.1.
165. Dio 54.6.1; Vell. Pat. 2.94.4.
166. Dio 54.7.1.
167. Cyprus and Gallia Narbonensis: Dio 54.4.1: τότε δ᾽ οὖν καὶ τὴν Κύπρον καὶ τὴν Γαλατίαν τὴν Ναρβωνησίαν ἀπέδωκε τῷ δήμῳ ὡς μηδὲν τῶν ὅπλων αὐτοῦ δεομένας. Illyricum: Dio 53.12.7, 54.34.3.
168. Dio 54.5.1.
169. Seneca, *De Ben.* 2.25.1.
170. Dio 52.42.4.
171. Dio 54.5.1–2.
172. Dio 54.5.3.
173. Orosius 6.21.6.
174. Dio 54.5.4; Strabo, *Geog.* 17.1.54.
175. Strabo, *Geog.* 17.1.54. Her full name and title was *Amnirense qore li kdwe li*, 'Ameniras, Qore and Kandake'. The name Kandake, the Greek form of the Nubian word, indicates she was a queen. She is mentioned in the Bible, *Acts* 8:26–27.
176. Strabo, *Geog.* 17.1.54. Opper (2014), p. 25.
177. Prince Akinidad is known from the stele, EA 1650 in the British Museum, which was found in building M 292 at Hamadab, located 3km south of Meroë. It is carved in Meroitic script. See Opper (2014), pp. 27–29, fig. 15.
178. Strabo, *Geog.* 17.1.54.
179. Dio 54.6.1–2.
180. Dio 54.6.2–3.
181. Dio 54.6.4: ἀγανακτήσας οὖν ἐπὶ τούτῳ ὁ Αὔγουστος, καὶ μήτε μόνῃ τῇ Ῥώμῃ σχολάζειν δυνάμενος μήτ᾽ αὖ ἄναρχον αὐτὴν καταλιπεῖν τολμῶν, ἐζήτει τινὰ αὐτῇ ἐπιστῆσαι, καὶ ἔκρινε μὲν τὸν Ἀγρίππαν ἐπιτηδειότατον ἐς τοῦτο εἶναι.
182. Dio 54.6.5.
183. Dio 54.6.6.
184. See 'New Clues as to the Whereabouts of the Lost Varus Inscription LWL-Römermuseum makes a surprise discovery during research for the "IMPERIUM"-exhibition', LWL-Römermuseum, Haktern am (online at http://www.lwl.org/varus-download/presse_imperium/Presseinformation_I_eng.pdf – accessed 29 February 2016).
185. See Hoff (1989), pp. 270–74.
186. See Hoff (1989) p. 269 for his interpretation of Dio 54.7.3.
187. Dio 54.7.2.
188. Aigina: Plutarch, *Reg. et imp. Apophth.* 207 f.; Samos: Dio 54.7.4.
189. Strabo, *Geog.* 17.1.54.
190. Dio 54.7.4.
191. Dio 54.7.6.
192. Dio 54.7.6.
193. Dio 54.9.2.
194. Dio 54.9.4; Jos., *Ant. Iud.* 15.105.

195. *Fasti Triumphales.*
196. Vell. Pat. 2.94.4.
197. Dio 54.9.4.
198. Dio 54.9.5.
199. Suet., *Tib.* 9.1; Vell. Pat. 2.94.4 calls the new regent by the name Artavasdes.
200. Vell. Pat. 2.94.4: *tanti nominis fama territus.*
201. Vell. Pat. 2.94.4; Strabo, *Geog.* 6.4.2; Eutrop., 7.9. Dio is less than flattering about Tiberius' contribution: *yet he assumed a lofty bearing, especially after sacrifices had been voted to commemorate what he had done, as though he had accomplished something by valour* | ὁ δ᾽ οὖν Τιβέριος, ἄλλως τε καὶ ἐπειδὴ θυσίαι ἐπὶ τούτῳ ἐψηφίσθησαν, ἐσεμνύνετο ὡς καὶ κατ᾽ ἀρετήν τι ποιήσας – Dio 54.9.5.
202. Dio 54.8.2–3: καὶ αὐτοὺς ἐκεῖνος ὡς καὶ πολέμῳ τινὶ τὸν Πάρθον νενικηκὼς ἔλαβε: καὶ γὰρ ἐπὶ τούτοις ἐφρόνει μέγα, λέγων ὅτι τὰ πρότερόν ποτε ἐν ταῖς μάχαις ἀπολόμενα ἀκονιτὶ ἐκεκόμιστο.
203. Dio 54.9.7–10.
204. Strabo, *Geog.* 17.53: Πετρώνιός τε ὕστερον τοῦ Ἀλεξανδρέων πλήθους τοσούτων μυριάδων ὁρμήσαντος ἐπ᾽ αὐτὸν μετὰ λίθων βολῆς, αὐτοῖς τοῖς περὶ ἑαυτὸν στρατιώταις ἀντέσχε, καὶ διαφθείρας τινὰς αὐτῶν τοὺς λοιποὺς ἔπαυσε.
205. Some historians assign this war to 19 BCE, the same year Balbus was in Rome celebrating his military award. This makes no sense given the date of his triumph, 27 March 19 BCE. Consistent with his whereabouts, the campaign must surely have been fought in his first or second year in office: I opt here for his second year.
206. Pliny, *Nat. Hist.* 5.5: *clarissimumque Garama, caput Garamantum.* For the list of cities see Ch. 2, n. 200. *Cf.* Cornelius Gallus' claim of capturing five cities in fifteen days, Ch. 1, n. 329.
207. Pliny, *Nat. Hist.* 5.5: *a Cornelio Balbo triumphata, unius omnium curru externo et Quiritum iure donato; quippe Gadibus genito civitas Romana cum maiore Balbo patruo data est.*
208. Dio 54.10.1.
209. Dio 54.10.2.
210. *Fasti Triumphales.*
211. Pliny, *Nat. Hist.* 5.5: *et hoc mirum, supra dicta oppida ab eo capta auctores nostros prodidisse, ipsum in triumpho praeter Cidamum et Garamam omnium aliarum gentium urbiumque nomina ac simulacra duxisse, quae iere hoc ordine: Tabudium oppidum, Niteris natio, Miglis Gemella oppidum, Bubeium natio vel oppidum, Enipi natio, Thuben oppidum, mons nomine Niger, Nitibrum, Rapsa oppida, Viscera natio, Decri oppidum, flumen Nathabur, Thapsagum oppidum, Tamiagi natio, Boin oppidum, Pege oppidum, flumen Dasibari, mox oppida continua Baracum, Buluba, Alasit, Galsa, Balla, Maxalla, Cizania, mons Gyri, in quo gemmas nasci titulus praecessit.*
212. Dio 54.10.1; Vell. Pat. 2.92.1–5.
213. Dio 54.20.3.
214. Dio 54.11.1–2. Dio calls the Germanic invaders by the name Κελτοί.
215. Dio 54.11.2: ταῖς Γαλατίαις προσετάχθη: ἔν τε γὰρ ἀλλήλοις ἐστασίαζον καὶ ὑπὸ τῶν Κελτῶν ἐκακοῦντο.
216. Strabo, *Geog.* 4.3.4, Tac., *Ann.* 12.27.1–2, *Germ.* 28.5, *cf. Hist.* 4.28, 4.63; and Suet., *Div. Aug.* 21.1.
217. Strabo *Geog.* 4.3.4: οὓς μετήγαγεν Ἀγρίππας ἑκόντας εἰς τὴν ἐντὸς τοῦ Ῥήνου. Cf. Suet., *Div. Aug.* 21.1.
218. Tac., *Germ.* 28. The archaeological evidence suggests that a Roman army was based here at different times over several years, but that the successive military encampments were probably sited some distance away from the civilian settlement. See Wells (1972), pp. 134–36.
219. During Iulius Caesar's Gallic War T. Labienus had defeated and killed their leader Indutiomarus and broken the Treveran resistance. Expelled from their strongholds, such as the hillfort at Hunnering – or 'Circle of the Huns' – located at Otzenhausen, St Wendel, in the Rhineland-Palatinate, this crushed nation had been largely left to its own devices.
220. Wightman (1971), p. 36.
221. *Cohors Ubiorum peditum et equitum*: Cheesman (1914), p. 29, and Haynes (2013), p. 44, both citing *CIL* X, 4862 = *ILS* 2690 dated to the end of Augustus' reign. *Ala Treverorum*: Cheesman (1914), p. 68, and Haynes (2013), p. 31.

222. Dio 54.11.2: οἱ γὰρ Κάνταβροι οἱ ζωργηθέντες τε ἐν τῷ πολέμῳ καὶ πραθέντες τούς τε δεσπότας σφῶν ὡς ἕκαστοι ἀπέκτειναν, καὶ πρὸς τὴν οἰκείαν ἐπανελθόντες πολλοὺς συναπέστησαν, καὶ μετ᾽ αὐτῶν χωρία καταλαβόντες καὶ ἐντειχισάμενοι τοῖς τῶν Ῥωμαίων φρουροῖς ἐπεβούλευον.

223. CIL II, 3414 (Carthago Nova).

224. Dio 54.11.3: ἐπ᾽ οὖν τούτους ὁ Ἀγρίππας ἐπιστρατεύσας ἔσχε μέν τι καὶ πρὸς τοὺς στρατιώτας ἔργον: πρεσβύτεροι γὰρ οὐκ ὀλίγοι αὐτῶν ὄντες καὶ τῇ συνεχείᾳ τῶν πολέμων τετρυχωμένοι, τούς τε Καντάβρους ὡς καὶ δυσπολεμήτους δεδιότες, οὐκ ἐπείθοντο αὐτῷ.

225. Augustus forbade his legates to use the term *comilitiones*, insisting on *milites*: *After the civil wars he never called any of the troops 'comrades', either in the assembly or in an edict, but always 'soldiers'; and he would not allow them to be addressed otherwise, even by those of his sons or stepsons who held military commands, thinking the former term too flattering for the requirements of discipline, the peaceful state of the times, and his own dignity and that of his household* | *Neque post bella civilia aut in contione aut per edictum ullos militum 'commilitones' appellabat, sed 'milites', ac ne a filiis quidem aut privignis suis imperio praeditis aliter appellari passus est, ambitiosius id existimans, quam aut ratio militaris aut temporum quies aut sua domusque suae maiestas postularet* – Suet., *Div. Aug.* 25.1.

226. Dio 54.11.4: ἀλλ᾽ ἐκείνους μέν, τὰ μὲν νουθετήσας τὰ δὲ παραμυθησάμενος τὰ δὲ καὶ ἐπελπίσας, διὰ ταχέων πειθαρχῆσαι ἐποίησε.

227. Dio 54.11.4: πρὸς δὲ δὴ τοὺς Καντάβρους πολλὰ προσέπταισεν. Roddaz (1984), pp. 405–10, questions Dio's account, beginning with the date. He believes the rebellion began in 20 BCE and only after appreciating the gravity of the situation did Agrippa intervene in the spring of the following year. He posits that the captives turned rebels could not have been held far beyond the conflict zone, perhaps at the mines in northwestern Spain, which would explain the speed of the uprising so soon after the war supposedly ended. He further suggests that the entire region, in particular the mountainous areas, had not been subdued in that war. This difficult terrain was unsuited to the Roman style of war fighting, the effect of which was to degrade the morale of the legionaries who perceived the conflict as a war without end.

228. Dio 54.11.4: καὶ γὰρ ἐμπειρίᾳ πραγμάτων, ἅτε τοῖς Ῥωμαίοις δεδουλευκότες, καὶ ἀπογνώσει τοῦ μὴ ἂν ἔτι σωθῆναι ἁλόντες ἐχρῶντο.

229. Strabo, *Geog.* 3.4.17.

230. Dio 54.11.5: ἀποβαλὼν τῶν στρατιωτῶν, συχνοὺς δὲ καὶ ἀτιμώσας ὅτι ἡττῶντο τά τε γὰρ.

231. Dio 54.11.5. Augustus came down hard on recalcitrant units – Suet., *Div. Aug.* 24. It is possible *Legio* I was removed to Aquitania or Belgica where it was reconstituted, suggests Syme (1933), p. 16.

232. Dio 54.11.5: τέλος δέ ποτε συχνοὺς μὲν ἀποβαλὼν τῶν στρατιωτῶν ... τούς τε ἐν τῇ ἡλικίᾳ πολεμίους πάντας ὀλίγου διέφθειρε καὶ τοὺς λοιποὺς τά τε ὅπλα ἀφείλετο καὶ ἐς τὰ πεδία ἐκ τῶν ἐρυμνῶν κατεβίβασεν.

233. Strabo, *Geog.* 3.3.8: ἀλλὰ νῦν, ὡς εἶπον, πέπαυται πολεμοῦντα πάντα: τούς τε γὰρ συνέχοντας ἔτι νῦν μάλιστα τὰ λῃστήρια Καντάβρους καὶ τοὺς γειτονεύοντας αὐτοῖς κατέλυσεν ὁ Σεβαστὸς Καῖσαρ.

234. Hor., *Ep.*1.12.26–27: *Cantaber Agrippae ... virtute ... cecidit*; Vell. Pat. 2.90.1; Strabo, *Geog.* 3.3.8, 6.4.2; Suet., *Div. Aug.* 21.1.

235. Dio 54.11.6: οὐ μὴν οὔτε ἐπέστειλέ τι τῇ βουλῇ περὶ αὐτῶν, οὔτε τὰ ἐπινίκια καίτοι ἐκ τῆς τοῦ Αὐγούστου προστάξεως ψηφισθέντα προσήκατο, ἀλλ᾽ ἔν τε τούτοις ἐμετρίαζεν ὥσπερ εἰώθει.

236. Aul. Gell., *Noct. Att.* 5.6.8; Livy, *AUC* 26.4. Maxfield (1981), pp. 76–79.

237. *Aureus*: BMCRE I 110. *Denarius*: BMCRE I 121, RIC I 414.

238. Pliny, *Nat. Hist.* 4.34; Pomponius Mela 3.13; Ptolemy, *Geog.* 2.6.3. See Fishwick (1987), Part 1, pp. 141–44. Syme (1934a), p. 316, advances Albinianus as the successor of Carisius; an alternative theory by Diego Santos (1975), p. 541, posits he he succeeded P. Silius Nerva in 14 BCE.

239. On the *auxilia* raised in the Iberian Peninsula see Roxan (1973).

240. Suet., *Verg.* 125–28. The hurriedly erected circular *monopteros* temple in front of the Parthenon on the Acropolis of Athens was dedicated to *Roma et Augustus* and temporarily housed the *aquilae* and *signa* recovered from Parthia (Rose (2005), pp. 50–52).

241. Avery (1957), p. 228.

242. Suet., *Verg.* 26–27, 50–52.

243. Suet., *Verg.* 22, 152–65.

244. Ver., *Aen.* 1.278–83: *His ego nec metas rerum nec tempora pono;* | *imperium sine fine dedi. Quin aspera Iuno,* | *quae mare nunc terrasque metu caelumque fatigat,* | *consilia in melius referet, mecumque fovebit* | *Romanos rerum dominos gentemque togatam:* | *sic placitum.* (Trans. Theodore C. Williams).
245. *RG* 12.
246. Dio 54.10.4: *cf.* Suet., *Div. Aug.* 53.2.
247. Dio 54.10.3. One of these was the *curator legum et morum summa potestate solus,* 'sole and pleni-potentiary guardian of law and order' (*RG* 6).
248. *RG* 11; *Fast. Amit. ad IV Id. Oct. et ad XVIII Kal. Ian; Fast. Cum. ad XVIII Kal. Ian.*; Prop. 4.3.71; Dio 54.10.3. Suet., *Div. Aug.* 29; Pliny, *Nat. Hist.* 36.50; Prop. 4.3.71. The altar is depicted on a *denarius, BMC* 4; *RIC* 322.
249. Dio 54.8.3: καὶ προσέτι καὶ ἐπὶ κέλητος ἐς τὴν πόλιν ἐσήλασε καὶ ἁψῖδι τροπαιοφόρῳ ἐτιμήθη.
250. The silver coins bear the legend SIGNIS RECEPTIS: e.g. *RIC²* 86b (*Colonia* Patricia). The same mint issued a denarius the following year showing on the obverse a *toga picta* over *tunica palmate* between *aquila* on the left and wreath on the right, and the legend SPQR PARENT (above) *CONS SVO* (below), and on the reverse a triumphal *quadriga* facing right, ornamented with two Victories and surmounted by four miniature galloping horses, and the legend CAESARI (above) AVGVSTO (below): *RIC* I 99.
251. *RG* 29. Cf. Dio 54.8.3: *in honour of this success he commanded that sacrifices be decreed and likewise a temple to Mars Ultor on the* Capitolium, *in imitation of that of Iupiter Feretrius, in which to dedicate the* signa; *and he himself carried out both decrees.* | ἀμέλει καὶ θυσίας ἐπ᾽ αὐτοῖς καὶ νεὼν Ἄρεως Τιμωροῦ ἐν τῷ Καπιτωλίῳ, κατὰ τὸ τοῦ Διὸς τοῦ Φερετρίου ζήλωμα, πρὸς τὴν τῶν σημείων ἀνάθεσιν καὶ ψηφισθῆναι ἐκέλευσε καὶ ἐποίησε. Coins show the recovered *signa* standing in a domed temple. See Appendix 4.
252. *RG* 21; Suet., *Div. Aug.* 56.2.
253. Hor., *Carm.* 4.15.4–16: *Tua, Caesar, aetas* | *fruges et agris rettulit uberes* | *et signa nostro restituit Iovi* | *derepta Parthorum superbis* | *postibus et vacuum duellis* | *Ianum Quirini clausit et ordinem* | *rectum evaganti frena licentiae* | *iniecit emovitque culpas* | *et veteres revocavit artes* | *per quas Latinum nomen et Italae* | *crevere vires famaque et imperi* | *porrecta maiestas ad ortus* | *solis ab Hesperio cubili* – trans. John Conington. Cf. Hor. *Epist.* 1.3.1ff, 1.12.26; Prop., 4.6.79f; Ov. *F.* 5.567ff; *Anth. Pal.* 9.219, 16.61; Verg., *Aen.* 7.604ff.
254. Dio 54.10.4, *cf.* 53.28.3.
255. Hor., *Carm.* 1.35.29–32: *Serves iturum Caesarem in ultimos* | *orbis Britannos et iuvenum recens* | *examen Eois timendum* | *partibus Oceanoque rubro* – trans. John Conington. The poem was published in 23 BCE.
256. Dio 54.10.5: ἐπειδή τε μηδὲν ὡμολόγει ὅσα τε ἀπόντος αὐτοῦ στασιάζοντες καὶ ὅσα παρόντος φοβούμενοι ἔπρασσον, ἐπιμελητής τε τῶν τρόπων ἐς πέντε ἔτη παρακληθεὶς δὴ ἐχειροτονήθη, καὶ τὴν ἐξουσίαν τὴν μὲν τῶν τιμητῶν ἐς τὸν αὐτὸν χρόνον τὴν δὲ τῶν ὑπάτων διὰ βίου ἔλαβεν, ὥστε καὶ ταῖς δώδεκα ῥάβδοις ἀεὶ καὶ πανταχοῦ χρῆσθαι, καὶ ἐν μέσῳ τῶν ἀεὶ ὑπατευόντων ἐπὶ τοῦ ἀρχικοῦ δίφρου καθίζεσθαι. For a discussion of the measures of 19 BCE see Ferrary (2001), pp. 103–10.
257. This despite what Augustus claims in *RG* 34. For an in-depth discussion of the *summum imperium auspiciumque* see Vervaet (2014). In an email to me dated 24 October 2014, Frederik Vervaet explained his choice of 19 BCE as the crucial year: 'this was when he [Augustus] completed and consolidated his constitutional domination of the old republican machinery of state as he assumed prioritary (*sic*) consular powers for life, as a proconsul, becoming in all but in name a third consul, with legally defined precedence over the two nominal consuls. Outward symbols of his new position: the right to carry the fasces always and anywhere (normally the consuls alternated these in Rome on a monthly basis, the consul holding the *fasces* having the right of initiative) as well as to sit in between the consuls, like before Augustus, the triumvirs *r.p.c.* and possibly the dictators. So, in a very real way, that's when the old Republic was definitively extinguished in Rome, after it had already been killed in the provinces by virtue of the sweeping settlements of 27 and 23.' For a critical review see Berthelet and Dalla Rosa (2015).
258. Dio 54.12.3.

Chapter 3: On the Offensive

1. Strabo, *Geog.* 17.3.25; Dio 54.12.4: see Ch. 2, n. 12.
2. Dio 54.12.4.
3. Dio 54.12.5.
4. Dio 54.13.1; *cf.* 52.42.
5. Dio 54.13.2.
6. Dio 54.13.2–4.
7. Dio 54.14.2–3: καὶ Λικίνιός τέ τις Ῥήγουλος, ἀγανακτήσας ὅτι τοῦ τε υἱέος καὶ ἄλλων πολλῶν, ὧν κρείσσων εἶναι ἠξίου, διειλεγμένων ἀπαλήλιπτο, τήν τε ἐσθῆτα ἐν αὐτῷ τῷ βουλευτηρίῳ κατερρήξατο, καὶ τὸ σῶμα γυμνώσας τάς τε στρατείας κατηριθμήσατο καὶ τὰς οὐλὰς προσεπέδειξέ σφισι. The dramatic incident highlights the premium Romans placed on having served in a military capacity even for a political role.
8. Dio 54.14.4–5.
9. Dio 54.12.3.
10. Dio 54.15.1.
11. Dio 54.15.3–4; *cf.* Dio 54.3.5.
12. For conventions on distributions of war spoils see Shatzman (1972).
13. For a discussion of the economic motives for war and expansion in the Republic see Harris (2006), esp. pp. 54–104.
14. Dio 54.18.2: καὶ τοῖς τὰ ἐπινίκια πέμπουσιν ἔργον ἐκ τῶν λαφύρων ἐς τὴν τῶν πράξεων μνήμην ποιεῖν προσέταξε; *cf.* Suet., *Div. Aug.* 29.4. See Shatzman (1972) pp. 185–86.
15. Zosimus, 2.
16. Tac., *Ann.* 11.11.
17. Roepke (2008), p. 142.
18. Hor., *Carm. Saec.* 45–48: *di, probos mores docili iuventae,* | *di, senectuti placidae quietem,* | *Romulae genti date remque prolemque* | *et decus omne.*
19. Hor., *Carm. Saec.* 53–60: *iam mari terraque manus potentis* | *Medus Albanasque timet securis,* | *iam Scythae responsa petunt, superbi* | *nuper et Indi.*| *iam Fides et Pax et Honos Pudorque* | *priscus et neglecta redire Virtus* | *audet adparetque beata pleno* |*Copia cornu.*
20. Hor., *Carm. Saec.* 65–68: *si Palatinas videt aequos aras,* | *remque Romanam Latiumque felix* | *alterum in lustrum meliusque semper* | *prorogat aevum.*
21. Suet, *Div. Aug.* 64.1; Dio 54.18.1.
22. Strabo, *Geog.* 7.1.4; Dio 54.32.1; Suet., *Tib.* 9.1.
23. Florus 2.30: *Inde validissimas nationes Cheruscos Suebosque et Sicambros pariter adgressus est, qui viginti centurionibus in crucem actis hoc velut sacramento sumpserant bellum, adeo certa victoriae spe, ut praedam in antecessum pactione diviserint.* According to Florus: *The Cherusci had chosen the horses, the Suebi the gold and silver, the Sicambri the captives* | *Cherusci equos, Suebi aurum et argentum, Sicambri captivos elegarant; sed omnia retrorsum.*
24. Strabo, *Geog.* 7.1.4: ἤρξαντο δὲ τοῦ πολέμου Σούγαμβροι πλησίον οἰκοῦντες τοῦ Ῥήνου, Μέλωνα ἔχοντες ἡγεμόνα. *Cf. RG* 32: Augustus spells the chief's name Maelo.
25. Caes., *Bell. Gall.* 35.
26. Dio 54.20.5.
27. Dio 54.20; Vell. Pat. 2.92.1.
28. Dio 54.19.1, 54.19.6.
29. Dio 54.20.4: ὁ δὲ δὴ μέγιστος τῶν τότε συμβάντων τοῖς Ῥωμαίοις πολέμων, ὅσπερ που καὶ τὸν Αὔγουστον ἐκ τῆς πόλεως ἐξήγαγε, πρὸς τοὺς Κελτοὺς ἐγένετο. *Cf.* 54.20.6.
30. Suet., *Div. Aug.* 23.1.
31. Dio 54.20.6: μαθὼν οὖν ταῦτα ὁ Αὔγουστος ὥρμησε μὲν ἐπ᾽ αὐτούς· οὐ μέντοι καὶ ἔργον τι πολέμου ἔσχεν: οἱ γὰρ βάρβαροι τόν τε Λόλλιον παρασκευαζόμενον καὶ ἐκεῖνον στρατεύοντα πυθόμενοι ἔς τε τὴν ἑαυτῶν ἀνεχώρησαν καὶ σπονδὰς ἐποιήσαντο, ὁμήρους δόντες.
32. The so-called 'Neuss A' was a 6.5 hectare fort with double ditch: see Wells (1972), pp. 127–28, fig. 6. *Cf.* Rüger (1996), p. 525.
33. For the evidence for a fort at Folleville see Keppie (1998), p. 156 and fig. 40. In the preface to the second edition Keppie mentions the fort at Aulnay-de-Saintonge near Saintes in what was then

province Aquitania, citing Tassaux *et al* (1983, 1984) and Tronche in Reddé (1996). A later paper by Lignereux and Peters assisted by Tassaux and Tronche (1997) dates the 6-hectare fort convincingly to 20–30 CE – Tiberius' principate – based on finds of animal and poultry bones.

34. Dio 54.21.1; Suet., *Div. Aug.* 23.1.
35. Caes., *Bell. Gall.* 20; Strabo, *Geog.* 4.1.4; Pliny, *Nat. Hist.* 4.108–09. Suet., *Tib.* 9.1: *discord among the leaders | principum discordia inquietam.* For a discussion of violent conflicts in Gaul under Augustus see Reddé (2011).
36. Craftiness: Vell. Pat. 2.102.1; *cf.* Pliny, *Nat. Hist.* 9.58. Deceitfulness: Hor., *Carm.* 4.9, 34–44.
37. Suet., *Tib.* 9.1.
38. Dio 54.20.1.
39. Dio 54.11.2–6, 54.20.2. Gruen (1996), p. 169; Dio 54.20.1; *Legio* VIIII *Hispana* may have been a participant in the campaign as it may have been stationed in Aquileia or Siscia.
40. Dio 54.20.2. The nations, often referred to as Pannonii, formed a confederacy comprising the Breuci, Andizetii, Ditiones, Peirustae, Mazaei and the Daesitiatae: Strabo, *Geog.* 7.5.3.
41. Dio 54.20.2–3.
42. Dio 54.20.3.
43. Dio 54.19.6.
44. Powell (2015), pp. 161–64.
45. Pliny, *Nat. Hist.* 23.58.
46. Dio 54.19.6, 54.23.7.
47. Dio 54.11.2–6, 54.20.2. See Curchin (1995), pp. 53.
48. Strabo, *Geog.* 3.4.
49. Morillo (2011), pp. 17–18.
50. Strabo, *Geog.* 3.1.6.
51. Strabo, *Geog.* 3.1–2.1, 3.2.15. An alternative date of 13 BCE is proposed: see Rich (2002), p. 159, n. 82.
52. *CIL* II, 4697–734. See Frothingham (1915), pp. 160–61.
53. The most complete survey of Roman gold mines in northwest Spain in English are Lewis and Jones (1970), pp. 169–85, and Jones and Bird (1972), pp. 59–74. See also Domergue (1978) and Richardson (1976), pp. 140–41.
54. Blázquez (1992).
55. E.g. *Alae* II *Asturum*: Haynes (2013), pp. 174; *Cohors* V *Asturum*: Haynes (2013), pp. 220.
56. Dio 54.22.1. The Raeti lived in the great sweep of what is now southern Bavaria, Tyrol and eastern Switzerland, reaching down to Lombardy in northern Italy, just north of Verona and Comum.
57. Dio 54.22.2: πᾶν δὲ δὴ τὸ ἄρρεν τῶν ἁλισκομένων, οὐχ ὅτι τὸ φαινόμενον ἀλλὰ καὶ τὸ ἐν ταῖς γαστράσιν ἔτι τῶν γυναικῶν ὃν μαντείαις τισιν ἀνευρίσκοντες, ἔφθειρον. The invocation of the supernatural seems designed to mark the behaviour of the Raeti out as particularly wicked and inhuman.
58. *CIL* X.6087.
59. Vell. Pat., 2.97.2: *cura deinde atque onus Germanici belli delegata, Druso Claudio.* His youngest stepson may even have proposed that he should be given the chance to command, suggests Th. Mommsen (1996), p. 106.
60. Vell. Pat. 2.97.2: *Druso Claudio, fratri Neronis, adulescenti tot tantarumque virtutum, quot et quantas natura mortalis recipit vel industria perficit. Cuius ingenium utrum bellicis magis operibus an civilibus suffecerit artibus, in incerto est.*
61. Strabo, *Geog.* 4.6.8; *RG* 26; Hor., *Carm.* 4.14.10ff; P. Silius Nerva had already subdued the three eastern Alpine tribes the previous year: Dio 54.20.1–2. See Ch. 3, n. 39.
62. Strabo, *Geog.* 4.6.9.
63. Florus 2.22 (drawing from Livy's account); Strabo, *Geog.* 4.6.8; Hor., *Carm. Saec.* 4.14.34ff.
64. Dio 54.22.3: δι᾽ οὖν ταῦτα ὁ Αὔγουστος πρῶτον μὲν τὸν Δροῦσον ἐπ᾽ αὐτοὺς ἔπεμψε· καὶ ὃς τοὺς προαπαντήσαντάς οἱ αὐτῶν περὶ τὰ Τριδεντῖνα ὄρη διὰ ταχέων ἐτρέψατο. These mountains were named after the nearby city of Tridentum (Trento). See Wolff (1996), p. 535.

65. For a survey of archaeological finds of the first century BCE from the Alpine region including weapons see Martin-Kilcher (2011).
66. For a full discussion of the route taken along the Reschen-Scheideck Pass by Drusus see Powell (2011), pp. 40–42 and maps 2 and 3. Wells (1972), p. 67, argues for advances along *both* the Brenner and Reschen-Scheideck Passes.
67. At 410km (250 miles) in length, the Adige is the second longest river in Italy, after the River Po with 652km (405 miles).
68. Polybius 34.10.
69. Chevalier (1976), p. 137.
70. A Roman *milia passum* equates to 1,478 metres (4,849ft).
71. Florus 2.22: he seems disinclined to see it as a desperate last act of defiance in the defence of their homeland, but it may also be a trope of the barbarian intended to portray the Raeti as uncivilized savages.
72. In 1997 traces of a barn belonging to a poststation of the imperial courier service (*cursus publicus*) were discovered in the Wiese northeast of Biberwier near Lermoos in sight of the spectacular Zugspitze, modern Germany's highest mountain at 2,962 metres. Suet., *Div. Aug.* 49 mentions that Augustus established posting stations with carts or wagons (*vehicula*) to replace young men (*iuvenes*) as relay runners, who not only delivered the messages but could find themselves interrogated about their contents.
73. Dio 54.22.3: τῆς μὲν Ἰταλίας ἀπεκρούσθησαν; *Cons. Liv.* 15–16; Vell. Pat. 2.39.3; Liv., *Per.* 138; Florus 2.22; Orosius 6.21, 22; Eutrop. 7.9; Strabo, *Geog.* 4.6.9.
74. Dio 54.22.3.
75. Wells (1972), p. 67. See Powell (2011), pp. 42–43 and map 3.
76. Strabo, *Geog.* 4.3.3 mentions that part of the territory in which the Raeti and Vindelici lived was marshland and near a lake that fed the Rhine.
77. Dio 54.22.4: ἐσβαλόντες οὖν ἐς τὴν χώραν πολλαχόθεν ἅμα ἀμφότεροι, αὐτοί τε καὶ διὰ τῶν ὑποστρατήγων; *cf.* Vell. Pat. 2.95.1: *Quippe uterque e diversis partibus Raetos Vindelicosqueadgressi.*
78. Vell. Pat. 2.95.2.
79. See Powell (2011), pp. 42–43 and map 3. Dio 54.22.4 simply mentions that Tiberius crossed 'the lake' (λίμνης) without actually naming it. The footnote in the Loeb translation on p. 339 identifies this lake as Lacus Venetus (Lake Garda), which was first recorded by Pomponius Mela around 43 CE, but the identification with this lake puts the site of the battle back in the vicinity of Tridentum. Other commentators – such as Wells (1972), p. 67 – associate Dio's location with Bodensee (Lake Constance to the English). However, if he had been following the course of the Rhône River from Lugdunum it would have taken him to Lake Geneva, which is the largest natural freshwater lake in western Europe at 582km² (225 sq. miles). All that can safely be said is that the ancient sources are too obscure to make a definite identification of the lake in question.
80. Strabo, *Geog.* 4.6.8.
81. Livy, *Peri.* 138.
82. Dio 54.22.5: ἐπειδή τε ἐπολυάνδρουν καὶ ἐδόκουν τι νεωτεριεῖν, τό τε κράτιστον καὶ τὸ πλεῖστον τῆς ἡλικίας αὐτῶν ἐξήγαγον, καταλιπόντες τοσούτους ὅσοι τὴν μὲν χώραν οἰκεῖν ἱκανοὶ νεοχμῶσαι δέ τι ἀδύνατοι ἦσαν.
83. E.g. *Cohors* II *Raetorum*: Cheesman (1914), p. 130.
84. Vell. Pat. 2.104.4.
85. Strabo, *Geog.* 4.6.8.
86. Strabo, *Geog.* 4.6.8: Strabo uses the word *poleis* by which he is likely referring to fortified hilltops, the Latin for which is *oppida*. Many were built with strong defensive ditches and banks surmounted by parapets, such as Berching/Pollanten, Bullenheimer Berg (Wuerzburg), Burgberg (Donaustauf), Fentbach (Weyarn), Hesselberg (Dinkelsbuehl), Manching and Michelsberg (Kehlheim): see Wolff, *CAH*, p. 537.
87. Vell. Pat. 2.95.2: *multis urbium et castellorum oppugnationibus.*
88. Strabo, *Geog.* 4.6.8: he classifies the Genauni as Illyrici not Raeti.
89. Hor., *Carm.* 4.14.34ff; 1st August was also the 'natal day' of the temples of Victoria and Victoria Virgo on the Palatinus Hill. Futrell (1997), pp. 81–82.

90. Eutrop. 7.9.
91. Vell. Pat. 2.104.4.
92. See Ch. 3, n. 40 and 41. Cunliffe (1997), pp. 217–18.
93. 1,058 metres (3,471ft.).
94. Strabo, *Geog.* 4.6.9. On the status of Noricum see Cunliffe (1994), pp. 426–27, and Alfödy (1974), pp. 62–77.
95. Florus, 2.22: *Noricis animos Alpes dabant, quasi in rupes et nives bellum non posset ascendere.* Cf. Strabo, *Geog.* 4.6.8–9.
96. Strabo, *Geog.* 4.6.9. He notes they were still pacified at the time he was writing his geography, thirty-three years later; cf. Livy, *Peri.* 138.
97. Strabo, *Geog.* 4.6.9: πάντας δ᾽ ἔπαυσε τῶν ἀνέδην καταδρομῶν Τιβέριος καὶ ὁ ἀδελφὸς αὐτοῦ Δροῦσος θερείᾳ μιᾷ, ὥστ᾽ ἤδη τρίτον καὶ τριακοστὸν ἔτος ἐστὶν ἐξ οὗ καθ᾽ ἡσυχίαν ὄντες ἀπευτακτοῦσι τοὺς φόρους (He says they had paid tribute consistently for thirty years at the time of his writing).
98. E.g. *Ala Noricorum*, Cheesman (1914), frontispiece, p. 149 and 176; Haynes (2013), p. 244. *Cohors I Noricorum Equitata* Cheesman (1914), p. 154 and 176.
99. For Drusus and Tiberius as examples of Roman heroes see A. Rogerson, 'Heroes Today: Creating a Champion with Horace (Odes 4.4)', 135th Annual Meeting of the American Philological Association (APA) in San Francisco, California, 3 January 2004.
100. Gold *aureus*: *RIC* I 164a, C. 132, *BMC* 443; silver *denarius*: *RIC* I 165b, C. 135, BMC 448. The branches look almost like branches from pine trees, which would be appropriate for the Alps.
101. Hor., *Carm.* 4.14.1–24: *Quae cura patrum quaeve Quiritium | plenis honorum muneribus tuas, | Auguste, virtutes in aevum | per titulos memoresque fastus | aeternet, o qua sol habitabilis | inlustrat oras maxime principum? | quem legis expertes Latinae | Vindelici didicere nuper | quid Marte posses. Milite nam tuo | Drusus Genaunos, inplacidum genus, | Breunosque velocis et arces | Alpibus impositas tremendis | deiecit acer plus vice simplici. | Maior Neronum mox grave proelium | commisit immanisque Raetos | auspiciis pepulit secundis, | spectandus in certamine Martio, | devota morti pectora liberae | quanti fatigaret ruinis, | indomitas prope qualis undas | exercet Auster Pleiadum choro | scindente nubes, impiger hostium | vexare turmas et frementem | mittere equum medios per ignis.* – trans. John Conington.
102. Hor. *Carm.* 4.4.17–28: *videre Raeti bella sub Alpibus | Drusum gerentem; Vindelici – quibus | mos unde deductus per omne | tempus Amazonia securi | dextras obarmet, quaerere distuli, | nec scire fas est omnia – sed diu | lateque victrices catervae | consiliis iuvenis revictae | sensere, quid mens rite, quid indoles | nutrita faustis sub penetralibus | posset, quid Augusti paternus | in pueros animus Nerones* – trans. John Conington.
103. Hor., *Carm* 4.4.73–76: *Nil Claudiae non perficient manus, | quas et benigno numine Iuppiter | defendit et curae sagaces | expediunt per acuta belli* – trans. John Conington. Compare Horace's lofty praise to the derision expressed in Mommsen (1996), p. 109.
104. Suet., *Tib.* 9.1.
105. Wells (1972), p. 67.
106. The precise locations of their winter camps is not known – they may include Auerberg, Augsberg-Oberhausen, Bregenz, Chur, Dangstetten, Gauting, Lorenzberg at Epfach and Kempten. See Wells (1972), pp. 57–58 and 74–89; Rüger, (1996), map 9 on pp. 518–19 and map 10 on p. 536. Evidence from inscriptions suggests the legions stayed until redeployed out of the area between 12BCE and 12CE. See M.C. Wells (1972), pp. 79–89.
107. Wells (1999), p. 69: the site, dated to 15BCE, has produced over 300 Roman weapons including two daggers as well as native weapons, personal effects and an assortment of tools. For the bent iron-tipped bolt from a catapult stamped with its legion number found during excavations in 1992 and 1993 see Zanier (1994).
108. Wells (1972), pp. 147–48.
109. Dio 53.12.4; Strabo, *Geog.* 17.3.25.
110. Tac., *Ann.* 3.48: *impiger militiae.*
111. Strabo, *Geog.* 17.3.23.
112. Florus 2.31: *Potuit et ille redire Marmaricus, sed modestior in aestimanda victoria fuit.*
113. Tac., *Ann.* 3.48: Quirnius was elected consul for 12 BCE.

114. Powell (2015), p. 168.
115. Powell (2015), p. 170.
116. Dio 54.24.4–5.
117. Dio 54.24.4 explains that after the death of Asander, Scribonius married Asander's wife, named Dynamis, who was really the daughter of Pharnakes and the granddaughter of Mithradates VI and had been entrusted with the regency by her husband, and thus he was holding Bosporus under his control.
118. Dio 54.24.4–5; Lucian, *Macrobioi* 17; Strabo, *Geog.* 11.2.3.
119. Dio 54.24.6; Strabo, *Geog.* 11.2.3.
120. Joseph., *Ant. Iud.* 16.20.
121. Joseph., *Ant. Iud.* 16.21.
122. Dio 54.24.6.
123. Dio 54.24.6: καὶ ἐνίκησε μέν, οὐ μὴν καὶ παρεστήσατό σφας πρὶν τὸν Ἀγρίππαν ἐς Σινώπην ἐλθεῖν ὡς καὶ ἐπ᾽ αὐτοὺς στρατεύσοντα. οὕτω δὲ τά τε ὅπλα κατέθεντο καὶ τῷ Πολέμωνι παρεδόθησαν.
124. Orosius 21.28: *Bosforanos vero Agrippa superauit et signis Romanis, quae illi quondam sub Mithride sustulerant, bello recuperatis victos ad deditionem coegit.* Eutrop. 7.9. The *signa* were captured when Mithridates beat L. Licinius Murena in the Second Mithridatic War of 83–81 BCE.
125. Dio 54.26.6. A *praefectus cohortis Bosporanorum* is mentioned on an inscription found at Antiocheia in Pisidia and dated to 8–7 BCE: see Cheesman (1913).
126. Dio 54.24.6.
127. For an archaeological survey of the Cheronesos see Carter (2003).
128. Dio 54.24.7: οὔτε γὰρ ἔγραψεν ἀρχὴν ἐς τὸ συνέδριον ὑπὲρ τῶν πραχθέντων οὐδέν, ἀφ᾽ οὗ δὴ καὶ οἱ μετὰ ταῦτα, νόμῳ τινὶ τῷ ἐκείνου τρόπῳ χρώμενοι, οὐδ᾽ αὐτοί τι τῷ κοινῷ ἔτ᾽ ἐπέστελλον.
129. Dio 54.24.8: ἐδέξατο· καὶ διὰ τοῦτο οὐδ᾽ ἄλλῳ τινὶ ἔτι τῶν ὁμοίων αὐτῷ, ὥς γε καὶ ἐγὼ κρίνω, ποιῆσαι τοῦτο ἐδόθη, ἀλλὰ μόναις ταῖς ἐπινικίοις τιμαῖς ἐγαυροῦντο.
130. Flor. 2.24; *ILS* 8965.
131. Suet., *Tib.* 9.1; Vell. Pat. 2.96.2.
132. Flor. 2.24: *In hos domandos Vinium misit. Caesi sunt in utrisque fluminibus.*
133. Livy, *Peri.* 138.
134. Dio 54.31.1. For a discussion of the *Concilium Galliarum* see Powell (2011a), p. 56.
135. E.g. an *optio carceris*, a deputy to a centurion in charge of a prison, is recorded both in Rome and Lugdunum (*CIL* IX, 1617 = *ILS* 2117; *CIL* XIII, 1833 = *ILS* 2116; and *CIL* VI, 531 = *ILS* 3729 (238–244).
136. Vel Pat. 2.97.2; *cf.* Strab., *Geog.* 6.4.2; *Florus 2.30.*
137. Florus 2.30: *Sed quatenus sciebat patrem suum C. Caesarem bis transvectum ponte Rhenum quaesisse bellum, in illius honorem concupierant facere provinciam.*
138. See Ch. 3, nos 31 and 32.
139. Sommer (2009) argues that the placement of forts on many sites on the Danube River was not intended to control access points such as roads and bridges, since they do not offer good lines of surveillance, but to give the army the best vantage to control lengths of the river.
140. Florus 2.30: *In Rheni quidem ripa quinquaginta amplius castella dixerit.* Contra: Wells (1972), p. 97, and Petrikovits (1961), pp. 33–34, express doubt about the claim based on current archaeology. *Pro*: Reed (1975), p. 97, argues that, instead of discounting Florus' claim we should be prepared to accept it until the evidence – or confirmed absence of it – categorically refutes it, i.e. just because we have not found all of them does not mean they are not there.
141. Florus 2.30: *Bonam et Gesoriacum pontibus iunxit classibusque firmavit.* These locations have confounded modern historians. For a discussion on the identification of Borma or Bonna and Gesoriacum see Wells (1972), pp. 136–37.
142. For a strategic overview see Kühlborn (2004), pp. 27–29; Petrikovits (1961), pp. 15–17 and fig. 1 on p. 17; Powell (2011), pp. 61–63; Rüger (1996), p. 525; and Wells (1972), pp. 95–96 and fig. 1 on p. 17. For comparative ground plans to scale see Petrikovits (1961), fig. 5 on p. 25.
143. Rüger (1996), p. 525.
144. Wells (1972), p. 97; Bingen: Wells (1972), Appendix II, p. 283; Bonn: Wells, (1972), pp. 136–37; Koblenz: Wells (1972), pp. 137–38; Strasbourg: Wells (1972), pp. 147–48.

145. On the archaeological evidence see Wells (1972), pp. 138–46 and fig. 7 on p. 139.

146. Wells (1972), p. 146.

147. Wells (1972), p.146, notes that great numbers of *amphorae*, the large two-handled pottery jars used in the Roman era for shipping dried fruits, grain, wine, oil and fish sauce (*garum*, *liquamen*), as well as quantities of the waxy red *terra sigillata* ware that took pride of place on a Roman's dinner table, have been found there.

148. Tact, *Germ.* 28.

149. Tac., *Ann.* 1.31.3 confirms two legions were based here in 14 CE. On the archaeological evidence see Petrikovits (1961), p. 33; Wells (1972), pp. 134–36: the graffito *PRIN. LEG. XIX* has been found scratched into a fragment of red *sigillata* ware.

150. On the archaeological evidence see Petrikovits (1961), pp. 17–33; Wells (1972), pp. 127–34 and fig. 6 on p. 129.

151. Wells (1972), p. 128.

152. Wells (1972), p. 132. A civilian settlement (*cannabae*) grew up alongside the fort, the remains of which have been found at Selssche Ziegelei, along with pieces of pottery and some 3,000 coins, mostly dating to the reign of Augustus.

153. Wells (1972), p. 132.

154. Vetera may have been a soldier's colloquial or affectionate term for an army base: a *castra vetera* is mentioned in the war against Pompeius Magnus by Iulius Caesar in *Bell. Civ.* 3.66. On the archaeological evidence for Vetera at Xanten see Petrikovits (1961), pp. 32–33; Wells (1972), pp. 123–27 and fig. 5 on p. 125.

155. Tac., *Ann.* 1.45 confirms two legions were based here in 14 CE.

156. On the archaeological evidence see Wells (1972), pp. 116–23 and fig. 4 on p. 117. Jona Lendering (livius.org) remarks that the Hunerberg fortress was 'very, very large'. Measuring 650 metres by 650 metres, it could accommodate at least two – possibly three – legions. (Attested by epigraphic evidence are *legiones* I *Germanica* and XIII *Gemina*). The base was surrounded by two ditches and a large wall, with towers placed every 24 metres. The *principia* has been identified, but not yet excavated. The houses of the senior officers, however, have been examined: they measure between 240 square metres and 540 square metres; and the *praetorium*, measuring 35.5 metres by 36.5 metres, was more than double the size. Located to the east of the legionary fortress at Kops Plateau, there was a second, independent military installation. The roughly oval shaped fortification offered accommodation for one cavalry *ala*, contained within a double ditch. The *praetorium* inside measured about 60 metres by 35 metrss and had the elaborate floorplan of an Italianate villa. A granary has also been identified, but no barrack buildings. The stables were located to the south of the fort, outside the walls.

157. Wells (1972), p. 123.

158. Tac., *Germ.* 29.

159. Dio 55.24.7, 60.20; Tac., *Germ.* 29.

160. Tac., *Germ.* 29. Their unfailing reliability and ruthlessness in a battle against the Caledonii is described in Tac., *Agr.* 36. The Kops Plateau/Hunerberg site in Nijmegen has produced several spectacular Roman cavalry helmets and facemasks in recent years, which have been dated to the Augustan era: see Willems (1992), pp. 57–66; and Enckevort (1994), pp. 125–37.

161. Tac., *Ann.* 4.12. E.g. *Ala Batavorum* Haynes (2013), p. 122 and 197; *Ala I Batavorum Milliaria* Haynes (2013), p. 232; *Ala I Batavorum Milliaria* Haynes (2013), p. 297; *Cohortes* I–IX *Batavorum* see Cheesman (1914), p. 72, 78 n. 2, 92 n. 2, 147, 151, 154, 157 and 173; *Cohors* I *Batavorum Milliaria* Haynes (2013), p. 116, 129 and 333; *Cohors* III *Batavorum Milliaria Equitata* Haynes (2013), p. 116, 297 and 335.

162. Rollo (1938), p. 49.

163. Suet., *Claud.* 1.5.2: *Is Drusus ... transque Rhenum fossas navi et immensi operis effecit, quae nunc adhuc Drusinae vocantur*; cf. Tac., *Ann.* 2.8.1.

164. Tac., *Ann.* 13.53, *Hist.* 5.19. Its design and function is not well understood and, despite attempts to find the structure, it has remained elusive. For a range of hypotheses see Huisman (1995), pp. 188–94; Makaske *et al* (2008), pp. 323–37; and Wells (1972), pp. 101–16.

165. Wells (1972), p. 105, see also map as fig. 3 on p. 102, 107–08 and 110 cites *CIL* XIII.8811, 8810, 8815 and 12086a. Traces of a fort have been found by archaeologists sited right next to the course of the old Vecht River. While numismatic evidence from the site suggests that Fectio was founded the during the later campaigns of 4/5 CE, building a fort at this location (or close by) at the same time as constructing the *fossa Drusiana* seems a strong possibility.

166. Dio 54.24.3: καὶ αἱ Ἄλπεις αἱ παραθαλασσίδιοι ὑπὸ Λιγύων τῶν κομητῶν καλουμένων ἐλευθέρως ἔτι καὶ τότε νεμόμεναι ἐδουλώθησαν.

167. *Cohors* I *Ligurum* and *Cohors* II *Ligurum* are known: see Cheesman (1914), p. 37, 69, 150 and 186. They were initially stationed in Alpes Maritimae (Tac., *Hist.* 2.14). Livy, *AUC* 42.35 records that 2,000 were recruited – probably by forced levy – for the Macedonian campaign of 171 BCE by consul P. Licinius.

Chapter 4: Into the Unknown
1. Dio 54.25.1.
2. Dio 54.25.1–2.
3. Dio 54.25.3.
4. *RG* 4; Dio 54.25.4.
5. Dio 54.25.5.
6. Dio 54.25.6.
7. Dio 54.25.6.
8. Dio 54.25.5–6.
9. Dio 54.25.6: ταῦτα δὲ ἐκείνοις μὲν οὔθ᾽ ἡδονὴν οὔτ᾽ ὀργὴν ἔν γε τῷ τότε παρόντι ἐνεποίησε διὰ τὸ μήτε πάντων ὧν ἐπεθύμουν τυχεῖν μήτε πάντων διαμαρτεῖν, τοῖς δὲ δὴ ἄλλοις ἀγαθὰς ἐλπίδας τοῦ μηκέτι τῶν κτημάτων ἀφαιρεθήσεσθαι.
10. *RG* 12. This is one of the first official uses of the term.
11. Dio 54.26.3.
12. Dio 54.26.3–4.
13. Dio 54.26.8–9: τότε δὲ αὐτὸς πάντας αὐτοὺς ἐξήτασε, καὶ τὰ μὲν τῶν ὑπὲρ πέντε καὶ τριάκοντα ἔτη γεγονότων οὐκ ἐπολυπραγμόνησε, τοὺς δὲ ἐντός τε τῆς ἡλικίας ταύτης ὄντας καὶ τὸ τίμημα ἔχοντας βουλεῦσαι κατηνάγκασε, χωρὶς ἢ εἴ τις ἀνάπηρος ἦν. καὶ τὰ μὲν σώματα καὶ αὐτός που αὐτῶν ἑώρα, περὶ δὲ δὴ τῶν οὐσιῶν ὅρκοις ἐπιστοῦτο αὐτῶν τε ἐκείνων καὶ ἑτέρων συνομνύντων σφίσι καὶ λογισμὸν τῆς τε ἀπορίας ἅμα καὶ τοῦ βίου διδόντων.
14. Dio 54.28.1: μεῖζον αὐτῷ τῶν ἑκασταχόθι ἔξω τῆς Ἰταλίας ἀρχόντων ἰσχῦσαι ἐπιτρέψας; Dio 55.6.1 inferred. The power is usually presumed to be the *imperium proconsulare* but the statement 'greater authority than the officials outside Italy *ordinarily* possessed' could logically be interpreted to be the *summum imperium auspiciumque*, granted to Augustus in 19 BCE, and now extended to his partner Agrippa – see Ch. 2. n. 257.
15. Powell (2015), pp. 202–03.
16. *RG* 12. See Goudineau (1996), p. 489. Further north a hoard of *asses* has been found at Port Haliguen, Quiberon, in which the portrait of Augustus on every coin is scored: Giard (1967); *cf.* Gaillou and Jones (1991), p. 77.
17. Many historians place this event in 13 BCE, but Dio 54.34.5–7 clearly sets it in the context of 11 BCE.
18. Dio 54.34.5.
19. Florus 2.27: *Ille barbaros et signis militaribus et disciplina, armis etiam Romanis adsueverat.*
20. Where was the governor of Macedonia, asks Syme (1986), p. 334.
21. Vell. Pat. 2.96.2; Dio 55.28.1–2.
22. Dio 54.28.2: καὶ ὃς τὴν μὲν στρατείαν καίτοι τοῦ χειμῶνος, ἐν ᾧ Μᾶρκος τε Οὐαλέριος καὶ Πούπλιος Σουλπίκιος ὑπάτευον, ἐνεστηκότος ἐποιήσατο, ἐκπλαγέντων δὲ τῶν Παννονίων πρὸς τὴν ἔφοδον αὐτοῦ καὶ μηδὲν ἔτι νεωτερισάντων ἐπανῆλθε.
23. A *denarius* struck at Rome in 12 BCE by Cossus Cornelius Lentulus shows the bare head of Augustus with the legend AVGVSTVS on the obverse, an equestrian statue (facing right) of a helmeted M. Agrippa bearing a trophy over his left shoulder, on pedestal, ornamented with two

prows with the legend COSSVS CN F LENTVLVS, *RIC* I 412; *RSC* 418; *BMCRE* 122–3 = *BMCRR* Rome 4672–3; *BN* 551–4.

24. Dio 54.28.2.
25. Dio 54.28.3.
26. Dio 54.28.4. The fragment of the eulogy in Greek is *P. Köln* 249 (Inv. Nr. 4701 + 4722 Recto). For the text see http://www.uni-koeln.de/phil-fak/ifa/NRWakademie/papyrologie/Karte/VI_249.html (accessed 29 February 2016) and a translation see Powell (2015), p. 181 and n. 14–16.
27. Dio 54.28.5.
28. Dio 54.31.1.
29. Dio 54.31.2.
30. Suet., *Tib.* 7.2.
31. Dio 54.31.2; Suet., *Tib.* 7.3.
32. Dio 54.29.5n, 55.22.4, 55.32.1–2n. On the name of M. Agrippa's posthumous son see Pappano (1941) who notes that the *cognomen* Postumus does not appear on any surviving inscriptions.
33. Dio 54.31.2.
34. Strabo, *Geog.* 7.5.2.
35. Dio 54.31.3.
36. Dio 54.31.3: καί σφας ὁ Τιβέριος, πολλὰ μὲν τῆς χώρας πορθήσας πολλὰ δὲ καὶ τοὺς ἀνθρώπους κακώσας, ἐχειρώσατο.
37. Dio 54.31.3: καὶ τά τε ὅπλα σφῶν ἀφείλετο, καὶ τῆς ἡλικίας τὸ πλεῖον ἐπ᾽ ἐξαγωγῇ ἀπέδοτο. *cf.* Ch. 3, n. 81, Dio 54.22.5.
38. Dio 54.36.2.
39. Joseph., *Ant. Iud.* 16.4.
40. Dio 54.31.2: καὶ αὐτῷ διὰ ταῦτα ἡ μὲν βουλὴ τά γε ἐπινίκια ἐψηφίσατο, ὁ δ᾽ Αὔγουστος ταῦτα μὲν οὐκ ἐπέτρεψεν ἑορτάσαι, τὰς δὲ τιμὰς τὰς ἐπινικίους ἀντέδωκε.
41. Dio 54.32.1.
42. Dio 54.32.1; *cf.* Strabo, *Geog.* 7.1.3.
43. Dio 54.32.2: ἔς τε τὸν ὠκεανὸν διὰ τοῦ Ῥήνου καταπλεύσας τούς τε Φρισίους ὠκειώσατο.
44. As the crow flies, the distance between Batavodurum and the way to the open sea (Ostium Flevum) was around 143 nautical miles (230km). Travelling 25 nautical miles per day, assuming no problems *en route*, the fleet could have reached the Mare Germanicus in a little under six days.
45. Pliny, *Nat. His.* 16.2–4.
46. Dio 54.32.2: Φρισίους ὠκειώσατο. *cf.* Tac., *Germ.* 34.
47. Dio 54.32.2; Tac., *Germ.* 34.
48. Tac., *Ann.* 4.72.
49. Strabo, *Geog.* 7.1.3: ὧν ἐστι καὶ ἡ Βυρχανίς, ἣν ἐκ πολιορκίας εἷλε. The identity of Burchanis is often interpreted to be Borkum, which is today the largest and westernmost of the East Frisian Islands in the North Sea. Bant, a large island which has since receded into the Wadden Sea, is another contender. The Romans nicknamed it Fabaria, meaning 'Bean Island', because of the wild beans (*fabae*) that grew there. Who opposed Drusus is not specified, though faced with several hundred warships, many equipped with artillery weapons mounted on turrets, resistance would not have lasted long.
50. Suet., *Claud.* 1.5.2: *deinde Germanici belli Oceanum septemtrionalem primus Romanorum ducum navigavit.*
51. Tac., *Germ.* 34: *Nec defuit audentia Druso Germanico, sed obstitit Oceanus in se simul atque in Herculem inquiri. Mox nemo temptavit, sanctiusque ac reverentius visum de actis deorum credere quam scire.* Cf. Pliny, *Nat. Hist.* 3.67 and Suet., *Claud.* 1.5.3.
52. The Ems River was known to Pliny, *Nat. Hist.* 4.14; Tac., *Ann.* 1.60; Pomponius Mela, 3.3; Strabo, *Geog.* 7.1.3; and Ptolemy, *Geog.* 2.10: by the name *Amisia, Amasia, Amasios* or *Amisius*.
53. Dio 54.32.2: καὶ ἐς τὴν Χαυκίδα. Tac., *Germ.* 35; Pliny, *Nat. Hist.* 16.1–2.
54. Strabo, *Geog.* 7.1.3: ὧν ἐν τῷ Ἀμασίᾳ Δροῦσος Βρουκτέρους κατεναυμάχησε.
55. Dio 54.32.2.
56. Dio 54.32.3.
57. Dio 54.32.3.

58. Strabo, *Geog.* 4.1.3.
59. On the Roman road network in the region see Chevalier (1976), p. 137.
60. Dio 54.34.6; Florus 2.27.
61. Hor., *Carm.* 2.12; Tac., *Ann.* 6.10.
62. Vell. Pat. 2.98.2–3: *De quo viro hoc omnibus sentiendum ac praedicandum est, esse mores eius vigore ac lenitate mixtissimos et vix quemquam reperiri posse, qui aut otium validius diligat aut facilius sufficiat negotio et magis quae agenda sunt curet sine ulla ostentatione agendi.*
63. Dio 54.34.6.
64. Dio 54.26.1; Suet., *Div. Aug.* 43. The *Lusus Troiae* were reintroduced by Cornelius Sulla, then revived by Iulius Caesar and again by Agrippa in 40 and 33 BCE (Dio 48.20.2). Augustus ensured their continuation. They are mentioned in Ver., *Aen.* 5.545–603, and associated with the founding of the city of Rome.
65. *Cf.* Dio 49.43.3. In 28 BCE Ti. Claudius Nero – then 15 years old – was *ductor turmae puerorum maiorum*, commanding a group of the biggest boys (Suet., *Tib.* 6).
66. Suet., *Div. Aug.* 43: *Sed et Troiae lusum edidit frequentissime maiorum minorumque puerorum, prisci decorique moris existimans clarae stirpis indolem sic notescere.*
67. Suet., *Div. Aug.* 43: *rursus commissione ludorum, quibus theatrum Marcelli dedicabat, evenit ut laxatis sellae curulis compagibus caderet supinus.*
68. Dio 54.33.2: ἐν ὀργῇ σχόντες πανδημεὶ ἐπ᾽ αὐτοὺς ἐξεστράτευσαν, κἂν τῷ καιρῷ τούτῳ ἔλαθε τὴν χώραν αὐτῶν διεξελθών.
69. Kühlborn (2004), p. 33; Wells (1972), pp. 161–62 and 319–20. The site shows evidence of multiple occupations with marching camps preceding the building of the main fortress (the so-called *Hauptlager*). The last base in the series to be built, large enough for up to two legions, measured 900 metres by 650 metres.
70. Kühlborn (2004), pp. 30–32; *cf.* Wells (1972), pp. 174–77 and 246–47. As Wells (1972), p. 163 and fig. 8, notes, the site was occupied multiple times. The earliest was a marching camp, the so-called *Feldlager*. It is associated with Drusus' campaign. Built on the slopes of the Silverberg ('Silver Mountain'), the single ditch and bank suggest the inner space was used for tents. The so-called *Anlegeplatz* at the Wiegel may be a supply dump. There are four successive bases built one on top of the other at Haltern proper. The age and function of the Annaberg fort is not well understood; it has a circumference of 1,050 metres with a revetment at the front only, and inside archaeologists found a well: see Wells (1972), pp. 165–66 and 170–74.
71. Wells (1972), p. 221. It measured 230 metres by 250 metres. For the press release from Landschaftsverband Westfalen-Lippe (LWL) on the excavations of 2011 see http://www.lwl.org/pressemitteilungen/mitteilung.php?25644 (accessed 29 February 2016).
72. Dio 54.33.1: τόν τε Λουπίαν ἔζευξε καὶ ἐς τὴν τῶν Συγάμβρων ἐνέβαλε. Wells (1972), p. 165, notes that footings of a structure have been found near Haltern but it has not been excavated or securely dated.
73. It measured 188 metres by 88 metres. For archaeological reports see Kühlborn (1990), Kühlborn (2004), p. 29, and Wells (1972), pp. 220–22.
74. It measured 840 metres by 640 metres. For archaeological reports see Kühlborn (1990 and 1991) and Wells (1972), pp. 211–20 and location map fig. 11 on p. 212.
75. See Kühlborn (1990) and Wells (1972), p. 223.
76. Wells (1972), pp. 226–30 argues the fort was built as early as 12 BCE, but not later than 11, and was located in territory of the friendly Mattiaci tribe – see Tac., *Germ.* 29 – whose capital was at Bad Nauheim to collect tribute in kind. Nearby is *Lager am Goldstein*, a marching camp measuring 300 metres by 700 metres, encompassing a space of 1.5 hectares, which may date from this period, perhaps for soldiers building the Rödgen facility. It lies 700 metres west of Rödgen identified from air photography: see Köhler and Schnurbein (2003), Lindenthal and Nickel (2005) and Wigg (1999).
77. Obsequens 72: *In Germania in castris Drusi examen apium in tabernaculo Hostilii Rufi, praefecti castrorum, consedit ita ut funem praetendentem praefixamque tentorio lanceam amplecteretur.* *Cf.* Dio 54.33.2: *and, besides, a swarm of bees been seen in his camp* | καὶ ὁ χειμὼν ἐνέστη καί τι καὶ σμῆνος ἐν τῷ στρατοπέδῳ αὐτοῦ ὤφθη; and Pliny, *Nat. Hist.* 11.18, see note below.

78. Obsequens 72: *Multitudo Romanorum per insidias subiecta est.*
79. Dio 54.33.2.
80. Dio 54.33.3.
81. Tac., *Germ.* 6: *hastas vel ipsorum vocabulo frameas gerunt angusto et brevi ferro.*
82. Powell (2014), pp. 16–17 and 58.
83. Dio 54.33.3–4: οἱ γὰρ πολέμιοι ἄλλως τε ἐνέδραις αὐτὸν ἐκάκωσαν, καί ποτε ἐς στενὸν καὶ κοῖλον χωρίον κατακλείσαντες ὀλίγου διέφθειραν, κἂν πασσυδὶ ἂν ἀπώλεσαν, εἰ μὴ καταφρονήσαντές σφων ὡς καὶ ἑαλωκότων καὶ μιᾶς ἐπικοπῆς ὄντων ὁμόσε αὐτοῖς ἀσύντακτοι ἐχώρησαν. νικηθέντες γὰρ ἐκ τούτου οὐκεθ᾽ ὁμοίως ἐθρασύνοντο, ἀλλὰ πόρρωθεν μέν σφας παρελύπουν, ἐγγὺς δὲ οὐ προσῄεσαν.
84. Pliny, *Nat. Hist.* 11.18: *sedere in castris drusi imperatoris, cum prosperrime pugnatum apud Arbalonem est, hautquaquam perpetua haruspicum coniectura, qui dirum id ostentum existimant semper.*
85. Dio 54.33.5.
86. Florus, 2.30: *Praeterea in tutelam provinciae praesidia atque custodias obique disposuit per Mosam flumen, per Albin, per Visurgim.*
87. Dio 54.33.4: The site of the fort – ὅ τε Λουπίας καὶ ὁ Ἐλίσων συμμίγνυνται φρούριόν τί σφισιν ἐπιτειχίσαι – which is usually referred to as Aliso, is unknown; similarly the location of ἕτερον ἐν Χάττοις παρ᾽ αὐτῷ τῷ Ῥήνῳ. Cf. Florus 2.30. For a 'Special Study on the Location of Aliso' see Delbrück (1990), pp. 131–48; cf. Kühlborn (2004), p. 29; Swan (2004), pp. 267–68; and Wells (1972), pp. 152–53, who, proposing hypothetically that it was the fort at Annaberg on the site, remarks 'but we can say that if Haltern is *not* Aliso, then we have no idea where Aliso was' (his emphasis). It is entirely possible that the site of Aliso still remains to be discovered by archaeologists in Germany.
88. Wells (1972), pp. 218–20 argues for 10/9 BCE. Specimens of a variety military equipment including *pila* have been found at the site, attesting to the presence of regular *caligati*.
89. Dio 54.33.5: διὰ μὲν οὖν ταῦτα τάς τε ἐπινικίους τιμὰς καὶ τὸ ἐπὶ κέλητος ἐς τὸ ἄστυ ἐσελάσαι, τῇ τε τοῦ ἀνθυπάτου ἐξουσίᾳ, ἐπειδὰν διαστρατηγήσῃ, χρήσασθαι ἔλαβε. Suet., *Claud.* 1.5: *For these exploits he received the honour of an ovatio with the triumphal ornaments | res ovandi ius et triumphalia ornamenta.*
90. Dio 54.33.5.
91. Dio 54.34.3.
92. Dio 54.34.4: κἀκ τούτου καὶ ἡ Δελματία τῇ τοῦ Αὐγούστου φρουρᾷ, ὡς καὶ ὅπλων τινῶν ἀεὶ καὶ δι᾽ ἑαυτὴν καὶ διὰ τὴν τῶν Παννονίων γειτονίαν δεομένη, παρεδόθη.
93. Dio 54.34.6; Livy, *Peri.* 140.
94. Dio 54.34.7: καὶ τότε τοὺς μὲν ἐθελοντὰς προσθέμενος τοὺς δ᾽ ἄκοντας ἐκπλήξας, τοῖς δὲ καὶ ἐκ παρατάξεως συνενεχθείς, πάντας αὐτοὺς ὑπηγάγετο, καὶ μετὰ τοῦτο νεοχμώσαντάς τινας αὐτῶν αὖθις κατεδουλώσατο. On Piso's willingness to compromise see Tac., *Ann.* 6.10.
95. Florus 2.27: *Quippe cum catenas morsibus temptaret, feritatem suam ipsi puniebat.*
96. Vell. Pat. 2.98.2: *virtus compressit (quippe legatus Caesaris triennio cum iis bellavit gentesque ferocissimas plurimo cum earum excidio nunc acie, nunc expugnationibus in pristinum pacis redigit modum) eiusque patratione Asiae securitatem, Macedoniae pacem reddidit.*
97. Dio 54.35.1.
98. Dio 54.35.1.
99. Dio 54.36.3.
100. Dio 54.36.2: οἵ τε γὰρ Δακοὶ τὸν Ἴστρον πεπηγότα διαβάντες λείαν ἐκ τῆς Παννονίας ἀπετέμοντο, καὶ οἱ Δελμάται πρὸς τὰς ἐσπράξεις τῶν χρημάτων ἐπανέστησαν. Eutrop. 7.9.
101. Dio 54.36.3.
102. Dio 54.36.3; Florus 2.30.
103. Tac., *Germ.* 30; Strabo, *Geog.* 7.1.3.
104. Tac., *Germ.* 30.
105. Florus 2.30.
106. Livy, *Peri.* 141: *In quo inter primores pugnaverunt Chumstinctus et Avectius, tribuni ex civitate Nerviorum.*

107. Suet., *Claud.* 1: *Fuisse autem creditur non minus gloriosi quam civilis animi; nam ex hoste super victorias opima quoque spolia captasse summoque saepius discrimine duces Germanorum tota acie insectatus.* On Augustus and the *spolia opima* see Harrison (1989), McPherson (2009) and Rich (1999).
108. See Ch. 1, n. 235.
109. Its dimensions are 320 metres by 150 metres. Straddling the Burgberg its 760 metre long circuit of palisade and ditch enclosed an area of 3.2 hectares plus an additional two outer enclosures beyond it. For details of the archaeology of the site see Grote (2005 and 2012) and online at http://www.grote-archaeologie.de/roemer.html (accessed 29 February 2016).
110. Dio 54.36.4.
111. Livy, *Peri.* 139.
112. Livy, *Peri.* 139 records that the first *sacerdotus* was C. Iulius Vericondaribunus of the Aedui nation. For a description of the site see Powell (2011), pp. 97–99. *Aes* (*RIC* 230 and 233) and *sestertii* (*RIC* 231), *dupondii* (*RIC* 232) and *semis* (*RIC* 234) minted at *Colonia* Copia Felix Munatia shows the great altar on inauguration day.
113. Strabo, *Geog.* 7.3.12–13.
114. Florus 2.28: *Visum est Caesari Augusto gentem aditu difficilem summovere.*
115. See Syme (1986), pp. 287–99 on the identity of the Lentulus mentioned in Florus 2.28.
116. Strabo, *Geog.* 7.3.12.
117. Florus 2.28: *Misso igitur Lentulo ultra ulteriorem perpulit ripam; citra praesidia constituta. Sic tum Dacia non victa, sed summota atque dilata est.*
118. Florus 2.29: *Tanta barbaria est, ut nec intellegant pacem.*
119. Dio 55.1.1. *Inscr. It.* 13.2.117: See Powell (2011), p. 165.
120. Ovid, *Fasti* 1.709–22.
121. *RG* 12. See Ch. 4, n. 10.
122. Ryberg (1940), pp. 85–88, Stern (2006), pp. 177–81.
123. Her identity is uncertain: she may be Iulia, or Livia or Octavia or she may even be an eastern princess.
124. Another suggestion is that he is a barbarian child from the East as he wears the style of shoes and a diadem wrapped tightly around his forehead that would be worn in the Bosporus or Parthia. See Crawford (1922).
125. The symbolic message may be that the primary crafters of the new *Pax Augusta*, Agrippa and Augustus, are connected through Iulia and the two boys who represent the next generation. On the importance and meaning of the *Ara Pacis* and its relation to the earlier *Ara Fortuae Reducis* see Torelli (1982), pp. 27–61.
126. Dio 55.1.1; Suet., *Claud.* 1.5.3; Livy, *Peri.* 140.
127. Florus 2.30.
128. Dio 55.1.2.
129. Dio 55.1.2: τήν τε ἐν ποσὶν οὐκ ἀταλαιπώρως χειρούμενος καὶ τοὺς προσμιγνύντας οἱ οὐκ ἀναιμωτὶ κρατῶν.
130. Dio 55.1.3; Eutrop. 7.9.
131. Florus 2.30: *Nam Marcomannorum spoliis et insignibus quendam editum tumulum in tropaei modum excoluit.* The reference to the Marcomanni is curious as these resided far to the south.
132. Ptolemy, *Geog.* 2.10: 'Trophy of Drusus, 33° 45', 52° 45'' | Τρόπαια Δρούσου, λγ΄δ΄΄, νβ΄δ΄΄.
133. Dio 55.1.3: γυνὴ γάρ τις μείζων ἢ κατὰ ἀνθρώπου φύσιν ἀπαντήσασα αὐτῷ ἔφη 'ποῖ δῆτα ἐπείγῃ, Δροῦσε ἀκόρεστε; οὐ πάντα σοι ταῦτα ἰδεῖν πέπρωται. ἀλλ᾽ ἄπιθι· καὶ γάρ σοι καὶ τῶν ἔργων καὶ τοῦ βίου τελευτή. Cf. Suet., *Claud.* 1.5.2.
134. Dio 55.1.5. For interpretations, supernatural and scientific, see Powell (2011), pp. 104–05.
135. Dio 55.1.1; Livy, *Peri.* 140.
136. Strabo, *Geog.* 7.1.3.
137. Suet., *Claud.* 1.3.
138. Dio 55.2.4; Eutrop. 7.9.
139. Livy, *Peri.* 142; Pliny, *Nat. Hist.* 7.20.
140. Dio 55.1.1; Livy, *Peri.* 142; Vell. Pat. 2.97.3.
141. Dio 55.2.1.

142. Suet., *Claud.* 1.3.
143. Suet., *Tib.* 7.2; Val. Max. *Fact. et Dict.* 5.5.3.
144. Suet., *Claud.* 1.5.3.
145. Dio 55.2.2.
146. Dio 55.2.2, 55.5.1.
147. Suet., *Claud.* 1.5.5: *ut deos precatus sit, similes ei Caesares suos facerent sibique tam honestum quandoque exitum darent quam illi dedissent*; Dio 55.2.3; Livy, *Peri.* 140.
148. Dio 55.2.3.
149. Dio 55.2.3; Livy, *Peri.* 140.

Chapter 5: Trouble in the East

1. Dio 55.5.1, *cf.* 54.25.4 and *RG* 4. On the laurels see Dio 53.5.1–2: Iulius Caesar had been permitted to have lictors who always carried laurel on their fasces, a right which Augustus inherited.
2. Dio 55.5.2: καὶ αὐτὸς μὲν οὐδεμίαν ἐπὶ τούτοις ἑορτὴν ἤγαγε, πολὺ πλεῖον ἐν τῷ τοῦ Δρούσου ὀλέθρῳ ἐζημιῶσθαι ἢ ἐν ταῖς νίκαις ὠφελῆσθαι νομίζων.
3. Suet., *Claud.* 1.4–5; *cf.* Suet., *Tib.* 50.1.
4. Suet., *Div. Aug.* 72.2; *Claud.* 1.5. Not a word of either survives.
5. Dio 55.2.3; Suet., *Claud.* 1.5; Livy, *Peri.* 142; *Tabula Hebana*.
6. After 8 BCE Germanicus Claudius Drusus; after 4 CE Germanicus Iulius Caesar.
7. Suet., *Claud.* 1.5: *Ceterum exercitus honorarium ei tumulum excitavit, circa quem deinceps stato die quotannis miles decurreret Galliarumque civitates publice supplicarent*; *cf.* Dio 55.2.3.
8. For a description of the monument see Panter (2007).
9. Dio 55.6.1; *cf.* 54.12.5.
10. Dio 55.6.1: μετὰ δὲ δὴ ταῦτα τήν τε ἡγεμονίαν, καίπερ ἀφιείς, ὡς ἔλεγεν, ἐπειδὴ τὰ δέκα ἔτη τὰ δεύτερα ἐξεληλύθει, ἄκων δῆθεν αὖθις ὑπέστη, καὶ ἐπὶ τοὺς Κελτοὺς ἐστράτευσε.
11. Suet., *Tib.* 16.1; Vell. Pat. 2.97.4; Strabo, *Geog.* 6.4.2.
12. Vell. Pat. 2.97.4: *quod is sua et virtute et fortuna administravit peragratusque.*
13. Suet., *Tib.* 21.2, 68.3; *cf.* Dio 57.1.1.
14. Dio 55.6.4.
15. Dio 55.6.1–2.
16. Dio 55.6.2–3: ἔπεμψαν μὲν γὰρ καὶ οἱ Σύγαμβροι πρέσβεις, τοσούτου δὲ ἐδέησαν διαπράξασθαί τι ὥστε καὶ ἐκείνους πάντας, καὶ πολλοὺς καὶ ἐλλογίμους ὄντας, προσαπολέσθαι· ὅ τε γὰρ Αὔγουστος συλλαβὼν αὐτοὺς ἐς πόλεις τινὰς κατέθετο, καὶ ἐκεῖνοι δυσανασχετήσαντες ἑαυτοὺς κατεχρήσαντο. κἀκ τούτου χρόνον μέν τινα ἡσύχασαν, ἔπειτ᾽ ἐπὶ πολλῷ τὸ πάθημα σφων τοῖς Ῥωμαίοις ἀνταπέδοσαν.
17. Vell. Pat. 2.97.4: *quod praecipue huic duci semper curae fuit.*
18. *RG* 32; Eutrop. 7.9.
19. Tac., *Ann.* 4.47.4. E.g. *Cohors* I *Sugambrorum Veterana*: Cheesman (1914), p. 48 and 162; *Cohors* IV *Sugambrorum*: Cheesman (1914), p. 166.
20. Kühlborn (2004), p. 29; Wells (1972), p. 191 and p. 219.
21. See Ch. 4, n. 70.
22. Wells (1972), pp. 163–211. It measured 370 metres by 485 metres with a later extension adding a further 50 metres, or 18 hectares in total.
23. Wells (1972), p. 186. One of these buildings, sited at the east gate, may have been an *armamentarium* to judge by the finds of some sixty arrowheads and several *pilum*-heads, and thousands of *ballista*-bolts.
24. Dio 55.6.4–5. Augustus now counted XIV acclamations.
25. Dio 55.6.4. The *aureus* (*BMC* 498–9; *RIC* 198) and *denarius* (*BMC* 500; *RIC* 199), showing the figure of C. Caesar wearing a *bulla* riding past military standards, may have been minted to mark this event; *contra* this dating see Romer (1978).
26. Dio 55.7.1–5.
27. Dio 55.8.1.
28. Dio 55.8.2. *Fast. Consul. (fasti magistrorum vici).*

29. Dio 55.9.1: τοσαῦτα μὲν ἐν τῷ ἔτει τούτῳ ἐπράχθη: ἐν γὰρ δὴ τῇ Γερμανίᾳ οὐδὲν ἄξιον μνήμης συνέβη.
30. Suet. *Tib.* 19.1: *Sed re prospere gesta non multum afuit quin a Bructero quodam occideretur, cui inter proximos versanti et trepidatione detecto tormentis expressa confessio est cogitati facinoris.* Extracting confessions and information using torture was the responsibility of specialist soldiers called *speculatores*.
31. Syme (1986), p.68.
32. Dio 55.9.1; alternatively he may have been Vetus' son.
33. Dio 55.9.1.
34. Dio 55.9.4.
35. Dio 55.9.4n, 55.10.20n.
36. Dio 55.9.5–7.
37. Dio 55.9.8, *cf.* 55.10.17.
38. Vell. Pat. 2.105.1. On the difficulty of precise dating of provincial assignments see Atkinson (1958) and Syme (1986), pp. 85–86. An alternative date for his transfer to Germania is 3 CE, placing him after L. Domitius Ahenobarbus.
39. Vell. Pat. 2.105.1: *Sentium Saturninum ... praefecisset.*
40. The construction of roads and towns began around this time, Dio 56.18.1–2.
41. Vell. Pat. 2.105.2.
42. For a full description of the monument see Broomwich (1993), pp. 270–75.
43. Pliny, *Nat. Hist.* 3.24 (3.136): IMP • CAESARI DIVI FILIO AVG • PONT • MAX • IMP • XIIII • TR • POT • XVII • S • P • Q • R • QVOD EIVS DVCTV AVSPICIISQVE GENTES ALPINAE OMNES QVAE A MARI SVPERO AD INFERVM PERTINEBANT SVB IMPERIVM P • R • SVNT REDACTAE • GENTES ALPINAE DEVICTAE TRVMPILINI • CAMVNNI • VENOSTES • VENNONETES • ISARCI • BREVNI • GENAVNES • FOCVNATES • VINDELICORVM GENTES QVATTVOR • COSVANETES • RVCINATES • LICATES • CATENATES • AMBISONTES • RVGVSCI • SVANETES • CALVCONES • BRIXENETES • LEPONTI • VBERI • NANTVATES • SEDVNI • VARAGRI • SALASSI • ACITAVONES • MEDVLLI • VCENNI • CATVRIGES • BRIGIANI • SOGIONTI • BRODIONTI • NEMALONI • EDENATES • VESVBIANI • VEAMINI • GALLITAE • TRIVLLATI • ECDINI • VERGVNNI • EGVI • TVRI • NEMATVRI • ORATELLI • NERVSI • VELAVNI • SVETRI = *AE* 1973, 323. 136 letter fragments survive.
44. *RG* 26. Goudineau (1996), p. 471–72 argues that its location mirrors the monument erected by Pompeius Magnus on the same road linking the Hispania Citerior on the Col de Panissars to Italy.
45. Syme (1986), pp. 85–86 and p. 253 n. 76, citing *Inst. Iust.* 2.25.
46. Dio 55.9.9.
47. *Cf. CIL* II, 3828, VI, 897, IX, 3343, XI, 1421 *et al.* It apparently did not include *augur*, despite *CIL* II, 2422.
48. Dio 55.9.9. See Appendix 3.1(b).
49. Suet., *Div. Aug.* 38.3.
50. Strabo, *Geog.* 14.5.24.
51. Tac., *Ann.* 3.48; Strabo, *Geog.* 12.6.5, 24; *CIL* XIV, 3613 'Lapis Tiburtinus' – some believe it refers to Quinctilius Varus. On the war with the Homonadeis see Broughton (1933) and Ramsay (1917).
52. This is the so-called *Hauptlager*: see Wells (1972), pp. 177–211. Within its oval-shaped double ditch and rampart enclosing a 20-hectare space several wooden buildings have been excavated. These include the HQ (*principia*), houses for senior officers, barracks, bathhouse, granaries and a warehouse. A lead ingot stamped 'LEG XIX' attests to the presence of that legion at the site.
53. Joseph., *Ant. Iud.* 17.6.4. The year is based on working back from the death of Philip the Tetrarch after a thirty-seven-year reign in the twentieth year of Tiberius' principate (34 CE). Some scholars believe he died in 1 CE, which is the traditional date. The month is based on Josephus' claim that there was an eclipse at the time of his death: one is known for 13 March 4 BCE, though there were three other eclipses between 5 and 1 BCE; for a discussion see Bernegger (1983).
54. Joseph., *Ant. Iud.* 17.6.4: Josephus calls it Herodes' Evil.

55. Joseph., *Bell. Iud.* 1.33.9.
56. On the importance of the relationship see McCane (2008).
57. *Cf.* Dio 54.27.1, 55.9.1–5.
58. Joseph., *Bell. Iud.* 2.1.3.
59. Joseph., *Bell. Iud.* 2.1.3: πρὸς ὃ δείσας Ἀρχέλαος πρὶν δι᾿ ὅλου τοῦ πλήθους διαδραμεῖν τὴν νόσον ὑποπέμπει μετὰ σπείρας χιλίαρχον προστάξας βίᾳ τοὺς ἐξάρχοντας τῆς στάσεως κατασχεῖν. πρὸς οὓς τὸ πλῆθος ἅπαν παροξύνεται καὶ τοὺς μὲν πολλοὺς τῆς σπείρας βάλλοντες λίθοις διέφθειρον, ὁ δὲ χιλίαρχος ἐκφεύγει τραυματίας μόλις. ἔπειθ᾿ οἱ μὲν ὡς μηδενὸς δεινοῦ γεγονότος ἐτρέποντο πρὸς θυσίαν:οὐ μὴν Ἀρχελάῳ δίχα φόνου καθεκτὸν ἔτι τὸ πλῆθος ἐφαίνετο.
60. Joseph., *Bell. Iud.* 2.1.3: τὴν δὲ στρατιὰν ἐπαφίησιν αὐτοῖς ὅλην, τοὺς μὲν πεζοὺς διὰ τῆς πόλεως ἀθρόους, τοὺς δὲ ἱππεῖς ἀνὰ τὸ πεδίον: οἳ θύουσιν ἑκάστοις ἐξαίφνης προσπεσόντες διαφθείρουσι μὲν περὶ τρισχιλίους, τὸ δὲ λοιπὸν πλῆθος εἰς τὰ πλησίον ὄρη διεσκέδασαν. εἴποντο δὲ Ἀρχελάου κήρυκες κελεύοντες ἕκαστον ἀναχωρεῖν ἐπ᾿ οἴκου, καὶ πάντες ᾤχοντο τὴν ἑορτὴν ἀπολιπόντες.
61. Joseph., *Ant. Iud.* 17.5.2.
62. Joseph., *Bell. Iud.* 2.2.1–2.
63. Joseph., *Bell. Iud.* 2.3.1.
64. Joseph., *Bell. Iud.* 2.2.2, 2.3.1.
65. Joseph., *Bell. Iud.* 2.3.2: αὐτὸς δὲ ἐπὶ τὸν ὑψηλότατον τοῦ φρουρίου πύργον ἀναβάς, ὃς ἐκαλεῖτο Φασάηλος ἐπώνυμον ἔχων ἀδελφὸν Ἡρώδου διαφθαρέντα ὑπὸ Πάρθων, ἐντεῦθεν κατέσειεν τοῖς ἐν τῷ τάγματι στρατιώταις ἐπιχειρεῖν τοῖς πολεμίοις: δι᾿ ἔκπληξιν γὰρ οὐδ᾿ εἰς τοὺς σφετέρους καταβαίνειν ἐθάρρει. παραπεισθέντες δὲ οἱ στρατιῶται προπηδῶσιν εἰς τὸ ἱερὸν καὶ μάχην καρτερὰν τοῖς Ἰουδαίοις συνάπτουσιν, ἐν ᾗ μέχρι μὲν οὐδεὶς καθύπερθεν ἐπήμυνεν περιῆσαν ἐμπειρίᾳ πολέμου τῶν ἀπείρων: ἐπεὶ δὲ πολλοὶ Ἰουδαίων ἀναβάντες ἐπὶ τὰς στοὰς κατὰ κεφαλῆς αὐτῶν ἠφίεσαν τὰ βέλη, συνετρίβοντο πολλοὶ καὶ οὔτε τοὺς ἄνωθεν βάλλοντας ἀμύνεσθαι ῥᾴδιον ἦν οὔτε τοὺς συστάδην μαχομένους ὑπομένειν.
66. Joseph., *Bell. Iud.* 2.3.3.
67. Joseph., *Bell. Iud.* 2.3.4.
68. Joseph., *Bell. Iud.* 2.3.5.
69. Joseph., *Bell. Iud.* 2.4.1: ἐν δὲ Σεπφώρει τῆς Γαλιλαίας Ἰούδας υἱὸς Ἐζεκία τοῦ κατατρέχοντός ποτε τὴν χώραν ἀρχιληστοῦ καὶ χειρωθέντος ὑφ᾿ Ἡρώδου βασιλέως συστήσας πλῆθος οὐκ ὀλίγον ἀναρρήγνυσιν τὰς βασιλικὰς ὁπλοθήκας καὶ τοὺς περὶ αὐτὸν ὁπλίσας τοῖς τὴν δυναστείαν ζηλοῦσιν ἐπεχείρει.
70. Joseph., *Bell. Iud.* 2.4.2; *cf.* Tac., *Ann.* 5.9.
71. Joseph., *Bell. Iud.* 2.4.3.
72. Joseph., *Bell. Iud.* 2.4.3: καὶ τὸ κτείνειν αὐτοῖς προηγούμενον ἦν Ῥωμαίους τε καὶ τοὺς βασιλικούς, διέφευγεν δὲ οὐδὲ Ἰουδαίων εἴ τις εἰς χεῖρας ἔλθοι φέρων κέρδος. ἐτόλμησαν δέ ποτε Ῥωμαίων λόχον ἄθρουν περισχεῖν κατ᾿ Ἀμμαοῦντα: σῖτα δ᾿ οὗτοι καὶ ὅπλα διεκόμιζον τῷ τάγματι. τὸν μὲν οὖν ἑκατοντάρχην αὐτῶν Ἄρειον καὶ τεσσαράκοντα τοὺς γενναιοτάτους κατηκόντισαν, οἱ δὲ λοιποὶ κινδυνεύοντες ταὐτὸ παθεῖν Γράτου σὺν τοῖς Σεβαστηνοῖς ἐπιβοηθήσαντος ἐξέφυγον. πολλὰ τοιαῦτα τοὺς ἐπιχωρίους καὶ τοὺς ἀλλοφύλους παρ᾿ ὅλον τὸν πόλεμον ἐργασάμενοι μετὰ χρόνου οἱ μὲν τρεῖς ἐχειρώθησαν, ὑπ᾿ Ἀρχελάου μὲν ὁ πρεσβύτατος, οἱ δ᾿ ἑξῆς δύο Γράτῳ καὶ Πτολεμαίῳ περιπεσόντες: ὁ δὲ τέταρτος Ἀρχελάῳ προσεχώρησεν κατὰ δεξιάν.
73. Joseph., *Bell. Iud.* 2.5.1.
74. Joseph., *Bell. Iud.* 2.5.2.
75. Joseph., *Bell. Iud.* 2.5.2: Οὔαρος δὲ κατὰ μοῖραν τῆς στρατιᾶς ἐπὶ τοὺς αἰτίους τοῦ κινήματος ἔπεμψεν περὶ τὴν χώραν, καὶ πολλῶν ἀγομένων τοὺς μὲν ἧττον θορυβώδεις φανέντας ἐφρούρει, τοὺς δὲ αἰτιωτάτους ἀνεσταύρωσεν περὶ δισχιλίους.
76. Joseph., *Bell. Iud.* 2.5.3.
77. Timbers excavated at the site have been dated dendrochronologically to 4 BCE. On the archaeological research conducted at Waldgirmes see Rasbach and Becker (2004), Becker and Rasbach (2007) and von Schnurbein (2004), p. 37. A magnificent gilt bronze head of an equestrian statue, probably of Augustus, was discovered at the site in 2010. For a discussion of businesses in Germania under Augustus see Rothenhöfer (2003).
78. Dio 55.22.3.

79. Syme (1986), p. 253 citing *Inst. Iust.* 2.25.
80. Tibullus, *Carm.* 2.5.17–18, 119–20; Röpke (2008), p. 941.
81. Dio 55.22.3.
82. He would not have received the command of a *turma* of *iuniores* or a priesthood, such as granted to Caius (see ch. 5, n. 47 and 48) or Lucius (ch. 5, n. 92). On the markedly different treatment of Agrippa Postumus see Allen (1947), Jameson (1975) and Pappano (1941).
83. On the lacuna see Swan (2004), p. 36 and 91–93. The loss of an entire section of Dio's *History* recalls the caveat in Syme (1934c), p. 113 quoted in the preface.
84. Dio 55.22.3.
85. Dio 54.20.3: ἔπειτα δὲ Λούκιος Γάιος Σαυρομάτας ἐκ τῆς αὐτῆς αἰτίας κρατήσας ὑπὲρ τὸν Ἴστρον ἀπεώσατο.
86. *Denarius:* BMC 128; *RIC* I 416.
87. Dio 55.10.9.
88. Suet., *Div. Aug.* 51: '*Quod bonum,*' inquit, '*faustumque sit tibi domuique tuae, Caesar Auguste! Sic enim nos perpetuam felicitatem rei p. et laeta huic urbi precari existimamus: senatus te consentiens cum populo R. consalutat patriae patrem.*' Cui lacrimans respondit Augustus his verbis (ipsa enim, sicut Messalae, posui): '*Compos factus votorum meorum, patres conscripti, quid habeo aliud deos immortales precari, quam ut hunc consensum vestrum ad ultimum finem vitae mihi perferre liceat?*'
89. Other honorees included the fourth century BCE M. Furius Camillus, the first century BCE C. Marius and consul M. Tullius Cicero after the Catilinian Conspiracy: see Richardson (2012), p. 154.
90. Dio 55.9.10.
91. *ILS* 132 (Rome); *cf. CIL* II, 2109, VI, 898, IX, 3914, XI 1420 *et al.*
92. Dio 55.10.7; *cf.* Suet., *Div. Aug.* 43.
93. See Ch. 1. n. 326.
94. Ovid, *Fasti* 5.545–98; *cf.* Dio 55.101a–8 stating 1 August. On the date of the dedication of the Temple of Mars Ultor see Simpson (1977).
95. On the building as described by Dio see Swan (2004), pp. 93–99. For a full discussion of the architecture of the *Forum Augustum* see Claridge (1998), pp. 158–61, and Galinsky (1996), pp. 197–213; and Kockel (1995).
96. Suet., *Div. Aug.* 29; *CIL* VI.8709; Ovid, *Fast.* 5.569–78. 1 August: Dio 55.10; 55.5.3; Vell. Pat. 2.100.2; 12 May: Ovid, *Fast.* 5.551 ff.
97. *RG* 21.1; Macrobius, *Sat.* 2.4.9; Suet., *Div. Aug.* 29.1.
98. The arrangement of the statuary is preserved in the *Ara Pietatis Augustae.*
99. The scene is depicted on a *sestertius* of Antoninus Pius, *RIC* 1003 and 1004.
100. Pliny, *Nat. Hist.* 36.24, written some seventy years after the inauguration of the *Forum Augustum.*
101. *RG* 26; Ovid, *Fast.* 5.551–52, 555–68; *Trist.* 2.295–96; Tac., *Ann.* 3.18; 13.8; Suet., *Cal.* 24; Pliny, *Nat. Hist.* 7.183, 34.48, 34.141, 35.27, 93–94; Serv. *Aen.* 1.294; Paus. 8.46.1.4.
102. Pliny, *Nat. Hist.* 35.27 and 93–94.
103. Suet., *Div. Aug.* 31.1; Ovid, *Fast.* 5.563–66; Dio 55.10.3; Pliny, *Nat. Hist.* 22.13; Aul. Gell., *Noct. Att.* 9.11.10; *Hist. Aug.* Alex. Sev. 28.6, states the statues were marble. On the *summi viri* see Itgenshorst (2004) and Shaya (2013). For the literary connection with Vergil, *Aen.* 6 see Galinsky (1996), pp. 210–12, Pandey (2014), pp. 92–94, and Rowell (1941).
104. Many of the inscriptions have survived: *CIL* I² pp. 186–202; *BC* 1889, 26–34, 73–79, 481–82; 1890, 251–59; *NS* 1889, 15–16, 33–34; 1890, 318–20. On the *elogia* see Frisch (1980).
105. Dio 55.10.6; likely as *duumviri aedibus dedicandis.*
106. Romer (1978) argues that this is the scene depicted on the *aureus* (BMC 498–9; *RIC* 198) and *denarius* (BMC 500; *RIC* 199). However, the coins clearly show a boy wearing a *bulla* around his neck and the inscription at the top states *C. CAES*, which is consistent with him going on tour with Tiberius and the troops in 8 BCE.
107. The *suovetaurilia* was closely associated with Mars: Festus, 189 and 293a; Livy, *AUC* 8.10; Serv., *ad Aen.* 9.627.
108. *RG* 29; Suet., *Vit.* 8.1; *CIL* I² p. 318.
109. Dio 55.10.7.

110. Vell. Pat. 2.100.2: *quo magnificentissimis gladiatorii muneris naumachiaeque spectaculis divus Augustus*; cf. Dio 55.10.7. Suet., *Div. Aug.* 43 reveals the location of the 'naval fight': *for which he excavated the ground near the Tiber, where there is now the Grove of the Caesars | item navale proelium circa Tiberim cavato solo, in quo nunc Caesarum nemus est.*
111. Dio 55.10.8.
112. Suet., *Div. Aug.* 43: *Quibus diebus custodes in urbe disposuit, ne raritate remanentium grassatoribus obnoxia esset.*
113. Romer (1978).
114. Dio 55.10.17; Vell. Pat. 2.101.1. Swan (2004), p. 111, suggests this could mean any location in Illyricum, Raetia or Thracia Macedoniaque.
115. Dio 55.10.17.
116. Dio 55.10.9.
117. Suet., *Div. Aug.* 49; cf. *Tib.* 37; Tac., *Ann.* 4.2.1; Paullus *Dig.* 1.15.3 pr. The other *Praetoriani* may have been stationed at barracks in Aquileia, Brundisium, Ravenna and Ticinum where Augustus was a frequent visitor.
118. Dio 55. 24.9.
119. Dio 55.10.18.1; Vell. Pat. 2.100.1; Tac., *Ann.* 2.4.1 mentions the king's ouster: *not without heavy Roman losses | et non sine clade nostra deiectus.* See Swan (2004), pp. 112–17.
120. Tac., *Ann.* 2.4.1.
121. Dio 55.10.20; Suet., *Div. Aug.* 54.1, *Tib.* 12.2. The last person to hold the position was his own natural father, M. Agrippa. There is a suggestion in Pliny, *Nat His.* 6.141, that a certain Isodoros from Charax was sent on a mission ahead – *ad commentanda omnia* – of C. Caesar to gather intelligence about Parthia and the coasts of Arabia, but as Healy (2000), p. 43, n. 8, points out, this is based on the assumption Pliny misnamed the Greek as 'Dionysios'.
122. Suet., *Tib.* 12.2: *Comes et rector.*
123. Suet., *Div. Aug.* 23.1; Vell. Pat. 2.97.1; Horace, *Carm.* 4.9.37f.
124. See Swan (2004), p. 121.
125. Vell. Pat. 2.101.1; cf. Suet., *Div. Aug.* 64.1. Sources attest to visits to Athens (*IG* 112 3250 = *EJ* 64), Assos (*IGRR* IV 248), Samos (Suet., *Tib.* 12.2) or Chios (Dio 55.10.19).
126. Dio 55.10a.2: *Somewhat earlier Domitius, while still governing the districts along the Ister | ἕως ἔτι τῶν πρὸς τῷ Ἴστρῳ χωρίων ἦρχε.* Historians have argued over the precise meaning of the phrase. Swan (2004), p. 123, notes Dio in using the word πρὸς explicitly separates Ister/Danube from the Rhine command and the complete phrasing implies Ahenobarbus had recently been *legatus* of Illyricum before coming to Germania. Considering the distance and geography involved I have placed the encounter with Hermunduri in 1 BCE and the succeeding events in 1 CE.
127. Dio 55.10a.2.
128. Tac., *Ann.* 4.44.
129. Presumably the Langobardi.
130. The statement implies the Elbe, in which case the new altar would complement the *Tropaeum Drusi* on the other side; but Dio may be confusing the location with the Rhine where an altar was erected to Roma and Augustus at Ara Ubiorum.
131. Cf. Dio 55. 9.1. A lower limit of 33 was often applied against the traditional minimum age of 42, but Caius was just 20 years old.
132. Dio 55.10a.4.
133. Syme (1986), p. 103.
134. Dio 55.10.20–21.
135. Dio 55.10a.4.
136. Vell. Pat. 2.101.1–3: *Cum rege Parthorum, iuvene excelsissimo, in insula quam amnis Euphrates ambiebat, aequato utriusque partis numero coiit. Quod spectaculum stantis ex diverso hinc Romani, illinc Parthorum exercitus, cum duo inter se eminentissima imperiorum et hominum coirent capita, perquam clarum et memorabile sub initia stipendiorum meorum tribuno militum mihi visere contigit.*
137. Dio 55.10a.4–6.
138. Pliny, *Nat. Hist.* 9.118; Vell. Pat. 2.102.1.
139. Tac., *Ann.* 3.48.

140. Dio 55.10a.9.
141. See Campbell (1993), pp. 223–28.
142. Dio 55.10a.5.
143. Vell. Pat. 2.102.2; *ILS* 140, lines 9–10 = *EJ* 69.
144. Dio 55.10.9, *cf.* 55.10.17; Tac., *Ann.* 1; Suet., *Div. Aug.* 64.1; Vell. Pat. 2.102.3. Why Augustus chose the Iberian Peninsula for him and not Germania is not disclosed in the extant sources.
145. Dio 55.10a.1. See Swan (2004), pp. 120–21.
146. *Cf.* Dio 55.10.19.
147. Dio 55.10a.3.
148. *Civitas Ubiorum*: Tac., *Ann.* 1.36–37.
149. Tac., *Ann.* 1.63.4. Its location has not been identified.
150. Dio 55.10a.3.
151. Suet., *Nero* 4.
152. *Cf.* Florus 2.30: *Therefore our joy was short-lived; for the Germans had been defeated rather than subdued, and under the rule of Drusus they respected our moral qualities rather than our arms* | *Quippe Germani victi magis quam domini erant, moresque nostros magis quam arma sub imperatore Druso suspiciebant.*
153. Dio 55.10a.5.
154. Dio 55.10a.5–6; *cf.* Seneca *Polyb.* 15.4.
155. Seneca, *Polyb.* 15.4: *in aparatu Parthici belli.* cf. Florus 2.32.
156. Dio 55.10.19n; Suet., *Tib.* 13.2.
157. Dio 55.11.1–2; Suet., *Tib.* 13.2.
158. Suet., *Tib.* 13.2.
159. *RG* 14; Dio 55.10a.9n; Vell. Pat. 2.102.3; Tac., *Ann.* 1.3.3; *cf.* Suet., *Div. Aug.* 64.1.
160. Dio 55.10a.10.
161. Dio 55.10a.9; *cf.* Vell. Pat. 2.102.3; Tac., *Ann.* 1.3.3; Suet., *Div. Aug.* 64.1.
162. Dio 55.12.1; *Fast. Ostienses* [Praha, 1982], 40; *cf.* 56–57.
163. A marble inscription found in Kempten is dedicated to L. Caesar: see Zanier (2004), p. 15 (fig. 12).
164. Strabo, *Geog.* 7.3.10. For a discussion of the identity and career of Aelius Catus see Syme (1934c), pp. 126–28.

Chapter 6: World in Tumult

1. Dio 55.12.2–3; *cf.* 55.13.5.
2. Seneca, *Polyb.* 15.4.
3. Dio 55.10a.6n. The location of Artagira is not known.
4. Strabo 11.14.6 mentions 'the strong fortresses Babyrsa, and Olani' and says 'there were others also upon the Euphrates' – φρούρια ἐρυμνά, Βάβυρσά τε καὶ Ὀλανή· ἦν δὲ καὶ ἄλλα ἐπὶ τῷ Εὐφράτῃ – which may have been attacked by C. Caesar's army prior to Arteigira (Ἀρτάγειρα).
5. For a discussion of Rome's conflicts with Parthia over Armenia see Gregoratti (2012).
6. Strabo 11.14.6.
7. Dio 55.10a.6; Vell. Pat. 2.102.2.
8. Florus 2.32: *Quippe Donnes, quem rex Artageris praefecerat, simulata proditione adortus virum intentum libello, quem ut thensaurorum rationes continentem ipse porrexerat, stricto repente ferro subiit. Et tunc quidem Caesar recreatus est ex volnere in tempus et [lacuna] Ceterum barbarus undique infesto exercitu oppressus gladio et pyra, in quam se percussus inmisit, superstiti etiam nunc Caesari satisfecit.*
9. Ruf. Fest. 19.
10. Dio 55.10a.7. The fate of Adon or Donnes is not recorded.
11. Dio 55.10a.7: this was Augustus' sixteenth acclamation.
12. Dio 55.19a.7.
13. *Fasti Cuprenses IIt* 13.1.245: *C. Caesar Aug(usti). f(ilius) ... V Eid. Sept. bellum cum [hostibus P(opuli) R(omani) gerens] in Armenia percuss[us est, dum obsiet Ar]ta[g]iram, Ar[meniae oppidum].* See Lott (2012), p. 199.
14. Dio 55.10a.8; Vell. Pat. 2.102.3.

15. Scarborough (1968), p. 257 and 260 citing Tiberius' treatment of the wounded in Vell. Pat. 2.114.1–3. See also Davies (1989), pp. 212–14.
16. Dio 55.30.4 and 55.33.2.
17. See Syme (1986), p. 338.
18. *RG* 14; Dio 55.10a.9; *Fasti Cuprenses IIt* 13.1.245: [*VIIII k. Mart. C. Caesar*] *Aug(usti) f. dec[essit in Lycia agens XXI]II.*
19. Vell. Pat. 2.102.3. An inscription was erected in the Portico that bore his and his brother's names in the *Forum Romanum* next to an arch that straddled a newly constructed spur of the *Via Sacra* – Suet., *Div. Aug.* 29.4; Dio 56.27.5.
20. Gordon (1983), p. 106.
21. Dio 55.12.1. Their shields and spears were depicted on the *aureus RIC* I 206, Lyon 81, Calicó 176a and *denarius RIC* I 207, Lyon 82, *RSC* 43.
22. Dio 55.13.2; Vell. Pat. 2.104.1; *cf.* Suet., *Div. Aug.* 65.1, *Tib.* 15.2.
23. Vell. Pat. 2.104.2; *cf.* Aul. Gell., *Noct. Att.* 5.19.6 who gives these words to Augustus.
24. Dio 55.13.1; *cf. RG* 6.2, Suet., *Tib.* 16.1, which states the term was for five years.
25. Dio 55.13.3.
26. Dio 55.13.6.
27. Dio 55.14.1; *cf.* earlier plots in Ch. 1, n. 173, Ch. 2, nos 163 and 164, Ch. 3, n. 10; Seneca, *Clem.* 1.9.1–12 describes the same event but places it at a different time, between 23 and 13 BCE – see Swan (2004), pp. 147–50.
28. Dio 55.22.1.
29. Suet., *Tib.* 16.1: *delegatus pacandae Germaniae status. Cf.* Dio 55.13.1; Vell. Pat. 2.103.3, 2.104.2. On his way he stopped at Bagacum-Bavay where a local official marked the visit by setting up an inscription, *CIL* XIII, 3570.
30. Vell. Pat. 2.104.3.
31. Vell. Pat. 2.104.4: *At vero militum conspectu eius elicitae gaudio lacrimae alacritasque et salutationis nova quaedam exultatio et contingendi manum cupiditas non continentium protinus quin adiicerent. 'Videmus te, Imperator?' 'Salvum recepimus?' 'Ac deinde ego tecum, imperator, in Armenia.' 'Ego in Raetia fui.' 'Ego a te in Vindelicis' 'Ego in Pannonia' 'Ego in Germania donatus sum'; neque verbis exprimi et fortasse vix mereri fidem potest.*
32. Vell. Pat. 2.105.1.
33. Saturninus: Vell. Pat. 2.105.1–2; Dio 55.27.6, 55.28.6. See Ch. 5, nos 38–41.
34. Vell. Pat. 2.105.1.
35. Excavated during 2008–2012 finds included a 7.3cm section of chain mail decorated with animal-shaped bronze terminals, iron blades from two Roman spears, fragments of millstones for grinding grain, sixty coins of Roman and Celtic mints and several brooches. See Kröger and Best (2011).
36. Vell. Pat. 2.105.3: *in cuius mediis finibus ad caput Lupiae fluminis hiberna digrediens princeps locaverat.* The claim that he was 'the first Roman to winter there' is wrong as Nero Claudius Drusus Germanicus had established at least two forts on German soil in 11 BCE.
37. Discovered in 1967, the fortresses' dimensions are 500 metres by 700 metres. The *principia* alone measured 71 metres by 47 metres. For archaeological site reports see Kühlborn (1990; 1995; 2004, pp. 32–33; and 2014) and von Schnurbein (2002).
38. Wells (1972), p. 222. The Anreppen site is 10km (6 miles) northwest of modern Paderborn.
39. Vell. Pat. 2.105.3.
40. Dio 55.28.5; Vel. Pat. 2.106.2–3.
41. Vell. Pat. 2.107.3.
42. Vell. Pat. 2.106.3: *cum plurimarum gentium victoria parta cum abundantissima rerum omnium copia exercitui Caesarique se iunxit. Cf.* Dio 55.27.5–6.
43. Dio 55.28.6. *Cf. ILS* 107 = *EJ* 67; Dio 55.10a.7n.
44. Vell. Pat. 2.107.1–2: *Cum citeriorem ripam praedicti fluminis castris occupassemus et ulterior armata hostium virtute fulgeret, sub omnem motum conatumque nostrarum navium protinus refugientium, unus e barbaris aetate senior, corpore excellens, dignitate, quantum ostendebat cultus, eminens, cavatum, ut illis mos est, ex materia conscendit alveum solusque id navigii genus temperans ad medium processit fluminis et petiit, liceret sibi sine periculo in eam, quam armis tenebamus, egredi ripam ac videre Caesarem. Data*

petenti facultas. Tum adpulso lintre et diu tacitus contemplatus Caesarem, 'nostra quidem,' inquit, 'furit iuventus, quae cum vestrum numen absentium colat, praesentium potius arma metuit quam sequitur fidem. Sed ego beneficio ac permissu tuo, Caesar, quos ante audiebam, hodie vidi deos, nec feliciorem ullum vitae meae aut optavi aut sensi diem.' Impetratoque ut manum contingeret, reversus in naviculam, sine fine respectans Caesarem ripae suorum adpulsus est.

45. Vell. Pat. 2.106.1: *Perlustrata armis tota Germania est, victae gentes paene nominibus incognitae ... Omnis eorum iuventus infinita numero, immensa corporibus, situ locorum tutissima, traditis armis una cum ducibus suis saepta fulgenti armatoque militum nostrorum agmine ante imperatoris procubuit tribunal.*

46. Dio 55.28.5–6: ταῦτά τε ἅμα ἐγίγνετο, καὶ ἐπὶ τοὺς Κελτοὺς ἐστράτευσαν μὲν καὶ ἄλλοι τινές, ἐστράτευσε δὲ καὶ ὁ Τιβέριος. καὶ μέχρι γε τοῦ ποταμοῦ, πρότερον μὲν τοῦ Οὐισούργου, μετὰ δὲ τοῦτο καὶ τοῦ Ἀλβίου, προεχώρησεν, οὐ μέντοι καὶ ἀξιομνημόνευτόν τι τότε γε ἐπράχθη.

47. The fortress encompassing 37 hectares was discovered in 1985. Finds of pottery at the site have been dated to 5–9 CE. While the palisade and ditch – measuring 2.25km in length – and several interior buildings – the headquarters, three centurions' houses, granaries and kilns – were completed, the camp seems, like Haltern, never to have been fully occupied. A smaller 9 hectare fort erected on top of the hill appears to have been the temporary home of the engineers building the larger fortress. See Pietch, Timpe and Wamser (1991); Pietch (1993); von Schnurbein (2000 and 2004), pp. 34–35 and fig. 26.

48. Vell. Pat. 2.110.1. The press release announcing the discovery, entitled 'The First Romans in Carununtum: Earliest Roman military camps discovered in Carnuntum by georadar measurements', states: 'Carnuntum is the largest archaeological landscape in Central Europe. Almost the entire Roman town, which covered more than ten square kilometres of area in antiquity, is still preserved under fields and vineyards some 40km to the east of Austria's capital Vienna. Since 2012 the Ludwig Boltzmann Institute for Archaeological Prospection and Virtual Archaeology (LBI ArchPro) together with ZAMG and their international partners have been exploring the subsurface of this vast area on behalf of the County of Lower Austria ... Outside the western gate of the Roman town the [georadar] surveys have revealed an extensive street village located alongside the Roman road to Vindobona (Vienna). Underneath the remains of this village – hidden in the deeper layers of the digital data volumes – the scientists of the LBI ArchPro discovered a typical fortification ditch of a Roman military camp placed directly adjacent to the river Danube, enclosing an area of more than six football pitches (57,600m^2). Due to the superposition with buildings, the researchers conclude that this camp has been one of the earliest military camps constructed during the Roman occupation of the Carnuntum area' (http://archpro.lbg.ac.at/press-release/first-romans-carnuntum – accessed 29 February 2016). The spelling Karnuntum is Celtic.

49. Dio 55.22.4. See Ch. 5, nos 81 and 82.

50. Dio 55.23.1: χαλεπῶς δὲ δὴ τῶν στρατιωτῶν πρὸς τὴν τῶν ἄθλων σμικρότητα διὰ τοὺς πολέμους τοὺς τότε ἐνεστηκότας οὐχ ἥκιστα ἐχόντων, καὶ μηδενὸς ἔξω τοῦ τεταγμένου τῆς στρατείας σφίσι χρόνου ὅπλα λαβεῖν ἐθέλοντος.

51. Swan (2004), p. 158, citing Keppie (1973). See Ch. 4, nos 7–9.

52. Dio 55.23.1: ἐψηφίσθη τοῖς μὲν ἐκ τοῦ δορυφορικοῦ πεντακισχιλίας δραχμάς, ἐπειδὰν ἑκκαίδεκα ἔτη, τοῖς δὲ ἑτέροις τρισχιλίας, ἐπειδὰν εἴκοσι στρατεύσωνται, δίδοσθαι. Cf. the grievances of soldiers of the Rhine Army in 14 CE in Tac., *Ann.* 1.17.

53. Dio 56.22.3–4. Asprenas may have been with his uncle in Syria as a *tribunus militum*, suggests Syme (1986), p. 314, citing W. John.

54. Dio 56.18.3.

55. Dio 56.18.3; Florus 2.30. For a discussion of the mission of Varus in the region see Dreyer (2009), pp. 106–18; Wolters (2008), pp. 71–74 and 84–86; and Wells (1972), p. 239, who notes 'in Germany he [Varus] was not expected to fight a major campaign'.

56. Not all Germania was under Roman control as Dio 56.18.1 admits: *The Romans were holding portions of it – not entire regions, but merely such districts as happened to have been subdued* | εἶχόν τινα οἱ Ῥωμαῖοι αὐτῆς, οὐκ ἀθρόα ἀλλ᾽ ὥς που καὶ ἔτυχε χειρωθέντα.

57. Dio 56.18.2: καὶ στρατιῶταί τε αὐτῶν ἐκεῖ ἐχείμαζον καὶ πόλεις συνῳκίζοντο, ἔς τε τὸν κόσμον σφῶν οἱ βάρβαροι μετερρυθμίζοντο καὶ ἀγορὰς ἐνόμιζον συνόδους τε εἰρηνικὰς ἐποιοῦντο. Ptolemy's

geography lists several settlements by name. The only one that has been found is Waldgirmes, the Roman name of which is not known: see Ch. 5, n. 77.

58. Dio 55.28.1–2: κἀν τοῖς αὐτοῖς τούτοις χρόνοις καὶ πόλεμοι πολλοὶ ἐγένοντο. καὶ γὰρ λῃσταὶ συχνὰ κατέτρεχον, ὥστε τὴν Σαρδὼ μηδ᾽ ἄρχοντα βουλευτὴν ἔτεσί τισι σχεῖν, ἀλλὰ στρατιώταις τε καὶ στρατιάρχαις ἱππεῦσιν ἐπιτραπῆναι· καὶ πόλεις οὐκ ὀλίγαι ἐνεωτέριζον, ὥστε καὶ ἐπὶ δύο ἔτη τοὺς αὐτοὺς ἐν τοῖς τοῦ δήμου ἔθνεσι, καὶ αἱρετούς γε ἀντὶ τῶν κληρωτῶν, ἄρξαι· τὰ γὰρ τοῦ Καίσαρος καὶ ἄλλως ἐπὶ πλείω χρόνον τοῖς αὐτοῖς προσετάττετο. οὐ μέντοι καὶ περὶ πάντων αὐτῶν ἀκριβῶς ἐπεξάξω. Sardinia and Corsica now needed a military presence to maintain law and order and, consequently, switched from being a Province of the People to a Province of Caesar (Strabo, *Geog.* 17.840): see Swan (2004), p. 189, on T. Pompius Proculus, the equestrian official curiously entitled *pro legato* placed in charge of it and shown on a milestone (*ILS* 105 = *EJ* 232a, dated 13–14 CE). Dio goes on to state in the quoted passage that he simply recorded the events worthy of mention, and very briefly at that, except for 'those of greatest importance'; the implication is that many events were omitted from his account, and lost to history because of his editorial decisions; on this point see Swan (2004), p.190.

59. Dio 55.28.3.
60. Dio 55.28.3–4.
61. Flor. 2.31; Vell. Pat. 2.116.2; Orosius 6.21.18; Dio 55.28.3–4; *ILS* 120 El-Lehs; *IRT* 521, 301 (Lepcis).
62. *Matthew* 2.22 implies that Joseph and Mary were afraid to travel to the territories under King Archelaus, deciding to settle, instead, in Galilee. For a discussion of Iudaea after Herodes and relations with the Romans see Fischer (2011).
63. Dio 55.27.6; Strabo, *Geog.* 16.765; Joseph., *Bell. Iud.* 2.111, *Ant. Iud.* 17.344.
64. Dio 55.27.6.
65. Joseph., *Ant. Iud.* 18.1–2; *Bell. Iud.* 2.117.
66. Joseph., *Ant. Iud.* 18.4: Ἰούδας δὲ Γαυλανίτης ἀνὴρ ἐκ πόλεως ὄνομα Γάμαλα Σάδδωκον Φαρισαῖον προσλαβόμενος ἠπείγετο ἐπὶ ἀποστάσει, τήν τε ἀποτίμησιν οὐδὲν ἄλλο ἢ ἄντικρυς δουλείαν ἐπιφέρειν λέγοντες καὶ τῆς ἐλευθερίας ἐπ᾽ ἀντιλήψει παρακαλοῦντες τὸ ἔθνος.
67. Joseph., *Ant. Iud.* 18.1; cf. *Acts* 5, 36, where the leader is called Theudas.
68. None are listed in the summary in Tac., *Ann.* 5.9 or in Dio 55.28.
69. *Acts* 5.37.
70. Strabo, *Geog.* 7.1.3; Vell. Pat. 2.108.2; Tac., *Ann.* 2.63. See Dobiáš (1960), pp. 155–66; Pitts (1989), pp. 46–47.
71. Strabo, *Geog.* 7.1.3.
72. Vell. Pat. 2.109.1–2. Strabo, *Geog.* 7.1.3 lists the coalition partners as the Luji, Zumi, Gutones, Mugilones, Sibini and the Semnones of the Suebi (or Suevi) federation.
73. Vell. Pat. 2.109.5; Tac., *Ann.* 2.63.
74. Suet., *Tib.* 16.1; Vell. Pat. 2.110.1.
75. On the historical and archaeological challenges of documenting the campaign see Salač (2006).
76. Dio 55.28.7n; Vell. Pat. 2.109.5.
75. See Ch. 2, nos 55 and 56.
78. Vell. Pat. 2.110.1–2: *Praeparaverat iam hiberna Caesar ad Danubium admotoque exercitu non plus quam quinque dierum iter a primis hostium aberat, legionesque quas Saturninum admovere placuerat, paene aequali divisae intervallo ab hoste intra paucos dies in praedicto loco cum Caesare se iuncturae errant.*
79. See Swan (2004), pp. 197–98, citing as source Kolník (1991), pp. 71–84.
80. The remains of marching camps have been identified at Mušov-Burgstall on the Dyje (Thaya) River, a tributary of the March in Moravia, Czech Republic, some 90km north of Carnuntum, the earliest of which may date to this period. (See Swan (2004), p. 198, citing Bálek and Sedo (1996), pp. 399–414). Most, however, have been dated using stratigraphy to the later Marcomannic Wars of M. Aurelius (166–180 CE).
81. Vell. Pat. 2.110. 2.
82. Dio 55.29.3.
83. Vell. Pat. 2.110.6: *Oppressi cives Romani, trucidati negotiatores, magnus vexillariorum numerus ad internecionem ea in regione, quae plurimum ab imperatore aberat, caesus.*

84. Vell. Pat. 2.110.6: *occupata armis Macedonia, omnia et in omnibus ocis igni ferroque vastata.*
85. Dio 55.29.3.
86. Dio 55.29.1.
87. Dio 55.29.1–2.
88. Vell. Pat. 2.110.4.
89. Dio states the rebellion broke out *before* Tiberius launched his German War. Mócsy (1983), pp. 173–74, argues that the cause of the rebellion was, in fact, Tiberius' mishandling of the situation by insisting Messallinus recruit men from Illyricum and bring them. The men of Illyricum, however, refused to endanger their lives in foreign lands across the Danube in a war that did not serve their best interests.
90. Appian's estimate (*Ill.* 22) is that the Pannonii – the name given to the tribes of Illyricum living close to the Danube – could field 100,000 armed men. For an assessment see Dzino (2005), p. 147.
91. Strabo, *Geog.* 7.5.4: καὶ ζειᾷ καὶ κέγχρῳ τὰ πολλὰ τρεφομένων· ὁ δ᾽ ὁπλισμὸς Κελτικός· κατάστικτοι δ᾽ ὁμοίως τοῖς ἄλλοις Ἰλλυριοῖς καὶ Θρᾳξί. On Iron Age 'Celtic' arms, armour and modes of fighting see Powell (2011) pp. 34–38.
92. The Pannonian warriors – those who could afford them – wielded iron swords measuring 0.55–0.57 metres (1.80–1.87ft) in length with a pointed end best suited for cutting and chopping rather than thrusting.
93. Ennius, *Ann.* 5.540.
94. *Cf.* The fighting style of the Cantabri – see Ch. 2, nos 65 and 66.
95. Of these fortifications the eastern section of the town walls – built out of huge stone blocks with the door surrounded by octagonal towers ('Porta Caesarea') dating from the time of Augustus – still stands to the present day.
96. Dio, 55.29.4. On improvised weapons see Cowan (2009).
97. Dio 55.29.4.
98. Vell. Pat. 2.110. 6: *Quin etiam tantus huius belli metus fuit, ut stabilem illum et firmatum tantorum bellorum experientia Caesaris Augusti animum quateret atque terreret.*
99. Vell. Pat. 2.111.1: *Habiti itaque dilectus, revocati undique et omnes veterani, viri feminaeque ex censu libertinum coactae dare militem. Audita in senatu vox principis, decimo die, ni caveretur, posse hostem in urbis Romae venire conspectum. Senatorum equitumque Romanorum exactae ad id bellum operae, pollicitati.*
100. Vell. Pat. 2.111.2: *The res publica, therefore, requested of Augustus to give command in that war to Tiberius, as their best defender | Itaque ut praesidium ultimum res publica ab Augusto ducem in bellum poposcit Tiberium.*
101. Dio 55.28.7.
102. Vell. Pat. 2.110.3; Dio 55.28.6.
103. Dio 55.28.6–8; Vell. Pat. 2.97.4. The first two times followed the military campaigns of 4 and 5 CE, the special treaty with the Marcomanni was a third peace: Vell. Pat. 2.110.3; Tac., *Ann.* 2.26.3, 2.46.2. See Ch. 6, n. 103.
104. Dio 55.30.1–2. The home base of *Legio* XX was Burnum in Dalmatian Illyricum.
105. Swan (2004), p. 247.
106. Suet., *Tib.* 16: *quod gravissimum omnium externorum bellorum post Punica.*
107. Dio 55.30.2.
108. Dio 55.30.3.
109. Dio 55.30.3–4. See Ch. 4, n. 19.
110. Dio 55.30.4.
111. Dio 55.30.4, 55.33.2. This is the M'. Ennius of Tac., *Ann.* 1.38.1–2.
112. Vell. Pat. 2.111.3. He waived the opportunity of a provincial governorship to accept the military position.
113. Vell. Pat. 2.111.4.
114. Vell. Pat. 2.112.2.
115. Suet., *Tib.* 20; Vell. Pat. 2.112.2: *ornamenta* took the form of an *ovatio* in which the honoree could ride a horse, rather than a chariot as in a full triumph, at the head of his victorious troops.

116. Dio 55.30.5; Vell. Pat. 2.112.1.
117. Dio 55.30.5–6.
118. Dio 55.30.5–6.
119. Vell. Pat. 2.111.1.
120. See Ch. 1, n. 23.
121. Dio 55.31.1.
122. Suet., *Tib.* 21.4: *Vale, iucundissime Tiberi, et feliciter rem gere, ἐμοὶ καὶ ταῖς μούσαις στρατηγῶν. Iucundissime et ita sim felix, vir fortissime et dux νομιμώτατε, vale. Ordinem aestivorum tuorum ego vero laudo, mi Tiberi, et inter tot rerum difficultates καὶ τοσαύτην ἀποθυμίαν τῶν στρατευομένων non potuisse quemquam prudentius gerere se quam tu gesseris, existimo.* [*H*]*ii quoque qui tecum fuerunt omnes confitentur, versum illum in te posse dici: unus homo nobis vigilando restituit rem.* In the quote Augustus adapts Enn., *Ann.* 370 V^2 to switch *cunctando* with *vigilando*.
123. Tac., *Ann.* 1.4; Vell. Pat. 2.112.7.
124. Dio 55.32.1–2; Suet., *Div. Aug.* 65.4. His mother, Iulia Caesaris, was banished here for the alleged crime of adultery in 2 BCE. Any chance that he might succeed Augustus was now extinguished. Barbara M. Levick (1972, p. 696), observes that Augustus deposited the young man's confiscated property in the *aerarium militare* and, by doing so, avoided the charge that he had embezzled it.
125. Dio 55.31.1.
126. Nero Claudius Drusus was 23 years old in 15 BCE. See Ch. 3, n. 58.
127. Dio 55.31.1. Slaves were not normally considered fit for military service: Pliny the Younger, *Epist.* 10.29–30.
128. See Brunt (1974), Orth (1978) and Speidel (1976). For a discussion of the *Cohortes Voluntariorum* see Appendix 3.6.
129. Vell. Pat. 2.110.6: *Quin etiam tantus huius belli metus fuit, ut stabilem illum et firmatum tantorum bellorum experientia Caesaris Augusti animum quateret atque terreret.*
130. Dio 55.31.4.
131. Dio 55.31.2.
132. For estimates of fodder needed to feed cavalry horses on campaign see Herz (2007), p. 317.
133. *RG* 17; Dio 54.25.2.
134. Dio 54.25.3.
135. Dio 54.25.4.
136. Dio 54.25.5: *συναγαγὼν δὲ ἐκ τούτου τὸ βουλευτήριον αὐτὸς μὲν οὐδὲν εἶπεν ὑπὸ βράγχου, τὸ δὲ δὴ βιβλίον τῷ ταμίᾳ ἀναγνῶναι δοὺς τά τε πεπραγμένα οἱ κατηριθμήσατο, καὶ διέταξε τά τε ἔτη ὅσα οἱ πολῖται στρατεύσοιντο, καὶ τὰ χρήματα ὅσα παυσάμενοι τῆς στρατείας, ἀντὶ τῆς χώρας ἣν ἀεί ποτε ᾔτουν, λήψοιντο, ὅπως ἐπὶ ῥητοῖς ἐκεῖθεν ἤδη καταλεγόμενοι μηδὲν τούτων γε ἕνεκα νεωτερίζωσιν.*
137. Dio 54.25.1, 54.25.6.
138. Suet., *Div. Aug.* 25.2, 30.1; Dio 55.26.1, 4–5; Tac., *Ann.* 13.27.1. For a discussion of the *Vigiles Urbani* see Appendix 3.8.
139. Suet., *Div. Aug.* 25.2; Dio 52.33.1, 55.26.4, 58.9.3; Dig. 1.2.2.33.
140. *Cf.* Dio 55.26.4 on the *praefectus*' duties.
141. Dio 55.33.4, 55.26.5.
142. Vell. Pat. 2.113.1: *unctis exercitibus, quique sub Caesare fuerant quique ad eum venerant, contractisque in una castra decem legionibus, septuaginta amplius cohortibus, decem alis et pluribus quam decem veteranorum milibus, ad hoc magno voluntariorum numero frequentique equite regio, tanto denique exercitu*; Suet., *Tib.* 16.1 states fifteen legions and an equal number of auxiliaries were involved. Saeger (1972), p. 42, asserts this is 'far more than he really needed' but this underestimates the difficulty of the terrain in the Western Balkans and the refusal of the rebels to fight in the open.
143. Vell. Pat. 2.113.1: *quantus nullo umquam loco post bella fuerat civilia, omnes eo ipso laeti erant maximamque fiduciam victoriae in numero reponebant.*
144. Florus 2.27: *Ille barbaros et signis militaribus et disciplina, armis etiam Romanis adsueverat.*
145. Vell. Pat. 2.112.4–5: *apud signa quoque legionum trepidatum.*
146. Vell. Pat. 2.112.6.

147. Vell. Pat. 2.112.5: *Sed Romani virtus militis plus eo tempore vindicavit gloriae quam ducibus reliquit, qui multum a more imperatoris sui discrepantes ante in hostem inciderunt, quam per explora,tores, ubi hostis esset, cognoscerent.*
148. Vell. Pat. 2.112.6: *Iam igitur in dubiis rebus semet ipsae legiones adhortatae, ... invasere hostes nec sustinuisse contenti perrupta eorum acie ex insperato victoriam vindicaverunt.*
149. Dio 55.32.3.
150. Dio 55.32.3: καὶ τοὺς μὲν ἔξω τοῦ ταφρεύματος ἐφόβησαν καὶ κατήραξαν ἐς αὐτό, δεξαμένων δέ σφας τῶν ἔνδον ἡττήθησαν.
151. Dio 55.32.3–4. Dio may be referring to *vexillarii* or 'vexillations', which were smaller often mixed units brought together temporarily for a tactical mission, *cf.* Vell. Pat. 2.110.6.
152. Vell. Pat. 2.112.3; Pliny, *Nat. Hist.* 3.28 places Mons Claudius between the Scordisci and Taursici.
153. See Šašel Kos (2011), p. 114 and plan in fig. 5.
154. Dio's account for 7 CE is light on details, so our understanding of events may miss important events.
155. Dio 55.32.4.
156. Strabo, *Geog.* 7.5.1.
157. Dio 55.32.4: ὁ δὲ δὴ Γερμανικὸς Μαζαίους Δελματικὸν ἔθνος μάχῃ νικήσας ἐκάκωσεν.
158. Dio 55.33.3.
159. See Ch. 6, n. 62.
160. Dio 56.11.1. The exact identity of this location is not known.
161. Evans (1883).
162. Dio 56.11.1: καίπερ τῇ τε φύσει ἰσχυρὸν ὂν καὶ τοῖς τείχεσιν εὖ πεφραγμένον τούς τε ἀμυνομένους παμπληθεῖς ἔχον.
163. Dio 56.11.1: οὔκουν οὔτε μηχαναῖς οὔτε προσβολαῖς ἠδυνήθη τι ἐξεργάσασθαι.
164. Dio 56.11.2: Πουσίων ἱππεὺς Κελτὸς λίθον ἐς τὸ τεῖχος ἀφεὶς οὕτω τὴν ἔπαλξιν διέσεισεν ὥστε αὐτήν τε αὐτίκα πεσεῖν καὶ τὸν ἄνδρα τὸν ἐπικεκλιμένον οἱ συγκατασπάσαι. γενομένου δὲ τούτου ἐκπλαγέντες οἱ ἄλλοι καὶ φοβηθέντες τό τε τεῖχος ἐκεῖνο ἐξέλιπον καὶ ἐς τὴν ἀκρόπολιν ἀνέδραμον.
165. Dio 56.11.2.
166. Dio 56.11.1, 56.11.3. Raetinium may be the Rataneum of Pliny, *Nat. Hist.* 3.26. The modern location might be Bihać on the Una River.
167. Dio 56.11.3–7: οἱ γὰρ ἐναντίοι βιαζόμενοι τῷ πλήθει σφῶν, καὶ μὴ δυνάμενοι ἀντέχειν, πῦρ ἐθελούσιοι ἔς τε τὸν κύκλον πέριξ καὶ ἐς τὰ οἰκοδομήματα πλησίον αὐτοῦ ἐνέβαλον, μηχανησάμενοι ὅπως ὅτι μάλιστα μὴ παραχρῆμα ἐκλάμψῃ ἀλλ᾽ ἐπὶ χρόνον τινὰ διαλάθῃ. καὶ οἱ μὲν τοῦτο ποιήσαντες ἐς τὴν ἄκραν ἀνεχώρησαν· ἀγνοοῦντες δὲ οἱ Ῥωμαῖοι τὸ πεπραγμένον ἐπεσέπεσον ὡς καὶ αὐτοβοεὶ πάντα διαρπάσοντες, καὶ εἴσω τε τῆς τοῦ πυρὸς περιβολῆς ἐγένοντο, καὶ οὐ πρότερον εἶδον αὐτό, πρὸς τοὺς πολεμίους τὸν νοῦν ἔχοντες, πρὶν πανταχόθεν ὑπ᾽ αὐτοῦ περιληφθῆναι. τότε δὲ ἐν παντὶ κινδύνου ἐγένοντο, ἄνωθεν μὲν ὑπὸ τῶν ἀνθρώπων βαλλόμενοι, ἔξωθεν δὲ ὑπὸ τῆς φλογὸς κακούμενοι, καὶ μήτε κατὰ χώραν ἀσφαλῶς μεῖναι μήτε πῃ διαπεσεῖν ἀκινδύνως δυνάμενοι. εἴτε γὰρ ἔξω βέλους ἀφίσταντο, πρὸς τοῦ πυρὸς ἀναλοῦντο, εἴτ᾽ ἀπὸ τῆς φλογὸς ἀπεπήδων, πρὸς τῶν βαλλόντων ἐφθείροντο· καί τινες ἔν τε στενοχωρίᾳ ἀπ᾽ ἀμφοτέρων ἅμα ἀπώλοντο, τῇ μὲν τιτρωσκόμενοι τῇ δὲ καιόμενοι. οἱ μὲν οὖν πλείους τῶν ἐσελθόντων οὕτως ἀπήλλαξαν· ὀλίγοι δέ τινες νεκροὺς ἐς αὐτὴν τὴν φλόγα ἐμβαλόντες, καὶ δίοδόν σφισι δι᾽ αὐτῶν καθάπερ ἐπὶ γεφύρας ποιήσαντες, διέφυγον. οὕτω γάρ που τὸ πῦρ ἐπεκράτησεν ὥστε μηδὲ τοὺς ἐν τῇ ἀκροπόλει ὄντας κατὰ χώραν μεῖναι, ἀλλὰ τῆς νυκτὸς αὐτὴν ἐκλιπεῖν καὶ ἐς οἰκήματα κατώρυχα κατακρυφθῆναι.
168. Swan (2004), p. 247, argues the actual number in 8 CE was eight legions.
169. Dio 56.12.2: καὶ φοβηθεὶς μὴ καὶ καθ᾽ ἓν ὄντες στασιάσωσι, τριχῇ διεῖλεν αὐτούς, καὶ τοὺς μὲν τῷ Σιλουανῷ τοὺς δὲ Μάρκῳ Λεπίδῳ προστάξας ἐπὶ τὸν Βάτωνα μετὰ τῶν λοιπῶν σὺν τῷ Γερμανικῷ ὥρμησε.
170. Dio 55.34.5–6.
171. Dio 55.34.6: καὶ αὐτοῖς ὁ Σιλουανὸς ἐπιστρατεύσας τούς τε Βρεύκους ἐνίκησε καὶ τῶν ἄλλων τινὰς ἀμαχεὶ προσεποιήσατο.
172. Vell. Pat. 2.114.4–5. See Wilkes (1969), p. 553.
173. Dio 55.34.7.

174. Vell. Pat. 2.115.4; Dio 56.13.5, *cf.* description of *saltus Teutoburgiensis* in 56.20.1.
175. Dio 55.12.4.
176. Dio 56.12.5: καὶ προσέτι καὶ τὴν σιτοπομπίαν τῶν Ῥωμαίων ἐνεδρεύοντες ἐκώλυον, ὥστε τὸν Τιβέριον, πολιορκεῖν σφας δοκοῦντα, αὐτὸν τὰ τῶν πολιορκουμένων πάσχειν.
177. Suet., *Tib.* 16.2.
178. Dio 55.33.1.
179. Dio 55.33.2, 56.15.2. On the Pannonian deserters see Dzino (2005), pp. 154–55.
180. Dio 56.13.2.
181. Dio 56.13.1.
182. Dio 56.13.3.
183. Dio 56.13.4.
184. Dio 56.14.1.
185. Dio 56.14.5.
186. Dio 56.14.6.
187. *Cf.* Vell. Pat. 2.115.2.
188. Dio 56.14.7.
189. Dio 56.15.1.
190. The modern location is not known: see Swan (2004), pp. 245–46.
191. Dio 56.15.1–2.
192. Dio 56.15.2.
193. Dio 56.15.3.
194. Dio 56.16.1.
195. Dio 56.16.2.
196. Dzino (2005), p. 155.
197. Dio 56.16.2–3.
198. Suet., *Tib.* 17.2.
199. Suet., *Tib.* 9.2.
200. Vell. Pat. 2.116.1; Dio 56.17.2; Suet., *Tib.* 20.1.
201. Dio 56.24.2–5 meticulously records the catalogue of signs and portents that presaged a disaster. The Temple of Mars in the *Campus Martius* was struck by lightning. There was a plague of locusts. There were reports that the Alps exploded like volcanoes. Comets had blazed across the night sky. Additionally: *spears seemed to dart from the north and to fall in the direction of the Roman camps; bees formed their combs about the altars in the camps; a statue of Victory that was in the province of Germania and faced the enemy's territory turned about to face Italia; and in one instance there was a futile battle and conflict of the soldiers over the eagles in the camps, the soldiers believing that the barbarians had fallen upon them* | καὶ δόρατα ἀπ᾽ ἄρκτου φερόμενα πρὸς τὰ τῶν Ῥωμαίων στρατόπεδα προσπίπτειν ἐδόκει, μέλισσαί τε περὶ τοὺς βωμοὺς αὐτῶν κηρία ἀνέπλασσον, καὶ Νίκης τι ἄγαλμα ἔν τε τῇ Γερμανίᾳ ὂν καὶ πρὸς τὴν πολεμίαν βλέπον πρὸς τὴν Ἰταλίαν μετεστράφη· καὶ ποτε καὶ περὶ τοὺς ἀετοὺς τοὺς ἐν τοῖς στρατοπέδοις, ὡς καὶ τῶν βαρβάρων ἐπ᾽ αὐτοὺς ἐσπεπτωκότων, μάχη καὶ ἀγωνισμὸς τῶν στρατιωτῶν διὰ κενῆς ἐγένετο.
202. Dio 56.19.2; Vell. Pat. 2.118.2; Tac., *Ann.* 1.55.2–3, 58.2–3, 2.10.3, 2.88.1–2; Florus 2.30.32; Strabo, *Geog.* 7.292. See Ch. 5, n. 15.
203. Vell. Pat. 2.118.2.
204. Powell (2014), p. 35; *cf.* Murdoch (2006), p. 108.
205. Vell. Pat. 2.117.1. *Legiones* XIIX and XIX are known with certainty to have been part of his army group and XVII is presumed to have been the other since it is attested nowhere else: Manlius 1.900; Strabo, *Geog.* 7.291; Tac., *Germ.* 37.4, *Ann.* 1.61.2; Suet., *Div. Aug.* 23.1, *Tib.* 17.1. His starting point is unknown. It is possible it was the temporary marching camp dating to this period – found at Barkhausen, Porta Westfalica: see Ch. 6, n. 36.
206. At full strength it would consist of 16,800 legionaries including 360 mounted scouts, 3,072 cavalry (based on 512 men per *ala*) and 2,880 infantry auxiliaries (assuming 480 men per *cohors peditata*). Some men would have remained at the winter camps – Batavodurum, Vetera, Novaesium, Ara Ubiorum and Mogontiacum on the Rhine, as well as Anreppen, Haltern and other forts on the Lippe – to ensure they were maintained and stocked with provisions, while

others would have been seconded to the provincial administration running the legal and military affairs of province Germania. Following the troops was an unknown number of motley non-combatants – slaves, slave traders, merchants and personal-service providers – who made a living from trading with the soldiers and local tribes people they encountered. Murdoch (2006), p. 105, suggests 18,000 legionaries, 900 cavalry and 3,600 auxiliaries.

207. Dio 54.33.3–4.
208. Dio 56.19.2.
209. Vell. Pat. 2.118.4: *Id Varo per virum eius gentis fidelum clarique nominis, Segesten, indicatur.*
210. Dio 56.19.3: καὶ ἐκείνους διαβάλλουσιν, ἐπανίστανταί τινες πρῶτοι τῶν ἄπωθεν αὐτοῦ οἰκούντων ἐκ παρασκευῆς.
211. Dio 56.19.4.
212. Dio 56.19.4.
213. Dio 56.20.2.
214. Dio 56.20.4.
215. *Saltus Teutoburgiensis* is mentioned only by Tac., *Ann.* 1.60.3. *Saltus* is often translated as forest, but this ambiguous Latin word can also mean glade, pasture, pass, ravine or woodland. The location of the battle has been argued over for centuries and there some 700 modern theories as to its exact whereabouts: see Powell (2014), p. 31. For the case *pro* Kalkriese see Schlüter (1999) and Rost (2005; 2009), *contra* see Schoppe (2006).
216. Dio 56.19.1.
217. For a full discussion of the Battle of Teutoburg Pass and the arms, armour, strategies and tactics of the opposing sides, see Powell (2014), pp. 4–40.
218. Dio 56.20.4.
219. Tac., *Ann.* 1.64.2; cf. Dio 38.49.1.
220. Dio 56.20.4.
221. Dio 56.20.3: the sudden appearance of a storm may be a trope rather than an actual meteorological event. No other Roman historian mentions the weather during this battle.
222. Dio 56.20.5.
223. Dio 56.21.1.
224. *Cf.* Tac., *Ann.* 1.63–64.
225. Tac., *Ann.* 1.61.2.
226. Dio 56.21.2.
227. Dio 56.21.1.
228. Dio 56.21.2; cf. 56.20.5, 71.7.3.
229. Vell. Pat. 2.119.4.
230. Dio 56.21.3.
231. Tac., *Ann.* 1.60 locates the final stage of the ambush 'not far' from a region between the Ems and Lippe rivers in the lands of the Bructeri: *distrahendo hosti per Bructeros ad flumen Amisiam mittit.*
232. Vell. Pat. 2.119.4.
233. *CIL* 13.8648. His brother Publius erected the headstone.
234. Vell. Pat. 2.119.4.
235. Vell. Pat. 2.120.6.
236. Crinagoras, *Palatine Anthology* 7.741.
237. Florus 2.30.38.
238. Vell. Pat. 2.119.4.
239. Florus 2.30.37: '*vipera, sibilare desisti*'.
240. Dio 56.21.5; Suet., *Div. Aug.* 23.1. His father had also taken his life.
241. Vell. Pat. 2.119.5.
242. Vell. Pat. 2.119.5.
243. One *aquila* went to the Bructeri (Tac., *Ann.* 1.60), one to the Chauci (Dio 56.8.7) and the third to the Marsi (Tac., *Ann.* 2.25).
244. Florus, 2.30.
245. Dio 56.22.2a; Tac., *Ann.* 2.7.1–3. Some historians identify Aliso as the 'Hauptlager' of Annaberg at Haltern: see Ch. 4, n. 87.

246. Dio 56.22.2a; *cf.* Tac., *Ann.* 2.16, 17.4.6.
247. Dio 56.22.2b.
248. Dio 56.22.2b; Vell. Pat. 2.120.4.
249. Frontinus, *Strat.* 4.7.8.
250. Frontinus, *Strat.* 3.15.4: *horrea tota nocte circumduxerunt captivos, deinde praecisis manibus dimiserunt: hi circumsedentibus suis persuaserunt, ne spem maturae expugnationis reponerent in fame Romanorum, quibus ingens alimentorum copia superesset. Cf.* Dio 56.23.2b.
251. Dio 56.23.2b.
252. Dio 56.22.2: τὸ μὲν πρῶτον τό τε δεύτερόν σφων φυλακτήριον παρῆλθον, ἐπεὶ δὲ πρὸς τῷ τρίτῳ ἐγένοντο, ἐφωράθησαν, τῶν τε γυναικῶν καὶ τῶν παίδων συνεχῶς τοὺς ἐν τῇ ἡλικίᾳ διά τε τὸν κάματον καὶ διὰ τὸν φόβον τό ε σκότος καὶ τὸ ψῦχος ἀνακαλούντων.
253. Dio 56.23.3.
254. Vell. Pat. 2.120.4: *ad suos.*
255. Dio 56.22.2b.
256. Vell. Pat. 2.120.3: *there are those, however, who believed that, though he had saved the lives of the living, he had appropriated to his own use the property of the dead who were slain with Varus, and that inheritances of the slaughtered army were claimed by him at pleasure* | *Sunt tamen, qui ut vivos ab eo vindicatos, ita iugulatorum sub Varo occupata crediderint patrimonia hereditatemque occisi exercitus, in quantum voluerit, ab eo aditam.*
257. Vell. Pat. 2.117.1.; *cf.* Dio 56.18.1.
258. Dio 56.22.2b.
259. Suet., *Div. Aug.* 49.1: *Quintili Vare, legiones redde! Cf.* Dio 56.23.1; Oros. 6.21.27.
260. Dio 56.23.4: ἐπειδή τε συχνοὶ ἐν τῇ Ῥώμῃ καὶ Γαλάται καὶ Κελτοί, οἱ μὲν ἄλλως ἐπιδημοῦντες οἱ δὲ καὶ ἐν τῷ δορυφορικῷ στρατευόμενοι, ἦσαν, ἐφοβήθη μή τι νεοχμώσωσι, καὶ τούτους μὲν ἐς νήσους τινὰς ἀπέστειλε, τοῖς δ᾽ ἀόπλοις ἐκχωρῆσαι τῆς πόλεως προσέταξε.
261. Dio 56.23.1: καὶ πένθος μέγα ἐπί τε τοῖς ἀπολωλόσι καὶ ἐπὶ τῷ περί τε τῶν Γερμανιῶν καὶ περὶ τῶν Γαλατιῶν δέει ἐποιήσατο, τό τε μέγιστον ὅτι καὶ ἐπὶ τὴν Ἰταλίαν τήν τε Ῥώμην αὐτὴν ὁρμήσειν σφᾶς προσεδόκησε.
262. Suet., *Div. Aug.* 23.1.
263. Suet., *Div. Aug.* 23.1.
264. Dio 56.24.1.
265. Suet., *Div. Aug.* 23.2.
266. Suet., *Tib.*, 9.2, 17.2; *cf.* Vell. Pat. 2.121.2. His return from Illyricum is attested by the *Fasti Praenestini*, CIL I, 230 = *AE* 1937, 4 = *EJ* p. 45.
267. On the role of gods in war see Powell (2010).
268. Dio 56.22.2.
269. Dio 56.23.2–3: ὄφελος ἦν, ἐκεκάκωτο. ὅμως δ᾽ οὖν τά τε ἄλλα ὡς ἐκ τῶν παρόντων παρεσκευάσατο, καὶ ἐπειδὴ μηδεὶς τῶν τὴν στρατεύσιμον ἡλικίαν ἐχόντων καταλεχθῆναι ἠθέλησεν, ἐκλήρωσεν αὐτούς, καὶ τῶν μὲν μηδέπω πέντε καὶ τριάκοντα ἔτη γεγονότων τὸν πέμπτον, τῶν δὲ πρεσβυτέρων τὸν δέκατον ἀεὶ λαχόντα τήν τε οὐσίαν ἀφείλετο καὶ ἠτίμωσε. καὶ τέλος, ὡς καὶ πάνυ πολλοὶ οὐδ᾽ οὕτω τι αὐτοῦ προετίμων, ἀπέκτεινέ τινας. ἀποκληρώσας δὲ ἔκ τε τῶν ἐστρατευμένων ἤδη καὶ ἐκ τῶν ἐξελευθέρων ὅσους ἠδυνήθη, κατέλεξε, καὶ εὐθὺς σπουδῇ μετὰ τοῦ Τιβερίου ἐς τὴν Γερμανίαν.
270. Suet., *Div. Aug.* 24.1, *cf. Tib.* 8. There were precedents: for enslavement, Dig. 49.16.10; for confiscation of property, Val. Max. 6.3.4.
271. Dio 56.24.1.
272. Oros. 6.21.27; *cf.* Suet., *Div. Iul.* 67.2.
273. Suet., *Div. Aug.* 24.2.
274. Vell. Pat. 2.119.5.
275. Dio 56.24.1.
276. Dio 56.25.1n. The dedication of the temple is attested by the *Fasti Praenestini*, CIL I, 230 = *Ilt.* 13.2.114–115 = *EJ* p. 45.
277. Dio 56.24.6: ὁ δὲ Τιβέριος διαβῆναι τὸν Ῥῆνον οὐκ ἔκρινεν, ἀλλ᾽ ἠτρέμιζεν ἐπιτηρῶν μὴ οἱ βάρβαροι τοῦτο ποιήσωσιν. ἀλλ᾽ οὐδ᾽ ἐκεῖνοι διαβῆναι ἐτόλμησαν γνόντες αὐτὸν παρόντα. Vell. Pat. 2.120.1–2.

278. Dio 56.22.4.
279. Vell. Pat. 2.121.1.
280. In 15 CE Germanicus Caesar built a camp at a point along it, Tac., *Ann.* 1.50: *at Romanus agmine propero silvam Caesiam limitemque a Tiberio coeptum scindit.* It predates the so-called *Limes Germanicus* by seventy-five years.
281. Dio 56.24.1.
282. Tac., *Ann.* 1.31, 3.41, 4.73, 13.53.
283. Vell. Pat. 2.121.1: *cum res Galliarum maximae molis accensasque plebis Viennensium dissensiones coercitione magis quam poena mollisset.*
284. It was still referred to as Illyricum in 14 CE: *CIL* III, 1741 (Ragusae) = *ILS* 938; Vell. Pat. 2.125.5.
285. *Cf. ILS* 2280 = *EJ* 265.
286. Dio 56.25.2–3: οὐ μέντοι οὔτε μάχῃ τινὶ ἐνίκησαν ἐς γὰρ χεῖρας οὐδεὶς αὐτοῖς ᾔει οὔτε ἔθνος τι ὑπηγάγοντο· δεδιότες γὰρ μὴ καὶ συμφορᾷ αὖθις περιπέσωσιν, οὐ πάνυ πόρρω τοῦ Ῥήνου προῆλθον.
287. Dio 56.25.6: καὶ τῷ ὑπηκόῳ προσπαρήγγειλε μηδενὶ τῶν προστασσομένων αὐτοῖς ἀρχόντων μήτε ἐν τῷ τῆς ἀρχῆς χρόνῳ μήτε ἐντὸς ἑξήκοντα ἡμερῶν μετὰ τὸ ἀπαλλαγῆναί σφας τιμήν τινα διδόναι, ὅτι τινὲς μαρτυρίας παρ' αὐτῶν καὶ ἐπαίνους προπαρασκευαζόμενοι πολλὰ διὰ τούτου ἐκακούργουν. See Swan (2004), pp. 281–82.
288. Dio 56.26.2: καὶ μετὰ τοῦτ' ᾐτήσατο παρ' αὐτῶν, ἐπὶ τῇ τοῦ Κελτικοῦ πολέμου προφάσει, μήτ' οἴκοι αὐτὸν ἀσπάζεσθαι μήτ' ἀγανακτεῖν εἰ μηκέτι συσσιτοίη σφίσι.
289. Dio 56.27.4.
290. Dio 56.17.1; Suet., *Tib.* 17.2.
291. Suet., *Tib.* 20; Ovid, *Epistulae Ex Ponto* 2.1, 2.2, 3.3.85ff. Seager (1972), p. 45 n. 6, points out that the day is certain but the year is not, though there is more evidence in support of 12 CE.
292. Vell. Pat. 2.116.1; Dio 56.17.2; Suet., *Tib.* 20.1.
293. Dio 55.8.2.
294. Ovid, *Epistulae Ex Ponto* 2.1.25ff.
295. Vell. Pat. 2.121.2; *cf.* Suet., *Tib.* 17.2, which appears to relate to 9 CE. A silver *denarius*, minted in Lugdunum in 13 CE, shows Tiberius standing right in triumphal *quadriga*, holding an eagle-tipped sceptre: *RIC* I 222, *RSC* 300, *BMC* 512.
296. Suet., *Tib.* 16.2: *Ac perseuerantiae grande pretium tulit, toto Illyrico, quod inter Italiam regnumque Noricum et Thraciam et Macedoniam interque Danuuium flumen et sinum maris Hadriatici patet, perdomito et in dicionem redacto.*
297. Suet., *Tib.* 20.
298. The *Gemma Augustea*, now in the Kunsthistorisches Museum, Vienna, is cut from double-layered Arabian onyx and is roughly square in shape; jewel measures 19cm (7.5in) high by 23cm (9in) wide. The engraver, believed to be master craftsman Dioskurides or one of his pupils, carefully cut the top white layer down to the bluish-brown stone beneath, leaving low-relief figures in high contrast. The engraver created two tiers of parallel scenes. In the upper tier Augustus appears as Iupiter, seated on a curule chair holding the lituus, a symbol of his high command: Tiberius' victory was won under the auspices of Augustus. He is being crowned with a *corona civica* of oak leaves – for saving Roman lives – by Oikumene. Oceanus or Neptunus and Gaia sit beside her. The three figures are personifications of the world and the surrounding seas over which Rome has dominion, and the world yet unconquered beyond. To Augustus' right sits Roma wearing a helmet and clasping a spear, but she is lightly touching a sword as if to indicate Rome is always ready to defend herself. To her right stands a man wearing the armour of a commanding officer and distinctive *paludamentum*. Most scholars identify this youthful figure as Germanicus Caesar. To his right, Tiberius descends from a chariot clutching a staff in one hand as a winged victory stands behind him. In the lower tier, soldiers heave as they hoist up a *trophaeum*, while bound barbarian captives look on dejectedly. This artwork may have been given as a gift to a wealthy friend of the *princeps* or to a client king after Tiberius' day of public recognition.
299. Grant (1970), p. 190; Goldsworthy (2006), p. 468.
300. Suet., *Tib.* 20; *cf.* 37.4.

301. Dio 56.25.1.
302. Dio 56.27.5. This building may be the *basilica* referred to in *RG* 20.3; *cf.* Suet., *Div. Aug.* 29.4. See Swan (2004), pp. 291–93.

Chapter 7: Limits to Empire

1. Dio 56.28.1: τήν τε προστασίαν τῶν κοινῶν τὴν δεκέτιν τὴν πέμπτην ἄκων δὴ ὁ Αὔγουστος ἔλαβε.
2. Dio 55.33.5: τὰς δὲ δὴ πρεσβείας τάς τε παρὰ τῶν δήμων καὶ τὰς παρὰ τῶν βασιλέων ἀφικνουμένας τρισὶ τῶν ὑπατευκότων ἐπέτρεψεν, ὥστ᾽ αὐτοὺς χωρὶς ἕκαστον καὶ διακούειν τινῶν καὶ ἀπόκρισιν αὐτοῖς διδόναι, πλὴν τῶν ὅσα ἀναγκαῖον ἦν τήν τε βουλὴν καὶ ἐκεῖνον ἐπιδιακρίνειν; and 56.25.7.
3. Vell. Pat. 2.121.1: *ut aequum ei ius in omnibus provinciis exercitibusque esset*; Suet., Tib. 21.1; *cf.* Dio 55.13.2n.
4. He had held it since 4 CE.
5. Suet., *Tib.* 9.2; *cf.* Vell. Pat. 2.121.1–2.
6. Dio 57.3.1.
7. Drinkwater (1983), p. 21.
8. *Tab. Siar.* Frag. 1.12: *ordinato statu Galliarum.*
9. *Tab. Siar.* Frag. 1.12; Suet., *Cal.* 8.3; Vell. Pat. 2.123.1. See Syme (1978), p. 58 and n. 5 and 6.
10. See Syme (1978), pp. 58–61;
11. Vell. Pat. 2.123.1: *Quippe Caesar Augustus cum Germanicum nepotem suum reliqua belli patraturum misisset in Germaniam.*
12. Vell. Pat. 2.123.1: *Tiberium autem filium missurus esset in Illyricum ad firmanda pace quae bello subegerat.*
13. Suet., *Div. Aug.* 97.3.
14. Dio 56.29.2.
15. Suet., *Div. Aug.* 98.2: *Forte Puteolanum sinum praetervehenti vectores nautaeque de navi Alexandrina, quae tantum quod appulerat, candidati coronatique et tura libantes fausta omina et eximias laudes congesserant, per illum se vivere, per illum navigare, libertate atque fortunis per illum frui.* Presumably his personal German guard and a cohort of Praetorians attended him.
16. Suet., *Div. Aug.* 98.
17. Suet., *Div. Aug.* 98.1 and 98.5; Dio 56.29.2.
18. Suet., *Div. Aug.* 98.5.
19. Suet., *Div. Aug.* 100.1: his natural father, C. Octavius Thurinus, also died in the room.
20. Suet., *Div. Aug.* 98.5; *cf.* Dio 56.31.1, who says Tiberius was already in Dalmatia according to some reputable sources, but that others insist he was actually with Augustus in his last hours, which is the version favoured by Suet., *Div. Aug.* 98.5, *Tib.* 21.1; Vell. Pat. 2.123.1–2; Tac., *Ann.* 1.5.3–4.
21. Dio 56.30.3; Suet., *Div. Aug.* 99.1.
22. Dio 56.29.5; *cf.* Dio 51.1.1. Suet., *Div. Aug.* 100.1 reverses the numbers to state Augustus would have been 76 had he lived another 35 days. On the dating see Swan (2004), pp. 304–05.
23. Dio 56.31.1: Dio relates the allegation that the news of Augustus' death was withheld until Tiberius arrived. Tac., *Ann.* 1.5.3–4 alleges Livia worked secretly to ensure her son's succession was trouble-free.
24. Suet., *Div. Aug.* 99.2: *Unum omnino ante efflatam animam signum alienatae mentis ostendit, quod subito pavefactus a quadraginta se iuvenibus abripi questus est. Id quoque magis praesagium quam mentis deminutio fuit, siquidem totidem milites praetoriani extulerunt eum in publicum.*
25. Suet., *Div. Aug.* 100.2; Dio 56.31.2.
26. Suet., *Div. Aug.* 100.2; Dio 56.34.2–3.
27. Suet., *Tib.* 23. See Levick (1976), p. 69–70 and n. 4.
28. Dio 56.31.3.
29. Dio 56.32.1. Suet., *Div. Aug.* 101.1: with Augustus, Polybius and another freedman Hilarion had each handwritten parts of the will.
30. Suet., *Div. Aug.* 101.2: *praetorianis militibus singula milia nummorum, cohortibus urbanis quingenos, legionaris trecenos nummos: quam summam repraesentari iussit, nam et confiscatam semper repositamque habuerat.* Cf. Dio 56.32.2: καὶ τοῖς στρατιώταις τοῖς μὲν δορυφόροις κατὰ πεντήκοντα καὶ διακοσίας

δραχμάς, τοῖς δ᾽ ἀστικοῖς τὴν ἡμίσειαν, τῷ τε λοιπῷ τῷ πολιτικῷ πλήθει πέντε καὶ ἐβδομήκοντα δοθῆναι ἐκέλευσε. For the estimate see Champlin (1989), p. 160.

31. Dio 56.33.1–6 says there were four books; Suet., *Div. Aug.* 101.4 says there were three; Tac., *Ann.* 1.11.1–4 mentions just two.

32. Tac., *Ann.* 1.11.1–4 does not mention this document.

33. Dio 56.33.1; *cf.* Tac., *Ann.* 1.11.1–4 does not mention this document.

34. Suet., *Div. Aug.* 101.4: *tertio breviarium totius imperii.*

35. Dio 56.33.2: τὸ τρίτον τά τε τῶν στρατιωτῶν καὶ τὰ τῶν προσόδων τῶν τε ἀναλωμάτων τῶν δημοσίων, τό τε πλῆθος τῶν ἐν τοῖς θησαυροῖς χρημάτων, καὶ ὅσα ἄλλα τοιουτότροπα ἐς τὴν ἡγεμονίαν φέροντα ἦν; *cf.* Tac, *Ann.* 1.11.4: *sua manu perscripserat.* It was read out – perhaps for a second time – on 17 September: see Swan (2004), pp. 314–18, for a review of issues in reconciling the various accounts into a cogent chronology.

36. App., *Bell. Civ.* 1.105–106.

37. Dio 56.34.2.

38. Dio 56.34.2–3. The *imago* of Iulius Caesar was absent because he was a divinity. As Swan (2004), p. 340, notes, the use of *designati* as pall bearers was unique. Equestrians had carried the body of Nero Claudius Drusus: see Ch. 4, n. 145.

39. Dio 56.34.4; *cf.* Polyb. 6.54.1–2.

40. Dio 56.34.1–41.9; Suet., *Div. Aug.* 100.3.

41. Suet., *Div. Aug.* 100.3 says the body was carried *on the shoulders of senators | ac senatorum umeris delatus.* The bier normally followed the procession of the *imagines, cf.* Tac., *Ann.* 3.76.2.

42. Suet., *Div. Aug.* 100.2; *cf.* Arce, *Funus* 46–47. C. Asinius Gallus, consul 8 BCE, had proposed the route.

43. Dio 56.34.2.

44. Suet., *Div. Aug.* 100.2; Tac., *Ann.* 1.8.3. The *Porta Triumphalis*, 'Triumphal Gate', has never been located. On the distinction between the sphere where civilian law (*domi*) and martial law (*militiae*) applied see Drogula (2015), pp. 47–56.

45. Dio 56.42.2; Strabo, *Geog.* 5.236.

46. See Swan (2004), pp. 341–42, for different interpretations of Dio 56.42.2.

47. Dio 56.42.2; *cf.* Suet., *Div. Iul.* 84.4. For Roman military decorations see Maxfield (1981), pp. 55–100.

48. Dio 56.42.3 states that an eagle was released at this moment, but the story is problematic: neither Suetonius nor Tacitus mention it in their accounts. Instead Suet., *Div. Aug.* 100.2: *a man of pretorian rank affirmed upon oath, that he saw his spirit ascend from the funeral pile to heaven | nec defuit vir praetorius, qui se effigiem cremati euntem in caelum vidisse iuraret.* See Swan (2004), pp. 343–44.

49. Dio 56.42.4; *cf.* Suet., *Div. Aug.* 100.4. The ashes of Augustus joined those of Marcellus (Dio 53.30.5), Nero Claudius Drusus Germanicus (54.28.5) and M. Agrippa (55.2.3).

50. Suet., *Tib.* 24.1: the *statione militum* was presumably one or more units of the Praetorian Cohorts, though it could have possibly been the *Germani Corporis Custodes; cf.* Dio 57.2.3.

51. Suet., *Tib.* 24.1; *cf. Tib.* 26.2.

52. Tac., *Ann.* 1.11.

53. See Corbett (1974), pp. 95–96.

54. Tac., *Ann.* 1.12–13; Suet., *Tib.* 25.3 and 38. See Charlesworth (1923).

55. Suet., *Tib.* 22.

56. Suet., *Tib.* 25.1, 25.3.

57. Suet., *Tib.* 25.1, 25.3.

58. Tac., *Ann.* 1.14.

59. Tac., *Ann.* 1.31, 1.37.

60. Tac., *Ann.* 1.31, 1.37–39, 1.45.

61. Tac., *Ann.* 1.35.

62. Tac., *Ann.* 1.36.

63. Tac., *Ann.* 1.34.

64. Tac., *Ann.* 1.35.

65. Tac., *Ann.* 1.35; Suet., *Tib.* 25.2.

66. Tac., *Ann.* 1.36.
67. Tac., *Ann.* 1.31: *vernacula multitudo, nuper acto in urbe dilectu.* From them it had spread to the other legions. *Cf.* Dio 57.5.4.
68. Dio 57.5.3; Tac., *Ann.* 1.37.
69. Tac., *Ann.* 1.45.
70. Suet., *Tib.* 25.2.
71. This Blaesus was not the suffect consul of 10 CE. Tac., *Ann.* 1.16. See Syme (1986), p. 144, n. 19.
72. Tac., *Ann.* 1.18–19.
73. Tac., *Ann.* 1.18–19.
74. Tac., *Ann.* 1.20.
75. Tac., *Ann.* 1.21–2.
76. Tac., *Ann.* 1.23.
77. Tac., *Ann.* 1.23.
78. Tac., *Ann.* 1.24.
79. Tac., *Ann.* 1.25.
80. Tac., *Ann.* 1.26–27.
81. Tac., *Ann.* 1.28.
82. Tac., *Ann.* 1.28–29.
83. Tac., *Ann.* 1.30.
84. Tac., *Ann.* 1.39.
85. Dio 57.5.6.
86. Dio 57.5.6; Tac., *Ann.* 1.39.
87. Tac., *Ann.* 1.39.
88. Tac., *Ann.* 1.41; Suet., *Calig.* 9.
89. Dio 57.5.7; Tac., *Ann.* 1.44.
90. Tac., *Ann.* 1.48.
91. Tac., *Ann.* 1.49.
92. Tac., *Ann.* 1.49.
93. *CIL* XIV, 3602 (Tibur) = *ILS* 950.
94. Tac., *Ann.* 1.50. See Ch. 6, n. 281.
95. Tac., *Ann.* 1.51.
96. *Cf.* Suet., *Div. Iul.* 67.2; Frontinus, *Strategemata* 1.9.4.
97. Suet., *Calig.* 4.
98. Dio 57.4.2, 57.6.4–5; Tac., *Ann.* 1.52.

Chapter 8: Assessment
1. *RG* 13.
2. 'Autocrat': Levick (2010), p. 311. 'Between citizen and king': Wallace-Hadrill (1982). 'Monarch': Alston (2015), p. 299; Bleicken (2015), pp. 612–13; the term preferred by Dio 53.17.1–2 but detested by the Romans themselves. Kienast (2009). 'Military dictator': Goldsworthy (2014), p. 478. 'Rome's first emperor': Everett (2006). 'Warlord': Goldsworthy (2014), pp. 480–81; Fuhrmann (2010), p. 123. 'Monarchy': Alston (2015), p. 299; Bleicken (2015), p. 613. 'Military regime': Alston (2015), pp. 242–43.
3. Bleicken (2015), p. 613.
4. Dio 53.17.4; Tac., *Ann.* 1.1. See Ch. 2, n. 148.
5. Syme (1939a), pp. 311–13.
6. Alston (2015), p. 300.
7. Annals in Latin available to Augustus in his youth would have likely included those of Q. Fabius Pictor, Cn. Gellius, P. Mucius Scaevola and Sempronius Asellio. Their books, now mostly lost, only survive as fragments or as references in other written accounts. The works of Livy and Sallust were yet to be written. Augustus could also read Greek and would likely have had access to Herodotus and Thucydides. The influential Greek philosopher and natural scientist Aristotle wrote there was truth in the saying that he who has never learned to obey cannot be a good commander (Aristotle, *Politics* 3.1277b).

388 *Augustus at War*

8. Polybius, *Hist.* 31.29.1: λοιποῦ δ᾽ ὄντος τοῦ κατὰ τὴν ἀνδρείαν μέρους καὶ κυριωτάτου σχεδὸν ἐν πάσῃ μὲν πολιτείᾳ μάλιστα δ᾽ ἐν τῇ Ῥώμῃ, μεγίστην ἔδει καὶ τὴν ἄσκησιν περὶ τοῦτο τὸ μέρος ποιήσασθαι.

9. E.g. Asklepiodotos' *Taktika*. For a discussion of ancient military handbooks see Campbell (1987).

10. Plutarch, *Sulla* 6.6, 14.1, 14.6, 17.1, 23.2, 37.1. The greatest extant Roman war reports are, without doubt, Iulius Caesar's *Commentaries on the Gallic War* and *Commentaries on the Civil War*.

11. Listed as leadership traits by the Army of the United States in FM 6–22 (2006), pp. 2–4.

12. Army Regulations 600–100 (2007), p. 1. For a discussion of leadership in war see Vermillion (1987).

13. Galinsky (2012), pp. 23, 48 and 179.

14. For a discussion of the importance of the allusion for Augustus to Aeneas see Alston (2015), pp. 294–97; Galinksy (2012), pp. 144–48; and Hard (2003), p. 594.

15. Wardle (2005), pp. 190–91.

16. Tac., *Ann.* 1.9–10.

17. For a discussion of how the image of Kleopatra changed under Augustus see Wyke (2009).

18. Gruen (1996), p. 189.

19. *RG* 34: *postquam bella civilia oxstinxeram, perconsensum universorum potitus rerum omnium, rem publicam ex pea potestate in senatus populique Romani arbitrium transtuli.*

20. On the evolution of the legal meaning of the term *provincia* see Drogula (2015), esp. pp. 346–68.

21. Drogula (2015), p. 308, notes this extended command also had precedents in Scipio Africanus (203 BCE), Antonius Creticus (74 BCE), Pompeius Magnus (77 BCE) and Acilius Glabrio (67 BCE).

22. *RG* 3.

23. Adapted from Peter Feaver, 'What is Grand Strategy and Why Do We Need it?', *Foreign Policy*, 8 April 2009 (online at http://foreignpolicy.com/2009/04/08/what-is-grand-strategy-and-why-do-we-need-it/ (accessed 29 February 2016))

24. Dio 53.19.2–4: πρότερον μὲν γὰρ ἔς τε τὴν βουλὴν καὶ ἐς τὸν δῆμον πάντα, καὶ εἰ πόρρω που συμβαίη, ἐσεφέρετο· καὶ διὰ τοῦτο πάντες τε αὐτὰ ἐμάνθανον καὶ πολλοὶ συνέγραφον, κἀκ τούτου καὶ ἡ ἀλήθεια αὐτῶν, εἰ καὶ τὰ μάλιστα καὶ φόβῳ τινὰ καὶ χάριτι φιλίᾳ τε καὶ ἔχθρᾳ τισὶν ἐρρήθη, παρὰ γοῦν τοῖς ἄλλοις τοῖς τὰ αὐτὰ γράψασι τοῖς τε ὑπομνήμασι τοῖς δημοσίοις τρόπον τινὰ εὑρίσκετο. ἐκ δὲ δὴ τοῦ χρόνου ἐκείνου τὰ μὲν πλείω κρύφα καὶ δι᾽ ἀπορρήτων γίγνεσθαι ἤρξατο, εἰ δέ πού τινα καὶ δημοσιευθείη, ἀλλὰ ἀνεξέλεγκτά γε ὄντα ἀπιστεῖται· καὶ γὰρ λέγεσθαι καὶ πράττεσθαι πάντα πρὸς τὰ τῶν ἀεὶ κρατούντων τῶν τε παραδυναστευόντων σφίσι βουλήματα ὑποπτεύεται. καὶ κατὰ τοῦτο πολλὰ μὲν οὐ γιγνόμενα θρυλεῖται, πολλὰ δὲ καὶ πάνυ συμβαίνοντα ἀγνοεῖται, πάντα δὲ ὡς εἰπεῖν ἄλλως πως ἢ ὡς πράττεται διαθροεῖται. καὶ μέντοι καὶ τὸ τῆς ἀρχῆς μέγεθος τό τε τῶν πραγμάτων πλῆθος δυσχερεστάτην τὴν ἀκρίβειαν αὐτῶν παρέχεται.

25. Millar (1982), p. 2; Kagan (2006), pp. 352–54.

26. Livy, *AUC* 36.7.21: *de ratione universi belli*. For a discussion on terminology see Wheeler (1993b), pp. 217–18.

27. Harris (1979), p. 252.

28. Harris (1979), p. 253.

29. Harris (1979), p. 254. Mary Beard notes, 'it was a culture in which it wasn't war that broke out; it was peace that broke out' (online at https://www.youtube.com/watch?v=wCIfRY8wzfE – accessed 29 February 2016).

30. E.g. Plut., *Crass.* 18. For a discussion see Harris (1979), p. 252.

31. *RG* 1; *cf.* 35.

32. Gruen (1996), p. 188.

33. For a discussion of critical views of Luttwak see Wheeler (1993a and 1993b) discussing works by Issacs (1990), Mann (1974), Millar (1982) and Whittaker (1994).

34. Evolving strategy: Galinsky (2012), p. 89; Rich (2002), p. 164. Pragmatism: Gruen (1996), critiqued by Galinsky (2012), p. 88.

35. Gruen (1996), p. 188.

36. Luttwak (1996), pp. 7–50. For critiques of his 'three system' model see Campbell (2010); Kagan (2006); and Wheeler (1993a and 1993b).

37. Luttwak (1976), pp. 49–50.
38. Luttwak (1976), p. 192.
39. For other authors supporting this view see Gruen (1996), p. 194, n. 255.
40. Wheeler (1993a), p. 24.
41. Syme (1934b), p. 353; Wells (1972), p. 249.
42. For a discussion of Roman frontiers see Elton (1996), esp. p. 4 and 111; *cf.* Wheeler (1993a), p. 25.
43. *RG* 26: *Omnium provinciarum populi Romani, quibus finitimae fuerunt gentes quae non parerent imperio nostro, fines auxi.*
44. Galinsky (2012), p. 88; Gruen (1996), p. 189. On the role of policy in grand strategy see Kagan (2006), p. 348.
45. For a discussion of the comparison see Adams Holland (1947) and Avery (1957).
46. Gruen (1996), pp. 188–89.
47. Galinsky (2012), p. 89; Rich (2002), p. 154.
48. Tac., *Ann.* 1.9: *mari Oceano aut amnibus longinquis saeptum.*
49. Tac., *Ann.* 1.11: *addideratque consilium coercendi intra terminos imperii.*
50. For a full discussion of Augustus' diplomacy with Parthia see Campbell (1993), pp. 213–28.
51. App., *Bell. Civ.* 2.110. Plut., *Brut.* 25; *Caes.* 58. Suet., *Div. Iul.* 44.
52. Joseph., *Ant. Iud.* 18.39–43. The slave girl Musa (or Mousa) was elevated by Frahâta to the status of most favoured wife; she bore him a son, known as Frahâtak or Phraataces ('Little Phraates') – an ancient romance with a fairy tale ending.
53. *RG* 27: *Armeniam maiorum, interfecto rege eius Artaxe, cum possem facere provinciam, malui maiorum nostrorum exemplo regnum id Tigrani, regis Artavasdis filio, nepoti autem Tigranis regis, per Ti. Neronem trader, qui tum mihi privignus erat. Et eandem gentem postea desciscentem et rebellantem domitam per Gaium filium meum regi Ariobarzani, regis Medorum Artabazi filio, regendam tradidi et post eius mortem filio eius Artavasdi. Quo interfecto, Tigranem qui erat ex regio genere Armeniorum oriundus, in id regnum misi.*
54. Mattern (1999), p. 122 and 171; Gruen (1996), pp. 192–97.
55. Mattern (1999), pp. 217–18; Dobson (2009), p. 25; Rich (2002), pp. 161–62.
56. Dobson (2009), p. 25. Hostages: Caes., *Bell. Gall.* 2.35.1, 3.27.1–2, 4.21.5, 4.27.1 and 5–6, 4.31.1, 4.38.3, 5.22.4, 5.23.1. *Obses* also means a guarantee. Weapons: Caes., *Bell. Gall.* 1.27.3, 2.13.1, 2.31–33 (*cf.* 2.28.3), 3.22.1, 3.23.1, 7.12.3–4, 7.89.3.
57. *RG* 32; Suet., *Div. Aug.* 43.4. Significantly, 'in his *Res Gestae* he wrote more about the pacification of Armenia and Parthia than of his policies in any other region' notes Rose (2005), pp. 21–22.
58. Powell (2016).
59. Mattern (1999), pp. 175–76.
60. Mattern (1999), pp. 175–76 and 184–85.
61. Cicero, *Off.* 1.36: *Ex quo intellegi potest nullum bellum esse iustum, nisi quod aut rebus repetitis geratur aut denuntiatum ante sit et indictum.*
62. For a discussion of fetial law and ceremonial see Wiedemann (1986) and Powell (2010).
63. Suet., *Div. Aug.* 21.2: *Nec ulli genti sine iustis et necessariis causis bellum intulit, tantumque afuit a cupiditate quoquo modo imperium vel bellicam gloriam augendi, ut quorundam barbarorum principes in aede Martis Ultoris iurare coegerit mansuros se in fide ac pace quam peterent, a quibusdam vero novum genus obsidum, feminas, exigere temptaverit, quod neglegere marum pignora sentiebat; et tamen potestatem semper omnibus fecit, quotiens vellent, obsides recipiendi. Neque aut crebrius aut perfidiosius rebellantis graviore umquam ultus est poena, quam ut captivos sub lege venundaret, ne in vicina regione servirent neve intra tricensimum annum liberarentur.*
64. *RG* 3: *Externas gentes, quibus tuto ignosci potuit, conservare quam excidere malui.*
65. *RG* 27.
66. *RG* 26: *Omnium provinciarum populi Romani, quibus finitimae fuerunt gentes quae non parerent imperio nostro, fines auxi. Gallias et Hispanias provincias, item Germaniam qua includit Oceanus a Gadibus ad ostium Albis fluminis pacavi. Alpes a regione ea, quae proxima est Hadriano mari, ad Tuscum pacari feci. nulli genti bello per iniuriam inlato. Cf. Tac., Ann.* 1.9.
67. *RG* 26: *Classis mea per Oceanum ab ostio Rheni ad solis orientis regionem usque ad fines Cimbrorum navigavit, ~ quo neque terra neque mari quisquam Romanus ante id tempus adit, Cimbrique et Charydes*

et Semnones et eiusdem tractus alii Germanorum populi per legatos amicitiam mean et populi Romani petierunt.

68. *RG* 27: *Aegyptum imperio populi Romani adieci.*

69. Tac., *Ann.* 1.11: *solam divi Augusti mentem tantae molis capacem: se in partem curarum ab illo vocatum experiendo didicisse quam arduum, quam subiectum fortunae regendi cuncta onus. proinde in civitate tot inlustribus viris subnixa non ad unum omnia deferrent: plures facilius munia rei publicae sociatis laboribus exsecuturos.*

70. Africa, Asia and Europe.

71. The insight is credited to A.D. Chandler Jr. (1962), *Strategy and Structure: Chapters in the History of the American Industrial Enterprise*, Cambridge, Mass: MIT Press.

72. Drogula (2015), pp. 368–69. See also Ch. 2, n. 18. On the differences in duties of a deputy commander and his commander-in-chief see Caes., *Bell. Civ.* 3.51: 'The duties of a legate and of a commander are different: the one ought to do everything under direction, the other should take measures freely in the general interest.' | *Aliae enim sunt legati partes atque imperatoris: alter omnia agere ad praescriptum, alter libere ad summam rerum consulere debet.*

73. Drogula (2015), pp. 306–09 and 336.

74. Drogula (2015), pp. 310, 332–37.

75. Drogula (2015), pp. 309–10, who notes the Senate preferred to divide wars among several commanders with smaller jurisdictions, especially of those which could be lucrative, to avoid one man becoming wealthy from the assignment.

76. Dio 53.12.1–2, 53.13.4–7, 53.14.1–4; Strabo, *Geog.* 17.3.25; Suet., *Div. Aug.* 47.

77. Dio 53.13.2–3. Suet., *Div. Aug.* 36 notes Augustus introduced regulations that 'magistrates should not be sent to the provinces immediately after laying down their office; that a fixed sum should be allowed the proconsuls for mules and tents, which it was the custom to contract for and charge to the State' | *ne magistratus deposito honore statim in provincias mitterentur, ut proconsulibus ad mulos et tabernacula, quae publice locari solebant.*

78. Dio 53.13.3.

79. Ulpian, *Dig.* 1.18.13.pr. *Pacata atque quieta.*

80. Dio 53.13.5–6.

81. For a discussion of the army as a police force see Fuhrmann (2011), pp. 4–8.

82. Joseph., *Bell. Iud.* 2.117.

83. Dio 53.13.2–3; *cf.* Dio 55.28.1–2. Suet., *Div. Aug* 23.1.

84. Dio 53.13.2–4. Six *fasces* were normally the mark of a praetor. On the scholarly debate about the number of *lictores* assigned see Drogula (2015), pp. 335 and 369.

85. Dio 53.13.2–3.

86. Dio 53.13.2.

87. Joseph., *Bell. Iud.* 2.117, *Ant. Iud.* 18.1–2.

88. Drogula (2015), p. 370.

89. Tac., *Ann.* 1.3.

90. Syme (1939a), p. 360 and pp. 366–67.

91. Vell. Pat. 2.127.1–2: *quibus novitas familiae haut obstitit quominus ad multiplicis consulatus triumphosque et complura eveherentur sacerdotia. Etenim magna negotia magnis adiutoribus egent interestque rei publicae quod usu necessarium est, dignitate eminere utilitatemque auctoritate muniri.*

92. Tac., *Ann.* 1.3: *domi res tranquillae, eadem magistratuum vocabula; iuniores post Actiacam victoriam, etiam senes plerique inter bella civium nati: quotus quisque reliquus qui rem publicam vidisset?*

93. Syme (1939a), p. 328.

94. *RG* 8. See Syme (1939a), p. 362.

95. Suet., *Div. Aug.* 38.2: *Liberis senatorum, quo celerius rei p. assuescerent, protinus a virili toga latum clavum induere et curiae interesse permisit militiamque auspicantibus non tribunatum modo legionum, sed et praefecturas alarum dedit; ac ne qui expers castrorum esset, binos plerumque laticlavios praeposuit singulis alis.*

96. Syme (1939a), pp. 356–357 and 367.

97. Suet., *Div. Aug.* 46: *Ac necubi aut honestorum deficeret copia aut multitudinis suboles, equestrem militiam petentis etiam ex commendatione publica cuiusque oppidi ordinabat.*

98. Dio 52.25.7.
99. Suet., *Div. Aug.* 38.3.
100. Dio 55.9.10.
101. Suet., *Div. Aug.* 43.2: *Sed et Troiae lusum edidit frequentissime maiorum minorumque puerorum, prisci decorique moris existimans clarae stirpis indolem sic notescere. In hoc ludicro Nonium Asprenatem lapsu debilitatum aureo torque donavit passusque est ipsum posterosque Torquati ferre cognomen.*
102. Suet., *Div. Aug.* 25.4: *Nihil autem minus perfecto duci quam festinationem temeritatemque convenire arbitrabatur. Crebro itaque illa iactabat: Σπευδε βραδέως. Ἀσφανς γὰρ ἐστ᾿ ἀμείνον ἡ θρασὺς στρατηλάτης. Et: sat celeriter fieri quidquid fiat satis bene.*
103. Suet., *Div. Aug.* 51.1.
104. Cic., *Ad Att.* 6.2.4; *Cael.* 18.42; *de Nat. Deor.* 2.37.92; 3.35.85; *de Off.* 3.25.96.
105. Agrippa: Powell (2015), p. 129, 150, 188 and 211. Tiberius: Cowan (2009), pp. 480–81, Levick??
106. Suet., *Nero* 4: *Verum arrogans, profusus, immitis censorem L. Plancum via sibi decedere aedilis coegit; praeturae consulatusque honore equites R. matronasque ad agendum mimum produxit in scaenam. Venationes et in Circo et in omnibus urbis regionibus dedit munus etiam gladiatorium, sed tanta saevitia, ut necesse fuerit Augusto clam frustra monitum edicto coercere.*
107. Suet., *Div. Aug.* 48. For the role of client kings see Braund (1984b), pp. 10–12 and 40–45.
108. Suet., *Div. Aug.* 38.1: *Nec parcior in bellica virtute honoranda, super triginta ducibus iustos triumphos et aliquanto pluribus triumphalia ornamenta decernenda curavit.*
109. Syme (1939a), p. 327.
110. E.g. *ILS* 918 (Tibur) = *EJ* 199.
111. Tac., *Ann.* 1.3.
112. For a discussion of the issues see Syme (1939a), pp. 308–09.
113. Suet., *Div. Aug.* 24.1: *Disciplinam severissime rexit.* Augustus frowned upon allowing officers to bring family members into army camps: 'it was with great reluctance that he allowed even his *legati* to visit their wives, and then only in the winter season.' | *ne legatorum quidem cuiquam, nisi gravate hibernisque demum mensibus, permisit uxorem intervisere* (Suet., Div. Aug. 24.1). Nevertheless, it seems Livia Drusilla often accompanied him on his travels.
114. Drogula (2015), pp. 48–49.
115. Suet., *Div. Aug.* 24.2: *Decimam legionem contumacius parentem cum ignominia totam dimisit, item alias immodeste missionem postulantes citra commoda emeritorum praemiorum exauctoravit. Cohortes, si quae cessissent loco, decimatas hordeo pavit. Centuriones statione deserta, itidem ut manipulares, capitali animadversione puniit, pro cetero delictorum genere variis ignominis adfecit, ut stare per totum diem iuberet ante praetorium, interdum tunicatos discinctosque, nonnumquam cum decempedis, vel etiam cespitem portantes.*
116. Suet., *Div. Aug.* 25.1: *Neque post bella civilia aut in contione aut per edictum ullos militum commilitones appellabat, sed milites, ac ne a filiis quidem aut privignis suis imperio praeditis aliter appellari passus est, ambitiosius id existimans, quam aut ratio militaris aut temporum quies aut sua domusque suae maiestas postularet. Cf.* Iulius Caesar's use of *quirites* ('citizens') reported by Suet., *Div. Iul.* 70.
117. Suet., *Div. Aug.* 53.1; Orosius, *Against the Pagans* 6.22: *domini appellationem ut homo declinauit.*
118. Suet., *Div. Aug.* 67.1: *Patronus dominusque non minus severus quam facilis et clemens multos libertorum in honore et usu maximo habuit, ut Licinum et Celadum aliosque.* Though it should be noted Augustus never invited his freedman to dine with him, with the exception of one Menas: Suet., *Div. Aug.* 74.1.
119. Suet., *Div. Aug.* 51.1.
120. *RG* 3: *victorque omnibus veniam petentibus civibus peperci.*
121. Suet., *Div. Aug.* 67.1: *Cosmum servum gravissime de se opinantem non ultra quam compedibus coercuit.*
122. Suet., *Div. Aug.* 67.1.
123. Suet., *Div. Aug.* 66.2.
124. Suet., *Div. Aug.* 66.3.
125. Suet., *Div. Aug.* 25.4: *Proelium quidem aut bellum suscipiendum omnino negabat, nisi cum maior emolumenti spes quam damni metus ostenderetur. Nam minima commoda non minimo sectantis discrimine similes aiebat esse aureo hamo piscantibus, cuius abrupti damnum nulla captura pensari posset.*

126. Tac., *Germ.* 2: *Quis porro, praeter periculum horridi et ignoti maris, Asia aut Africa aut Italia relicta Germaniam peteret, informem terris, asperam caelo, tristem cultu adspectuque, nisi si patria sit?*
127. Tac., *Germ.* 1: *Germania omnis a Gallis Raetisque et Pannoniis Rheno et Danuvio fluminibus, a Sarmatis Dacisque mutuo metu aut montibus separatur: cetera Oceanus ambit, latos sinus et insularum inmensa spatia complectens, nuper cognitis quibusdam gentibus ac regibus, quos bellum aperuit. Rhenus, Raeticarum Alpium inaccesso ac praecipiti vertice ortus, modico flexu in occidentem versus septentrionali Oceano miscetur.*
128. On what is known about ancient maps see Brodersen (1995) and Syme (1988).
129. Pliny, *Nat Hist.* 3.17. For a discussion of the *Orbis Terrarum* see Powell (2015), pp. 135–37 and 185–86.
130. Pliny, *Nat. Hist.* 4.98: *Toto autem mari ad Scaldim usque fluvium Germaniae accolunt gentes, haud explicabili mensura: tam inmodica prodentium discordia est. Graeci et quidam nostri | XXV | oram Germaniae tradiderunt, Agrippa cum Raetia et Norico longitudinem DCXXXVI, latitudinem CCXLVIII, Raetiae prope unius maiore latitudine, sane circa excessum eius subactae; nam Germania multis postea annis nec tota percognita est.*
131. E.g. Strabo, *Geog.* 7.5.2–12.
132. Dzino (2008c), p. 699.
133. Tac., *Ann.* 4.5.
134. Dio 55.34.3: πρὸς μέντοι τὰς τῶν πολέμων διαχειρίσεις οὕτως ἔρρωτο ὥσθ᾽, ἵν᾽ ἐγγύθεν καὶ ἐπὶ τοῖς Δελμάταις καὶ ἐπὶ τοῖς Παννονίοις πᾶν ὅ τι χρὴ συμβουλεύειν ἔχῃ, πρὸς Ἀρίμινον ἐξώρμησε.
135. Tac., *Ann.* 1.46. Suet., *Div. Aug.* 47.
136. Suet., *Div. Aug.* 49.3: *Et quo celerius ac sub manum adnuntiari cognoscique posset, quid in provincia quaque gereretur, iuvenes primo modicis intervallis per militaris vias, dehinc vehicula disposuit. Commodius id visum est, ut qui a loco idem perferunt litteras, interrogari quoque, si quid res exigant, possint.*
137. Seneca, *Epp.* 83.14. Millar (1982), p. 9.
138. Suet., *Div. Aug.* 84.1–2.
139. Suet., *Div. Aug.* 88: *Quotiens autem per notas scribit, B pro A, C pro B ac deinceps eadem ratione sequentis litteras ponit; pro X autem duplex A.* Cf. Dio 51.3.7. According to Suet., *Div. Iul.* 56.6 Caesar used a shift of three cipher.
140. Suet., *Div. Aug.* 50: *In diplomatibus libellisque et epistulis signandis initio sphinge usus est, mox imagine Magni Alexandri, novissime sua, Dioscuridis manu scalpta, qua signare insecuti quoque principes perseverarunt. Ad epistulas omnis horarum quoque momenta nec diei modo sed et noctis, quibus datae significarentur, addebat.*
141. Dio 51.3.5–6.
142. Suet., *Div. Aug.* 50: *Ad epistulas omnis horarum quoque momenta nec diei modo sed et noctis, quibus datae significarentur, addebat.*
143. Iulius Caesar submitted written reports in the form of a notebook rather than as a scroll according to Suet., *Div. Iul.* 56.6.
144. *RG* 31–33; Strabo, *Geog.* 4.5.3. See Millar (1982), pp. 11–12.
145. Keaveney (2007), pp. 71–77.
146. *RG* 3.
147. *RG* 28: *Italia autem XXVIII colonias, quae vivo me celeberrimae et frequentissimae fuerunt.*
148. For a discussion of the function of *coloniae* see Yeo (1959).
149. *RG* 15.
150. Caes., *Bell. Gall.* 1.52.
151. Goldsworthy (1996), pp. 140–41.
152. Dio 53.15.1.
153. Suet., *Div. Aug.* 38.2.
154. Tac., *Ann.* 1.9.
155. Tac., *Hist.* 1.55.
156. For the breakdown of the elements of the reconstructed budget see Alston (2014), p. 318.
157. Campbell (1984), pp. 162–63; cf. Alston (2014), pp. 316–17.
158. Duncan-Jones (1982), p. 6.

159. Duncan-Jones (1990), p. 44.
160. *RG* 17.
161. The *centesima rerum venalium* was introduced after the Civil War, the *quinta et vicesima venalium mancipiorum* was introduced in 7 CE and the *vicesima hereditatum* funded the *Aerarium Militare* of 6 CE.
162. Hispania Citerior: Jones (1972 and 1976); Noricum: Alföldy (1974), pp. 34, 37 and 50.
163. For a discussion of the political significance of the reforms see Raaflaub (2009), pp. 203–28.
164. Gilliver (2007), p. 185, cites legions raised in 86 BCE by Valerius Flaccus to fight Mithridates who had served twenty years when Pompeius Magnus arrived to assume command, whereas Metellus Creticus' legions, formed to combat pirates in 68 BCE, served only three years.
165. Alston (2015), p. 317. Raising the length of service to twenty-five years would reduce the number still further to 110 men and cost just HS1.3 million (saving 32 per cent).
166. Keaveney (2007), p. 98.
167. Suet., *Div. Aug.* 49: *ne aut aetate aut inopia post missionem sollicitari ad res novas possent.*
168. Gilliver (2007), p. 186.
169. *RG* 16.
170. Gilliver, (2007), p. 190.
171. Webster (1994), p. 117.
172. Tac., *Ann.*1.20.
173. Vell. Pat. 2.120.3.
174. For a discussion of the positioning of forts along rivers see Sommer (2009), p. 111.
175. Dobson (2009), pp. 26–29.
176. For a discussion of site, topography and gates see von Schnurbein (2000), pp. 29–31.
177. For a discussion of internal buildings see von Schnurbein (2000), pp. 30–37.
178. *CIL* XIV, 3602 (Tibur) = *ILS* 950.
179. For a discussion of helmet evolution see D'Amato (2009), pp. 109–21; Bishop (2006), pp. 100–06.
180. For a discussion of body armour evolution see D'Amato (2009), pp. 122–44; Bishop (2006), pp. 95–100.
181. Suet., *Div. Aug.* 25.3: *Dona militaria, aliquanto facilius phaleras et torques, quicquid auro argentoque constaret, quam vallares ac murales coronas, quae honore praecellerent, dabat; has quam parcissime et sine ambitione ac saepe etiam caligatis tribuit.*
182. Suet., *Div. Aug.* 38.1.
183. *CIL* X, 4862 (Venafrum) = *ILS* 2690.
184. *CIL* V, 4365.
185. Pliny, *Nat. Hist.* 34.139; Dio 42.29.2, 44.51.1.
186. Ulpian, *Dig.* 48.6.1; *cf.* Dion. Hal., *Ant. Rom.* 4.48.1. On Roman law relating to ownership and carrying of weapons and the law of *vis* see Nippel (1995), p. 55.
187. Dio 52.21.1–2; Tac., l.c.; Suet., *Div. Aug.* 37.
188. Suet., *Div. Aug.* 43.1.
189. Suet., *Div. Aug.* 23.1.
190. *RG* 25.
191. Grünewald (2004), pp. 14–17; Shaw (1984), p. 6.
192. Suet., *Div. Aug.* 32.1: *Pleraque pessimi exempli in perniciem publicam aut ex consuetudine licentiaque bellorum civilium duraverant aut per pacem etiam exstiterant. Nam et grassatorum plurimi palam se ferebant succincti ferro, quasi tuendi sui causa, et rapti per agros viatores sine discrimine liberi servique ergastulis possessorum supprimebantur, et plurimae factiones titulo collegi novi ad nullius non facinoris societatem coibant.*
193. Suet., *Div. Aug.* 32.1: *Igitur grassaturas dispositis per opportuna loca stationibus inhibuit, ergastula recognovit, collegia praeter antiqua et legitima dissolvit.*
194. Dio 54.22.1–3.
195. Vell. Pat. 2.126.3. *Cf.* Epictetus 3.13.9. For a discussion of philosophers' attitudes to war see Sidebottom (1993).
196. Orosius, *Against the Pagans* 6.22.
197. Gruen (2006), p. 188.
198. Praeneste: *CIL* XIV, 2898. Other examples: *ILS* 3787, 3789; *IGRR* IV, 1173.

199. Altar: *CIL* XII, 4335; for a discussion see Weinstock (1960), p. 56 and fig. 1 (p. 54). *Colonia*: Strabo, *Geog.* 3.2.15; this may be Pax Iulia (modern Beja) in Lusitania.
200. *RG* 13: *Ianum Quirinum, quem clausum esse maiores nostri voluerunt, cum per totum imperium populi Romani terra marique esset parta victoriis pax.*
201. *RG* 13: *cum prius quam nascerer, a condita urbe bis omnino clausum fuisse prodatur memoriae, ter me principe senatus claudendum esse censuit.* See Ch. 1, n. 284.
202. Orosius, *Against the Pagans* 6.22.
203. Baetican inscription: *EJ* 42 = *ILS* 103: *Imp. Caesari Augusto P. P. Hispania Ulterior Baetica quod beneficio eius et perpetua cura provincia pacata est. Auri P. C.* Koinon: *EJ* 98 line 36 = *OGIS* 458.
204. Dio 56.30.3.
205. For a more detailed guided tour of Augustan Rome see Favro (1996), pp. 252–80.
206. Wallace-Hadrill (1993), pp. 53–55 and fig. 17: he notes 'there was no room on the plaque for future names, and the list was a museum piece'. For a full discussion of the architecture of the *Forum Romanum* at the time of Augustus see Gorski and Packer (2015), pp. 3–36.
207. Suet., *Div. Aug.* 29.
208. For a discussion of the verticality of Augustan architecture see Favro (1996), pp. 150–55.
209. For the significance of the *Horologium-Solarium Augusti* see Holliday (1990). The 21.79m (71.5 ft)-high obelisk was the *gnomon of the solarium* – a sundial for marking the hours of the day – designed by the mathematician Facundus Novius (Pliny, *Nat. Hist.* 36.72). It was erected in Rome in 10 BCE on the twentieth anniversary of Augustus' conquest of Egypt. In contrast to the hieroglyphs covering the obelisk itself, the rose-coloured Aswan granite base is inscribed in Latin. The last phrase of the inscription reads: 'With Aegyptus having been brought under the control of the Roman People, he [Augustus] gave this gift to the Sun' | *Aegypto in potestatem Populi Romani redacta Soli donum dedit.* It was originally erected in Heliopolis, Egypt in the early 6th century BCE by Neferibra Psamtik II. The monument is now known as Obelisk of Montecitorio.
210. *RG* 12: *Cum ex Hispania Galliaque, rebus in iis provincis prospere gestis, Romam redi Ti. Nerone P. Quinctilio consulibus, aram Pacis Augustae senatus proreditu meo consacrandam censuit ad campam Martium, in qua magistratus et sacerdotes et virgines Vestales anniversarium sacrificium facere decrevit.*
211. *Pax Augusta*: De Grummond (1990), but Gruen (1996), p. 194, n. 253, is unconvinced. For the identification with Venus see Galinsky (1966), for Italia see Van Buren (1913). For advocates for Tellus and Ceres see De Grummond (1990), p. 663, n. 2.
212. De Grummond (1990), pp. 674–76 notes that the relief from Carthage in the Louvre, long recognized as closely related to the *Ara Pacis* in Rome, also shows *Pax* without the *Horae*, but with similar seasonal allusions, for which see Spaeth (1994) who argues for an identification with Ceres in both sculptures.
213. Gruen (1996), p. 194.
214. For the case for Numa see Rehak (2001).
215. For the processions and sacrifices associated with the *Ara Pacis* see Elsner (1991).
216. Verg,. *Aen.* 8.678–713.
217. Hor., *Carm.* 1.36.
218. Kleiner (2005), pp. 207–17.
219. For a discussion about the statue and its meanings see Zanker (1990), pp. 188–92. For the claim that the provenance of the statue is disputed see Klynne and Liljenstolpe (2000).
220. On the hand gesture see Graf (1991), p. 41 citing Quintilian, 11.100: 'Wonder is best expressed as follows: the hand turns slightly upwards and the fingers are brought in to the palm, one after the other, beginning with the little finger; the hand is then opened and turned round by a reversal of this motion'. | *est admirationi conveniens ille gestus, quo manus modice supinata ac per singulos a minimo collecta digitos redeunte flexu simul explicatur atque convertitur.* Galinsky (2013), p. 76 suggests the statue shows Augustus addressing the troops at an *adlocutio*. Reeder (1997), pp. 90–94 suggests the right hand may once have held a laurel branch.
221. A later *dupondius* coin minted at Rome by Caligula (*RIC* I 57) depicts Germanicus Caesar in exactly this pose: standing, bare-headed and cuirassed, right-hand raised and the left holding an *aquila*. The inscription reads: 'SIGNIS RECEPT DEVICTIS GERM S C'. Germanicus would seem to be presented mimicking his grandfather. In the Second Century CE, Florus identified the return of military standards from Parthia in 20 BCE as *the* turning point in the struggle for the

Pax Augusta: 'The Parthians too, as though they repented of their victory, voluntarily returned the standards which they had won at the time of Crassus' defeat. Thus everywhere throughout the inhabited world there was firmly-established and uninterrupted peace or truce.' | *Parthi quoque, quasi victoriae paeniteret, rapta clade Crassiana signa ultro rettulere. Sic ubique certa atque continua totius generis humanis aut pax fuit aut pactio* (Florus, 2.34; cf. Forus, 2.21 and Dio 54.8.2–3).

222. Tac., *Ann.* 1.9.5; 1.10.4: *pacem sine dubio … verum cruentam.*
223. *RG* 4: *Ob res a me aut per legatos meos auspicis meis terra marique prospere gestas quinquageniens et quinquiens decrevit senatus supplicandum esse dis immortalibus.*
224. Compare maps in Cairns (1970), p. 25 and 42.
225. Woolf (1993), p. 186 and pp. 189–90.

Bibliography

Ancient Authors

Appian, *Bellum Civilum* (*Civil War*).

Appian, Ἰλλυρική (*Illyrike, Illyrian Wars*).

Ammianus Marcellinus, *Res Gestae a Fine Corneli Taciti* (*Roman History*).

Augustus, *Res Gestae* (*Deeds of Augustus*).

Aulus Gellius, *Noctes Atticae* (*Attic Nights*).

Caesar, *Commentarii de Bello Gallico* (*The Gallic War*).

Cassiodorus, Χρονικῶν (*Chronicles*).

Cassius Dio, Ῥωμαϊκὴ Ἱστορία (*Roman History*).

Cicero, *De Oratore* (*On Oratory*).

Cicero, *Epistulae ad Atticum* (*Letters to Atticus*).

Cicero, *De Legibus* (*On Law*).

Cornelius Nepos, *Corneli Nepoti Attici* (*Life of Atticus*).

Crinagoras, *Anthologia Palatina*.

Eutropius, *Breviarium Historiae Romanae* (*Brief History of the Romans*).

Florus, *Epitome de T. Livio Bellorum Omnium Annorum* (*Epitome of Livy*).

Frontinus, *De Aqueductu Urbis Romae* (*The Aqueducts of Rome*).

Frontinus, *Strategemata* (*On Generalship*).

Horace, *Carmina* (*Odes*).

Horace, *Carmen Saecularum* (*Century Ode*).

Horace, *Saturae* (*Satires*).

Josephus, *Antiquitates Iudaicae* (*Antiquities of the Jews*).

Josephus, *Bellum Iudaicum* (*Jewish War*).

Josephus, *Contra Apionem* (*Against Apion*).

Josephus, Ἱστορία Ἰουδαϊκοῦ Πολέμου πρός Ῥωμαίους (*Wars of the Jews* or *The History of the Destruction of Jerusalem*).

Livy, *Ab Urbe Condita* (*History from the Foundation of Rome*).

Livy, *Periochae* (*Extracts*).

Macrobius, *Saturnalia*.

Nikolaos of Damaskos, Βίος Καῖσαρος (*Life of Caesar*).

Obsequens, *Ab Anno Urbis Conditae Du Prodigiorum Liber* (*Book of Prodigies Since the Foundation of the City*).

Orosius, *Historiarum Adversum Paganos* (*History Against the Pagans*).

Ovid (?), *Consolatio ad Liviam* (*Poem of Consolation to Livia on the Death of Her Son Nero Drusus*).

Ovid, *Epistulae Ex Ponto* (*Letters from Pontus*).

Pliny, *Naturalis Historia* (*Natural History*).

Plutarch, Ἀντωνίος (*Life of Antonius*).

Plutarch, Βροῦτος (*Life of Brutus*).

Plutarch, Καῖσαρος (*Life of Iulius Caesar*).

Plutarch, Κράσσος (*Life of Crassus*).

Plutarch, Κικέρωνος (*Life of Cicero*).

Plutarch, Πομπήϊος (*Life of Pompeius Magnus*).

Plutarch, *De Invidia et Odio* (*On Envy and Hate*).

Polybius, Οἱ Ἱστορίες (*The Histories*).

Propertius, *Elegiae* (*Elegies*).

Ptolemy, Γεωγραφικὴ Ὑφήγησις (*Geography, Cosmographia*).

Seneca the Younger, *Controversiae* (*Debates*).

Seneca the Younger, *Epistulae* (*Letters*).

Servius, *In Vergilii Carmina Commentarii* (*Commentaries on Vergil's Poems*).

Strabo, Γεωγραφικά (*Geography*).

Suetonius, *Caligula* (*Life of Caligula*).

Suetonius, *Divus Augustus* (*Life of the Divine Augustus*).

Suetonius, *De Grammaticis et Rhetoribus* (*On Teachers of Grammar and Rhetoric*).

Suetonius, *Divus Claudius* (*Life of the Divine Claudius*).

Suetonius, *Divus Iulius* (*Life of the Divine Iulius Caesar*).

Suetonius, *Nero* (*Life of Nero*).

Suetonius, *Tiberius* (*Life of Tiberius*).

Tacitus, *Ab Excessu Divi Augusti* (*Annales, The Annals*).

Tacitus, *De Origine et Situ Germanorum* (*Germania*).

Vergil, *Aeneid* (*Aeneid*).

Ulpian, *Digesta* (*Digest*).

Valerius Maximus, *Factorum et Dictorum Memorabilium* (*Memorable Deeds and Sayings*).

Velleius Paterculus, *Historiae Romanae* (*Compendium of Roman History*).

Zonaras, Ἐπιτομὴ Ἱστοριῶν (*Extracts of History*).

Modern Authors

AA.VV. (1990), *Il bimillenario di Agrippa*, Atti delle XVII Giornate Filologiche Genovesi 1989, Genoa.

Abbott, F.F., Johnson, A.C. (1926), *Municipal Administration in the Roman Empire*, Princeton: Princeton University Press.

Abday, R., Harling, N. (2005), 'Two Important New Roman Coins', *The Numismatic Chronicle* (1966–) 165, 175–178.

Adams Holland, L. (1947), 'Aeneas-Augustus of Prima Porta', *Transactions and Proceedings of the American Philological Association* 78, 276–84.

Adler, W. (1993), *Studien zur germansichen Bewaffnung: Waffenmitgabe und Kampfesweise im Niederelbegebiet und im Freien Germanien um Christi Geburt*, Bonn: Saarbrücker Beiträge zur Altertumskunde.

Africa, T.W. (1971), 'Urban Violence in Imperial Rome', *Journal of Interdisciplinary History* 2.1, 3–21.

Alföldi, A. (1976), *Oktavians Aufstieg zur Macht*, Bonn: Habelt.

Alföldy, G. (1974), *Noricum*, London: Routledge and Kegan Paul.

Alföldy, G. (1996), 'Spain', in Bowman, A.K., Champlin, E., Lintott, A. (eds), *The Cambridge Ancient History Volume X: The Augustan Empire, 43 B.C.–A.D. 69* (Second Edition), Cambridge: Cambridge University Press, 449–63.

Alföldy, G. (2000a), 'Das neue Edikt des Augustus aus El Bierzo in Hispanien', *Zeitschrift für Papyrologie und Epigraphik* 131, 177–205.

Alföldy, G., Dobson, B., Eck, W. (2000b), *Kaiser, Heer und Gesellschaft in der Romischen Kaiserzeit*, Heidelberger Althistorische Beitrage Und Epigraphische Studien (Book 31), Stuttgart: Franz Steiner Verlag.

Allen, G.H. (1908), 'The Advancement of Officers in the Roman Army', *Supplementary Papers of the American School of Classical Studies in Rome* 2, 1–25.

Allen, S., Reynolds, W. (2001), *Celtic Warrior, 300BC–AD100*, Oxford: Osprey Publishing.

Allen, W. Jr. (1947), 'The Death of Agrippa Postumus', *Transactions and Proceedings of the American Philological Association* 78, 131–39.

Allison, J.E., Cloud, J.D. (1962), 'The *lex Julia Maiestatis*', *Latomus* 21.4 (October–December), 711–31.

Almagro-Gorbea, M., Lorrio, A.J. (2004), 'War and Society in the Celtiberian World', in Alberro, M. and Bettina Arnold, B. (eds), *Journal of Interdisciplinary Studies* 6: The Celts in the Iberian Peninsula, 73–112 (online at http://www4.uwm.edu/celtic/ekeltoi/volumes/vol6/6_2/gorbea_lorrio_6_2.pdf – accessed 29 February 2016).

Alonso-Núñez, J.M. (1987), 'An Augustan World History: The *Historiae Philippicae* of Pompeius Trogus', *Greece & Rome (Second Series)* 3.1 (April), 56–72.

Alston, R. (1994), 'Roman Military Pay from Caesar to Diocletian', *Journal of Roman Studies* 84, 113–23.

Alston, R. (2014), *Aspects of Roman History, 31 BC–AD 117* (Second edition), London: Routledge.

Ando, C. (2000), *Imperial Ideology and Provincial Loyalty in the Roman Empire*, Berkeley: University of California Press.

Army Regulation 600–100 (2007), *Army Leadership* (8 March), Washington, DC: Headquarters Department of the Army (online at http://armypubs.army.mil/epubs/pdf/r600_100.pdf – accessed 29 February 2016).

Atkinson, K.M.T. (1958), 'The Governors of the Province Asia in the Reign of Augustus', *Historia: Zeitschrift für Alte Geschichte* 7.3 (July), 300–30.

Austin, N.E., Rankov, N.B. (1995), *Exploratio: Military and Political Intelligence in the Roman World from the Second Punic War to the Battle of Adrianople*, London: Routledge.

Avery, W. T. (1957), 'Augustus and the "Aeneid"', *Classical Journal* 52.5 (Feb.), 225–29.

Baatz, D., Herrmann, F.-R. (eds) (2002), *Die Römer in Hessen*, (revised edition), Hamburg: Nikol Verlag.

Bacevic, A.J. (2005), *The New American Militarism: How Americans Are Seduced by War*, Oxford: Oxford University Press.

Badian, E. (1980), 'Notes on the *Laudatio* of Agrippa', *Classical Journal* 76.2 (December 1980–January 1981), 97–109.

Bálek, M, Šedo, O. (1996), 'Das Frühkaiserzeitliche Lager bei Mušov – Zeugnis eines augusteischen Feldzugs ins Marchgebiet?', *Germania* 74, 399–414.

Balsdon, J.P.V.D. (1933), 'The Successors of Augustus', *Greece & Rome* 2.6 (May), 161–69.

Balsdon, J.P.V.D. (1979), *Romans and Aliens*, London: Duckworth.

Bannon, C.J. (1997), *The Brothers of Romulus: Fraternal Pietas in Roman Law, Literature, and Society*, Princeton: Princeton University Press.

Barker, D. (1996), '"The Golden Age Is Proclaimed"? The *Carmen Saeculare* and the Renascence of the Golden Race', *Classical Quarterly New Series* 46.2, 434–46.

Barnes, T.D. (1974), 'The Victories of Augustus', *Journal of Roman Studies* 64, 21–26.

Barrett, A.A. (2002), *Livia: First Lady of Imperial Rome*, New Haven: Yale University Press.

Barrett, A.A. (2005), 'Aulus Caecina Severus and the Military Woman', *Historia: Zeitschrift für Alte Geschichte* 54.3, 301–14

Barrett, A.A. (2006), 'Augustus and the Governor's Wives', *Rheinisches Museum für Philologie* 149, 129–47.

Barton, C. (2007), 'The Price of Peace in Ancient Rome' in Raaflaub, K.A. (2007), *War and Peace in the Ancient World*, Oxford: Blackwell Publishing.

Bay, A. (1972), 'The Letters SC on Augustan *Aes* Coinage', *Journal of Roman Studies* 62, 111–22.

Beacham, R.C. (1999), *Spectacle Entertainments of Early Imperial Rome*, New Haven: Yale University Press.

Bean, G.E. (1979), *Aegean Turkey*, Second Edition, London: Ernest Benn.

Beard, M. (2007), *The Roman Triumph*, Cambridge, Mass.: Harvard University Press.

Becker, A., Rasbach, G. (2007), 'Neue Forschungsergebnisse der Grabunged in Lahnau-Walgirmes in Hessen', in Wamser, L., Flügel, C., Ziegaus, B. (2004), *Die Römer zwischen Alpen und Nordmeer*, Düsseldorf: Patmos Verlag, 38–40.

Becker, A., Rasbach, G. (2007), '*Städte in Germanien: Der Fundplatz Waldgirmes*' in Wiegels, R. (ed.): *Die Varusschlacht. Wendepunkt der Geschichte?* (Archäologie in Deutschland), Stuttgart: Theiss, 102–16.

Bell, S. (2008), 'Role Models in the Roman World', in *Memoirs of the American Academy in Rome. Supplementary Volumes* 7. Identity and Assimilation, 1–39.

Bell, M.J.V. (1965), 'Tactical Reform in the Roman Republican Army', *Historia: Zeitschrift für Alte Geschichte* 14.4 (October), 404–22.

Berke, S., Bérenger, D., Ilisch, P., *et al.* (2009), *Corpus der römischen Funde im europäischen Barbaricum, Deutschland, 7: Land Nordrhein-Westfalen, Landesteile Westfalen und Lippe*, Bonn: Habelt.

Bernegger, P.M. (1983), 'Affirmation of Herod's Death in 4 B.C.', *Journal of Theological Studies* 34, 526–31.

Berthelet, Y., Dalla Rosa, A. (2015), '*Summum imperium auspiciumque*. Une lecture critique', *Revue historique de droit français et étranger 2* (April–June), 267–84.

Besteman, J.C., Bos, J.M., Gerrets, D.A., Heidinga, H.A., de Koning, J. (1999), *The Excavations at Wijnaldum: Reports on Frisia in Roman and Medieval Times, Volume 1*, Rotterdam: Balkema.

Bingham, S.J. (1997), *The Praetorian Guard in the Political and Social Life of Julio-Claudian Rome*, University of British Columbia (unpublished doctoral thesis online at https://open.library.ubc.ca/cIRcle/collections/ubctheses/831/items/1.0099480 – accessed 29 February 2016).

Birch, R.A. (1981), 'The Settlement of 26 June A.D. 4 and Its Aftermath', *Classical Quarterly (New Series)* 31.2, 443–56.

Bishop, M.C. (2002), *Lorica Segmentata Volume I: A Handbook of Articulated Roman Plate Armour*, Chirnside: The Armatura Press (online at https://www.academia.edu/513011/Lorica_Segmentata_Volume_I_A_Handbook_of_Articulated_Roman_Plate_Armour – accessed 29 February 2016).

Bishop, M.C., Coulston, J.C.N. (2006), *Roman Military Equipment from the Punic Wars to the Fall of Rome*, Oxford: Oxbow Press.

Blázquez, J.M (1992), 'The Latest Work on the Export of Baetican Olive Oil to Rome and the Army', *Greece & Rome (Second Series)* 39.2 (October), 173–88.

Bleicken, J. (2015), *Augustus: The Biography*, London: Allen Lane.

Boatwright, M.T. (2000), *Hadrian and the Cities of the Roman Empire*, Princeton: Princeton University Press.

Borzsák, S. (1969), 'Das Germanicusbild des Tacitus', *Latomus* 28, 588–600.

Boschung, D. (1993), 'Die Bildnistypen der iulisch-claudischen Kaiserfamilie: ein kritischer Forschungsbericht', *Journal of Roman Archaeology* 6, 39–79.

Bosworth, B. (1999), 'Augustus, the *Res Gestae* and Hellenistic Theories of Apotheosis', *Journal of Roman Studies* 89, pp. 1–18.

Botsford, G.W. (1908), 'The *Lex Curiata*', *Political Science Quarterly* 23.3 (Sep.), 498–517.

Botsford, G.W. (1918), 'Roman Imperialism', *American Historical Review* 23.4 (July), 772–78.

Bowersock, G. (1964), 'Augustus on Aegina', *Classical Quarterly* 14, 120–21.

Bowersock, G. (1984), 'Augustus in the East: The Problem of the Succession', in Fergus Millar and Erich Segal (eds) *Caesar Augustus: Seven Aspects*, Oxford, 169–88.

Bowman, A.K., Champlin, E., Linott, A. (1996) (Second Edition), *The Cambridge Ancient History Vol. X: The Augustan Empire, 43BC–AD69*, Cambridge: Cambridge University Press.

Boyce, A.A. (1942), 'The Origin of *ornamenta triumphalia*', *Classical Philology* 37.2 (April), 130–41.

Brandon, C., Hohlfelder, R.L., Oleson, J.P. (2008), 'The Concrete Construction of the Roman Harbours of Baiae and Portus Iulius: The ROMACONS 2006 field season', *International Journal of Nautical Archaeology* 37.2 (September), 374–79.

Braund, D.C. (1984a), 'North African Rulers and the Roman Military Paradigm', *Hermes* 112.2 (Second Quarter.), 255–56.

Braund, D.C. (1984b), *Rome and the Friendly King: The Character of Client Kingship*, Beckenham: Croom Helm.

Braunert, H. (1957), 'Der römische Provinzialzensus und der Schätzungsbericht des Lukas-Evangeliums', *Historia: Zeitschrift für Alte Geschichte* 6, Stuttgart: Franz Steiner Verlag, 192–214.

Breeze, D.J. (1969), 'The Organization of the Legion: The First Cohort and the *Equites Legionis*', *Journal of Roman Studies* 59.1/2, 50–55

Breeze, D.J. (1976), 'A Note on the Use of the Titles *Optio* and *Magister* below the Centurionate during the Principate', *Britannia* 7, 127–33.

Brent, B.D. (1990), 'Bandit Highlands and Lowland Peace: The Mountains of Isauricia-Cilicia', *Journal of the Economic and Social History of the Orient* 33.3, 237–70.

Brodersen, K. (1995), *Terra Incognita: Studien zur römischen Raumerfassung*, Spudasmata 59, 268–87.

Brogan, O. (1936), 'Trade between the Roman Empire and the Free Germans', *Journal of Roman Studies* 26 Part 2, 195–222.

Broomwich, J. (1993), *The Roman Remains of Southern France: A Guidebook*, London: Routledge.

Broughton, T.R.S (1933), 'Some Notes on the War with the Homonadeis', *American Journal of Philology* 54.2, 134–44.

Broughton, T.R.S. (1935), 'Some Non-Colonial *Coloni* of Augustus', *Transactions and Proceedings of the American Philological Association* 66, 18–24.

Brunt, P.A. (1962), 'The Army and the Land in the Roman Revolution', *Journal of Roman Studies* 52 Parts 1 and 2, 69–86.

Brunt, P.A. (1963), 'Review of *Die Aussenpolitik des Augustus und die Augusteische Dichtung* by Hans D. Meyer', Journal of Roman Studies 53, Parts 1 and 2, 170–76.

Brunt, P.A., Moore, J.M. (1967), Res Gestae Divi Augusti: *The Achievements of the Divine Augustus*, Oxford: Oxford University Press.

Brunt, P.A. (1971), *Italian Manpower, 225 B.C–A.D. 14*, Oxford: Oxford University Press.

Brunt, P.A. (1974), 'C. Fabricius Tuscus and an Augustan *Dilectus*', *Zeitschrift für Papyrologie und Epigraphik* 13, 161–85

Brunt, P.A. (1975), 'The Administrators of Roman Egypt', *Journal of Roman Studies* 65, 124–47.

Brunt, P.A. (1983), '*Princeps* and *Equites*', *Journal of Roman Studies* 73, 42–75.

Brunt, P.A. (1984), 'The Role of the Senate in the Augustan Regime', *Classical Quarterly (New Series)* 34.2, 423–44.

Bruun, P. (1999), 'Coins and the Roman Imperial Government', in Paul, G.M., Ierardi, M. (eds) *Togo Salomon Papers II*, Ann Arbor: University of Michigan Press, 19–40.

Bryce, T. (2014), *Ancient Syria: A Three Thousand Year History*, Oxford: Oxford University Press.

Buchan, J. (1937), *Augustus*, Boston: Houghton Mifflin Co.

Burn, A.R. (1952), *The Government of the Roman Empire from Augustus to the Antonines*, London: Historical Association.

Butcher, K. (2003), *Roman Syria and the Near East*, London: The British Museum Press.

Cairns, F. (1995), 'M. Agrippa in Horace "Odes" 1.6', *Hermes* 123.2, 211–17.

Cairns, T. (1970), *The Romans and Their Empire* (Cambridge Introduction to the History of Mankind: Book 2), Cambridge: Cambridge University Press.

Campbell, B. (1975), 'Who Were the *Viri Militares*?', *Journal of Roman Studies* 65, 11–31.

Campbell, B. (1987), 'Teach Yourself How to Be a General', *Journal of Roman Studies* 77, 13–29.

Campbell, B. (1993), 'War and Diplomacy: Rome and Parthia, 31 BC–AD 235', in Rich J., and Shipley G. (eds), *War and Society in the Roman World*, London: Routledge, 213–40.

Campbell, B. (1994), *The Roman Army 31BC–AD337: A Sourcebook*, London: Routledge.

Campbell, J.B. (1984), *The Emperor and the Roman Army 31BC–AD235*, Oxford: Oxford University Press.

Campbell, J.B. (1987), 'Teach Yourself How to Be a General', *Journal of Roman Studies* 77, 13–29.

Campbell, D.B. (2006), *Roman Legionary Fortresses 27BC–AD378*, Oxford: Osprey Publishing.

Campbell, D.B. (2010), 'Did Rome Have a Grand Strategy?', *Ancient Warfare* 4.1, 44–49.

Campbell, D.B. (2009), 'Secrets from the Soil: The Archaeology of Augustus' Military Bases', in Oorthuys, J. (ed.), *Ancient Warfare*, Special Issue 1, 10–16.

Campbell, D.B. (2010), 'Women in Roman forts: residents, visitors or barred from entry?', in Oorthuys, J. (ed.) *Ancient Warfare* 6.6, 48–53.

Carey, S. (2003), *Pliny's Catalogue of Culture: Art and Empire in the Natural History*, Oxford: Oxford University Press.

Carpenter, R. (1973), *Beyond the Pillars of Hercules; The Classical World Seen Through the Eyes of its Discoveries*, London: Tandem.

Carroll. M. (2001), *Romans, Celts and Germans: The German Provinces of Rome*, Stroud: The History Press/Tempus Publishing.

Carter, J.E. (2003), *Crimean Chersonesos: City, Chora, Museum and Environs*, Austin: Institute of Classical Archaeology, University of Texas at Austin.

Carter, J.M (1970), *The Battle of Actium: The Rise and Triumph of Augustus Caesar*, New York: Weybright and Talley.

Cartledge, P. (1975), 'The second thoughts of Augustus on the *res publica* in 28/7 B.C.', *Hermathena* 119, 30–40.

Caspari, M.O.B. (1911), 'On the *Ivratio Italiae* of 32 B. C. [On the *Iuratio Italiae* of 32 B. C.]', *Classical Quarterly* 5.4 (October), 230–35.

Casson, L. (1974), *Travel in the Ancient World*, Baltimore: The Johns Hopkins University Press.

Chadwick, N. (1970), *The Celts*, London: Penguin Books.

Champlin, E. (1989), 'The Testament of Augustus', *Rheinisches Museum für Philologie, Neue Folge* 132. Bd., H. 2, 154–65.

Champlin, E. (2009), Itinera Tiberi, *Working Papers in Classics*, Princeton: Princeton/Stanford.

Charlesworth, M.P. (1923), 'Tiberius and the Death of Augustus', *American Journal of Philology* 44.2, 145–57.

Cheesman, G.L. (1913), 'The Family of the Caristanii at Antioch in Pisidia', *Journal of Roman Studies* 3, 253–66.

Cheesman, G.L. (1914), *The Auxilia of the Roman Imperial Army*, Oxford: Oxford University Press.

Chevalier, R. (1976), *Roman Roads*, London: B.T. Batsford.

Christ, K. (1977), 'Zur augusteichen Germanienpolitik', *Chiron*, 149–205.

Chrissanthos, S.G. (2001), 'Caesar and the Mutiny of 47 B.C.', *Journal of Roman Studies* 91, Society for the Promotion of Roman Studies, 63–75.

Christopherson, A.J. (1968), 'The Provincial Assembly of the Three Gauls in the Julio-Claudian Period', *Historia: Zeitschrift für Alte Geschichte* 17.3, Stuttgart: Franz Steiner Verlag, 351–66.

Cilliers, L., Retief, F.P. (2000), 'Poisons, Poisoning and the Drug Trade in Ancient Rome', *Akroterion* 45, 88–100.

Claridge, A. (1998), *Rome: An Oxford Archaeological Guide*, Oxford: Oxford University Press.

Clark, M.A. (1983), '*Spes* in the Early Imperial Cult: "The Hope of Augustus"', *Numen* 30.1 (July), 80–105.

Clark, M.D.H. (2010), *Augustus. Caesar's Web – Power and Propaganda in Augustan Rome* (Bristol Phoenix Press Greece and Rome Live), Liverpool: Liverpool University Press.

Clausewitz, C. von (1832), *Vom Kriege*, Berlin: Dümmlers Verlag.

Cohen, S.T. (2008), 'Augustus, Julia and the Development of Exile *Ad Insulam*', *Classical Quarterly (New Series)*, 58.1, 206–17.

Colmenero, R. (1979), *Augusto e Hispania: Conquista y organizacion del norte peninsular*, University of Deusto.

Coltman Brown, I. (1981), 'Tacitus and a Space for Freedom', *History Today* 31. 4 (online at http://www.historytoday.com/irene-brown/tacitus-and-space-freedom – accessed 29 February 2016).

Connolly, P. (1975), *The Roman Army*, London: Macdonald.

Connolly, P. (1978), *Hannibal and the Enemies of Rome*, London: Macdonald.

Connolly, P. (1998), *Greece and Rome at War*, London: Macdonald.

Cooley, A.E. (2009), Res Gestae: *Text, Translation and Commentary*, Cambridge: Cambridge University Press.

Cooley, M.G.L. (ed.) (2013), *The Age of Augustus*, LACTOR 17, London (Second Edition).

Cooper, F. (1979), *Roman Realities*, Detroit: Wayne State University Press.

Corbet, J.H. (1974), 'The Succession Policy of Augustus', *Latomus* 33.1 (January–March), 87–97.

Cordingley, R.A., Richmond, I.A. (1927), 'The Mausoleum of Augustus', *Papers of the British School at Rome* 10, Rome, 23–35.

Cornell, T. (1993), 'The End of Roman Imperial Expansion', in Rich, J. and Shipley, G. (eds), *War and Society in the Roman World*, London: Routledge.

Cowan, E. (2009), 'Tiberius and Augustus in Tiberian Sources', *Historia: Zeitschrift für Alte Geschichte* 58.4, 468–85.

Cowan, R. (2003), *Roman Legionary 58BC–AD69*, Oxford: Osprey Publishing.

Cowan, R. (2007), *Roman Battle Tactics 109BC–AD313*, Oxford: Osprey Publishing.

Cowan, R. (2009), 'Sticks and Stones: Low tech and improvised weapons', in Oorthuys, J. (ed.), *Ancient Warfare* 6.6, 44–47.

Cowell, F.R. (1962), *Cicero and the Roman Republic*, London: Penguin Books (Second Edition).

Crawford, J.R. (1922), 'A Child Portrait of Drusus Junior on the Ara Pacis', *American Journal of Archaeology* 26, 307–15.

Crook, J.A. (1967), *Law and Life of Rome*, London: Thames and Hudson.

Crook, J.A. (1996), 'Political History, 30 B.C. to A.D. 14', in Bowman, A.K., Champlin, E., Lintott, A. (eds), *The Cambridge Ancient History Volume X: The Augustan Empire, 43 B.C.–A.D. 69* (Second Edition), Cambridge: Cambridge University Press , 70–112.

Cuff, D.B. (2010), *The* Auxilia *in Roman Britain and the Two Germanies from Augustus to Caracalla: Family, Religion and 'Romanization'*, Doctoral Thesis, University of Toronto.

Cunliffe, B.W. (1975), *Rome and the Barbarians*, London: The Bodley Head.

Cunliffe, B.W. (ed.) (1994), *Oxford Illustrated Prehistory of Europe*, Oxford: Oxford University Press.

Cunliffe, B.W. (1997), *The Ancient Celts*, Oxford: Oxford University Press.

Cunliffe, B.W. (1998), *Greeks, Roman and Barbarians: Spheres of Influence*, London: The Bodley Head.

Cunliffe, B.W. (2001), *Facing the Ocean: The Atlantic and Its Peoples 8000BC–AD1500*, Oxford: Oxford University Press.

Cunliffe, B.W. (2008), *Europe Between The Oceans: 9000BC–AD1000*, New Haven: Yale University Press.

Cüppers, H., Bernhard, H., Boppert, W. (eds) (1990), *Die Römer in Rheinland-Pfalz*, Stuttgart: Thomas Theiss Verlag.

Curchin, L.A. (1986), 'Marcus Agrippa's Gout', *American Journal of Philology* 107.3 (Autumn), 406.

Curchin, L.A. (1995), *Roman Spain*, New York: Barnes and Noble Books.

D'Amato, R., Sumner, G. (2009a), *Arms and Armour of the Imperial Roman Soldier: From Marius to Commodus*, Barnsley: Frontline Books.

D'Amato, R., Sumner, G. (2009b), *Imperial Roman Naval Forces 31 BC–AD 500*, Oxford: Osprey Publishing.

Daitz, S.G. (1960), 'Tacitus' Technique of Character Portrayal', *American Journal of Philology* 81, 30–52.

Dalzell, A. (1956), 'Maecenas and the Poets', *Phoenix* 10.4 (Winter), 151–62.

Daniel, R. (1933), *M. Vipsanius Agrippa: Eine Monographie*, Breslau.

Daugherty, G.N. (1992), 'The Cohortes Vigilum and the Great Fire of 64 AD', *The Classical Journal* 87.3 (Feb.-Mar.), 229–40.

David, J-M. (1996), *The Roman Conquests of Italy*, Oxford: Blackwell.

Davies, R. (1989), *Service in the Roman Army*, Edinburgh: Edinburgh University Press.

Davis, P.J.E. (2004), *Death and the Emperor: Roman Imperial Funerary Monuments from Augustus to Marcus Aurelius*, Austin: University of Texas Press.

De la Gravière, J. (1885), *La marine des Ptolémées et la marine des Romans*, Paris.

DeGrassi, A. (1947), *Consulares et Inscriptiones Italiae* XIII, 1 *Triumphales*, 567–70.

Delbrück, H. (1990), *History of the Art of War: The Barbarian Invasions*, Volume 2, Lincoln: University of Nebraska Press.

Deming, D. (2010), *Science and Technology in World History, Volume 1: The Ancient World and Classical Civilization*, Jefferson: McFarland.

Desbat, A. (2005), *Lugdunum: Naissance d'une Capitale: Dossier de Presse*, Lyon-Fourvière: Rhône Le Département.

Detweiler, R. (1970), 'Historical Perspectives on the Death of Agrippa Postumus', *Classical Journal* 65.7 (Apr.), 289–95.

Dilke, O.A.W. (1998), *Greek and Roman Maps*, Baltimore: Johns Hopkins University Press.

Dixon, K.R., Southern, P. (1992), *The Roman Cavalry from the First to the Third Century AD*, London: B.T. Batsford.

Dobiáš, J. (1960), 'King Maroboduus as a Politician', *Klio* 38, 155–66.

Dobson, B. (2009), 'The Rôle of the Fort', in Hanson, W.S. (ed.) *The Army and Frontiers of Rome: Papers Offered to David J. Breeze, Journal of Roman Archaeology* Supplement 74, 25–32.

Domergue, C. (1978), *Mines d'or romaines en Espagne*, Toulouse.

Dörrenberg, O. (1909), *Römerspuren und Römerkriege im nordwestlichen Deutschland*, Leipzig: Kommissions-Verlag der Dieterich'schen Verlagsbuchhandlung Theodor Weicher.

Downey, G. (1983), 'Tiberiana', in Wolfgang Haase (ed.), *Aufstieg und Niedergang der römischen Welt* 2, Stuttgart: de Gruyter, 109–10.

Dreyer, B. (2009), *Arminius und der Untergang des Varus. Warum die Germanen keine Römer wurden*, Stuttgart: Klett-Cotta.

Drinkwater, J.F. (1983), *Roman Gaul: The Three Provinces, 58BC–AD260*, London: Croom Helm.

Drogula, F.K. (2011), 'Controlling Travel: Deportation, Islands and the Regulation of Senatorial Mobility in the Augustan Age', *Classical Quarterly (New Series)* 61.1 (May), 230–66.

Drogula, F.K. (2015), *Commanders and Command in the Roman Republic and Early Empire* (Studies in the History of Greece and Rome), Chapel Hill: The University of North Carolina Press.

Duncan-Jones, R.P. (1982), *The Economy of the Roman Empire: Quantitative Studies* (second edition), Cambridge: Cambridge University Press.

Duncan-Jones, R.P. (1990), *Structure and Scale in the Roman Economy*, Cambridge: Cambridge University Press.

Durry, M. (1938), *Les Cohortes Prétoriennes*, Paris: E. de Boccard.

Dušanić, S. (1994), 'Roman Mining in Illyricum: Historical Aspects', *Dall' Adriatico al Danubio: L'Illirico nell'età greca e romana. Cividale del Friuli*, 47–70.

Dušanić, S. (2008), 'The Valle Ponti Lead Ingots: Notes on Roman Notables, Commercial Activities in Free Illyricum at the beginning of the Principate', *Starinar* 58, 107–18.

Dzino, D. (2005), *Illyrian Policy of Rome in the Late Republic and Early Principate*, Doctoral Thesis, University of Adelaide (online at http://hdl.handle.net/2440/37806 – accessed 29 February 2016).

Dzino, D. (2008a), 'Strabo 7, 5 and imaginary Illyricum', *Athenaeum: Studi periodici di letteratura e storie dell'Antichità* 96.1, 173–92.

Dzino, D. (2008b), 'Deconstructing Illyrians: Zeitgeist, Changing Perceptions and the Identity of Peoples from Ancient Illyricum', in *Croatian Studies Review*, 43–55.

Dzino, D. (2008c), 'The "Praetor" of Propertius 1.8 and 2.16 and the Origins of the Province of Illyricum', *Classical Quarterly (New Series)* 58.2 (December), 699–703.

Dzino, D. (2010), *Illyricum in Roman Politics: 229BC–AD68*, Cambridge: Cambridge University Press.

Dzino, D. (2012), '*Bellum Pannonicum*: The Roman armies and indigenous communities in southern Pannonia 16–9 BC', *Actes du Symposium international: Le livre. La Romanie. L'Europe* 3 (20–23 September 2011), 461–80 (fourth edition).

Earl, D.C. (1968), *The Age of Augustus*, London: Paul Elek Productions.

Ebel-Zepauer, W. (2003), 'Die augusteischen Marschlager in Dorsten-Holsterhausen', *Germania* 81, 539–55.

Ebel-Zepauer, W. (2005), 'Römer und Germanen in Dorsten-Holsterhausen', in H.-G. Horn *et al.* (eds) *Von Anfang an. Archäologie in Nordrhein-Westfalen (Schriften zur Bodendenkmalpflege in Nordrhein-Westfalen)* 8, 367–368.

Echols, E. (1958), 'The Roman City Police: Origin and Development', *Classical Journal* 53.8 (May), 377–85.

Eck, W. (2003), *The Age of Augustus*, Oxford: Blackwell Publishing.

Eck, W. (2009), *Augustus und seine Zeit*, München: Verlag C.H. Beck (fifth edition).

Edmondson, J. (ed.) (2009), *Augustus*, Edinburgh: Edinburgh Readings on the Ancient World.

Edwards, C. (2007), *Death in Ancient Rome*, New Haven: Yale University Press.

Eggers, H.J. (1976), 'Zur absoluten Chronologie der Kaizerzeit im freien Germanien', in H. Temporini, W. Haase (eds) *Aufstieg und Niedergang der römischen Welt: Geschichte und Kultur Roms im Spiegel d. neueren Forschung* II.5.1, Stuttgart: de Gruyter, 3–64.

Ehrenberg, V. (1953), '*Imperium Maius* in the Roman Republic', *American Journal of Philology* 74.2, 113–36.

Ehrenberg, V., Jones A.H.M. (1955), *Documents Illustrating the Reigns of Augustus and Tiberius*, Oxford: Clarendon Press (Second Edition).

Eilers, C. (2004), 'The Date of Augustus' Edict on the Jews (Jos. AJ 16.162–165) and the Career of C. Marcius Censorinus', *Phoenix* 58.1/2 (Spring-Summer), 86–95.

Elbe, J. von (1977), *Die Römer in Deutschland: Ausgrabungen, Fundstätten, Museen*, Gütersloh: Bertelsmann.

Elsner, J. (1991), 'Cult and Sculpture: Sacrifice in the *Ara Pacis Augustae*', *Journal of Roman Studies* 81, 50–61.

Elton, H. (1996), *Frontiers of the Roman Empire*, Bloomington: Indiana University Press.

Engelmann, H. (2004), 'Marcus Agrippa in Patara (*SEG* 44, 1208)', *Zeitschrift für Papyrologie und Epigraphik* 146, 129.

Engels, D., (1990), *Roman Corinth: An Alternative Model for the Classical City*, Chicago: University of Chicago Press.

Erdkamp, P. (2005), *The Grain Market in the Roman Empire: A Social, Political and Economic Study*, Cambridge: Cambridge University Press.

Erdkamp, P. (ed.) (2007), *A Companion to the Roman Army*, Oxford: Blackwell Publishing.

Esmonde-Cleary, S. (2007), *Rome in the Pyrenees: Lugdunum and the Convenae from the First Century B.C. to the Seventh Century A.D.*, London: Routledge.

Eubel, P.K. (1906), *Geschichte der Kölnischen Minoriten-ordensprovinz*, Köln: J. and W. Boisserée Buchhandlung.

Evans, Sir A.J. (1883), 'An Investigation of the Roman Road-Lines from Salonae to Scupi, and the Municipal Sites and Mining Centres in the Old Dalmatian and Dardanian Ranges', *Antiquarian Researches in Illyricum*, Part 3, from *The Archaeologia* 58, London: Nichols and Sons, 1–78.

Evans, R. (2011), *Roman Conquests: Asia Minor, Syria and Armenia*, Barnsley: Pen & Sword Books.

Everitt, A. (2001), *Cicero: The Life and Times of Rome's Greatest Politician*, New York: Random House.

Everitt, A. (2006), *Augustus: The Life of Rome's First Emperor*, New York: Random House.

Fagan, G.F. (2011), *The Lure of the Arena: Social Psychology, Spectatorship and the Roman Games*, Cambridge: Cambridge University Press.

Fantham, E. (2006), *Julia Augusti: The Emperor's Daughter*, London: Routledge.

Favro, D. (1992), '*Pater urbis*: Augustus as City Father of Rome', *Journal of the Society of Architectural Historians* 51.1 (Mar.), 61–84.

Favro, D. (1996), *The Urban Image of Augustan Rome*, Cambridge: Cambridge University Press.

Favro, D., Johanson, C. (2010), 'Death in Motion: Funeral Processions in the Roman Forum', *Journal of the Society of Architectural Historians* 69, no. 1: 12–37.

Feeny, D. (2007), *Caesar's Calender: Ancient Time and the Beginnings of History*, Berkeley: University of Califormia Press.

Feldman, L.H. (1993), *Jew and Gentile in the Ancient World: Attitudes and Interactions from Alexander to Justinian*, Princeton: Princeton University Press.

Ferrary, J.-L. (2001), 'The Powers of Augustus', in Edmondson, J. (ed.), *Augustus*, Edinburgh: Edinburgh Readings on the Ancient World (2009), 90–136.

Ferris, I.M. (2000), *Enemies of Rome: Barbarians Through Roman Eyes*, Stroud: Sutton/The History Press.

Field Manual No. 6–22 (2006), *Army Leadership: Competent, Confident, and Agile* (12 October), Washington, DC: Headquarters, Department of the Army (online at http://usacac.army.mil/cac2/Repository/Materials/fm6–22.pdf – accessed 29 February 2016).

Fields, N. (2009), *The Roman Army of the Principate 27BC–AD117*, Oxford: Osprey Publishing.

Figuera, T.J., Brennan, T.C., Sternberg, R.H. (2001), *Wisdom of the Ancients: Leadership Lessons from Alexander the Great to Julius Caesar*, New York: Withrop.

Finley, M.I. (1985), 'The battle of Actium', *The Listener*, 17 September, 372–75.

Finley, M.I. (1985), *Ancient History: Evidence and Models*, London: Chatto and Windus.

Fischer, M. (2011), 'Rome and Judaea during the First Century CE: A strange *modus vivendi*', in Moosbauer, G., Wiegels, R. (eds), *Römische Okkupations- und Grenzpolitik im frühen Principat Beiträge zum Kongress ,Fines imperii – imperium sine fine?' in Osnabrück vom 14. bis 18. September 2009*, Osnabrücker Forschungen zu Altertum und Antike-Rezeption 14, Diepholz: Druckhaus Breyer, 143–56.

Fischer, T. (2012), *Die Armee der Caesaren*, Regensburg: F. Pustet Verlag.

Fishwick, D. (1987), *The Imperial Cult in the Latin West: Studies in the Ruler Cult of the Western Provinces of the Roman Empire, Volume 1, Parts 1 and 2*, Boston: Brill Academic Publishers.

Fishwick, D. (1988), 'Dated inscriptions and the *Feriale Duranum*', *Syria* 65 fascicule 3–4, 349–61.

Fishwick, D. (1992), 'On the Temple of *Divus* "Augustus"', *Phoenix* 46.3 (Autumn), 232–55.

Fishwick, D. (1999), 'Coinage and Cult: The Provincial Momuments at Lugdunum, Tarraco and Emertita', in Paul, G.M, Ierardi, M. (eds), *Roman Coins and Public Life: E. Togo Salomon Papers II*, Ann Arbor: University of Michigan Press, 95–121.

Fishwick, D. (2002), *The Imperial Cult in the Latin West: Studies in the Ruler Cult of the Western Roman Empire, Volume 3, Part 1*, Boston: Brill Academic Publishers.

Fishwick, D. (2003), *The Imperial Cult in the Latin West: Studies in the Ruler Cult of the Western Provinces of the Roman Empire, Volume 3, Part 3*, Boston: Brill Academic Publishers.

Flower, H.I. (1996), *Ancestor Masks and Aristocratic Power in Roman Culture*, Oxford: Oxford University Press.

Flower, H.I. (2006), *The Art of Forgetting: Disgrace and Oblivion in Roman Political Culture*, Chapel Hill: The University of North Carolina Press.

Flower, H.I. (2011), *Roman Republics*, Princeton: Princeton University Press.

Frandsen, P.S. (1835), *Über die Politik des Marcus Agrippa*, Altona.

Frank, T. (1921), 'The *Carmen Saeculare* of Horace', *American Journal of Philology* 42.4, 324–29.

Fraschetti, A. (1980), 'La mort d'Agrippa et l'autel du Belvedere: Un certain type d'hommage', *Mélanges de L'École Française de Rome* 92, 957–76.

Freis, H. (1967), *Die* Cohortes Urbanae. (*Epigraphische Studien 2, Beihefte der Bonner Jahrbücher* 21), Cologne: Böhlau-Verlag.

Freisenbruch, A. (2010), *Caesar's Wives: Sex, Power and Politics in Ancient Rome*, New York: Free Press.

Frisch, P. (1980), 'Zu den Elogien des Augustusforums', *Zeitschrift für Papyrologie und Epigraphik* 39, 91–98.

Frothingham, A.L. (1915), 'The Roman Territorial Arch', *American Journal of Archaeology* 19.2 (April–June), 155–74.

Fuhrmann, C.J. (2011), *Policing the Roman Empire: Soldiers, Administrators, and Public Order*, Oxford: Oxford University Press.

Fulford, M. (1992), 'Territorial Expansion and the Roman Empire', *World Archaeology* 23.3, Archaeology of Empires (February), 294–305.

Fullerton, M. (1985), 'The *Domus Augusti* in Imperial Iconography of 13–12 B.C.', *American Journal of Archaeology* 89, 473–83.

Futurell, A. (1997), *Blood in the Arena: The Spectacle of Roman Power*, Austin: University of Texas Press.

Gabba, E. (1971), 'The Perusine War and Triumviral Italy', *Harvard Studies in Classical Philology* 75, 139–60.

Gabriel, R.A. (2006), *Soldiers' Lives through History – The Ancient World*, Santa Barbara: Greenwood Press.

Gaillou, P., Jones, M (1991), *The Bretons*, Oxford: Blackwell.

Galinsky, G.K. (1968), 'Aeneid V and the Aeneid', *American Journal of Philology* 89.2 (Apr.), 157–85.

Galinsky, K. (1966), 'Venus in a Relief of the *Ara Pacis Augustae*', *American Journal of Archaeology* 70.3 (July), 223–43.

Galinsky, K. (1967), 'Sol and the *Carmen Saeculare*', *Latomus* 26.3, 619–33.

Galinsky, K. (1996), *Augustan Culture: An Interpretive Introduction*, Princeton: Princeton University Press.

Galinsky, K. (ed.) (2012), *Augustus: Introduction to the Life of an Emperor*, Cambridge: Cambridge University Press.

Galinsky, K. (2015), 'Augustus' *Auctoritas* and *Res Gestae* 34.3', *Hermes* 143.2, 244–49.

Garnsey, E.R. (1924), 'The Fall of Maecenas', *The Sewanee Review* 32.2 (April), 146–61.

Garnsey, P.D.A., Whittaker, C.R., (eds) (1978), *Imperialism in the Ancient World*, Cambridge: Cambridge University Press.

Garnsey, P. (1988), *Famine and Food Supply in the Graeco-Roman World: Responses to Risk and Crisis*, Cambridge: Cambridge University Press.

Gebauer, G.C., Sommersberg, F.W. von (1717), *De M. Agrippa*, Leipzig: Zeidler.

Giard, J.-B. (1967), 'Le trésor de Port-Haliguen: Contribution à l'étude du monnayage d'Auguste', *Revue Numismatique* 6.9, p.121.

Gilliam, J.F. (1954), 'The Roman Military *Feriale*', *Harvard Theological Review* 47.3 (July), 183–96.

Gilliver, K. (2007), 'The Augustan Reform and the Structure of the Imperial Army', in Erdkamp, P. (ed.), *A Companion to the Roman Army*, Oxford: Blackwell Publishing, 183–200.

Goldsworthy, A. (1996), *The Roman Army at War 100BC–AD200*, Oxford: Oxford University Press.

Goldsworthy, A. (2000), *Roman Warfare*, London: Cassell.

Goldsworthy, A. (2000), *The Punic Wars*, London: Cassell.

Goldsworthy, A. (2003), *In the Name of Rome: The Men Who Won the Roman Empire*, London: Weidenfeld and Nicholson.

Goldsworthy, A. (2006), *Caesar: The Life of a Colossus*, London: Weidenfeld and Nicolson.

Goldsworthy, A. (2010), *Antony And Cleopatra*, New Haven: Yale University Press.

Goldsworthy, A. (2014), *Augustus: First Emperor of Rome*, Yale: Yale University Press.

Golz Huzar, E. (1978), *Mark Antony: A Biography*, Minneapolis: University of Minnesota Press.

Goodman, M. (1996), 'Judaea', in Bowman, A.K., Champlin, E., Lintott, A. (eds), *The Cambridge Ancient History Volume X: The Augustan Empire, 43 B.C.–A.D. 69* (Second Edition), Cambridge: Cambridge University Press, 737–80.

Gordon, A.E. (1968), 'Notes on the *Res Gestae* of Augustus', *California Studies in Classical Antiquity* 1, 125–38.

Gordon, A.E. (1983), *Illustrated Introduction to Latin Epigraphy*, Berkeley: University of California Press.

Gordon, R., Reynolds, J., Beard, M., Roueché, C. (1997), 'Roman Inscriptions', *Journal of Roman Studies* 87, 206–40.

Gorski, G.J., Packer, J.E. (2015), *The Roman Forum: A Reconstruction and Architectural Guide*, Cambridge: Cambridge University Press.

Goudineau, C. (1996), 'Gaul', in Bowman, A.K., Champlin, E., Lintott, A. (eds), *The Cambridge Ancient History Volume X: The Augustan Empire, 43 B.C.–A.D. 69*, Cambridge: Cambridge University Press, 464–502.

Goudineau, C., Rebourg, A. (eds) (1985), *Les villes Augustéennes de Gaule* (Actes du Coloque international d'Autun 6–8 juin 1985), Autun.

Graf, F. (1991), 'Gestures and conventions: the gestures of Roman actors and orators' in *A Cultural History of Gesture: From Antiquity to the Present Day*, Bremmer, J.N, Roodenburg, H. (eds), Cambridge: Cambridge University Press, 1991, pp. 36–58.

Grant, M. (1949), 'The Augustan "Constitution"', *Greece & Rome* 18.54 (October), 97–112.

Grant, M. (1958), *Roman History from Coins*, Cambridge: Cambridge University Press.

Grant, M. (1970), *Julius Caesar*, London: Weidenfeld and Nicolson

Grant, M. (1974), *The Army of the Caesars*, New York: M. Evans and Company.

Grapin, C. (2003), 'Tiberius Turus/Turos, un Celtibère au service de la VIᵉ légion mort à Metz', *Latomus* 62.3 (July–September), 635–41.

Gray, E.W. (1970), 'The *Imperium* of M. Agrippa. A Note on P. Colon. inv. nr. 4701', *Zeitschrift für Papyrologie und Epigraphik* 6, 227–38.

Green, P. (1989), *Classical Bearings: Interpreting Ancient History and Culture*, Berkeley: University of California Press.

Gregoratti, L. (2012), 'Between Rome and Ctesiphon: the problem of ruling Armenia', in Армения – Иран: *Proceedings of the Conference Armenia – Iran: History. Culture. The modern perspectives of progress, 28 June, 2010*, Moscow.

Griffin, M.T. (1985), *Nero: The End of a Dynasty*, New Haven: Yale University Press.

Griffin, M.T. (1997), 'The Senate's Story', *Journal of Roman Studies* 87, 249–53.

Grote, K. (2005), *Römerlager in Hedemünden*, Heimat- u. Geschichtsverein Sydekum.

Grote, K. (2012), *Römerlager in Hedemünden. Der augusteische Stützpunkt, seine Außenanlagen, seine Funde und Befunde*, Niedersächsisches Landesmuseum Hannover, Sandstein Verlag.

Gruen, E. (1996), 'The Expansion of the Empire', in Bowman, A.K., Champlin, E., Lintott, A. (eds), *The Cambridge Ancient History Volume X: The Augustan Empire, 43 B.C.–A.D. 69* (Second Edition), Cambridge: Cambridge University Press, 147–97.

Gruen, E. (2003), 'The Emperor Tiberius and the Jews', T. Hantos (ed.), *Laurea Internationalis: Festschrift für Jochen Bleicken zum 75 Geburstag*, 298–312.

Gruen, E. (2005), 'Augustus and the Making of the Principate', in K. Galinsky, *The Cambridge Companion to the Age of Augustus*, Cambridge: Cambridge University Press (2005), 33–52.

Grummond, N.J. de (1990), '*Pax Augusta* and the *Horae* on the *Ara Pacis Augustae*', *American Journal of Archaeology* 94.4 (October), 663–77.

Grünewald, T. (2004), *Bandits in the Roman Empire: Myth and Reality*, London: Routledge.

Gurval, R.A., (1995), *Actium and Augustus: The Politics and Emotions of Civil War*, Ann Arbor: The University of Michigan Press.

Güven, S. (1998), 'Displaying the *Res Gestae* of Augustus: A Monument of Imperial Image for All', *Journal of the Society of Architectural Historians* 57.1 (March), 30–45.

Haas, R.N. (2009), *War of Necessity; War of Choice: A Memoir of Two Iraq Wars*, New York: Simon and Schuster.

Habicht, C. (1991), 'Was Augustus a Visitor at the Panathenaia?', *Classical Philology* 86, 3 (July), 226–28.

Habicht, C. (2005), 'Marcus Agrippa *Theos Soter*', *Hyperboreus* 11, 242–46.

Haight, E.H. (1922), 'Reconstruction in the Augustan Age', *Classical Journal* 17.7 (April), 355–76.

Haley, E.W. (2003), *Baetica Felix: People and Prosperity in Southern Spain from Caesar to Septimius Severus*, Austin: University of Texas Press.

Hammond, M. (1965), 'The Sincerity of Augustus', *Harvard Studies in Classical Philology* 69, 139–62.

Hanson, A.E. (1980), 'Juliopolis, Nicopolis, and the Roman Camp', *Zeitschrift für Papyrologie und Epigraphik* 37, 249–54.

Hanson, A.E. (1982), 'Publius Ostorius Scapula: Augustan Prefect of Egypt', *Zeitschrift für Papyrologie und Epigraphik* 47, 243–53.

Hanson, W.S. (ed.), (2009), 'The Army and the Frontiers of Rome', *Journal of Roman Archaeology Supplementary Series* 74.

Hard, R. (2003), *The Routledge Handbook of Greek Mythology: Based on H.J. Rose's Handbook of Greek Mythology*, London: Routledge.

Hardy, E.G. (1887), 'The Movements of the Roman Legions from Augustus to Severus', *English Historical Review* 2.8 (October), 625–56.

Hardy, E.G. (1889), 'Dr. Mommsen on the Recruiting System for Legionaries and Auxiliaries under the Empire in Hermes XIX', *Classical Review* 2.3 (March), 112–14.

Hardy, E.G. (1920), 'Augustus and His Legionaries', *Classical Quarterly* 1, 14.3/4 (July–October), 187–94.

Harley, B., Woodward, D. (1987), *The History of Cartography: Cartography in Prehistoric, Ancient and Medieval Europe and the Mediterranean* 1, Chicago: University Of Chicago Press.

Harrer, G.A. (1919), 'Rome and Her Subject Peoples', *Classical Journal* 14.9 (June), 550–56.

Harris, W. (2006), *War and Imperialism in Republican Rome 327–70BC*, Oxford: Oxford University Press.

Harrison, S.J. (1989), 'Augustus, the Poets, and the *Spolia Opima*', *Classical Quarterly (New Series)* 39.2, 408–14.

Haslam, M.W. (1980), 'Augustus' Funeral Oration for Agrippa', *Classical Journal* 75.3 (February–March), 193–99.

Haverfield, F. (1914), 'Legions and *Auxilia*', *Classical Review* 28.7 (November), 226–27.

Haynes, H. (2003), *The History of Make-Believe: Tacitus on Imperial Rome*, Berkeley: University of California Press.

Haynes, I.P. (1993), 'The Romanisation of Religion in the "*Auxilia*" of the Roman Imperial Army from Augustus to Septimus Severus', *Britannia* 24, 141–157.

Haynes, I.P. (2013), *Blood of the Provinces: The Roman Auxilia and the Making of Provincial Society from Augustus to the Severans*, Oxford: Oxford University Press.

Healy, J. (2000), *Pliny on Science and Technology*, Oxford: Clarendon Press.

Heinrichs, J. (1999), 'Zur Verwicklung Ubischer Gruppen in den Ambiorix-Aufstand d. J. 54 v. Chr.: Eburonische und ubische Münzen im Hortfund Fraire-2', *Zeitschrift Für Payrologie und Epigraphik* 127, 275–93.

Henderson, M. I. (1963), 'The Establishment of the *Equester Ordo*', *Journal of Roman Studies* 53, 1 and 2, 61–72.

Heinrichs, J. (2000), 'Römische Perfidie under germanischer Edelmut? Zur Umsiedlung protocugernischer Gruppen in den Raum Xanten 8 v. Chr.', T. Grünewald, H.J. Schalles (eds) *Germania Inferior: Beiträge des deutschen-niederländischen Kolloquiums in Regionalmuseum Xanten 21.–24. September 1999*, Berlin: Walter de Gruyter, 54–92.

Heiss, A. (1870), *Description générale des monnaies antiques de l'Espagne*, Paris.

Hekster, O. (2008), *Rome and its Empire, AD193–284*, Edinburgh: Edinburgh University Press.

Henig, M. (1970), 'The Veneration of Heroes in the Roman Army: The Evidence of Engraved Gemstones', *Britannia* 1, 249–65.

Herm, G. (1977), *The Celts: The People Who Came Out of the Darkness*, New York: St Martin's Press.

Herz, P. (1984), 'Das Kenotaph von Limyra. Kultische und juristische Voraussetzungen', *Mitteilung des Deutschen Archäologischen Instituts* (Istanbul) 35, 178–192.

Herz, P. A (2007), 'Finances and Costs of the Roman Army', in Erdkamp, P. (ed.), *Companion to the Roman Army*, London: Blackwell, 306–22.

Hickson, F.V. (1991), 'Augustus *Triumphator*: Manipulation of the Triumphal Theme in the Political Program of Augustus', *Latomus* 50.1 (January–March), 124–38.

Hill, Sir G.F, (1899), *A Handbook of Greek and Roman Coins*, London: MacMillan.

Hinge, G., Krasilnikoff, J.A. (eds) (2009), *Alexandria: A Cultural and Religious Melting Pot (Aarhus Studies in Mediterranean Antiquity)*, Aarhus: Aarhus University Press.

Hoff, M.C. (1989), 'Civil Disobedience and Unrest in Augustan Athens', *Hesperia: Journal of the American School of Classical Studies at Athens* 58.3 (July–September), 267–76.

Hoffmann, F., Minas-Nerpel, M., Pfeiffer, S. (eds) (2009), *Die dreisprachige Stele des C. Cornelius Gallus: Übersetzung und Kommentar*, Berlin: De Gruyter.

Hoffman, M.W. (1952), 'The college of *Quindecimviri* (*Sacris Faciundis*) in 17 B.C.', *American Journal of Philology* 73, 289–94.

Holder, P.F. (1980), *Studies in the* Auxilia *of the Roman Army from Augustus to Trajan* (BAR international series), Oxford: Archaeopress.

Holland, L.A. (1947), 'Aeneas-Augustus of Prima Porta', *Transactions and Proceedings of the American Philological Association* 78, 276–84

Holliday, P.J. (1990), 'Time, History, and Ritual on the *Ara Pacis Augustae*', *The Art Bulletin* 72.4 (December), 542–57.

Holmes, T.R. (1928), *The Architect of the Roman Empire*, Oxford: Clarendon.

Hölscher, T. (1985), 'Monuments of the Battle of Actium: Propaganda and Response', in Edmondson, J. (ed.), *Augustus*, Edinburgh: Edinburgh Readings on the Ancient World (2009), 310–33.

Hölscher, T. (2003), 'Images of War in Greece and Rome: Between Military Practice, Public Memory, and Cultural Symbolism', *Journal of Roman Studies* 93, 1–17.

Hope, V.M. (2003), 'Trophies and Tombstones: Commemorating the Roman Soldier', *World Archaeology* 35.1, *The Social Commemoration of Warfare* (June), 79–97.

Horden, P., Purcell, N. (2000), *The Corrupting Sea: A Study of Mediterranean History*, London: Blackwell.

Hurlet, F. (1994), 'Recherches sur la durée de l'"*imperium*" des "co-régents" sous les principats d'Auguste et de Tibère', *Cahiers du Centre Gustave Glotz* 5, 255–89.

Hurlet, F. (1997), *Les collègues du prince sous Auguste et Tibère*. (Collection de l'École française de Rome 227), Rome: École française de Rome.

Hurlet, F. (2011), 'Consulship and Consuls Under Augustus', in Beck, H., Duple, A., Jehne, M., Polo, F.P. (eds), *Consuls and* Res Publica: *Holding High Office in the Roman Republic*, Cambridge: Cambridge University Press: 319–35.

Huzar, E.G. (1995), 'Emperor Worship in Julio-Claudian Egypt', in *Aufstieg und Niedergang der römischen Welt: Geschichte und Kultur Roms im Spiegel der neuren Forschung*, Volume 1, Berlin: Walter de Gruyter, 3092–3143.

Huzar, E.G. (1978), *Mark Antony: A Biography*, Beckenham: Croom Helm.

Illarregui, E. (2005), 'Cantabrian Weapons' in Kocsis, L. (ed.), *Journal of Roman Military Equipment* 16, The Enemies of Rome: Proceedings of the 15th International Roman Military Equipment Conference, Budapest 2005, 81–105.

Isaac, B. (1990), *The Limits of Empire: The Roman Army in the East*, Oxford: Clarendon.

Isaac, B. (2006), *The Invention of Racism in Classical Antiquity*, Princeton: Princeton University Press.

Itgenshorst, T. (2004), 'Augustus und der republikanische Triumph: Triumphalfasten und *summi viri*-Galerie als Instrumente der imperialen Machtsicherung', *Hermes* 132.4, 436–58.

Jacobson, D.M., Kokkinos, N. (eds) (2008), *Herod and Augustus: Papers Presented at the IJS Conference, 21st–23rd June 2005*, Brill: Leiden.

Jahnkun, H. (1976), 'Siedlung, Wirtschaft und Gesellschaftsordnung der germanischen Stämme in der Zeit der römischen Angriffskriege', Temporini, H., Haase, W. (eds) *Aufstieg und Niedergang der römischen Welt: Geschichte und Kultur Roms im Spiegel d. neueren Forschung*, Vol II.5.1, Stuttgart: de Gruyer, 65–126.

James, H. (1989), *A German Identity: 1770–1990*, New York: Routledge.

Jameson, S. (1968), 'Chronology of the Campaigns of Aelius Gallus and C. Petronius', *Journal of Roman Studies* 58, Parts 1 and 2, 71–84.

Jameson, S., Jameson, S. (1969), '22 or 23?', *Historia: Zeitschrift für Alte Geschichte* 18.2 (April), 204–29.

Jameson, S. (1975), 'Augustus and Agrippa Postumus', *Historia: Zeitschrift fr Alte Geschichte* 24.2 (2nd Qtr.), 287–314.

Johne, K.-P. (2006), *Die Römer an der Elbe: Das Stromgebiet der Elbe im geographischen Weltbild und im politischen Bewusstsein der griechisch-römischen Antike*, Berlin: Akademie Verlag.

Jomini, A.H. (1862), *The Art of War*, Westport: Greenwood Press.

Jones, A.H.M. (1950), 'The *Aerarium* and the *Fiscus*', *Journal of Roman Studies* 40.1/2, 22–29.

Jones, A.H.M. (1951), 'The *Imperium* of Augustus', *Journal of Roman Studies* 41, Parts 1 and 2, 112–19.

Jones, R.F.J., Bird, D.G. (1972), 'Roman Gold-Mining in North-West Spain, II: Workings on the Rio Duerna', *Journal of Roman Studies* 62, 59–74.

Jones, R.F.J. (1976), 'The Roman Military Occupation of North-West Spain', *Journal of Roman Studies* 66, 45–66.

Jorgensen, L. *et al.* (eds) (2003), *The Spoils of Victory: The North in the Shadow of the Roman Empire*, Copenhagen: National Museum of Denmark.

Judge, E.A, Harrison, J.R. (eds) (2008), *The First Christians in the Roman World: Augustan and New Testament Essays*, Tübingen: Mohr Siebeck.

Junkelmann, M. (2006), Panis militaris, *Die Ernährung des römischen Soldaten oder der Grundstoff der Macht*, Mainz: Verlag Philipp von Zabern.

Junkelmann, M. (2014), *Die Legionen des Augustus*, München: Herbert Utz Verlag.

Kagan, K. (2006), 'Redefining Roman Grand Strategy', *Journal of Military History* 70.2 (April), 333–62.

Kalfoglou-Kaloteraki, V. (2003), 'Μάρκῳ Ἀγρίππᾳ', *Hellenika* 53, 299–303.

Kaufman, D.B. (1932), 'Poisons and Poisoning Among the Romans', *Classical Philology* 27.2, 156–67.

Keaveney, A. (2007), *The Army in the Roman Revolution*, Abingdon: Routledge.

Keay, S.J. (1988), Roman Spain, London: British Museum Publications.

Keay, S.J. (2003), 'Recent Archaeological Work in Roman Iberia (1990–2002)', *Journal of Roman Studies* 93, 146–211.

Keegan, J. (2003), *Intelligence in War: From Napoleon to Al-Qaeda*, New York: Alfred A. Knopf.

Kennedy, D.L. (1983), 'Military Cohorts: The Evidence of Josephus, *BJ*, III.4.2(67) and of Epigraphy', *Zeitschrift für Papyrologie und Epigraphik* 50, 253–63.

Kennedy, D. (1996a), *The Roman Army in the East. Journal of Roman Archaeology Supplementary Series no. 18*, Ann Arbor, Michigan.

Kennedy, D. (1996b), 'Syria', in Bowman, A.K., Champlin, E., Lintott, A. (eds), *The Cambridge Ancient History Volume X: The Augustan Empire, 43 B.C.–A.D. 69* (Second Edition), Cambridge: Cambridge University Press, 703–36.

Keppie, L.J.F. (1971), 'A Note on the Title *Actiacus*', *Classical Review* 21.3 (December), 329–30.

Keppie, L.J.F. (1973), '*Vexilla Veteranorum*', *Papers of the British School at Rome* 41, 8–17.

Keppie, L. (1984), 'Colonisation and Veteran Settlement in Italy in the First Century AD', *Papers of The British School at Rome* 52, 77–114.

Keppie, L. (1996), 'The Army and The Navy', in Bowman, A.K., Champlin, E., Lintott, A. (eds), *The Cambridge Ancient History Volume X: The Augustan Empire, 43 B.C.–A.D. 69* (Second Edition), Cambridge: Cambridge University Press, 371–96.

Keppie, L. (1998), *The Making of the Roman Army From Republic to Empire*, Norman: University of Oklahoma Press (Second Edition).

Keppie, L. (2002), 'The Origins and Early History of the Second Augustan Legion', in Brewer, R.J. (ed.), *The Second Augustan Legion and the Roman Military Machine*, Cardiff: National Museum of Wales (2002).

Kienast, D. (1966), *Untersuchungen zu den Kriegsflotten der römischen Kaiserzeit*, Bonn: Habelt.

Kienast, D. (2009), *Augustus: Prinzeps und Monarch*, Darmstadt: Primus Verlag (fourth edition).

Kiessel, M., Weidner, M. (2009), 'Defining Roman, Celtic and Germanic Ethnicity through Archaeological Monuments. Examples from Roman Provinces in North-western Europe', *GAU Journal of Social and Applied Sciences* 5, 35–51.

King, A. (1990), *Roman Gaul and Germany*, London: British Museum Publications.

Kiss, Z. (1975), *L'iconographie des princes julio-claudiens au temps d'Auguste et de Tibère*, Warsaw: Travaux du Centre d'archéologie méditerranéenne de l'Académie polonaise des sciences.

Kleineburg, A. *et al.* (2010), *Germania und die Insel Thule: Die Entschlüsselung von Ptolemaios' 'Atlas der Oikumene'*, Darmstadt: Wissenschaftliche Buchgesellschaft.

Klein, M. (2005), 'Roman Decorated Daggers and Figural Sword Fittings from Mainze-*Mogontiacum* (Germania Superior)' in Kocsis, L. (ed.), *Journal of Roman Military Equipment* 16, The Enemies of Rome: Proceedings of the 15th International Roman Military Equipment Conference, Budapest 2005, 237–48.

Kleiner, D.E.E. (1978), 'The great friezes of the *Ara Pacis Augustae*. Greek Sources, Roman Derivatives and Augustan Social Policy', *Mélanges de l'Ecole française de Rome. Antiquité* 90–2, 753–85.

Kleiner, D.E.E. (2005), 'Semblance and Storytelling in Augustan Rome', in Galinsky, K. (2005), *The Cambridge Companion to the Age of Augustus*, Cambridge: Cambridge University Press, 197–233.

Klynne, A., Liljenstolpe, P. (2000), 'Where to Put Augustus? A Note on the Placement of the Prima Porta Statue', *American Journal of Philology* 121.1, 121–128.

Knight, D.J. (1991), 'The Movements of the *Auxilia* from Augustus to Hadrian', *Zeitschrift für Papyrologie und Epigraphik* 85, 189–208.

Kockel, V. (1995), '*Forum Augustum*', in Steinby, E.V. (ed.), *Lexicon Topographicum Urbis Romae II*, Rome: Quasar, 289–95.

Koepfer, C. (2009a), 'Arming the Warrior: Archaeological Evidence', in Oorthuys, J. (ed.), *Ancient Warfare*, Special Issue 1, 48–51.

Koepfer, C. (2009b), 'The Legionary's Equipment: Archaeological Evidence', in Oorthuys, J. (ed.), *Ancient Warfare*, Special Issue 1, 37–41.

Köhler, H.J, von Schnurbein, S. (2003), 'Die Römer kommen! Die Lagerspuren auf dem Goldberg', in *Sole und Salz schreiben Geschichte. 50 Jahre Landesarchäologie. 150 Jahre Archäologische Forschung Bad Nauheim*. Mainz, 279–81.

Köhne, E., Ewigleben, E. (eds) (2000), *Gladiators and Caesars*, Berkeley: California University Press.

Kolník, T. (1991), 'Zu ersten Römern und Germanen an der mittleren Donau im Zusammenhang mit den geplanten römischen Angriffen gegen Marbod 6 n. Chr.', in *Die römische Okkupatzion nördlich der Alpen zur Zeit des Augustus*, Münster, 71–84.

Kondoleon, C. (ed.) (2000), *Antioch: The Lost Ancient City. Exhibition Catalogue, Worcester Art Museum, 7 October, 2000–4 February, 2001; The Cleveland Museum of Art, 18 March–3 June, 2001; The Baltimore Museum of Art, 16 September–30 December, 2001*, Princeton: Princeton University Press.

Kornemann, E. (1930), *Doppelprinzipat und Reichsteilung im Imperium Romanum*, Teubner: Leipzig.

Kornemann, E. (1980), *Tiberius*, Frankfurt (Main): Societäts-Verlag (reprint of Stuttgart 1960 edition).

Kösters, K. (2009), *Mythos Arminius. Die Varusschlacht und ihre Folgen*, Münster: Aschendorf Verlag.

Kraft, K. (1967), 'Der Sinn des Mausoleums des Augustus', *Historia: Zeitschrift für Alte Geschichte* 16.2 (April), 189–206.

Krebs, C.B. (2011), 'Tacitus: The Continuing Message', *History Today* 61.9 (online at http://www.historytoday.com/christopher-krebs/tacitus-continuing-message – accessed 29 February 2016).

Kröger, H., Best, W. (2011), *Porta Westfalica-Barkhausen Ein Gang durch die Jahrtausende*, Förderverein Römerlager Barkhausen Porta Westfalica e.V. in Zusammenarbeit mit dem LWL – Archäologie für Westfalen, (online at http://www.roemerlager-porta.de/wp-content/Grabungsbroschüre.pdf – accessed 29 February 2016).

Kromayer, J. (1899), 'Kleine Forschungen zur Geschichte des zweiten Triumvirats VII: der Feldzug von Actium und der sogennanten Verrath der Cleopatra', *Hermes* 34, 1–54.

Kruta, V. (ed.) (1999), *The Celts*, New York: Rizzoli International.

Kühlborn, J.S. (1989), 'Oberaden', in Trier, B. (ed.) *2000 Jahre Römer in Westfalen*, Mainz: Zabern.

Kühlborn, J.S. (1990), 'Die augusteischen Militärlager an der Lippe', in Horn, H.-G. (ed.) *Archäologie in Nordrhein-Westfalen. Geschichte im Herzen Europas*, Mainz: Zabern, 169–86.

Kühlborn, J.S. (1991), 'Die Lagerzentren der römischen Militärlager von Oberaden und Anreppen', in Asskamp, R., Berke, S. (eds): *Die römische Okkupation nördlich der Alpen zur Zeit des Augustus.* Münster: Aschendorff, 129–40.

Kühlborn, J.S. (ed.) (1995), *Germania pacavi: Germanien habe ich befriedet: Archäologische Stätten august-eischer Okkupation*, Münster: Westfälisches Museum für Archäologie – Amt für Bodendenkmalpflege.

Kühlborn, J.S. (1996), *Das römische Uferkastell Beckinghausen*, Museum der Stadt Lünen. Informationen aus dem Museum der Stadt Lünen, 1–4 (online at www.luenen.de/medien/archiv/dok/Uferkastell.pdf – accessed 29 February 2016).

Kühlborn, J.S. (2004), 'Frühe Germanienpolitik: Schlagkraft. Die Feldzüge unter Augustus und Tiberius in Nordwestdeutschland', in Wamser, L., Flügel, C., Ziegaus, B. (2004), *Die Römer zwischen Alpen und Nordmeer*, Düsseldorf: Patmos Verlag, 27–33.

Kühlborn, J.S. (2014), 'Römer im Paderborner Land. Anreppen, das Hauptquartier des Tiberius', in *Führer zur Vor- und Frühgeschichte der Hochstiftkreise Paderborn und Höxter* 3 (Marsberg), 1–42.

Kunić, A.D. (2006), 'Posljednja faza osvajanja Ju'ne Panonije', *VAMZ*, 3.s., XXXIX, 59–164.

Kurkjian, V.M. (1958), *A History of Armenia*, New York: Armenian General Benevolent Union of America.

Kuttner, A.L. (1995), *Dynasty and Empire in the Age of Augustus: The Case of the Boscoreale Cups*, Berkeley: University of California Press.

Lacey, W.K. (1974), 'Octavian in the Senate, January 27 B.C.', *Journal of Roman Studies* 44, 176–84.

Lacey, W.K. (1996), *Augustus and the Principate: The Evolution of the System (ARCA (Classical & Medieval Texts, Papers & Monographs))*, Francis Cairns Publications.

Lange, C.H. (2008), 'Civil War in the *Res Gestae Divi Augusti*: Conquering the World and Fighting a War at Home', in Bragg, E., Hau, L.I., Macaulay-Lewis, E. (eds), *Beyond the Battlefields: New Perspectives on Warfare and Society in the Graeco-Roman World*, Cambridge: Cambridge Scholars Publishing, 185–204.

Lange, C.H. (2009a), Res Publica Constituta*: Actium, Apollo and the Accomplishment of the Triumviral Assignment*, Brill: Leiden.

Lange, C.H. (2009b), 'The Battle of Actium and the "slave of passion"' in Moore, J., Morris, I., Bayliss, A.J. (eds) *Reinventing History: The Enlightenment Origins of Ancient History*, London: Centre for Metropolitan History, 115–36.

Lange, C.H. (2011), 'The Battle of Actium: A Reconsideration', *Classical Quarterly* 61.2, 608–23.

Lange, C.H. (2015), 'Augustus' Triumphal and Triumphal-like Returns', in Ostenberg, I., Malmberg, S., Jonas Bjørnebye, J. (eds) *The Moving City: Processions, Passages and Promenades in Ancient Rome*, Bloomsbury Academic, 133–44.

Langguth, A.J. (1994), *A Noise of War: Caesar, Pompey, Octavian and the Struggle for Rome*, New York: Simon and Schuster.

Le Bohec, Y. (1994), *The Imperial Roman Army*, London: B.T. Batsford.

Le Bohec, Y. (2011), 'La violence et la guerre chez les Romains au temps d'Auguste', in Moosbauer, G., Wiegels, R. (eds) *Römische Okkupations- und Grenzpolitik im frühen Principat Beiträge zum Kongress ,Fines imperii – imperium sine fine?' in Osnabrück vom 14. bis 18. September 2009*, *Osnabrücker Forschungen zu Altertum und Antike-Rezeption* 14, Diepholz: Druckhaus Breyer, 239–52.

Lehman, G.A., 1991, 'Das Ende der römischen Herrschaft über das "Westelbische" Germanien: Von der Varus-Katastrophe zur Abberufung des Germanicus Caesar 16/7 n. Chr.', *Zeitschrift für Papyrologie und Epigraphik* 86, 79–96.

Lendering, J., Bosman, A. (2010), *De Rand van het Rijk: De Romeinen en de Lage Landen*, Amsterdam: uitgeverij Atheneum.

Lepper, F., Frere, S. (1988), *Trajan's Column*, Gloucester: Alan Sutton, 1988.

Lesquier, J. (1918), *L'Armée romaine d'Égypte d'Auguste à Dioclétien*, Cairo: L'Institut Française.

Letta, C. (1976), 'La dinastia dei Cozii e la romanizzazione delle Alpi occidentali', *Athenaeum* 54, 37–76.

Levick, B. (1972), 'Tiberius' Retirement to Rhodes in 6 B.C.', *Latomus* 31, 779–813.

Levick, B. (1976), *Tiberius the Politician*, London: Routledge.

Levick, B. (1985), *Government of the Roman Empire: A Source Book*, Beckenham: Croom Helm.

Levick, B. (1990), *Claudius*, London: B.T. Batsford.

Levick, B. (1999), 'Messages on Roman Coinage: Types and Inscriptions', in Paul, G.M., Ierardi, M. (eds), *Roman Coins and Public Life: E. Togo Salomon Papers II*, Ann Arbor: University of Michigan Press, 41–60.

Levick, B. (2010), *Augustus: Image and Substance*, Harlow: Pearson Education.

Levick, B.M. (1972), 'Abdication and Agrippa Postumus', *Historia: Zeitschrift fr Alte Geschichte* 21.4 (4th Qtr.), 674–697.

Lewis, M.J.T. (2001), 'Railways in the Greek and Roman World', in Guy, A., Rees, J., (eds) *Early Railways. A Selection of Papers from the First International Early Railways Conference*, 8–19 (10–15).

Lewis, P.R., Jones, G.D.B. (1970), 'Roman Gold-Mining in North-West Spain', *Journal of Roman Studies* 60 (1970), 169–85.

Lewis, R.G. (1993), 'Imperial Autobiography, Augustus to Hadrian', *Aufstieg und Niedergang der römischen Welt* 2.34.1, Berolini: De Gruyter, 629–706.

Lignereux, Y., Peters, J., Tassaux, F., Tronche, P. (1997), 'Viandes, volailles et fruits de mer à la table des legions romaines d'Aunedonnacum, 20–30 après Jésus-Christ (Aulnay-de-Saintonge, Charente-Maritime)', *Revue de Médecine Vétérinaire* 148.5, 399–412.

Lindemann, K., (1967), *Der Hildesheimer Silberfund: Varus und Germanicus*, Hildesheim: Lax.

Lindenthal, J.R., Nickel, R. (2005), 'Römische Lager Am Goldstein in Bad Nauheim', *Hessen Archäologie 2004*. Stuttgart, 86–88.

Linderski, J. (1984), 'Rome, Aphrodisias and the *Res Gestae*: The *Genera Militiae* and the Status of Octavian', *Journal of Roman Studies* 74, 74–80.

Lindsay, H. (1995), 'A Fertile Marriage: Agrippina and the Chronology of her Children by Germanicus', *Latomus* 54, 3–17.

Lintott, A. (1993), *Imperium Romanum: Politics and Administration*, London: Routledge.

Lobur, J.A. (2008), *Consensus, Concordia and the Formation of Roman Imperial Ideology*, London: Routledge.

Lott, J.B. (2012), *Death and Dynasty in Early Imperial Rome: Key Sources, with Text, Translation, and Commentary*, Cambridge: Cambridge University Press.

Lucas, H. (1904), *Zur Geschichte der Neptunsbasilica in Rom*, Berlin.

Luden, H. (1825), *Geschichte Des teutschen Volkes*, Volume 1, Gotha: Justus Perthes.

Luttwak, E.N. (1976), *The Grand Strategy of the Roman Empire: From the First Century A.D. to the Third*, Baltimore: The Johns Hopkins University Press.

MacKendrick, P. (1970), *Romans on the Rhine: Archaeology in Germany*, New York: Funk and Wagnalls.

MacKendrick, P. (1971), *Roman France*, London: Bell.

MacKenzie, D.C. (1983), 'Pay Differentials in the Early Empire', *The Classical World* 76.5 (May–June), 267–73.

MacMullen, R. (1984a), 'The Roman Emperors' Army Costs', *Latomus* 43.3 (July–September), 571–80.

MacMullen, R. (1984b), 'The Legion as a Society', *Historia: Zeitschrift für Alte Geschichte* 33.4 (Fourth Quarter), 440–56.

MacMullen, R. (2000), *Romanization in the Time of Augustus*, New Haven: Yale University Press.

Maddison, A. (2007), *Contours of the World Economy 1–2030 AD: Essays in Macro-Economic History*, Oxford: Oxford University Press.

Magie, D. (1908), 'The Mission of Agrippa to the Orient in 23 BC', *Classical Philology* 3.2 (Apr.), 145–52.

Magie, D. (1920), 'Augustus' War in Spain', *Classical Philology* 15.4 (October), 323–39.

Malloch, S.J.V. (2004), 'The end of the Rhine mutiny in Tacitus, Suetonius, and Dio', *Classical Quarterly (New Series)* 54, 198–210.

Mallory, J.P. (1989), *In Search of Indo-Europeans: Language, Archaeology and Myth*, London: Thames and Hudson.

Mann, J.C. (1963), 'The Raising of New Legions during the Principate', *Hermes* 91.4, 483–89.

Mann, J.C. (1974), 'The Frontiers of the Principate', *Aufstieg und Niedergang der römischen Welt* 2, 508–33.

Manning, W.H. Scott, I.R. (1979), 'Roman Timber Military Gateways in Britain and on the German Frontier', *Britannia* 10, 19–61.

Marañón, G. (1956), *Tiberius: The Resentful Caesar*, New York: Duell, Sloan and Pearce.

Marlowe, J. (1971), *The Golden Age of Alexandria: From its Foundation by Alexander the Great in 331BC to its Capture by the Arabs in 642AD*, London: Victor Gollancz.

Martin-Kilcher, S. (2011), 'Römer und *gentes Alpinae* im Konflikt – archäologische und historische Zeugnissedes 1. Jahrhunderts v. Chr.', in Moosbauer, G., Wiegels, R. (eds) *Römische Okkupations- und Grenzpolitik im frühen Principat Beiträge zum Kongress* ,Fines imperii – imperium sine fine?' *in Osnabrück vom 14. bis 18. September 2009, Osnabrücker Forschungen zu Altertum und Antike-Rezeption* 14, Diepholz: Druckhaus Breyer, 27–62.

Martino, E. (1982), *Roma Contra Cántabros y Astures. Nueva Lectura de las Fuentes*, Santander.

Matei-Popescu, F. (2013), 'The Roman Auxiliary Units of Moesia', in *Il Mar Nero: Annali di archeologia e storia* 8 (2010–11), 207–230.

Matijević, K. (2006), *Zur augusteischen Germanienpolitik*, Osnabrücker Online – Beiträge zu den Altertumswissenschaften.

Mattern, S.P. (1999), *Rome and the Enemy: Imperial Strategy in the Principate*, Berkeley: The University of California Press.

Mattingly, D.J., Hitchner, R.B. (1995), 'Roman Africa: An Archaeological Review', *Journal of Roman Studies* 85, 165–213.

Mattingly, D.J. (2013), *Imperialism, Power, and Identity: Experiencing the Roman Empire* (Miriam S. Balmuth Lectures in Ancient History and Archaeology), Princeton: Princeton University Press.

Mattingly, H. (1960), *Roman Coins: From the Earliest Times to the Fall of the Western Empire*, London: Methuen (Second Edition).

Matyszak, P. (2006), *The Sons of Caesar: Imperial Rome's First Dynasty*, London: Thames and Hudson.

Maxfield, V.A. (1981), *The Military Decorations of the Roman Army*, London: B.T. Batsford.

Mayor, A. (2009), *Greek Fire, Poison Arrows and Scorpion Bombs: Biological and Chemical Warfare in the Ancient World*, New York: Overlook Press.

McAllen Green, W. (1927), 'Notes on the Augustan Deities', *Classical Journal* 23.2 (November), 86–93.

McCall, J.B. (2002), *The Cavalry of the Roman Republic: Cavalry Combat and Elite Reputations in the Middle and Late Republic*, London: Routledge.

McCane, B.R. (2008), 'Simply Irresistible: Augustus, Herod, and the Empire', *Journal of Biblical Literature* 127.4 (Winter), 725–35.

McCullough, D.W. (ed.) (1998), *Chronicles of the Barbarians; Firsthand Accounts of Pillage and Conquest, From the Ancient World to the Fall of Constantinople*, New York: History Book Club.

McDermott, W.C. (1970), '*Milites Gregarii*', *Greece & Rome* (Second Series) 17.2 (October) 184–96.

McDonnell-Staff, P. (2009), 'The Other Invader Over the Alps: Watershed of the Second Punic War', in Oorthuys, J. (ed.), *Ancient Warfare* 3.4 (August/September), 36–41.

McPherson, C. (2009), 'Fact and Fiction: Crassus, Augustus, and the *Spolia Opima*', *McGill Journal of Classical Studies* 8, 21–34.

Melchior, A. (2009), 'What Would Pompey Do? *Exempla* and Pompeian Failure in the *Bellum Africum*', *Classical Journal* 104.3 (February–March), 241–57.

M'Elderry, R.K. (1909), 'The Legions of the Euphrates Frontier', *Classical Quarterly* 3.1 (January), 44–53.

Mennelli, G. (1978), 'Ipotesi sull'iscrizione dei re Cozii nel teatro di Augusta Taurinorum', *RIL* CXII, 96–100.

Metzger, E. (2004), 'Roman judges, case law, and principles of procedure', *Law and History Review* 22, 243–75.

Meyer, A. (2013), *The Creation, Composition, Service and Settlement of Roman Auxiliary Units Raised on the Iberian Peninsula* (British Archaeological Reports International Series).

Meyer D. (1961), *Die Aussenpolitik des Augustus und die Augusteische Dichtung*, Cologne: Böhlau Verlag.

Miles, G.B. (1990), 'Roman and Modern Imperialism: A Reassessment', *Comparative Studies in Society and History* 32.4 (October), 629–59.

Millar, F. (1966), 'The Emperor, the Senate and the Provinces', *Journal of Roman Studies* 56, Parts 1 and 2, 156–66.

Millar, F. (1973), 'Triumvirate and Principate', *Journal of Roman Studies* 63, 50–67.

Millar, F. (1982), 'Emperors, Frontiers and Foreign Relations, 31 B.C. to A.D. 378', *Britannia* 13, 1–23.

Millar, F. (1988), 'Government and Diplomacy in the Roman Empire during the First Three Centuries', *The International History Review* 10.3 (August), 345–77.

Millar, F. (1992), 'The Augustan Monarchy. Review of *Between Republic and Empire: Interpretations of Augustus and his Principate* by Kurt A. Raaflaub; Mark Toher', *Classical Review (New Series)* 42.2, 378–81.

Mitchell, S. (1976), '*Legio* VII and the Garrison of Augustan Galatia', *Classical Quarterly (New Series)* 26.2, 298–308.

Mócsy, A. (1983), 'Civilized Pannonians', in Hartley, B., Wacher J. (eds), *Rome and Her Northern Provinces*, 169–78.

Momigliano, A. (1942), 'The Peace of the *Ara Pacis*', *Journal of the Warburg and Courtauld Institutes* 5, 228–31.

Mommsen, T.E. (1954), 'Augustus and Britain: A Fragment from Livy?', *American Journal of Philology* 75.2, 175–83.

Mommsen, T., Demandt, A. (1996), *A History of Rome Under the Emperors*, London: Routledge.

Monteil, M. (2008), *La France gallo-romaine*, Paris: Editions La Découverte.

Morillo, A., García-Marcos, V. (2002), 'Twenty Years of Roman Military Archaeology in Spain', in Freeman, P. *et al.* (eds), *Limes XVIIIth International Congress of Roman Frontier Studies held in Amman, Jordan* (Sept. 2000), Oxford, 2002, 779–89.

Morillo, A. (2011), 'The Roman occupation of the north of *Hispania*: war, military deployment and cultural integration', in Moosbauer, G., Wiegels, R. (eds) *Römische Okkupations- und Grenzpolitik im frühen Principat Beiträge zum Kongress ,Fines imperii – imperium sine fine?' in Osnabrück vom 14. bis 18. September 2009*, Osnabrücker Forschungen zu Altertum und Antike-Rezeption 14, Diepholz: Druckhaus Breyer, 11–26.

Mueller, H-F. (2002), *Roman Religion in Valerius Maximus*, London: Routledge.

Müller, K. (1874), *Fragmenta Historicorum Graecorum* 3, Paris.

Newark, T., McBride, A. (1985), *The Barbarians: Warriors and Wars of the Dark Ages*, Poole: Blandford Press.

Newark, T., McBride, A. (1986), *Celtic Warriors 400BC-AD1600*, Poole: Blandford Press.

Newark, T., McBride, A. (1998), *Celtic Warriors*, Hong Kong: The Military Book Club/Concord Publications.

Newlands, C.E. (1995), *Playing with Time: Ovid and the* Fasti, New York: Cornell University Press.

Nicholls, J.J. (1967), 'The Content of the *Lex Curiata*' in *American Journal of Philology* 88.3 (Jul.), 257–278.

Nicolet, C. (1984), 'Augustus, Government, and the Propertied Classes', in Millar, F., Segal, E. (eds) *Caesar Augustus: Seven Aspects*, Oxford, 89–128.

Nicolet, C., Gautier Dalché, P. (1986), 'Les quatre sages de Jules César et la mesure du monde selon Julius Honorius', *Journal des Savants* (October–December), 157–218.

Nicolet, C. (1991), *Space, Geography, and Politics in the Early Roman Empire*, Ann Arbor: University of Michigan Press.

Nigdélis, P.M. (1994), 'M. Insteius L.f. αὐτοκράτωρ et la province de Macedoine au debut du second triumvirat. À propos d'une inscription inédite d'Europos', *Bulletin de correspondance hellénique*, 118.1, 215–228.

Nippel, W. (1995), *Public Order in Ancient Rome*, Cambridge: Cambridge University Press.

Nock, A.D. (1952), 'The Roman Army and the Roman Religious Year', *Harvard Theological Review* 45.4 (October), 187–252.

Nony, D. (1982), 'Sur quelques monnaies impériales romaines', *Mélanges de l'Ecole française de Rome: Antiquité* 94–2, 893–909.

North, J.A. (1981), 'The Development of Roman Imperialism', *Journal of Roman Studies* 71, 1–9.

Ober, J. (1982), 'Tiberius and the Political Testament of Augustus', *Historia: Zeitschrift für Alte Geschichte* 31.3 (Third Quarter), 306–28

Oberziner, G. (1900), *Le guerre di Augusto contro i populi Alpini*, Trento: Roma E. Loescher.

Odiorne, G.S. (1961), *How Managers Make Things Happen*, Englewood Cliffs: Prentice-Hall.

Oldfather, W.A. (1916), 'The Varus Episode', *Classical Journal* 11.4 (January), 226–36.

Oliver, J.H. (1989), *Greek Constitutions of Early Roman Emperors from Inscriptions and Papyri* no. 295, Philadelphia: American Philosophical Society.

Oliver, R.P. (1951), 'The First Medicean MS of Tacitus and the Titulature of Ancient Books', *Transactions and Proceedings of the American Philological Association* 82, 232–61.

Opper, T. (2014), *The Meroë Head of Augustus*, London: The British Museum.

Orejas, A., Sánchez-Palencia, F.J. (2002), 'Mines, Territorial Organization, and Social Structure in Roman Iberia: Carthago Noua and the Peninsular Northwest', *American Journal of Archaeology* 106.4 (October), 581–99.

Orth W. (1978), 'Zur Fabricius-Tuscus-Inschrift aus Alexandreia/Troas', *Zeitschrift für Papyrologie und Epigraphik* 28, 57–60.

Osgood, J. (2011), *Claudius Caesar: Image and Power in the Early Roman Empire*, Cambridge: Cambridge Unversity Press.

Östenberg, I. (2014), 'War and remembrance. Memories of defeat in ancient Rome', in Alroth, B., Scheffer, C. (eds), *Attitudes towards the past in Antiquity: Creating identities?*, papers held at the Conference at Stockholm University 15–17 May 2009, 255–65.

Pandey, N.B. (2014), 'Reading Rome from the Farther Shore: *Aeneid* 6 in the Augustan Landscape', *Vergilius* 60, 85–116.

Panter, A. (2007), 'Der Drususstein in Mainz und dessen Einordnung in die römische Grabarchitektur seiner Erbauungszeit', *Mainzer Archäologische Schriften* 6, Generaldirektion Kulturelles Erbe Rheinland-Pfalz, Direktion Landesarchäologie.

Pantle, C. (2009), *Die Varusschlacht: Der germanische Freiheitskrieg*, Berlin: Ullstein Buchverlage.

Pappano, A.E. (1941), 'Agrippa Postumus', *Classical Philology* 36.1 (Jan.), 30–45.

Parchami, A. (2009), *Hegemonic Peace and Empire: The* Pax Romana, Britannica *and* Americana, Abingdon: Routledge.

Parker, H.M.D. (1928), *The Roman Legions*, Oxford: Clarendon Press.

Paul, G.M. Ierardi, M. (eds) (1999), *Roman Coins and Public Life Under the Empire: E. Togo Salmon Papers II*, Ann Arbor: University of Michigan Press.

Pelling, C.B.R (1988), *Plutarch: Life of Antony*, Cambridge: Cambridge University Press.

Pelling, C.B.R. (1996), 'The Triumviral Period', in Bowman, A.K. *et al* (ed.), *CAH* 10² Cambridge: Cambridge University Press, 1–69.

Perowne, S. (1956), *The Life and Times of Herod the Great*, London: Hodder and Stoughton.

Petrikovits, H. (1960), *Das römische Rheinland Archäologische Forschungen seit 1945*, *Beihefte der Bonner Jahrbücher* Band 8, Köln: Westdeutcher Verlag.

Pettegrew, D.K. (2011), 'The *Diolkos* of Corinth', *American Journal of Archaeology* 115.4, 549–74.

Pietsch, M., Timpe, D., Wamser, L. (1991), 'Das augusteische Truppenlager Marktbreit. Bisherige archäologische Befunde und historische Erwägungen', *Bericht der Römisch-Germanischen Kommission* 72, 263–324.

Pietsch, M. (1993), 'Die Zentralgebäude des augusteischen Legionslagers von Marktbreit und die *Principia* von Haltern', *Germania* 71, 355–68.

Piruli, S. (1980), 'Osservazioni sul feriale di Spello', *Tituli* 2, 47–80.

Pitassi, M. (2011), *Roman Warships*, Woodbridge: The Boydell Press.

Pitts, L.F. (1989), 'Relations between Rome and the German "Kings" on the Middle Danube in the First to Fourth Centuries A.D.', *Journal of Roman Studies* 79, 45–58.

Platner, S.B. (as completed and revised by T. Ashby) (1929), *A Topographical Dictionary of Ancient Rome*, London: Oxford.

Pleket, H.W. (1958), *The Greek Inscriptions in the* Rijksmuseum van Oudheden *at Leyden*, Leiden.

Polo, F.P. (2011), *The Consul at Rome: The Civil Functions of the Consuls in the Roman Republic*, Cambridge: Cambridge University Press.

Posluschny, A. (1977), 'Die hallstattzeitliche Siedlung auf dem Kapellenberg bei Marktbreit, Unterfranken', *Bayerische Vorgeschichtsblätter* 62, 29–113.

Potter, T.W. (1987), *Roman Italy*, London: Guild Publishing/British Museum Publications.

Powell, A. (ed.) (2013), *Roman Poetry and Propaganda in the Age of Augustus* (Bristol Classical Paperbacks), London: Bloomsbury.

Powell, A., Smith, C. (eds) (2008), *The Lost Memoirs of Augustus and the Development of Roman Autobiography*, Swansea: Classical Press of Wales.

Powell, A., Welch, K. (eds) (2002), *Sextus Pompeius*, Swansea: Classical Press of Wales.

Powell, L. (1988), 'The Mood of the Armies: Morale and Mutiny in the Roman Army of the First Century AD', *Exercitus* 2.4, 61–64.

Powell, L. (2009), '*Bella Germaniae*: The German Wars of Drusus the Elder and Tiberius', in Oorthuys, J. (ed), *Ancient Warfare*, Special Issue 1, 10–16.

Powell, L. (2010), 'Fighting for the Gods: Historical Introduction', in Oorthuys, J. (ed.), *Ancient Warfare* 4.5, 2–5.

Powell, L. (2011), *Eager for Glory: The Untold Story of Drusus the Elder*, Barnsley: Pen & Sword Books.

Powell, L. (2013), *Germanicus: The Magnificent Life and Mysterious Death of Rome's Most Popular General*, Barnsley: Pen & Sword Books.

Powell, L. (2014), *Combat: Roman Soldier v. Germanic Warrior*, Oxford: Osprey Publishing.

Powell, L. (2015), *Marcus Agrippa: Right-Hand Man of Caesar Augustus*, Barnsley: Pen & Sword Books.

Powell, L. (2016), 'A Trophy Proud to Thee: Celebrating Victory the Augustan Way', in Brouwers, J. (ed.), *Ancient Warfare* 9.6, 16–20.

Pratt, K.J. (1955), 'Roman Anti-Militarism', *Classical Journal* 51.1 (October), 21–25.

Raaflaub, K.A. (2007), *War and Peace in the Ancient World*, Oxford: Blackwell Publishing.

Raaflaub, K. A. (2009), 'The political significance of Augustus' military reforms', in Edmondson, J. (ed.), *Augustus*, Edinburgh Readings on the Ancient World, Edinburgh (2009), 203–28.

Ramage, E.S. (1985), 'Augustus' Treatment of Julius Caesar', *Historia: Zeitschrift für Alte Geschichte* 34. 2 (second quarter), 223–45.

Ramsey, J.T., Licht, A.L., Marsden, B.G. (eds) (1997), *The Comet of 44 B.C. and Caesar's Funeral Games* (APA American Classical Studies, No. 39), Oxford: Oxford University Press.

Ramsey, W.M. (1916), 'Colonia Caesarea (Pisidian Antioch) in the Augustan Age', *Journal of Roman Studies* 6, 83–134.

Ramsey, W.M. (1917), 'Studies in the Roman Province Galatia: I. The Homanadeis and the Homanadensian War', *Journal of Roman Studies* 7, 229–83.

Ramsey, W.M. (1922), 'Studies in the Roman Province Galatia', *Journal of Roman Studies* 12, 147–86.

Ramsey, W.M. (1924), Studies in the Roman Province Galatia. VI. – Some Inscriptions of Colonia Caesarea Antiochea', *Journal of Roman Studies* 14, 172–205.

Rankov, B., Hook, R. (1994), *The Praetorian Guard*, London: Osprey Publishing.

Rasbach, G., Becker, A. (2003), 'Die spätaugusteische Stadtgründung in Lahnau-Waldgirmes. Archäologische, architektonische und naturwissenschaftliche Untersuchungen', in *Germania* 81, 147–99.

Reddé, M. (2011), 'L'armée romaine et les peuples gaulois de César á Auguste', in Moosbauer, G., Wiegels, R. (eds) *Römische Okkupations- und Grenzpolitik im frühen Principat Beiträge zum Kongress 'Fines imperii – imperium sine fine?' in Osnabrück vom 14. bis 18. September 2009*, Osnabrücker Forschungen zu Altertum und Antike-Rezeption 14, Diepholz: Druckhaus Breyer, 63–74.

Reed, N. (1975), 'Drusus and the Classis Britannica', *Historia: Zeitschrift für Alte Geschichte* 24.2, 315–23.

Reeder, J.C. (1997), 'The Statue of Augustus from Prima Porta, the Underground Complex, and the Omen of the Gallina Alba', *American Journal of Philology* 118.1 (Spring), 89–118.

Regev, E. (2010), 'Herod's Jewish Ideology Facing Romanization: On Intermarriage, Ritual Baths, and Speeches', *Jewish Quarterly Review* 100.2 (Spring), 197–222.

Rehak, P. (2001), 'Aeneas or Numa? Rethinking the Meaning of the *Ara Pacis Augustae*', *The Art Bulletin* 83.2 (June), 190–208.

Reinhold, M. (1933), *Marcus Agrippa: A Biography*, New York: The W.F. Humphrey Press.

Reinhold, M. (1972), 'Marcus Agrippa's Son-in-Law P. Quinctilius Varus', *Classical Philology* 67.2 (Apr.), 119–21.

Reinking, L. (1855), *Die Niederlage des Quintilius Varus und Germanicus Kriegszug Durch das Bructerer-land: Eine Prüfung der bisherigen Ansichten*, Warendorf: J. Schnell.

Reinmuth, O.W. (1935), *The Prefect of Egypt from Augustus to Diocletian*, Leipzig: Dieterich'schen Verlagsbuchhandlung.

Retsö, J. (2000), 'Where and What Was "Arabia Felix"?', *Proceedings of the Seminar for Arabian Studies* 30, papers from the thirty-third meeting of the Seminar for Arabian Studies held in London, 15–17 July 1999, 189–92.

Retsö, J. (2003), 'When Did Yemen Become "Arabia Felix"?', *Proceedings of the Seminar for Arabian Studies 33*, papers from at the thirty-sixth meeting of the Seminar for Arabian Studies held in London, 18–20 July 2002, 229–35

Rettinger, E. (ed.) (2003), *2000 Jahre Mainz: Geschichte der Stadt digital*, (CD-ROM), Institut für Geschichtliche Landeskunde an der Universität Mainz, Mainz.

Reynolds, J. (1996), 'Cyrene', in Bowman, A.K., Champlin, E., Lintott, A. (eds), *The Cambridge Ancient History Volume X: The Augustan Empire, 43 B.C.–A.D. 69* (Second Edition), Cambridge: Cambridge University Press, 619–40.

Rich, J, Shipley, G. (eds) (1993), *War and Society in the Roman World*, London: Routledge.

Rich, J.W. (1998), 'Augustus's Parthian Honours, the Temple of Mars Ultor and the Arch in the Forum Romanum', *Papers of the British School at Rome* 66, 71–128.

Rich, J.W. (1999), 'Drusus and the *Spolia Opima*', *Classical Quarterly (New Series)* 49.2, 544–55.

Rich, J.W. (2002), 'Augustus, War and Peace', in Edmondson, J. (ed.), *Augustus*, Edinburgh Readings on the Ancient World, Edinburgh (2009), 137–64.

Richardson, J.S. (1976), 'The Spanish Mines and the Development of Provincial Taxation in the Second Century B.C.', *Journal of Roman Studies* 66, 139–52.

Richardson, J.S. (2012) *Augustan Rome 44 BC to AD 14: The Restoration of the Republic and the Establishment of the Empire* (The Edinburgh History of Ancient Rome), Edinburgh: Edinburgh University Press.

Richardson, P. (1996), *Herod: King of the Jews and Friend of the Romans*, Columbia SC: University of South Carolina.

Richmond, I.A. (1933), 'Commemorative Arches and City Gates in the Augustan Age', *Journal of Roman Studies* 23, 149–74.

Riese, A. (1878), *Geographi latini minores collegit, recensuit, prolegomenis instruxit*, Heilbronn: Henninger Bros.

Ritchie, W.F, Ritchie, J.N.G. (1985), *Celtic Warriors*, Aylesbury: Shire Archaeology.

Robinson, H.R. (1975), *The Armour of Imperial Rome*, London: Arms and Armour Press.

Rodà de Llanza, I. (2003), in Morillo, A., Aurrcoecha, J. (eds), *The Roman Army in Hispania*, Leon, pp. 53–63.

Roddaz, J.-M. (1984), *Marcus Agrippa*, Rome: École Française de Rome, Palais Farnèse.

Rogers, K. (2008), 'Sextus Pompeius: Rebellious Pirate or Imitative Son', *Chrestomathy* 7, 199–226.

Rogers, R.S. (1940), 'Tiberius' Reversal of an Augustan Policy', *Transactions and Proceedings of the American Philological Association* 71, 532–36.

Rogers, R.S. (1941), 'Augustus the Man', *Classical Journal* 36.8 (May), 449–63.

Rogers, R.S. (1967), 'The Deaths of Julia and Gracchus, A.D. 14', *Transactions and Proceedings of the American Philological Society* 98, 383–90.

Roller, D.W. (1998), *The Building Program of Herod the Great*, Berkeley: University of California Press.

Rollo, W. (1938), 'The Franco-German Frontier', *Greece & Rome* 8.22 (October), 36–49.

Romeo, I. (1998), *Ingenuus Leo. L'immagine di Agrippa*, Rome: L'Ermadi Bretschneider.

Romer, F.E. (1978). 'A Numismatic Date for the Departure of C. Caesar?', *Transactions of the American Philological Association (1974–)* 108, 187–202.

Romer, F.E. (1985), 'A Case of Client-Kingship', *American Journal of Philology* 106.1 (Spring 1985), 75–100.

Röpke, G. (2008), *Fasti Sacerdotum: A Prosopography of Pagan, Jewish, and Christian Religious Officials in the City of Rome, 300 BC to AD 499*, Oxford: Oxford University Press.

Rosborough, R.R. (1920), *An epigraphic commentary on Suetonius's Life of Caius Caligula*, Philadelphia, Penn.

Rose, C.B. (1990), '"Princes" and Barbarians on the *Ara Pacis*', *American Journal of Archaeology* 94.3 (Jul.), 453–67

Rose, C.B. (1997), *Dynastic Commemoration and Imperial Portraiture in the Julio-Claudian Period*, Cambridge: Cambridge University Press.

Rose, C.B. (2005), 'The Parthians in Augustan Rome', *American Journal of Archaeology* 109.1 (January), 21–75.

Ross, A. (1970), *Everyday Life of the Pagan Celts*, London: B.T. Batsford.

Rossini, O. (2007), *Ara Pacis*, Rome: Mondadori Electa (collana Musei in Comune).

Rosso, E. (2000), 'Vie d'un groupe statuaire julio-claudien à Mediolanum Santonum', *Labyrinthe* 7, 103–122 (online at http://labyrinthe.revues.org/index805.html – accessed 29 February 2016).

Rost, A. (2005), 'Conditions for the Preservation of Roman Military Equipment on Battlefields – the Example of Kalkriese' in Kocsis, L. (ed.), *Journal of Roman Military Equipment* 16, The Enemies of Rome: Proceedings of the 15th International Roman Military Equipment Conference, Budapest 2005, 219–224.

Rost, A. (2009), 'The battle between Romans and Germans in Kalkriese: interpreting the archaeological remains from an ancient battlefield', in Morillo, A., Hanel, N., Martin, E. (eds), *Limes XX*, *Roman Frontier Studies*. Anejo de Gladius 13, 1339–45.

Roth, J.P. (1994), 'The Size and Organization of the Roman Imperial Legion', *Historia: Zeitschrift für Alte Geschichte* 43.3 (Third Quarter), 346–62.

Roth, J.P. (1999), *The Logistics of the Roman Army at War (264 BC-AD 235)*, Boston: Brill Academic Publishers.

Rothenhöfer, P. (2003), 'Geschäfte in Germanien. Zur Ausbeutung von Erzlagerstätten unter Augustus in Germanien', *Zeitschrift für Papyrologie und Epigraphik* 143, 277–86.

Rowe, G. (2002), *Princes and Political Cultures: The New Tiberian Senatorial Decrees*, Ann Arbor: The University of Michigan Press.

Rowell, H.T. (1941), 'Vergil and the Forum of Augustus', *American Journal of Philology* 62.3, 261–76.

Roxan, M.M. (1973), *The auxilia of the Roman Army raised in the Iberian Peninsula*. Unpublished doctoral thesis, University of London (online at http://discovery.ucl.ac.uk/1318033/ – accessed 29 February 2016).

Roymans, N. (2000), 'The Lower Rhine *Triquetrum* Coinages and the Ethnogenesis of the Batavi', Grünewald, T., Schalles, H.J. (eds) *Germania Inferior: Beiträge des deutschen-niederländischen Kolloquiums in Regionalmuseum Xanten 21.–24. September 1999*, Berlin: Walter de Gruyter, 93–145.

Roymans, N. (2004), *Ethnic identity and imperial power: the Batavians in the early Roman Empire*, Amsterdam: Amsterdam University Press.

Roymans, N., Aarts, J. (2009), 'Coin use in a dynamic frontier region. Late Iron Age Coinages in the Lower Rhine area', *Journal of Archaeology in the Low Countries* 1–1 (May) (online at http://dpc.uba.uva.nl/cgi/t/text/get-pdf?c=jalc;idno=0101a02 – accessed 29 February 2016).

Rüger, C. (1996), 'Germany', in Bowman, A.K., Champlin, E., Lintott, A. (eds), *The Cambridge Ancient History Volume X: The Augustan Empire, 43 B.C.–A.D. 69* (Second Edition), Cambridge: Cambridge University Press, 517–34.

Rüpke, J. (2008), *Fasti Sacerdotum: A Prosopography of Pagan, Jewish, and Christian Religious Officials in the City of Rome, 300BC to AD499*, Oxford: Oxford University Press.

Rutledge, S.H. (2001), *Imperial Inquisitions: Prosecutors and Informants from Tiberius to Domitian*, London: Routledge.

Ryan, F.X. (1998), *Rank and Participation in the Republican Senate*, Stuttgart: Franz Steiner Verlag.

Ryberg, I.S. (1949), 'The Procession of the Ara Pacis', *Memoirs of the American Academy in Rome* 19, 77–101.

Sabin, P. (2000), 'The Face of Roman War', *Journal of Roman Studies* 90, 1–17.

Saddington, D.B. (1982), *The Development of the Roman Auxiliary Forces from Caesar to Vespasian (49B.C.–A.D.79)*, Harare: University of Zimbabwe.

Saddington, D.B. (1990), 'The Origin and Nature of the German and British Fleets', *Britannia* 21, 223–32.

Saddington, D.B. (1996), 'Early Imperial *praefecti castrorum*', *Historia: Zeitschrift für Alte Geschichte* 45.2 (Second Quarter), 244–52.

Salač, V. (2006), '2000 let od římského vojenského tažení proti Marobudovi Naše nejstarší historické výročí a metodologické problémy studia starší doby římské', *Archeologické rozhledy* 58, 462–85.

Salmon, E.T. (1956), 'The Evolution of Augustus' Principate', *Historia: Zeitschrift für Alte Geschichte* 5.4 (November), 456-78.

Sampson, G.C. (2007), *The Defeat of Rome in the East: Crassus, The Parthians and the Disastrous Battle of Carrhae, 53 BC*, Barnsley: Pen & Sword Books.

Sanders, H.A. (1941), 'The Origin of the Third Cyrenaic Legion', *American Journal of Philology* 62.1, 84–87.

Santosuosso, A. (1997), *Soldiers, Citizens, and The Symbols of War: From Classical Greece to Republican Rome, 500–167BC*, Boulder: Westview Press.

Šašel Kos, M. (1995), 'The 15th Legion at Emona: Some Thoughts', *Zeitschrift für Papyrologie und Epigraphik* 109, 227–44.

Šašel Kos, M. (2011), 'The Roman conquest of Dalmatia and Pannonia under Augustus – some of the latest research results', in Moosbauer, G., Wiegels, R. (eds) *Römische Okkupations- und Grenzpolitik im frühen Principat Beiträge zum Kongress 'Fines imperii – imperium sine fine?' in Osnabrück vom 14. bis 18. September 2009*, *Osnabrücker Forschungen zu Altertum und Antike-Rezeption* 14, Diepholz: Druckhaus Breyer, 107–18.

Sauer, E. (1999), 'The Augustan coins from Bourbonne-les-Bains (Haute-Marne): A mathematical approach to dating a coin assemblage', *Revue Numismatique* 6 (154), 145–82.

Savage, J.J.H. (1968), 'The *Aurea Dicta* of Augustus and the Poets', *Transactions and Proceedings of the American Philological Association* 99, 401–17.

Sayles, W.G. (2007) (Second Edition), *Ancient Coin Collecting III: The Roman World – Politics and Propaganda*, Iola: Krause Publications.

Scarborough, J. (1968), 'Roman Medicine and the Legions: A Reconsideration', in *Medical History* 12.3, 254–61.

Scheid, J. (2001), 'To Honour the *Princeps* and Venerate the Gods: Public Cult, Neighbourhood Cults, and Imperial Cult in Augustan Rome', Edmondson, J. (ed.), *Augustus*, Edinburgh: Edinburgh Readings on the Ancient World (2009), 275–309.

Scheidel, W. (2009), 'Disease and Death in the ancient city of Rome', in *Princeton/Stanford Working Papers in Classics* (available online at www.princeton.edu/~pswpc/pdfs/scheidel/040901.pdf).

Schiller, A.A. (1978), *Roman Law: Mechanisms of Development*, Berlin: de Gruyter Mouton.

Schlüter, W. (1999), 'The Battle of the Teutoburg Forest: archaeological research at Kalkriese near Osnabrück', in Creighton, J.D., Wilson, R.J.A. (eds), *Roman Germany: Studies in Culural Interaction*, *Journal of Roman Archaeology*, Supplementary Series 32, 125–59.

Schmitthenner, W. (1962), 'Augustus' spanischer Feldzug und der Kampf um den Prinzipat', *Historia: Zeitschrift für Alte Geschichte* 11.1 (January), 29–85.

Schmitthenner, W. (1979), 'Rome and India: Aspects of Universal History during the Principate', *Journal of Roman Studies* 69, 90–106.

Schneider, H. (ed.) (2006), *Feindliche Nachbarn: Rom und die Germanen*, Wien: Böhlau Verlag.

Schnurbein, S. von (1971), 'Ein Bleibarren der XIX. Legion aus dem Hauptlager von Haltern', in *Germania* XLIX, 132–36.

Schnurbein, S. von (1974), *Die römischen Militäranlagen bei Haltern: Bericht über die Forschungen seit 1899*, Münster: Verlag Aschendorff.

Schnurbein, S. von (1985), 'Die Funde von Augsburg-Oberhausen und die Besetzung des Alpenvorlandes durch die Römer', in Bellot, J., Czysz, W., Krahe, G. (eds), *Forschungen zur provinzial-römschen Archäologie in Bayerisch-Schwaben*, Augusburg, 15–44.

Schnurbein, S. von, Köhler, H.-J. (1994), 'Dorlar: Ein augusteisches Römerlager im Lahntal', in *Germania* 72, 193–703.

Schnurbein, S. von (2000), 'The Organization of the Fortresses in Augustan Germany', in Brewer, R.J. (ed.), *Roman Fortresses and their Legions: Papers in Honour of George C Boon*, London/Cardiff: Society of Antiquaries of London/National Museums and Galleries of Wales, 29–39.

Schnurbein, S. von (2002), 'Neue Grabungen in Haltern, Oberaden und Anreppen', in Freeman, P. et al. (eds), *Limes XVII: Proceedings of the XVIIIth International Congress of Roman Frontier Studies*, Oxford, 527–33.

Schnurbein, S. von (2004), 'Die augusteischen Stützpunkte in Mainfranken und Hessen', in Wamser, L., Flügel, C., Ziegaus, B. (2004), *Die Römer zwischen Alpen und Nordmeer*, Düsseldorf: Patmos Verlag, 34–37.

Schön, F. (1986), *Der Beginn der römischen Herrschaft in Rätien*, Sigmaringen: Thorbecke.

Schönberger, C. (1969), 'The Roman Frontier Policy in Germany: An Archaeological Survey', *Journal of Roman Studies* 59 1/2, 144–97.

Schönberger, H., Simon, H.G. (1976), *Römerlager Rödgen* (Limesforschungen 15), Berlin: Gebr. Mann Verlag.

Schumacher, L. (1985), 'Die imperatorischen Akklamationen der Triumvirn und die *auspicia* des Augustus', *Historia: Zeitschrift für Alte Geschichte* 34.2 (Second Quarter), 191–222.

Schußmann, M. (1993), *Die Kelten in Bayern*, Treuchtlingen-Berlin: wek-Verlag.

Seager, R. (1972), *Tiberius*, Berkeley: University of California Press.

Ségolène, D. (1992), *Prosopographie des chevaliers romains julio-claudiens (43 av. J.-C. – 70 ap. J.-C.)*, (Publications de l'École française de Rome, 153), Rome: École Française de Rome.

Seibert, J. (1970), 'Der Huldigungseid auf Kaiser Tiberius', *Historia: Zeitschrift für Alte Geschichte* 19.2 (April), 224–31.

Severy, B. (2003), *Augustus and the Family at the Birth of the Roman Empire*, London: Routledge.

Shatzman, I. (1972), 'The Roman General's Authority over Booty', *Historia: Zeitschrift für Alte Geschichte* 21.2 (2nd Qtr.), 177–205.

Shaw, B.D. (1984), 'Bandits in the Roman Empire', *Past and Present* 105 (November), 3–52.

Shaw-Smith, R. (1971), 'A Letter from Augustus to Tiberius', *Greece & Rome* (Second Series) 18.2 (October), 213–14.

Shaya, J. (2013), 'The Public Life of Monuments: The *Summi Viri* of the Forum of Augustus', *American Journal of Archaeology* 117.1 (January), 83–110.

Sherk, R.T., (1974), 'Roman Geographical Exploration and Military Maps', *Aufstieg und Niedergang des Römisches Welt* 2.1, 534–62.

Shero, L.R. (1941), 'Augustus and His Associates', *Classical Journal* 37.2 (November), 87–93.

Shirley, E. (2001), *Building a Roman Legionary Fortress*, Stroud: The History Press/Tempus.

Shotter, D. (1992), *Tiberius Caesar*, London: Routledge.

Sidebotham, S.E. (1986), 'Aelius Gallus and Arabia', *Latomus* 45.3 (July–September), 590–602.

Sidebottom, H. (1993), 'Philosphers' Attitudes to Warfare Under the Principate', in Rich, J., Shipley, G. (eds), *War and Society in the Roman World*, London: Routledge, 241–64.

Signon, H. (1978a), *Marcus Agrippa: Freund und Mitregend des Kaisers Augustus*, Frankfurt (Main): Frankfurter Societäts-Druckerei.

Signon, H. (1978b), *Agrippa: Freund und Mitregent des Kaisers Augustus*, Frankfurt (Main): Societäts-Verlag.

Simkins, M. (1984), *The Roman Army from Caesar to Trajan*, London: Osprey Publishing.

Simpson, C.J. (1977), 'The Date of Dedication of the Temple of Mars Ultor', *Journal of Roman Studies* 67, 91–94

Simpson, C.J. (1988), 'The Change in *Praenomen* of Drusus Germanicus', *Phoenix - Journal of the Classical Association of Canada* 42.2, 173–75.

Simpson, C.J. (2005), 'Rome's "Official Imperial Seal"? The Rings of Augustus and His First Century Successors', *Historia: Zeitschrift für Alte Geschichte* 54.2, 180–88

Sitwell, N.H.H. (1986), *Outside the Empire: The World the Romans Knew*, London: Paladin.

Smith, W. (ed.) (1867), *The Dictionary of Greek and Roman Biography and Mythology*, Boston: Little, Brown.

Sommer, C.S. (2009), 'Why There? The Positioning of Forts Along the Riverine Frontiers', *Journal of Roman Archaeology* Supplement 74, 103–14.

Souza, P. (2008), '*Parta victoriis pax*: Roman emperors as peacemakers', in Souza, P., France, J. (eds), *War and Peace in Ancient and Medieval History*, Cambridge: Cambridge University Press, pp. 76–106.

Spaeth, B.S. (1994), 'The Goddess Ceres in the Ara Pacis Augustae and the Carthage Relief', *American Journal of Archaeology* 98.1 (January), 65–100.

Spaul, J. (2000), *Cohors²*. *The Evidence for and a Short History of the Auxiliary Infantry Units of the Imperial Roman Army*, BAR International Series 841, Oxford: Oxford Archaeopress.

Speidel, M. (1976), 'Citizen Cohorts in the Roman Imperial Army. New Data on the *Cohorts Apula*, Campana, and III Campestris', *Transactions of the American Philological Association (1974–)* 106, 339–48.

Speidel, M. (1982), 'Augustus's Deployment of the Legions in Egypt', *Chronique d'Egypte* 57.113, 120–24.

Speidel, M. (1992a), 'Roman Army Pay Scales', *Journal of Roman Studies* 82, 87–106.

Speidel, M. (1992b), '*Exploratores*: Mobile Elite Units of Roman Germany', *Roman Army Studies* II, *Mavors* 8, 89–104.

Speidel, M.P. (1994), *Riding for Caesar: The Roman Emperor's Horseguard*, London: B.T. Batsford.

Speidel, M.P. (2004), *Ancient Germanic Warriors: Warrior Styles from Trajan's Column to Icelandic Sagas*, Abingdon, Oxfordshire: Routledge.

Staccioli, R.A. (1986), *Guida di Roma Antica*, Milan: RCS Rizzoli Libri.

Starr, C.G. (1941), *The Roman Imperial Navy 31BC–AD324*, Cornell Studies in Classical Philology 26, New York: Cornell University Press.

Starr, C.G. (1956), 'How Did Augustus Stop the Roman Revolution?', *Classical Journal* 52.3 (December), 107–12.

Starr, C.G. (1969), 'Review of *Untersuchungen zu den Kriegsflotten der romischen Kaiserzeit* by Dietmar Kienast', *American Journal of Philology* 90.1 (January), 120–22.

Stern, G. (2006), *Women, Children, and Senators on the* Ara Pacis Augustae: *A Study of Augustus' Vision of a New World Order in 13 BC*, Berkeley: University of California.

Steuer, H. (2006), 'Warrior Bands, War Lords and the Birth of Tribes and States in the First Millenium AD in Middle Europe', in Otto, T., Thrane, H., Vandkilde, H. (eds) *Warfare and Society: Archaeological and Social Anthropological Perspectives*, Aarhus: Aarhus University Press, 227–236.

Stobart, J.C. (1908), 'The Senate under Avgvstvs [The Senate under Augustus]', *Classical Quarterly* 2.4 (October), 296–303.

Stone, S.C. (1983), 'Sextus Pompey, Octavian and Sicily', *American Journal of Archaeology* 87, 11–22.

Stout, S.E. (1921), 'Training Soldiers for the Roman Legion', *Classical Journal* 16.7 (April), 423–31.

Strahl, E. (2009), 'Die Dame von Bentumersiel an der Ems – Römischer Luxus für das Jenseits', *Archäologie in Niedersachsen* 12, 63–66.

Strahl, E. (2009), 'Germanische Siedler – Römische Legionäre. Die Siedlung Bentumersiel im Reiderland', *Varus-Kurier* 11, 12–15.

Strassmeir, A., Gagelman, A. (2009), *Das Heer des Arminius: Germanische Krieger zu Beginn des 1. nachchristlichen Jahrhunderts (Heere & Waffen)*, Berlin: Zeughaus Verlag.

Strassmeir, A., Gagelman, A. (2011), *Das Heer des Varus: Römische Truppen in Germanien 9 n. Chr. Teil 1: Legionen und Hilfstruppen, Bekleidung, Trachtzubehör, Schutzwaffen (Heere & Waffen)*, Berlin: Zeughaus Verlag.

Strassmeir, A., Gagelman, A. (2012), *Das Heer des Varus: Römische Truppen in Germanien 9 n. Chr. Teil 2: Waffen, Ausrüstung, Feldzeichen, Reiterei, Verbände und Einheiten (Heere & Waffen)*, Berlin: Zeughaus Verlag.

Strauss, B. (2012), *Masters of Command: Alexander, Hannibal, Caesar and the Genius of Leadership*, New York: Simon and Schuster.

Strothmann, M. (2000), *Augustus – der Vater der* res publica: *zur Funktion der drei Begriffe* restitutio, saeculum, pater patriae *im augusteischen Prinzipat*, Stuttgart: Steiner.

Sumi, G. (2005), *Ceremony and Power: Performing Politics in Rome between Republic and Empire*, Ann Arbor: University of Michigan Press.

Sumner, G. (2009), *Roman Military Dress*, Stroud: The History Press.

Sumner, G.V. (1967), 'Germanicus and Drusus', *Latomus* 26, 421–33.

Sumner, G.V. (1970a), 'The Legion and the Centuriate Organization', *Journal of Roman Studies* 60, 67–78.

Sumner, G.V. (1970b), 'The Truth About Velleius Paterculus: Prolegomena', *Harvard Studies in Classical Philology* 74, 257–97.

Sumner, G.V. (1971), 'The *Lex Annalis* under Caesar', *Phoenix* 25.3 (Autumn), 246–71.

Sutherland, C.H.V. (1934), 'Aspects of Imperialism in Roman Spain', *Journal of Roman Studies* 24, 31–42.

Sutherland, C.H.V. (1938), 'Two "Virtues" of Tiberius: A Numismatic Contribution to the History of His Reign', *Journal of Roman Studies* 28, Part 2, 129–40.

Sutherland, C.H.V. (1978), *Coinage in Roman Imperial Policy: 31 B.C.–A.D. 68*, New York: Numismatic Publications.

Swan, M. (1967), 'The Consular Fasti of 23 B.C. and the Conspiracy of Varro Murena', *Harvard Studies in Classical Philology* 71, 235–47.

Swan, P.M. (2004), *The Augustan Succession: An Historical Commentary on Cassius Dio's Roman History Books 55–56 (9BC–AD14)*, Oxford: Oxford University Press.

Swoboda, E. (1932), *Octavian and Illyricum*, Wien: Höfels.

Syme, R. (1933a), 'Some Notes on the Legions Under Augustus', *Journal of Roman Studies* 23, 14–33.

Syme, R. (1933b), 'M. Vinicius (Cos. 19 BC)', *Classical Quarterly* 27, No. 3/4 (Jul.–Oct.), 142–48.

Syme, R. (1934a), 'The Spanish War of Augustus (26–25 B.C.)', *American Journal of Philology* 55.4, 293–317.

Syme, R. (1934b), 'The Northern Frontier under Augustus', in *Cambridge Ancient History* Volume X, Cambridge: Cambridge University Press, 358–64.

Syme, R. (1934c), 'Lentulus and the Origin of Moesia', *Journal of Roman Studies* 24, 113–37.

Syme, R. (1939a), *The Roman Revolution*, Oxford: Clarendon Press.

Syme, R. (1939b), 'Review of *Les Cohortes Prétoriennes* by Marcel Durry', *Journal of Roman Studies* 29, Part 2, 242–48.

Syme, R. (1958a), *Tacitus*, Oxford: Oxford University Press.

Syme, R. (1958b), 'Imperator Caesar: A Study in Nomenclature', in Edmondson, J. (ed.), *Augustus*, Edinburgh: Edinburgh Readings on the Ancient World (2009), 40–59.

Syme, R. (1959), 'Livy and Augustus', *Harvard Studies in Classical Philology* 64, 27–87.

Syme, R. (1978), *History in Ovid*, Oxford: Oxford University Press.

Syme, R. (1979), 'Some Imperatorial Salutations', *Phoenix* 33.4 (Winter), 308–29.

Syme, R. (1984a), *Roman Papers*, Oxford: Oxford University Press.

Syme, R. (1984b), 'Lurius Varus, a Stray Consular Legate', *Harvard Studies in Classical Philology* 88, 165–69.

Syme, R. (1986), *The Augustan Aristocracy*, Oxford: Oxford University Press.

Syme, R. (1988), 'Military Geography at Rome', *Classical Antiquity* 7.2 (October), 227–51.

Syme, R., Birley, A.R. (eds) (1999), *The Provincial at Rome: And Rome and the Balkans 80BC–AD14*, Exeter: University of Exeter Press.

Talbert, R.J.A. (1996), 'The Senate and Senatorial and Equestrian Posts', in Bowman, A.K., Champlin, E., Lintott, A. (eds), *The Cambridge Ancient History Volume X: The Augustan Empire, 43 B.C.–A.D. 69* (Second Edition), Cambridge: Cambridge University Press, 324–43.

Talbert, R.J.A. (2000), *Map-by-Map Directory*, Princeton: Princeton University Press.

Talbert, R.J.A. (2001), 'Review of *Rome and the Enemy: Imperial Strategy in the Principate* by Susan P. Mattern', *American Journal of Philology* 122.3 (Autumn), 451–54.

Tameanko, M. (1999), *Monumental Coins: Buildings and Structures on Ancient Coins*, Iola, Wis.: Krause Publications.

Tarn, W.W. (1931), 'The Battle of Actium', *Journal of Roman Studies* 21, 173–99.

Tarn, W.W. (1932), 'Antony's Legions', *Classical Quarterly* 26.2 (April), 75–81.

Tarn, W.W. (1934), 'The Actium Campaign', in Cook, S.A. *et al.* (eds) *CAH* 10, Cambridge, 100–06.

Tarver, J.C. (1902), *Tiberius the Tyrant*, London: Archibald Constable.

Taylor, L.R. (1920), 'The Worship of Augustus in Italy during His Lifetime', *Transactions and Proceedings of the American Philological Association* 51, 116–33.

Taylor, L.R. (1929), 'Tiberius' Refusals of Divine Honors', *Transactions and Proceedings of the American Philological Association* 60, 87–101.

Taylor, L.R. (1957), 'The Centuriate Assembly before and after the Reform', *American Journal of Philology*, 78.4, 337–54.

Taylor, M.J. (2009), 'Hit and Run: The Germanic Warrior in the First Century AD', in Oorthuys, J. (ed.), *Ancient Warfare*, Special Issue 1, 42–47.

Tenney, F. (1933), 'On Augustus and the *Aerarium*', *Journal of Roman Studies* 23, 143–48.

Thompson, E.A. (1958), 'Early Germanic Warfare', *Past and Present*, 14.1, 2–22.

Thorburn, J.E., Jr. (2008), 'Suetonius' *Tiberius*: A Proxemic Approach', *Classical Philology* 103.4 (October), 435–48.

Thorley, J. (1969), 'The Development of Trade between the Roman Empire and the East under Augustus', *Greece & Rome (Second Series)* 16.2 (October), 209–23.

Thornton, M.K. (1992), 'Damage-Control in the *Aeneid*: or Rescuing the Military Reputation of Augustus', *Latomus* 51.3 (July–September), 566–70.

Timpe, D. (1998), 'Germanen, Germania, Germanische Altertumskunde', *Reallexikon der Germanischen Altertumskunde* 11. Berlin, 181–245.

Timpe, D. (2006), *Römisch-germanische Begegnungen in der späten Republik und frühen Kaiserzeit. Voraussetzungen – Konfrontationen – Wirkungen. Gesammelte Studien*, München/Leipzig: Sauer.

Todd, M. (2009), *The Early Germans* (The Peoples of Europe), Oxford: Wiley-Blackwell.

Toll, K. (1997), 'Making Roman-Ness and the "Aeneid"', *Classical Antiquity* 16.1 (Apr.), 34–56.

Torelli, M. (1982), *Topology and Structure of Roman Historical Reliefs*, Ann Arbor: University of Michigan Press.

Torres-Martínez, J.F, Martínez Velasco, A., Pérez Farraces, C. (2012), 'Augustan Campaigns in the Initial Phase of the Cantabrian War and Roman Artillery Projectiles from the Monte Bernorio *Oppidum* (Villarén, Prov. Palencia)', *Sonderdruck aus Archäologisches Korrespondenzblatt* 42.4, Römisch-Germanisches Zentralmuseum, Mainz, 525–41.

Toynbee, J.M.C. (1961). 'The *Ara Pacis Augustae*', *Journal of Roman Studies* 51, Parts 1 and 2, 153–56.

Trillmich, W. (1978), *Familienpropaganda der Kaiser Caligula und Claudius: Agrippina Maior und Antonia Augusta auf Münzen*, Berlin: Walter de Gruyter.

Trillmich, W. (1990), '*Colonia Augusta Emerita*, Capital of Lusitania', in Edmondson, J. (ed.), *Augustus*, Edinburgh: Edinburgh Readings on the Ancient World (2009), 427–67.

Tully, G.D. (1998), 'The στρατάρχης of *Legio* VI Ferrata and the Employment of Camp Prefects as Vexillation Commanders', *Zeitschrift für Papyrologie und Epigraphik* 120, 226–32

Turpin, W. (1994), '*Res Gestae* 34.1 and the Settlement of 27 B.C.', *Classical Quarterly*, New Series 44.2, 427–37.

Vanvinckenroye, W. (1985), *Tongeren: Romeinse Stad*, Tielt: Uitgeverij Lannoo.

Vermillion, Maj. J.M. (1987), 'The Pillars of Generalship', *Parameters* (Summer) 2–17 (online at http://www.au.af.mil/au/awc/awcgate/au-24/vermillion.pdf – accessed 29 February 2016).

Van Buren, A.W. (1913), 'The *Ara Pacis Augustae*', *Journal of Roman Studies* 3 Part 1, 134–41.

Van Nostrand, J.J. (1915), *The Reorganization of Spain by Augustus*, University of California Press: Berkeley.

Vervaet, F.J. (2014), *The High Command in the Roman Republic: The Principle of the Summum Imperium Auspiciumque from 509 to 19 BCE*, Stuttgart: Franz Steiner Verlag.

Vishnia, R. F. (2002), 'The Shadow Army: The *Lixae* and the Roman Legions', *Zeitschrift für Papyrologie und Epigraphik* 139, 265–72.

Vulić, N. (1934), 'The Illyrian War of Octavian', *Journal of Roman Studies* 24, 163–67.

Walker, S, Higgs, P. (eds) (2001), *Cleopatra of Egypt: From History to Myth*, Princeton: Princeton University Press.

Wallace-Hadrill, A. (1982a), '*Civilis Princeps*: Between Citizen and King', *Journal of Roman Studies* 72, 32–48.

Wallace-Hadrill, A. (1982b), 'The Golden Age and Sin in Augustan Ideology', *Past and Present* 95.1, 19–36.

Wallace-Hadrill, A. (1986), 'Image and Authority in the Coinage of Augustus', *Journal of Roman Studies* 76, 66–87.

Wallace-Haddrill, A. (1993), *Augustan Rome* (Classical World Series), London: Bristol Classical Press.

Walser, G. (1994), *Studien zur Alpengeschichte in antiker Zeit*, Stuttgart: Franz Steiner Verlag.

Wamser, L., Flügel, C., Ziegaus, B. (2004), *Die Römer zwischen Alpen und Nordmeer*, Düsseldorf: Patmos Verlag.

Ward-Perkins, J.B. (1970), 'From Republic to Empire: Reflections on the Early Provincial Architecture of the Roman West', *Journal of Roman Studies* 60, 1–19.

Wardle, D. (2005), 'Suetonius and Augustus' "Programmatic Edict"', *Rheinisches Museum für Philologie, Neue Folge* 148 H. 2, 181–201.

Wardle, D. (2014), *Suetonius: Life of Augustus*: Oxford: Oxford University Press.

Watkins, T.H. (1983), '*Coloniae* and *Ius Italicum* in the Early Empire', *Classical Journal* 78.4 (April–May), 319–336.

Watson, G.R. (1969), *The Roman Soldier*, London: Thames and Hudson.

Weinrib, E.J. (1968), 'The Family Connections of M. Livius Drusus Libo', *Harvard Studies in Classical Philology* 72, 247–78.

Weinstock, S. (1960), '*Pax* and the "Ara Pacis"', *Journal of Roman Studies* 50, Parts 1 and 2, 44–58.

Wells, C.M. (1971), 'The Supposed Augustan Base at Augsburg-Oberhausen: A New Look at the Evidence', *SJ*, XXVII, 63–72.

Wells, C.M. (1972), *The German Policy of Augustus: An Examination of the Archaeological Evidence*, Oxford: Oxford University Press.

Wells, C.M. (1984), *The Roman Empire*, Cambridge: Harvard University Press.

Wells, P.S. (1999), *The Barbarians Speak: How the Conquered Peoples Shaped Roman Europe*, Princeton: Princeton University Press.

Werner, W. (1997), 'The largest ship trackway in ancient times: the *Diolkos* of the Isthmus of Corinth, Greece, and early attempts to build a canal', *International Journal of Nautical Archaeology* 26.2 (May), 98–119.

Weski, T. (1982), *Waffe in germanischen Gräbern der älteren römischen Kaiserzeit südlich der Ostsee*, Oxford: British Archaeological Reports International Series 147.

Wheeler, E.L. (1993a), 'Methodological Limits and the Mirage of Roman Strategy: Part I', *Journal of Military History* 57.1 (January), 7–41.

Wheeler, E.L. (1993b), 'Methodological Limits and the Mirage of Roman Strategy: Part II', *Journal of Military History* 57.2 (April), 215–40.

Whitby, M. (1995), 'Old Frontiers: Modern Models. Review of *Frontiers of the Roman Empire. A Social and Economic Study* by C.R. Whittaker', *Classical Review (New Series)* 45.2, 338–39.

White, K.D. (1984), *Greek and Roman Technology*, Ithaca, New York: Cornell University Press.

White, L.M. (2005), 'Herod and the Jewish Experience of Augustan Rule', in Galinsky, K., *The Cambridge Companion to the Age of Augustus*, Cambridge: Cambridge University Press, 361–88.

White, P. (1988), 'Julius Caesar in Augustan Rome', *Phoenix* 42.4 (Winter), 334–56.

Whittaker, C.R. (1996a), 'Roman Africa', in Bowman, A.K., Champlin, E., Lintott, A. (eds), *The Cambridge Ancient History Volume X: The Augustan Empire, 43 B.C.-A.D. 69* (Second Edition), Cambridge: Cambridge University Press, 586–618.

Whittaker, C.R. (1996b), *Frontiers of the Roman Empire: A Social and Economic Study*, Baltimore: The John Hopkins University.

Wiedemann, T. (1986), 'The *Fetiales*: A Reconsideration', *Classical Quarterly* 36.2 (1986), 478–90.

Wigg, A. (1999), 'Neu entdeckte halternzeitliche Militärlager in Mittelhessen', in Schlüter, W., Wiegels, R. (eds), *Rom, Germanien und die Ausgrabungen von Kalkriese*, Osnabrück: Rasch, 419–36.

Wightman, E.M. (1971), *Roman Trier and the Treveri*, New York: Praeger.

Wightman, E.M. (1977), 'Military Arrangements, Native Settlements and Related Developments in Early Roman Gaul', *Helinium* 17, 105–26.

Wilbers-Rost, S. (2009), 'The site of the Varus Battle at Kalkriese. Recent results from archaeological research', in Morillo, A., Hanel, N., Martin, E. (eds), *Limes XX, Roman Frontier Studies*, Anejo de Gladius 13, 1347–52.

Wilcox, P. (1982), *Rome's Enemies: Germanics and Dacians*, London: Osprey Publishing.

Wilhelm, A.B. (1826), *Die Feldzüge des Nero Claudius Drusus in nördlichen Deutschland*, Halle: Verlag von Friedrich Kuff.

Wilkes, J.J. (1963), 'A Note on the Mutiny of the Pannonian Legions in A. D. 14', *Classical Quarterly (New Series)* 13.2 (November), 268–71

Wilkes, J.J. (1969), *Dalmatia: History of the Roman Provinces*, London: Routledge and Kegan Paul.

Wilkes, J.J. (1992), *The Illyrians*, Oxford: Blackwell.

Wilkes, J.J. (1996), 'The Danubian and Balkan Provinces', in Bowman, A.K., Champlin, E., Lintott, A. (eds), *The Cambridge Ancient History Volume X: The Augustan Empire, 43 B.C.–A.D. 69* (Second Edition), Cambridge: Cambridge University Press, 545–85.

Willems, W.J.H. (1980), 'Arnhem-Meinerswijk: een Nieuw *Castellum* aan de Rijn', *Westerheem* 29, 334–48.

Willems, W.J.H. (1989), 'Early Roman Camps on the Kops Plateau at Nijmegen (NL)', in Maxfield, V.A. *et al.* (ed.), *Proceedings of the XVth International Congress of Roman Frontier Studies*, University of Exeter Press, 210–14.

Willems, W.J.H. (1992), 'Roman Face Masks from the Kops Plateau, Nijmegen, The Netherlands', in *Journal of Roman Equipment Studies*, Armatura Press 3, 57–66.

Willems, J.H.W., Enckevort, H. van (2009), 'Vlpia Noviomagus: Roman Nijmegen, The Batavian Capital at the Imperial Frontier', Supplement 73, *Journal of Roman Archaeology*, Portsmouth, Rhode Island.

Williams, D. (1998), *Romans and Barbarians*, London: Constable.

Wiseman, T.P. (1970), 'The Definition of *Eques Romanus* in the Late Republic and Early Empire', *Historia: Zeitschrift für Alte Geschichte* 19.1 (January), 67–83.

Wolff, H. (1996), 'Raetia', in Bowman, A.K., Champlin, E., Lintott, A. (eds), *The Cambridge Ancient History Volume X: The Augustan Empire, 43 B.C.–A.D. 69* (Second Edition), Cambridge: Cambridge University Press, 535–44.

Wolfram, H. (1997), *The Roman Empire and Its Germanic Peoples*, Berkeley: University of California Press.

Wolters, R. (1990), *Römische Eroberung und Herrschaftsorganisation in Gallien und Germanien*, Bochum: Brockmeyer Verlag.

Wolters, R. (2008), *Die Schlacht im Teutoburger Wald: Arminius, Varus und das römische Germanien*, München: Verlag C.H. Beck.

Woodman, A.J. (1998), *Tacitus Reviewed*, Oxford: Clarendon Press.

Woolf, G. (1993), 'Roman Peace', in Rich, J., Shipley, G. (eds), *War and Society in the Roman World*, London: Routledge, 171–94.

Woolf, G. (1997), 'Beyond Romans and Natives', *World Archaeology* 28.3, Culture Contact and Colonialism (Feb.), 339–50.

Woolf, G. (1998), *Becoming Roman: The Origins of Provincial Civilization in Gaul*, Cambridge: Cambridge University Press.

Wright, F.A. (1937), *Marcus Agrippa: Organizer of Victory*, Edinburgh: T. and A. Constable.

Wyke, M. (2009), '*Meretrix regina*: Augustan Cleopatras', in Edmondson, J. (ed.), *Augustus*, Edinburgh: Edinburgh Readings on the Ancient World, 334–80.

Yeo, C.A. (1959), 'The Founding and Function of Roman Colonies', *The Classical World* 52.4 (January), 104–07, 129–30.

Zanier, W. (1994), 'Eine römische Katapultpfeilspitze der 19. Legion aus Oberammergau: Neues zum Alpenfeldzug des Drusus im Jahr 15 v. Chr.', *Germania* 72, 587–96.

Zanier, W. (2004), 'Die Besetzung des Alpenvorlandes: Der Alpenfeldzug 15 v. Chr. Und die augusteische Okkupation in Süddeutschland', in Wamser, L., Flügel, C., Ziegaus, B., *Die Römer zwischen Alpen und Nordmeer*, Düsseldorf: Patmos Verlag, 11–17.

Zanker, P. (1990), *The Power of Images in the Age of Augustus*, Ann Arbor: University of Michigan Press.

Ziegaus, B. (2004), 'Der frühkaiserzeitliche Münzumlauf zwischen Alpen, Donau und Iller', in Wamser, L., Flügel, C., Ziegaus, B., *Die Römer zwischen Alpen und Nordmeer*, Düsseldorf: Patmos Verlag, 18–23.

Index

A Roman citizen is listed under his or her *nomen gentile*, or *cognomen* where it is not known. A military unit is listed under its respective designation *ala*, *classis*, *cohors* or *legio*. A military campaign is listed under the designation *bellum* or *clades* when there is a contemporary Roman title, or under 'battle' or 'siege' when there is not.

Moesian War: *see Bellum Moesum*
Mogontiacum, 82, 84, 94, 98, 100–101, 105, 133, 158
Moneyers: *see Tres viri monetales*
Mons Claudius, 144
Mons Vindius (or Vinnius), 43
Morale, 85, 206
Morini, 25, 34
mos maiorum, 173
Moselle River, 30, 63
Mount Angel, 109
Mucius Scaevola, C., 70
Munatius Plancus, L., Appendix 2.1(a), 39, 74, 169, 215
municipium, 74, 203
Musa (or Mousa), 181
Mutiny at Actium, 20
Mutiny in Germania Inferior, 167–8
Mutiny in Germania Superior, 168
Mutiny in Hispania Citerior, 63, 206
Mutiny in Illyricum, 146, 180, 206
Myrus Harbour, 51
Mysia, 57, 213

Nabataea, 50, 192
Nabataean Troops, 49
Napata, 56
Narbo Martius, 213
Nasamones, 79–80
Nasidius, Q., 11
National Strategy: *see Grand Strategy*
Nauportus, 168
Navy: *see Classis*
Neapolis, 163
Negrani, 50
Nervii, 98
Neuss: *see Novaesium*
Neuss A: *see Novaesium*
Neuss B: *see Novaesium*
New Testament, 132
Niedersachsen, 91
Nijmegen-Hunerberg: *see Batavodunum*
Nikarchos, 19
Nikopolis ('Victory City'), Egypt, 24, 214
Nikopolis ('Victory City'), Epirus, 19–20, 24, 214
Nile Delta: *see Nile River*
Nile River, 22, 24, 35, 50–1, 56
nobiles, 86, 166
Nola, 163
Non-citizen army: *see Auxilia*
Nonius Asprenas Torquatus, L., Appendix 2.1(a), 131, 156, 189

Nonius Gallus, M., Appendix 2.1(a), 30, 194
Norican War: *see Bellum Noricum*
Norici, 73–4, 77, 179, 183
Noricum
conquest of: *see Bellum Alpium*
geography of, 197–8
and trade and industry, 77
tribes of:
see Norici
North Sea, 84, 91, 131, 158, 197
Novaesium, 72, 82–4, 158, 207
Novellius Torquatus Atticus, 170, 209
novus homo, 5, 10, 48, 115, 119, 186
Numa, 217
Numidia, 37, 132
Numonius Vala, 154

Oath: *see Sacramentum*
Oberaden, 94, 97, 106, 158, 207
Oberammergau, 79
Obodas, 50
obses, 27, 53, 72, 122, 152, 158, 182, 192, 198, 212
Octavia (sister of Augustus), 1, 32, 42, 53, 98
Octavian (heir of Iulius Caesar): *see Augustus*
Octavius Thurinus, C. (heir of Iulius Caesar): *see Augustus*
Octavius, M. (cousin of Augustus), 15–16, 19
Octavius, P., Appendix 2.1(b)
Odrysae, 28, 54
officium, 201
Olfen, 94
Opheion, 35
Oppidum Ubiorum, 63, 82, 84, 120, 122
Oppius, C., 5, 172
Order of battle, Appendix 3, 42, 89, 153, 167
Ordo Equester, Appendix 2.1(b), 20–1, 23–4, 104, 119, 132, 137, 152, 163, 166, 186, 207
Orienti Praepositus, 119
Orosius, 11, 13, 16, 81, 213
Osnabrück, 153
Ostia, 122
Ostorius Scapula, Q., Appendix 2.1(b), 119
Ouologaisis, 86–7, 92
ovatio, 192

pacere, 171
Pacification, 40, 46, 77, 88, 109, 114, 121, 123, 126, 152, 180, 184, 189, 197–9, 203–204, 215, 219
pactio, 171, 182